MACARTHUR

HIS RENDEZVOUS

WITH HISTORY

BY MAJOR GENERAL

COURTNEY WHITNEY

GREENWOOD PRESS, PUBLISHERS
WESTPORT, CONNECTICUT

Library of Congress Cataloging in Publication Data

Whitney, Courtney.
   MacArthur : his rendezvous with history.

   Reprint of the 1956 ed. published by Knopf, New York.
   Includes index.
     1. MacArthur, Douglas, 1880-1964. 2. Generals--
United States--Biography.
[E745.M3W48 1977]   973.91'092'4 [B]   77-2965
ISBN 0-8371-9564-0

Originally published in 1956 by Alfred A. Knopf, Inc.,
New York

Reprinted with the permission of Alfred A. Knopf, Inc.

Reprinted in 1977 by Greenwood Press, Inc.

Library of Congress catalog card number 77-2965

ISBN 0-8371-9564-0

Printed in the United States of America

TO JAMES H. RAND,

INDUSTRIAL PIONEER, WHO HAD THE VISION

TO GUIDE MACARTHUR'S BRILLIANT MIND

TOWARD NEW HORIZONS AFTER A WILLFUL

PRESIDENT FORECLOSED THE OLD

Preface

"The only history worth reading," John Ruskin points out in his *Stones of Venice*, "is that written at the time of which it treats, the history of what was done and seen, heard out of the mouths of the men who did and saw." I fully agree with this sage aphorism. To record my impressions, therefore, of MacArthur's role in the climactic events which have surged across Asia since the advent of World War II, I have sought, insofar as the record will permit, to let his own voice and pen speak for themselves and bear contemporary witness concerning his strategic decisions and social and political philosophy, in order that those of this and future generations may accurately formulate their impressions of the titanic influence he has had and, if permitted, still might have upon the course of events in Asia.

C. W.

Contents

Part I WORLD WAR

Part II JAPAN

Contents

Part III   Korea

Part IV   America

List of Maps

Maps drawn by Rafael Palacios

Part I

WORLD WAR

". . . An army of free men that has brought your people once again under democracy's banner, to rededicate their churches, long desecrated, to the glory of God and public worship; to reopen their schools to liberal education; to till the soil and reap the harvest without fear of confiscation; to reestablish their industries that they may again enjoy the profit from the sweat of their own toil; and to restore the sanctity and happiness of their homes, unafraid of violent intrusion . . ."

City of Manila—February 26, 1945

Chapter I "These islands must and will be defended."

The pre-dawn of Manila's Sunday morning on July 27, 1941, seemed like the pre-dawn of any other Manila morning. The weather was as hot and sultry as usual. South of the Luneta, the Army and Navy Club was shrouded in silence that had fallen over it only a few hours before. The Manila Hotel Pavilion slumbered after the last echo of the popular Tirso's band, which had quieted even later than the gaiety at the Army and Navy Club.

Yet beneath that normal surface, unknown to all but a few telegraphers at their stations, an event of great importance and lasting significance was already taking place. For the air waves between Manila and Washington, ten thousand miles away, were crackling with messages and directives. Before the sun now bursting over the Noveliches watershed set in its silent melody of brilliant hues behind the Mariveles horizon, the first steps would have been taken to muster the infant Philippine army into the service of the U.S., thereby forming the largest segment of American forces in the Far East. Its leader was to be Douglas MacArthur, retired general of the U.S. Army by act of Congress, Field Marshal of the Philippine Army by act of the Philippine Assembly, now recalled to active service by the President of the United States.

The full significance and importance of these messages of July 27, 1941, can be seen only in retrospect. For at that time none could surmise the chain of historical events they were to set in motion. An uneasy peace ruled the Pacific, and gathering war storms were beginning to cast their shadows. But even MacArthur could not foresee the magnitude of the destiny that was to put his military judgment to the acid test and challenge his capacity for resourceful leadership in an all but impossible situation. MacArthur had been called to a rendezvous with history.

He was having breakfast in his penthouse quarters atop the Manila

3

Hotel when the cables were brought to him. One was from President Roosevelt, ordering the Philippine army mobilized under MacArthur, who was returned to active service as a lieutenant general. The other, from the Pentagon, elaborated on the President's terse directive. With his customary calm MacArthur read the colorless military language that would so profoundly influence his own life and the lives of the nations and the peoples surrounding him. He promptly summoned Major General Richard Sutherland, his chief of staff, from an early-morning round on the golf course, and the two set to work. As he worked, MacArthur's senses quickened at the prospect of once more taking active field command.

No man was more suited to the task before him. When Douglas MacArthur retired from active service at fifty-five, he had already given his country one of the most illustrious military careers in history: the most brilliant West Point student in a quarter of a century; praised by Secretary of War Baker in 1918 as "the bravest front line general in the war"; acclaimed for reforming and modernizing West Point as its superintendent; Chief of Staff of the Army for a longer term than anyone else; and now Field Marshal of the Philippine army with thirty-eight years of experience and an intimate knowledge of Asia and the Asians.

He had come to the Philippines because he, almost alone, had foreseen that a strong defensive position there was vital to the preservation of peace in the Pacific. He, almost alone, had fully realized and assessed the U.S.'s moral and legal obligations to protect the Philippines. He, almost alone, had fully comprehended the importance of a friendly Philippine government and people to the security of the continental United States. He, almost alone, had fully understood the vulnerability of our Western seaboard should our outpost of friendly islands in the Pacific fall into enemy hands. In short, he, almost alone, then saw that U.S. security was as much a Pacific as an Atlantic problem.

Because he had been unable to convince the Europe-first policy-planners in Washington, MacArthur had accepted the earnest invitation of President Manuel Quezon to go to the Philippines and do what he could —again almost alone, as far as official Washington was concerned—to prepare the Islands for military self-reliance. By law, the Philippines were to be separated from the sovereign protection of the U.S. on July 4, 1946.

It was a heart-breaking task, especially since some of the biggest obstacles were thrown in his path by his own government. In Washington the administration and the Congress only listlessly considered the need for defenses in the Pacific. Congress, for example, turned down an ap-

4

"These islands must and will be defended."

propriation for five million dollars which would have made Guam an almost impregnable fortress. Largely responsible for this refusal to supply military defenses in the Pacific was the belief, almost universal in Washington, that any Pacific war would be the Navy's private war—a belief abetted by the Navy's carefully fostered argument that the U.S. fleet could quickly smash the Japanese fleet in its first engagement.

Refusing to put a single dollar into the Pacific defense effort, the U.S. government finally and reluctantly consented to provide the Filipinos with a few obsolete World War I Enfield rifles, some old 75-mm. guns for artillery training, and a limited supply of Lewis and Browning machine guns. MacArthur had only a token supply of heavy weapons and practically no naval defenses. He was forced to purchase from England the engines to power the two motor torpedo boats that his limited budget had provided. Faced with official neglect, he had to keep revising downward his over-all plans for the size of the defense structure—from the originally planned 40,000-man increase per year to 30,000, to 20,000 and less.

Even in those early days when he had first started building the Philippines' defenses, U.S. officials had harassed him right in Manila. Frank Murphy, as High Commissioner of the Philippines, betrayed his jealousy of MacArthur's stature in the Islands by initiating a personal campaign of pressure on President Roosevelt to cause the General's removal, a campaign that ended only when MacArthur voluntarily retired from active service. The President accepted his retirement reluctantly and with the accolade: "Your service in war and peace is a brilliant chapter in American history." But accolades did not protect MacArthur from being sniped at, even after his retirement. For when he became military advisor to the Philippine government, he found himself facing a movement to supplant him even in this position, on the specious theory that as a retired officer he could not lawfully exercise authority over the active U.S. Army officers assigned to the military advisory group. The movement gained powerful support in Washington, but failed because of a greater support MacArthur had—the support of the Filipino government and people.

The MacArthur name had long shone like a beacon in the Philippines. General Arthur MacArthur, Douglas's father, had served there not only with distinction in freeing the Islands from the Spaniard, but also with such justice and compassion in the peace which followed that he had earned the love of all the Filipinos. His son followed in this tradition. With this heritage and through the magnetism of his own personal leadership,

5

MacArthur managed to organize a community of peacefully inclined agricultural workers, fishermen, and tradesmen into a military force. He impressed upon them the hard truth that U.S. military protection did not extend into perpetuity. And he persuaded them to swallow an even stronger pill: conscription for military training.

MacArthur accomplished this mostly through his unique ability to evoke in Filipino hearts the nobility of the soldier's mission. They remembered best his eloquence on this subject when he accepted the baton of Field Marshal from President Quezon at Malacanan Palace. "The military code," he said on that occasion, "has come down to us from even before the age of knighthood and chivalry. . . . The soldier, above all men, is required to perform the highest act of religious teaching—sacrifice. In battle and in the face of danger and death he discloses those divine attributes which his Maker gave when He created man in His own image. However horrible the incidents of war may be, the soldier who is called upon to offer and to give his life for his country, is the noblest development of mankind."

Moved by such eloquence, Filipinos began to respond to his call for military service. But the Philippine Assembly delayed on appropriations; some politicians tried to cut down the amounts MacArthur needed and even tried to postpone the defense effort entirely. Here again MacArthur had no weapon but the earnest persuasion of his own oratory. In a speech to the Assembly he outlined the philosophy on which he was building the defense establishment. He explained that it reflected "the lessons of history, the conclusions of acknowledged masters of warfare and of statesmanship, and the sentiments and aspirations of the Filipino people. It is founded on enduring principles that are fundamental to any plan applicable to our needs.

"The first of these principles is that every citizen is obligated to the nation's defense. . . . No man has the inalienable right to enjoy the privileges and opportunities conferred upon him by free institutions unless he simultaneously acknowledges his duty to defend with his life and with his property the government through which he acquires these opportunities and these privileges. To deny this individual responsibility is to reject the whole theory of democratic government. This principle knows of no limitation of time or condition. It is effective in war, in peace and for as long as the nation shall endure. . . .

"The second great principle is that our national defense system must provide actual security. Indeed, an insufficient defense is almost a contradiction in terms. A dam that crumbles under the rising flood is nothing more than a desolate monument to the wasted effort and lack of vision of its builders. . . .

"The next principle to which I hold is the insistent need for current and future economy. Although there are no costs of peace comparable to those that would surely follow defeat in war, it is nevertheless incumbent upon the government to avoid unnecessary expenditure. . . ."

Patriotism, power, and economy thus became the three pillars upon which MacArthur planned his structure for the defense of the Islands. With the persuasion of blunt truths like these, the Assembly voted an allocation of ten million dollars a year for his program. But because political pressures on appropriations continued to limit the defensive power he was able to develop in the short time allotted him, he placed his greatest reliance upon the patriotism of the people. His plan provided for subdividing the Islands into military districts. It included a reserve force of universal-military-service trainees, supplementing a small core of regular professional soldiers. It allowed for an air component of 1,500–2,000 planes and an offshore patrol of 150–200 motor torpedo boats. The plan aimed not at invulnerability, but at a defensive posture that would render an invasion effort costly enough to discourage the attempt.

In the late afternoon of July 27, MacArthur, Chief of Staff Sutherland, and Deputy Chief of Staff Richard Marshall were still huddled over their maps and tables of organization, this time at MacArthur's GHQ, 1 Victoria Street. Headquarters were in a spacious old building in the ancient walled city. MacArthur's office was lined with his favorite books and pictures and decorated with inlaid cabinets and screens.

As MacArthur made his complicated arrangements for merging the Philippine army with the American troops already stationed in the Islands, he realized that his defense plan, envisioned for ten years, still had four years to go. What he did not realize that summer afternoon of 1941 was that Washington decisions were even then in the making to direct U.S. military resources, when war came, to the European theater and to sacrifice the U.S. position in the Western Pacific.

Indeed, MacArthur could only conclude that this important July 27 directive meant further support from the U.S.; surely the incorporation of Filipino forces into the U.S. Army would not be the logical step toward *less* support. Accordingly, he made sure that this rare gesture of U.S. interest in the Pacific was noticed by sensitive Asians; the Philippines would not be deserted. MacArthur announced: "The action of the American government in establishing this new command can only mean that it intends to maintain, at any cost, its full rights in the Far East. . . . To this end both American and Filipino soldiers can be expected to give their utmost."

So, on the afternoon of that significant day of July 27, MacArthur plunged into the job of integrating his Philippine troops into the U.S. Army and speeding up his defense plan. As they worked, Sutherland looked at him across the table and said, with a sense of foreboding: "You know, General, it adds up to an almost insurmountable task." MacArthur glanced up from his map and answered simply: "These islands must and will be defended. I can but do my best."

Then he paused in his work long enough to stare musingly out the window of his office and across the roofs of the city toward the blue waters of Manila Bay. Wistfully and with something of the mysticism of the Far East, where he had served so long, he almost whispered: "Destiny, by the grace of God, sometimes plays queer pranks with men's lives."

Destiny would indeed play its part in the life of Douglas MacArthur. He then had less than five months before the Japanese attack.

CHAPTER II   "The enemy has committed himself
in force."

◤ During the days that flew by in that autumn of 1941 MacArthur bombarded Washington with requests for more men and munitions with which to rush the Philippine defenses. He had some success, though always the time seemed too short and the distances too long. Ships from both the east and west coasts of the U.S. belatedly sailed for the Pacific outposts. But it takes forty-five days for the average cargo ship to go from New York to Manila. To MacArthur, working against time and watching the Japanese become more and more belligerent, every ship seemed to crawl.

By the end of November, though, he could take some satisfaction in this balance sheet of his military resources:

►10 partially mobilized Philippine army divisions, with approximately 100,000 unseasoned Filipino reservists, and 20,000 regulars, including 12,000 Philippine scouts—all in addition to 19,000 American officers and enlisted men. These latter included Army Air Corps personnel and the 31st Infantry Regiment, long stationed in the city of Manila (total American strength amounted to less than one division).

►200 combat planes. About two thirds of these were operational, including 35 recently arrived B-17's and 100 P-40's.

There was also the possibility of naval support—a reinforced U.S. Asiatic fleet, consisting primarily of 3 cruisers, 13 destroyers, 29 submarines, 3 submarine-tenders, 1 submarine-rescue vessel, 6 PT boats, and an air patrol wing composed of 30 PBY's and 4 seaplane-tenders. This force was not under MacArthur's command.

Hardly an adequate defense force, MacArthur realized. But over the horizon were promised reinforcements that would give him much greater strength: a convoy then on the high seas carried 18 P-40's, 52 dive bombers, 20 75-mm. guns, 500,000 rounds of .50-caliber ammunition, 600 tons of bombs, 9,000 drums of aviation fuel, other heavy equipment and supplies. The convoy also carried 4,600 troop reinforcements; two field-artillery regiments and the ground echelon of the 7th Heavy Bombardment Group. Other shipments were being readied for sailing, and the total reinforcement amounted to more than one million ship tons. But fate—and procrastinations in Washington—had already wiped out these reinforcements, so far as MacArthur was concerned. Those on the high seas would be diverted before reaching their destination. The others were not due to arrive in Manila before April 1942.

Meanwhile, MacArthur was doing his best with the meager forces he had. On November 28 he received an "alert" warning from the War Department: "Negotiations with Japan appear to be terminated to all practical purposes, with only the barest possibility that the Japanese government might come back and offer to continue. Japanese future action unpredictable but hostile action possible at any moment. If hostilities cannot be avoided the United States desires that Japan commit the first overt act."

MacArthur already had a regular air reconnaissance; he now increased it. The pilots began to report nightly contacts with groups of hostile aircraft only twenty to fifty miles out at sea. He strengthened his beach defenses. He ordered the B-17's at Clark Field in Luzon to fly south to fields in Mindanao, to be out of reach of the Japanese Formosa-based planes. He met with U.S. High Commissioner Francis Sayre and Admiral Thomas Hart, who commanded the naval forces in the Philippines, to confirm the final details of co-operation between Army, Navy, and Philippine forces when the attack came. He then sent Washington a message which combined a warning that his forces might be insufficient with a promise that they would do their utmost: "Within the limitations imposed by present state of development of this theater of operations," he said, "everything is in readiness for the conduct of a successful defense."

Within these limitations of which he was careful to remind Washington, MacArthur had organized his defenses. They were grouped into three principal commands: the North Luzon Force, which was the most important, but to which MacArthur could give only three Philippine divisions (it was commanded by Jonathan Wainwright, soon to be made famous by the tragedies of war); the South Luzon Force; and the Visayan-Mindanao Force. A reserve force was held under control of GHQ in Manila, ready to be sent in whichever direction it should be needed.

"The enemy has committed himself in force."

With his troops stationed, his aircraft constantly scouting the area around the Islands, and his plans ready for immediate implementation, MacArthur could only wait for the enemy to show his hand. He did not have long to wait. Ten days after the "alert" from Washington, the Japanese struck.

The enemy's first big attack on the Philippines, ten hours after the strike at Pearl Harbor, was at Clark Field. There some of the new B-17's were caught on the ground. One wave of Japanese bombers plastered the runways so accurately that not a bomb fell more than two hundred feet away from the field. The bombers were followed by a swooping attack of fighters strafing everything in sight and destroying seventeen of the B-17's.

In contrast to the punishment MacArthur was to inflict on enemy planes under comparable circumstances, this was not an important incident. But there has been debate—and misrepresentation—about it ever since it happened. And this is as good a place as any to set the record straight.

MacArthur had, as I mentioned earlier, ordered all the B-17's sent south to Mindanao, out of range of the Japanese planes. Some of them were sent south, but this force had not yet left Clark Field. Many of Mac-Arthur's friends have pointed out that, once he had given the order, it should have been carried out immediately by his air commander. But he has always refused to accept this easy excuse, however justified it might be, and has sought to have historical judgment of the incident based on all the circumstances involved.

The air commander in the Philippines was Major General Lewis H. Brereton. His was the over-all responsibility for tactical security. But when criticism of Brereton was brought to MacArthur's attention in 1943, he quickly retorted with the true and extenuating circumstances of the situation: "General Brereton had in the Philippines only a token force which, excluding trainers and hopelessly obsolete planes, comprised but 35 bombers and 72 fighters. He was further greatly handicapped by the lack of airdromes, there being only one on Luzon, Clark Field, that was usable by heavy bombers and only five usable by fighters. Many air-dromes were under construction in the Philippines, but they were not completed and available by December 7. . . . A number of our airplanes were destroyed on the ground while landing for gas or while down for essential maintenance—but never as a result of negligence."

This explanation politely omitted detailing some of the other reasons behind the Clark Field incident. Although MacArthur had pleaded con-stantly for radar equipment, he had received only seven sets for all the

Philippines. And they had arrived so recently that there had been time to put only one in commission; there had not been time to ready the one intended for Clark Field. He had received so few anti-aircraft guns, of such poor performance, that their defense hardly bothered the Japanese attackers. The anti-aircraft shells exploded two thousand to four thousand feet short of their targets. Worst of all was the three-inch-gun ammunition that had been shipped out to the 200th Coast Artillery. The newest of this ammunition had been made in 1932; fuses were corroded, and one observer claimed that five out of every six shells were duds. There had not even been enough equipment to enlarge the airfields so that they could be used by the bombers. Only one field on Mindanao, Del Monte, could take heavy bombers, and Brereton reasoned that if he put all his B-17's down there, the new bombers supposedly en route from the United States by way of Australia would be unable to land.

As for the protection of Clark Field, the same familiar reasons applied. Most of the newly arrived P-40's could not be flown until their engines had been broken in. There were no spare parts for most of the fighters, none at all for the bombers, and not a single extra airplane engine in the Philippines. And the tenor of Washington had quickly been made evident to General Brereton when he had put the maintenance and repair depots on two shifts; he had received a strong letter of protest from the Civil Service Commission.

So MacArthur's bombers were confined to one airfield on Luzon and one on Mindanao because supplies and equipment still had not come from the U.S. in sufficient quantity. Enough had been promised, but it was too late. Within days of the time the war started in the Pacific this was to become a refrain that must have haunted official Washington.

In certain biased circles the strategic value of these seventeen bombers has been exaggerated to the extent that one would think an entire Air Corps wing had been destroyed. The statement has been made that the destruction of these planes was a vital, if not determining, factor in the defense of the Philippines. Such an argument overlooks the fact that the air force at MacArthur's disposal was doomed as long as it was provided with no spare parts and confined to so few airfields.

Meanwhile the Japanese attacked with flights of from forty to fifty planes at a time. The B-17's that had been sent to Mindanao returned and tried to stem the enemy tide, sometimes having to stay aloft all day in order not to be destroyed on the ground. The fighters that had not been put out of action for lack of parts went into battle with odds of ten to one against them. Their plight was as hopeless as their spirit was game.

"The enemy has committed himself in force."

Some of the pursuit planes stayed on until they were shot to pieces. Within a few days of the first attack by the enemy, all the U.S. bombers were forced to retreat to Australia. They never returned.

One more myth about MacArthur's air force at the time needs to be corrected. It was said that, immediately after the news from Pearl Harbor, MacArthur refused a request by General Brereton to hit the enemy on Formosa before he could bomb the Philippines. Only recently MacArthur was asked about this by the historical section of the Army. His answer is illuminating:

"My orders were explicit not to initiate hostilities against the Japanese. The Philippines, while a possession of the U.S., had, so far as war was concerned, a somewhat indeterminate international position in many minds, especially the Filipinos and their government. While I personally had not the slightest doubt we would be attacked, great local hope existed that this would not be the case. Instructions from Washington were very definite to wait until the Japanese made the first 'overt' move.

"Even without such a directive, practical limitations made it unfeasible to take the offensive. . . . Our only aggressive potential consisted of about 36 B-17's. Their only possible target was the enemy's fields on Formosa. Our advance fields in Luzon were still incomplete, and our fighters from other fields in Luzon were too far away from Formosa to protect our bombers in a Formosa attack. . . . The enemy's air force, based on excellent fields, outnumbered ours many times. In addition, he had a mobile force based on carriers which we entirely lacked. Our basic mission directive had confined our operations to our own national waters, so no outside reconnaissance had been possible. The exact location of enemy targets was therefore not known. . . . An attack under such conditions would have been doomed to total failure. In my opinion it would have been suicidal as well as in direct defiance of my basic directive."

Post-war examination of Japanese records and interrogation of qualified Japanese personnel have borne out the wisdom of that decision. The evidence shows that any such daylight attack on Formosa at the time would have been met by overwhelming enemy interception alerted for just such a situation. None of our planes could have reached their targets, much less returned to their Philippine bases. Had the first air battles over the Philippines gone in our favor, MacArthur contemplated a surprise night raid; but under the circumstances it could have been little more than a nuisance attack, and it could never have been repeated.

So the enemy immediately took command of the air. On the third day the Cavite Navy Yard was subjected to a massive bombing that left it practically in a shambles. In a sense, though, the enemy was too late, because the command of the sea had already been given to him as well.

This was the first tragedy of divided U.S. command. Admiral Thomas C. Hart, Commander of the Asiatic Fleet, was responsible to Admiral H. R. Stark, Chief of Naval Operations in Washington. Hart's mission was clearly worded: "to support the defense of the Philippines as long as that defense continues." But, unlike MacArthur, Hart assumed that the fall of the Philippines was inevitable, and he was apparently supported in this view by Stark in Washington. The Navy's strategy of the war in the Pacific was one of engaging the Japanese fleet in driving across the center of the ocean, and in these plans the Philippines were of no importance. When the attack on the Philippines came, it turned out that Admiral Hart had already disposed of most of the surface elements of his Asiatic Fleet to place them beyond the path of immediate action. The flagship *Houston* was at Iloilo in the central Philippines, 415 miles south of Manila; the *Boise* was at Cebu, 355 miles away; and with the exception of five destroyers, submarines, and some miscellaneous elements of the fleet, all the rest of his forces had already been sent south to safety. Because Hart was not under MacArthur's command, he did not notify MacArthur that most of his fleet, far from patrolling the area around the Philippines, was out of reach.[1] The surface elements of the Asiatic Fleet joined the Dutch fleet in the approaches to the East Indies and two months later were destroyed by the Japanese in the Battle of the Java Sea.

Undeterred, the enemy landed troops at Aparri in the north and Vigan in the northwest, the same day as the bombing of the Cavite Navy Yard. Two days later, on December 12, more troops landed at Legaspi in the south. Some of the local U.S. commanders nervously urged MacArthur to attack these forces, but he sensed that they were diversionary thrusts and held his fire. He could not now defend all the beaches, he explained, and thus it was necessary to hold back "until the enemy has committed himself in force." He even knew where the main attack would come: in Lingayen Gulf. There two divisions of the Philippine army waited behind their beach defenses. And there, on December 22, the main blow did indeed fall.

They came in a swarming fleet of transports and supporting naval units. With no opposition save the feeble attempts of the few planes left

---

[1] Neither did Hart tell MacArthur that the Navy Department had ordered him to place under MacArthur's immediate command all naval and Marine Corps personnel left in the Philippines. MacArthur did not learn of this until a month after Hart had returned home, and only then when he urged the necessity of such action.

on the Islands, the Japanese swept ashore and established firm beachheads.

In his command post at 1 Victoria Street, MacArthur studied the dismaying intelligence reports as they came in. Looking at the map and shaking his head slowly, he said to General Sutherland: "What a target this would have been for the submarines." He did not then realize the irony behind his remark. Although Admiral Hart's surface fleet was small compared to the full weight of warships which the Japanese could throw at him, he did have an unusually large complement of submarines. There were twenty-nine in his fleet, including some of the newest types just delivered, plus three submarine-tenders and one submarine-rescue vessel. Furthermore, when the Japanese bombed the Cavite Navy Yard and Manila Bay, they inexplicably seemed to concentrate on surface craft and installations, destroying only one submarine. When Hart sent nearly all the rest of his fleet south, he ordered his submarines to continue the defense of the Philippines. But although the Lingayen landings had been expected, there was only one submarine cruising off Lingayen Gulf when the Japanese invasion armada appeared.

As if to compound the irony, the radio of that one submarine went out of commission; it could receive, but it could not transmit. The submarine was called in, and another was sent to cruise this vital area. By the time the second submarine got to its station, it was too late. She radioed back on December 21 that the Japanese ships had already reached the shallow, reef-protected inner gulf, where submarine attacks were all but impossible. Four more submarines—all that seemed to be left in the area from Hart's original twenty-nine—were rushed to Lingayen Gulf. Their attack was ineffectual.

It was only later that MacArthur learned what an opportunity had been missed and what a target the Japanese had indeed provided for the submarines. For hours before entering the Gulf, the enemy invasion force had been spread out in a long line extending twenty miles, open to what could have been a disastrous submarine attack. But those hours happened to be the time when no submarine was cruising the area where the big landing-force was expected to come. With not enough planes for reconnaissance and only a few for a feeble attack on the transports, with no surface fleet for patrols and with nearly all the submarines somewhere else, MacArthur had to wait helplessly while the enemy landed his biggest invasion force on the beaches of Lingayen Gulf.

The picture elsewhere in the Pacific was even more dismal than in the Philippines. Guam had fallen December 10, and Wake Island, after the Marines' intrepid defense, on the 22nd. The line of communications between Hawaii and the Philippines was cut. Midway, the nearest base still in American hands, was 4,500 miles away. Most of the battle force of the U.S. Pacific Fleet had been destroyed at Pearl Harbor, and Britain's proudest warships, the *Prince of Wales* and the *Repulse*, had been sunk off Malaya. These disasters left all naval commanders ill-disposed to venture far in the Pacific, despite their commitments to aid the defense of the Philippines. As for the Far Eastern resources of the other Allies, they were fully employed against the Japanese in Indochina, Malaya, Hong Kong, and in the Netherlands East Indies.

Surveying the strategic situation in the Pacific in those first days after Pearl Harbor, MacArthur could only conclude that he was isolated. He would have to defend the Philippines on his own, with no help from the United States until our naval power could be regrouped and major forces dispatched to his aid. Instinctively he knew that that aid would be delayed, and he planned his strategy accordingly as he took his stance to hold until relief arrived. He little dreamed that he was destined to wait in vain.

The Filipino defenders on the beaches at Lingayen Gulf fought heroically in their first baptism of fire. But they were confronted with sweeping hordes of highly trained, battle-seasoned Japanese troops. The first major landing was at Agoo, on the east side of the Gulf. As the Filipinos tried to defend the beach, they were hit by a flanking attack by Japanese forces that had landed previously at Vigan, to the north. The weary defenders gave ground, and thus the beachhead was rapidly expanded.

Then, in the early morning of December 24, another Japanese convoy entered Lamon Bay, to the east of Manila, and in a three-pronged landing put ashore a considerable force at Atimonan, Mauban, and Siain. They were hit by crossfire from Filipino troops dug in on the beaches and strafed by American planes, but their size and power were irresistible. The battle was joined in both North and South Luzon, and the campaign for the Philippines was on.

Now came the time for a major decision of strategy. Both the North and South Luzon forces faced a well-seasoned enemy in superior numbers, with supporting tanks, heavy artillery, superior firepower, and dominant air support. As the Japanese northern force swept steadily down the approach to the Central Luzon Plain, the southern force headed over the Tayabas Mountains; both were on courses that would converge directly before the city of Manila. MacArthur saw that the enemy expected him to fight it out on both approaches, finally converging his forces north of Manila for a showdown. But he had another plan.

Actually, he had two plans. The first, for which he had argued long and determinedly with Washington before obtaining approval, was for an "offensive defense": he would surprise and attack the Japanese troops right at the beaches and drive them back into the sea, wherever they landed. The plan was naturally dependent on full air and naval support. But now both were gone. That was why he had had to hold back and wait for the major enemy landings. And it was why, when the major landings did come, they were met on the beaches by the Filipino defenders. But with no air or naval power to aid them, the defenders were falling back before the enemy's superior force. So MacArthur had to switch to his second plan.

It was based on a defense strategy worked out long before and officially labeled War Plan ORANGE 3. It called for retirement to Bataan peninsula for a delaying-action, thereby denying the enemy the use of Manila Bay and pinning down his expeditionary force until reinforcements could arrive from the United States. But it had been predicated on the defenders' having the necessary time to carry out this complicated maneuver.

At this point, with the enemy ashore in force and with no air or naval protection, MacArthur was forced to make the maneuver under the worst possible conditions. The powerful and fast-moving Japanese pincers threatened to close upon the defending forces and destroy them before the juncture on Bataan could be accomplished. The South Luzon Force would have to withdraw with great speed in order to sideslip into Bataan, while Wainwright's North Luzon Force would have to take a stand at some point on the Central Plain and hold the enemy until the Southern Force had passed safely by.

The critical point, the place of possible entrapment, was San Fernando, where the South Luzon Force would have to round the top of Manila Bay. If the enemy reached that point first, he could either destroy the two defending forces in detail or compress them into one group and annihilate them. It was a daring gamble; if it paid off, MacArthur would have snatched his defending forces right out from under the grasp of the Japanese pincers. In short, all depended on how fast he could move his troops.

This he knew, and this he had been preparing for ever since he had first begun readying the Philippines' defenses. Indeed, as far back as 1935, in his valedictory as he left the office of Chief of Staff of the Army,

MacArthur had said that "to gain surprise, nothing is more important than superiority in mobility. The constant trend in the modern world is toward greater and greater speed. An army that fails to keep in step with this trend is, far from making progress toward modernization, going steadily and irrevocably backward. . . . Nothing is more important to the future efficiency of the army than to multiply its rate of movement." MacArthur, who is credited with the leadership in the mechanization of the American Army to achieve maximum mobility, had also concentrated on mobility in his Philippine defense forces, to the fullest extent permitted by the trickle of equipment sent him from the United States. Now, as he had expected, mobility would spell the difference between success and failure; and now he was prepared.

He personally took the field, riding along the dusty Philippine roads in an old Chrysler sedan as he visited the command posts. In a series of rapid maneuvers, involving forced marches and holding-actions, he moved his southern troops northwestward to round the corner into Bataan. Meanwhile, he designated the several lines for Wainwright to stage his delaying-actions across the great Central Plain. Hard-pressed as Wainwright's forces were, it was essential that they hold the enemy back from San Fernando until the coast was clear.

The plan focused on one small bridge just south of San Fernando— the Calumpit Bridge. Two spans, one carrying the single track of the railroad and another carrying a two-lane road, crossed the swirling Pampanga River and its surrounding marshes. Through this difficult defile all the troops and equipment and supplies would have to pass. Every available piece of civilian transportation—cars, trucks, and even horse-drawn vehicles—were commandeered to speed the maneuver. All day and night they formed endless columns along the narrow Philippine roads as they moved men and munitions and military stores from Manila to Bataan. The scene was reminiscent of that critical point in World War I when every taxicab in Paris was mobilized to rush troops to the front to defend the Marne.

Such a huge logistical movement could not long be kept secret from the enemy, which was one reason why all elements had to act with such speed. By December 27 the Japanese commander, General Masaharu Homma, had discovered MacArthur's strategy. He reacted immediately and with reckless violence. The Japanese forces were driven forward desperately in an all-out attempt to cut across the road above and below and make a trap of the Calumpit Bridge. MacArthur had troops, artillery, and tanks ready for the desperate attack.

18

"The enemy has committed himself in force."

The next three days were crammed with suspense, and even had an almost split-second climax on the last day. The deadline for blowing the Calumpit Bridge was set for six a.m. on New Year's Day, 1942. On December 31 a big Japanese attack was massing at the road junction just below the bridge, preparing to cut off the escape route before all the South Luzon force had got through. U.S. tanks that had been held in GHQ reserve were rushed to the rescue, and in a crashing battle in the late afternoon the attackers were temporarily driven off. It was 2:30 a.m. on New Year's Day before the last U.S. tank had crossed the bridge onto the safe side of the Pampanga. The other defending forces quickly followed, one group of infantry piling into trucks and roaring out of the town nearest Calumpit under fire from the advancing Japanese. The last infantryman crossed the bridge at five a.m.

General Wainwright, about to give the order to blow the bridge, was warned that a platoon of demolition engineers was still on the other side. In the dark they waited for the demolition men. At 5:45, with still no sign of them, Wainwright postponed the touch-off time from six to 6:15. Just after six, dawn broke. Rifle fire could be heard from the direction in which the Japanese were coming. Wainwright could jeopardize the entire withdrawal no longer. He gave the order: "Blow it."

Both spans of the Calumpit Bridge went up in a crashing shower of steel and mortar just as the vanguard of the enemy came into sight on the opposite bank. With the Japanese cut off by the racing Pampanga River, the withdrawal onto Bataan was secure.

On the first day of 1942, MacArthur announced that the sideslip into Bataan had been successfully completed. He had outsmarted—and moved faster than—the enemy, and the entire defense force had slipped out of the great Japanese pincers. From Washington, General Pershing, MacArthur's old commander in World War I, congratulated his comrade-in-arms for "one of the greatest moves in all military history. It was a masterpiece." His view was confirmed later by captured Japanese records. The Imperial Japanese Headquarters called the maneuver "a great strategic move." The attackers "never planned for or expected a withdrawal to Bataan. The decisive battle had been expected in Manila. The Japanese commanders could not adjust to the new situation." MacArthur's move also weakened Japanese morale. "Politically," the captured records revealed, "it stood as a symbol—there was a spiritual influence exerted by the American resistance on Bataan."

More than a week after their initial landings, the only prize the Japanese had to show for their marching and fighting was the city of

Manila. And, as MacArthur pointed out in his announcement, the city, "because of complete evacuation of our forces previously, has no practical military value." For on December 27 he had declared Manila an open city. Enemy air attacks had at that point been confined to military targets, but he was afraid that as the battle lines drew closer the Japanese would become less discriminate, bringing tragedy and suffering to the Filipino populace and destruction to the city's homes, churches, and monuments to Philippine history and culture. Also, Manila was too near sea level for air-raid shelters to be dug. His proclamation read: "In order to spare the metropolitan area from possible ravages of attack either by air or ground, Manila is hereby declared an open city without the characteristics of a military objective. In order that no excuse may be given for a possible attack, the American High Commissioner, the Commonwealth Government and all combatant military installations will be withdrawn from its environs as rapidly as possible. The municipal government will continue to function with its police force, reinforced by constabulatory troops, so that the normal protection of life and property may be preserved. Citizens are requested to maintain obedience to constituted authorities and continue the normal processes of business."

The next day the Japanese bombed Manila heavily, concentrating on the residential districts and killing 40 and wounding at least 150. In one church the people were at their prayers when the bomb hit; they never had a chance. MacArthur's headquarters announced bitterly that night: "Until Manila was declared an open city it was noticeable that the Japanese did not attempt to attack civilian installations from the air, but as soon as the army, including anti-aircraft protection, was withdrawn, they immediately raided, hitting all types of civilian premises including churches, convents, the cathedral, business houses and residences." After the savage air attack MacArthur studied the reports on the ruin of the ancient city and publicly called on the American government for retaliation at the proper time and place.

Not only retaliation, but the life of the Philippines waited on American forces. MacArthur had won the first round, but he realized that all he could do with his slender resources was fight for time. Only the arrival of aid from the United States could save the Philippines now.

CHAPTER III   "I don't want to *see* your 155's, Jim,
I want to *hear* them."

❧ Even before World War II there was magic in the word Bataan. To the sailors it is towering breakwater, extended to shelter Manila from the lashing of the South China Sea. To the geographer it is a fantastic conglomeration of tangled jungle, open plains, sea-beaten cliffs, and quiet, sandy bays. To the tourist the sun setting over the saddle of Mariveles Mountain is one of the glorious sights of the Pacific. To the Filipino, watching that same brilliant sunset at the end of the day's work, Bataan is a gentle reminder that this land is indeed the "Pearl of the Orient."

It was to Bataan that the colorful revolutionary Aguinaldo and his band had fled from the pursuit of General Arthur MacArthur a generation before. It was to Bataan that American and Filipino soldiers now looked as the battlefield where they would face the supreme test of valor and faith, under the leadership of Arthur MacArthur's son, General Douglas McArthur.

MacArthur knew Bataan well, long before he took his stand there against the Japanese. In 1903, when he had been stationed in the Philippines as assistant to the chief engineer officer of the Philippine Division, he had surveyed part of the peninsula. So he knew that Bataan, only thirty miles long and fifteen miles wide at its base, was an excellent place for a tactical defense. For the defender there was cover in the jungle fastness of gum trees, ipils, and the famous hard-grain Philippine mahogany, all entangled with enormous vines. The banyan trees were so large that protective shelters could be carved out of their trunks. Only one flank, the South China Sea coastline, was exposed to the enemy. So much of it was booby-trapped with sharp coral outcroppings that amphibious landings were difficult, and the sheer drop along almost the entire western and southern approaches, as much as one hundred feet, made envelopment by sea all but impossible. For the attacker the jungle inland was a green hell, clotted with fibrous undergrowth, cogon grass, inhabited by pythons, and indented by rock cliffs and treacherous rivers. Astride the enemy's route of advance lay the precipitous Zambales mountain range, running from 4,222-foot-high Mount Natib in the north to 4,722-foot-high Mount Mariveles in the south. MacArthur knew that Bataan had its liabilities for defender as well as attacker. But it was the best choice—indeed, the only choice—for a final stand that would give him the time he needed so desperately.

At the tip of Bataan—actually thirty miles out in Manila Bay, but a part of Bataan as far as his defense set-up was concerned—stood Corregidor. MacArthur established his headquarters there for the battle of Bataan. With him went his family, just as his mother, his brother, and young Douglas had accompanied Arthur MacArthur to an isolated and dangerous outpost in those frontier days when army garrisons stood vigil over the westward advance of American civilization. To Jean Faircloth MacArthur this was normal army life. To their child, Arthur, who was almost four, it was little more than an adventure; he took with him a favorite stuffed rabbit (which he still clutched in his arms when he arrived in Australia two months later).

MacArthur also took to Corregidor Arthur's governess, Ah Cheu (to save her from certain torture and death), U.S. High Commissioner Francis Sayre and his wife, and Philippines President Manuel Quezon and his family. President Quezon was suffering from tuberculosis and barely able to walk, but he bore up stubbornly and cheerfully under the rigors of life on Corregidor. It was a moving scene when, on December 30, just outside MacArthur's headquarters in Malinta Tunnel and to the accompaniment of Japanese bombs, Quezon was sworn in for his second term as President of the Commonwealth of the Philippines.

Thus the seat of government of the Philippines was a five-mile-long island best described by its nickname, the "Rock." On Corregidor's three terraces, Topside, Middleside, and Bottomside, were some barracks, two small schools and their playgrounds, an Army club, tiny Kindley Air Field, and a few gun positions. There was little more above ground. Below, intertwined tunnels had been drilled in the solid rock. Some of the corridors contained small trolleys; all of them were strung with communications wires. In the bigger rooms were a hospital, a storeroom, some living-quarters, and a war office.

At first MacArthur chose for his residence a cottage perched on the rocks of Topside. But Japanese bombing destroyed it, and at the insistent pleading of his staff he moved to safer quarters, a little gray cottage

"I don't want to see your 155's, Jim, I want to hear them."

at Bottomside, a quarter of a mile from Malinta Tunnel. Here he and his family settled down, on half-rations, for the duration of the battle of Bataan.

His routine was little changed from what it had been at his office in Manila. Dressed in light khaki trousers and shirt, his four stars (he was now a full general) and his brown shoes brightly shined, he had a light breakfast with Chief of Staff Sutherland. Smoking a Lucky Strike in his long black holder, he walked briskly to his office, where his desk and Sutherland's were placed side by side. The first business of the day was reading the cables from the U.S., reviewing the night's developments on Bataan and whatever might have happened in the rest of the Philippine Islands. Then he studied the news from the rest of the world—in the North African desert, the British, reinforced by U.S. tanks, were beating Rommel; on the Oka River, Russian troops, aided by bitter winter weather and reinforced by U.S. Lend-Lease, were blocking the *Panzers* of Hitler's crack tank general, Heinz Guderian; in the Pacific, with no U.S. reinforcements, Allied soldiers were falling back before the enemy in Indochina, Malaya, Borneo, and Burma. Only in the Philippines had the Japanese been stopped.

After studying these dispatches, MacArthur turned his attention back to Bataan. As he planned his strategy, he paced up and down his small office, thinking out loud and occasionally giving an order to Sutherland or another of the officers who gathered for this morning conference. The orders came fast, and were as simple and direct as they were urgent.

MacArthur regrouped his Bataan defense into two corps, placing the First Corps, under Wainwright, on the western side and the Second Corps, under Major General George M. Parker, on the eastern side. He improvised new artillery regiments by gathering up miscellaneous elements, in an effort to reduce the enemy's great artillery superiority. He had two runways hastily constructed at the southern end of the peninsula, to serve as a base for the few remaining P-40's. He had a new hospital established at Cabcaben, to supplement the hospital facilities he had had set up earlier in anticipation of the battle of Bataan. He arranged for emergency provisions for the care of the thousands of civilian refugees who had swarmed onto Bataan with the troops; isolated as Bataan was, the job of providing food, transportation, and medical care for the peninsula's swollen civilian populace was staggering. This multitude of problems confronted MacArthur every day, and he disposed of them in typical fashion, discussing them with his staff and calmly issuing orders as he paced up and down in his office inside the "Rock."

His lunch would have been light even if he had not been on half-rations. Sometimes he ate it with members of his staff, calling them by their first names as the discussions went on. Sometimes he ate with Mrs. MacArthur, at a picnic table outside his office, under the speckled shade of the camouflage nets. After lunch came the only relaxation in his long day: with his black cigarette-holder in his mouth, he sprawled on a settee and listened to the news over the radio. This usually lasted only ten or fifteen minutes.

But always his thoughts came back to Bataan. What galled him more than almost anything else about the battle of Bataan was that, by its very nature, he could not be there personally. Not only was there no way to supervise the over-all strategy from any command post save Corregidor, but the shifting battle positions in the peninsula's pathless jungle made a comprehensive inspection of front-line positions physically impossible.

When he made the effort, however, he learned details that would never have reached his Corregidor command post. At a tiny air-strip hacked out of the jungle, sweating mechanics were cannibalizing wrecked P-40's; that meant his pitiful air force would have two more planes to fly by the next day. Along the rifle pits of an outpost line, where machine guns and monkeys chattered alternately and thick dust filled everyone's eyes and throat, the stench of dead Japanese a few yards away in the steaming jungle told him that another attack had been stopped. At a command post hidden in a valley a sweat-streaked officer told him that the enemy was resorting to incendiary bombs, but their phosphorus was inferior, and the green, tropical growth of the jungle was not so inflammable as it looked from the air, even in the dry season. At a hospital station, marked with an enormous red cross but bombed by the Japanese just the same, he learned that the malarial mosquito was causing more casualties than enemy bullets; another natural enemy was gas gangrene, maiming hundreds because there was not enough vaccine to combat it. Against the Japanese the troops were doing better than against disease. Outnumbered ten to one at some points, they were holding the line, despite fanatical troops who set off firecrackers and beat drums during attacks and snipers who were masters at silent camouflage.

But more important than all the information MacArthur could get on his visit to Bataan was the stimulus that it gave to his weary men. Their morale was good partly because it was MacArthur who led them—a heroic figure who would fight the Japanese, if need be, alone. They passed among themselves sayings attributed to him: When a Japanese submarine shelled California, MacArthur told Sutherland: "Wire them that if

24

"I don't want to see your 155's, Jim, I want to hear them."

they can hold out for thirty days, we'll send help." When his aides asked that the flag be removed from atop his GHQ because it was a perfect target for Japanese bombers, he said: "Take every precaution, but keep the colors flying." This was the kind of talk that struck a responsive chord in men fighting in the jungles of Bataan. The effect was even greater when he actually appeared among them.

Unexpectedly, at a front-line position they looked up and there he was. The famous cap, the brown walking-stick, the corncob pipe, the ribbonless but sharply pressed shirt, the plain leather jacket, the khaki trousers and shining shoes—these constituted his trademark. The sight of him suddenly in the jungle gave his troops the lift they needed, and MacArthur knew it. His flair for mixing the dramatic appearance with the dignity of command was never so effective as on Bataan. Even where the battle had been going badly, he flashed his wide smile of reassurance, and his men smiled back. Despite the weight of responsibilities and worry on his shoulders, he walked straight as a ramrod, looked twenty years under his actual age, and was seemingly unconcerned and confident of victory. And everywhere he pressed the fight harder against the enemy. When he asked Wainwright where his 155's were, Wainwright offered to show them to him. MacArthur answered: "Jim, I don't want to *see* them; I want to *hear* them."

His men already knew his reputation for utter fearlessness, and on Bataan he proved it. When a flight of Japanese bombers came over and the troops broke for cover, they looked back, found MacArthur still standing there studying the planes through binoculars, and climbed sheepishly out of their slit trenches. Despite repeated warnings, MacArthur refused to skulk from cover to cover, even in the no-man's-land of the front. His men, watching him, knowing that snipers were everywhere and knowing their marked preference for officers, admired MacArthur more than ever and fought harder than ever for him. It has always been this kind of leadership that has enabled him to get more out of his men than any other general, and on Bataan he was at his best. Part of the glory of Bataan will always be the personal glory of MacArthur.

Back on Corregidor for supper and a cigar, MacArthur spent the evening reviewing what he had read in the dispatches and what he had seen on Bataan and trying to fit all the pieces together. As he thought, sometimes out loud to Sutherland or another staff officer, he continued his pacing, up and down his office. He has walked as much as five miles a day just in his office, in the endless pacing that he finds helps him think most clearly.

25

MacArthur could take pride in the fact that the battle of Bataan was going better than anyone had expected, despite a total lack of outside support. Literally inspired by his leadership, the Americans and Filipinos were taking everything thrown at them by thoroughly seasoned enemy troops. His troops were inflicting four casualties on the enemy for every one of their own. General Masaharu Homma, the plump commander of the Japanese attack on the Philippines, had been enraged at the way Mac-Arthur had given him the slip and maneuvered onto Bataan. He threw the full weight of his forces against MacArthur's lines, and was sent reeling back with sickening casualties. Finally, by killing thousands of his men, he forced the defenders back, only to have MacArthur counterattack in a brilliant stroke that broke the Japanese advance again. MacArthur, incidentally, celebrated his birthday with this counterattack—just the kind of gesture to amuse and please his men. Homma, fought to a standstill, outmaneuvered and outfoxed by MacArthur, waited for the best reinforcements that Tokyo could send him, which arrived in due course. Meanwhile, MacArthur waited too. But Washington sent him no reinforcements.

CHAPTER IV   "I plan to fight to the complete
destruction of our forces. . . ."

▰ While MacArthur, alone of all commanders in the Pacific, was stopping
the enemy in his tracks, he was being sacrificed in Washington. The administration, deliberately or not, subjected him and his men to one of the
cruelest deceptions of the war. Not only were no large reinforcements
sent to the Philippines, but, more important, the administration *never intended to send them and concealed the fact that they would not be sent.*

Every morning in his Corregidor office MacArthur studied the dispatches that told him the progress of World War II. He realized that the
enemy was apparently trying to seal him off and thereby increase Washington's difficulty in sending help. But he knew that the Japanese "blockade" was much more a paper blockade than enemy propaganda (and,
evidently, Washington) made it out to be. He also knew that Lend-Lease
supplies were pouring across the Atlantic to places like North Africa for
seesaw tank battles in the desert wastes, to places like England for an invasion that was not planned for three years, and to places like Communist
Russia. He also knew that, despite its Pearl Harbor losses, the U.S. Fleet,
if concentrated, was still large enough to cut a path through the Japanese
ships supposedly surrounding the Philippines and thereafter keep open
the line of supply across the Pacific.

What he did not know was that in the Pentagon and the White House
the decision had already been made to fight "Europe first." Instead, this is
what he had been told:

On December 28, after three weeks of World War II, President Roosevelt issued a message addressed and broadcast to the people of the
Philippines. "News of your gallant struggle against the Japanese aggressors," it said, "has elicited the profound admiration of every American.
As President of the United States, I know that I speak for all our people
on this solemn occasion. The resources of the United States, of the British

Empire, of the Netherlands East Indies, and the Chinese Republic have been dedicated by their people to the utter and complete defeat of the Japanese warlords . . . I give to the people of the Philippines my solemn pledge that their freedom will be redeemed and their independence established and protected. The entire resources in men and materials of the United States stand behind that pledge. . . .

"I give you this message from the Navy," the broadcast went on. "The Navy Department tonight announced the Japanese government is circulating rumors for the obvious purpose of persuading the United States to disclose the location and intentions of the American Pacific Fleets. It is obvious that these rumors are intended for, and directed at, the Philippine Islands. The Philippines may rest assured that, while the United States Navy will not be tricked into disclosing vital information, the Fleet is not idle. The United States Navy is following an intensive and well-planned campaign against Japanese forces which will result in positive assistance to the defense of the Philippine Islands."

MacArthur accepted the message at face value. It said simply and plainly that the U.S. Navy was following a campaign that would "result in positive assistance to the defense of the Philippine Islands."

If MacArthur was misled by this message, he was far from alone. When President Quezon read it in his quarters in Corregidor's Malinta Tunnel, where he fought against his tuberculosis, he came to the same conclusion. His elation at the news is recorded in his memoirs, *The Good Fight*. "On reading the message," he writes, "I was instantly electrified and thrilled. The dungeon, where my sick body was lying, lost its depressing gloom. I asked to be taken out to the open space, for the world was too small to contain the emotions that almost burst my heart. . . . I held a cabinet meeting and read it to them. Giving vent to my feelings, I told my colleagues that the sacrifices our country was making were not in vain. . . . The Philippines would not only be independent and free, but its independence and freedom were to be protected and safeguarded by the 'entire resources in men and materials of the United States.'"

In order to reassure the worrying Filipino people, Quezon issued a proclamation: "The President of the United States . . . solemnly pledged that the freedom of our country will be preserved. . . . You are therefore fighting with America because America is fighting for our freedom. . . . America will not abandon us. Her help will not be delayed. . . . We must resist further advance of the enemy until assistance arrives, which will be soon." The significance of this proclamation could not possibly have been lost on Washington. Had the message intended to hedge on this vital point, had President Roosevelt meant even to suggest that help might be delayed, someone in the government should have informed MacArthur or Quezon that the message had been misinterpreted. No one did.

Even if this was an oversight, the administration had enough further opportunity to correct any misinterpretation. U.S. High Commissioner Sayre, in a statement broadcast from Manila by the National Broadcasting Company and carried in the American press, made the same positive declaration that the government had promised reinforcements. "Help is surely coming," Commissioner Sayre announced, "help of sufficient adequacy and power that the invader will be driven from our midst and he will be rendered powerless to ever threaten us again." This was the statement of the official representative of President Roosevelt in the Philippines. But no one in Washington indicated that Commissioner Sayre had been misled.

If this was a misinterpretation of the President's message, it was repeated right at home, in the *New York Times* of December 29. The *Times* story ran under a banner headline that read: "ALL AID PROMISED. PRESIDENT PLEDGES PROTECTION. NAVY SAYS OUR FLEET IS NOT DESTROYED AND WILL HELP DEFENSE." The account, written by Thomas J. Hamilton, repeated the President's and the Navy's assurances, and quoted William D. Hassett, White House Secretary, as explaining that the message was designed "to offset false propaganda from Tokyo," adding that "the Japanese have been saying the American Fleet has been sunk and a lot of lies." And the *New York Times* story concluded with a paragraph that, in the light of what has happened since, is of utmost importance. "Some comment was aroused," the paragraph read, "by the President's use of the phrase to 'redeem' the freedom of the Philippines, *which might be interpreted to mean that their temporary loss was expected. But Mr. Hassett summarily rejected all suggestions that the message could be regarded as any kind of a valedictory over the defenders of the Philippines."* [1]

The next day, the *Times* reported, presidential aide Stephen Early told reporters that they might be reading "too much of the immediate rather than the ultimate" into the President's message, adding that the problem of getting help to the Philippines would take time. "You must consider distances," he cautioned. But Early then carefully made it clear that he did not expect the Philippines to fall for lack of reinforcements. The *Times* account states: *"The Presidential secretary insisted, however, that he saw nothing in the President's statement that would justify an interpretation that Mr. Roosevelt was preparing the nation for the loss of*

[1] Italics in this chapter have been added by me.

the Philippines." To be absolutely certain, a reporter asked Early again *if the "redeemed" phrase was intended to hint that aid would get there too late to prevent the loss of the Philippines. Early said: "No, I shouldn't think so. I saw nothing in the statement to justify that."*

In other words, if President Roosevelt meant, or was even implying, that relief could not reach the Philippines before they fell, he was keeping this fact even from his own White House secretaries.

On New Year's Day, MacArthur received a query from General George C. Marshall, Army Chief of Staff, inquiring as to the possibility of evacuating President Quezon and his official family from Corregidor to the Southern Islands. Quezon's response to this suggestion, which MacArthur transmitted immediately, was to inquire, politely but directly, whether or not reinforcements were coming. "I am willing to do what the government of the United States may think that will be more helpful for the successful prosecution of the war," he said. "My immediate concern, however, is to secure prompt and adequate help from the United States because our soldiers at the front and the Filipino people in general have placed their trust in this indispensable help coming from America, especially after the proclamation of the President and the announcement by the Navy which gave them the impression that help is forthcoming."

There could have been no plainer notice served on Washington that Quezon expected "prompt and adequate" help from America. But Washington did nothing to disabuse him of the idea. In fact, no one deigned to answer his question.

MacArthur promptly put his own query to Washington, outlining the strategic situation as he saw it at the time and pointing out what Washington should have known already: "I wish to re-emphasize," he said, "my firm belief that . . . yielding of the Philippines by default and without a major effort would mark the end of white prestige and influence in the East. In view of the Filipinos' effort the United States must move strongly to their support and promptly, or withdraw in shame from the Orient." To appreciate the prophecy of that statement one need only read the newspapers and consider the extent of American prestige in the Orient today.

Characteristically, MacArthur made this plea for more troops not in the form of predictions of defeat, but in a plan for action and victory. Mindanao, he pointed out, could be readied for an expeditionary force, with its Del Monte airfield providing a base for supporting planes. The relief action would start with attacks by the bombers that had had to flee to Australia and the new planes that had joined them there. "Our air force bombardment missions from the south should quickly eliminate hostile air from Davao," he wired, "and our pursuit should go into Del Monte without delay. Establishment of air force will permit immediate extension into Visayas and attacks on enemy forces in Luzon. . . . An Army corps should be landed in Mindanao at the earliest possible date. . . . Enemy appears to have tendency to be overconfident, and time is ripe for brilliant thrust with air carriers."

Here was the succinct outline of a carefully planned surprise counterattack intended to do for the strategy of the entire Pacific war what Mac-Arthur had been doing day after day on Bataan. It was a plan that Mac-Arthur still thinks would have reversed the course of the war in that area. It was the product of many hours' sweat and study by MacArthur's hard-pressed staff on Corregidor, the product of many hours' pacing by Mac-Arthur, far into the night in his office inside the "Rock."

But Washington evidently did not even dignify the plan with any kind of careful study. Worse than that, Washington's response was to continue the deception. Certainly this was a point at which MacArthur should have been informed that, for whatever opinion sincerely if erroneously held at the time, the plan could not be implemented because no troops or planes could be sent. Instead, the reply to Corregidor was hedging but still hopeful. General Marshall wired that he and all the other officials "have been studying every possibility looking forward to *the quick development of strength in the Far East so as to break the enemy's hold on the Philippines. . . . Every day of time you gain is vital to the concentration of overwhelming power necessary for our purpose."*

But time went on, Americans and Filipinos died on Bataan, and still no reinforcements came. President Quezon tried again to get a clear answer from Washington. In a note addressed to MacArthur but later conceded in his memoirs to have been intended primarily for President Roosevelt, Quezon first reiterated the fact that no people deserved support more than the Filipinos. Fighting with nothing but promises from the U.S., they were still fiercely resisting the blandishments of the Japanese. Even the so-called quislings who, the enemy announced, had accepted posts in an occupation government were loyal to the country that had so far let them down. "I have no direct information," Quezon said, "concerning the veracity of the news broadcasts from Tokyo that a commission composed of some well-known Filipinos has been recently organized in Manila to take charge of certain functions of civil government. The organization of such a Commission, if true, can have no political significance, not only because it is charged with purely administrative functions, but also because the acquiescence by its members to serve on the Commission was evidently for the purpose of safeguarding the welfare of the civilian population and can in no way reflect the sentiments of the Filipinos toward the enemy. . . ."

Then Quezon, confidentially to MacArthur but still intended for President Roosevelt, repeated the question he had asked before in vain. This time his plea, though still clear and to the point, was also an eloquent expression from a great leader in sorrow over the slaughter of his people. "I am going to open my mind and my heart to you," he wrote. "We are before the bar of history, and God only knows if this is the last time that my voice will be heard before going to my grave. My loyalty and the loyalty of the Filipino people to America has been proven beyond question. . . . But it seems to me questionable whether any government has the right to demand loyalty from its citizens beyond its willingness or ability to render actual protection. . . . We have done the best we could. . . . But how long are we to be left alone? *Has it already been decided in Washington that the Philippine front is of no importance as far as the final result of the war is concerned and that, therefore, no help can be expected here in the immediate future, or at least before the power of resistance is exhausted?* If so, I want to know, because I have my own responsibility to my countrymen whom, as President of the Commonwealth, I have led into a complete war effort. I am greatly concerned as well regarding the soldiers I have called to the colors and who are now manning the firing line. I want to decide in my own mind whether there is justification for allowing all these men to be killed when, for the final outcome of the war, the shedding of their blood may be wholly unnecessary. . . ."

The question could not have been put more directly or movingly. MacArthur passed it on to President Roosevelt immediately. Roosevelt's reply to Quezon stated that "I appreciate completely your position." "I solemnly state," he promised, "that I would never ask of you and [your countrymen] any sacrifice that I believed was without hope. . . ." He praised "the superb defense" of the men on Bataan as "a definite contribution in bringing about an eventual and complete overwhelming of the enemy in the Far East." He apologized for the "deficiency which now exists in our offensive weapons" and explained that early in the war "reverses, hardships and pain are the price that democracy must pay" for being peaceful nations.

The message went on in such vein at length, carefully avoiding a direct answer to Quezon's direct question. Then he gave a half-answer:

"I plan to fight to the complete destruction of our forces. . . ."

"Although I cannot at this time state the day that help will arrive in the Philippines, *I can assure you that every vessel available is bearing to the southwest Pacific the strength that will eventually crush the enemy and liberate your native land.* Vessels in that vicinity have been filled with cargos of necessary supplies and have been dispatched to Manila. Our arms, together with those of our Allies, have dealt heavy blows to enemy transports and naval vessels and are most certainly retarding his movement to the south. By the trans-African route and lately by the Pacific route our heavy bombers are each day joining General Wavell's command. A continuous stream of fighters and pursuit planes is traversing the Pacific; already 10 squadrons of the foregoing types are ready for combat in the southwest Pacific area. Extensive arrivals of troops are being guarded by adequate protective elements of our Navy. The heroes of Bataan are effectively assisting by gaining invaluable time, and time is the vital factor in reinforcing our military strength in this theater of war."

Perhaps apologists for Roosevelt can interpret this message to mean that all these troops and arms were going everywhere but the Philippines; that they were being massed, not to relieve the desperate men on Bataan, but to "liberate" the Philippines in a year or two, by which time the Islands would most certainly have fallen. The answer to that argument is that if President Roosevelt meant that aid could not come to the Philippines for many months, all he had to do was say so. Faced with the direct question, he not only refused to answer frankly, but misled those whose fate hung in the balance.

Perhaps apologists for Roosevelt can argue that he hedged on his answer because he did not yet know, because there was still a chance to get reinforcements to the Philippines in time. The answer to that argument is that there was not enough time. And he did know.

The proof that he knew, and that this was intentional deception, is contained in Dwight Eisenhower's book, *Crusade in Europe*. During this period Eisenhower was a brigadier general in the War Department's plans-and-operations division. As he relates in his book, he reported on the prospects of the Philippines to his superior, General Marshall.

"General," Eisenhower said, "it will be a long time before major reinforcements can go to the Philippines, *longer than the garrison can hold out with any driblet assistance.*"

Marshall replied: "I agree with you."

This conference took place on December 14, 1941, two weeks before President Roosevelt's first message of reassurance and the Navy's promise of aid to the Philippines. During all the rest of December and January, while President Roosevelt and General Marshall kept promising that help was on the way, they knew that by formal policy already worked out with Churchill and the Joint Chiefs of Staff meeting in Washington, the priority would go to Europe first. It was that simple; they had handed MacArthur the stewardship of a military disaster. And what made it one of the cruelest deceptions of the war was that they not only did not tell MacArthur, but instead tried with every circumlocution possible to pretend the opposite of the truth.

There *was* a convoy of reinforcements which might have helped, small though it was in comparison with MacArthur's needs. Seven ships, carrying some troops, artillery, fighter planes, anti-aircraft guns, ammunition, and miscellaneous equipment, were en route to the Philippines when the war broke out. The convoy was directed into Suva, in the Fijis, where it sat for four days while the Army and Navy in Washington wrangled over whether it should go on to the Philippines or return to Pearl Harbor. It was finally directed to Brisbane, Australia. By that time the Japanese had thrown their blockade around the Philippines.

As soon as he learned of the decision, MacArthur met with Admiral Hart and asked him if he could furnish, with his Asiatic Fleet and help from the Allies, enough naval and air protection to get these vital supplies through. Hart knew about this convoy. Admiral Stark had wired him from Washington, telling him of its existence but saying nothing about its being a reinforcement for the Philippines. In fact, Stark had hinted that the artillery and aircraft in the convoy would "be very important for the defense of Port Darwin [Australia], and vicinity." Hart said that the Allied navies were too busy defending Singapore and the Malay Barrier, and he dared not attempt to pierce the Japanese blockade with his own fleet alone.

In Washington, Admiral Stark backed up Hart's decision. This was at a time when in the Atlantic convoys were still running to Murmansk, despite casualties up to eighty per cent. Not a ship, a gun, or a bullet from that convoy reached the Philippines. Nor did any more bombers come up from Australia, though there was even less risk for them.

Meanwhile, planning his desperate strategy on Corregidor and walking among his desperate men on Bataan, MacArthur could only believe what Washington told him. But he could see that the GI's and Filipinos were beginning to believe that they would be betrayed. Every time he talked with his subordinate commanders, he was confronted with the same question: "How much longer? When will the reinforcements arrive?" His soldiers were fighting on quarter-rations, dropping with tropi-

cal disease, watching their ranks thin day by day. They had had to fall
back to the second major line of defense.

The enemy was attacking them with a highly developed campaign of
psychological warfare. A constant barrage of leaflets was dropped on
them, alternately cajoling and threatening, but all urging the futility of
further resistance. Radio broadcasts from Tokyo and Manila, some by
Americans forced into so unpleasant a task, beamed a steady flow of the
same propaganda at the troops. One such broadcast from Tokyo even
depicted a playlet in which MacArthur, defeated and taken prisoner, was
publicly executed in the park overlooking the Imperial Palace. The theme
was always the same: "America is not sending help. You have been left to
die."

Generally, the soldiers' morale stood up well against this campaign.
As usual with GI's in adversity, they were partly sustained by a wry sense
of humor. On a tree in the jungle someone nailed a calendar painting of a
sailing-ship loafing along before a gentle breeze; under it was the notice:
"WE TOLD YOU SO. HELP IS ON THE WAY." Some of the men organized
a "Bomber for Bataan" fund. One soldier asked a war correspondent to
deliver a message to the President: "DEAR PRESIDENT ROOSEVELT, OUR P-40
IS FULL OF HOLES. PLEASE SEND US ANOTHER."

Despite such evidences of sturdy morale so far, MacArthur knew
that half-starved, fever-ridden men can keep fighting only while they
still have hope. So on January 15 he published a general order to his
troops, repeating Washington's promise of help and adding: "it is a question now of courage and determination. . . . I call upon every soldier in
Bataan to fight in his assigned position, resisting every attack. This is the
only road to salvation. If we fight we will win, if we retreat we will be
destroyed." Again he inspired his men. It was after this message that they
stopped the enemy's all-out attack on the second line of defense and drove
the Japanese back all along the line.

This message to the troops had its effect in Washington, too, it later
developed. Eleven years after the event an apologist for Roosevelt made
one more vicious stab at MacArthur. William D. Hassett, former White
House Secretary, was quoted in his diary in the *Saturday Evening Post*
(October 17, 1953) as saying that Roosevelt had decried MacArthur's
message of hope. The entry is dated July 11, 1942. The President, it recalled, "said MacArthur's assurances to his men early in December—after
the Japanese attack—that ample reinforcements of men, planes, tanks,
and matériel were on the way and would reach the Philippines very soon,
in ample time to relieve shortages—were unjustifiable. MacArthur knew

this was not true. He [the President] said it was justifiable to give incorrect information in some circumstances in time of war, but criminal to raise false hopes—hopes that MacArthur knew could not be fulfilled."

This is a strange statement indeed. MacArthur gave no assurance to his troops that help was coming "early in December"; he gave none until the General Order he published on January 15. This in itself casts doubt upon the entry. MacArthur did *not* know that no help was coming, as I have just documented. Not only had President Roosevelt given his and the Navy's assurances of prompt aid, but it was the same William D. Hassett (this is more than irony) who, as representative of the President, had publicly rejected any interpretation of Roosevelt's message other than that of a promise of reinforcements. The President's choice of July 1942 for an observation of this kind is incongruous. It was six months after the fact and two months after he had personally awarded MacArthur the Congressional Medal of Honor, the highest decoration in the U.S.

Certainly President Roosevelt more than anyone else, with the possible exception of General Marshall, knew who was the deceiver and who the deceived. The question arises whether Roosevelt made such a statement. It is strange that Hassett, who had given newspapermen assurances of aid to the Philippines, would let such a remark by the President go unchallenged; if he were afraid to speak up in Roosevelt's presence, certainly he would comment on it later when noting it in his diary. All this permits the inference that President Roosevelt never made such a deliberately defamatory reference to MacArthur.

The deception practiced on MacArthur brought tragedy to thousands of Americans and more thousands of Filipinos. And the basis for this deception, the global planning behind it, has brought tragedy to the world. At that time in Europe the British were at least temporarily withstanding General Rommel's threat to the Middle East, and the Russian armies were digging in for their successful defense of Stalingrad. Our earliest target date for attack on Europe from the west was still two to three years off. In the Pacific, despite the U.S. naval losses at Pearl Harbor and the British loss of the *Prince of Wales* and the *Repulse*, we still had enough naval power to engage any Axis fleet. We proved this only six months later when, with practically no new major elements added to our naval arm, we scored decisive victories in the battles of Coral Sea and Midway. But we chose to withhold our punch in the Pacific.

It was a major strategic blunder, one for which we have already paid dearly and one for which we will continue to pay for a long time to come. It established the basic "Europe-first" concept that not only set up an automatic military priority for Europe but also assumed unnecessary defeats in other vital areas of the world.

It shaped our military-political policy then, and its shadow does today. It led to an isolation in military planning which completely ignored the relative strategic values in the struggle for world dominance. It set in motion a chain of events whose disastrous effect has perhaps never been equaled in the modern world. It not only permitted but encouraged the marauding conquests of the Japanese in the rest of the Pacific Basin. It helped Japan ravish the Philippines and other friendly lands in the Southwest Pacific, down to the very threshold of Australia. It was the motivating influence behind the political blunders of General Marshall which did so much to lose the Chinese mainland to Communism. Later on it was responsible for the inane policy of "priorities" which prevented us from mounting maximum strength against an enemy we were fighting in Korea because men and materials were siphoned off for stationing opposite an enemy we were not fighting in Europe—and one we openly conceded we would not be able to fight for two years at the earliest.

Had we elected to stop Japan's advance at the outset, when MacArthur wanted us to (and had a plan for doing it), we would have avoided the costly tragedy of the long-drawn-out Pacific war. Japan's Axis partners, stymied at that time in the Middle East and on the eastern front, would have suffered a psychological setback of major proportions. And we would have preserved Asia from the ravages of Communist imperialism. Thus, even apart from the cruel deception practiced on our defending forces and the Philippine people, our decision to start the Pacific war by losing it was one of the most tragic ever made in the history of the nation.

As for the immediate situation on Corregidor and Bataan, that decision led to three messages between MacArthur and his Commander-in-Chief in February 1942, messages that are eloquent in their simplicity and in the deep significance behind them.

The first was a routine, dispassionate report from MacArthur: "My estimate of the military situation here," he wired, "is as follows: the troops have sustained practically 50% casualties from their original strength. Divisions are reduced to the size of regiments, regiments to battalions, battalions to companies. Some units have entirely disappeared. The men have been in constant action and are badly battle worn. They are desperately in need of rest and refitting. Their spirit is good, but they are capable now of nothing but fighting in place on a fixed position. All our supplies are scant, and the command has been on half rations for the past month. It is possible for the time being that the present enemy force might temporarily be held, but any addition to his present strength will ensure the destruction of our whole force. We have pulled through a number of menacing situations, but there is no denying of the fact that we are near done. Corregidor itself is extremely vulnerable. This type of fortress, built prior to the days of air power, when isolated is impossible of prolonged defense. . . . Since I have no air or sea protection, you must be prepared at any time to figure on the complete destruction of this command. . . ."

The reply from Roosevelt, for MacArthur's eyes only, was peremptory and read like a farewell. It forbade surrender "as long as there remains any possibility of resistance. . . . It is mandatory that there be established once and for all in the minds of all peoples complete evidence that the American determination and indomitable will to win carries on down to the last unit. I, therefore, give you this most difficult mission in full understanding of the desperate situation to which you may shortly be reduced. The service that you and the American members of your command can render to your country in the titanic struggle now developing, is beyond all possibility of appraisement. . . ."

The third message, from MacArthur to Roosevelt, sounded the death knell of the men on Bataan—and American prestige in Asia. It read: "I plan to fight to the complete destruction of our forces on Bataan and then to do the same on Corregidor. . . ."

CHAPTER V   "It's time to mount up, Jeannie."

⚜ In the same message in which he promised his Commander-in-Chief that he would fight "to the complete destruction" of his forces, MacArthur added a note that was in keeping with his soldier's faith and in the stern tradition of his soldier's family. "I will remain and share the fate of the garrison," he said. "My family, with whom I have consulted, wish to remain with me to such end and I will not interfere with their decision."

This statement was partly in answer to an earlier query from General Marshall, one that had shocked MacArthur for two reasons. In the first place, it was only by way of an offhand question that official Washington finally revealed to MacArthur the all-important decision to surrender the Philippines temporarily to the enemy. No announcement of this decision was sent to the man responsible for the defense of the Philippines. Instead, the news was merely hinted at in a message from Marshall. After inquiring about the future disposition of Filipino troops, the Chief of Staff went on: "The most important question concerns your possible movements should your forces be unable longer to sustain themselves in Bataan and there should remain nothing but the fortress defense of Corregidor. Under these conditions the need for your services there might be less pressing than at other points in the Far East.

"There seem to be but two possible courses of action: the first is that you, at least initially, proceed to Mindanao. How long you would remain there would depend on the good you might do toward stimulating guerrilla operations in the Visayas and Mindanao. . . . From there you could later proceed south to resume command of the United States forces in the Far East. The alternative would be for you to proceed south direct without pause in Mindanao. . . . The purpose of this message is to secure from you a highly confidential statement of your own views. It is understood that in case of your withdrawal from immediate leadership of your

39

beleaguered forces is to be carried out, it will be by direct order of the President to you. What I want are your views in advance of a decision."

Then General Marshall added a strange conclusion: "No record is being made of this message within the War Department, and I have arranged that your reply labeled personal to General Marshall for his eyes only, will come direct from the decoding clerk to me with no copy retained and no other individual involved."

This was the second surprise in Marshall's message—the statement that MacArthur's order to leave the Philippines would come from the President himself, coupled with the curious note about extra secrecy (an assurance, by the way, that is belied by the fact that I found a copy in the War Department files last year). Was Marshall threatening ahead of time to "use the Commander-in-Chief on him"? If so, why then was he asking for MacArthur's views? And why the precautions about copies of the message, an unprecedented precaution that went far beyond the normal requirements of military security? Was Marshall making the gratuitous implication that his subordinate could thus speak freely? Was he setting any kind of trap? MacArthur could only guess at the answers.

There is, incidentally, in all this the suggestion that MacArthur was not always subordinate in his messages to his Washington superiors. This slur is part of the carefully repeated legend that his messages to the Pentagon and the White House were sometimes intemperate and that they were given special treatment when received. Not only is this incompatible with MacArthur's character and training as a soldier, but it has no basis in the record. I have been given free access to his official and personal correspondence, and, despite a careful search, I have found nothing even slightly resembling the type of bristling messages he is reported to have sent. Incisive, yes; positive in his estimates and firm in his recommendations, yes; but unfailingly subordinate in tone. Nothing has ever been produced to support the myth of MacArthur as an argumentative, insolent, and insubordinate field officer.

While the question of MacArthur's departure was still being discussed in the messages radioed back and forth between Washington and Corregidor, he was handed a message for President Roosevelt from President Quezon. It reflected all the bitter resentment that had welled up in Filipino hearts because of the failure of American protection. But it also contained a concrete suggestion. After pointing out that America promised aid and never sent it, Quezon made it clear that the Filipinos were "concerned with what is to transpire during the next few months and years as well as with our ultimate destiny. There is not the slightest doubt in our

minds that victory will rest with the United States, but the question before us now is: shall we further sacrifice our country and our people in a
hopeless fight? I voice the unanimous opinion of my War Cabinet, and I
am sure the unanimous opinion of all Filipinos, that under the circumstances we should take steps to preserve the Philippines and the Filipinos
from further destruction."

The steps Quezon had in mind were bold and surprising ones, occa-
sioned both by Filipino reaction to the failure of U.S. aid and a recent
Japanese offer to grant the Philippines independence. "I deem it my duty,"
Quezon went on, "to propose my solution." This was his solution:

"The government of the United States," he pointed out, "under the
Tydings-McDuffie law is committed to grant independence to the Philippines in 1946, and the same law gave authority to the President of the
United States to begin parleys for the neutralization of the Philippines.
On the other hand, the Premier of the Imperial Government of Japan, ad-
dressing the Diet, stated that the Imperial Government of Japan was
ready to offer the Filipino people independence with honor. On the
strength of these commitments, and impelled by a sincere desire to put
an end to the suffering and sacrifice of our people, and to safeguard their
liberty and welfare, I propose the following program of action: that the
government of the United States and the Imperial Government of Japan
recognize the independence of the Philippines; that within a reasonable
period of time both armies, American and Japanese, be withdrawn,
previous arrangements having been negotiated with the Philippine government; that neither nation maintain bases in the Philippines; that the
Philippine army be at once demobilized, the remaining force to be a
constabulary of moderate size; that at once upon the granting of freedom,
trade agreements with other countries become solely a matter to be settled by the Philippines and the nations concerned; that American and
Japanese noncombatants who so desire be evacuated with their own
armies under reciprocal and appropriate stipulations.

"It is my earnest hope that, moved by the highest considerations of
justice and humanity, the two great powers which now exercise control
over the Philippines will give their approval in general principle to my
proposal. If this is done, I further propose, in order to accomplish the details thereof, that an armistice be declared in the Philippines and that I
proceed to Manila at once for necessary consultations with the two governments concerned."

It is a measure of MacArthur's subordination as a soldier that, much
as he disliked any such easy way out of American commitments, and

vitally concerned as he was with the decision to be made, he passed Quezon's revolutionary proposal along to Washington with no political suggestions of his own. Instead, he let High Commissioner Sayre make the recommendations, and attached them to Quezon's message. Sayre's statement was: "If the premise of President Quezon is correct that American help cannot or will not arrive here in time to be available, I believe his proposal for immediate independence and neutralization of the Philippines is the sound course to follow." MacArthur then gave his estimate of the military situation, adding: "So far as the military angle is concerned, the problem presents itself as to whether the plan of President Quezon might offer the best possible solution of what is about to be a disastrous debacle. . . . Please instruct me."

(Are these, incidentally, the words of a testy, insubordinate commander?)

The military reply from Roosevelt to MacArthur we have seen; it was to keep fighting in the Philippines as long as "any possibility of resistance" remained. His political reply to Quezon resounded with lofty phrases about the forty-year-old U.S. pledge to the Philippines "to help them succeed, however long it might take, in their aspirations to become a self-governing and independent people. . . . May I remind you now," Roosevelt went on, that the U.S. program of helping a territory toward independence "has been unique in the history of the family of nations." He had only scorn for the Japanese offer of independence, and asked, with ill-disguised contempt for Quezon's apparent gullibility, "is it any longer possible for any reasonable person to rely upon a Japanese offer or promise?"

In refusing to approve Quezon's suggestion, Roosevelt reiterated the promise of U.S. aid to the Philippines. But this time, and for the first time, he mentioned a clear difference: "Whatever happens to the present American garrison, we shall not relax our efforts until the forces we are now marshaling outside of the Philippine Islands return to the Philippines and drive the last remnant of the invaders from your soil."

There it was for the first time, the admission that American reinforcements would not get there. The message was received on Corregidor with dismay. It blasted the last hope that, under any circumstances or responsive to any argument, help would be dispatched to the Philippines to support the battle then being waged by the defending garrison.

This shocker was followed by further urging from Marshall that MacArthur make plans to evacuate his family. Disaster seemed to be closing rapidly on MacArthur and his embattled men. "I think it very

important," Marshall wired, "that you have in mind the possibility that
your personal withdrawal might be ordered at such time as would not
jeopardize continued defense. . . . As such a movement would certainly
be at a much later date than withdrawal of the Filipino officials and the
Sayres and inevitably under more hazardous conditions, should not your
family be evacuated with the others, leaving you free to accept whatever
perilous course might later be found necessary? . . . You may find yourself in grave embarrassment should you receive orders for your withdrawal under conditions impossible for them."

The next day, as if by afterthought, Marshall asked MacArthur to
consider seriously "the possibility that some later situation might require
duty from you that would compel separation from them under circumstances of greatly increased peril. . . ." Besides painting a rather dismal
picture of the immediate future, Marshall's messages indicated that official Washington still had an exaggerated notion of the Japanese blockade.

MacArthur's reply was typical: a plan for attack. "The opportunities
still exist," he wired, "for a complete reversal of the situation." He thereupon proposed another plan for cutting Japan's vital lines of communication. But, like his other positive plans, it was apparently overwhelmed
by the tide of negativism then running in Washington. At this point, War
Department spokesmen were announcing loudly that the Philippines were
all but gone, and any suggestion that they might still be saved was met
with derision.

On the night of February 20, Douglas MacArthur and Manuel Quezon grasped hands in farewell. The Philippine president, his family, and
his war cabinet filed into a submarine to be taken to the Visayan Islands,
160 miles to the south. The two embattled leaders were both touched by
the scene. Each in his own way had fought hard to preserve the freedom
and integrity of the Philippines. Each knew that it might well be a final
parting. Yet both ignored personal considerations; their last words to each
other on the dark wharf were of how the war would go, and how and
when America would fulfill her promise.

The submarine's hatch clanked shut. MacArthur gave a final wave.
Only two days later, following orders from Washington, High Commissioner Sayre and his family also bade MacArthur good-by and climbed
down the conning-tower of the same submarine, to go to Australia. As
they parted, MacArthur said: "When you see the sun again, it will be a
different world." Now that the last of the political leaders was in the
submarine, slipping beneath the waters of Manila Bay for the run past
the thin line of blockading Japanese warships, the defense of Corregidor

was purely a soldier's business. MacArthur walked up the dock to face the grave responsibilities alone.

In the submarine with Quezon was a small foot locker addressed to the Riggs National Bank of Washington, with instructions that it be held in safekeeping until MacArthur or his legally authorized representative called for it. The foot locker duly arrived at the bank, was held there throughout the rest of the war, and was returned to MacArthur at Tokyo. Meanwhile, its contents became the subject of wild speculation. Assertions were made then, and have been made since, that it contained the documentation of the interchange of messages between Washington and Corregidor, and that MacArthur was keeping these records for the sole purpose of embarrassing the Administration. It was even implied that he had rifled official records and taken for his personal use documents to which he had no right.

I like mystery thrillers as much as anyone else, and in some circles the mystery of the foot locker seems to have reached almost thriller proportions. But a historical record must hold to the truth, and accordingly I must report that the infamous foot locker contained none of the documentation it was alleged to be hiding. It held those personal effects that any husband and wife, father and mother, would want to preserve when facing peril and possible death. In the foot locker were a wedding certificate, a large number of baby pictures of Arthur MacArthur, his baptismal certificate, his first baby shoes, the last wills and testaments of both General and Mrs. MacArthur, personal securities, less than a hundred dollars in currency, some military decorations won by MacArthur and his father, and some articles on the general which his wife had clipped from several magazines and hastily tucked into the foot locker just before it was closed and sealed. I happen to know what the contents were because I did what no one else did: I asked him. Although fantastic legends about that foot locker were told and retold for years, no one bothered to ask MacArthur the simple question, which he would have answered just as plainly as he did to me.

The day after Quezon's departure, MacArthur received another wire from Marshall on the subject of leaving Corregidor. "The President is considering the advisability of ordering you to Mindanao to continue the command of the Philippines from that locality," Marshall said. "There is now the further consideration of the effect of the transfer of the Philippine government in the person of President Quezon to the Southern Islands and the fact that it is the opinion here that the future of the Philippines would be greatly influenced by the continuance of American resistance in

Mindanao. . . ." This seemed to indicate a tentative Washington decision for MacArthur *not* to leave the Philippines, but to change his command post from Corregidor to Mindanao and continue the fight from there. Whether the new decision also included giving him any help in this fight, Washington evidently was not ready to tell him. MacArthur mentally filed away this new suggestion with the others he had received in the past few days, while he waited for the promised presidential directive. That directive was not long in coming, and, despite the previous warnings, it caught him with shocking suddenness.

It arrived in two days, on February 23, and it read: "The President directs that you make arrangements to leave Fort Mills [on Corregidor] and proceed to Mindanao. You are directed to make this change as quickly as possible. The President desires that in Mindanao you take such measures as will ensure a prolonged defense of that region—this especially in view of the transfer of President Quezon and his government to the southern Philippines and the great importance the President attaches to the future of the Philippines by prolonging, in every way possible, the continued defense by United States troops and the retention of the active support of the Philippine government and people."

Then came the news for which Marshall's advisory wire of two days before had not prepared him. The President's directive went on: "From Mindanao you will proceed to Australia where you will assume command of all United States troops. . . . Because of the vital importance of your assuming command in Australia at an early date, your delay in Mindanao will not be prolonged beyond one week, and you will leave sooner if transportation becomes available. . . ."

Evidently Washington policy had switched again, and MacArthur was to go on to Australia as soon as possible. That he could do little to set up any kind of well-organized defense in the Southern Islands in only one week Washington surely must have known, and doubtless this part of the message was intended for President Quezon's eyes and for propaganda purposes later. The importance of the message, of course, was in the order that MacArthur leave Corregidor. This meant leaving the men who still fought for him so bravely on Bataan when even they knew now that it was in vain.

How should he respond to such an order? His soldier's reaction, long trained in the rigidity of discipline that demanded strict obedience, told him that he must leave. But his soldier's heart shrank from the thought of leaving his men. At Natchez in 1813, Andrew Jackson disobeyed direct orders to desert his men, stayed with them, and won his nickname of "Old

45

Hickory." At Copenhagen in 1801, Admiral Nelson put his telescope to his blind eye, thus ignored the signal to retreat, and thereby beat the Danish fleet. On Corregidor in 1942, MacArthur considered, for the first and only time in his military career, whether he should refuse to obey an order.

He called a meeting of his staff. When they assembled in his office, he paced up and down the room while he outlined his dilemma to them. They could see that he had been pacing for many hours before he called them in. He explained that he had been working on a plan for a daring breakthrough to the north and an assumption of guerrilla operations in the mountains of Central Luzon. Even without carrying out that plan, he was anticipating a fresh enemy attack. He expected it to be a major assault, aimed at splitting his two corps apart. It should come within three weeks, and he wanted to be there, directing his planned defense, when it came. But, on the other hand, a soldier's orders were orders.

His staff members knew that, and they urged on him the necessity for obedience, however distasteful it might be for him personally. They pointed out that defiance of the President's orders could only provoke disciplinary action. If he were not superseded by a subordinate officer, at best Washington would cast such a cloud on his position as to materially reduce the effectiveness of his command functions.

Then they produced the clincher. This order might be the best hope for salvaging the military situation in the Philippines after all. They reminded him of the Washington messages that described the massing of power in the southwest Pacific. They quoted President Roosevelt's assurances to President Quezon that "every vessel available is bearing to the southwest Pacific the strength that will eventually crush the enemy. . . . Our heavy bombers are each day joining General Wavell's command. A continuous stream of fighters and pursuit planes is traversing the Pacific; already 10 squadrons of the foregoing types are ready for combat in the southwest Pacific area. Extensive arrivals of troops—" and so on and on. Thus they conjured up a massive force already poised near Australia for major offensive operations that could stop the Japanese advance and relieve the Philippines—possibly while the defenders of Bataan and Corregidor still held on. This was the force that awaited the right kind of leader, a bold, aggressive-minded leader who appreciated the strategic importance of the Philippines to the Japanese advance. And MacArthur was the President's choice as this leader. They argued that there could be no question about it; not only was he sworn to obey the orders he received, but he would be accomplishing more with the swelling forces at his disposal in Australia than he could with the worn-out men left on Bataan and Corregidor.

MacArthur quietly heard them out. He had to agree with the logic of their arguments, but he could not bring himself to leave his men quite yet. He compromised in his decision. In his reply to Marshall he stated that he would do as ordered, but he asked that the time for his departure be left to his discretion. He cited the expected enemy assault, and asked that he be allowed to see it through with his men.

Marshall replied: "Your message of February 24th has been carefully considered by the President. He has directed that full decision as to the timing of your departure and details of method be left in your hands. . . ."

The anticipated attack was launched by the enemy almost immediately, and MacArthur was ready. He had expected the full force to come against the hinge between his two corps and had prepared his defense accordingly. It came exactly there, and the enemy was met with such heavy artillery fire that he was thrown back with bloody losses.

From President Quezon in the Southern Islands came a message of exultation: "The most glorious chapter in the history of our country is being written in Bataan and Corregidor on the epic stand of our armies. . . . I urge every Filipino to be of good cheer, to have faith in the patriotism and valor of our soldiers in the field and, above all, to trust America. . . . I know she will not fail us." The exultation in the Allied camp was matched by the gloom on the Japanese side. The February victories had bolstered the morale of MacArthur's troops while destroying that of the Japanese. The enemy had dug in, waiting for the reinforcements *they* knew were coming, and thus the fighting temporarily became positional warfare, while the soldiers of both sides watched each other across a thin strip of no-man's-land. For the time being, at least, the front was reasonably stabilized.

On March 6 MacArthur got a further nudge from Washington: "The situation in Australia indicates desirability of your early arrival there." He could wait no longer. On the 9th he made his decision.

It was clear to him that he was merely shifting his command post to Australia, just as Washington had originally intended him to shift south only to Mindanao. He would retain command of the Philippines from his Australian headquarters. Nevertheless, he felt it necessary to reorganize his defense forces. He split the Visayan-Mindanao command, placing the defense of the Visayan Islands under Major General Bradford Chynoweth. Major General William Sharp had commanded both, but Mac-

Arthur now ordered him to concentrate his attention on Mindanao, which he regarded as the final bastion for the defense of the Philippines and the ultimate springboard for the counteroffensive. He left Corregidor and the harbor defenses under Major General George Moore, who had held this command since the sideslip into Bataan. On Luzon, MacArthur grouped his scattered forces and put them under the command of Major General Jonathan Wainwright.

In addition, he established under Brigadier General Lewis Beebe on Corregidor an advance echelon of his own headquarters, through which he would issue his orders from Australia. All this gave him a cohesive command set-up that he could manage from a distance, so he would not have to relinquish command over the officers and men who had fought so well for him and who might otherwise feel that he was letting them down. He did not assign anyone to assume command after his departure.

So at noon on March 10 General Wainwright came across to Corregidor from Bataan to be told the news. In his book, *General Wainwright's Story*, he writes that he had no idea what MacArthur wanted to talk to him about. He was met in the office in Malinta Tunnel by General Sutherland, who told him of MacArthur's directed withdrawal and of the new command set-up. Then Sutherland took Wainwright to the little gray house where MacArthur lived, a quarter of a mile away from the tunnel.

MacArthur came out on the porch to meet him. The two old friends shook hands and sat down. MacArthur reiterated that he was leaving only because of repeated orders from the President; he had no other course, and he wanted everyone in his command to know that he was obeying his orders under protest. After going over the new commands and discussing the worsening situation on Bataan, he said: "We're alone, Jim; [2] you know as well as I. If I get through to Australia, you know I'll come back as soon as I can with as much as I can."

He then cautioned Cavalryman Wainwright about the need for greater defense in depth and the fullest possible use of artillery—the kind of tactics which had just smashed the last Japanese attack. Wainwright agreed.

In the momentary silence that followed, they could hear the thunder of Bataan across the bay. Wainwright broke the silence by saying: "You'll get through."

The lines around MacArthur's mouth tightened. With the steely note of dedicated determination in his voice, he answered:

"—and back."

[2] As far as I know, MacArthur was the only man who called Wainwright by this nickname.

"It's time to mount up, Jeannie."

Two days later darkness was settling over Manila Bay when four PT boats idled up to the dock at Corregidor. Although President Quezon and High Commissioner Sayre had left by submarine, MacArthur chose PT boats for a number of reasons. They had been his idea for part of the defense of the Islands, and they had worked even better than he had thought they would. They had slipped into protected harbors, sunk Japanese shipping, and roared away before the enemy could catch them. They had sneaked through the blockade countless times with desperately needed provisions. Once they had even successfully engaged a flight of enemy planes, their gunners firing so accurately that three Japanese aircraft were destroyed. Now they were providing MacArthur with a method of transportation which would show Washington, and especially the Navy, that the much-vaunted Japanese blockade was penetrable, and at the same time allow him figuratively to thumb his nose at the enemy as his parting gesture. MacArthur knew the Japanese, and he knew what a defiant gesture like this would do to the morale of the enemy command.

A messenger brought word to his house that the boats were ready. MacArthur walked onto the porch, where his wife and son sat waiting. "It's time to mount up, Jeannie," he said quietly. They went down to the dock where the PT boats rose and fell and tugged at their hawsers, their 4,000-horsepower Packard engines muttering and snorting beneath them. MacArthur, his family, and the members of his staff he was taking with him quickly climbed into the boats. The lines were cast off, the engines' muttering rose to a throaty roar, the boats planed over the tops of the waves, and Corregidor receded rapidly in the darkness.

Those who were on the PT boat with him will never forget the sight of MacArthur standing there looking back at Corregidor, obviously recalling all that he was leaving behind and at the same time considering the perilous and strenuous ordeal that lay ahead. On his lips was a prayer for the defenders, and in his heart was an invincible resolve to return. So much depended on his getting through. So much depended on his getting back—in time. With that knowledge and appreciation he has always had for the drama and significance of the great event, he knew that he now faced a rendezvous with history. The feeble light astern had all but disappeared in the dark distance when he raised his cap to Corregidor and Bataan, in a final salute that came from deep in his soldier's heart.

CHAPTER VI   "I came through, and *I shall return.*"

🏛 "Departed from Corregidor at dark on 12th, with party of 22 . . . traveling on four United States Navy torpedo boats. Afternoon air reconnaissance revealed one hostile cruiser and one destroyer off west coast of Mindoro, but we slipped by them in the darkness. Passed following day in shelter of uninhabited island but risked discovery by air and started several hours before dark in order to approach Mindanao at dawn. Sighted enemy destroyer at 15,000 yards but escaped unseen, making scheduled run despite heavy seas and severe buffeting. Upon arrival Mindanao learned that of four planes despatched only one had arrived and that, without brakes or supercharger and being unfit for mission, had already departed. Brett selected three more planes for trip, of which one developed mechanical trouble and two arrived safely, taking entire party out. Safe arrival and departure forced us to pass latitude at Ambon at dawn but course set somewhat to eastward enabled party to escape interception. Landed Batchelor Field while Darwin was under raid."

This almost cryptic report to Marshall was MacArthur's own description of his famous dash from Corregidor to Australia. Never before had such a perilous trip through twenty-five hundred miles of enemy territory been made by a commanding general and his staff. Yet MacArthur confined himself to the barest details.

He said nothing of the fact that the PT boats should long ago have had a complete overhaul, and that they were able to make only half their usual speed. He said nothing of the fact that the boats were literally floating blockbusters, with twenty steel drums piled on their decks, each filled with fifty gallons of 100-octane gasoline for the long run to Mindanao. He said nothing about the suspense as they picked their way through the minefields outside Manila Bay and watched the silhouettes of the blockading ships against the horizon while enemy signal fires on shore announced that the PT boats must have been seen. He said nothing about the worry as the motors of one PT boat faltered and the four became separated.

He did not describe the hushed tension aboard his boat when a Japanese destroyer came over the horizon at dusk on the first day; with engines stilled, the little craft bobbed in the seas while the enemy warship steamed majestically and blindly off to the west. He did not mention that at a rendezvous one PT-boat gunner mistook the General's boat for the enemy and was on the point of opening fire when someone spotted MacArthur's familiar silhouette at the bow. He did not mention the loss of one of these worn-out little craft, and the crowding of its occupants into the remaining boats.

He did not mention that enemy fighters rose to attack the two unprotected B-17's over Timor but missed them in the darkness. He did not mention that in Australia he had to leave Batchelor Field and head inland as soon as he had landed because a heavy force of Japanese planes was on the way. "It was close," he admitted privately to one of his companions, "but that's the way it is in war. You win or lose, live or die—and the difference is just an eyelash." Nor did he mention, as he might have, that his trip by PT boat had proved his contention that the Japanese had only a paper "blockade" around the Philippines.

He did mention in his report to Marshall that he had to wait in Mindanao for the planes supposed to have been sent for him, without detailing any of the anxiety he and his staff went through during their three-day wait while a Japanese force, aware of the great prize, made a frenzied drive to take the Del Monte airport from its desperate defenders. But what MacArthur did not include in his reference to the planes' delay was its cause. Lieutenant General George H. Brett, then U.S. Army commander in Australia, had tried to borrow three of the brand-new B-17's that had just arrived, consigned to the Navy. Brett's bombers were in such a beaten-up condition that he did not think one of them could make it to the Philippines and back. He went to Vice Admiral Herbert Fairfax Leary, Navy commander in the area, and made his plea. Leary said that the planes could not be spared "for a ferry job." So Brett sent the best of his worn-out planes. Only after two had turned back and one had crashed into the sea (killing two of its crew) did Leary lend Brett the Navy bombers that finally got MacArthur and his staff out of the trap closing on him in Mindanao.

Of course MacArthur's terse report passed over all such personal touches as are recalled by his fellow passengers: young Arthur, soaking wet and seasick but still game, thrusting his chin out exactly like his father; Jean MacArthur, taking advantage of a layover in a quiet bay, sunning herself on deck and looking healthy in contrast to the seasick men all around her; the General pacing the deck, lost in his thoughts; Arthur running about with General Tojo, the cook's monkey; Jean MacArthur caring for both her son and the nurse, when he came down with a high fever and Ah Cheu was too seasick to move; the General, waking from a sound sleep as the dock at Mindanao was sighted, springing up, shaking the water out of his famous cap and tossing it onto his head, ready and eager for the next leg of the journey; the crowded plane, with MacArthur in the radio-operator's seat and Mrs. MacArthur, Arthur, and Ah Cheu under the waist gun. These trivialities, lost though they may be in the large canvas of the war, will never be forgotten by those who made that perilous trip with MacArthur.

The journey's end was like coming out into the sunlight from a darkened room. While the trip from Corregidor had been a tense, secret race against death in a dark, heaving sea, its end was a riotous welcome from thousands of Australians in the sun-warmed street outside Melbourne's railroad station. The Australians were merely echoing the cheers that had gone up throughout the free world at the news that he had come through safely. In the U.S. there was a near-chorus of "By God, they got him out!" In England a correspondent reported that Londoners were comparing MacArthur to Lord Nelson and Sir Francis Drake. Back in Australia a newspaper headlined: "THE MAN OF THE MOMENT." Newborn babies were named after him, and restaurant chefs named special dishes for him. At Alice Springs, where MacArthur changed trains during the grueling five-day trip across the desolate center of Australia to Melbourne, he was met by some reporters. They asked him for a statement, and he scribbled one on the back of a used envelope. He especially asked that it be published to the troops still fighting in the Philippines and to the Filipino people.

"The President of the United States," the statement read, "ordered me to break through the Japanese lines and proceed from Corregidor to Australia for the purpose, as I understand it, of organizing the American offensive against Japan, a primary object of which is the relief of the Philippines."

And then he added a sentence that was directed to the men in the foxholes of Bataan, to the soldiers, sailors, and nurses on Corregidor, and to the eighteen million people of the Philippine Islands. But the sentence also stirred the imagination of free men everywhere in the world because

"*I came through, and* I shall return."

of its message of hope in these times of despair in the Pacific. It was a pledge that helped sustain every Filipino when the darkness of enemy occupation later settled on their homeland. It became the keystone of the guerrilla movement, the slogan of the Filipino fighting-man by day and the essence of the Filipino mother's lullaby at night. It was painted on the walls, scratched out on the rocks of the beaches, whispered in the nightly prayers. It became the symbol for a nation in its time of greatest need. And to the rest of the world it became one of the most famous battle cries of history.

It was: "I came through and *I shall return.*"

At that moment in history the free world, and especially Australia, needed precisely the tonic MacArthur could give. For Australians the initial shock of war had been followed by four months of news that was invariably black, news of the enemy moving ever nearer their doorstep. In all that news, one, and only one, man stood out as a shining figure of defiance against the enemy's might, and that figure now appeared before them at the railroad station in Melbourne. The six thousand Australians strung around the station found a reception committee of bemedaled generals, admirals in white and gold, a guard of honor in crisp khaki and shining leather. Everyone—the generals, the admirals, the honor guard, the audience of civilians, and even some white-legginged Filipinos lately evacuated by hospital ship—waited expectantly while the occupants emerged. Then Melbourne echoed to the cheers. They were cheers of welcome, but they were also cheers of hope and eventual victory.

Amid the resplendent array of the welcoming delegation, and spotlighted by the contrast, MacArthur wore his plain, open-necked shirt, with no medals—nothing but the four stars of his rank. His khaki trousers were still sharply pressed, and the well-worn, well-known gold-starred cap was perched on his head with the same air of confidence which had inspired the men on Bataan.

MacArthur now inspired the Australians. His words were carefully suited to the occasion—half warning that the road ahead would be difficult, half assurance of ultimate victory. He said: "I have every confidence in the ultimate success of our joint cause; but success in modern war requires something more than courage and willingness to die; it requires careful preparation, sufficient troops, sufficient materials. . . . No general can make something out of nothing. My success or failure will depend primarily upon the resources which our respective governments place at my disposal. My faith in them is complete. In any event I shall do my best. I shall keep the soldier's faith."

A reporter, as reporters will, asked MacArthur to repeat the last sentence. As if for emphasis, MacArthur agreed and stepped back to the microphone. "I shall keep the soldier's faith."

The honors came thick and fast, and MacArthur responded with the friendliness, the assurance, the determination, and the eloquence that the Australians had been waiting for. He was asked to address the Australian Parliament, and he gave them his pledge:

"There is a link which binds our countries together which does not depend upon written protocol, upon treaties of alliance, or upon diplomatic doctrine. It is that indescribable consanguinity of race which causes us to have the same aspirations, the same hopes and desires, the same ideals and the same dreams of future destiny. My presence here is tangible evidence of our unity. I have come as a soldier in a great crusade of personal liberty as opposed to perpetual slavery. My faith in our ultimate victory is invincible, and I bring you tonight the unbreakable spirit of the free man's military code in support of our just cause. . . . Under its banner the free men of the world are united today. We shall win or we shall die, and to this end I pledge the full resources and all the mighty power of my country and all the blood of my countrymen."

Australia went wild, and their faith in him never waned thereafter.

From the United States came the greatest honor its government can bestow: President Roosevelt, in behalf of the Congress, awarded MacArthur the Medal of Honor. The citation summed up what Americans, as well as Australians, thought of him: "For conspicuous leadership in preparing the Philippine Islands to resist conquest, for gallantry and intrepidity above and beyond the call of duty in action against invading Japanese forces, and for the heroic conduct of defensive and offensive operations on the Bataan Peninsula. He mobilized, trained and led an army which has received world acclaim for its gallant defense against a tremendous superiority of enemy forces in men and arms. His utter disregard of personal danger while under heavy fire and aerial bombardment, his calm judgment in each crisis, inspired his troops, galvanized the spirit of resistance of the Filipino people and confirmed the faith of the American people in their armed forces."

This, incidentally, was the third time that Douglas MacArthur had been recommended for the Medal of Honor. He had won it for action at Vera Cruz in 1915 and on the fields of France in World War I. Both times technicalities had kept him from receiving it—once because war had not been declared against Mexico, and the other time because the war had just ended and it was decided not to make the award to any general officer. His receipt of this decoration made a unique case of father and son; Arthur MacArthur won the Medal of Honor for leading the charge of Sheridan's division up Missionary Ridge in the Civil War. This medal, the nation's greatest, has been given to no other father and son.

Yet through all this acclaim and applause MacArthur moved with a heavy heart, and it was difficult for him to share the jubilation of the Australians who welcomed him. For his mind was still on the Philippines, and each day's dispatch told of the disintegration of the Islands' defense. On March 21, immediately after his arrival in Melbourne, he had wired Marshall, detailing the changes he had made in the command set-up in the Philippines. Following Washington's orders, as he understood them, to move his command post to Australia, he had made arrangements to co-ordinate all operations on the Islands through advance headquarters on Corregidor, and he had left a special staff behind for this job. To his astonishment, Marshall in effect removed the Philippines from Mac-Arthur's command. Wainwright was named commander-in-chief of all forces in the Philippines, and MacArthur's role was changed to one of general strategic supervision as the theater commander.

This decision upset a carefully laid plan for continuing the defense of the Philippines. MacArthur had contemplated another of the surprises with which he had bamboozled the Japanese attackers for so long. This surprise was to be a massive breakthrough as soon as the supplies on Bataan and Corregidor were near exhaustion. It was obvious now that nothing more was coming through from the United States, and it followed with cruel military certainty that Bataan and Corregidor would fall unless some ingenious maneuver could be used to throw the enemy off balance. MacArthur had just such a maneuver worked out, and he quickly outlined it to Marshall.

His plan, he explained, included "an ostentatious artillery preparation on the left by I Corps as a feint and a sudden surprise attack on the right by the II Corps—taking the enemy's Subic Bay positions in reverse simultaneously with a frontal attack by the I Corps. If successful, the supplies seized at this base would permit them to operate in Central Luzon, where food could be obtained and where they could still protect Bataan and the northern approaches to Corregidor. If the movement is not successful and our forces defeated, many increments thereof, after inflicting important losses upon the enemy, could escape through the Zambales mountains and continue guerrilla warfare in conjunction with forces now operating in the north."

In this message MacArthur also pointed out that "the pressure on this situation could be immeasurably relieved if a naval task force with its own air protection could make some kind of threat in that general direction"—no major engagement, not even an attempt to slip through the "blockade," but simply a feint with some ships and planes; considering that this was only three months before the all-aircraft Battle of the Coral Sea, it was not asking a great deal. And as if there were any doubt about the importance MacArthur attached to this plan, he said: "I would be glad, if you believe it advisable, to attempt to rejoin this command temporarily and take charge of this movement."

Perhaps the Pentagon generals considered the plan impractical. If so, they must have ignored—or refused to believe—the many past assurances from MacArthur and his staff that the Filipinos would never cease their guerrilla warfare until the Japanese were driven from their homeland. These assurances were later to be proved true many times over by the defiant, unremitting fighting of guerrilla armies composed of Filipinos and U.S. Army and Navy personnel who had avoided capture. In any case, MacArthur's plan for a breakthrough and continued resistance was vetoed by Marshall.

A more likely reason for this decision, in retrospect, might be the defeatism that seemed to be infecting the Pentagon at that time, as far as the Philippines were concerned. Only a month before, Roosevelt had wired MacArthur on Corregidor forbidding surrender "as long as there remains any possibility of resistance. . . . It is mandatory," Roosevelt had said, "that there be established once and for all in the minds of all peoples complete evidence that the American determination and indomitable will to win carries on down to the last unit. . . ." Evidently that indomitable will no longer existed in Washington—only on Bataan and Corregidor and in MacArthur's headquarters in Australia. MacArthur thought he was carrying out and confirming his orders when he concluded the outline of his breakthrough plan with the emphatic words: "I am utterly opposed, under any circumstances or conditions, to the ultimate capitulation of this command." But those orders of a month before, it seemed, had been changed.

Either with cavalier disregard for a field commander or by fantastic oversight, Washington did not even bother to tell MacArthur that the tactical Philippine command had been taken from him. The day before MacArthur was able to give Washington the details of the new command set-up he had worked out for continuing the Philippine defense, notice was sent to Wainwright that he was now commander-in-chief in the Philippines. MacArthur received no word of this, and indeed found out only from Wainwright. As Wainwright notes with unconcealed surprise in his book, he had to send MacArthur the text of the War Department order.

This might have been enough to make many a field commander sit back and let the Pentagon generals learn their lesson. But MacArthur knew that they were going to learn their lesson at the expense of the death and torture of his Bataan boys, of his beloved Filipino scouts, and of his comrade-in-arms, "Jim" Wainwright. MacArthur did not need any great perception, nor did Washington, to see that these sick, starved men, forced to fight a continuous delaying-action without supplies and without even being allowed by the Pentagon to use aggressive ingenuity, were doomed. And he could easily foresee what would happen to Wainwright and his men when they were captured. Now that Washington had appointed him commander-in-chief, Wainwright had the authority to surrender *all* forces in the Philippines, including those already fighting guerrilla actions on Mindanao and the other islands. Certainly the hysterically vindictive General Homma contemplated ingenious tortures to force the surrender order from Wainwright and at the same time revenge the disgrace that MacArthur, Wainwright, and the men of Bataan had inflicted on him. This was part of the reason why MacArthur had kept the over-all tactical Philippine command in his own hands; no field commander in the Philippines would then have the authority to surrender any but his own local forces. But official Washington, for whatever reasons, could not see this logic. Wainwright, like a good soldier, took the command.

MacArthur continued to warn Marshall, however, of the fast deteriorating situation in the Philippines, as Wainwright faithfully reported it to him. On April 8, MacArthur wired Marshall that "the enemy has driven a wedge between the first and second corps and is still advancing. . . . I regard the situation as extremely critical and feel you should anticipate the possibility of disaster there very shortly." Marshall's reply was curt and amounted to an order to "mind your own business."

The next day Bataan was gone.

MacArthur was not surprised when he received the news, but there was no alleviating the shock of its finality. As he put the message on his desk, his lips were drawn into a tight line, his face a mask. He canceled appointments for the rest of the day. Those who came to see him found a closed door and, knowing why, went quietly away. Those who had offices under his could faintly hear the unbroken sound of his constant pacing back and forth all afternoon in the solitude of his office. He never told me, but I am sure that he also prayed.

Finally the pacing stopped as MacArthur sat at his desk. The buzzer sounded in the outer office, and an aide answered it. He came out with a sheet of white paper on which this was written:

"The Bataan force went out as it would have wished, fighting to the end in its flickering, forlorn hope. No army has ever done so much with so little, and nothing became it more than its last hour of trial and agony. To the weeping mothers of its dead, I can only say that the sacrifice and halo of Jesus of Nazareth has descended upon their sons, and that God will take them unto Himself."

The aide reported that MacArthur's face was still set in the same grim lines—but that his cheeks were streaked with tears.

The fall of Corregidor was now only a matter of time. President Roosevelt finally clarified the fact that he had indeed modified his instructions to fight to the end. He sent to MacArthur a message for Wainwright on Corregidor, asking politely that it be forwarded, "if you concur both as to substance and timing." MacArthur had no choice, but he later discovered that the message had already been sent to Wainwright anyway. Roosevelt's orders gave Wainwright "complete freedom of action and of my full confidence in the wisdom of whatever decision you may be forced to make." Wainwright was not, however, free to give the tactical command back to MacArthur. Corregidor fell on May 6, and Wainwright sent his last message to MacArthur: "We are sad but not ashamed . . . good-bye, general. . . ." The Japanese thereupon did precisely what MacArthur had feared.

When he surrendered Corregidor, Wainwright tried to remedy the Pentagon's mistake with the only device left to him: he announced that he was releasing the Visayan-Mindanao forces, the largest potential guerrilla army, from his command and instructed their commander, General Sharp, to report direct to MacArthur for instructions. Sharp wired MacArthur, in a pitiful attempt to save his men from capture and death. MacArthur could only hope that the maneuver would work. He quickly replied: "Orders emanating from General Wainwright have no validity. If possible, separate your force into small elements and initiate guerrilla operations." And in a last desperate endeavor to give Sharp the freedom of operation which Washington had denied him, MacArthur added to his wire: "You, of course, have full authority to make any decision that immediate emergency may demand."

But it was too late. General Homma's men had General Wainwright's men lined up in front of their guns on Corregidor. Homma simply pointed to the document he held in his hand, a copy of the official War Department order placing Wainwright in tactical command of *all* Philippine forces. And Wainwright had no difficulty imagining what would happen to the Corregidor garrison if he did not surrender all the troops in the Philippines. In the ensuing confusion some of Sharp's officers and men managed to get away; their guerrilla operations during the three black years that followed helped keep large sections of the Southern Islands free. But the bulk of the Visayan-Mindanao forces could only march off to the horror of the Japanese prison camp.

The fact that most of this force might have continued fighting merely added gall to MacArthur's cup. He had had his say after the fall of Bataan, and he intended to add nothing more. But the press kept after him to "make a comment" on Corregidor. Finally, with bowed head, he replied:

"Corregidor needs no comment from me. It has sounded its own story at the mouth of its guns. It has scrolled its own epitaph on enemy tablets. But through the bloody haze of its last, reverberating shot, I shall always seem to see a vision of grim, gaunt, ghastly men, still unafraid."

CHAPTER VII   The defense of Australia is in New Guinea.

⚜ It was not because of the Philippines alone that MacArthur moved through Melbourne's festivities with a heavy heart. Another reason was that he had already learned appalling news about his command.

Any elation that he may have felt over the manner in which he had outfoxed the enemy by successfully reaching Australia was nullified by what he discovered when he got there. He had left the Philippines because he believed the promises contained in Roosevelt's message to the Filipino people on December 28: "I give to the people of the Philippines my solemn pledge that their freedom will be redeemed and their independence established and protected. The entire resources in men and materials of the United States stand behind that pledge. . . ." That statement had been backed up by one from the Navy: "The United States Navy is following an intensive, well-planned campaign against Japanese forces which will result in positive assistance to the defense of the Philippine Islands." And Roosevelt had followed up these pledges with a message to Quezon that was larded with impressive references to strong forces being sent out across the Pacific: "heavy bombers," "continuous stream of fighters," "extensive arrivals of troops." It all added up to a massive concentration of air, sea, and ground forces, with which MacArthur would be able to rescue his men on Bataan and Corregidor.

As soon as he had landed near Darwin, MacArthur sent Brigadier General Richard Marshall, his deputy chief of staff, ahead by air to get a preliminary estimate of the size of his new command. Marshall was waiting for MacArthur's train at Adelaide, where the railroad changed from narrow to wide gauge and where MacArthur changed cars. He had unbelievable news: the massive force that MacArthur had been led to believe was gathered in Australia, the armies supposedly waiting for a leader to hurl the enemy back and relieve the Philippines, were completely non-

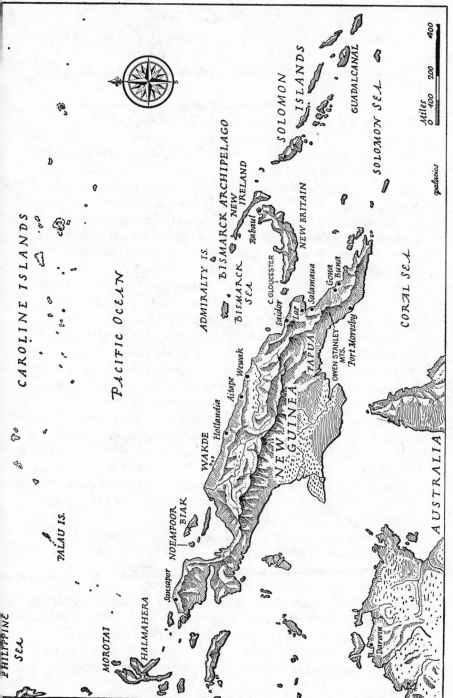

New Guinea and the Southwest Pacific

existent. MacArthur's mind went back to the golden promise of Roosevelt's message as he listened to the ugly truth of the situation:

Roosevelt had said: "Our heavy bombers are each day joining General Wavell's command."

The fact was that there were only about seventy bombers in Australia when MacArthur arrived. They were supplemented by the few Navy bombers that General Brett had had such a hard time getting even on loan. The old B-17's that Brereton had rescued from the downfall of Java were all undergoing repairs. Of MacArthur's heavy bombers only twelve could fly because so many were either being repaired or waiting for such essential parts as propellers and wheels. Some supplies and spare parts had arrived in Australia, but they were in southern Australia, while the planes were a thousand miles away, and there were not enough transportation facilities to rush the parts north. Even four months later MacArthur's effective bomber command consisted of *six* planes.

Roosevelt had said: "A continuous stream of fighters and pursuit planes is traversing the Pacific; already 10 squadrons of the foregoing types are ready for combat in the southwest Pacific area."

The fact was that there were 177 U.S. pursuit planes, but most of them were in patches. The convoy that had been caught at sea by the outbreak of the war and sent to Australia carried 52 A-24's and 18 P-40's. They were still smeared with mud from maneuvers the year before in Louisiana. There were no trigger motors for many of the planes' guns; these had been sent separately aboard some B-17's, but the B-17's had not been allowed beyond Hawaii. There were also some elements of the Royal Australian Air Force; their planes were fabric-covered Gypsy Moths that had to be started by whirling the propellers by hand, and open-seater Wirraways. Most of these planes were grounded for parts or repairs also.

Roosevelt had said: "Extensive arrivals of troops are being guarded by adequate protective elements of our Navy."

The fact was that there was only one American division in Australia, and it needed more training before it would be ready for combat. Of the less than 25,000 Americans in Australia, many were service troops. The best of the Australian fighting-men at this stage were, of all places, in the Middle East. Only one weak and weary Australian division was currently spread around northern Australia and New Guinea. As for the American-Australian Navy, it was a pitiful force with not even one landing-barge, and the co-operation of its commander, could be judged by the experience of General Brett when he had tried to borrow planes from the Navy.

The defense of Australia is in New Guinea.

General Brett returned to the United States soon thereafter. He has since written down his experiences, in which he gives this picture of the state of affairs in Australia at the time of MacArthur's arrival:

"We had flown what was left of our planes out of Java, just as Brereton had flown his out of the Philippines. I took over as Commander of the American forces. The situation was, to put it mildly, muddled and unhappy. Australia's defenses were weak, and Australia expected an invasion. There are no better fighting men in the world than the hard-bitten soldiers of the island continent, but there were too few of them. The Royal Australian Air Force was equipped with almost obsolete planes and was lacking in engines and spare parts, as well as personnel. We had only one American infantry division, and that was incompletely trained. When MacArthur arrived he was extremely disappointed in what he found. He had not wanted to leave the Philippines. . . . However, his better judgment prevailed, influenced by reports that a great American army was being gathered in Australia for him to lead. It did not take long for him to find out how erroneous those reports had been. There was no great army; the airmen found it difficult to understand why their country, the greatest industrial nation on earth, could not give them the tools with which to fight. Nothing much came through in those dreary months. . . . On my way back Stateside, everywhere I went I saw bombers and fighters stacked up waiting to move to Australia. Many had been waiting a long time."

To MacArthur's friends it looked as though he had been transferred from one forlorn hope to another. Apparently he had been selected to leave his beleaguered forces on Bataan for a dash through the enemy blockade to assume command of what, for all he could fathom, was a phantom army. Not only could he no longer count on any quick relief of the Philippine defenders, but he would have a difficult enough time stopping the enemy who was already on the threshold of Australia itself. The force of this blow was immeasurable; probably never before or since has MacArthur's resourcefulness been put to so great a test. Yet his resilience proved equal to it. He discarded pessimistic post-mortems and set about making a realistic survey of what he could do with what he had. And by the time his train reached Melbourne he had revised his entire strategy.

Belatedly he received a message from Washington in which Marshall explained that commitments to other theaters and a scarcity of shipping would prevent the build-up of a powerful striking-force in the southwest Pacific area. Consequently, his mission would be strictly limited. Two divisions of American troops would be allocated to him, and the air units assigned him would be built up to authorized strength; but beyond this he could expect little more.

Marshall may have expected MacArthur's mission to be limited, but meanwhile the enemy's was not. Besides overrunning most of the Philippines, the Japanese had taken Hong Kong, Singapore, Borneo, Java, and Indochina. Washington's abandonment of the Philippines gave the enemy full sway over everything from Japan south to New Guinea, and New Guinea was the doorstep to Australia. By January, New Britain, just above New Guinea, had gone, and there was no doubt about the direction of Japan's next drive. Already Japanese bombers were making regular attacks on Port Moresby in New Guinea, and on Darwin, Australia. They came over at twenty-two thousand feet, too high for the old P-40's and P-39's to intercept them.

To meet this seemingly overwhelming threat, the Australian Chiefs of Staff had set up small defenses at such perimeter stations as Tasmania, Darwin, Port Moresby, Thursday Island, and Townsville. But none of them was strong enough to oppose any major assault, and there were not sufficient troops to reinforce them. So the Australian Chiefs had drawn a line across the continent just above Brisbane, and they planned to defend that line to the death. They intended to abandon New Guinea and to scorch the earth above this "Brisbane Line." Power-generating facilities in northern Australia were to be blown up, military installations destroyed, and docks and harbors incapacitated.

MacArthur was in complete disagreement. "Such a concept," he said to the Chiefs at his first meeting with them, "is fatal to every possibility of ever assuming the offensive, and even if tactically successful will bottle us up on the Australian continent, probably permanently. I am determined to abandon the plan completely."

He had made a characteristic decision; he had decided to attack.

The decision, bold almost to the point of desperation, was to move forward more than a thousand miles into eastern Papua, in New Guinea. He planned to stop the Japanese advance on the Owen Stanley mountain range of New Guinea. Then he would take the offensive. With whatever small forces he could gather, with patched-up planes and—if necessary —without landing-craft, he would counterattack. It was exactly the opposite of what the Japanese, surging forward under the impetus of their own momentum and the psychological booster of continued victories, would expect him to do. Here were shades of Bataan; here, too, was a preview of Inchon, Korea.

The defense of Australia is in New Guinea.

History has shown that this was one of the world's greatest decisions of military strategy. Not only did it save Australia, but it was also the foundation upon which was built our victory over Japan. In his conferences with the Australian Chiefs, MacArthur would listen to no more talk about defense lines in Australia; instead, he insisted upon an aggressive policy of attacking in New Guinea.

The Australians received a tremendous lift from the decisions and actions of MacArthur. They regarded his defense of the Philippines as an epic. They understood his repudiation of any thought of yielding any part of Australia to Japanese conquest; they understood his determination to fight to win. And they understood his complete dedication to the task at hand. Understanding these things, they instantly responded to him with devotion and rallied to his leadership of their war effort.

MacArthur and John Curtin, their Prime Minister, became warm and fast friends and established an alliance unparalleled in the wartime relationship of any other political and military leaders. From the start, they brought such synchronized pressure upon the British and American governments that in the end they were able to secure at least some of the much-needed supplies for the defense of Australia.

Evidently MacArthur was not receiving as hearty support in Washington as he was in Australia. In the first place, some of Roosevelt's military strategists had advised him that Japan might now invade the Indian Ocean area rather than push on through the Pacific, that the enemy's course of conquest might turn west against India instead of south and east against Australia and the U.S.-Australia supply line. If this were the case, Roosevelt explained in a personal message to MacArthur just following the fall of Corregidor, the flow of help should go to India rather than to the Pacific. He asked for MacArthur's viewpoint.

MacArthur replied at once: "The fall of Corregidor and the collapse of resistance in the Philippines, with the defeat of Burma, brings about a new situation. . . . At least two enemy divisions and all the air force in the Philippines will be released for other missions. Japanese troops in Malaya and the Netherlands East Indies are susceptible of being regrouped for an offensive effort elsewhere since large garrisons will not be required. . . . The Japanese Navy is as yet unchallenged and is disposed for further offensive effort. A preliminary move is now under way, probably initially against New Guinea and the line of communications between the United States and Australia. The series of events releases an enormously dangerous potential in the Western Pacific. That the situation will remain static is most improbable. I am of the opinion that the Japa-

65

nese will not undertake large operations against India at this time. That area is undoubtedly within the scope of their military ambitions, but it would be strategically advisable for them to defer it until a later date. On the other hand, the enemy advance toward the south has been supported by the establishment of a series of bases while his left is covered from the Mandated Islands. He is thus prepared to continue in that direction. Moreover, operations in these waters will permit the regrouping of his naval and air forces from the East. Such is not the case in a movement towards India. He must thrust into the Indian Ocean without adequate supporting bases, relinquishing the possibilities of concentrating his naval strength in either ocean. The military requirements for a decisive Indian campaign are so heavy that it cannot be undertaken under those conditions. On the other hand, a continuation of his southern movement at this time will give added safety for his eventual move to the West. . . .

"In view of this situation I deem it of the utmost importance to provide adequate security for Australia and the Pacific area, thus maintaining a constant frontal defense and a flank threat against further movement to the southward. This should be followed at the earliest possible moment by offensive action. . . . The first step in the execution of this conception is the strengthening of the position in this area. . . . If serious enemy pressure were applied against Australia, the situation would be extremely precarious. The extent of territory is so vast and the communication facilities are so poor that the enemy, moving freely by water, has a preponderant advantage. . . . I consider it essential for the security of this country that it be reinforced as follows—two aircraft carriers—an increase from 500 to 1,000 front line planes in the U.S. air forces—one U.S. Army corps of three first-class divisions capable of executing a tactical offensive movement. . . . We must anticipate the future or we will find ourselves once more completely outnumbered."

Had he looked into a magic crystal ball, he could not have "anticipated the future" more accurately.

MacArthur heard no more about diverting shipments to India; but neither was he promised anything like the forces he outlined as necessary for his own operations. At this time the Washington planners were preparing for the invasion of North Africa, evidently on the principle that it was more important to chase about in the desert thirty-five hundred miles from the heart of the German enemy than it was to put up a strong defense in the very face of the Japanese enemy. Into the North African landings went eight aircraft-carriers, seventeen hundred planes, and five divisions, almost twice what MacArthur asked for in order to defend Australia against the rapidly approaching Japanese. But, for the time being, his plea fell upon deaf ears.

In fact, MacArthur was not even officially appointed Supreme Commander of the Southwest Pacific Theater until April 18, a whole month after his arrival in Australia. When Washington did manage to get this important matter through the red tape of confirmation by the other Allied governments, a courier from the Joint Chiefs delivered to him his mission. It was defensive in every respect, and only by implication did it promise future offensive operations. Even so, it was a large order. He was directed to hold the key military areas of Australia as bases for future offensive action and to stop or slow the enemy advance by destroying Japanese shipping, aircraft, and bases in the Netherlands East Indies, New Guinea, and the Solomon Islands. He was to attempt to maintain the position in the Philippines, protect communications, and support Allied operations in the South Pacific and Indian oceans.

It is no wonder that at this time MacArthur cabled the pastor of the Little Rock (Arkansas) Episcopal Church, where he had been baptized: "At the altar where I first joined the sanctuary of God, I ask that you seek divine guidance for me in the great struggle that looms ahead." Nor is it any wonder that after surveying the vast territorial expanse which he was supposed to defend with his meager forces, MacArthur cabled Marshall:

"With the limited forces at my disposal the missions assigned must be construed in large measure as a pattern for future development. None of the three elements of naval, air or ground strength are at present adequate. . . . The naval force has no direct air support due to the absence of a carrier and is therefore suitable only for operations of a minor and subsidiary character. The Australian Air Force will require many months for its development. . . . The U.S. Air Corps strength . . . will require at least four months of the most intensive effort to reach a satisfactory condition. The ground troops are not prepared. . . . In view of the assigned mission and the size and composition of the forces now available I find myself in need of additional information. . . ."

He did not get it, nor did he get any sizable increase in the promised forces. But he refused to sit back and let the Japanese sweep down on an undefended Australia. He kept up his pleas for "at least one carrier, however small," or even as few as "nine additional B-17's." In complete agreement with MacArthur that more strength was vital, Curtin matched his requests with his own to London, asking repeatedly for more troops and naval units, particularly an aircraft-carrier. Finally, on May 4, Churchill sent Curtin a curt rebuff:

"Conditions for diverting divisions to Australia are invasion of Australia by eight or ten Japanese divisions but there are no signs of such mass invasion. Danger to India," he added, "increased by events in Burma and situation Eastern Fleet. UK government would act wrongly if it sent troops needed for invaded India to uninvaded Australia. Arrangements proposed for temporary diversion to Australia of British divisions pending return of Australian Forces in the Middle East would involve maximum expenditure and dislocation of shipping. It is hoped to relieve Australian troops in Ceylon by British units by end of May. . . . To remove CV *Illustrious, Formidable,* or *Indomitable* from the Eastern Fleet would destroy its chance of action this summer. Had hoped to send *Hermes* but she is sunk. No prospect of increasing British shipping on Australia-America run because all engaged in shipping ammunition to Russia and in heavy convoys around the Cape."

But Curtin, too, refused to give up. He knew as well as MacArthur that once Japan invaded Australia, it would be too late to send help from England. At MacArthur's urging he went to London personally in an attempt to persuade Churchill of the danger threatening Great Britain's dominion at a time when soldiers who should be defending that dominion were giving their lives near El Alamein, halfway around the world. The conference between the two prime ministers was at times tense, and its failure was summed up in the message Curtin sent MacArthur from London.

"The grand strategy of the United Nations," it read, "appears to be the defeat of Germany, after which Italy is expected to collapse and the defeat of Japan to soon follow. A cardinal principle of this strategy, as agreed upon by the President and Prime Minister Churchill, is that only the minimum force necessary for the safeguarding of vital interests in other theaters should be diverted from Germany. . . . No effort will be made to divert land forces to Australia until the Japanese intention to invade is reasonably clear." In other words, as Curtin added in a note to Acting Prime Minister Herbert Evatt, "General MacArthur does not have the forces necessary to carry out a single part of his directive."

Churchill evidently did not explain to Curtin just how the grand strategists intended to determine the "Japanese intentions to invade" before the Japanese had invaded. Nor did he seem to understand that the only effective defense of Australia was an offense. At MacArthur's suggestion, Curtin went on to Washington, where he was received genially but evasively by President Roosevelt.

Meanwhile, an extremely important battle had taken place in the

Coral Sea on May 8, between elements of the U.S. and Japanese navies. It was one of the strangest naval engagements in history, because not a ship fired a shot and the entire action was fought by carrier-based planes. Three Japanese carriers were lost to our one, and the enemy fleet was turned back from its destination. That destination was Port Moresby, and as soon as the enemy had thus disclosed his intentions, MacArthur realized that, reinforcements or not, he must move at once and decisively. He must secure Port Moresby. This village, with its big deep-water harbor, was only 350 miles across the Coral Sea from Australia. It was the key to New Guinea, and in enemy hands would be the springboard for an invasion of Australia. One of the first requirements for its defense was the construction of airfields for fighter planes and heavy bombers, first within range of Papua and then on Papua itself.

The problems of logistics in this campaign seemed almost impossible to solve. A report written later in MacArthur's headquarters gives a good indication of the difficulties: "The magnitude of the Southwest Pacific Theater can best be appreciated against a background of comparative geographic distance. If a map of the United States is superimposed upon one of the Southwest Pacific, the continental area of the United States will fit roughly between Australia and the Philippines. . . . Against this geographical background it is evident that the logistical difficulties of the Southwest Pacific Theater in the conduct of the war were tremendous. Not only was the line of communication from the United States to the scene of operation one of the longest the world has ever seen, but the entire route was by water at a time when the Japanese Navy was undefeated and roaming the Pacific almost at will.

"The time factor alone demanded more than usual foresight in logistical planning and required the application of methods not taught in any of the American service schools. The shortage of water transportation for supplies and equipment as well as for troops was probably the most difficult problem. There was not sufficient shipping available to mount operations adequately and then to support the troops in widely dispersed locations. Allowances for supplies and equipment accompanying troops into battle and also the amounts to be sent later for their maintenance had to be curtailed—at times to the danger point. Factors used for the computation of these requirements in the Southwest Pacific were less than those used in many other theaters or areas of the world; at times they were less than half the usual figure."

MacArthur well knew it would be a long and tortuous road back. But he was determined to get on with it and minimize the time element involved. He was pledged to defend Australia at one end and to redeem the Philippines at the other. These two objectives were inseparable. Fail in one and he would fail in the other.

By late spring the promised two U.S. divisions—the 32nd and the 41st—had arrived in Australia, helping to fill in what had been paper forces. But this did not diminish MacArthur's need for the further reinforcements essential to offensive action. On June 6 the famous naval and air victory at Midway demonstrated that the Japanese fleet was vulnerable—that the U.S. had the means for victory if we had the will. Within forty-eight hours MacArthur wired Marshall, calling for "prompt exploitation of this victory" by offensive action in the Southwest Pacific:

"The first objective should be the New Britain–New Ireland area, against which I would move immediately if the means were available," his message read. "I have the 32nd and 41st Infantry Divisions and the 7th Australian Division which can be used in support of a landing force but which cannot be employed in initial attack due to lack of specialized equipment and training. . . . Recommend one division trained and equipped for amphibious operations and a task force, including two carriers, be made available to me at earliest practical date. With such force I could retake that important area, forcing the enemy back 700 miles to his base at Truk with manifold defensive and offensive advantages. Speed is vital. Not possible for me to act quickly if I must build equipment and train my divisions. Cannot urge too strongly that time has arrived to use the force, or a portion of it, which you have informed me to be 40,000 men, on the west coast in training for amphibious operations. . . ."

After some delay, Marshall wired MacArthur that the Navy had raised certain objections to this plan. One objection was that the operation would penetrate enemy territory too deeply; the Navy was wary—or afraid—of risking its ships in waters controlled by the Japanese. MacArthur explained his plan in greater detail in a wire to Marshall on June 24. Pointing out that the Navy appeared to be under a misconception, he said: "My plan contemplates a progressive movement involving primary action against the Solomons and the north coast of New Guinea in order to protect the naval surface forces and to secure airfields from which essential support can be given to the forces participating in the final phase of the operation."

This seemed to answer the Navy's first objection. But the second one was more important. As described in Marshall's wire to MacArthur, the Navy objected to lending support to the New Guinea–New Ireland opera-

70

tion unless these supporting ships could be under naval command in Hawaii.

Here was the old problem of divided command again, the same kind of divided command which had been so disastrous in the Philippines. In his own theater he had noticed that Admiral Herbert Leary was receiving orders direct from Admiral King in Washington. He knew that the Navy, still smarting from the Pearl Harbor disaster and still determined to make the Pacific war a naval war, wanted to fight the enemy in its own way, meanwhile trying to relegate MacArthur and the Army and Air Corps to a minor holding-action in Australia. He realized that under such circumstances the only command which could seize the initiative from the Japanese right away was his own, and he knew that in an enormously complicated action like the one he planned, an Army and Navy working independently could achieve nothing but catastrophe.

His answer minced no words. "The very purpose of the establishment of the SWPA area," he reminded Marshall, "was to obtain unity of command, and any campaign, other than a mere isolated operation such as that carried out by a task force, can be handled only by the commander-in-chief of this area, who is charged with such duties and responsibilities and who operates through land, sea and air commanders. The personnel and the means necessary for the preparation of detailed plans of attack against all objectives in this area are located here, and the various elements that are to be employed should be co-ordinated under my immediate command. . . . Have noted that operational directives apparently come from Admiral King to Admiral Leary. This is not only contrary to channels prescribed in my main directive . . . but also is in violation of all proper command procedure. If correct procedure is not followed. it makes a mockery of the unity of command theory which was the basis of the organizational plan applied to the Pacific Theater."

A more timid commander would not have raised this issue at this time in so definite a manner, but instead would have let matters drift to the point of threatened conflict and confusion. Not so MacArthur. He clearly saw the danger immediately. Only with the proper authority could he implement his strategy of taking the offensive away from the enemy, and it was vital that his authority be plainly defined at the outset. Avoiding the issue would not only serve no fruitful purpose; it could be disastrous.

The self-evident merit of this point, and of MacArthur's strategy, finally convinced Washington. On July 2, 1942, a directive was issued assigning tasks to the Central Pacific and South Pacific commanders as well as to MacArthur, with specific provision made that operations within MacArthur's Southwest Pacific area would be under his direction. Thus, MacArthur's unity-of-command concept was accepted and affirmed. And thus did the Joint Chiefs of Staff turn to thinking and planning in terms of offense rather than defense.

Japanese records examined after the war disclose the shock with which the enemy military leaders came to realize that MacArthur was not to remain in a posture of passive defense, but was instead to move to the offense, with the north coast of New Guinea as his immediate objective. This threw their whole strategic plan out of gear and necessitated thinking and planning in terms of defending and consolidating what they then held. Had not MacArthur insisted upon departure from the mission of defense originally assigned him, the Japanese would have been able to extend and strengthen their positions, and dislodging them eventually would have cost infinitely more in blood and material.

MacArthur wasted no time implementing the directive. His headquarters was a scene of intense activity. Fired with the enthusiasm of taking the initiative again, the staff worked with a will—and a precision—unmatched in any other theater. New members were added: Major General George Kenney, for example, arrived at the end of July to replace General Brett. Kenney immediately set about reorganizing the air command from top to bottom, promoting youngsters who deserved it and sending home officers who did not deserve to stay on the team. He grounded every bomber until enough could be put in good condition for effective missions, cannibalizing wrecked planes to use even the skin for patching the ones that would fly. As more planes arrived, MacArthur asked for and received the designation of the Fifth Air Force, in honor of his old fighter-bomber command in the Philippines. More and heavier bombing-missions went out against the Japanese strongholds at Lae and Salamaua. Meanwhile, the ground troops were toughened for the hard fighting ahead. The flow of supplies increased slightly. In headquarters, at the air and naval bases and among the troops getting ready, there was a new atmosphere. The heady scent of vengeance was in the air.

On July 20, only four months after he had left the Philippines, MacArthur moved his advance headquarters up to Port Moresby, New Guinea. He was on the road back.

CHAPTER VIII   "Put a finger on the enemy's heart."

❧ I do not intend here to chronicle in detail the incidents of the campaign in New Guinea. I leave that to the military historian. It *is* my purpose, however, to attempt to trace the mark of MacArthur's leadership, the impact of his personality and the clarity of his decisions upon the succession of hard-won but decisive victories which lay ahead. For, once he had shifted strategic planning from the defense to the offense, he no longer doubted the issue; he only doubted how much his operations might be retarded by the meagerness of his resources.

Commanding through a staff imbued with his confidence, inspired by his vision, and animated by devotion to his leadership, which was well co-ordinated by his brilliant chief of staff, General Richard K. Sutherland, MacArthur made his decisions with clock-like precision. And the soundness of none of those decisions has been subject to controversy or challenge. This is important, especially when it is historically reflected against the backdrop of such decisions in Europe as the doubtful North African invasion, the bloody "Anzio Beachhead," the "Battle of the Bulge," the withdrawal from the Elbe, the partition of Germany, the Soviet occupation of Eastern Europe, and the encirclement by the Soviet forces of American troops occupying Berlin. Not only are these decisions of the European war the subjects of sharp controversy even today, but the problems and international tensions that they brought to the post-war world remain unresolved, despite U.S. expenditures of billions of dollars for European stability and the maintenance of a large American army on the Continent. All this is in sharp contrast to MacArthur's decisions in the Southwest Pacific campaigns. They met the issue of war decisively and left in their wake no unresolved post-war problems to plague the United States.

It was July 20 when MacArthur moved his main headquarters from

73

Melbourne to Brisbane and established his advance headquarters at Port Moresby. And on the very next day, July 21, the Japanese made a large amphibious landing in force at Buna and Gona on the other side of New Guinea. Immediately the Japanese started overland with the intention of crossing the towering Owen Stanley range along the Kokoda trail and attacking Port Moresby from the rear. At Awala, about thirty miles inland, they met a small Australian force, and the clash that followed was the first ground action in New Guinea.

The Australians, badly outnumbered, were forced to give ground, fighting desperately all the way. Reinforcements were rushed by both sides, but the Japanese had superior reserves and were able to maintain a stronger force in numbers. On July 28 they took the vital airstrip on the Kokoda plateau. Still greatly outnumbered by the Japanese, the Australians were forced back to within ten miles of Kokoda. Here the Japanese dug in to establish forward bases and await further reinforcements. These reinforcements were not long in coming, for the main strength of the Japanese South Seas Detachment now landed near Buna and moved rapidly toward the Kokoda position. Meanwhile, supplies were flown into the enemy-held Kokoda airstrip.

MacArthur, on the other hand, with no amphibious equipment and not enough troops, found that as soon as he was able to send a detachment into a battle area, enemy pressures immediately placed it on the defensive. Yet he realized that if he failed to stop the enemy advance somehow, he would not only lose Port Moresby but would be plunged into the death struggle for Australia itself.

Every day that the black, looming clouds over the Owen Stanleys would let them through, his planes blasted all the enemy concentrations they could find on the north side of New Guinea, so that no parachute operations could be organized to attack Port Moresby. Meanwhile, MacArthur turned his attention to the spot where he thought the next attack would come.

At the southeastern tip of New Guinea lay Milne Bay, with its naval harbor and an airfield. Until July 1942 it had been left practically undefended because of the shortage of troops. But MacArthur recognized its vital importance in the defense of New Guinea, so he sent the Seventh Australian Brigade to garrison and protect its airfield. He now secretly reinforced this garrison by another Australian brigade, the 18th, and some thirteen hundred American combat and service troops.

It was just in time. The Japanese had also recognized this as a key point and were racing to seize it and turn the flank of Port Moresby. They

74

believed it to be undefended, and so they were taken completely by surprise when they ran into heavy fire. The battle lasted for a week, and the Japanese were decisively defeated. By September they had evacuated the remnants of their force, leaving seven hundred of their number dead and practically all of their equipment on shore.

This was our first ground victory in the Pacific, and it sent a thrill throughout not only Australia but the entire Allied world. MacArthur used the occasion to sum up the enemy's fruitless attempts at Port Moresby: "This citadel is guarded by the natural defense line of the Owen Stanley range. The first effort was to turn its left flank from Lae and Salamaua, which proved impracticable. The enemy then launched an attack in large convoy force against its rear. This was repulsed and dispersed in the Coral Sea. He then tried to pierce the center by way of Buna-Gona-Kokoda, subjecting himself to extraordinary air losses because of the extreme vulnerability of his exposed position. His latest effort was to turn the right flank by a surprise attack at Milne Bay. The move was anticipated, however, and . . . the enemy fell into the trap with disastrous results to him."

Meanwhile, on the Kokoda trail the fighting continued bitterly and unrelentingly on into September. In the swirling cloud banks that almost perpetually enshroud the mountain passes, the Australians and Japanese fought as much a "battle of lungs" as a battle of bullets; and the Australians were accustomed to the dry air of the desert. The enemy kept advancing, up to the passes, through the equatorial rain forests, and over the steep limestone ledges. The Japanese soldiers were veterans and picked troops. They painted their faces, bodies, arms, and legs green and, monkey-like, infiltrated everywhere. Bribing and torturing natives into improvising supply lines for them, they slithered over the tops of the Owen Stanleys and down the other side, toward Port Moresby. Never relaxing their pressure, they repeatedly forced the Australians to fall back to new lines of defense. Australian reinforcements and intense Allied air attacks on enemy concentrations and movements had little decisive effect upon this constant enemy pressure.

MacArthur could see that he was in for one of the fights of his life. The Japanese were determined to take New Guinea, no matter what it cost them in matériel and men. His intelligence reports from Rabaul indicated an ominous build-up in strength, and the increasing convoys and reinforcements to New Guinea clearly showed the enemy's intentions. In Australia five months before he had said: "We shall win or we shall die." Here in New Guinea, on the jagged precipices of the Owen Stanleys and in the stinking swamplands along their base, he and his men would win or die.

He had only one man for every five of the enemy. He had the defensive advantage of one of the greatest obstacles of terrain in the world, the supposedly impassable Owen Stanleys. His reserve troops had never fought an enemy before anywhere, much less a highly trained enemy in the world's worst jungle. His air force was finally beginning to get its strength, and was hurting the Japanese more each day. By any textbook of military strategy, MacArthur should have put everything he had into an overwhelming defense, pouring his reserve troops onto those narrow trails and plastering the advancing supply lines with every plane he could use.

MacArthur had read the textbooks, but he had a better idea. He would counterattack.

He explained his plan to Washington and tried again to get some of the necessary help. He said that he was making his appeal "with greatest reluctance and impelled by gravest sense of duty." He pointed out that the enemy had appeared to "shift the center of gravity of his forces to this general area, his main battle front being now definitely in the Southwest and South Pacific. His potential—air, sea and land—is increasing and his relative strength is rapidly growing greater than that of the Allied potential in these areas." Trying to make it clear that he, too, was considering the over-all situation, he said: "I comprehend entirely the strategy adopted, assigning present missions as holding ones to enable concentrations to be made elsewhere. It is fundamental, however, that holding areas have sufficient forces actually to hold and that the strength of holding forces, with the initiative in the enemy's hands, can be determined only by a constantly changing and accurate appraisal of the enemy's power. . . . Unless steps are taken to match the heavy air and ground forces the enemy is assembling, I predict the early development of a situation similar to those that have overwhelmed our forces in the Pacific since the beginning of the war. I beg of you most earnestly to have this momentous question reviewed by the President and the Chief of Staff lest it become too late."

A week later he made another appeal for the equipment he needed and reiterated his plan: "Enemy is continually infiltrating from the north in ever increasing pressure. . . . Urgently request additional naval facilities to dispatch large ground reinforcements to New Guinea, as lack of shipping prevents me from doing now. My objective is a counter infiltration to the north, while at the same time making creeping advances along the north coast with small vessels and Marine amphibious forces." Having had no results from his first plea, he could not resist adding: "If New Guinea goes, the result will be disastrous." It did him no good; this request was in vain.

MacArthur could not help being saddened by Washington's seeming indifference when he went to the front and saw the misery and death to which it committed his men. His advance headquarters in Port Moresby was a big, rambling wooden house that had been the home of the Australian governor before the war. From this close vantage point he could see at first hand what it was like to fight in New Guinea.

It was like no other ground fighting in the world, and it was worse. A wilder, fiercer terrain could not be found anywhere. New Guinea's area is three times that of the Philippines, more than one tenth that of the United States, and its altitude varies so much that while the equatorial jungle simmers below, ice forms on the wings of a plane flying over the Owen Stanleys. On the mountainsides the going is so tough that sometimes the troops made only half a mile in an entire day. At one spot on the mountainside, called "The Golden Staircase," fifteen hundred steps went down one side of a narrow gorge and twenty-five hundred up the other. At the end of a day's march, the advance guard, climbing up the cliff, could shout across to the main body of troops sliding down the other side. The coral soil in the jungle below, eroded by torrential rains, supports nothing but pestiferous vegetation whose sickly green contrasts with the ugly yellow of the razor-sharp, man-high kunai grass.

The forest is a tangle of bamboos, palms, and rotting undergrowth. Stink lilies fill the air with a smell like that of rotted beef. Creeping liana vines form overhead mats that shut out the light. The narrow trails are booby-trapped by twisted roots and surrounded by acres of waist-deep, stinking slop. This is during good weather; when it rains, the hot soil steams, trails become millraces, and the best ground is a juicy morass. In the U.S. the average rainfall is 29 inches a year; in the New Guinea jungle the 1943 rainfall was 170 inches.

Everywhere the air was filled with clouds of mosquitoes and flies, so much so that a constant waving of the hand in front of the food at mealtime was known as "the New Guinea salute." The ground swarmed with chiggers, fleas, biting ants, poisonous spiders, and huge, vivid butterflies that drank the sweat off a man's arm. The trees and vines of the jungle were alive with beautifully colored birds, as well as with huge bats. In the swamps, crocodiles and enormous snakes waited for the unwary soldier. So did disease—dengue fever, blackwater fever, bacillary and amœbic dysentery, scrub typhus, ringworm, hookworm, and the yaws. Insect bites itched until the soldier scratched them, and then turned into ulcerating sores. Every man sweated away at least fifteen to twenty pounds. Hardest to fight of all the natural enemies was malaria, which was everywhere. At one point every man in an entire company had his temperature taken; every one had a fever.

Still every man fought on, in a hunter-and-hunted warfare, stalking the enemy as troops under MacArthur's father had stalked the American Indian, but in much worse terrain. And the Japanese sniper tried out some new tricks on the men who fought in New Guinea. A sniper would rig a dummy on pulleys in a tree near him, fire at an Allied soldier, and then jerk the dummy enough to draw the answering fire. Snipers would let patrols pass by a given spot for two or three days without firing a shot, and then slaughter a particularly big patrol, sometimes using explosive bullets. After one of New Guinea's downpours snipers would watch for soldiers floundering in the chest-deep trails and send a fusilade into them, leaving nothing but a red tide washing down to the river and the Solomon Sea.

As the fresh troops sloshed up to relieve their comrades, they had to squeeze past dismaying lines of the wounded, their green uniforms begrimed with gray mud and the dull brown of dried blood, their faces fever-yellowed and swollen from insect bites. Sometimes the ones too badly wounded to walk were carried on litters by the slow-moving, splay-footed, but perpetually patient natives, while other natives held big banana leaves over the heads of the wounded to shield them from the scorching sun.

Clearly, under such conditions, the only way to beat the enemy was to outfox him, and MacArthur had already set about doing that. He was matched against General Tomatore Horii, one of Japan's best amphibious experts. With practically no amphibious equipment of his own, he would have to rely upon delicate timing; he would have to hit General Horii and his troops at the moment when their supply lines were extended to the farthest over the mountains and before enough reinforcements had arrived to consolidate the recently won gains. MacArthur calculated that this time would come at about the first of October, and he planned a three-way counteroffensive. While the Australians increased their pressure along the mountain trails, other Allied troops, mostly the American reserves training under General Eichelberger in Australia, would strike from the flank and rear, along the mountains and the northern New Guinea coast.

"Put a finger on the enemy's heart."

Yet how could he double back on an enemy ensconced on these formidable mountains without doing it by sea? Could he possibly beg or borrow some landing-barges in time for this maneuver? Once again he tried to impress his plight upon Marshall. "A golden opportunity is being lost," he pointed out, "in not anticipating the enemy through clearing the coast as far as Buna by trained amphibious combat teams. . . . Earnestly request reconsideration of previous decision not to make available such forces. . . ." This time he was promised some landing-craft—but not until November. He knew that would be too late. He had no choice but to make do with what he had.

Every kind of river boat, tug, and coastal ferry which could be drafted was pressed into action. Warships of the fleet in MacArthur's area were temporarily converted into troop-carriers for the fourteen-hundred-mile voyage from Brisbane to Port Moresby. More Australian troops, with more arms, were flown across to the south side of the mountains, to start pushing the Japanese back across the mountains. But all of this was not enough; and in order to ensure the success of his envelopment, MacArthur made the decision that made history.

He could not get enough troops to the north coast of New Guinea with the few ferries he had been able to enlist. So he decided to fly them there; not only that, he would supply them by air as well. This was a revolutionary idea. Never before had so large an attacking force been landed by air, and never had an entire battle area been supplied by air, certainly not one 650 miles from the nearest base. When MacArthur put this proposal before his staff, some members frankly voiced their opinions that it could not be done. MacArthur turned to his air commander, General Kenney, and asked him if he thought it was possible. Kenney's answer was blunt and to the point: "Give me a few days to prepare and I'll move a whole goddamned division, if you want it." MacArthur thanked his other staff members politely for their advice, but this time he did not take it. He told Kenney to go ahead and land the troops and supplies by air.

The operation was a huge success, transporting two divisions and more than a million tons of food and ammunition, including light artillery. The battle-worn old B-17's of Kenney's air fleet flew in load after load of soldiers day and night, some of whom were surprised to find MacArthur greeting them on the airstrip as they arrived. When storms closed down on the peaks of the Owen Stanleys, the pilots described them by saying: "Those clouds are full of rocks today"—but they kept flying in the troops and supplies, with practically no losses. Even a 105-mm. howitzer was taken apart and fitted into a B-17, to be followed by more how-itzers, wagons for them, and even horses to pull them, along with all the food, equipment, and arms needed by the soldiers. Some of it was dropped by parachute, and a system was worked out for blind delivery of supplies. To accomplish this, Kenney commandeered every plane he could get his hands on, including those of Australia's civil airlines, and every crew he could muster, including some American ferry pilots who dropped in on a special mission. They were from Boeing Aircraft Company, and when they landed at an Australian field and asked where the nearest town was, Kenney told them that the next town they would see would be Port Moresby, because their new B-17's were now in the ferrying business. The civilian crews gladly pitched in, taking a new load of soldiers into New Guinea every twenty-four hours.

Meanwhile, Kenney's planes had to keep attacking the enemy, both to protect the new landings and to stall the Japanese drive. In one day, for example, while troops and supplies were still being flown into battle, thirty-five tons of bombs and thirty-three thousand rounds of ammunition plastered Buna; on another day MacArthur's and Kenney's bombers flew through the anti-aircraft fire and the corrosive volcanic-dust clouds of Rabaul to drop another thirty tons of bombs. From the start of the counteroffensive until its final victory, the Japanese lost 418 planes, 24 warships, 86 transports, and 150 landing-barges in the New Guinea area alone.

General Horii was finding in MacArthur the same inspired ingenuity that had so frustrated General Homma on Bataan. While major strategic maneuvers like this envelopment were catching thousands of Japanese like rats in a trap, even minor tactics were giving the enemy some nasty surprises. Fragmentation bombs were rigged to parachutes and exploded overhead at Buna, slaughtering hundreds of troops in one attack. B-25's were armed with so many guns for strafing that the recoil shook some of the rivets out of the skins of the planes; but meanwhile the hugely increased firepower mowed enemy lines like wheat. MacArthur would not attempt to take credit for such technical innovations himself—though a list of the ones he personally suggested would be surprisingly large—but the point is that he encouraged and inspired this kind of ingenuity in everyone who worked with him.

The enemy tried to rush reinforcements to Buna. The ships were met and sunk by more bombers. A discouraged Japanese soldier wrote in his diary (which was found after the war) that MacArthur's planes "fly above our positions as if they own the skies." This air superiority was established despite the fact that MacArthur was still not getting nearly the number of planes and amounts of material he needed and had asked for. There were enough bombsights for only about one third of his planes. When a squadron of new B-24's finally arrived on October 22, the nose-wheel collar of every one was cracked. Replacements were rushed by air, but these were cracked, too. For two weeks, while new ones were being made in Australia, the B-24's sat on the ground. Meanwhile, as though MacArthur had nothing else to do, Pentagon officers were cabling him for explanations of various tactical maneuvers.

Despite shortages, the world's worst terrain for an offensive, seemingly malevolent weather, and senseless, time-consuming queries from Pentagon generals, MacArthur accomplished the unheard-of feat of placing two divisions of troops exactly where he wanted them and supplying them almost solely by air. This entirely new concept of warfare brought from all the Allied world cheers as loud as the screams of rage from the outwitted enemy. Of this kind of co-ordinated attack MacArthur said: "We can outguess, outmaneuver and out-think the enemy; we can put a finger right on his heart and paralyze him with surprise." The history-making counterattack on New Guinea not only surprised the enemy; it put him to rout.

Virtually surrounded, cut off from all supplies, reeling under the fresh attacks of the Australians on the mountain passes and the Americans along the coast, the Japanese retreated to the jungles around Buna and Gona. Here a formidable defense fortress had been prepared, and here occurred some of the most savage fighting of World War II.

The Japanese regarded the defense of Buna and Gona as a face-saving battle. Had MacArthur been given a strong enough force early enough, the enemy might have been driven out of Buna before he could dig in so thoroughly; but the Japanese had had four months to prepare their last redoubt, and they had used the time well.

Buna was protected by rivers and the sea on both sides and a swamp that stretched almost all the way across its front. All the dry areas were fortified, and approaching trails were covered by an enfilade of machine-gun fire. Everywhere were sunken fortresses lined with sand-filled gasoline drums and covered with palm trunks and bags of coral sand, camouflaged with vines and palm leaves so that they were invisible only a few yards away. Usually they were built at the edge of neck-deep swamps, so there was no way to bypass their murderous fire; the only way was to assault them, one by one. Over most of these bunkers, and hidden all through the surrounding jungle, were the ever-present hornets' nests of snipers.

It was siege warfare under the worst possible conditions, and the Japanese fought more fanatically than ever. Artillery, mortar fire, grenades, and small-arms fire would reduce a bunker to a smoking ruin, and still its occupants would fight to the death. In one pocket, when it was finally taken, the attackers found six Japanese, knee-deep in bodies of their dead and wearing gas masks because of the smell, but still fighting. When enemy bombers sneaked over, they concentrated on the hospitals; in one attack twenty-one bombers subjected a plainly marked hospital tent to both high-level and dive bombing, wounding and killing forty of the patients. The Buna-Gona defense was one of desperation; but it was slowing the attack in some places and stopping it in others.

MacArthur could see that the combination of the desperate defense, the enervating heat, and the effects of malaria was hurting the morale of his men to such an extent that the whole counteroffensive was endangered. It would, of course, have been a simple tactical matter to turn the Japanese flank by sea, land in their rear, and wipe out their force; but this maneuver required amphibious equipment, and Washington still had not sent what he had so frequently and urgently requested. So all he could do was use the resources at hand.

One of those resources was a brilliant field general, Lieutenant General Robert Eichelberger, who had been in Australia training the troops who were flown in against the Japanese. MacArthur sent for Eichelberger, who promptly reported to the Government House headquarters in Port Moresby.

On the wide screened-in veranda where MacArthur and Sutherland had placed their desks to catch whatever cooling breeze there might be, Eichelberger found a sober welcome. MacArthur, pacing up and down the veranda, did not have his usual smile of greeting. Equally grim-faced was Sutherland, who had just returned from the Buna front with the news that the attack there was getting nowhere. Only the irrepressible airman Kenney had a welcoming grin for Eichelberger.

MacArthur wasted no time on preliminaries. Continuing his striding, he said: "Bob, I'm putting you in command at Buna." He explained that with the command went freedom of action to do anything Eichelberger considered necessary to relieve the situation. "I'm sending you in, Bob," he went on, "and I want you to remove all officers who won't fight. Relieve regimental and battalion commanders; if necessary, put sergeants in charge of battalions and corporals in charge of companies—anyone who will fight." MacArthur made it clear that any measures Eichelberger wanted to take were approved in advance, so long as the result was the only important one: "Take Buna."

That was November 30, 1942. By eleven the next morning, after a long night of staff conferences, Eichelberger stepped out of his plane at the front and set out to "take Buna." As MacArthur suggested, he sent back officers who did not fight and replaced them with men who would, regardless of rank. He stopped the fighting for two days while he reorganized the entire command set-up. He stepped up the hour-by-hour front-line intelligence, improved the food and medical situation, and devised new tactics of attack. Most of all, he gave his men the kind of leadership they could fight for.

Following the example of MacArthur on Bataan, he wore his stars instead of hiding his rank from the snipers as his predecessors had done. He went up to the front and personally led his men forward through enemy fire. Of the four generals at the Buna front, three were injured, and only Eichelberger seemed impervious to the Japanese bullets. Taking a machine gun, Eichelberger killed some Japanese snipers himself. Watching this display of military leadership, MacArthur cheered Eichelberger on and gave him unlimited support. When, for example, a sergeant named Herman Bottcher led eighteen men through Japanese lines to the Buna beach, Eichelberger sent a commendatory note about him to MacArthur. MacArthur responded by giving Sergeant Bottcher the Distinguished Service Cross and making him a captain on the spot.

With this kind of backing and appreciation, the men of Buna began to fight like the men on Bataan. The tide was turned. By December 14, only two weeks after he had changed commanders, MacArthur could announce: "Buna Village has been taken. It was occupied by our troops at 10 o'clock this morning."

The fall of Buna Village did not bring the battle for the Buna area to a close, but the Allies now pushed on against weakening enemy resistance. It was three weeks before the Buna area fell and another three weeks before the last remaining Sanananda defensive position was reduced and the Japanese army was destroyed. A key point of this Sanananda defense was the town of Gona, where the frenzied Japanese resistance was epitomized by a captured order from the enemy commander which read as follows: "It is not permissible to retreat even a step from each unit defensive position. I demand that each man fight until the last. As previously instructed, those without firearms or sabers must be prepared

83

to fight with sharp weapons such as knives or bayonets tied to sticks, or with clubs." But Gona and Sanananda did fall in a rout of the enemy so complete that the only Japanese left on Papua were small isolated groups fleeing or swimming along the coast toward Salamaua.

MacArthur took this occasion to point out publicly the lessons that the Papuan campaign had taught. "The destruction of the remnants of the enemy forces in the Sanananda area concludes the Papuan campaign," he said. "The Horii army has been annihilated. The outstanding military lesson of this campaign was the continuous calculated application of air power, inherent in the potentialities of every component of the air forces, employed in the most intimate tactical and logistical union with ground troops. The effect of this modern instrumentality was sharply accentuated by the geographical limitations of this theater. . . . A new form of campaign was tested, which points the way to ultimate defeat of the enemy in the Pacific. The offensive and defensive power of the air in the adaptability, range and capacity of its transport in an effective combination with ground forces, represents tactical and strategical elements of a broadened conception of warfare that will permit the application of offensive power in swift, massive strokes, rather than the dilatory and costly island-to-island advance that some have assumed to be necessary in a theater where the enemy's far-flung strongholds are dispersed throughout a vast expanse of archipelagos. Air forces and ground forces were well knit together in Papua and when in sufficient strength and proper naval support, their indissoluble union points the way to victory through new and broadened strategic conceptions."

The Japanese made two more desperate attempts to halt MacArthur's advance. One was at Wau, once the center of a small gold rush but now a ghost town with an airfield left behind by the prospectors. A small Australian force had held the Wau airfield against the enemy since early 1942. Not only was it a strong outpost in the defense of Port Moresby; it was also a constant threat to the Japanese airfields at Lae and Salamaua. So the enemy made a strong attack on Wau. Greatly outnumbered, the defending forces fell back toward the airfield.

MacArthur saw that he could not get reinforcements to Wau in time by land, so once again he took to the air. The result was reminiscent of the famous last-minute arrival of the cavalry in the old West. By the time the first planes came down with their troops, the Japanese had reached one end of the airstrip, and some of the Australian troops were actually shooting as they came out of their planes. When the first planeload of reinforcements landed on January 29, there were only two hundred men defending the airstrip. By noon of the 30th, the Japanese attackers had been sent fleeing in disorder into the jungle.

The enemy's second attempt came when the Japanese tried to sneak an armada of reinforcements to New Guinea's north coast. MacArthur knew all about this maneuver ahead of time, and had made special preparations for it. Kenney and his pilots had perfected a new method of attack—skip bombing, in which the pilot swept low over his target and aimed his bomb to skip across the water toward the broad target of a ship's hull. Skip bombing had the advantages of both torpedo and dive bombing without many of the disadvantages of these methods, and Kenney and his pilots practiced this ingenious new maneuver against the rusted hulks littering the New Guinea shores. So when the reinforcement armada made its run for New Guinea, it rushed straight toward its own destruction.

Eight transports and eight destroyers steamed out of Rabaul on February 28. By March 1 the convoy had been spotted. What followed was the famous Battle of the Bismarck Sea, which lasted three days and in which MacArthur, with land-based air, gave the enemy a lesson in protecting a convoy. The weather conditions were so bad during this battle that varying estimates of damage were reported to headquarters, both by Kenney and by the enemy. And, in fact, some slighting comments were made back in the U.S. about MacArthur's statement that our victory assumed "the proportions of a major disaster to the enemy." But Japanese records found after the war proved the critics wrong. Of the more than 7,000 Japanese soldiers in the armada, only 850 got through; and airplane and motor fuel, together with four months' supply of food for 20,000 men, went to the bottom of the Bismarck Sea.

Thus two attempts by the enemy to stop MacArthur had completely failed. The Papuan campaign was won. It was less than a year since the dark night when MacArthur had looked back with raised cap in a parting tribute to Corregidor and Bataan; and now he had won his first campaign on the road back. Congratulatory messages had poured in from everywhere. Marshall had cabled: "Congratulations. . . . The amount that has been accomplished with the very limited means available is a tribute to your leadership and to the fortitude and fighting qualities of the Australian and American soldiers. Quite evidently the wonderful support given by the Air Forces contributed in large measure to the success of the operations." Pondering this message, MacArthur wondered whether an appreciation of the success he was achieving on this limited offensive would help to gain for him the means for a sustained offensive against the enemy on a broad front. He could only hope that it would.

The Marshall message had been followed by one from Secretary of War Stimson: ". . . Have followed your masterly campaign with close interest and much gratification. . . . It is a tremendous satisfaction to feel that American fortunes in SWPA are in such skillful hands. I am in constant touch with President Quezon here [1] and we are both beginning to think with encouragement of the time, which now really seems approaching, when we shall redeem our promise to the Filipinos. . . ."

It was difficult to tell from this message whether it augured well for a kinder reception of MacArthur's requests to Washington for greater resources. While the tenor of it showed that the tension and uncertainty of the early days of the war had eased in Washington as a result of MacArthur's successes, it also seemed to pass over rather gingerly a long, tortuous road that MacArthur knew lay ahead. But he was glad to see a spirit of eager anticipation permeating Washington thinking and hoped that it might presage an easing of the barrier to needed men and supplies.

The most heartwarming congratulatory message MacArthur received in this period was from his old friend Prime Minister Curtin, whose country MacArthur's victory had now made safe. "I would express to you," Curtin wired, "your commanders and all ranks of Australian and American forces, the thanks and admiration of the Australian people and the government for their magnificent services. The campaign has been fought under most trying conditions in one of the most difficult regions in the world. The forces under your command have not only overcome these immense natural difficulties but have decisively defeated a tenacious and stubborn foe. The campaign has been a demonstration of comradeship in arms and cooperation between the forces of the United States and Australia which I am sure will continue till the common foe is totally defeated."

Congratulations were indeed in order, because this was a historic occasion. For the first time, after more than a year of apparent invincibility, the Japanese had been stopped, and the Allies had started to fight their way back. MacArthur had, incidentally, accomplished all this with surprisingly small losses. Despite the fact that a commander expects twice as many casualties as the enemy when he is on the offensive, MacArthur's casualties in the Papuan campaign were less than half those of

---

[1] At MacArthur's urging, Quezon had gone to Australia and then on to the U.S. to establish his government in exile.

"Put a finger on the enemy's heart."

the Japanese. Neither the Japanese enemy nor the natural enemy of disease had been able to defeat him. Against the multitudinous infections, illnesses, and disorders endemic to New Guinea swamplands, MacArthur had fought a medical battle, armed with the latest drugs even though in small quantity; and he had won.

MacArthur's victory in the Papuan Peninsula came seventeen days before the final victory on Guadalcanal. That campaign, which the Navy had insisted on fighting in conjunction with MacArthur's New Guinea operation, had gone badly. MacArthur had foreseen this; when, in July 1942 he and Vice Admiral Robert L. Ghormley met in Australia to plan their joint operation, both men warned Washington that to attack the Lower Solomons too soon was to court disaster. But the Joint Chiefs of Staff in Washington could not wait. Admiral King himself later admitted that "because of the urgency of seizing and occupying Guadalcanal, planning was not up to the usual thorough standard." Support lent by Mac-Arthur's bombers kept the Guadalcanal landings from being opposed by enemy planes. But the Japanese quickly poured reinforcements onto the island, and the Navy was unable, or unwilling, to fight it out with that portion of the Japanese fleet. Throughout the Guadalcanal campaign MacArthur's planes, and even some ships from his pitifully small naval force, supported the Navy's operations at the same time that they were fighting their own war in New Guinea. But what the Navy strategists had estimated as a brief surprise action turned into a grueling six-month siege.

Its comparison with Buna is interesting. At Buna the Allies had to work their way through the equatorial jungle while the enemy was dug in along the cooler stretches of the beach. At Guadalcanal the situation was reversed. Yet when the Papuan campaign was won, the Guadalcanal fighting was bogged down in complete stalemate. Only after Admiral William Halsey took command of the South Pacific Theater was Guadalcanal finally won—and even then it took four more months.

But won it was, and MacArthur and Halsey promptly planned to coordinate in a gigantic envelopment operation against the Japanese. The two men developed a mutual respect and admiration for each other which grew into a warm friendship. Their meeting was the beginning of a totally new kind of warfare.

MacArthur spelled out this new kind of warfare as he finished up the Papuan campaign and turned his thoughts once again toward the Philippines. His own forces were depleted and exhausted, and the slow trickle of replacements from the U.S. provided only the minimum essentials for immediate operations. But he already knew what strategy he would use in his future operations against the Japanese.

"My strategic conception for the Pacific Theater," he said, "contemplates massive strokes against only main strategic objectives, utilizing surprise and air-ground striking power supported and assisted by the fleet. This is the very opposite of what is termed 'island-hopping,' which is the gradual pushing back of the enemy by direct frontal pressure with the consequental heavy casualties which will certainly be involved. Key points must of course be taken, but a wise choice of such will obviate the need for storming the mass of islands now in enemy possession. 'Island-hopping' with extravagant losses and slow progress . . . is not my idea of how to win a war as soon and as cheaply as possible. New conditions require for solution and new weapons require for maximum application new and imaginative weapons. Wars are never won in the past."

This principle was later popularly referred to as MacArthur's "hit-'em-where-they-ain't" concept, and it became the unfailing guide to all subsequent strategic planning. Because of it and because of MacArthur's accurate estimates of timing and his concern for each life entrusted to his command, thousands of veterans of his campaigns are alive today who might otherwise lie beneath the white crosses that dot the wake of war. Yet when MacArthur recently was asked by a historical section of the Army to comment on how the system of "bypassing or leapfrogging" developed, he refused to take credit for it.

"The system is as old as war itself," he answered. "It is merely a new name, dictated by new conditions, given to the ancient principle of envelopment. It was the first time that the area of combat embraced land and water in such relative proportions. Heretofore, either one or the other was predominant in the campaign. But in this area the presence of great land masses separated by large sea expanses with the medium of transportation of ground troops by ships as well as land transport seemed to conceal the fact that the system was merely that of envelopment applied to a new type of battle area. It has always proved the ideal method for success by inferior in number but faster moving forces."

But if MacArthur would not take credit for developing "hit-'em-where-they-ain't" strategy, he could certainly view with satisfaction his daring and magnificent accomplishment in saving Australia under such seemingly impossible circumstances. He had taken a great gamble in electing to defend Australia 650 miles north in New Guinea. He had committed all of his forces in this gamble. Had he lost, Australia would have been wide open for Japanese attack. And if ever in history there was a case of a campaign won with a minimum of manpower and a maximum of brainpower, it was the Papuan campaign. So the end of the fighting around Buna marked the turning-point of the war in the Pacific. As Mac-Arthur said in commenting on it many years later: "From this point on, I never doubted our full success." It was no longer a question of whether the Japanese would be beaten; now the only question was how.

CHAPTER IX   Intimate Glimpses

When the Buna campaign was won, MacArthur returned to his permanent headquarters in Brisbane. Those who had not been with him at Port Moresby naturally expected to see a weary figure bowed by the exhaustion of one of history's worst battles. Instead, MacArthur looked as if he had been vacationing. There was a sparkle in his eyes and a spring in his step. At a press conference he joked and laughed with correspondents. He had every reason to be exultant over the outcome at Buna because he had just won a great victory against seemingly impossible odds. But in the midst of the jocularity his expression changed to grimness and determination as he offered his only unrequested comment on the Papuan campaign. "The dead of Bataan," he said, "will rest easier tonight."

He had not forgotten, and he never would. His next targets would be Hollandia and the Admiralty Islands, Wewak and Wakde, Biak and Noemfoor. But his major objective was the Philippines. From the Philippines he could get his hands around the throat of the enemy and throttle him; in the Philippines he could redeem the prestige of the U.S. in Asia. The islands next on his planning agenda were but steppingstones on the route there.

I had been reminded of this fact with urgent clarity at the beginning of 1943. While MacArthur was applying the finishing touches to the Papuan campaign, I was in Washington making preparations to go to China. I had left the Philippines in the summer of 1940 to spend a short vacation with my wife and two sons, whom I had sent to the U.S. the year before in order to get them out of the path of the Japanese aggression that I sensed was coming. In the U.S., I was recalled to active duty in the Army Air Corps after a lapse of thirteen years, prior to which I had been a regular officer in that branch of the service. I was now preparing to report as intelligence officer for the 14th Air Force, which was about to be activated under General Clare Chennault. It was at this point that I received word that MacArthur had asked to have me on his staff. And it was his special job that emphasized to me his constant awareness of the major objective; he wanted me to organize and direct the activities of the Filipino guerrillas.

With undying faith in MacArthur's pledge to return, they were still resisting the Japanese despite a total lack of supply. MacArthur wanted them supported and their operations organized as well as could be done across thirty-six hundred miles and through enemy lines. I knew the Philippines and the Filipinos well from my fifteen years in the Islands, and I knew that these brave, faithful people needed only the inspiration of MacArthur's pledge to maintain a spiritual resistance to the Japanese efforts at pacification. But I knew, too, that they needed more if they were going to translate such spiritual resistance into guerrilla warfare and intelligence operations.

I canvassed Army sources in Washington for the most important fighting-arm of all—the portable radios so necessary if communications with isolated areas were to be established. The best transmitter that I could find weighed one ton, entirely too much for guerrillas to carry through the jungles. But I extended my search to London, where, through local British intelligence representatives, I finally located a British-made transmitter that could be carried on a man's back. I initially ordered dozens of them; I would be ordering hundreds before the war was over. Flying to the west coast, I made a study of two regiments of Filipino soldiers training there, and selected the best men I could find for the difficult assignment of slipping past the Japanese patrols and establishing an intelligence network to keep MacArthur informed of all enemy dispositions and movements throughout the Islands.

Upon my arrival in Brisbane on May 24, 1943, MacArthur greeted me in General Sutherland's office with his characteristic warmth of expression, emphasized by his firm handclasp. Then he motioned me into his adjoining office and, without further amenities, began to outline the task he had in mind. It was a concise and bold statement of objectives— the organization, supply, and co-ordination of guerrilla activities throughout the Philippines; the development of an intelligence network and corresponding communications facilities capable of keeping him informed of enemy troop movements; the countering of enemy propaganda designed to break the will of resistance of the Filipino people; and the preparation in the Islands of interior forces capable of striking behind the enemy's lines when the campaign of liberation began. Characteristically, too, he

91

made it clear that he left to my imagination and ingenuity the manner in which these objectives might be achieved. I knew that I would have his unqualified support as well as that of his chief of staff, General Sutherland; and I was gratified to be told that my channel of report would be direct to that office.

As he talked, my eyes roamed around MacArthur's office. It reminded me of his office in Manila. The broad, austere-looking desk was uncluttered by papers awaiting attention. There were a single leather couch, a few chairs, and one bookcase. The walls had no charts or maps on them; only pictures of Washington and Lincoln hung there. And the man pacing up and down in front of me was unchanged from the one I had last seen in Manila. If anything, he seemed even younger and more vigorous; it was difficult for me to believe that he was anywhere near sixty-three. As he paced, he described the job he had for me in vivid language and with intimate detail that showed that the smallest facet of it had not escaped his attention. He was the same positive, resolute, self-reliant man I had known as a friend, and as I now studied him as my commander I began to feel that sense of loyalty, devotion, and pride which I have heard described so many times by "MacArthur men" who have served under him and known him well. MacArthur, I remember thinking as I watched and listened to him, is the personification of the truism that great leaders are born, not made. This, I thought, must have been what it was like in a tent in Gaul with Cæsar; on the approaches to Cannæ with Hannibal; on the plains before Gaugamela with Alexander the Great; on the banks of the Delaware with Washington.

Then suddenly he was through. I arose to go, and as I did so I took a long chance. Looking directly at him, I said: "General, I will deliver you periodic reports from my own operatives in the city of Manila within three months." He looked his doubts and then laughed as he replied: "And what will the penalty be if you fail?" But there was to be no failure and no penalty. As I left, he called after me: "Oh, Court, drop by and see Jean any afternoon."

In the next few days, as I renewed acquaintances with the old members of the staff and met the new ones, I found that the business of headquarters proceeded with the same routine as when the Philippine defenses were being prepared. There was nothing hectic about the routine, but nothing lackadaisical either. MacArthur did not come to the office until ten a.m., but this fact was deceptive. He had been up since seven, and when he arrived at the office he had thoroughly digested every news item, every report from the front, every dispatch from other theaters, and every important cable from Washington. If he needed to consult a staff member, he would ask him to come to his quarters—or he might telephone him in the middle of the night. When he arrived at his office he expected the morning's staff work to be well under way and all papers for his attention to be waiting on his desk.

Reports, correspondence, directives, and all the other written details of a big army headquarters then came pouring from MacArthur's office. There were no periodic conferences; when he wanted to discuss something with a staff member, he sent for him. Or, more simply, he would wander into the other's office, muttering: "Say, what would you think if—" and start pacing up and down. One aide, Lieutenant Colonel Charles Morehouse, was an Army doctor and had an office directly across the corridor. MacArthur usually summoned him in a particularly direct fashion: "Hey, Doc!"

MacArthur had no private secretary; any one of the regular stenographic pool typed his letters and directives. His "memos" consisted of notes patiently written out in his tall, angular hand; a query was answered at the bottom or on the opposite side of the same piece of paper. When, during his pacing in a discussion with a staff member, he thought of something he wanted recorded, he suddenly said: "Make a note." We were always prepared for this and would jot down whatever it was, to be typed and placed in the files. He used the phone only in emergencies, principally when he had to talk to his chief of staff from his home, and never had one on his office desk.

By two p.m. he was gone again, having assigned enough work to keep the staff busy for the rest of the day. But he was back in his office by mid-afternoon, after lunch and a refreshing nap at home, and now the day's work really began. During this period, of course, it consisted mostly of planning for the next military operation. And planning in MacArthur's staff was like planning nowhere else in the world. For one secret of Mac-Arthur's success in battle was that everything was planned down to the minutest detail. There was no getting away with slipshod work; if the smallest mistake or oversight missed the hawk eyes of Chief of Staff Sutherland, it invariably was caught by MacArthur himself. He constantly astonished the various experts by knowing nearly as much about their specialties as they did—often more. When every detail of every group was assigned, the whole was co-ordinated with the intricacy of a fine machine. The result, especially for major operations, was a volume inches thick. Every commander thoroughly familiarized himself with his section of it; MacArthur knew it all. Therein lay the difference between the daring and the foolish commander. MacArthur made some seemingly long bets in World War II, but he always knew exactly what cards he held in his hand.

And he shrewdly estimated those of the enemy. "Expect only five per cent of an intelligence report to be accurate," he would say. "The trick of a good commander is to isolate the five per cent." To this there were no exceptions. Even the reports of his uncannily accurate chief of intelligence, Major General Charles A. Willoughby, to whom MacArthur frequently has referred as "the finest intelligence officer in the Army," came in for close scrutiny as MacArthur searched for the information on which he was satisfied he could place full reliance.

He would frequently order the preparation of alternate operational plans, each down to the smallest detail, and make his own selection just before giving the appropriate orders. Almost all plans returned to the planning staff with some alteration after passing the gamut of MacArthur's penetrating study. When an officer formerly with his planning group was recently given credit in a national magazine for conceiving and planning an important MacArthur thrust in the Southwest Pacific, one of the chief planners in that campaign made a snorting rejoinder: "Why, every operational plan coming out of general headquarters was a *MacArthur* plan. By the time he got through going over the proposals we sent up, they usually came back to us so radically altered as to be scarcely recognizable." This, of course, was an exaggeration. But it did reflect the degree of control which MacArthur, personally and through Chief of Staff Sutherland, exercised over the details of operational planning, even though he unhesitatingly rated his planning staff as professionally without peers and its shrewd leader, Major General Stephen J. Chamberlin, as a military strategist unexcelled in any other theater of operations.

Another secret of MacArthur's success was the organization he set up for the branches of the service under his command. He foresaw that to make the naval and air units merely subordinate arms of the Army in his theater would be unfair as well as inefficient; so he set up a command organization in which each arm was of equal and separate importance. (This was four years before the Army Air Corps achieved separate status as the Air Force.) So effective was this organization that in the summer of 1943 Marshall asked MacArthur for a description of it, explaining that Admiral Nimitz in the Central Pacific Theater was interested in incorporating some of its features in his own staff organization. MacArthur's answer is interesting to the layman because it not only described what became the standard American practice but also foreshadowed the National

Intimate Glimpses

Defense Act, which in 1947 established the Department of Defense with its separate branches of the service.

"Complete, thorough integration of ground, air and naval headquarters within general headquarters," he reported, "is the method followed with marked success in the Southwest Pacific area, rather than the assembly of an equal number of officers from those components into a general headquarters staff. Land, air and naval forces each operate under a commander with a completely organized staff. Naval and air commanders and their staffs are in the same building with general headquarters. The land commander and his staff are nearby. The commanders confer frequently with the commander-in-chief and principal members of the general headquarters. In addition to their complete functions as commanders, they operate in effect as a planning staff to the commander-in-chief. When operating in forward areas the same conditions exist." There were more details, of interest chiefly to the military student, but the essential point was that each arm was co-equal with the others, with all serving under, and in close physical contact with, general headquarters.

Of course it took more than that to make the successes MacArthur achieved. One factor was the complete loyalty he won from his subordinates, which stemmed largely from MacArthur's own loyalty to them. Opinions were sought on every decision of importance, and the idea that MacArthur preferred to have "yes-men" surrounding him is a canard. He always insisted on honest, sincere advice. Whether he always accepted it was another matter, but he did not long tolerate anyone who could contribute nothing more to a conference than fawning assent. He repaid his subordinates for good results in ways that made them even more dedicated to their jobs and to him. A brigadier general who had contributed greatly to the drive against Buna was wounded on December 5. MacArthur urged quick Washington approval to make him a major general, and on Christmas Day a MacArthur aide went to the hospital and pinned the new pair of stars on the wounded man's shoulders. Recalling it later, the officer said simply: "He does things like that." On the other hand, when things went wrong he accepted full responsibility for attendant decisions, whatever faulty information or opinions from subordinates had led him astray.

With his staff members MacArthur maintained an easy camaraderie that belied the myths about his aloofness. Many long evenings were spent in discussions of everything from the history of warfare to the details of the next campaign, especially during the times when MacArthur had taken up residence at an advance headquarters like Port Moresby or was

95

at sea en route to the next point of attack. On such trips he would have the members of his staff dine in his cabin with him, and frequently during these dinners would call for suggestions as to which of the motion pictures available should be shown in the cabin after dinner on the small portable screen brought along for the purpose. This discussion was usually accompanied by considerable banter in which MacArthur took the lead. Finally, when the projector was about to be turned on, he would break all naval tradition by calling the Marine sentry stationed at the door of his cabin to come in, sit down, and enjoy the movie with him. (At Port Moresby, as at every MacArthur headquarters throughout the war, the telephone exchange was pointedly named "Corregidor"; the headquarters building was called "Bataan," as was MacArthur's plane.)

MacArthur could almost always draw a story from the recesses of his mind to illustrate a point he was trying to make. For instance: Kenney had just prepared a communiqué on an air battle in which the Japanese had lost twenty-five planes and the U.S. none. MacArthur changed the last part of it to read: "Our losses were light." Kenney protested violently that we had not lost a single plane. MacArthur answered by telling a story.

It was one his father had told him, and it concerned a time when Arthur MacArthur was aide to General Sheridan in the Indian country of the frontier West. Sheridan was sent to confer with some Sioux chiefs who were threatening to go on the warpath. He met the chiefs, sat in a circle with them while they smoked their pipes, and addressed his interpreter, who happened to be Wild Bill Hickok.

"Bill, I want you to tell these chiefs that they shouldn't fight the white man. It wouldn't make any sense. The white man is too smart for them. He can do things they never heard of. Bill, tell them about the white man's railroad train. Tell them how it will haul all the buffalo meat they can shoot in a month and that it will haul it three times as fast as their fastest horses can run."

Hickok told them about the railroad train. They grunted a few times and were silent. "Well," asked Sheridan, "what did they say?"

"General," said Hickok, "they said they don't believe you."

"They don't?" said Sheridan. "All right, tell them about the steamboat. Tell them that the white man has invented a big boat that will go without paddles or sails and that it could carry the whole Sioux nation up and down all the rivers."

Hickok told the Indians about the steamboat. Again they grunted. "Well," said Sheridan, "what did they say?"

"General," said Hickok, "they said they don't believe you."

Sheridan played his last card. "Bill," he said, "tell them about the telegraph. Tell them that it's like their smoke signals, except that it is much better. Tell them that I have a little black box out here, and the Great White Father has a little black box in Washington. When I talk into my box the Great White Father hears me, and when the Great White Father talks into his box I hear him."

Hickok said nothing. "Well," said Sheridan impatiently, "go ahead, Bill. Tell them about the telegraph."

"General," said Hickok slowly, rolling his quid of tobacco in the hollow of his cheek, "now *I* don't believe you.". . . .

"So," MacArthur said to Kenney, "I know we didn't lose a plane. But I think we'd better say: 'Our losses were light.'"

But despite the companionship of his closest staff members, MacArthur was always alone, in the sense that any supreme commander is always thrown upon his own resources. After all the discussions and the reports and the advice, there is only one man who can make the decisions on which he will act and on which will depend victory or defeat. Only one man holds the responsibility, and that is the supreme commander. Those who were with MacArthur during this time, when nearly every day he had to make decisions on which rested the lives of thousands of men, know the soul-searing pressure under which he constantly lived. At Port Moresby his aides would wake in the night and hear his familiar pacing stride on the veranda below as he communed with himself and his God, making some decision that could shorten the war by months—or prolong it by even more. A soldier on guard duty outside the Port Moresby headquarters was once heard telling a friend how he had watched the general walking alone by himself in the garden, his hands full of papers and clasped behind his back. "He seemed to have a lot on his mind," said the soldier. He did indeed. MacArthur did much of his thinking in that garden, which was a beautiful, peaceful spot with a brilliant profusion of poincianas and frangipani. His solitude of command was summed up by another sentry who was talking to a correspondent. Pointing to the light burning in MacArthur's bedroom window one night, he said: "You know, that guy must be about the loneliest man in the world." He was indeed.

His loneliness was accentuated when he was at an advance post like Port Moresby and away from his wife and son. I will never forget a scene I witnessed there on the eve of the battle for Lae. The first major paratroop drop behind the enemy lines in the Pacific war had just been projected. All the multitudinous plans had been made, and the commanders had familiarized themselves with them. All the troops were poised. There remained nothing but the final briefing conference the night before the attack was to take place. My duties in directing guerrilla activities in the Philippines did not require me to move with MacArthur to advance head-quarters, but on this occasion he had sent for me to discuss a problem in my area. He had assigned me a bedroom in his own quarters, and after dinner I was sitting in the living-room browsing through some magazines. In a corner of the room MacArthur sat at a desk writing.

Just before eight o'clock the generals and admirals and senior staff officers began to arrive for a scheduled meeting. They entered and stood at one end of the room waiting for the meeting to start, but not interrupt-ing MacArthur, who did not look up. As the minutes passed, I watched the scene with increasing interest. The conferees spoke among themselves in soft whispers so as not to disturb MacArthur at his work; in the pauses I could almost detect the scratch of his pen on the paper. The hands of the clock went to 8:05, to 8:10, to 8:15—then to 8:30. Finally MacArthur finished writing, folded his paper into an envelope, and addressed it. Ris-ing from his desk, he came over and handed me the letter. "Court," he said, "when you return to Brisbane tomorrow, I'd appreciate it if you would deliver this." Replying: "Of course, General," I took it and glanced at the envelope. It read:

MASTER ARTHUR MacARTHUR

MacArthur turned to the assembled officers and apologized for keep-ing them waiting, and the important meeting proceeded.

Long before dawn and the beginning of the battle, I took off for Brisbane, trying to make myself comfortable for the nine-hour ride in the bucket seat of a C-47. It was a little after noon when I landed in Brisbane. I went straight to the MacArthurs' quarters in Lennon's Hotel, where I found a scene that made me smile at the memory of similar scenes with my own eldest son. Mrs. MacArthur was patiently but not very success-fully trying to coax Arthur to eat his lunch.

Putting on an air of great solemnity, I announced: "Arthur, a dis-patch from the General, your father, at the front." Arthur accepted the letter with a "Thank you, sir" of equal solemnity and handed it to his mother. She broke the seal and read it to him. In his letter the General commiserated with his son over the loss of a baby tooth, which Arthur had sent to him at the front.

Whenever I hear someone repeat the calumny that MacArthur is too great a man to be human, I think of this scene and others within the

Intimate Glimpses

privacy of his little family. Anyone who accuses MacArthur of being austere should have been present at 7:15 a.m. most mornings in the double suite of housekeeping rooms which served as the MacArthurs' home all the time they were in Australia. For at 7:15, when he was home, the General and five-year-old Arthur played the "boom-boom" game. It started with Father striding into the room and receiving a smart salute from Arthur. Then the two marched about the room, to the tune of "boomity, boomity, boom" shouted by both of them. When Arthur reached a certain chair, he knelt and hid his eyes until the General shouted a particularly loud "BOOM!" At that signal Arthur looked up to see what his morning surprise was—usually a pencil or some paper clips, but on special occasions a more valuable toy. Mrs. MacArthur kept strictly away from this morning ritual, as it was the one time of day when her son and his father could have any time alone together. But she did have to hide the "boom-boom presents" from the General and give them to him one at a time; otherwise, in a burst of generosity he would give Arthur a whole handful at once. Of all these little presents, Arthur's favorite was, to me, a touching one: a tiny American flag, symbol of the homeland he had never seen.

Occasionally these morning sessions erupted into bursts of song. "Arthur," the General admitted, "is the only one who can tolerate my singing." Arthur learned the old army songs fast, and Mrs. MacArthur would hurry breakfast along when she heard, down the hall, the bellowed duet of "Old soldiers never dieeee—" followed by shrieks of boyish laughter. Thus the Commander in Chief of the Southwest Pacific Theater prepared for another day.

Every meal in the MacArthur household in Brisbane was prepared by Mrs. MacArthur. Once in a while she used the General's car for shopping-trips, especially when they first arrived and she had to purchase entire new outfits for herself and Arthur. But she insisted on standing in line at banks, stores, and the post office. Some afternoons she took Arthur to a near-by park where he could ride his tricycle, but most of the time Arthur's companion on such jaunts was Ah Cheu, because Mrs. MacArthur let nothing interfere with what she regarded as her primary duty: having a warm meal and a restful home waiting for the General whenever he returned.

That could be at any time between noon and three p.m. for lunch, any time from eight to midnight for dinner. But the comforts of a normal home and family always awaited him, no matter how late the hour. And, no matter how late, his first move was to tiptoe into Arthur's room for a

99

glance at the sleeping form, which was usually curled up around a huge, bewhiskered toy rabbit. Like Arthur, the rabbit was a veteran of Corregidor and the harrowing trip to Australia; its name was "Old Friend."

It was the manifestation of this father-son relationship which caused all who knew MacArthur fully to understand his reply when informed that he had been selected as Father of the Year in 1942. For that reply exemplified the spirituality that is a part of their relationship. "By profession I am a soldier and take pride in that fact," MacArthur said. "But I am prouder —infinitely prouder—to be a father. A soldier destroys in order to build; the father only builds, never destroys. The one has the potentiality of death; the other embodies creation and life. And while the hordes of death are mighty, the battalions of life are mightier still. It is my hope that my son, when I am gone, will remember me not from the battle but in the home repeating with him our simple daily prayer, 'Our Father Who Art in Heaven.'"

Dinner at the MacArthurs' was almost never attended by anyone but the General and Mrs. MacArthur; this was his time for relaxation. And dinner was *not* preceded by a cocktail. MacArthur had liked an occasional drink when I knew him earlier in Manila. But from that July 27, 1941, when he was called back into active service, he became a teetotaler and remained one until the end of the war. The meal itself was simple to the point of being spartan, and MacArthur followed it with his single cigar of the day.

Frequently a guest was invited to lunch, but all invitations extended to the MacArthurs were politely declined. To Jean MacArthur, giving up all but a few friends and devoting every hour of every day to the General's welfare with never even Sunday off for rest was her own small contribution to add to his great one. A good soldier, she cherished a watch that her husband had given her right after their arrival in Australia; it was inscribed: "To my bravest." She did, however, sometimes achieve the distinction of being the only person in the Southwest Pacific Theater to flatly disobey an order, as when she took Arthur to the barber after the General had forbidden it because he was afraid Arthur would catch cold. Arthur caught cold.

Between young Arthur and his father has grown the ideal father-son relationship, possibly drawn closer by the sharing in common of the perils of battle. But there has been military tradition involved, too—tradition that caused MacArthur to call a family council, even including four-year-old Arthur, to discuss the question raised by Washington of evacuating mother and son from shell-torn Corregidor. It was in the same tradition that MacArthur thereafter replied simply: "My wife and son have decided to remain and share the fate of the garrison. I will not interfere with their decision." And in that tradition Mrs. MacArthur answered the invitation to accompany the Quezons on their departure with the words: "We three drink of the same cup."

No one can measure the important part this woman and this boy played by keeping MacArthur fit both physically and mentally for his superhuman task, day after day without cease for three years. It even seemed at times as if Arthur, at only five, understood his father's mission perfectly. One of the General's happiest moments came when Arthur, with no coaching whatsoever, fixed his father with an unblinking eye and asked:

"When are we going back to Manila?"

CHAPTER X   "Defeat now stares Japan in the face."

⚓ A few days before Christmas, 1943, Arthur MacArthur received a wire which read: "TERRIBLY SORRY BUT SANTA CLAUS HAS BEEN HELD UP IN NEW GUINEA FOR A FEW DAYS." It was not until two weeks later that Santa Claus had completed landings at Cape Gloucester and Saidor and could spare a day or two to return to Australia for a Christmas with his wife and son.

MacArthur spent a great deal of 1943 at his advance headquarters in New Guinea, because he was now busily engaged in two great strategic operations without which he could not continue his march toward the Philippines. The maneuvers were necessary to protect his right flank, and MacArthur conceived them as gigantic envelopments of the enemy's strongest bases in the Southwest Pacific.

The first of these envelopments was clamped on Rabaul, the northeast tip of New Britain Island and the nerve center of Japanese forces in the area. In Rabaul were mountains of supplies gathered for distribution to enemy troops in New Guinea and on all the islands of the Solomon and Bismarck seas. In Rabaul were five airfields, ninety-five thousand troops, and the biggest concentration of shipping south of the great Japanese naval base at Truk. In all the conferences on future plans, the intelligence officers made gloomy predictions that bloody fighting would be needed to reduce this mountain-girt fortress. Finally MacArthur announced his decision: he would render Rabaul impotent, but he would do it without wasting a single man's life on its coral ledges and sucking swamps. He would simply bypass it.

So began Envelopment Number One, in which MacArthur and Admiral Halsey worked together with flawless co-operation. Pacific operations were divided into North, Central and South theaters, under Nimitz, and a Southwest theater under MacArthur, the dividing-line being longitude 159. When Guadalcanal was finally won on February 8, 1943, Hal-

102

sey's operations moved across the line into MacArthur's theater and the Joint Chiefs of Staff in Washington placed Halsey under MacArthur's strategic command. Remembering the Navy's past attempts in Washington to undercut MacArthur and his theater, some may have entertained strong doubts about this relationship. But there were no misgivings on MacArthur's staff. Ever since Halsey had spent a few days with MacArthur in May 1943 and had later commented publicly: "There's a commander I would be honored to serve under at any time," we had come to understand the independent character of this fighting naval commander. As soon as the General and the Admiral got together, they hit it off perfectly. MacArthur promptly planned a joint maneuver in which his Army forces would close on Rabaul from New Guinea while Halsey's amphibious forces did the same along the Solomons.

As MacArthur worked out the details of these operations, he could take some comfort from the fact that he now had a little more strength than before. After being forced to win the Papuan campaign with no trained amphibious troops, he had finally received the 7th Amphibious Force, under the command of Rear Admiral Daniel Barbey, an ingenious, daring leader who, like Halsey, was MacArthur's kind of admiral. More Army and air troops had arrived in Australia, and MacArthur trained them also for amphibious warfare.

It was still a fact, however, that at the beginning of 1943, for reasons known only to the Pentagon planners, Admiral Halsey in the South Pacific area had been given 3,000 more *ground and air* troops than MacArthur had in his entire command; Nimitz, in the Central Pacific, had nearly 25,000 more. But, realizing that to wait for sufficient troops might mean waiting until the Japanese took over the Southwest Pacific, MacArthur proceeded to plan for the maximum use of his minimum resources.

His over-all strategy, as he designed it and refined it, was what later became famous as the "hit-'em-where-they-ain't" style of warfare.[1] Like Rabaul, most of the formidable centers of Japanese strength would be bypassed, as landings were made around, over, and under them, cutting them off and leaving them behind to "die on the vine."

It is not my purpose, as I have said before, to chronicle in detail the tactics and incidents of the campaigns that followed. But the isolation of Rabaul is a perfect demonstration of the strategic genius with which MacArthur won the fantastic string of victories in the months ahead.

It began with the attack on the Lae-Salamaua area which I mentioned in the last chapter (see map, page 61), the last-minute details of

[1] For MacArthur's description of it, see Chapter VIII, page 87.

which waited while MacArthur wrote a letter to his son. Here the bold-ness of his concept in the co-ordination of air with ground power again asserted itself. It was planned to move the Australian 7th Division by air from Port Moresby and land it in the Markham Valley to attack Lae from the west. First, however, a suitable landing-strip had to be secured. To ac-complish this, it was planned to drop the 503rd Parachute Regiment at Nadzab, across the Markham River, on September 5. Besides being an example of employing the maximum potential of land, sea, and air power, this was the first major jump of United States paratroopers in the Pacific war.

I had been called to Port Moresby the day preceding this assault. The staff was tense with expectancy as the time for attack drew closer. Mac-Arthur had announced his intention to observe personally the air drop and ensuing action from a command plane in order, as he expressed it to his staff, to provide "such comfort as my presence might bring to our para-troops who enter their first combat fraught with such hazard."

Shortly after I had taken off for Brisbane, MacArthur had arrived at the point of departure of the airborne regiment, shaking hands and wish-ing Godspeed to many of them as he walked toward his plane. Suddenly he was told that the plane intended for him was inoperable, but that a plane might be selected from a flight just then returning from a mission. He replied quietly: "Any plane will do, but I must get off in time to lead the flight into its destination."

A B-17 was soon selected. It had been badly shot up in the engage-ment from which it had just returned, but it was able to fly. MacArthur climbed aboard and surveyed the powder marks, the empty cartridge cases, and the blood-spattered interior that gave mute but grim evidence of the struggle in its last encounter. Soon after the take-off one of the engines sputtered and went dead. The pilot suggested that they return to the field, but MacArthur ordered him to proceed on the remaining three engines. In this manner he led the flight in and closely observed the drop and ground maneuvers until the forces had consolidated and seized the airstrip objective. When he left the scene, flame-throwers were al-ready burning away the tall kunai grass to prepare the field for the trans-ports. On schedule, planes bearing the 7th Division began to land and dis-charge their cargoes of men and matériel.

Meanwhile, Kenney's bombers were neutralizing Japanese air strength everywhere near by. Admiral Barbey's amphibious troops swarmed ashore at carefully selected beaches, where they encountered very little opposition. When the enemy moved to counter these landings,

"Defeat now stares Japan in the face."

MacArthur landed more troops in their rear, this time by air. So perfectly planned and rehearsed was this landing that it took exactly *one minute and ten seconds* for seventeen hundred paratroops to swing down onto the airfield and take the tiny town. Thus the two jaws of the mighty pincer movement clamped around the defenders of Lae. That night MacArthur wired his wife in Brisbane: "It was a honey."

Meanwhile, knowing that enemy planes from Rabaul would try to stop the Lae-Salamaua landings, MacArthur laid a trap. More than a hundred fighters rendezvoused over the area and waited, their backs to the sun, until the Rabaul dive bombers came on the scene. In one flashing dogfight every Japanese plane—forty-one in all—was shot down. The once-powerful Lae airfield was taken, and the MacArthur drive was 170 miles ahead of Buna in one jump.

The Japanese prepared for the next hop along the New Guinea coast, but, instead, MacArthur had Halsey strike 670 miles away in the Solomon Islands. Skipping past the fortress at Kolombangara, he leapfrogged all the way from Munda to Vella Lavella, almost halfway up the chain of the Solomons.

The next prize of these islands, and the next logical step, was Buin-Faisi, a big naval base just below the topmost island of Bougainville. But while the enemy prepared defenses there, MacArthur had Kenney's bombers plaster Rabaul in the worst aerial bombardment ever inflicted on that Southwest Pacific bastion. Mustering every plane in the theater, he sent them against Rabaul at midday, when such an attack would be least expected. The Japanese planes were caught on the ground and raked to pieces. In all, 177 planes—sixty per cent of the base's potential—were destroyed, making this one of the most destructive and successful air attacks in World War II. MacArthur summed up this operation in a message to Kenney: "Rabaul has been the center and very hub of the enemy's advanced air effort. I think we have now broken its back."

The enemy had not recovered from this devastating blow when MacArthur struck again. Instead of hitting the next logical objective, Buin-Faisi, he bypassed it and landed above it, in Empress Augusta Bay on Bougainville itself.

Reeling in the west in New Guinea and in the east in the Solomons, bleeding from the wounds of the air attack in the north at Rabaul, the Japanese now got it in the south. Eleven months earlier MacArthur had asked Washington for Lieutenant General Walter Krueger, an old friend and brilliant tactician, for command of the Sixth Army. Krueger sent his troops ashore at Arawe, near the other end of New Britain from Rabaul.

This, the first landing on the island on which Rabaul was situated, worried the enemy even more than the other landings, and the Japanese rushed strong forces to defend Arawe.

MacArthur promptly revealed that Arawe was a diversion, as he struck eighty miles away, at Cape Gloucester on the western tip of New Britain. Sure now that MacArthur was driving on Rabaul, the Japanese made elaborate preparations for defense of New Britain Island. No sooner had they done that than MacArthur jabbed at them again, assaulting and taking Green Island, on Rabaul's right, and Emirau Island, on Rabaul's left. The enemy's biggest Southwest Pacific base was virtually surrounded.

And the beauty of it all was that the Japanese would now expend all their resources preparing the strongest possible defense against an attack that would never come. Only as the ammunition and food supplies slowly disappeared would they realize that Envelopment Number One was already completed, and that MacArthur had completely outwitted them by cutting them off instead of attacking. Rabaul as a nerve center of enemy forces in the Southwest Pacific was through.

On New Britain, on New Ireland, down the chain of the Solomons, and on the constellation of islands in the Solomon and Bismarck seas, tens of thousands of Japanese were left to starve and die. Meanwhile, in complete co-operation, Admiral Nimitz, raiding through the Central Pacific, had worked his way across to the Marshalls and had blasted the major enemy base at Truk.

This lightning series of feints, jabs, and Sunday punches had seized eight hundred thousand square miles of enemy territory in less than a year, and MacArthur's fighter and bomber lines were advanced as much as sixteen hundred miles. Under MacArthur's command, Halsey had taken all the Solomons in two thirds of the time that had been required for Guadalcanal alone. MacArthur was making the final preparations for the Cape Gloucester landings just before Christmas of 1943. It would have been in the pattern of his previous attacks—striking at the place and time least expected—if he had picked Christmas Day for the landings. He could not bring himself to do it; the landings were made on December 26.

Envelopment Number Two took even less time. When MacArthur struck again, it was against Saidor, on New Guinea, and it put the finishing touches on the earlier Lae-Salamaua landings. Thus the Huon Peninsula was pinched off and the vital Vitiaz Strait was cleared for the convoys for further New Guinea landings. What the Japanese did not know was that Saidor was part of the second envelopment. They found out when the next squeeze came.

"Defeat now stares Japan in the face."

MacArthur was extremely anxious to secure the Admiralty Islands in the Bismarck Archipelago. They would provide him with fine natural harbors and airfields to support further operations along the New Guinea coast, while at the same time completing the encirclement of Japanese forces cut off on New Britain and in the Solomons and furthering the isolation and neutralization of Rabaul. He felt that he must move rapidly to exploit the enemy confusion in that general area.

So on February 24, against the counsel of many of his senior commanders and staff officers, he directed a landing at Hyane Harbor on eastern Los Negros by a reinforced squadron of the 5th Cavalry Regiment of the First Cavalry Division, supported by a light naval force of two cruisers and a dozen destroyers with air cover. As a precautionary measure, a strong auxiliary force was standing by at Finschhafen to be sent in two days after the initial landing to meet any powerful Japanese reaction. The strategic conception of this movement was one of the most daring and most brilliant of the war. Its complete success saved thousands of Allied lives and untold effort and expense, and materially shortened the war with Japan.

The situation was this: In order to move our naval forces forward, it was necessary to obtain and hold an advanced naval base. Truk and Rabaul with their excellent harbors were such bases, but were firmly held by the enemy. To attack either would involve staggering losses both in men and matériel. Manus, in the Admiralties, hundreds of miles behind them and hundreds of miles nearer the final objective, was not so strongly held because the enemy could not visualize a movement to his rear such as MacArthur contemplated. Manus had a magnificent harbor capable of holding the entire American fleet. MacArthur's plan was the epitome of his concept of deep envelopment to the rear of the enemy in order to achieve complete surprise and isolate the enemy's forces by severing his lines of supply. With no material resources, these forces would then, as he expressed it, "wither and die on the vine."

At one of his rare councils of war, held on the U.S.S. *Phoenix* before the departure, one of his commanders advised strongly against the movement. He argued that it was "a military gamble with the deck of cards in the enemy's hands as dealer." MacArthur quickly answered: "Yes, but a gamble in which I have everything to win, little to lose. I bet ten to win a million, if I hit the jackpot." And that is how it turned out.

As the troops went north to Los Negros through the night of February 28, 1944, MacArthur went with them. He was leaning at the rail of the *Phoenix*, looking out across the black, phosphorescent sea, as an aide,

Colonel Larry Lehrbas, made the cautionary remark that the 5th Cavalry troops, with no combat experience, might not do so well as hoped.

MacArthur replied softly: "When I was a little boy of four, Larry, my father was a captain in the 13th Infantry, stationed at Fort Selden in the Indian frontier of New Mexico. Geronimo, the Apache scourge, was loose, and our little infantry garrison was to guard the upper fords of the Rio Grande. A troop of this same 5th Cavalry . . . rode through to help us. I can still remember how I felt when I watched them clatter into the fort, their tired horses gray with the desert dust. They'd fight then—and they'll fight now. Don't worry about them."

Because of the extraordinary delicacy of the operation, MacArthur himself, accompanied by his naval commander, Vice Admiral Thomas C. Kinkaid, personally supervised the assault landings. Only minor resistance was encountered; as he had anticipated, the enemy was taken completely by surprise. Then he directed the 5th Cavalry to "dig in" and secure the beachhead they had taken.

His concern was so great that, in spite of all remonstrance, he personally reconnoitered the Momote airfield in front of our line to assure himself of its future potentiality and to estimate the strength of the enemy's reaction. He narrowly escaped destruction from the gathering enemy snipers only a hundred yards away in the high grass bordering the west side of the field. Surrounded by men in camouflage battle dress and steel helmets, he wore a light trench coat and his famous gold-embroidered cap.

A worried officer tried to steer him back toward the landing-barge. "Excuse me, sir," he said, pointing to a spot of jungle fifty yards away, "but we killed a Jap sniper in there only a few minutes ago."

"Fine," said MacArthur. "That's the best thing to do with them."

This incident so impressed General Krueger that he records in his book, *From Down Under to Nippon*, the following:

". . . Early on the 28th [I] reported to General MacArthur, who had just arrived at Cape Cretin on the Cruiser *Phoenix*. His visit could only mean that he intended to accompany the reconnaissance force and would probably go ashore in the objective area. This disturbed me greatly. I no doubt showed my apprehension when I reported to him and he insisted that I tell him what was troubling me. I finally did so and urged him earnestly not to accompany the reconnaissance force and, in any case, not to go ashore.

"He had expressly forbidden me to accompany our assault loadings and yet now proposed to do so himself. 1 argued that it was unnecessary and unwise to expose himself in this fashion and that it would be a calamity if anything happened to him. He listened to me attentively and thanked me, but added, 'I have to go.' He had made up his mind on the subject—and that was that.

"The reconnaissance in force was a brilliant strategic move and fortunately successful. But if it had not been, and General MacArthur had been killed or captured—by no means a far-fetched idea—it would have been a disaster. . . .

"When General MacArthur went ashore in Hyane Harbor about 1400 on the 29th, the Japanese reaction had not yet started in earnest and fortunately did not begin until after he had returned on board the *Phoenix*, which departed at 1730 for Cape Cretin. But the Japanese, who were there in considerable force only a few hundred yards away from where General MacArthur had been on Momote air strip, could easily have attacked early in the afternoon and might well have gotten him. Before leaving, General MacArthur decorated the first man to land on Los Negros—Lieutenant Marvin J. Henshaw, of the 5th Cavalry, with the Distinguished Service Cross." [2]

MacArthur then instructed General Chase, the cavalry commander, to "hold what you have taken, no matter against what odds. You have your teeth in him now—don't let go."

The enemy reacted with a powerful counterattack, but General Chase held his position stubbornly and brilliantly until the reinforcing elements arrived. Thereafter, the combined force met and defeated a determined attack by the Japanese garrison, heavily reinforced from Japanese on the outlying islands. By March 9 the entire island had been secured.

Meanwhile, assured of the success of the operation, MacArthur had returned to his New Guinea headquarters and reported: "We have landed in the Admiralty Islands which stand at the northern entrance to the Bismarck Sea almost due south of Guam and 1,300 miles from the Philippines. This marks a final stage in the great swinging move pivoting on New Guinea which has been the basic purpose of the operations initiated on June 29, 1943, when the Southwest Pacific area and South Pacific area were united under my command. The axis of advance has thereby been changed from the north to the west. This relieves our supply line of the constant threat of flank attack which has been present since the beginning of the Papuan campaign. This line, previously so precariously exposed, is now firmly secured not only by air coverage but by our own front to which it is perpendicular. The operation has been a delicate one,

[2] From *From Down Under to Nippon*, by General Walter Krueger (Washington: Combat Forces Press; 1953).

and its final success lays a strategically firm foundation for the future. Tactically it tightens the blockade of the enemy's remaining bases. Their supply lines are definitely and conclusively severed and only a minimum of blockade running, by submarine or individual surface craft, is now possible. In addition to the troops trapped in the Solomons, some 50,000 of the enemy, largely in New Britain and at Rabaul, are now enclosed. Their situation has become precarious and their ultimate fate is certain under blockade, bombardment and the increasing pressure of besieging ground forces. The end of the Bismarck campaign is now clearly in sight with a minimum of loss to ourselves."

If the Japanese had been befuddled and outsmarted by these two operations, their surprises were only beginning. Now MacArthur was free to leapfrog along the coast of New Guinea, and he was ready. It would seem that the enemy, knowing what the route of the advance must be— i.e., along the New Guinea coast—would not be fooled any more. But MacArthur was still too smart for him. What followed during the spring and summer of 1944 was a series of triphammer blows in such unexpected places and with such blinding speed that the Japanese were never able to recover from one in time to be prepared for another. Here is Mac-Arthur's timetable of victory in 1944:

APRIL 22. HOLLANDIA. Ever since the victory at Buna, MacArthur and his staff had planned that the next step after cutting off Rabaul and reducing the Admiralties would be the big New Guinea base at Wewak. Enemy planes from Wewak had been particularly annoying, and we felt that this Japanese stronghold would have to be wiped out before we could move ahead toward the Philippines. But here again MacArthur showed his genius for outwitting the enemy. After laying careful plans for the Wewak operation, he suddenly switched his target to an even bigger Japanese base, 450 miles farther along the New Guinea coast.

Hollandia, noted for little before the war except as a source for bird-of-paradise feathers, was becoming jammed with enemy shipping, troops, and supplies. With Rabaul useless, Hollandia had taken its place as the most important enemy base in the Southwest Pacific. But Hollandia was so far ahead of our lines of attack that landings there would have the element of utter surprise. So it became the next target.

Every kind of deception was used. Fake plans for attacking Wewak were carefully "leaked" to put the Japanese off guard. Kenney's bomber pilots shortened their range purposely, so that the Japanese would think the planes could not reach Hollandia. Then, on March 31, every bomber that could fly was sent against this big base in one smashing assault. The tactics were like those of Rabaul, and they were nearly as successful.

Meanwhile, the daring of the plan [3] had stimulated the imagination of Admiral Nimitz in the Central Pacific, and he promised the support of a complete naval task force. So on April 22, sixty-six thousand men went ashore at Hollandia, supported by a simultaneous landing at Aitape, 125 miles away. The surprise was complete.

The Hollandia landings marked the first time that MacArthur had strong naval task-force support. And Vice Admiral Marc A. Mitscher, who commanded the supporting fleet, had so many bombs left over that he staged a raid on Truk on the way home. So certain had the Japanese been that our landings would be at Wewak or Hansa Bay that Vice Admiral Yoshikazu Endo, commander of the Japanese Eighth and Ninth fleets, had been taken by submarine to Hollandia to escape the expected attack. When the landings did come, right on the beach below him, he sat in a chair and watched the U.S. forces swoop onto the island, then put on his dress uniform, walked off into the jungle, and killed himself.

The seizure of Hollandia cut the Japanese supply routes from the Philippines to all the bases in New Guinea. It isolated 60,000 more Japanese troops (besides killing 3,300 and capturing 700). The prize included what was probably the biggest supply dump ever captured in the Pacific, with tons of everything from sake to quinine. The capture of Hollandia also rescued 125 nuns and missionaries and many slave laborers imported from East India. It advanced MacArthur 450 miles nearer the Philippines and jumped his schedule ahead by many months. From Washington, General Marshall cabled that it was "a model of strategic and tactical maneuver."

MAY 17. WAKDE. Only three weeks after the Hollandia landings, MacArthur's troops went ashore on the Wakde Islands, 110 miles farther along the New Guinea coast and along the road to the Philippines. In the three days that followed, eight hundred Japanese were killed, at a cost of forty U.S. dead. A fine coral airstrip over a mile long was won at Wakde. The fate of the bypassed Japanese can be guessed from the gruesome reports MacArthur's staff received concerning the starved Japanese who had been cut off at Wewak; they were surviving only by cannibalism when they finally gave themselves up.

MAY 27. BIAK. The next blow of MacArthur's triphammer hit the enemy only ten days after the Wakde landings. The Biak defenders fought harder than any others in this period, holed up in the weird, five-story caves that honeycombed this island off the New Guinea coast. By June 28

[3] Its code name was "Reckless."

Biak had finally fallen. Here, however, the mopping-up operation was particularly bitter, and the attackers had to learn how to explode home-made gasoline-drum bombs inside the caves and literally blast the suicidal Japanese out of them. Within two weeks Biak had started to function as a huge supply base for MacArthur's forces.

The day after the assault, MacArthur revealed its significance: "We have landed on Biak Island. The capture of this stronghold will give us command domination of Dutch New Guinea except for isolated enemy positions. For strategic purposes this marks the practical end of the New Guinea campaign. The final stage has also been reached in the offensive . . . by the combined forces of the Southwest Pacific and South Pacific areas. It has resulted in the reconquest or neutralization of the Solomons, the Bismarcks, the Admiralties, and New Guinea. From the forward point reached by the Japanese we have advanced our front approximately 1,800 statute miles westward and approximately 700 miles to the north. Compared with the enemy our offensive employed only modest forces, and through the maximum use of maneuver and surprise we have incurred only light losses. The operations have effected a strategic penetration in the Southwest Pacific and have secured bases of departure for the advance to the vital areas in the Philippines and the Netherlands East Indies."

JULY 2. NOEMFOOR. Surprised again, the Japanese retreated before some twenty-three thousand of MacArthur's troops, who landed on Noemfoor Island by barge and parachute. Besides attaining another stepping-stone at very little cost, this landing rescued the loyal natives of the island, who had resisted the Japanese occupation and had therefore been the victims of typical, unspeakable Japanese atrocities.

JULY 30. SANSAPOR. This was an important staging-point on the ship route of the enemy along the New Guinea coast. But Sansapor meant more than that, because with Noemfoor it bracketed one of the biggest Japanese air bases, on Vogelkop Peninsula. The Japanese were on the run all along the New Guinea coast by now, completely dispirited by the war of nerves MacArthur had been waging against them. Every time they prepared their defense, MacArthur hit somewhere else, going around their fortresses and leaving them to rot away. Consequently, the enemy defenses crumbled everywhere. At Sansapor there was only minor resistance, and the price was well worth the effort. Engineers moved in right after the combat troops and soon had airfields functioning both at Vogelkop and Sansapor. What was important about these airfields was that they permitted MacArthur, for the first time since he had left the Philippines, to send American bombers over the Japanese in the Islands.

"Defeat now stares Japan in the face."

SEPTEMBER 15. MOROTAI. Here was another example of MacArthur's strategical fleetfootedness. The logical point after the last New Guinea steppingstone, the one directly in line with the Philippines, was Halmahera. The Japanese knew this as well as MacArthur did, and they had prepared strong defenses accordingly. So again MacArthur hit them where they weren't. Aided again by attacks on other islands in the area carried out by Nimitz's Central Pacific forces, he sent his troops ashore on Morotai. And again the Japanese were caught napping; there was practically no resistance. Halmahera, cut off from supplies and reinforcements, was doomed.

More important, the southernmost Philippine island now lay almost over the horizon to the northwest. On September 21, MacArthur was able to report with satisfaction: "We shall shortly have an air and light naval base here within 300 miles of the Philippines." He knew that the seizure of Morotai marked a penetration in the Halmahera-Philippine line and that the rolling-up of this line would cut off Japanese armies—an estimated two hundred thousand men—and isolate the Netherlands East Indies' great stores of oil resources from use on the Japanese mainland.

In twenty-two months MacArthur had fought his way back to within three hundred miles of the Philippines, along a road marked by some bitter fighting but more often by dazzling examples of outfoxing the enemy. From Buna and Lae to Aitape and Hollandia, Wakde, Biak and Noemfoor, Sansapor and Morotai—to say nothing of Gloucester and Los Negros and Empress Augusta Bay—MacArthur had strode back toward the Philippines with a speed that had never let the enemy catch up with him. Already he had taken more territory with a smaller loss of life than any commander since Darius the Great.

Although it was less spectacular, one of MacArthur's toughest fights, and in the end one of his greatest victories during the New Guinea campaign, was the defeat of the anopheles mosquito. He had learned from long experience that the effectiveness of military weapons, however cutting their edge or destructive their explosive power, was limited by the physical strength, the mental alertness, and the manipulating skill of those who controlled them. Casualty reports began to point to the malarial mosquito as a far more deadly enemy than even the Japanese, and as whole battalions and regiments became gaunt, fever-ridden ghosts of their former selves, MacArthur realized that this jungle enemy—elusive, treacherous, and deadly—had to be neutralized before victory could be won. So he mobilized all of the scientific skill at his command. Under the close supervision of his old friend and aide, Colonel Howard Smith, for

113

many years Public Health Officer and Chief of Quarantine Service in the Philippines, a systematic and relentless scientific war was declared against the mosquito.

Textbooks offered little help. Quinine, the recognized medication of long standing, was obtainable only in inadequate quantities, its main sources of supply being under enemy control. Coating stagnant pools with oil was impracticable in view of the vast reaches of tropical terrain, with almost impenetrable density of swamp and jungle growth. But then a synthetic quinine substitute was found. If taken with adequate regularity, it acted as a prophylactic to reduce materially the incidence of the disease. Additional precautionary measures extended control over the mosquito itself, such as the spraying of bivouac areas with DDT. Individual and troop discipline was tightened in order to make the control measures effective. Gradually the discovery and implementation of scientific methods began to produce progressive and heartening results. Eventually the reduction of casualty rate from jungle disease constituted the equivalent of heavy reinforcement of troops.

It was a decisive victory over a stubborn and destructive foe, and it gave malaria-infected areas of the world new hope in the never-ending fight against this enemy that attacks as relentlessly in peace as in war. This successful battle against disease provided added support to MacArthur's oft-stated admonition that "battles are not won by arms alone." The conquest of the anopheles mosquito in the jungles of New Guinea was, indeed, comparable to the victory of Gorgas over the scourge of yellow fever in Panama, enabling Goethals to complete the Panama Canal. And the contrast between Allied success and enemy failure against the mosquito emphasized MacArthur's statement: "Nature, with its concomitant of disease, is strictly neutral and impartial in war. But if by any artificial process its disasters can be ameliorated for one side and not for the other, it can be made into a powerful ally."

As important a reason for the small cost of victory in New Guinea was MacArthur's burning passion for the preservation of his men. By avoiding frontal assaults upon enemy concentrations and instead neutralizing them by strategic envelopment, he saved thousands of American lives. His first order of business in the daily routine was to examine the casualty reports; therein, to his mind, largely rested the balance between success or failure. And when Washington showed concern as to the disposition of the tens of thousands of enemy troops which now studded his rear area, MacArthur answered: "The enemy garrisons which have been by-passed in the Solomons and New Guinea represent no menace to present or future operations. Their capacity for organized offensive effort has passed. The various processes of attrition will eventually account for their final disposition. The actual time of their destruction is of little or no importance, and their influence as a contributing factor of the war is already negligible. The actual process of their immediate destruction by assault methods would unquestionably involve heavy loss of life, without adequate compensating strategic advantages. The present allotment of shipping and assault craft would not permit such operations except at the expense of those which are now scheduled."

A few days later MacArthur sent Washington some more revealing comments on the nature of the enemy he was battling—comments that presaged his success in the occupation of Japan. "Japanese ground troops will fight with the greatest tenacity," he reported. "The military quality of the rank and file remains the highest. Their officer corps, however, deteriorates as you go up the scale. It is fundamentally based upon a caste and feudal system and does not represent strict professional merit. Therein lies Japan's weakness. Her sons are strong of limb and stout of heart but weak in leadership. Gripped inexorably by a military hierarchy, that hierarchy is now failing the nation. It has had neither the imagination nor the foresighted ability to organize Japanese resources for a total war. Defeat now stares Japan in the face. Its barbaric codes have dominated Japanese character and culture for centuries and have practiced a type of national savagery at strange variance with many basic impulses of the Japanese people. Its successful domination has been based largely on the people's belief in its infallibility. When public opinion realizes that its generals and admirals have failed in the field of actual combat and campaign, the revulsion produced in Japanese thought will be terrific. Therein lies a basis for ultimate hope that the Japanese citizen will cease his almost idolatrous worship of the military and readjust his thoughts along more rational lines. No sophistry can disguise the fact from him that the military has failed him in his greatest hour of need. That failure may mark the beginning of a new and ultimately happier era for him; his hour of decision is close at hand."

MacArthur could now make his plans for the time, just thirty days ahead, when he would again stand on the soil of the Philippines. But meanwhile he emphasized his deep concern for moral responsibilities in the forthcoming campaign by issuing a stern warning to the commanders of the air, naval, and ground forces scheduled to participate, as well as to the Commander-in-Chief, Pacific Ocean Area (Nimitz), and the Commander Third Fleet (Halsey):

"One of the purposes of the Philippine campaign," he said, "is to liberate the Filipinos. They will not understand liberation if accompanied by indiscriminate destruction of their homes, their possessions, their civilization and their own lives. Humanity and our moral standing throughout the Far East dictate that the destruction of lives and property in the Philippines be held to a minimum compatible with the assurance of a successful military campaign. Indications are that in some localities the Japanese are evacuating cities, leaving Filipinos in residence, either failing to warn them or compelling them to stay. Aerial bombing causes the greatest destruction. Our objective in areas we are to occupy is to destroy totally hostile effort in order to ensure our own success; in other areas we neutralize, to weaken any hostile effort which may tend to increase resistance to our occupation objectives. In the latter areas, our attack objectives are primarily airfields and shipping, not metropolitan areas or villages or barrios. To the extent possible, we must preserve port facilities that we plan to use. The Commander Allied Air Forces will, and the Commander-in-Chief, Pacific Ocean Area is requested to issue general instructions in consonance with the above objectives of minimizing destruction of life and property of Filipinos."

In the United States, eleven thousand miles away from MacArthur as he made his plans for his return to the Philippines, Manuel Quezon lay dying. But with fading breath, Quezon whispered to his devoted wife: "Aurora, he's only three hundred miles away!"

CHAPTER XI   A Momentous Conference

⚑ In mid-August, when the issues of the campaign in the Southwest Pacific were no longer in doubt, MacArthur suddenly received the startling information that the British government was planning to send a force of its own into the area to operate independently of his command. This news came as a considerable surprise, for it had been the British who for so long had resisted the dislodgement of any forces or matériel from the European front to reinforce Pacific operations. But he realized at once the political implications underlying such a move.

London was becoming concerned over the growing signs of friendship of the Australian and New Zealand peoples for the United States, the natural result of close bonds forged in the common war effort. British leaders were viewing with increasing worry the future effect upon British political and economic interests in Asia and in the Pacific area if British Commonwealth peoples and others with economic ties to the British crown were liberated largely by American arms.

Prime Minister Curtin brought back from a Prime Ministers' conference in London full information on the British plan. MacArthur at once sent it on to Washington. In a message dispatched on August 27 he reviewed the whole situation. "The Prime Minister of Australia has told me that during the Prime Ministers' conference in London he was confronted with a plan to form a British force here composed of land, naval and air elements under a British commander; that it was contemplated that the forces involved would be completely independent of my command and that the scheme would be effectuated upon the establishment of Southwest Pacific area forces in the Philippines; that Australia and the area of the NEI and Borneo would be removed from the SWPA.

"Considerable pressure in advancing the proposal apparently was placed upon Curtin who expressed himself repeatedly in opposition to the concept . . . and that he feared there was a danger of the gravest misunderstandings with the United States if Australian forces were taken away from General MacArthur's direct command and placed under a new commander. . . . [He] pointed out that the decision on this issue could not be taken without consideration of the past. There was a heritage of successful association and collaboration between the Australian government and General MacArthur's headquarters. That was a fact which was bound to influence the Australian attitude in the matter."

MacArthur then explained the grave problems of military strategy involved: "The main attack is about to be resumed and will effect a decisive penetration in the center of the enemy's main defensive position by our landing in force in the Philippines. After the operation, the strategic situation will be entirely different. Having effected a penetration in the enemy's center, it will be possible to roll up either or both flanks from the advantageous position that has been gained. Under these circumstances it would manifestly be unsound to return to our initial line of departure in Australia and execute another frontal attack against the relatively light forces by attacking the enemy's rear. Every strategic consideration dictates that the campaign for the liberation of the NEI be launched from the Philippines.

"The addition of British forces would be welcome," MacArthur pointed out. "Every effort has been made, without avail, to secure their participation. . . . Additional naval forces should be available for the support of operations to the south and for necessary escort assignments. The British task force which has been contemplated would be admirably suited for this duty. British forces, however assigned, should come under the present setup. To attempt to segregate such a force into an entirely self-contained command consisting of ground, naval and air components would not only introduce a clash of command authority, but would require the complete reorganization of the present setup where Australian, New Zealand and American forces are amalgamated along service lines and coordinated under my immediate control. The basic organization which has been so successful in combining the forces in three classifications would have to be reconstituted along national rather than professional lines. The withdrawal of the Australian and New Zealand components would present a serious problem. Any forces assigned here should be unhampered in their use and control by the Supreme Commander.

"Under the agreement entered into by the 5 interested nations, the SWPA has operated under American command for more than two years. We have passed through dark days and are now on the threshold of decisive victory. It is appropriate that this command is maintained to the successful conclusion of the campaign. Entirely aside from any consideration of equity, the division of the area and the assignment of the major portion thereof under a British commander would be completely destructive of American prestige in the Far East and would have the most serious repercussions. It is my belief that such a line of action would not receive the approval of the American people and that if consummated, would give rise to a condition that would be prejudicial to the maintenance of cordial relations between the U.S. and Great Britain during the post war period. . . ."

Here MacArthur showed his deep concern for American commercial interests in the Far East—a concern that was later to cause him to resist, throughout his administration of Japan, British efforts to bring that unhappy land within the orbit of the Sterling Bloc. It is not to disparage the British to point to their efforts, both during and after the war, to exploit MacArthur's victories to their own economic advantage, as their geography demands maximum exploitation of the economic resources of others if the British are to live. It is, however, to MacArthur's credit that even in war he foresaw the threat of conflict between British and American commercial interests following a victorious peace, and that he sought firmly to defend the American economic position.

The logic of MacArthur's position was too impelling. The opposition of Australian public opinion was too forceful. The attitude of official Washington was lukewarm. Hence, despite the British efforts, the bonds of comradeship-in-arms between the Australian and New Zealand and American forces in the Southwest Pacific, welded in a "grand alliance" of political and military leaders of differing nationalities but with a singleness of purpose, withstood all assaults. Not until a year later, in August 1945, when the Philippine and Borneo campaigns had been successfully concluded and the decisions were made to launch a land attack against Japan proper, did the situation change. Then the strategic objective was altered. Operations in the NEI were secondary in importance and the need for mounting maximum force against Japan was primary, so MacArthur was relieved of further responsibilities in the area and assigned to be Supreme Commander of the invasion of Japan. And it is interesting to note that when the area of the NEI was ultimately transferred to Mountbatten's Southern Asia command, the Australian leaders declined to participate in the ensuing operations and instead pulled their forces back toward Australia.

Meanwhile, MacArthur was having to ward off another flank attack by his allies—this time from his own countrymen. On June 17 he received a disquieting message from the Joint Chiefs of Staff advising that the Chiefs were considering the possibilities of expediting the Pacific campaign by "(a) advancing the target for operations now scheduled through operations against Formosa; (b) by-passing presently selected objectives prior to operations against Formosa; and (c) by-passing previously selected objectives and choosing new objectives, including Japan proper." The message asked for MacArthur's views and recommendations along with those of Nimitz.

MacArthur understood at once the implications of this message. He had already made strong recommendations to the Joint Chiefs of Staff on October 31, nearly eight months before, wherein he had said: "An attack across the Pacific must be delivered against a position organized in great depth, which starts at the maximum distance from the objective and involves a succession of independent seaborne attacks, supported by carrier based aviation in opposition to land based air. Each successive operation contributes little to the next, and the loss of each successive point does not materially weaken the enemy beyond the immediate attrition he suffers in the process. Because of the successive and separate nature of the attacks and because of the inability of carrier based aviation to maintain an unrelenting pressure, the offensive can never achieve momentum. Taking these outposts of the enemy defense will not cut his lines of communication and curtail his potential. This course of action does not employ in effective combination the three essentials of modern combat: land, sea, and air power."

He had then gone on to explain the advantages of the course of attack he had been planning all along. "The attack from the Southwest Pacific area," he had said, "departs from the base that is closest to the objective and advances against the most lightly organized portion of the enemy's defenses, effecting a decisive penetration. It is the only plan that permits an effective combination of land, sea, and air power. The advance can be made by a combination of airborne and seaborne operations, always supported by the full power of land based aviation and assisted by the fleet operating in the open reaches of the Pacific. A penetration of the defensive perimeter along this line results in by-passing heavily defended areas of great extent which will fall, practically of their own weight, to mopping-up operations with a minimum of loss. These by-passed positions will be liabilities to the enemy because of attrition. This course of action will allow the Allied forces to capitalize on any weakness that may develop. It is capable of obtaining momentum."

Then he had pointed out why both operations, a direct attack across the Central Pacific and an attack from the Southwest Pacific up through to the Philippines, could not go on at once. "To attempt a major effort along each axis would result in weakness everywhere in violation of cardinal principles of war, and would result in failure to reach the vital, strategic objective at the earliest possible date, thus prolonging the war."

As to the abandonment of the Philippines as an objective in favor of a direct assault upon Formosa or even Japan proper by a drive across the Central Pacific, MacArthur replied: ". . . It is my most earnest conviction that the proposal to by-pass the Philippines and launch an attack directly against Formosa is unsound; that operation would have to be launched without appreciable support from land based aviation and be based upon the Hawaiian Islands at a distance of 5,000 miles; assuming the success of the Marianas operations, there still will be no bases west of Oahu along this line of advance. Under these conditions and with the enemy solidly established on Formosa, susceptible to rapid reinforcement from Japan or the mainland, with his air bases in a flanking position at effective range in Luzon, I do not believe the campaign would succeed. The hazards of failure would be unjustifiable when a conservative and certain line of action is open. The occupation of Luzon is essential in order to establish air forces and bases prior to the move on Formosa. Assault forces could then be launched at short range with effective air support and with every assurance of success.

"The proposal to by-pass all other objectives and launch an attack directly on the Japan mainland is in my opinion utterly unsound. There is available in the Pacific only enough shipping to lift about 7 divisions. That fact alone would preclude such an enterprise in the predictable future. Even with unlimited shipping I do not believe a direct assault without air support can possibly succeed. Since the initiation of our advance the enemy has executed delaying actions within his outpost positions. Our successes in these operations must not lead us into a suicidal direct assault without air support and with inadequate shipping and bases against heavily defended bastions of the enemy's main positions.

"In my opinion purely military considerations demand the reoccupation of the Philippines in order to cut the enemy's communications to the south and to secure a base for our further advance. Even if this were not the case, and unless military factors demanded another line of action, it would, in my opinion, be necessary to re-occupy the Philippines. It is American territory, where our unsupported forces were destroyed by the enemy. Practically all of the 17,000,000 Filipinos remain loyal to the

United States and are undergoing the greatest privation and suffering because we have not been able to support or succor them. We have a great national obligation to discharge. . . . I feel also that a decision to eliminate the campaign for the relief of the Philippines, even under appreciable military considerations, would cause extremely adverse reactions among the citizens of the United States. The American people, I am sure, would acknowledge the obligation."

He then concluded: "In this dispatch I have expressed my firm conviction with a mere outline of the military factors that enter the problem. If serious consideration is being given to the line of action indicated in your radio, I request that I be accorded the opportunity of personally proceeding to Washington to present fully my views." This was the only occasion, before or since, on which MacArthur ever requested his recall from a duty assignment to present his views personally. That he did so reflects the depth of his feeling in the matter and his determination to do everything within his power to prevent what he firmly believed to be an unsound—and possibly fatal—strategic course, as well as an immoral abandonment of the Philippines.

Marshall replied on June 24 with his own explanation of the reasoning behind this suggested change of strategy. ". . . I think it is important that you should have my comments without delay. In the first place the query to you and to Nimitz should have provided some background as to the factors leading to the further investigation of the matter by the JCS. All information we have received indicates a steady build up of Japanese strength in the area Mindanao, Celebes, Halmahera, Vogelkop, Palau. It is also apparent from the information that the Japanese are seriously limited in their capacity to re-deploy or re-arrange their troops due to limited shipping. The information available appears to indicate their expectation of an early attack on Palau as well as continued advances to the northwest by your forces. In other words, further advances in this particular region will encounter greatly increased Japanese strength in most localities. There will be less opportunity to move against his weakness and to his surprise, as has been the case in your recent series of moves.

"Involved in the immediate foregoing is also the critical factor, on which I have been insisting, that the great Pacific Fleet with its thousands of planes should be maintained in practically continuous employment, because of its mobility, its power to select objectives along a tremendous front and the great and rapidly increasing carrier forces available. . . . Whether or not such operations should be carried out before a heavy

blow is struck at the Japanese fleet is also of course a serious consideration. There is little doubt in my mind that, after a crushing blow is delivered against the Japanese fleet, then we should go as close to Japan and
as quickly as possible in order to shorten the war. . . ."

Then Marshall threw in an oblique and gratuitous reference to Mac-
Arthur's passionate desire to liberate the Filipinos and Americans from
the chains of enemy captivity. "With regard to the re-conquest of the
Philippines," he said, "we must be careful not to allow our personal feeling
and Philippine political considerations to over-rule our great objective. . . ."

Marshall concluded by acknowledging MacArthur's request to present his views in person if necessary. "As to your expressed desire to be
accorded the opportunity of personally proceeding to Washington to
present fully your views," he said, "I see no difficulty about that. If the
issue arises I will speak to the President, who, I am quite certain, would
be agreeable to your being ordered home for the purpose."

From this message, MacArthur knew where Marshall stood. He could
already see that the issue was perilously close to being lost unless he could
move the President.

Suddenly, in the midst of all this correspondence, MacArthur received orders to meet President Roosevelt at Pearl Harbor for a conference. He was not informed as to its purpose, and he departed immediately
with but a single aide, and with no reports, no charts, no plans, no maps,
nor any other type of reference data.

What followed was probably the most dramatic war council of World
War II. By the time MacArthur arrived at Pearl Harbor, the Joint Chiefs
of Staff, with Marshall's support, had already tentatively approved the
plan to bypass the Philippines. Thus, he had to do a great deal more than
argue his case; he had to so convince Roosevelt of the soundness of his
strategic viewpoint that the President would reject the recommendations
of virtually all his other chief military advisers.

Franklin Roosevelt had accepted his fourth-term nomination the day
before boarding the new heavy cruiser U.S.S. *Baltimore* to speed to Hawaii, where he had arrived with an escort of pursuit planes and PT boats.
On the broad sundeck of one of Hawaii's showplaces overlooking Waikiki, he had set up his temporary military headquarters. At this cream
stucco mansion the President called the conference before lunch on the
third day of his visit. He explained that the various plans for attack on
Japan had been narrowed down to two. One was to attack Formosa and

bypass the Philippines. The other was to liberate the Philippines and by-pass Formosa. MacArthur listened while Admiral Nimitz presented his arguments for the first plan. Then came his turn, his final opportunity to alter the U.S. course toward disaster in the Pacific.

Observers who witnessed this occasion credit MacArthur with being at his very best, and anyone who has heard him speak for any length of time knows what that means. His intuitive ability of expression, which has made so many of his phrases a part of the English language, is even more forceful when he speaks. He never shouts, but there are few who can spellbind a listener as MacArthur can. Indeed, when he speaks at length on a serious subject, he is sometimes carried away himself, and this only adds to the effect. I have long ceased to be surprised at the unsolicited comments made by nearly everyone who comes out of his office after a first conference or interview with him.

And his arguments were not wasted on Roosevelt. Despite the President's Europe-first orientation, he had long ago learned not to underestimate the validity of MacArthur's arguments. Some years before, when George Marshall had been a more or less obscure colonel and MacArthur had been Chief of Staff, President Roosevelt had often asked him to the White House for long discussions, many of which had little or nothing to do with military affairs. On one of these occasions MacArthur asked Roosevelt why he was soliciting the General's advice on civilian matters. "Douglas," the President replied, "to me you are a symbol of the conscience of America."

Now, in the living-room of the mansion overlooking Waikiki Beach, as the cooling tropical breezes swept in off the Pacific, MacArthur rose, took up a pointer, and walked to the map on the wall. Using no gestures but the graphic emphasis of distances on the map of the Pacific, he proceeded to destroy the argument that had been advanced. "I spoke of the high esteem and extraordinary admiration I felt for Admiral Nimitz and his naval associates," MacArthur told me later, "but I argued against the naval concept of frontal assault against the strongly held island positions of the enemy." He quickly went over the arguments that had already been advanced in his message to Washington; and then he presented, succinctly but eloquently, the undeniable strategic case for retaking the Philippines.

He placed the real emphasis where he knew it belonged: on the moral argument against abandoning the Philippines. As he related this later, he commented dryly: "I was also critical of what I regarded as a major blunder in originally abandoning all effort to relieve the Philippines. I stated that had we had the will to do so, we could have opened the way to reinforce Bataan and Corregidor garrisons and probably not only have saved the Philippines but thereby stopped the enemy's advance toward New Guinea and Australia. I felt that to sacrifice the Philippines a second time would not be condoned or forgiven."

He finished, placed the pointer on the rack below the map, turned and walked silently to his chair. President Roosevelt adjourned the meeting.

Later, MacArthur had a few minutes with the President alone. And this time he confined himself to a point which he was sure the President already knew and which only needed emphasizing. "Mr. President," he said quietly, "if your decision be to bypass the Philippines and leave its millions of wards of the United States and thousands of American internees and prisoners of war to continue to languish in their agony and despair—I dare to say that the American people would be so aroused that they would register most complete resentment against you at the polls this fall." But the President had already made his decision. "We will not bypass the Philippines," he replied. "Carry out your existing plans. And may God protect you."

MacArthur warmly replied: "Thank you, Mr. President. If it is all right with you, I shall take my leave and return to my theater at once."

"No," the President said, "I wish you would remain over and take a ride with me around the island tomorrow."

On the morning following the conference, MacArthur was waiting at the time appointed. He has told me of the events which followed. The President came out with Admiral Leahy and joined him on the veranda. They then went to the waiting car. MacArthur started to get into the front seat because of Admiral Leahy's seniority as Chief of Staff to the President, but Roosevelt asked him to ride in the back with him. "Bill won't mind riding up front," he added. The conversation between the President and MacArthur consisted mainly of reminiscences of the high points of their long association together, starting when MacArthur was a major on the General Staff in Washington and the President was Assistant Secretary to the Navy. This reminiscence continued throughout the ride.

When they approached the first of the many camps they visited that day, the President asked MacArthur if he thought he should address the troops and, if so, on what subject. MacArthur replied that by all means he should address them, adding that this could be done through a microphone without the President having to get out of the car. The subject of patriotism, he suggested, was always appropriate before troops.

Late that day, when the last camp had been visited and the return home completed, MacArthur and the President took leave of each other. "We parted," MacArthur told me recently, "in a spirit of deep mutual regard. I knew then that I would never see him again."

That night Admiral Nimitz asked MacArthur if he could drive him to the airport. As they started off, Nimitz at once expressed his amazement that—as was obvious from what MacArthur had said during the previous day's conference—he had not been briefed on the agenda for the President's conference before leaving his Brisbane headquarters. "I can hardly believe that General Marshall would instruct you to meet the President here without giving you full details on the subject matter to be discussed," he said.

MacArthur replied: "Well, that is the way it was. I was given no inkling that such a vital decision was to be in issue, although I did instinctively associate the conference with the recent exchange of messages on future Pacific strategy."

There have been many who have charged, then and since, that President Roosevelt's dramatic trip to Pearl Harbor to confer with a victorious general just before opening the election campaign for his fourth term was a political trick. It is true that on the day after the conference with MacArthur, Roosevelt held a press conference on the lawn of the estate (under palm trees, incidentally, from which the coconuts had been removed lest they fall on the Presidential head) and announced that MacArthur and U.S. fighting forces would return to the Philippines. It is true that this trip of the President's served to remind the voters that they were still electing a commander-in-chief. And it is true that two of Roosevelt's chief advisers on the trip were speech-writer Sam Rosenman and OWI Boss Elmer Davis. But, whether or not the President's trip was really necessary, I have never heard MacArthur associate himself with the viewpoint that it was more political than strategical.

He has always felt that a great issue had arisen between himself and the Joint Chiefs of Staff as to the conduct of the war. It was a moment of vital decision. He had asked for a hearing, and the President had granted it. MacArthur has ever been grateful that this opportunity was given him, and even more grateful that Roosevelt could understand what other military advisers apparently could not: that in war there are times when moral and psychological advantages are as important as military ones. This fact I felt most keenly when, on returning to Manila on its liberation, I talked with a few of the many thousands of Filipinos and American prisoners of war who will be eternally grateful that their lives were saved —by President Roosevelt, who made the decision not to bypass the Philippines, and even more by MacArthur, who stood alone to plead their cause when their own lips were silenced.

The conference at Waikiki was perhaps the most striking example during World War II of MacArthur's having to use diplomatic persuasion upon his friends and allies in order to avert military disaster. So well did he argue his case at Waikiki that Admiral Nimitz plunged wholeheartedly into support of the Philippine drive as soon as the Presidential decision for it had been made. In fact, what followed was called by one correspondent "probably the most productive liaison in American history." Another correspondent reported: "Let me emphasize again that relationships between MacArthur and Nimitz have been particularly good in the last six months, and that the Joint Chiefs of Staff have had a hard time keeping up with them."

MacArthur and Nimitz had had their first formal conferences four months earlier, when Nimitz had flown to Port Moresby to work out the Army-Navy co-ordination for the Hollandia landings. Like Halsey, Nimitz took to MacArthur immediately, and together the General and the Admiral worked out the attack that took the enemy so completely by surprise. MacArthur was grateful for the strong support that the Navy task force gave him at Hollandia, just as Nimitz was grateful for the support that MacArthur's ground and air forces had been giving him all through the Solomons campaign. The two men developed a mutual respect for each other's abilities, as well as a warm friendship. Statements by MacArthur's critics to the contrary notwithstanding, Nimitz found the General ready and willing not only to accept but to capitalize on suggestions from the Navy.

These two men formed the most powerful Army-Navy team the world has ever seen. And they lost no time in launching the attack for which MacArthur had argued so persuasively at Waikiki. On September 1, U.S. bombers thundered over Davao, in Mindanao. They were the first American planes the Filipinos had seen in two and a half years—a dramatic announcement that the campaign to liberate the Philippines was on.

CHAPTER XII   Behind the Enemy Lines

⚑ Actually, in a sense, the war in the Philippines had never stopped. And MacArthur had never ceased trying to penetrate the silence that had enshrouded that unhappy land in the dark days immediately following Corregidor's fall. He had hoped for and long planned an organized guerrilla resistance against the enemy's effort to conquer and pacify the Islands; and he felt sure that many of his former soldiers, who had refused to surrender, were still at large and eager to form the nucleus of such a movement. But even enemy propaganda failed to give any clue to events following the surrender. Information from the Philippines was as lacking as though the Islands had been physically blotted off the face of the map.

Then suddenly on July 10, 1942, a weak signal addressed to MacArthur was picked up by a patriot on the enemy-occupied island of Java and passed on. This partially lifted the shroud of silence. "Detachments of Fil-American Forces—we have not surrendered—are actively raiding northeast barrios and towns of Pangasinan including Dagupan [Central Luzon]," the message read. "Radio censorship by Jap very rigid resulting in almost complete ignorance of Filipinos of the true and correct status of the war. As remedy we disseminate information and words of encouragement through our pamphlet, *Bataan Fortnightly*, copies of which are distributed in several provinces including Manila. Jap penalty for possession of this pamphlet and other counter-propaganda is death. . . . Our people, nevertheless, are undaunted and continue to seek correct information. Your victorious return is the nightly subject of prayer in every Filipino home. [Signed] Lieut. Colonel Nakar."

Nakar had been a battalion commander of the 14th Infantry, which was operating in the Province of Nueva Vizcaya in North Luzon when Corregidor fell. Probably no message ever gave MacArthur more of an uplift. It dramatically informed him that the Filipinos' spiritual resistance to the enemy still continued long after their military bastions had crumbled, and that his soldiers who had avoided enemy capture still fought on. It confirmed his faith that they would. As he read and reread the passage: "Your victorious return is the nightly subject of prayer in every Filipino home," he knew at once that he still had a great and powerful ally behind the enemy's lines. It was the moral force of a Christian nation, the indomitable spirit of a Christian people, and he determined to do all in his power not only to support it but in time to exploit it as a powerful adjunct to Allied arms. There followed a radio exchange between MacArthur and Nakar, in which MacArthur learned information of value concerning enemy activity in Central Luzon and the disposition and condition of prisoners of war. The darkness and silence were penetrated.

On August 7 came an ominous warning from Nakar: "Intelligence report reveals that enemy has detected the existence of our radio station, possibly by geometric process, and detailed a large force to look for us." He then went on to give long and detailed instructions for codes and deceptive timing to fool the enemy, and to continue radio contact. It was an extraordinarily calm rehearsal of security precautions by one under imminent danger of capture. Unfortunately, it was too daring; silence followed this last report. We later learned that the enemy had captured Nakar and put him to death.

Such was the grim fate that was to be repeated time and time again, as devoted patriots, Filipino and American, rose to give militant leadership to the people's irrepressible resistance—and later to fall, many unknown and unsung. Many more were to fill the ranks of those who had fallen, and the movement was to grow in a crescendo until it encompassed the entire length and breadth of the Philippines. It was to force upon the Japanese the commitment of large numbers of troops for occupation duty, but, like the inexorable flow of the tides and the winds, it could not be stopped. It was to become a test such as the world has rarely known—brute force against human spirit, a spirit molded from Christian ideals and fortified by faith in the ultimate redemption of a soldier's pledge to return.

On November 2 another signal came through. A listening-post of the Royal Australian Air Force in northern Australia picked up a message from a Major Macario Peralta, Jr., who had fought in the 61st Division on the island of Panay. Peralta reported that he had assumed command of guerrilla forces in the Visayan Islands. "Fourth Philippine Corps," he advised MacArthur, "consists of 61st Division, strength 8,000 men fully reorganized on Panay. . . . Only about 800 enemy there in all provincial capitals. . . . Panay outfit controls all interior and west coast. Civilians and officials 99 per cent loyal. Supplies could be dropped anywhere away from towns, and subs could make coast anywhere more than 20 miles distant from capitals. . . . Puppet governor Hernandez of Capiz captured in guerrilla raid and sentenced to death by court-martial. Request confirmation of sentence. I have installed Governor Confessor, who refused surrender to enemy, as governor of whole island. I have declared martial law for Panay. Request information as to general policy finances. . . ."

MacArthur replied immediately: "Your action in reorganizing Philippine army units is deserving of the highest commendation and has aroused high enthusiasm among all of us here. You will continue to exercise command. Primary mission is to maintain your organization and to secure maximum amount of information. Guerrilla activities should be postponed until ordered from here. Premature action of this kind will only bring heavy retaliation upon innocent people. As our intelligence unit covering maximum territory you can perform great service. You cannot operate under provision of martial law in the Philippines, occupied as they are by the enemy. It is not practicable to issue money. You should issue to your men certificates showing that the United States owes them pay as accrued. Similar certificates can be used as required showing purpose. The United States will honor them in the due course of time." And he added: "The enemy is now under heavy pressure and victory will come. We cannot predict the date of our return to the Philippines, but we are coming."

Peralta answered with a simple message that in two sentences predicted the entire course of the guerrilla war and gave the reason why. The message brought back memories of brighter days, because it was addressed to "Field Marshal" MacArthur—the rank he had held as head of the Philippine army. And the message itself read: "Mission assigned us will be accomplished. Humblest soldier has blind faith in you."

By now the flow had increased. On January 3 a radio flash came in from still another area of the Philippines—the Cagayan Valley in north Luzon. It was signed by Captain Ralph B. Praeger, who had been commanding officer of Troop C of the 26th Cavalry at the time of Corregidor's surrender. Only part of the message was picked up. "Am conducting government with utmost care legally and morally devoid of politics and personal considerations. Military and civil authorities in perfect accord helping one another. I have provided all needs of the army composed of scouts, constabulary, and Philippine army in Cagayan and Apayo. . . . If I may be permitted, I can organize 5,000 able-bodied trainees, R.O.T.C.'s, and intelligence men provided we would be furnished arms and ammunition."

130

MacArthur quickly promised help as soon as possible. He was having difficulties enough then getting arms and ammunition in adequate supply for his forces in New Guinea, but he realized the extreme importance of this guerrilla activity in the Philippines, and he was already making plans to secure support for it.

In the interchange of messages with Praeger's radio station MacArthur received the news that Lieutenant Colonels Arthur Noble and Martin Moses, both from the 11th Philippine Division, had managed to escape from Bataan and were directing north Luzon guerrilla activities. Noble reported that he and Moses "have unified command and control approximately 6,000 guerrilla troops in provinces north of Manila." Further messages brought confirmation that the spirit of resistance was alive and vibrant, though badly in need of direction. "Large number of enemy motor vehicles and bridges have been destroyed by USFIP (United States Forces in the Philippines) troops. . . . Enemy telephone poles have been torn down, food dumps burned, and considerable enemy arms and ammunition have been captured. USFIP losses very small. Morale USFIP and behavior in action excellent. Thousands young Filipinos eager to join USFIP when arms available and our reinforcements imminent. Greatest need now is radio communication between our widely separated units and Allied propaganda to strengthen morale of civilian population. . . . The USFIP on Luzon is ready and eager to engage the enemy on your orders, and it is firmly believed that the mass of civilian population will aid us directly or indirectly by whatever means and whatever weapons are available."

So the messages poured in—from Dagupan, from Panay, from the Cagayan Valley. And now the southernmost island of Mindanao was heard from. Colonel Wendell W. Fertig, an engineer officer who had been with Sharp on Mindanao at the time of the surrender, reported that he had taken command of the guerrillas on Mindanao, and that he had "a strong force in being, with complete civilian support."

These radio contacts provided MacArthur with concrete evidence that the spirit of resistance was there: only a flickering spark, but one that could be fanned into a roaring flame. He saw in it a powerful moral force, erected upon faith and hope, which needed only his guidance and support.

There followed a campaign such as history has never before recorded. MacArthur had to project his leadership across thirty-five hundred miles through the most difficult channels of communication. Written messages depended upon the occasional submarine pick-up, and the multitudinous emergencies could be dealt with only by radio. So the information Mac-Arthur received was in abbreviated form and had to be supplemented by his encyclopedic knowledge of the Philippines and the Filipinos. Only across a bridge of faith could he communicate with those peril-bedeviled people. And only for MacArthur was there such a bridge; he could reach their eyes and ears because he had long since reached their hearts.

When I arrived in Australia, I was assigned to organize and direct this operation under his watchful eye. I moved into an office close to MacArthur's Brisbane headquarters and set to work. My operations were conducted in such secrecy that few in GHQ had the slightest inkling of what was going on. But MacArthur followed the project with the keenest interest, and personally directed or approved every major move that was made. Reports from our radio-operators in the Philippines were among the first things he picked up to read and evaluate when he arrived at his desk each morning.

We worked out countless separate codes to maintain the secrecy of our communications. I had selected five hundred men from Filipino units on the west coast of the United States and in Hawaii, and, at MacArthur's request, they were speeded to Australia. There they were organized into a special battalion in a camp about forty miles south of Brisbane, where they were put through a rigorous course of training in radio-operation and maintenance, intelligence, sabotage, and related subjects. Meanwhile, MacArthur had selected three gallant officers, well known to the Filipinos, to slip into the Islands by submarine to make preliminary surveys of the situation in the southern areas. Two of them were Americans: Lieutenant Commander Charles ("Chick") Parsons and Captain Charles Smith, who went into Mindanao. The third was a Filipino patriot who had become a hero to Filipinos and Americans alike when he won the Distinguished Service Cross as a daring pursuit pilot during the early days of the defense of the Philippines. He was Major Jesus Villamor, and he went into the Visayas.

At first, in order to move our supplies and trained personnel into the Philippines, we were forced to rely upon space available on submarines that were assigned missions in the Western Pacific and could stop briefly off the Philippine coast to discharge this type of cargo in rubber boats. But as soon as the Navy realized the advantages of having coast watchers with communications to report on weather and enemy naval activity in the area, a few submarines were assigned to the operation. The first was one of the Navy's two large cargo-carrying submarines, which accommodated a hundred tons of supplies and a dozen or more passengers.

Additional submarines later joined our outfit, including the second of the Navy's two big cargo-carriers.

From the start, MacArthur adhered to the policy that the operations of the organized guerrilla units would be confined to intelligence and communications. He well knew that, apart from the reprisals it would bring down upon the people, more aggressive action at that stage would only expose and endanger our intelligence operations and threaten destruction of our communications without contributing significantly to the ultimate liberation of the Philippines. His specific orders to this effect, however, were occasionally violated by overzealous guerrilla leaders.

The most difficult single task at this stage of the operation was to find a means of combating the propaganda with which the enemy had saturated the Philippines. The Japanese controlled all sources of internal propaganda—the press, the radio, the billboards, the schools, and every local medium for the dissemination of information. We had only a short-wave radio beamed from San Francisco, and this was of doubtful value, as few Filipinos possessed the equipment to receive short-wave broadcasts and those who did risked strong penalties for listening in. Not only was the weight of the enemy's false propaganda concerning the progress of the war bearing down heavily on Filipinos, but it was also hurting the morale of those Americans still at large. Time after time, in their radio messages to our headquarters, guerrilla leaders pleaded for Allied counter-propaganda.

On August 10, 1943, I suggested to MacArthur a possible solution to this problem. In a memorandum I proposed that various items known to be scarce in the Philippines, such as cigarettes, matches, chewing-gum, candy bars, sewing-kits, and pencils, be sent to the Islands by submarine in great quantity for widespread distribution. Each package would bear the crossed American and Philippine flags on one side, and on the other the quotation "I shall return"—printed over a facsimile of MacArthur's signature. I explained that this simple gesture might become an extremely effective method of counter-propaganda. He wrote his answer in pencil on the bottom of my memorandum: "No objection—I *shall* return—MacA."

Over the years there has been some ribbing about this phrase, "I shall return," and MacArthur himself has not been above using it with a humorous connotation. When he first wrote this phrase down, however, he was directing it at Asians who were fighting for their very homes and who saw in that simple, heartfelt pledge their only hope. Those three words became the slogan and the watchword of the guerrilla movement. The phrase's strength was in its simplicity. Although there are eighty-seven dialects in the Philippines, the English words "I shall return" were understood everywhere and never needed to be translated.

We sent millions of articles so inscribed into the Islands. We produced and distributed great numbers of a pictorial magazine entitled *Free Philippines,* which reviewed the progress of the war and which reproduced the phrase in large, bold letters on its cover. We prepared a progress map of the Southwest Pacific area, showing the most recent advances of Allied arms and carrying the quotation in big type. It was simple, direct, and understandable to all Filipinos regardless of dialect or literacy, and was to become understandable to the Japanese as well. It became a household phrase throughout the Islands. The Japanese found it posted everywhere they turned. Sooner or later every enemy garrison was to be confronted with the phrase—on bulletin boards, pasted on military buses and trains, at the entrances to stations and post offices, and nearly everywhere civilians might gather or enemy soldiers might pass. Threats and violent reprisal did nothing to stop this barrage of counter-propaganda or to dampen the ardor of the guerrillas in its exploitation.

By every means possible we flooded the Philippines with newspapers and periodicals from the United States. Again the reactions were even better than we had expected. A message from guerrilla leader Fertig in September 1943 is self-explanatory: "Advise that article about Ibn Saud, King of Saudi Arabia, in *Life* for 31 May, be reprinted for distribution among Mohammedans of the Celebes, Borneo, particularly Brunei and all the Moro provinces in Mindanao and Sulu. Expressions of friendship by the king for the U.S.A. are extremely important. Many Mindanao Moros have made pilgrimage to Mecca. That single issue of *Life* has destroyed much pro-Jap support in Lanao. Send me every copy of that issue of *Life* available and reprint if possible." Another intelligence report from Fertig said: ". . . Smuggled *Life* magazine rented at 25 pesos ($12.50) per hour." And another report: "Wrapper from 'I shall return—MacArthur' chewing gum now selling for 10 pesos ($5.00) each in Manila." Sometimes this operation worked little advantages in both directions. Another issue of *Life* listed one Corporal Reid C. Chamberlain, of El Cajon, California, as dead. On reading this, a guerrilla leader reported that Corporal Chamberlain "is on duty here." It gave me no small pleasure to pass this information on to Corporal Chamberlain's mother.

All these supplies of propaganda material, goods, arms, ammunition, and radio sets were carried into the Philippines by the submarines supplied by the Navy—for whom, in return, we provided reports on weather and enemy naval activity three times a day. With our tiny fleet we increased the thin trickle to a steady flow as soon as we found that submarine contact with the guerrilla forces could be made with a minimum danger of being compromised. In all our contacts, not a single rendezvous was ever betrayed to the enemy. In fact, the only submarine casualty in this entire operation came when one vessel, shortly after leaving Australia, was apparently mistaken for the enemy by our own planes and sunk.

Gradually, with the specially trained Filipino radio experts as a nucleus, we established a network of stations throughout the Philippines. This network together with guerrilla intelligence operatives, became MacArthur's eyes and ears in the Philippines and, in fact, the advance echelon in his campaign of liberation. It was a long, arduous campaign, and the guerrilla forces needed all the encouragement that we could give them by way of such radio contact. Virtually every message from our headquarters carried the reiterated assurance that the day of liberation was coming. But there were times when MacArthur felt the frustration of delay as keenly as the men who were waiting for him in the Island hills. One of the guerrilla messages, which detailed enemy activity against civilians in north Luzon, concluded with this remark: "The oldest man in Apayo wanted to know if MacArthur, the only American who fights Japs, will get back before he dies of old age." MacArthur permitted himself to write the wry comment to me on the bottom of this message: "Perhaps I, too, may die of old age before I am given resources to return.—MacA."

Even Filipino leaders living in the laps of the Japanese in Manila occasionally made the long and dangerous journey to a guerrilla headquarters to establish contact with MacArthur. As early as June 1943, Peralta advised him of the visit of some prominent Filipinos. Their purpose was to inform him of and establish contact with a secret organization operating in Central Luzon under the sponsorship of such prominent Manilans as Antonio Bautista, Lorenza Tanada, Cepriano Cid, Judge Jesus Barrera, Judge Richaro Nepomuceno, Amado Dayrit, Dr. Caseario Candoval, Dr. Restituto Yuson, and Attorney Juan Paulmo—all well known to MacArthur and to me. MacArthur at once wired: "Please convey to men referred to as sponsoring secret organization among the people of Luzon and all those who have joined with them, my warm personal wishes and my grateful acknowledgment of their loyal and unswerving devotion to the cause to which we are mutually pledged. . . . Tell them I counsel a period of quiet and cautious organization of men whose loyalty is unquestioned, against the time that my own personal representative will make contact with and direct them. Tell them that I have abiding confidence in the assurance of ultimate victory but that the time intervening of continued suffering under enemy oppression will depend in large measure on the support which they and other patriots give me when I call for it. Tell them that I trust Almighty God will give them the courage, the fortitude, and the will to meet the tests which lie ahead in the struggle for liberty."

Words of encouragement like these from MacArthur meant as much to the Filipino patriots as all the food and arms we were sending in to them. But this exchange of support was by no means one-sided, because simultaneously messages of inspiration were flowing from the pens of Filipino leaders everywhere. Two examples were given especially wide circulation in the Philippines at the time, and I quote from them at considerable length because they symbolize the spirit of resistance which burned so defiantly in the Islands during the entire Japanese occupation.

The first was written by a Christian Filipino political leader, Governor Tomas Confessor, of Iloilo, to Dr. Fermin Caram, in the same city, who had tried to get him to collaborate with the Japanese. Governor Confessor's letter was dated February 20, 1943, and said in part: "This struggle is a total war in which the issues between the warring parties are less concerned with territorial questions but more with forms of government, ways of life, and things that affect even the very thought, feelings and sentiments of every man. In other words, the question at stake with respect to the Philippines is not whether Japan or the U.S. should possess it but more fundamentally it is: what system of government should stand here and what ways of life; what system of social organization and code for morals should govern our existence.

"The burden of your so-called message to me consists of the entreaty that further bloodshed and destruction of property in Panay should stop and that our people be saved from further suffering and misery resulting from warfare and hostilities now existing between Japan and ourselves. The responsibility, however, of accomplishing this end does not rest upon us but entirely upon your friends who have sworn allegiance to Japan. For it was Japan that projected and created those conditions; Japan is the sole author of this holocaust in the Far East.

"You may not agree with me but the truth is that the present war is a blessing in disguise to our people and that the burden it imposes and the hardships it has brought upon us are a test of our character to determine the sincerity of our convictions and the integrity of our souls. In other words, this war has placed us in the crucible to assay the metal in our being. For as a people, we have been living during the last 40 years

136

under a regime of justice and liberty regulated only by universally accepted principles of constitutional government. We have come to enjoy personal privileges and civil liberties without much struggle, without undergoing any pain to attain them. They were practically a gift from a generous and magnanimous people—the people of the United States of America.

"Now that Japan is attempting to destroy those liberties, should we not exert any effort to defend them? Should we not be willing to suffer for their defense? If our people are undergoing hardships now, we are doing it gladly; it is because we are willing to pay the price for those constitutional liberties and privileges. You cannot become wealthy by honest means without sweating heavily. You very well know that the principles of democracy and democratic institutions were brought to life through bloodshed and fire. If we sincerely believe in those principles and institutions, as we who are resisting Japan do, we should contribute to the utmost of our capacity to the cost of its maintenance to save them from destruction and annihilation, and such contribution should be in terms of painful sacrifice, the same currency that other peoples paid for these principles. . . .

"You are decidedly wrong when you tell me that there is no ignominy in surrender. That may be true in the case of soldiers who were corralled by the enemy consisting of superior force, with no way of escape whatsoever. For when they gave themselves up they did not repudiate any principle of good government and the philosophy of life which inspired them to fight heroically and valiantly—to use your own words. Should I surrender, however, and with me the people, by your own invitation and assurance of guarantee to my life, my family and those who follow me, I should be surrendering something more precious than life itself: the principles of democracy and justice, and the honor and destiny of our people.

"I note you emphasized in your letter only peace and the tranquillity of our people. I do not know whether by omission or intentionally you failed to refer in any way to the honor and destiny of our race. You seem to have forgotten those noble sentiments already, despite the fact that Japan has hardly been a year in our country. It appears clearly evident, therefore, that there is a great difference between the manner in which we are trying to lead our people during these trying days. You and your fellow puppets are trying to give them peace and tranquillity by destroying their dignity and honor, without suffering, or if there is any, the least possible. On the other hand, we endeavor to inspire them to face difficulties and undergo any sacrifice to uphold the noble principles of popular rule and constitutional government, thereby holding up high and immaculate their honor and dignity at the same time. . . .

"You may have read, I am sure, the story of Lincoln who held firmly to the conviction that the secession of the southern states from the northern was wrong. Consequently, when he became the President and the southern states seceded he did not hesitate to use force to compel them to remain in the union. The immediate result was civil war that involved the country in the throes of a terrible armed conflict that, according to reliable historians, produced proportionately more loss of lives, hardships and miseries than the First World War. The sufferings of the people of the south were terrible but the union was saved and America has become thereby one of the strongest and most respected nations on the surface of the earth. If Lincoln had revised his convictions and sacrificed them for the sake of peace and tranquillity as you did, a fatal catastrophe would have befallen the people of America. With this lesson of history clearly before us, I prefer to follow Lincoln's example than yours and your fellow puppets. . . .

"I will not surrender as long as I can stand on my feet. The people may suffer now and may suffer more during the next months. To use the words of St. Paul the Apostle: 'The sufferings of the present are not worthy to be compared with the glory to come that shall be revealed in us.'"

The second letter was from a Moro of the Mohammedan faith. His name was Datu Manalao Mindalano, and he was at that time serving as a captain in the guerrilla force on Mindanao. His letter was dated July 3, 1943, and it was in answer to an attempt by Captain K. Takemoto to induce him to collaborate. "It gives me no surprise," wrote Datu, "to hear from you Japanese the same old alibi that you came to the Philippines with good intentions. What have you done in Lanao that is worth appreciating anyway? When you came, you kill the natives like chicken and attack towns and barrios who are innocent. Now that you cannot force us to submission and your doomsday is in sight, your note is sorrowful. . . .

"You can be very sure that I will continue to redouble my efforts in attacking places wherever I smell Japs. If I have been active when I was fighting by my own accord, you should expect a much more terrific attack from me now that I am following military orders and have taken oath reaffirming my allegiance to the Commonwealth of the Philippines and the United States of America. . . . If I were to choose between being a pro-Satan and a pro-Japanese, I would choose being the former just to be always against Japanism of all types in the Philippines. Had you been enlightened enough in the affairs, the psychology, the needs, and well-being of my people, THE MARANAOS, you will not keep on wondering why I will never be tempted by your persuasive propaganda and sugar-coated promises and why, in spite of a temporary collapse of U.S. Army resistance in the country on account of the surrender of the main USAFFE Forces in the Philippines, I have not only withstood the defense of my sector but have continued harassing your forces wherever we met until you became imprisoned in the fox holes of your garrisons. . . .

"Believe me: If there is any impossibility under the sun, it is a Philippine Independence granted by Japan. . . . Before this war, America promised the Philippines her independence in 1946. We honor American promises after a close observation of their character for over 40 years. But Japan's one-year commitment does not warrant honoring her promise of independence even if the date of that promise were to take effect tomorrow."

As MacArthur read these two messages—the one from a Christian and the other from a Mohammedan—he saw in them the symbolic welding of the people of the Philippines into a union such as had never before existed. He saw that, confronted with a common peril, the people had found a common purpose which far transcended any differences and which would help speed the day when he could redeem his pledge.

CHAPTER XIII   "And the truth shall make you
free."

☙ "I do solemnly swear that I shall obey orders from my superior officers;
that I shall fight the enemy of the Government of the Commonwealth of
the Philippines and the United States of America whosoever and wherever
he may be in the territory of the Philippines; that I shall never allow myself nor any arm or ammunition to be caught by the enemy; that I shall
never turn traitor to my country nor the United States of America; and
much less reveal to the enemy any secret of the army to which I honorably
belong; that I shall never abandon a wounded brother in arms; that I shall
join the united forces in the Philippines without personal or party interests, but with the determination to sacrifice myself and all that is mine
for FREEDOM and DEMOCRACY; that I shall protect the lives and property
of all loyal Filipinos everywhere.

"I make this LOYALTY OATH without mental reservation or purpose of
evasion.

"SO HELP ME GOD."

This, a typical guerrilla's oath in Leyte, reflects the spirit of those
who worked behind enemy lines for MacArthur while they waited for him
to return. The Filipino guerrillas, and the American army personnel who
had escaped the Japanese to add their leadership to the guerrilla movement, complemented this spirit with resourcefulness and ingenuity that
must have enraged the Japanese as much as they delighted MacArthur.

One example of this resourcefulness was reported to him in a message
received in August 1943, announcing that the critical fuel problem in the
Peralta district had been solved. To keep radio communication it was
necessary to charge batteries and power generators, but submarine delivery of gasoline and fuel oil could not possibly be adequate for this purpose. The solution was ingenious, to say the least.

"One hydroelectric plant constructed out of auto parts and lumber," the message read, "secured some semi-diesel engines run on coconut oil, abundant in this district. Constructed portable alcohol distilleries producing 96 per cent motor alcohol, out of galvanized sheets and GI pipes. Other parts are thermometers, gate vales and soldering materials. Now operating three distilleries supplying regional needs and three more under construction. Uses coconut tuba [local beer] as raw material. Each distillery has maximum output of five gallons per day. . . . Alcohol fuel substitute gasoline for motor generators used in all radio stations this district." All over the Philippines seemingly formidable obstacles like this were being overcome with the same kind of inspired inventiveness.

Sometimes, though, we on MacArthur's staff wished as much ingenuity and understanding prevailed in Washington. At the same time that the people on my staff and the brave operators in the Philippines were devoting nearly all of their energy to the single problem of combating Japanese propaganda, MacArthur received from Washington a message saying: "The President of the United States and President Quezon are much concerned over the progress of Japanese propaganda in the Philippine Islands and desire strong positive measures taken to counteract this poison without delay. The substance of the message of the President to Congress on October 6 should be impressed upon the minds of the Filipinos by every practical means in connection with the sure progress of Allied arms toward victory. . . . Text of the President's message is being sent you. . . ."

MacArthur forbore answering this wire by asking what Washington thought the Filipino guerrillas had been doing all this time, and instead replied that he would see that the President's message was given maximum distribution by radio as well as in printed copies distributed throughout the Philippines. He could not, however, remain silent in the face of any implication that the Filipinos would succumb to the blandishments of the Japanese. "Have no fear," he said. "The Filipino people will remain loyal at heart, and the day we set foot on the Islands, they will rally as a unit to our call."

The text of the President's message arrived in due time. But, while it contained reassuring promises for the future, it sadly neglected the present. What the Filipinos most wanted at the moment was to have the enemy lifted off their backs. They wanted relief from the perils that beset their daily lives. They wanted to see their women and their children relieved of the terror that had so long plagued their days and nights. The President's message did not mention any of these things, but MacArthur moved to fill the gap.

In radio broadcasts and by submarine delivery of tons of printed letters prepared on his official stationery over a facsimile of his signature, he passed on the text of the President's message and added these important words: "I am fully conscious of the heavy burden that is resting upon you during this trying period in Philippine history, and along with the President's proposals for your future postwar welfare and security, I take this opportunity to convey to you my personal assurances that our military operations, designed to effect your complete liberation, are proceeding successfully—and that foremost of my plans of action envisage the day that I shall return to Philippine soil to lead our combined forces in a destructive blow aimed at your permanent release from the threat of subjugation by the Japanese Empire." Again this assurance spread through the Philippines like wildfire, and the Japanese, who picked up many copies, were even more deeply concerned over the strange alliance of the spirit which seemed almost to neutralize the force of their arms.

MacArthur had confounded the Japanese even more by the fact that in broadcasting the text of Roosevelt's and his message to the Filipinos he had disdained radio codes and had made his announcements in the clear. Reversing all the rules of secrecy which are a part of guerrilla warfare, he enraged the enemy by treating their radio monitors as being beneath contempt. And on New Year's Day, 1944, he added insult to injury by sending an uncoded message flauntingly addressed: "To my commanders in the Philippines." The broadcast was at a prearranged time and on a prearranged frequency, and while nearly everyone in the Philippines—and many in Japan—listened, MacArthur sent his holiday greetings:

"With the dawn of a new year, please convey to your officers and men and to the civilians who are giving you their loyal support, my warm personal greetings and grateful acknowledgment of resolute past service of inestimable value to the joint cause of the American and Filipino people. Tell them that I confidently look to the coming year as a period in which every month will see significant and decisive gains toward the final and complete destruction of Japanese military power; and that in this period I require that every man shall adhere to the path of duty with that same courage and invincible determination that has characterized the spirit of Philippine resistance during the difficult and trying past. Tell them that as we enter the new year it is my fervent prayer that Almighty God will guide, strengthen, and protect them, and will speed the day of my return personally to direct operations aimed at the permanent expulsion of the invader from the Philippine soil and the restoration of peace, happiness and security to Philippine homes."

"And the truth shall make you free."

By this daring device he contrived simultaneously to inform the Filipinos that 1944 would bring decisive military action, and to cause the Japanese to lose face. Although some in the United States thought it a rash gesture on MacArthur's part, those behind the lines in the Philippines knew better. Filipinos everywhere were cheered as they had not been in more than two years.

MacArthur understood this spirit clearly, but, try as we would, we could not seem to convince the Washington planners of it. On one occasion, when President Quezon issued a message to the Filipino people, someone in Washington directed that it be printed in a tiny booklet so that it could be readily concealed in the palm of the hand. MacArthur took one look at it and exclaimed: "No! We will broadcast it to the Philippines in the clear and widely publish it throughout the Islands. But we must never transmit to the Filipino people the fear that such a miniature document at once suggests."

In this same spirit, I had my staff strike off a special stamp for the establishment of a "Guerrilla Postal Service." When these were sent into the Philippines, guerrillas in the free areas used them, and with added defiance the postmasters even issued token one-peso money orders on the Central Post Office in Manila, in favor of "General Douglas MacArthur." Such was the psychological warfare that the guerrillas under MacArthur's inspiration constantly waged against their would-be conquerors.

The Japanese were meanwhile using their own weapons, mainly of treachery. Offering bribes and rewards, they pursued a particularly relentless hunt for every American they could run down. Virtually every Filipino resisted this campaign, even at the sacrifice of life itself. The Japanese manhunt became more vicious than ever, the enemy going so far as to raze entire villages where American refugees had been given sanctuary. Because of this, and because of the constant peril to the life of every American in the Philippines, MacArthur decided to evacuate these refugees wherever possible.

Thus started a series of odysseys, each of which would make a story of high adventure in itself. Almost every submarine that went into the Philippines with supplies and personnel came out with Americans not needed in the resistance movement. Before the campaign was over, every American refugee south of Luzon had been taken to safety in Australia and was being rehabilitated under the care of the American Red Cross. And never during this entire operation was a hiding-place or a rendezvous betrayed by a Filipino.

By this time the traffic of Americans going into the Philippines was increasing, too. Besides the Filipinos I had selected and trained for this mission, there were also many U.S. soldier volunteers. One whom I remember in particular was a twenty-year-old corporal who was engaged in erecting a weather station in northern Samar. On August 7, 1944, he sent a dispatch addressed—as all such messages were—to MacArthur. The message, reflecting the corporal's impatience with the countless frustrations under which he had to work, read: "If this weather information is as important as I think it is and you say it is, then it deserves proper handling. It is getting just that at this end. If one radio set and good operators cannot be devoted to appointed frequency at the appointed time, we may as well stop running and hiding. No contact all day August 4, no contact this morning. . . . I volunteered to do a job and am doing it. Let us have some co-operation. Where the hell is station KAZ? Those operators must be rookies. . . . [Signed] Corporal William Becker III."

I could not resist passing this spirited message on to MacArthur, nor could he resist answering it personally. I was never able to find out, but I can imagine the surprise with which Corporal William Becker III, who probably thought his dispatch would get no further than some other man of equal rank, received this answer: "I am in receipt of your message of 6 August complaining that contact by KAZ with your station was not established on the 4th or 5th, and the matter is under investigation by the Chief Signal Officer. I understand the difficulties of your position, and everything possible will be done to insure prompt reception of your reports, which are of great value, but desire that in the future presentation of such matters, you endeavor to exercise the patience and disciplined restraint expected of us as soldiers and without which duty cannot be well done." The answer was signed "MacArthur."

Another agent who slipped past enemy lines into the Philippines filled me with great personal pride. Right after Pearl Harbor my eldest son, Courtney, Jr., left his classes at Yale in order to serve in the Army, and eventually found himself in the Pacific Theater. MacArthur soon discovered this fact. Partly because my son had been reared in the Philippines and was well acquainted with the country and its people, but more because MacArthur is so understanding and human, he assigned my son to my command. Inevitably there came the time for me to make an anguished decision: as soon as "Sonny," as he was nicknamed, became well trained for the task, he volunteered to go along on the first guerrilla landing on Luzon. It was a particularly dangerous mission, but the spirit of those gallant Filipinos and Americans was such that there were many volunteers for it, just as there were for all such operations. So even discounting my parental forebodings, I could see that whether I sent him or not I could be accused of favoritism.

I asked MacArthur's advice, and he neatly resolved the dilemma by saying: "Let him go along. You can't deny him the opportunity. I am sending messages to the guerrilla leaders on Luzon, and he can accompany the landing-party as a special courier from this headquarters." I had the orders issued at once.

My son went along. While the submarine was en route, we received at headquarters an urgent warning from London that some of the sabotage materials of British manufacture which we were using in our operations had been found to be subject to spontaneous combustion and should be destroyed at once. I knew without checking the operations reports that a supply of those defective explosives was aboard the submarine with a large complement of my best men and my own son. And radio silence prevented communication with the submarine until night, when it would surface to recharge batteries. We did send instructions that night, as soon as it was possible, to jettison the explosives. But the anxiety I always felt while awaiting reports from our missions in those enemy waters was aggravated in this case by the knowledge that the submarine on which I had sent my son might disintegrate in one violent explosion at any moment. Not until after the mission had been successfully accomplished did I learn that, although our instructions had been received, the brave skipper of the submarine and the commander of the landing-party, Commander Charles ("Chick") Parsons, had refused to jettison even so dangerous a cargo because they felt it would give at least some strength to the guerrillas on Luzon.

The explosives did not go off, and the submarine reached its rendezvous point off the rocky Luzon coast on a night selected because it was the dark of the moon. My son and Chick Parsons took off in a rubber boat to try to establish contact with the guerrillas on shore. As they edged up near the beach they were greeted by a sharp challenge. They slipped quietly into the water and, clinging to the back of the rubber boat, waited for the challenger to identify himself as friend or foe. The identification came almost at once—a long, low whistle, which was the prearranged signal.

Parsons identified himself in Spanish, and he and my son propelled the boat toward the rocky shore. Then Parsons did something for which I shall always be grateful. "Sonny," he said, "work around to the bow and pull." My son did, and at that moment became the first American soldier to arrive on the soil of Luzon since MacArthur's departure two years before.

Within five minutes the men and supplies were being unloaded, aided by the eager hands of guerrillas who were appearing from all directions

By this time not only the traffic of personnel, but also the traffic of radio messages had increased to a flood. All the areas south of Luzon had been organized into military commands and were reporting to MacArthur several times daily. In Luzon, Colonels Noble and Moses had taken one chance too many and the Japanese, by cruelly torturing a member of their staff, had captured and executed them. But another American officer in the organization, Lieutenant Colonel R. W. Volckmann, immediately took command. By the time our forces hit the beaches at Leyte we had 134 radio stations and 23 weather observatories behind the enemy lines, from southern Mindanao to northern Luzon, from western Palawan to eastern Samoa. All were in regular communication with our headquarters, giving testimony to the invincible loyalty of the Filipino people—a loyalty unmatched in comparable circumstances by any other people at any time.

Besides their regular operations in their own areas, nearly all the guerrilla leaders both in the south and in the north had active agents in Manila vying with one another—and sometimes crossing one another up —in the collection of intelligence. We sought to discourage this duplication, but it did provide some good cross-checking on the accuracy of the information transmitted.

This intelligence covered all kinds of enemy activity. Officials of the Manila railroad would report on military traffic movements to the south and to the north. A news commentator on Manila's main broadcasting-station would, in a coded closing remark, tip us off as to the approximate number and tonnage of enemy ships entering and leaving Manila Bay during the past twenty-four hours. Other reports kept us up to date on enemy garrison points and supply dumps. Employees in the Manila Hotel would report on Japanese guests as soon as they registered. For example: "Guests at Manila Hotel, 24th July . . . Commanders Nagoi Nakajima, Tiro, and Notoura. . . ." "29th July . . . Marshal Terauchi occupies Imperial Suite formerly of MacArthur. . . ." When I showed this report to MacArthur, he smiled and said: "Well, I am glad at least to know who is occupying my apartment. He should like it. It has a pair of vases given by the Emperor to my father in 1905."

As the efficiency of our sending- and receiving-facilities reached its

peak, we were able to co-ordinate effectively the guerrillas' requests for
supplies and increase the incoming traffic of matériel to all parts of the
Islands. By the time we landed at Leyte we had sent in hundreds of
thousands of arms of all types, including more than a hundred thousand
carbines and millions of rounds of ammunition, great quantities of radio
equipment, clothing, food, and medical supplies—all delivered by our
tiny fleet of submarines.

As happens in any large operation, there was an occasional slip-up,
not to say foul-up; but ingenuity both at headquarters and in the jungle
generally retrieved the situation. On one occasion several cases whose
markings indicated that they contained highly prized submachine guns
instead turned out to contain antiquated cavalry sabers; but many a
dead Japanese testified to the fact that the guerrillas had put even these
outmoded weapons to good use. We also experienced certain difficulties
at the points of transshipment from central to northern Australia. It
seemed almost impossible to get either whisky (medicinal, of course) or
pesos, two essential items, all the way into the Philippines, until we designed a plan of subterfuge. We wrapped these critical items so that they
looked like military rations. The plan worked: from then on we never lost
a bottle of whisky or a peso.

One of our greatest regrets was that few of the supplies of food and
medical items which we smuggled into the Philippines ever reached our
prisoners-of-war in the Islands. The Japanese guarded their captives too
well. That they also mistreated and, in fact, tortured them brutally we
heard from time to time. But it was not until early July 1943 that we
received the positive, heartbreaking truth.

Three Americans who had escaped from Davao Prison Camp were
rescued by the guerrillas and spirited to a rendezvous point with one of
our submarines. When they reached Brisbane, it fell to me to take their
full statements on the treatment of Allied prisoners by the Japanese—in
all its gruesome, agonizing details. This was our first authoritative account
of the Bataan death march and of the terror-filled prison camps to which
the survivors of the death march were committed.

I sent the full account to MacArthur immediately. The next morning
he called for me. When I first walked into his office, he did not look up,
but continued to study a sheet of paper which he held in his hand. As
I waited quietly for him to speak, he raised his eyes.

"Court," he said, "I have read your report on the prisoner-of-war
atrocities, and I have prepared this statement for release to the press
along with the report." He was deeply moved as he began to read. "This

unimpeachable record of savage and merciless brutality to captured prisoners-of-war fills me with unspeakable horror. It is violative of the most
sacred code of martial honor and stains indelibly the creed of the Japanese soldier.' "

It was as if no one else were in the room with him. His voice pulsed
as he read. " 'No other belligerent of modern times has so debased an
honorable service. . . . It will become my sacred duty at the appropriate
time to demand justice on those who have so barbarously violated all justice. God in His all-powerful righteousness will surely punish the dreadful
crimes visited upon the helpless officers and soldiers whom I had the signal honor to command in their noble and gallant struggle against overwhelming odds.' "

As he finished, he spoke almost in a whisper. He handed me the
statement, rose silently, and walked over to the window. He did not look
out, but stood there, his head bowed.

The statement was never published. That same day we received orders from Washington forbidding the release of any of the details of these
prisoner-of-war atrocities. The Administration was committed to a maximum Europe-first effort and did not want the American people aroused
to the point of demanding a greater effort against Japan until the war in
the European Theater had been concluded. I placed MaoArthur's statement among my personal records, and have kept it there ever since. But
I need nothing to remind me of that scene and of the figure of MacArthur,
head bowed and alone with his grief, outlined against the window of his
office.

Long before the planners in Washington had permitted Americans
on the home front to know about these atrocities, they were common
knowledge wherever in the Philippine Islands the guerrillas' "bamboo
telegraph" could reach. The news provoked among the guerrillas a reaction of outrage which led to the killing of many Japanese. It also prompted
the guerrillas to do everything within their power to protect other Americans from capture. Whenever a flier was forced down in the Islands, he
found many Filipinos ready and eager to conceal him by day and lead
him by night to the coastal areas where he could be rescued. An example
I recall was in early September 1944 when three pilots of the Third Fleet,
including one of their aces, were forced down near Manila. They were
found at once by local inhabitants, who led them across the island to the
east coast, were they were picked up by a Navy PBY. Admiral Halsey
flashed a characteristic message to MacArthur: "Third Fleet thanks you
for helping her pilots to live to fight another day."

But as the people of the Philippines worked and waited for Mac-

"And the truth shall make you free."

Arthur's return, one great Filipino finally succumbed. President Manuel Quezon had managed to live through Corregidor, the perilous trip through the Japanese lines, and the arduous journey across the Pacific to the U.S. On the first anniversary of the Japanese attack, he had sent MacArthur a message that evoked the stanch spirit of all Filipinos. "My memory goes back," he had said, "to the days when you and I, with anxious hearts, worked together to defend the liberty of the Filipino people, the integrity of their soil, and the honor of the American flag. . . . I recall with warm appreciation your years of devoted service to my people as military adviser to the government of the commonwealth, and I remember too the dark days and bomb-shattered nights through which you led our combined American and Filipino forces against the sweep of Japanese aggression over the Pacific area. You and I have been friends for many years. You and I have understood each other well in facing Philippine problems, both national and international. This war has sealed our personal friendship and our common understanding of the best interest of the United States and the Philippines in future years. I know that your only ambition is to return and liberate the Philippines. That is the one thing for which I live. We shall both attain this objective. We shall return to the Philippines together. Love to you and Mrs. MacArthur and the boy, and warm regards to all." But Quezon was never to see the Philippines again. On August 1, 1944, less than three months before the Leyte landing, he was dead of tuberculosis.

His place was taken by Vice President Sergio Osmeña, who had gone to Washington with Quezon. And as the time for the return finally approached, MacArthur invited President Osmeña to his Hollandia headquarters. I was at the headquarters when Osmeña arrived, and MacArthur asked me to brief him on the guerrilla operations, much of which had been so secret that we had not even been able to inform Osmeña and Quezon of them. Osmeña was accompanied by General Basilio Valdez, Chief of Staff of the Philippine army, and General Carlos Romulo, then Philippine Ambassador to the United States and its delegate to the United States House of Representatives.

I had just received an intelligence report from the city of Cebu, President Osmeña's home town, and thought I would read it as typifying the kind of intelligence we were receiving daily from the Philippines. I read: "B-1 report on enemy installations, supply depots and fuel dumps follows: Radio station located Mrs. Torres house, biggest house near Guadalupe Church, Cebu City. Radio station located Mr. Marcus Nagua's house northwest Catholic Cemetery, at Calambast, Cebu City. AA gun emplaced under tamarindo tree in front ex-USAFFE Lieutenant Pedro

Villaroso house Calambast. AA gun at so-called English resident, Calambast. Radio station located under big trees in Margarita Labre house, Calambast. Gasoline and ammunition dumped along left side Katipunan Street. Cebu City from Junction A. Lopez and Katipunan Street, facing Cebu City proper. Gasoline dumped from Junction A. Lopez St. and Road going Municipal Cemetery along right side. Gasoline placed under mango trees on both sides Gen. Maxilom St. from railroad crossing to bridge over creek crossing Gen. Maxilom St. Cebu City. Ten to twenty drums gasoline placed under each mango tree, and bomb shells stored in Mabola Convent, Cebu City. AA gun placed under mangrove near Subang Dacu estuary northeast Subang Dacu bridge. Food supplies unloaded from unidentified transport that arrived Cebu port October 1st were stored in Gotiaoco Bldg. Night truckloads of unestimated number of Japs from Banawa and Guadalupe area were embarked in unidentified transport that docked Cebu port October 1st and left port southbound. Unestimated number Japs occupy civilian houses along F Famos St. from junction of Gen. Maxilom and F Famos St. to junction of F Ramos St. and Junguera Extension, Cebu City. Unestimated number Japs occupy barracks around Rizal Memorial Library. Navy Staff and Gen. Yousioas Amahaso in left wing Capitol Building with Red Cross mark on roof. Gasoline dumped behind State Relita College near Redemptionist Convent."

The dispatch went on: "A-1 Report: Mines are stored Aronson residence. Lawaan, Minglanilla. C-3 Report: Waters from San Fernando to Mabaling, Cebu City, relayed with mines, verification and more details if raid mines laid will follow. B-2 Report: Quartermaster Depot corner Morini and Zulueta St., Cebu City. Toledo advance field depot in Ignico and Expinasa used and also in Angel Troeno house with food supplies and ammunition stored. Supplies and ammunition stored in five tunnels Lutopan mine. A-1 Report: Gasoline stored in Major Osmeña residence corner Gosobdo Ave. and Gen. Maxilom in Cebu City camouflaged with leaves—"

At this point, recognizing the name, President Osmeña broke in. "Why," he said, "that is my brother's house. Have it destroyed at once!"

This spontaneous reaction was typical. Wards of the United States for over forty years, the proud race of Filipinos were ready to sacrifice their homes and their lives. That they proved themselves unconquerable by Japanese arms or guile is to the lasting credit of their Christian teachings, of the wise tutelage of the American nation and, above all, of their faith in MacArthur and his faith in them.

Chapter XIV   "I have returned."

◢ In his State of the Union Message to Congress on January 6, 1945, President Roosevelt hinted at an important shift of strategy which had been made only a little over three months earlier. "Within the space of twenty-four hours," the President said, "a major change of plans was accomplished which involved Army and Navy forces from two different theaters of operations—a change which hastened the liberation of the Philippines and the final day of victory—a change which saved lives which would have been expended in the capture of islands which are now neutralized far behind our lines."

With World War II still on, President Roosevelt could say no more, but what had happened was this: As of the first week of September 1944, MacArthur's plans for the long-awaited return to the Philippines called for a landing at Sarangani Bay, Mindanao, on November 15. This landing was to be followed by another at Leyte Gulf on December 20. But then one of those surprises happened, as surprises will in the full tide of war. While conducting missions to support MacArthur's impending landings on Morotai, Admiral Halsey discovered a serious weakness in the Japanese air defense in the area over Mindanao. Very few enemy planes were encountered, and when Halsey tested the Visayan area farther north, he encountered only meager enemy reaction there, too. It appeared that the Japanese air shield had been weakened even more than expected. There followed one of the fastest changes of pace that occurred in all of World War II.

Halsey wired his findings and conclusions to MacArthur as well as to Nimitz at Pearl Harbor, recommending that the initial assault be made against Leyte Gulf as soon as possible. His message was promptly relayed to the Joint Chiefs of Staff, who were then participating in the Quebec conference between Roosevelt and Churchill. What followed is told in

General Marshall's Report to the Secretary of War (*July 1, 1943 to June 30, 1945*):

". . . General MacArthur's views were requested and two days later he advised us that he was already prepared to shift his plans to land on Leyte 20 October instead of 20 December as previously intended. It was a remarkable administrative achievement. The message from MacArthur arrived at Quebec at night and Admiral Leahy [Chief of Staff to the President], Admiral King, General Arnold, and I were being entertained at a formal dinner by Canadian officers. It was read by the appropriate staff officers who suggested an immediate affirmative answer. The message, with their recommendations, was rushed to us and we left the table for a conference. Having the utmost confidence in General MacArthur, Admiral Nimitz and Admiral Halsey, it was not a difficult decision to make. Within ninety minutes after the signal had been received in Quebec, General MacArthur and Admiral Nimitz had received their instructions to execute the Leyte operation on the target date 20 October, abandoning the three previously approved intermediary landings."

What with our extensive guerrilla operations throughout the Philippines, it was not news to us in MacArthur's headquarters that enemy air strength had fallen below par. We knew, moreover, that it did not follow that Japanese land forces on Leyte were also weak; in fact, our guerrilla intelligence network told us that we could prepare for heavy fighting everywhere in the Philippines. But the main problem concerning an initial landing at Leyte was that it would take us well out of range of our own land-based air support. So our strategy was in part dependent upon the Navy, and MacArthur knew that if the Navy could advance its own schedule to October 20 and provide air cover until airfields could be prepared on Leyte, certainly he could move up the landing-date. This dependence upon Navy air support was a hazardous gamble that we almost lost.

On the afternoon of October 16, 1944, I went aboard the cruiser *Nashville*, which had been selected as MacArthur's flagship for the Leyte landing. I had not seen him for about a week, because while he had been in Brisbane I had been in Hollandia establishing an advance base for the direction and co-ordination of guerrilla operations. As I approached his cabin, MacArthur came out. His face lit up and he strode over to me and put his hands on my shoulders. "Well, Courtney, my boy," he said, "had to rescue you, didn't I?"

For the moment, I was puzzled, but I soon learned the reason for his remark. When the staff had discussed the composition of the small group

THE PHILIPPINES

that was to accompany him on his flagship, my name had not been included. MacArthur had asked why, and had been told that my services would be needed in Hollandia during this critical period to co-ordinate guerrilla activities. This was a perfectly sound reason, but it was not good enough for MacArthur. He felt that my work directing the guerrillas had earned me the right to go along. My name was added to the list. The incident was interesting to me for two reasons: it not only reflected MacArthur's concept of staff loyalty, down as well as up, but it also revealed his realization of the historic importance of this occasion. I shall always be grateful to him for his thoughtfulness in making it possible for me to be present at one of the great moments in history.

At the time, MacArthur did little else to indicate the strains and anxieties induced by the momentous importance of this occasion. Although these three days preceding the Leyte landings were among the most poignant in his long life, his expression did not show a trace of the emotions that must have been stirring inside him. He had left the Philippines in a PT boat, thrashing through angry waves and dodging the menace of enemy warships. He was returning with a fleet of more than 650 battleships, aircraft-carriers, cruisers, destroyers, transports, and landing-craft. He had left the Philippines with none but a few staff members of his forces in the Islands. He was returning with many of these same men—and with a force of 150,000 more. He was indeed redeeming his pledge; he was redeeming it with a vengeance.

The *Nashville* kept on her steady, though zigzagging, course bound due north for Leyte Gulf. At three in the afternoon of October 18, just east of Palau, we met the main convoy sweeping across the horizon in a seemingly limitless array of power. But we were still reminded of the danger of our mission as the *Nashville* made an abrupt turn to avoid a floating mine. Meanwhile, a typhoon threatened to strike Leyte at about the time we were scheduled to arrive off the Gulf. Hour by hour we watched the course of this storm with mounting anxiety, and then with relief as it blew on past Leyte before A-day.

On the afternoon of the 19th, as MacArthur and I stood at the rail watching the other ships stretching in every direction as far as the eye could see, I observed: "General, it must give you a sense of great power having such a mighty armada at your command."

"No, Court, it doesn't," he replied. "I cannot escape the thought of the fine American boys who are going to die on those beaches tomorrow morning." It was to me a striking lesson in the depth of his feeling concerning the inevitable sacrifice of war. He was confident that he was on the eve of a great military victory; he was about to redeem the solemn pledge that he had made to his men in the foxholes of Bataan and to the Filipino people. Yet his exultation was overshadowed by his anguish for the American boys who would die on the morrow.

It was eleven p.m., and black as only the Pacific can get on a dark, starless night, when we reached our position off Leyte Gulf. We would lie off Leyte until dawn. The ships of the convoy were dark silhouettes gliding past us. On each of them, nervous soldiers, sailors, and marines fidgeted as the night wore on toward the dawn that might be their last. For the hundredth time rifles were checked, landing-nets were tested, maps were carefully folded and refolded. Each man was alone unto himself, his lips quietly moving as he repeated over and over again from memory his particular assignment for the morning. Fully 150,000 men and 1,500,000 tons of general equipment plus 235,000 tons of combat vehicles and 200,000 tons of ammunition were poised to strike. And in his bunk in his cabin aboard the *Nashville*, MacArthur had fallen asleep, an open Bible in his lap.

We awoke at dawn to the dull and distant rumble of naval bombardment. Already the increased vibration of the *Nashville* indicated that we were heading into Leyte Gulf. I went out on deck for a look. Great rolling clouds stretched all the way across the horizon, but they were gradually dissipating, their blackness changing to gray as the dawning sun cut into them. Leyte was still a hazy black outline on the horizon, but all around us ships of every size and description were headed toward it. And the action had started already. The *Nashville* dodged two floating mines. An enemy periscope was spotted near by, and two destroyers closed in on it, throwing depth charges right and left.

I went to MacArthur's cabin and entered just as he was slipping an old-fashioned revolver into his trouser pocket. "That, Court, belonged to my father," he said in explanation. "I take it merely as a precaution—just to insure that I am never captured alive." Then he started to reminisce about Leyte. He told how forty-one years ago he had entered this same port of Tacloban as a newly commissioned engineer lieutenant, making a survey of Tacloban's potentiality and needs in case of war. It had been his first assignment after leaving West Point. I could hardly believe my ears. The dramatic hour of redemption was at hand. The timetable of the whole Pacific war hung in the balance, and yet here, in the stateroom of a cruiser steaming into Leyte Gulf, MacArthur was quietly talking about a time forty-one years earlier.

As he reminisced, my eyes took in the collection of framed photographs which occupied the dresser and every table in the cabin—photographs of his wife and son, his father and mother, his brother whose death at forty-seven had cut short an impressive career in the Navy. And I realized that at every headquarters, even so temporary a one as on shipboard, MacArthur had his orderly first unpack these photographs and arrange them about him. Such is his devotion to family ties.

His reminiscence was interrupted by the stilling of the motors and the clank of the anchor chain, telling us that we had reached our appointed position in Leyte Harbor. Someone pounded on the stateroom door to warn us that the landing-barges were about to go in.

We went out onto the captain's bridge. There, two miles off our starboard bow, was the shore of Leyte, a long, flat beach set against black, brooding hills beyond. MacArthur calmly lit his corncob pipe and surveyed the pandemonium all around us. The roar was deafening, punctuated by the thunder of shells and the whistling shriek of rockets bursting against the shore. Clouds of black, swirling smoke rose in the air, and through it flew wave after wave of planes from our carriers. The sea sparkled under the hot tropical sun, which had replaced the black clouds of dawn. And, like thousands of giant waterbugs, the invasion barges raced for the beaches.

This was at Red Beach, Palo, Leyte. Other landings were simultaneously taking place, or were about to take place, at White Beach, San Jose, and the island of Panaon, and all along the eastern coast of Leyte Island. Here at Red Beach the amphibious troops met minor opposition and rapidly pushed inland. Puffing on his pipe as he looked on from the bridge of the *Nashville*, MacArthur watched with a growing sense of gratification that the enemy apparently had been outfoxed once again.

A correspondent came up and asked him how he thought it was going. "It's going fine," he said, and his expression hardened as he mentioned the enemy division against which he and his troops were now fighting. "It's the Sixteenth," he explained, "the outfit that did the dirty work at Bataan." His jaw set in a grim line. "They've been living off the fat of the land for more than two years," he went on, "and I believe they'll be a little softer now." His eyes narrowed as he looked past the correspondent's shoulder. "But, soft or not, we'll get them."

The third assault wave was ready to go in, and MacArthur decided to go with it. With him, besides some of his staff, he took Sergio Osmeña, the man who had succeeded Quezon as President of the Philippines. MacArthur sat high in the stern of the boat while it swung away from the ship and started for the beach. As the historic moment approached, I studied his face to see if he was still able to conceal the emotions that must be flooding his soul. He sat there watching the scene about him, his face expressionless under the familiar gold-leaf-decorated cap that he had worn as Field Marshal of the Islands to which he was now returning. It was as if this were a routine ride to shore instead of one of the most dramatic days of his life.

At this point I asked him to do me a favor. Just before leaving for Leyte, I had received from my wife a handsome, self-winding watch with a wide band made from the aluminum of a downed enemy fighter plane. She had sent it to me as a Father's Day gift, but it had only just arrived. And it happened that this day, October 20, was the anniversary of our wedding. I turned to MacArthur and, over the noise of the landing-craft's engine, told him of the anniversary. I slipped the watch from my wrist and asked him if he would wear it as he set foot on the Philippines, so that I might always wear it as a reminder of this great day. MacArthur has never worn a wrist watch, but he took this one in his hand, slipped it into his left shirt pocket, and said with a chuckle: "I can't guarantee you'll ever get it back, Court." If in news pictures of that historic occasion one has noticed a slight unmilitary bulge in MacArthur's left shirt pocket, that was my watch.

The only sound aboard our assault barge now was the steady rumble of its engine as we slowly plowed across the harbor toward Red Beach. Then, as we neared the shore, the rumble of the landing-boat gave way to the sounds of war—the snapping crackle of the coconut palms still burning after the bombardment, the swooping drone of planes flying low over the beach, and the blat of Japanese snipers' small-caliber rifles that sounded about a hundred yards inland. Suddenly there was a grinding bump as our barge came to a stop in the shallow waters fifty yards from the shoreline. The skipper of the landing-barge was about to back off and try to find a spot where our ramp could reach dry land; but Mac-Arthur did not wait. He ordered the ramp put down and stepped off into knee-deep water. President Osmeña and the rest of us followed. It took only a few strides for him to reach the dry coral sand. There he stopped, motionless and ramrod-stiff, and took a deep breath. Then, with the water squishing out of his shoes, he strode down the beach to a spot where a mobile broadcasting-unit was being set up. A few paces inland, as he walked by, soldiers crouched behind the wide trunks of the palm trees, intermittently firing into the undergrowth beyond the edge of the beach. As MacArthur went by one of these trees, a crouching GI nudged his companion, saying: "Hey! Look, there's General MacArthur!"

His friend did not even look around. Sighting along his rifle, he said: "Oh, sure. And I suppose he's got President Roosevelt with him, too."

During our trip in to the beach a dark cloud had been moving across the face of the sun. Now, as MacArthur stepped up to the microphone, rain began to fall. I remember that I barely noticed it, so moved was I by this climactic moment. How much more affected MacArthur must have been by this scene I could only imagine. But his face was as expressionless as ever, and his tone was calm and even as he spoke the words he had waited and worked for through two and a half years:

"I have returned."

Then emotion did begin to move him as he proclaimed the message that will ring down through the ages of Philippine and American history. His hand trembled as it held the microphone, and his frame tensed. "By the grace of Almighty God," he said, "our forces stand again on Philippine soil—soil consecrated in the blood of our two peoples. We have come, dedicated and committed to the task of destroying every vestige of enemy control over your daily lives, and of restoring, upon a foundation of indestructible strength, the liberties of your people.

"At my side is your President, Sergio Osmeña, a worthy successor of that great patriot Manuel Quezon, with members of his cabinet. The seat of your government is now, therefore, firmly re-established on Philippine soil.

"The hour of your redemption is here. Your patriots have demonstrated an unswerving and resolute devotion to the principles of freedom that challenge the best that is written on the pages of human history. I now call upon your supreme effort that the enemy may know from the temper of an aroused people within that he has a force there to contend with no less violent than is the force committed from without.

"Rally to me. Let the indomitable spirit of Bataan and Corregidor lead on. As the lines of battle roll forward to bring you within the zone of operations, rise and strike. Strike at every favorable opportunity. For your homes and hearths, strike! For future generations of your sons and daughters, strike! In the name of your sacred dead, strike! Let no heart be faint. Let every arm be steeled. The guidance of Divine God points the way. Follow in His name to the Holy Grail of righteous victory!"

His emotion-filled voice was resonant. We knew that every Filipino who could crowd around a radio anywhere in the Islands could hear him. Indeed, the eyes and ears of the free world were upon him on this day at this hour. And what did MacArthur do at this dramatic moment as he finished his speech? He turned, spotted me, reached into his shirt pocket, and called: "Court, you'd better come get this watch before something happens to it."

Taking President Osmeña by the arm, he then walked a short way inland, where they sat on a fallen log and for nearly an hour talked animatedly of the civil problems ahead, now that the military return had been accomplished. Meanwhile, at MacArthur's direction, two stripped palm trees served as flagpoles, and the American and Philippine flags fluttered up into the breeze.

While this American and this Filipino sat on a battle-scarred palm trunk and talked, I thought back to MacArthur's broadcast of a few minutes ago and imagined the reception that it had got all through the Philippines. In the years since then I have heard criticism of his message, mainly in the United States. But MacArthur was not talking to the people in the United States; he was talking to Filipinos who had been living with terror and death for two and a half years, and to whom nothing on earth was more important than the single fact that MacArthur and the might of American arms had returned. He was talking to guerrillas who had loyally and at great sacrifice withstood every Japanese blandishment and threat, and who had waited for this hour—and this signal—for vengeance. They understood his message, and they did indeed rally to him.

The most absurd criticism of the message I have heard concerned MacArthur's reference to the Almighty. It must surprise him to be criticized for giving the Lord His due. But it is characteristic of MacArthur that, while he turns to God in adversity, like most, he also turns to Him in victory, unlike most. And the best reply I can make to such criticism is the answer that MacArthur himself gave to an officer who suggested beforehand, when the message was being typed for distribution to the guerrillas and those Filipinos who could not hear it by radio, that this part of the statement might provoke ridicule. "In war," said MacArthur, "when a commander becomes so bereft of reason and perspective that he fails to understand the dependence of arms on Divine guidance, he no longer deserves victory."

By the time MacArthur and Osmeña had finished their conversation, enemy bombs were cracking around us. But I noticed that neither so much as looked up. The rain had stopped, and our troops were still tracking down snipers along the beach. In a jeep MacArthur and Osmeña inspected the forward perimeter of troops and the Tacloban airfield before returning to the landing-barge for the trip back to the cruiser *Nashville*. As we rumbled across the harbor, a Japanese torpedo bomber swooped low over our heads, got caught in a pattern of anti-aircraft fire, heeled over, and smashed into the cruiser *Honolulu*, our nextdoor neighbor. And as we boarded the *Nashville*, three more Japanese planes came in and strafed the beach where MacArthur had just been standing.

Already he was deep in his plans for the rest of the campaign on Leyte and the other Philippine Islands. That night, as we reviewed the eloquent events of the day, the signal for attack was going out through the hidden radio network to MacArthur's guerrillas in every corner of the Philippines: "The campaign of reoccupation has commenced. Although your area is not at present within the immediate zone of operations, it is desired that your forces be committed to limited offensive action with the specific mission of harassing the movement of enemy reserves within your area and as far as possible containing him to his present positions. Intelligence coverage must be intensified in order that I be fully and promptly advised of all changes in enemy dispositions or movement." The time had come for the brave and loyal Filipinos, as MacArthur had promised, to "rally as a unit to our call."

Other messages flooded the airwaves that night. It was a time for congratulations to pour in from all over the world. The one that summed up the sentiments of the United States came from President Roosevelt: "You have the nation's gratitude and the nation's prayers for success as you and your men fight your way back. . . ." But the message that summed up the sentiments of the Filipinos, and indeed the feelings of MacArthur and all of us, was embodied in the greeting of a Leyte farmer who had stood erect and proud by the roadside that day, watching the Americans go past. Finally he had stepped up to MacArthur's jeep, held out his hand, and said in the Visayan dialect: "Good morning, Sir General, glad to see you. It has been many years."

CHAPTER XV   "The greatest defeat . . . of the
Japanese Army"

⚑ The Japanese reacted to the landings at Leyte with a combination of arrogance and violence. They recognized it as the vital move and its defense as the vital struggle. General Tomoyuki Yamashita, their best strategist, had already been moved from a command in Manchuria to the Philippines. Famous as the "Tiger of Malaya" and the conqueror of Singapore, he announced as he took over his new command: "The only words I spoke to the British Commander during negotiations for the surrender of Singapore were, 'All I want to hear from you is yes or no.' I expect to put the same question to MacArthur." Lieutenant General Yasuji Tominaga, chief of the Japanese army air force in the Philippines, announced: "The Americans will surely be defeated in the face of terrifying Japanese assaults." MacArthur did not dignify this hysterical boasting with any reply.

When he moved his headquarters ashore, the Japanese continued their efforts to get him. One day, as he was working in his combination bedroom and office, an enemy plane came down low and strafed the area, sending two 50-caliber bullets through his open window and into the wall immediately over his desk. An aide rushed in and found him working unperturbedly at the desk. "Well," said the General, "what is it?" "Thank God, General," the aide said. "I thought you were killed." MacArthur did not even glance at a hole in the wall inches above his head. He replied simply: "Not yet. Thank you for coming in."

MacArthur was already certain of Japan's early defeat. In fact, on the day of his landing on Leyte, he had publicly analyzed the strategic result of the capture of the Philippines as "decisive." "The enemy's so-called Greater East Asia co-prosperity sphere," he pointed out, "will be cut in two. . . . His conquered empire to the south, comprising the Dutch East Indies and the British possessions of Borneo, Malaya and Burma, will be severed from Japan proper." Then he went on: "The great flow of transportation and supply upon which Japan's vital war industry depends will be cut, as will the counter-supply of his forces to the south. A half million men will be cut off without hope of support and with ultimate destruction at the leisure of the Allies a certainty. In broad strategic conception, the defensive line of the Japanese, which extends along the coast of Asia from the Japan Islands through Formosa, the Philippines, the East Indies to Singapore and Burma, will be pierced in the center, permitting an envelopment to the south and to the north. Either flank will be vulnerable and can be rolled up at will."

But there was still some fight left in the Japanese. And the enemy's most violent reaction to the Leyte landings was the one that brought him closest to success. This was the Battle of Leyte Gulf.

Admiral Soemu Toyoda, of the Japanese Imperial Navy, had his headquarters in Singapore. As soon as he learned of the Leyte landings, he mustered every ship he could get from what was left of the Japanese fleet. With this force, which amounted to nearly sixty per cent of the entire original Japanese fleet, Toyoda steamed for the Philippines.

On October 23, MacArthur, still on the *Nashville,* was informed by Admiral Kinkaid that the battle for the southern entrance to Leyte Gulf was imminent and that the cruiser *Nashville* was needed in the battle line. MacArthur listened attentively as Kinkaid unfolded his estimate of the situation—an anything but optimistic estimate, obviously intended as a convincing argument of the need for the *Nashville's* fire power. Then MacArthur said: "Of course, Tom, send her in."

"But I can't, General, if you are on board," Kinkaid remonstrated. "I would not be a party to sending the commander-in-chief into the coming naval engagement."

"Why, Tom," MacArthur replied, "don't be ridiculous. There is every reason why I should be present during such a crucial engagement. And besides," he added as an afterthought, "I have never been in a major naval engagement, and I am anxious to see one."

So the discussion continued. MacArthur had planned to retain the *Nashville* as his flagship until his headquarters, and particularly his communications, could be fully established ashore. Kinkaid returned to his own flagship.

The following morning, however, he was back on board the *Nashville* bright and early. The situation had worsened during the night, he reported. The Japanese had massed even greater strength, with their southern force approaching the Surigao Strait, and there was grave doubt as to the outcome of the coming battle. The presence of the *Nashville* might mean the difference between victory and defeat, but still he would not throw it into the battle line so long as the commander-in-chief was aboard. MacArthur capitulated with good grace. "All right, Tom," he said, "I will move ashore in order that the *Nashville* may add strength in the line of battle." But as he turned to us on his personal staff, I could read on his face the disappointment he felt.

Much has been written concerning the Battle of Leyte Gulf. But because of the crucial importance of the battle, and especially because of the potentialities of disaster for MacArthur's beachhead, I felt that the authoritative and heretofore unpublished account of it as recorded by MacArthur's headquarters is interesting and important.

"At Leyte, General MacArthur was completely dependent on forces not under his control to protect the landing operation. Should the naval covering forces allow either of the powerful advancing thrusts to penetrate into Leyte Gulf, the whole Philippine invasion would be placed in the gravest jeopardy. It was imperative, therefore, that every approach to the gulf be adequately guarded at all times and that an enemy debouchment via Surigao and San Bernardino Straits be blocked with adequate allied naval strength.

"The naval forces protecting the Leyte invasion were disposed in two main bodies. The Seventh Fleet, under Admiral Kinkaid, protected the southern and western entrances to Leyte Gulf while the stronger Third Fleet, under Admiral Halsey, operated off Samar to cover San Bernardino Strait and approaches from the north and east. Admiral Halsey's immediate superior was Admiral Nimitz in Hawaii; Admiral Kinkaid was responsible to General MacArthur. While it was realized that such a division of command entailed certain disadvantages, it was theoretically assumed that frequent consultation and co-operative liaison would overcome any difficulties in the way of proper co-ordination. The coming battle was to demonstrate the dangers involved in the lack of a unified command and the misunderstanding that can ensue during major operations in which the commander ultimately responsible does not have full control over all forces in the operation.

"As Admiral Kurita's Central Force threaded its way through the narrow, reef-filled waters of the Sibuyan Sea during the morning and afternoon of the 24th, it was kept under repeated and severe attack by planes of the U.S. Third Fleet. The *Musashi,* one of the newest and largest of Japan's battleships which mounted 18-inch guns, was sunk; its sister ship, the mighty *Yamato,* was hit; a heavy cruiser was crippled; other cruisers and destroyers were damaged. The increasing force of these aerial blows, together with the torpedoes of Seventh Fleet submarines, caused Admiral Kurita, who was operating without air cover, to reverse his course for a time in order to take stock of the situation and reform his forces. This temporary withdrawal, executed at 1530, was later reported by overly optimistic Allied pilots as a possible retirement of the Japanese Central Force. Admiral Kurita had no intention of abandoning his mission, however, and at 1714 he headed once more for San Bernardino Strait. Shortly thereafter, he received a message from Admiral Toyoda in Tokyo: 'All forces will dash to the attack, trusting in divine assistance.'

"In the meantime, Admiral Nishimura's Southern Force sailed doggedly on into the Mindanao Sea and passed Bohol despite the fact that it had been sighted and attacked off Cagayan Island. Amply forewarned by sightings, Admiral Kinkaid had dispatched almost the whole of the Seventh Fleet's gunnery and torpedo force under Rear Admiral Jesse B. Oldendorf, to intercept and destroy the approaching Japanese warships. Admiral Oldendorf took full advantage of both the geography of the battle area and his foreknowledge of the enemy's route of advance. PT squadrons were deployed at the entrance to Surigao Strait at a place where the Japanese would have to reform in column to negotiate the narrow passage. Behind the torpedo boats, covering the northern part of the strait, were posted the destroyer squadrons, cruisers and battleships to form the horizontal bar to a "T" of vast firepower which the enemy would be forced to approach vertically as he moved forward.

"The ambush worked perfectly. As Admiral Nishimura's forces pushed forward through the smooth waters of Surigao Strait in the early hours of 25 October, the PT boats, waiting in the darkness near Panaon Island, launched their torpedoes. Results were not clear, but some damage was inflicted. Three separate, co-ordinated attacks by U.S. Destroyer Squadrons 54, 24 and 56 followed in rapid succession as torpedo after torpedo found its mark. . . . At 0337 Admiral Nishimura's force was not only confused and slowed by the tempest of torpedoes, it was mortally crippled. Virtually every unit in the formation was either sunk or badly damaged.

"Despite this severe punishment, Admiral Nishimura's force steamed blindly ahead to its final doom in the death trap at the northern exit to Surigao Strait. There in full battle formation Admiral Oldendorf's cruisers and battleships eagerly awaited the ill-fated Japanese task force. At 0354 the battleships *West Virginia, Tennessee, California* and *Maryland* opened fire in quick succession, with range about 21,000 yards. The *Mississippi* followed with a single salvo at 0411. Within a matter of minutes the withering hail of steel from Admiral Oldendorf's main battle line virtually completed the annihilation of Admiral Nishimura's force. The Japanese admiral himself went down with his flagship, the *Yamashiro*, which rapidly disintegrated after numerous torpedo hits. Only one lone destroyer, the *Shigure*, managed to survive the incredible carnage.

"In the meantime Admiral Shima's cruiser and destroyer group, following some forty miles astern of Admiral Nishimura's Southern Force, entered Surigao Strait about 0300. The Southern Force had already suffered heavy losses inflicted by the U.S. Seventh Fleet and, from his flagship, the *Nachi*, Admiral Shima could see the smoke and flash of gunfire in the distance. After brief blinker contact with the single surviving destroyer of the Southern Force and a careless collision with one of its crippled cruisers, the *Mogami*, which was maneuvering with broken steering gear, Admiral Shima retired southeastward into the Mindanao Sea and headed for Coron Bay. He did not escape unscathed, however, for he was attacked en route by Allied planes and lost one of his cruisers which had been torpedoed earlier in the action.

"With the destruction of the Japanese Southern Force and the retirement of Admiral Shima's units, the Battle of Surigao Strait had ended. The Seventh Fleet had performed its mission with precision and effectiveness. The southern entrance to Leyte Gulf had been closed successfully and General MacArthur no longer had to fear a Japanese naval threat from the south.

"While Admiral Kinkaid was preparing to meet the Japanese in Surigao Strait, Admiral Halsey was still trying to locate the suspected Japanese carriers. In the late afternoon of the 24th, scout planes of the Third Fleet finally reported a large enemy task force, including several carriers, off the northeastern coast of Luzon about 300 miles from San Bernardino Strait. As Admiral Halsey plotted the position and strength of the newly sighted enemy carrier force, he continued to receive exaggerated reports of mounting damage inflicted by his attacking planes on the Japanese Central Force as it sailed through the Sibuyan Sea toward San Bernardino Strait. As later events proved, the pilots' reports were inaccurate as to the status of both enemy forces. The firepower of the Northern Force was initially overestimated as was the damage inflicted upon Admiral Kurita's Central Force. This faulty information was primarily responsible for several important subsequent decisions.

"The sighting of the carrier force presented a picture of three enemy fleets converging on the invasion area—the Northern Force moving southward in the Philippine Sea, the Central Force moving southeastward to

San Bernardino Strait, and the Southern Force moving eastward toward the Mindanao Sea and Surigao Strait. Admiral Halsey felt that Admiral Kinkaid's Seventh Fleet had ample strength with which to meet the advancing Southern Force in Surigao Strait. He judged from his aviators' optimistic reports that the Central Force had been greatly damaged, had perhaps retired, and in all likelihood had been removed as a serious menace. He reasoned that, in any event, its strength had been reduced to the point where any threat it presented would be satisfactorily overcome by Admiral Kinkaid's Seventh Fleet. He estimated that the Northern Force comprised the whole carrier strength of the Japanese and therefore constituted the most potent danger to be met. Influenced by these factors, Admiral Halsey decided to move his entire force northward as a unit and intercept the Japanese carriers.

"During the afternoon of 24 October, however, Admiral Halsey had organized Task Force 34 as a strong surface force comprising the battleships *Iowa, New Jersey, Washington* and *Alabama,* 2 heavy cruisers, 3 light cruisers, and 14 destroyers. According to Admiral Halsey, the dispatch forming Task Force 34 was not an executive dispatch but a tentitive battle order and was so marked. As everyone was greatly concerned about the Japanese Central Force, including Admiral Halsey who knew its position and formidable firepower, it was assumed that Task Force 34 would engage Admiral Kurita's force which was heading east through the Sibuyan Sea. In the early evening Admiral Halsey informed Admiral Kinkaid and others of the position of the Japanese Central Force and added that he was 'proceeding north with three groups to attack the enemy carrier forces at dawn.' Accordingly, on the evening of the 24th, he withdrew the battleships, carriers, and supporting ships of the Third Fleet from San Bernardino Strait. . . .

"As the fast battleships of the Third Fleet had been detached from the carrier groups and organized as Task Force 34, it was assumed that Task Force 34 was still guarding San Bernardino Strait. Although no definite statement had been made to this effect by Admiral Halsey, Admiral Kinkaid thought that the big battleships were standing by awaiting the Japanese Central Force and that Admiral Halsey was going after the Japanese Northern Force with carrier units. Actually, however, Admiral Halsey took his three complete task groups on his run to the north and left San Bernardino Strait open.

"Free passage through San Bernardino Strait was a pivotal point of the enemy's strategy in his daring scheme to strike the Allies in Leyte Gulf. Admiral Halsey did not know that . . . the Northern Force under

Admiral Ozawa, almost completely destitute of planes and pilots, had only one mission—to serve as a decoy and lure the most powerful units of the U.S. Fleet away from the Leyte area. It was expected that the Northern Force would probably be destroyed, but it was hoped that this desperate device would enable the Japanese Central Force to pass unmolested through San Bernardino Strait and move southward into Leyte Gulf, timing its approach to coincide with the arrival of the Southern Force from Surigao Strait.

"To accomplish his mission, Admiral Ozawa continually sent out radio messages in an effort to advertise his position to the U.S. Fleet. An undetected fault in his transmission system, however, prevented the Third Fleet from intercepting these signals. Equally important to later operations, communication difficulties and divided responsibility also prevented an adequate exchange of information between the enemy's Northern and Central forces.

"As the U.S. Third Fleet sought contact with the carriers of the Northern Force during the evening of the 24th, Admiral Kurita, in a remarkable feat of high-speed navigation, skillfully led his warships through the darkness southeastward into the treacherous passes of the Sibuyan Sea. Since he had received no message from Admiral Ozawa off Luzon, he was actually unaware that the main body of the U.S. Fleet had been drawn away from the mouth of San Barnardino Strait. Nevertheless, Admiral Kurita, in compliance with repeated orders from the Combined Fleet, continued on his original task, setting his course for Leyte Gulf. By midnight he was in the waters of San Bernardino Strait, and at approximately 0035 of 25 October he debouched into the Philippine Sea. About 0530, as he was coming down the coast of Samar, Admiral Kurita received word of the loss of Admiral Nishimura's two battleships and of the damage to the cruiser *Mogami*. Although he was unaware of the fact, his was now the only Japanese force within striking distance of Leyte. The task of destroying the U.S. invasion units rested solely in his hands.

"At dawn on 25 October, three groups of escort carriers under Admiral Thomas L. Sprague were disposed east of Samar and Leyte Gulf. The Northern CVE Group with 6 carriers, 3 destroyers, and 4 destroyer escorts was under the command of Rear Admiral Clifton A. F. Sprague. It was on a northerly course about fifty miles east of Samar and approximately halfway up the east coast of the Island, directly in the path of Admiral Kurita's oncoming force.

"Some twenty or thirty miles east southeast was the Middle CVE

Group with the same composition under Rear Admiral Felix B. Strump. Farther to the south off northern Mindanao was the Southern CVE Group consisting of 4 carriers, 3 destroyers and 4 destroyer escorts. This group was under the direct supervision of the over-all escort carrier commander, Admiral Thomas Sprague.

"Through a series of fatal misunderstandings directly attributable to divided command, ambiguous messages, and poor communication between the U.S. Third and Seventh fleets, neither Admiral Kinkaid at Leyte Gulf, nor Admiral Sprague off Samar, realized that the exit from San Bernardino Strait had been left unguarded. They had no reason to expect such a situation; previous commitments were firm. During the night of the 24th, however, Admiral Kinkaid became uneasy concerning the actual situation at San Bernardino Strait and decided to check on the position of Task Force 34. At 0412 on the 25th Admiral Kinkaid sent an urgent priority dispatch (241912) telling Admiral Halsey of the results in Surigao Strait and asking him the vital question: 'Is TF 34 guarding San Bernardino Strait?' The reply to Admiral Kinkaid's dispatch was not sent until 0704, by which time the first salvos of Admiral Kurita's battleships were reverberating across the waters off Samar. Admiral Halsey's answer said: 'Your 241912 negative. Task Force 34 is with carrier group now engaging enemy carrier force.'

"It was a dramatic situation, fraught with disaster. The forthcoming battle between the U.S. Seventh Fleet's slow and vulnerable 'jeep' carriers and the Japanese Central Force of greatly superior speed and firepower gave every promise of a completely unequal struggle. The light carriers of Admiral Sprague were no match for the giant battleships and heavy cruisers of the Japanese Central Force. Should the enemy gain entrance to Leyte Gulf, his powerful naval guns could pulverize any of the eggshell transports still present in the area and destroy vitally needed supplies on the beachhead. The thousands of U.S. troops already ashore would be isolated and pinned down helplessly between enemy fire from ground and sea. Then, too, the schedule for supply reinforcement would not only be completely upset, but the success of the invasion itself would be placed in grave jeopardy. The battleships and cruisers of the Seventh Fleet were over 100 miles away in Surigao Strait with their stock of armor-piercing ammunition virtually exhausted by the pre-landing shore bombardment and the decisive early morning battle with the Japanese Southern Force. Admiral Halsey's Third Fleet was almost 300 miles away still in hot pursuit of the Northern Force and could not possibly return in time to halt the progress of Admiral Kurita.

"Although Admiral Kurita's Central Force had suffered considerable damage in its course across the Sibuyan Sea, it was still a fleet when it broke through San Bernardino Strait and headed for Leyte Gulf. The main force consisted of the mighty *Yamato* and three other fast battleships, the *Kongo*, *Haruna*, and *Nagato*. These were supported by the six heavy cruisers *Chikuma*, *Haguro*, *Chokai*, *Tone*, *Kumano*, and *Suzuya*. The two light cruisers *Yahagi* and *Noshiro* and eleven destroyers completed Admiral Kurita's fast and powerful task force. In quest of big game, its guns and shell hoists were loaded down with armor-piercing projectiles as it steamed southward along the coast of Samar.

"First indication that the enemy might be approaching came at 0637 when the escort carrier *Fanshaw Bay* intercepted Japanese conversation on the interfighter director net. This was followed closely by sighting anti-aircraft bursts to the northwest about twenty miles distant. The final shock came at 0647 when a pilot aboard a plane from the *Kadashan Bay* frantically announced that a large enemy surface force of battleships, cruisers, and destroyers was closing in about twenty miles to the northwest at a speed of 30 knots. The frightful possibility had materialized; the Japanese Central Force had broken through San Bernardino Strait.

"Admiral Kurita had located the U.S. escort carrier force at 0644 and a few minutes later at 0658 he gave the order to join battle. The *Yamato*'s 18-inch guns fired first with the cruisers following as soon as they came within range. Never before had U.S. warships been subjected to such heavy-caliber fire. With the world's biggest guns blazing away, Admiral Kurita pressed the attack full speed.

"As soon as the enemy was sighted the Northern CVE Group changed course to 090° due east, and began launching all available aircraft. Scarcely had the planes been sent aloft when large-caliber shells began falling among the units of the formation. Admiral Kurita was closing rapidly, straddling the U.S. escort carriers with dye-marked salvos that landed with uncomfortable accuracy and bracketed their targets with red, yellow, green, and blue splashes. The situation was most critical and from this point on it was only a question of how to save the greatly outnumbered and out gunned U.S. ships from almost certain destruction.

"At 0701 the commander of the Northern CVE Group reported the alarming news that he was in contact with the enemy and urgently needed assistance. He then ordered a general retirement to the southwest in the hope of obtaining support from the heavy forces in Leyte Gulf. Admiral Kinkaid received the request for support at 0724 and promptly ordered Admiral Oldendorf 'to prepare to rendezvous his forces at the eastern end to Leyte Gulf'; the escort carrier planes were sent the same order, and a dispatch was transmitted to Admiral Halsey requesting immediate aid.

"Admiral Kurita pushed the attack vigorously. . . . Huge geysers of water erupted around Admiral Sprague's units as the big Japanese batteries began to find the range. As the battle developed, Admiral Kurita, intent on encircling the retiring U.S. ships, deployed several of his cruisers on the left flank from where they delivered the most troublesome fire of the battle. Several destroyers were also deployed on the right flank while the rest of his force pressed the attack from astern. Along with these surface attacks Japanese air units based in the Philippines launched a series of Kamikaze strikes against the U.S. carriers. In his great distress Admiral Kinkaid sent Admiral Halsey another dispatch: 'Urgently need fast BB's Leyte Gulf at once.' Admiral Halsey responded to the Seventh Fleet's appeal by ordering Vice Admiral John S. McCain, Commander of Task Group 38.1, which had been refueling to the east, to attack the enemy at San Bernardino as soon as possible. Meanwhile the Third Fleet continued to steam northward in hot pursuit of the Japanese carrier group.

"Admiral Sprague's escort carriers used every trick of sea fighting to escape the heavy fire of the Japanese Fleet and to inflict losses on the enemy. Evasive tactics were ordered; thick smoke screens were laid down, temporary refuge was sought in a providential rain squall. In a desperate effort to stem the enemy advance, the destroyers and destroyer escorts fought back furiously. Interposing themselves between the carriers and their adversary, they boldly closed the range and fired their five-inch guns and torpedoes at cruiser and battleship targets. Both the *Johnston* and the *Heerman* challenged the *Kongo*. The escort carriers also engaged with gunfire whatever units of the enemy came within range. At the same time their planes attacked the enemy continuously and succeeded in putting several of his cruiser units out of action. They were greatly handicapped, however, by the damage inflicted on the carriers. The pilots, seeing their carrier decks ripped open or their ships sunk, made forced landings on the already overcrowded airstrip at Tacloban. Some also landed on the Dulag strip, while others were compelled at the last minute to ditch their planes in Leyte Gulf. . . .

"With disaster staring him in the face, Admiral Kinkaid sent Admiral Halsey another urgent dispatch which the latter received at 0900: 'Our CVE's being attacked by 4 BB's 8 Cruisers plus others. Request Lee cover Leyte at top speed. Request fast carriers make immediate strike.' By this time ammunition aboard the escort carriers was running low; some of the destroyers had expended their torpedoes and the torpedo planes were reduced to the dire expedient of making dummy runs on the enemy ships. Both the screening force and the carriers sustained considerable damage. The *Bambier Bay* was hit hard and sank at 0911 with an enemy cruiser pumping shells into her at a range of less than 2,000 yards. The destroyer *Johnston,* which had been under continuous heavy fire, was fatally struck and had to be abandoned. She rolled over and sank at 1010. The destroyer *Hoel* and the destroyer escort *Roberts* were also sunk. Early damage was also inflicted on the escort carriers *Santee, Suwannee,* and *Sangamon.* At 0922 Admiral Halsey had received a dispatch sent by Admiral Kinkaid at 0725: 'Under attack by cruisers and battleships . . . request immediate air strikes. My OBB's low in ammunition.'

"Meanwhile, off Samar, victory lay within Admiral Kurita's grasp. After almost two and one-half hours of continuous battle the flanking enemy units began closing in, firing salvo after salvo at the escort carriers dodging desperately to avoid more damage. By 0920 the heavy cruiser *Tone* was within 10,000 yards of her target and on the starboard flank the Japanese 10th Destroyer Squadron pressed the attack with torpedoes. The situation had become virtually hopeless for Admiral Sprague's task group, and few expected to come out of the ordeal afloat. Once more Admiral Kinkaid sent an insistent plea to Admiral Halsey, this time in the clear: 'Where is Lee? Send Lee.' Almost simultaneously Admiral Halsey received an urgent dispatch from Admiral Nimitz in Pearl Harbor: 'The whole world wants to know where is Task Force 34.'

"Then, as if in answer to fervent prayer, the unexpected happened. Admiral Kurita broke off the engagement. His units had sustained no little damage, and like everyone else he was unaware of the true battle situation. He therefore ordered his forces to cease firing and reassemble to the north. For the U.S. carrier forces this retirement by the enemy meant a remarkable and completely unexpected escape. Admiral Sprague in summing up the results of the battle shortly thereafter stated: '. . . the failure of the enemy main body and encircling light forces to completely wipe out all vessels of this Task Unit can be attributed to our successful smoke screen, our torpedo counterattack, continuous harassment of the enemy by bomb, torpedo, and strafing air attacks, timely maneuvers, and the definite partiality of Almighty God!'

"The continuous and urgent dispatches from Admiral Kinkaid and the cryptic message from Admiral Nimitz finally led Admiral Halsey to change course and direct the bulk of his fleet southward toward Leyte. He accordingly directed Task Force 34 under Admiral Lee and Task Group

38.2 under Rear Admiral Gerald F. Bogan to proceed south toward San Bernardino Strait. At exactly 1115, when he was expecting the pagoda masts of Admiral Ozawa's force to appear over the horizon at any minute, he made the crucial decision to return to Leyte Gulf. He expected to arrive early the next morning.

"The other units of the Third Fleet, Admiral Mitscher's Task Force 38 with Task Group 38.3 under Admiral Sherman and Task Group 38.4 under Admiral Davison, were to continue against the enemy carrier force. Throughout the afternoon of 25 October, Third Fleet carrier planes struck Admiral Ozawa's force again and again. When the battle was over the Japanese had lost the famous carrier *Zuikaku* and three light carriers *Chitose, Chiyoda,* and *Zuiho.* One light cruiser and two destroyers were also sunk, but the two hermaphrodite battleship-carriers *Ise* and *Hyuga* escaped with minor damage. United States forces suffered no surface losses in the engagement.

"After regrouping his forces and evaluating the situation, Admiral Kurita decided to make one last attempt against Leyte Gulf. At 1120 he ordered his ships to change course toward the target area to the southwest. He was en route approximately one hour, however, and only 45 miles from his objective when he finally decided to give up the attempt. At 1236 he ordered his ships about. As he retraced his course to the northwest his force came under attack by planes from the Seventh and Third fleets. Although he had sustained considerable damage, Admiral Kurita managed to limp through San Bernardino Strait at 2130 on 25 October. Of his original force of 32 ships he escaped with 4 battleships, 4 cruisers and 7 destroyers. In the meantime Admiral Halsey came racing down from the north with his big battleships. They were not to fire a shot, however, for when they arrived it was too late. Admiral Kurita had escaped.

"In the evaluation of the battle, Admiral Sprague's humble recognition of divine intervention must be read in conjunction with Admiral Halsey's radio dispatch on the day of impending disaster: 'To prevent any misunderstanding concerning recent Third Fleet operations, I inform you as follows: It became vital on 23 October to obtain information of Japanese plans, so 3 carrier groups were moved to the Philippine coast off Polillo, San Bernardino and Surigao to search as far west as possible; on 24 October Third Fleet air struck at Japanese forces moving east through the Sibuyan and Sulu seas; apparently the enemy planned a co-ordinated attack, but their objective was not ascertained and no carrier force located until afternoon of 24 October; merely to guard San Bernardino Strait while the enemy was co-ordinating his surface and carrier air force would be time wasted, so 3 carrier groups were concentrated and moved north for a surprise dawn attack on the carrier fleet; estimated the enemy force in the Sibuyan Sea too damaged to threaten Com7thFlt, a deduction proved correct by events of 25 October off Surigao; the enemy carrier force, caught off guard, offering no air oposition over the target or against our force; evidently their air groups were land-based, arriving too late to fight; I had projected surface strike units ahead of our carriers in order to co-ordinate surface and air attacks against the enemy; Com7thFlt sent urgent appeal for assistance just when my overwhelming force was within 45 miles of the crippled enemy; no alternative but to head south in response to call, although I was convinced his opponents were badly damaged from our attack of 24 October, a conviction later justified by events off Leyte. . . .'

"The command decisions during the battle of Leyte Gulf require a realistic appraisal. The 'events off Leyte' were the free entry of Admiral Kurita's Force into the Leyte area to a point where the complete destruction of the U.S. transports and escort carriers was an immediate and frightful possibility. Except for the superb and sacrificial intervention of a covering force under Admiral Sprague, the brilliant operation of Admiral Oldendorf in Surigao Strait, and the fortunate decision of Admiral Kurita, the results of the battle would have been different.

"During the course of these critical naval operations, the Japanese air forces had intensified their attacks both on sea and shore. The Seventh Fleet was busily occupied in a struggle for survival, employing its air strength to fight off hordes of hostile planes attacking in co-ordination with enemy fleet units. Its problem was further complicated by the appearance of Kamikaze pilots whose novel suicide tactics initially caused considerable havoc.

"On land, General MacArthur's troops without adequate air cover were exposed to continuous and damaging raids by enemy planes. Bombing and strafing from tree-top levels interfered with the unloading of supplies and hampered the progress of the advance into Leyte. In addition, under cover of their naval operations the Japanese had succeeded in landing 2,000 troop reinforcements from Cagayan at Ormoc on 25 October.

"The Japanese admirals had played for high stakes and lost. Their plan missed success, however, by only a slim margin. Had the Central Force adhered to its mission and proceeded into Leyte Gulf, the American invasion would in all probability have experienced a setback of incalculable proportions. The enemy's heavy guns would have experienced little trouble in pounding the remaining transports and landing craft. Shore positions and troop installations could have been bombarded almost at leisure and Admiral Kurita could have then continued on toward Surigao Strait. At this stage of the game, the weakened escort carriers and the ammunition-depleted battleships of the Seventh Fleet could have offered only relatively minor opposition. The intervention of the Third Fleet was too far removed to cause immediate tactical concern.

"Within the narrow limits of a lost opportunity, the Japanese Navy, however, had suffered a crushing and fatal defeat. The enemy fleet as an integral unit was no longer to be reckoned as a major factor in future operations, and his carrier force especially was now known to be impotent. The greatest sea battle in history left the remaining units of the Japanese Navy increasingly vulnerable to future Allied naval and air strikes. Against the background of this decisive naval victory, the strong wedge of General MacArthur's ground forces was driven solidly into the vulnerable Japanese flank on Leyte. If he could establish his forces securely in the central Philippines, the Japanese would be powerless to prevent him from overrunning the rest of the archipelago and bisecting the Japanese Empire."

The battle was over; the Japanese Navy had not got through, and the Leyte beaches were safe. MacArthur wasted no time on recriminations. That night he sent a message to Nimitz: "At this time I wish to express to you and to all elements of your fine command my deep appreciation of the splendid service they have rendered in the recent Leyte operations. Their record needs no amplification from me, but I cannot refrain from expressing the admiration everyone here feels for their magnificent conduct. All of your elements—ground, naval and air—have alike covered themselves with glory. We could not have gone along without them. To you my special thanks for your sympathetic and understanding co-operation."

He also wired Halsey: "We have co-operated with you so long that we expect your brilliant successes. Everyone here has a feeling of complete confidence and inspiration when you go into action in our support." Years later Halsey recalled this message as being "particularly warming" at a time when many other fellow officers were not so broadminded. Three months later, when Halsey left the Third Fleet to return home, among the farewell messages he received was one from MacArthur which gave him no end of amusement. It said: "Your departure from this theater leaves a gap that can be filled only by your return." What amused Halsey about it was that in transmission the word "filled" was garbled and came out "fouled."

Chapter XVI Shades of Bataan

MacArthur never blamed Halsey personally for his actions during the naval engagement off Leyte which had left the entire beachhead virtually at the mercy of the enemy for many hours. But he always regarded it as a shining example of the danger of divided command. During the Leyte operation only the fleet of Admiral Kinkaid was under MacArthur's command. All the other naval forces, including Halsey's, were under the command of Admiral Nimitz, who was in Pearl Harbor five thousand miles away. As late as March 5, 1953, in response to an inquiry from the historical section of the Department of the Army, MacArthur made his position clear on this subject.

"Of all the faulty decisions of the war perhaps the most unexplainable one was the failure to unify the command in the Pacific. The principle involved is perhaps the most fundamental one in the doctrine and tradition of command. In this instance, it did not involve an international problem. It was accepted and entirely successful in the other great theaters. The failure to do so in the Pacific cannot be defended in logic, in theory or even in common sense. Other motives must be ascribed. It resulted in divided effort, the waste of diffusion and duplication of force and the consequent extension of the war with added casualties and cost. The generally excellent cooperation between the two commands in the Pacific supported by the good will, good nature and high professional qualifications of the numerous personnel involved was no substitute for the essential unity of direction by centralized authority. The handicaps and hazards unnecessarily resulting were numerous indeed, but by way of illustration I will elucidate the one which produced the greatest jeopardy.

"It developed in the course of the Leyte landing. After Morotai, my next jump was tentatively to seize the islands off Davao Bay to base our air to cover the following objective, which was Leyte. It was necessary to make this intermediate move because of the approximately 300-mile limit of air coverage. Any landing had to be within covering distance of our previous bases as it would take time to build or secure new bases and make them operative. Until this was done our beachheads were entirely dependent for air protection from the rear bases. This was the determining factor in each move of the envelopment—the so-called 'hit-'em-where-they-ain't' and 'leave-'em-die-on-the-vine' maneuver. It was based upon the concept of cutting in behind the enemy's bastions and severing his supply line.

"The high command after Morotai expressed the desire to speed up operations in the belief that Leyte was lightly held, a report somewhat confirmed by naval air reconnaissance but which later proved not entirely accurate. It was suggested that if I moved direct on Leyte, naval air would cover me in landing and sixteen little 'flat tops' would stay to cover the command until we could build local air fields and bring forward our own ground air. The hop was double the usual distance and violated my basic concept never to risk having my ground forces uncovered from ground-based air. Under the conditions, however, I decided on the movement. I believe this was probably the first time a ground commander ever placed his complete trust so absolutely in naval hands.

"The 7th Fleet was reinforced with the old battleships and the little carriers, and Halsey's fleet containing the new battleships and big carriers under Nimitz's command was ordered to operate in the same general waters to the north. I was on the cruiser *Nashville* accompanying her convoys. It early became evident to me that Halsey was too far to the north to properly cover the Gulf of Leyte, and I so radioed Nimitz asking him to drop Halsey back. This would not only insure my base but would insure his fleet being in the action, as the magnetic attraction of my point of landing would draw the enemy's fleet there. Three times, as I remember, I sent such dispatches but without results. Nimitz repeated to Halsey apparently without getting through and then finally authorized me to communicate directly with Halsey but it was then too late.

"In the meantime, the enemy's forces acted with great skill and cunning. A decoy drew Halsey further to the north, the Japanese attacked from the south in the Mindanao Sea and drew our battleships and cruisers there to match his force, and then, evading our air reconnaissance, came through the San Bernardino Straits and moved on our base and rear naval echelons in the bay off Tacloban. Probably two hundred or more vessels were there exposed. We instantly threw in our little flat tops, which gallantly and successfully repulsed the attacking Japanese force. In doing so, however, the planes were practically destroyed, and my potential air umbrella to protect my ground forces and operations disappeared.

"For the following month I was thereby in gravest danger, as the Japanese under General Yamashita regarded this as the crucial point of the action. Actually, with the failure to hold the so-called 'Yamashita Line,' which collapsed with our Ormoc envelopment, the Emperor afterward told me, the Japanese admitted defeat and all their efforts were to accomplish an end without internal explosion. Leyte came out all right, but the hazards would have all been avoided by unity of command."

On Leyte it early became evident that the Japanese were trying to steal a page from MacArthur's book; the defense of Luzon, it appeared, was going to be fought in Leyte. Thousands upon thousands of Japanese reinforcements were rushed to the island. As soon as a fifteen-hundred-yard airstrip could be finished at Tacloban, Kenney's P-38's were rushed in. As they landed, the surprised pilots were met by MacArthur, who shook their hands and patted their backs, saying: "You don't know how glad I am to see you." Most of the carriers had to leave Leyte at this time, either for refueling or repairs. Despite the most heroic efforts of Kenney's airmen and the support of the carrier planes that had stayed, Japanese troops continued to pour ashore in the north of Leyte. After the war, Major General Toshi Nishimura, of the Fourteenth Area Army, claimed that during the battle for Leyte more than forty-five thousand troops and ten thousand tons of matériel were landed, despite the fact that U.S. planes sank *eighty per cent* of the Japanese vessels in this operation.

Here were shades of Bataan. General Yamashita tried attacks in force; he tried infiltration; he even tried paratroops. Some of these paratroops wore civilian clothes; others wore leggings that were U.S. Army surplus after World War I. They also carried papers on which were printed useful phrases in English, such as: "I am chief commander on Japanese besant paratroop army. All the airdrome of —— has been taken by the Japanese army. It is resistless, so you must surrender. Answer yes or no. All the Japanese army have done great attack."

But, as on Bataan, MacArthur outsmarted his opponent. Most of the Japanese forces were landed at Ormoc, on the western side of Leyte. When they flooded across the island, prepared for a frontal assault, MacArthur sent his 77th Division around to the west coast of the island in a surprise amphibious landing and struck them in their rear. As he explained it in a communiqué on December 8, right after the landing: "By this maneuver we have seized the center of the Yamashita Line from the rear and have split the enemy's force in two, isolating those in the valley to the north from those along the coast to the south. Both segments are now caught between our columns, which are pressing in from all fronts." Two days later, after severe fighting, Ormoc fell to the 77th Division. Most of Yamashita's force was trapped. On Christmas Day the last connecting road from the enemy's chief remaining port of entry for reinforcements and supply was severed. And the next day MacArthur could declare that all organized resistance had ceased on Leyte. "General Yamashita," he said, "has sustained perhaps the greatest defeat in the military annals of the Japanese army."

Meanwhile, MacArthur had been concerning himself with problems other than military. I think nothing better illustrates the depth of his concern for the protection of the civil power of government against undue pressure from the military than the speed with which he moved to restore the processes of civil government to those charged with its administration in the Philippines. On October 23, just three days after he had set foot on the beach at Leyte, MacArthur and President Osmeña were in Tacloban, the capital of the province. The interior of the capitol building had been reduced to wreckage by the Japanese, so we stood on the steps in front of the building. In solemn ceremony the flags of the United States and the Philippines were raised, and MacArthur formally restored to President Osmeña all of his constitutional power within the area.

As the citizens of Tacloban gathered about him, he concluded with stirring emphasis: "On behalf of my government I restore to you a constitutional administration by countrymen of your confidence and choice. As our forces advance, I shall in like manner restore the other Philippine cities and provinces until throughout the entire land you may walk down life's years erect and unafraid, each free to toil and to worship according to his own conscience, with your children's laughter again brightening homes once darkened by the grim tragedy of conquest." At the termination of the ceremony he turned to President Osmeña and took his leave, with a simple parting statement that was punctuated by the steady roar of artillery fire from the near-by battle line. "Now, Mr. President, my officers and I shall withdraw and leave you to discharge your responsibilities."

I could see on the faces of President Osmeña and the members of his cabinet grouped around him expressions of complete surprise. They had not anticipated so sudden a restoration of political power. They had expected to return to Washington while the issues of battle were being decided, leaving to the military full power over government. But they had reckoned without MacArthur's philosophy; for he believed, even in war, in maintaining a distinct separation of the powers—leaving to the civil authority the political responsibility in the affairs of government, and, conversely, to the military authority the responsibility to devise and implement military strategy and tactics. Thus, the ensuing campaign of liberation was carefully synchronized to the progressive restoration of the civil power, so that when the military campaign was to be brought to a successful conclusion just ten months later, all influence of military authority upon civil affairs was to be simultaneously terminated.

MacArthur has, whenever possible, put into action what others have been inclined to view as mainly rhetoric: "the wise and necessary subordination of the military to the civil power." Yet, conversely, he has viewed with alarm the growing tendency by the civil authority to interfere in military strategy and tactics, even after the military authority has been called upon to implement political policy by force of arms. He looks upon that tendency and its corollary—centralizing in Washington, even though in the hands of a military staff, full authority over strategic and tactical decisions in the conduct of military operations in the field—as a sure basis for future defeat.

MacArthur had been through all this only recently—in one of those side issues with which he was always having to concern himself while trying to concentrate on the prosecution of the war. Harold Ickes was then Secretary of the Interior. And because insular possessions, including the Philippines, were under the administrative responsibility of the Interior Department, Ickes had insisted that in the absence of a regularly appointed High Commissioner he should assume the reins of the Philippine government. He had made it clear that he wished to take power as soon as the campaign of liberation got under way. Furthermore, he had already insisted, with enviable self-assurance, that he knew who the "puppets" had been during the Japanese occupation and that he intended to arraign them immediately for treason.

It was obvious that he intended the prompt mass execution of all Filipino leaders who had co-operated with the Japanese occupation authorities, regardless of motive. For reasons that included a regard for common humanity, MacArthur took uncompromising exception to Ickes's recommendations. He believed, and so pointed out to Washington, that the mere holding or assumption of public office under the enemy regime did not in itself establish a case of disloyalty and that only the Filipinos themselves could justly evaluate the conduct of their leaders; that only the Filipinos themselves should pass judgment upon these men. Mac-

Arthur said that he intended to take all those accused of disloyal collaboration into custody to protect them from mob violence and hold them for the action of the Philippine government once the constitutional procedures had been fully restored.

Ickes had, of course, never set foot in the Philippines. But Secretary of War Henry Stimson had served in the Islands, and therefore understood and completely supported MacArthur's arguments. So convincing were they that President Roosevelt supported Stimson and MacArthur. Thus, the collaboration issue was settled by the Filipinos themselves according to their own constitutional processes and the true facts as they had known them, and civil government was restored to the people without falling under the domination of an eccentric who was proud of his self-styled nickname, "The Old Curmudgeon." Characteristically, Ickes never forgave MacArthur, and never stopped sniping at him.

MacArthur's decision to restore the powers of civil government to the people progressively proved a wise one. It brought into clear focus the blessings of constitutional government; it re-established the responsibility for civil administration; it revived dignity and independence of thought which had been long suppressed under enemy occupation; and it gave dynamic meaning to the campaign of liberation.

Meanwhile, with the battle for Leyte still in progress, MacArthur landed an American task force on the southwest coast of Mindoro. It moved rapidly inland, securing the airstrip at San Jose against minor opposition. His purposes were to develop airfields in closer proximity to Luzon; to provide flank protection for his movement north; and, through tactics of deception, to try to draw the enemy's Luzon force into the south. To accomplish this, he seized towns along the east coast of Mindoro all the way to Calapan, directly opposite Batangas in southern Luzon. Adjacent Marinduque Island was then occupied. Many photographic missions were flown over Batangas, and the guerrillas in southern Luzon were called upon for aggressive action against the enemy. These tactics of deception worked. The enemy was tricked into rushing a division of troops from its northern force to Batangas and another division to Bataan.

Mindoro was not in a direct line from Leyte to Manila, yet from Mindoro you could actually see Manila on a clear day. MacArthur had bypassed half a dozen islands between Leyte and Luzon, and was now within easy bombing-range of Manila—and Bataan and Corregidor. He was almost home.

Chapter XVII   "I'm a little late, but we finally came."

Luzon posed MacArthur with a peculiarly difficult and dangerous problem, for the Japanese ground forces, under General Yamashita, were numerically greater than his own. But MacArthur's strategy was, in his own words, as follows:

"With my 8th Army off the southern coast of Luzon, with a firm hold on Mindoro, I will threaten landings at Legaspi, Batangas and other southern ports and draw the bulk of the Japanese into the south. This done, I will land the 6th Army in an amphibious enveloping movement on the exposed northern shore, thus cutting off the enemy's supplies from Japan. This would draw the enemy back to the north, leaving the 8th Army to land against only weak opposition on the south coast in another amphibious movement. Both forces ashore, with but minor loss, will then close like a vise on the enemy deprived of supplies and destroy him." It was to work like a charm.

On January 5, 1945, the Cruiser *Boise*, flying a five-star ensign (MacArthur had been made a General of the Army on December 18, 1944), cut through the deep blue waters off the west coast of the Philippines. Only the sound of her engines and blower system and the wash of the sea broke the quiet. The *Boise* was under complete radio silence. At their stations, sailors and officers alike looked anxiously out across the sea toward the distant ships moving in convoy with them. The atmosphere was one of stillness, but of tension rather than peacefulness. Only the erect, khaki-clad figure with the familiar cap, the dark glasses, and the old corncob pipe paced leisurely on deck as though the ship were not sailing through enemy waters at all.

The air suddenly crackled with the call over the cruiser's loudspeaker: "*General quarters, general quarters, all hands man your battle stations, prepare for submarine attack! All hands man your battle stations, prepare for submarine attack!"* The ominous white wake of a torpedo streaked across the water, dead on course for the *Boise*. With a surge of speed, the cruiser lurched to starboard, barely easing out of the path of the white streak as it went by. Already a destroyer was steaming into the area, dumping depth charges into the water. Soon a Japanese midget submarine surfaced, black and dripping in the distance like a tiny whale. With a crunching lunge the destroyer rammed it and sent it bubbling to the bottom.

Still calmly puffing on his corncob, MacArthur watched and then resumed his pacing.

Next morning the cruiser's loudspeaker blared again! *"General quarters, general quarters, all hands man your battle stations, prepare for air attack! All hands man your battle stations, prepare for air attack!"* In a whining dive, an enemy plane plunged for the *Boise*, missed it, and dropped its bomb in the water midway between the cruiser and a near-by destroyer. The plane seemed hardly to have disappeared when another came into view, hovered directly over the *Boise*, and then flew away as black puffs of anti-aircraft fire materialized in the sky all around it. Thereupon the guns of eight ships cut loose in a staccato blast against another bomber. It was hit and thundered into the sea only a hundred yards from the *Boise*.

Bareheaded this time, but still puffing on his familiar corncob, MacArthur hardly interrupted his pacing to watch these frantic enemy attempts to get him. On a gun battery near "captain's country" where he paced, a sailor jerked his thumb in his direction and said to his companion: "That guy's all right. He stands out here on deck like the rest of us and takes it."

In one sense, these were days of anticlimax for MacArthur. The planning was already done and the first phase of action was under way. The battleships and carriers of the fleet were already fighting their way through desperate air attacks and driving into Lingayen Gulf to blast the beaches. For the moment, all MacArthur could do was sit on the flag bridge and look out across the expanse of rolling blue South China Sea and fleecy clouds, or pace the deck, stopping now and then to watch a bit of enemy action.

But in another sense, and a more important one, this was to be the most climactic of all his giant strides from Milne Bay back across the Pacific. For the *Boise* sailed close enough for all aboard to see the old familiar landmarks: Mariveles . . . Manila . . . Corregidor . . . Bataan. And as she steamed northward, part of a majestic and mighty fleet that was the biggest in the history of the Pacific, MacArthur was at the rail almost constantly, looking, just looking—standing tall and still, alone with his thoughts and his memories. As he passed by the long-remembered scenes of his past—and his father's past—he left me an unforgettable picture of loneliness, of sorrow, and of sacrificial dedication.

It was a hazardous trip. Besides the submarine and bombing attacks, the fleet was subjected to violent Kamikaze attacks. The escort carrier *Ommaney Bay* was damaged so badly that she had to be sunk. The *Louisville, Stafford, Manila Bay, Savo Island,* and H.M.A.S. *Arunta* and *Australia* all were hit. There were heavy casualties to ships and personnel. Admiral J. B. Oldendorf's flagship, the *California*, was seriously damaged; so were the battleship *New Mexico* and the cruiser *Columbia*. This kind of suicide attack, with the Japanese pilot turning himself and his plane into a huge, sacrificial bomb, was virtually impossible to stop, and the only defense against it was evasive action. The most massive wall of steel sent up by anti-aircraft fire seemed completely ineffective. It was a fearsome thing to witness. Watching it, I recognized yet another virtue of MacArthur's argument against bypassing the Philippines; had we tried to attack Japan from Formosa or the China coast, the multitude of airfields on the Philippines would have provided bases for so many Kamikaze planes that we might well have been stopped in our tracks until we had retaken the Philippines after all.

At dawn on the 9th we arrived in Lingayen Gulf and stood in toward shore, in the identical position of the Japanese invasion fleet more than three years before. And by 9:30 the first assault landings were going in to the beaches. Five hours after the first wave, MacArthur went ashore in a landing-craft.

Again, as at Leyte, the boat grounded before reaching the beach and MacArthur had to wade ashore. The scene was bedlam. More than twenty-five hundred landing-craft swarmed through the water or lay on the shoreline like beached fish. Almost a thousand amphibious tanks, tractors, and "ducks" chugged and snorted about above the high-tide line. Through a cloudless sky, occasional stubby Japanese fighter planes snarled over the fleet. But they were met with curtains of anti-aircraft fire and gangs of carrier-based U.S. pursuit planes, and were quickly sent booming and splashing into the Gulf.

Through this holocaust MacArthur strode to shore, studying the scene through his dark glasses and puffing on his corncob pipe. At the beach the troops were still on alert. The beachmaster commandeered a jeep, and MacArthur climbed aboard and headed for the nearest divisional command post. Soon, however, the jeep broke down, and the driver yanked up the hood and fumbled madly at the controls. MacArthur got out and proceeded across the sand dunes in long, even strides.

He had achieved exactly the surprise he had intended, and a wide, deep beachhead was firmly established. The first phase was completed, and the second was already started. All of his commanders were veteran fighters against the Japanese. His ground forces of the Sixth Army were under General Krueger, his naval forces of the Seventh Fleet and Australian Squadron were under Admiral Kinkaid, and his air forces of the Far East Air Force were under General Kenney. The Third Fleet, under Admiral Halsey, was acting in co-ordinated support. To the south was his Eighth Army, and in New Guinea was the First Australian Army under General Sir Thomas Blamey.

Simultaneously with the landings, a message from President Osmeña was air-dropped in leaflet form by the millions of copies all over the Philippines. "In a series of brilliantly conceived blows," it read, "General MacArthur's forces of liberation have successively, in but a short span of time, destroyed the enemy army defending Leyte, seized firm control of Mindoro, and now stand defiantly on the soil of Luzon at the very threshold to our capital city. Thus are answered our prayers of many long months—thus is the battle for the liberation of the Philippines fully joined and the hour of our deliverance at hand—yet in that hour it is incumbent upon us that we rise to our majestic heights as a freedom-loving people to acquit ourselves with courage and honor in the tests which lie ahead. General MacArthur has called upon us to rally to him—I look to every patriot to heed that call. . . ."

The guerrillas of northern Luzon had already been hard at work supporting the invasion. They had prepared maps detailing towns and even specific buildings where enemy arms and fuel were stored. Using these maps, U.S. pilots were able to avoid needlessly destroying the other towns and buildings. The guerrillas also cut enemy supply and communication lines, ambushed patrols, and destroyed supply dumps themselves. General Krueger said later that the northern Luzon guerrillas, led by Lieutenant Colonel Russell W. Volckmann, were worth at least one division of troops to the U.S. As calmly as any man reporting for duty, Colonel Volckmann strode into my office in the beachhead area only forty-eight hours after the landings, with a full report of what he and his guerrilla force had accomplished during the two and a half years of living and fighting in the hills and of what they were now prepared to do to support the invasion. We had plenty for them to do, because the Japanese were resisting desperately. They made the most of Luzon's difficult terrain; their positions were heavily fortified with mutually supporting tunnel and cave systems, fully supplied with weapons and ammunition. In close support of the infantry, tanks buried deep in the ground were used as pillboxes. Every Japanese soldier was fighting to the death. Aided by the initial surprise, our attack had quickly reached the Central Plain and had got as far as Tarlac, halfway to Manila, by January 21. But beyond here the going became much harder, as the enemy threw huge numbers of reinforcements into the battle. As the drive approached Clark Field, the rage of battle reached its highest tempo.

Explaining the extraordinary initial speed of the operation, MacArthur said later: "There was no fixed timetable. I hoped to proceed as rapidly as possible, especially as time was an element connected with the release of our prisoners. I have always felt, however, that to endeavor to formulate in advance details of a campaign is hazardous, as it tends to warp the judgment of a commander when faced with unexpected conditions brought about by the uncertainties of enemy reaction or enemy initiative. I therefore never attempted fixed dates for anything but the start of operations. The rate of progress in this operation was fast and more than fulfilled all hopes and expectations." And he added: "No greater danger can confront a field commander than too close 'backseat driving' and too rigid 'timetables' of operations from those above. There is a natural limit on a command due to its inherent strengths and weaknesses which place a bracket upon its operation which only its own commander can know and which even he at times has to estimate. Any arbitrary violation either way by those not present in the theater of operations might well prove disastrous."

One element of the campaign, however, did require a timetable, and that was supply. Engineers' and shipping schedules had all been upset by the changes in the original target dates for the Mindanao and Leyte landings. General Hugh Casey, MacArthur's brilliant chief engineer since Bataan days, later wrote: "Not the least of the factors involved in all planning was the normal 90/150-day gaps—five months—between the requisition of supplies and the delivery. For example, virtually no stocks existed in the Southwest Pacific of such matériel as Bailey bridging and floating equipage. While there was an impressive bulk of engineer tonnage in the theater, it was not in well-balanced depots, and could not be shipped forward from rear bases on Australia and New Guinea because of chaotic shipping and port facilities."

But MacArthur, who started his service as an engineer, foresaw these problems and prepared in advance to meet them. In conference with all the commanders involved, he stipulated that "airfields must be constructed within six days after landing; top priority to be given for the unloading of treadway bridging equipment; landings directly seaward of airdrome areas were to be avoided; landing mats on at least five ships to begin unloading on the second day were to be provided." Many other stipulations that he made ahead of time meant the narrow difference between success and failure.

Faced as he was with such a formidable supply problem, MacArthur was astonished at the order he received from Washington at this critical moment: one hundred of his transport ships were to be withdrawn immediately, to be used to carry munitions and supplies across the North Pacific to the Soviet forces in Vladivostok. He protested bitterly, but, as usual, his protests were ignored. The Washington planners were determined to bring Russia into the war against Japan, and this consideration evidently was more important than the possibility of losing thousands of men then fighting in north Luzon. MacArthur realized that the abrupt removal of these transport ships jeopardized his entire Philippine campaign, and he was utterly opposed to the entry of Russia into the war against Japan at this late date. No attention was paid to his warnings, however, with the result that tremendous quantities of munitions and supplies of all kinds were rapidly stacked up in Siberia. Later, of course, they were the basis of Soviet military support of North Korea and Red China.

Meanwhile, not only did MacArthur lose a hundred transport ships, but Admiral Nimitz desperately needed units of his fleet for his planned attack on Okinawa. MacArthur's estimate of the situation that had developed and his plans to meet it are recorded in his own words: "The only place the enemy could hope to counterattack successfully, except on the actual battle line, was at Lingayen itself to cut my line of supply. My beachhead and harbor base were exposed to attack from Formosa and the north. The 7th Fleet had been reinforced from the Central Pacific by battleships with accessories, and as long as these defended the Lingayen roadsteads I felt my naval supply line, though somewhat attenuated, was secure. Admiral Nimitz was preparing for the Okinawa attack, however, and he felt these ships must be recalled as soon as possible. I therefore decided to bring the XI Corps of the 8th Army, commanded by General Hall, forward by sea and throw it in on the Zambales coast of west Luzon so that if Lingayen, in its weakened naval state, became jeopardized I could shift my supply line to a more secure geographical position.

"I'm a little late, but we finally came."

"In addition, the movement, a complete surprise to the enemy, would place Hall's forces so as to threaten the flank of the enemy's resistance in the Manila plains and would effectively bar any movement of the enemy to or from the Bataan Peninsula. I then intended, when the resistance in the plains crumbled, to suddenly envelop from the other flank with the 1st Cavalry Division, which I was bringing up via Lingayen for that purpose. Manila would thus be enveloped by this movement from the east, by simultaneous attack from the south by the 8th Army, and by direct drive from the north by the main forces of the 6th Army."

The plan worked perfectly, mainly because of the resourcefulness of the commanders and the indomitable courage of the troops. MacArthur was especially lavish in his praise of General Krueger. "I have known all of our great army commanders of this century," he said, "and in over-all accomplishment rate him at the top of the list." In conjunction with the landing of the XI Corps, the Zambales guerrillas captured the airstrip at San Marcelino, which dominated the beachhead. Their leader, Colonel Magsaysay, is now President of the Philippine Republic. The Vice President, Carlos Garcia, was also a guerrilla leader, operating on the island of Bohol.

The enemy fought with desperation, but MacArthur fought with dedication. His advance headquarters was at the town of San Miguel, thus providing a unique situation in which the supreme commander's headquarters on the drive to capture Manila was fifty miles closer to the front than that of his army commander. This reflected MacArthur's anxiety for speed in the drive on Manila and not any fault of the army commander, who had to correlate the tactical operations on all sectors in which the army was engaged. Men at the front line ceased to be surprised at the sight of MacArthur's Philippine Field Marshal's cap and his outsized pipe. One evening General Kenney dropped in to report to him at his advance headquarters. They sat down to dinner together, but Kenney noticed that MacArthur ate practically nothing. To his question, MacArthur replied: "George, I'm so darn tired I can't eat." But he insisted on conferring far into the night. Next morning, before dawn, Kenney asked the duty officer to explain to MacArthur that he was sorry that he had to leave and could not wait to say good-by. "Oh," the officer replied, "General MacArthur left for the front two hours ago."

One compelling reason for MacArthur's driving himself almost to exhaustion was the news he had received about the prisoners-of-war. There were thousands of prisoners—civilian as well as military, women and children as well as men, British and Filipino as well as American—penned

187

up at Cabanatuan, at Santo Tomás University, at Bilibid in Manila, and at Los Baños on Laguna de Bay. Through guerrillas and other intelligence agents, MacArthur had discovered that, as his troops approached, the Japanese prison guards increased their savagery. The longer the delay, the more of these pitiful people would die. The thought of their destruction after so many years and with deliverance so near, struck him to the soul. Despite the tremendous enemy pressure on all fronts, a special operation was devised and planned by the Army for rescuing the prisoners. In a stunning series of surprise raids, well co-ordinated between selected men from the Sixth Army's ranger battalion and local guerrillas, the enemy's lines were penetrated at all four points and the prisoners liberated without the loss of a single prisoner's life. It was perhaps the most brilliant exhibition of tactics of this kind in the entire history of warfare. MacArthur viewed it with satisfaction. Not for nothing was he a student of the raiding tactics of the Civil War.

When one works intimately with MacArthur and accompanies him nearly everywhere, one becomes accustomed to the highly emotional scenes into which destiny seems so often to project him. It was my fortune to be with MacArthur at Port Moresby and Hollandia, at Leyte and Lingayen, and later at Tokyo and on all of his trips to Korea. I cannot remember a more moving scene on even these historic occasions than when MacArthur first visited the newly freed prisoners. At Santo Tomás, Japanese artillery shells were still falling in the compound. Apparently the survivors knew he was coming, because as he stepped out of his car he was greeted by a thundering roar of cheers from every window. Inside the main building he was mobbed as more than three thousand milling, shouting, crying people tried to kiss him, embrace him, or simply touch his sleeve.

At Bilibid, where eight hundred people had somehow survived for three years on wormy corn, rice, and soybeans, scarecrow figures fought and scratched at one another to get close enough to grasp MacArthur's hand. Others threw their arms around him and had to be gently pried loose. A weeping woman held up her son for him to touch. MacArthur put his arm around the boy's shoulder, saying: "Hello, sonny. I've got a boy at home just your size."

In contrast to the pandemonium in the civilian section of Bilibid was the scene when he entered the military section of the prison. As in the other part, floors and entryways were still littered with old clothing, bottles, and tin cans, once valued belongings in prison life but now discarded. But here, instead of shrieking mobs, were lines of silent men—emaciated,

"I'm a little late, but we finally came."

unkempt, but nearly every one standing at attention beside his cot. The only sound was the occasional sniffle of a grown man who could not fight back the tears. Here was what was left of MacArthur's men of Bataan and Corregidor. As he passed slowly down the scrawny, thin column, a murmur accompanied him as each man greeted him with "You're back" or "You made it" or "God bless you." MacArthur's reply, hoarse with emotion, was: "I'm long overdue. I'm long overdue."

Near the end of the column a man in dirty long drawers and a torn undershirt hobbled forward. He introduced himself as a major who had fought at Bataan. "Awfully glad to see you, sir," he said. "Sorry I'm so unpresentable."

MacArthur stopped and shook his hand. "Major," he said, "you never looked so good to me."

The reception at the prisons was only a foretaste of the near-riot that broke out when MacArthur entered Manila. Throughout the city, streets swarmed with men, women, and children shouting "Veektory!" and *"Mabuhay!"* (Tagalog for "Hurray!"). Trying to press gifts on their liberators, but stripped of everything by the Japanese, Filipinos broke into enemy-owned stores, shops, and breweries and then went swirling through the city offering their new-found riches to every American they saw. For MacArthur this was indeed his rendezvous with history. It was the end of a four-thousand-mile road and of the dedication of his life. He had reversed the old aphorism, "They never come back." At his insistence, however, there was no formal ceremony—merely a salute to the colors and a handshake to the man, Brigadier General William C. Chase, who had led the first charge into the city. MacArthur said simply: "I'm a little late, but we finally came."

Next: Corregidor. At MacArthur's orders, General Kenney unleashed against the holdouts on this island fortress a saturation of more than four thousand tons of bombs. Then, in a spectacular demonstration of pinpoint paratroop landing, 2,065 men floated down onto the "Rock." Corregidor's six thousand defenders surrendered. There was a touch of romance as well as of drama in the way he returned to the island personally. Assembling four PT boats, he gathered every member of his staff who had originally left Corregidor with him.[1] With a smartly dressed honor guard in the foreground and the gaunt silhouettes of parachutes draped over jagged tree stumps in the background, MacArthur congratulated and

[1] That he included me, the only staff member who had not accompanied him in the departure from Corregidor, was an honor for which I shall always be grateful. For it permitted me to witness at first hand the high drama of his return.

189

decorated Colonel George Madison Jones, the youthful commander of the forces that had retaken Corregidor. Then he said: "I see that the old flagpole still stands. Have your troops hoist the colors to its peak, and let no enemy ever haul them down." He could not but pay tribute to the original defense of Bataan and Corregidor. "Bataan, with Corregidor the citadel of its integral defense," he said, "made possible all that has happened here. History, I am sure, will record it as one of the decisive battles of the world. Its long-protracted struggle enabled the Allies to gather strength. Had it not held out, Australia would have fallen, with incalculable disastrous results. Our triumphs today belong equally to that dead army. Its heroism and sacrifice have been fully acclaimed, but the great strategic results of that mighty defense are only now becoming fully apparent. It was destroyed due to its dreadful handicaps, but no army in history more fully accomplished its mission. Let no man henceforth speak of it other than as of a magnificent victory."

Within Manila itself the enemy made a desperate stand before the city could be cleared. Burning and blasting everything they could, some twenty-five hundred of them made a last-ditch fight in Intramuros, which (as its name implies) is the ancient walled city. With them, virtually as hostages, they had four thousand men, women, and children whom they refused to release. When the attack on Intramuros slowed, General Kenney asked MacArthur's permission to bomb the area to knock out enemy gun emplacements that were taking a heavy toll among our forces. Because of the Filipino civilians inside the walls, MacArthur refused. Kenney argued that, judging by previous Japanese performance, the enemy would probably kill most of the Filipinos anyway and fight to the death themselves.

War is war, and most generals undoubtedly would have agreed that Intramuros must be bombed. MacArthur's answer, however, was: "No, such a thing is unthinkable. Knock out the enemy guns by counter-battery fire. I intend to save those Filipinos." And he did. Intramuros was nearly destroyed; the Japanese defenders were completely annihilated; but more than three thousand of the hostages were saved.

This concern for the welfare and protection of the Filipinos is equally reflected in the outline of MacArthur's philosophy of civil administration of the post-war Islands, which he gave to Major General John Hilldring, director of the civil affairs of the War Department. "It is essential," he said, "in any plans for the control of civil affairs that the measure of freedom and liberty given to the Filipino people be at least comparable to that enjoyed under the commonwealth government before Japanese occupation. It would be a matter of gravest concern if instructions were imposed, whether by direct or by individual means, in excess of those existing before the war. If any impressions were created that the United States is curtailing rather than expanding liberties, the most unfortunate repercussions might be expected. The only restrictions which might be imposed are the minimum required by military necessity, and these should be removed as quickly as possible. . . . I repeat, utmost care should be taken that an imperialist policy not be introduced into the situation under the guise of military operations and necessity. . . ."

As he had promised on the steps of the capitol at Tacloban the day after the Leyte landing, MacArthur had restored constitutional government under elected representatives all through the Philippines as soon as each area was secure from enemy interference. He had continually resisted the arguments of Filipino leaders who had wanted him to suspend such action until the end of the war, declaring that only by assuming political responsibility could they regain political self-reliance. It was no surprise, therefore, when on February 27 he made his way through rubble-strewn Manila streets to Malacañan Palace for formal ceremonies to restore the full powers of constitutional government to the Filipinos' own leaders. The air that morning was still filled with the stench of decomposing, unburied dead. Once-famous buildings were now shells. Some familiar landmarks were obliterated, and one proceeded by sense of direction rather than by sight. The proud trees that had once sheltered Manila's streets were splintered trunks, gaunt under the tropical sun. Yet Malacañan itself was virtually untouched; its stained windows, elaborate carvings, and even its richly embroidered hangings and large crystal chandeliers were still there.

MacArthur entered and strode through crimson-brocaded draperies into the state reception room, bathed in the glare of photographers' floodlights. Flanked by his senior commanders and his staff, he stood before a battery of microphones which would carry his voice not only to the people of the Philippines but to all corners of the world. Facing him was President Osmeña, with his cabinet and other senior officials of the Philippine government. The atmosphere was charged with suspense and expectancy, for all present knew that they were about to witness the unusual spectacle of a soldier divesting himself of power, where other great captains of history under similar conditions had sought to assume even greater power.

For MacArthur himself, it must have been a soul-wrenching moment. Nearly every surviving figure of the Philippines was there. But what memories that palace held for him—of his father, who had lived there as

191

governor general and helped the Filipinos along the road to becoming a modern nation; of Quezon, Osmeña, Roxas, Romulo, Quirino, and so many other Filipino leaders; of governor generals who had succeeded his father —William Howard Taft, Leonard Wood, Henry Stimson, Dwight Davis, Theodore Roosevelt, Jr. Near Malacañan, MacArthur's mother had died; he had courted his wife; his son had been born. Before just such a gathering as this, MacArthur had, not so long ago, become the first and only American to be made Field Marshal of the Philippine army. Now there was not a sound in the great room as he prepared to speak.

"Mr. President," he began slowly and evenly, "more than three years have elapsed—years of bitterness, struggle, and sacrifice—since I withdrew our forces and installations from this beautiful city that, open and undefended, its churches, monuments, and cultural centers might, in accordance with the rules of warfare, be spared the violence of military ravage. The enemy would not have it so, and much that I sought to preserve has been unnecessarily destroyed by his desperate action at bay— but by these ashes he has wantonly fixed the future pattern of his own doom."

His voice broke. His bronze features blanched and whitened. For a moment he could not go on. As I watched him, struggling to retain my own composure, I thought of a remark he had once made to me while inspecting a hospital: "It kills something inside me to see these men die." I thought back, too, to the aide who had gone into his office the day Bataan fell and had seen those cheeks streaked with tears. I thought back to the evening when he had kept his generals and admirals waiting for the Lae briefing while he wrote to his son; to the picture of him standing in front of his office window, his head bowed, after he received the news of the Bataan death march; to the moment when he had stood, seemingly alone despite the men all around him, on the beach at Leyte; to the afternoon when he had walked down that column of gaunt, silent men who had been waiting for him in Bilibid Prison ever since Bataan.

In a moment of victory and monumental personal acclaim, MacArthur could see only a panorama of physical and spiritual disaster. Here was an emotion reflecting strength, not weakness—an emotion born of outrage that spiritual values had been so wantonly ravaged. Here, in deeper and more lasting significance, an emotion portrayed better than the pen of a historian or the brush of an artist the spiritual bond that had been welded over the generations of common effort between the American and Filipino peoples.

He recovered almost instantly, and his resonant voice resumed:

"I'm a little late, but we finally came."

"Then we were but a small force struggling to stem the advance of overwhelming hordes, treacherously hurled against us behind the mask of professed friendship and international good will. That struggle was not in vain. God has indeed blessed our arms. The girded and unleashed power of America, supported by our allies, turned the tide of battle in the Pacific and resulted in an unbroken series of crushing defeats of the enemy, culminating in the redemption of your soil and the liberation of your people. My country has kept the faith. . . .

"On behalf of my government I now solemnly declare, Mr. President, the full powers and responsibilities under the constitution restored to the commonwealth, whose seat is here re-established as provided by law. Your country, thus, is again at liberty to pursue its destiny to an honored position in the family of free nations. Your capital city, cruelly punished though it be, has regained its rightful place—citadel of democracy in the East."

Chapter XVIII   "Defender—Liberator"

⚑ The congratulatory messages poured into MacArthur's headquarters. From the U.S. Senate came its unanimous Resolution 75, of February 12, expressing "its thanks and gratitude to General Douglas MacArthur and his gallant men for their glorious victory in liberating the Philippines and retaking Manila, its historic capital." It was followed by a similar resolution from the U.S. House of Representatives, and by honors from Australia and other governments of the Far East.

One of the most moving of the accolades came from Douglas Southall Freeman, the late distinguished historian and authority on Lee, the other generals of the Confederacy, and Washington. Freeman reminded MacArthur that General "Stonewall" Jackson is reported to have said, in appraising Lee: "The true worth of a commander-in-chief is only tested and proved under adversity. Any commander can win when he has superior force and unlimited resources on his side, but your real captain is the one who faces desperate odds, is not destroyed, comes back to fight again, and mayhap to win, even with the odds against him." Aware of how this standard measured MacArthur as much as it did Lee or Jackson, Freeman said: "The immortal mantle of Lee and Jackson has fallen on your shoulders."

But MacArthur barely had the time to express his gratitude, because the battle still went on. The fall of Manila by no means ended the fighting on Luzon. On the contrary, MacArthur was to find some of the most stubborn resistance in the north, where General Yamashita made his last-ditch defense. Balete Pass, entrance to the Cagayan Valley, proved to be the toughest position to crack. In the south, too—in Batangas and on Bicol Peninsula—strong enemy forces still had to be overcome.

A revealing description of MacArthur's resourcefulness in Luzon was made later by the Japanese General Muto, Yamashita's chief of staff. "Based on previous concepts of tactics," Muto wrote, "the terrain features of these areas provided impregnable fortification. However, the Americans started attacking in the beginning of February and kept it up incessantly. The superior enemy bombardment and shelling gradually obliterated the jungle. Bulldozers accomplished the impossible. Tanks and artillery appeared in positions where we had thought they would never penetrate. Our front-line troops destroyed bulldozers, tanks, and artillery by valiant hand-to-hand fighting. However, the enemy advanced inch by inch, capturing this mountain, taking that hill. . . ."

It was not until June 28—four months of hard fighting after the fall of Manila—that MacArthur was able to report: "Our northern and southern columns have joined forces, securing the entire length of the Cagayan Valley, heart of northern Luzon. . . . Battered enemy remnants have been driven into rugged mountain ranges to the east and west, cut off from all sources of supply. Except for isolated operations, this closes the major phases of the Northern Luzon Campaign, one of the most savage and bitterly fought in American history. No terrain has ever presented greater logistical difficulties and none has ever provided an adversary with more naturally impregnable strongholds. . . . The entire island of Luzon, embracing 40,420 square miles and a population of 8,000,000, is now liberated. . . ."

Meanwhile, President Roosevelt had died and Harry Truman had succeeded him. President Truman now wired MacArthur: "My sincere congratulations to you and your command on the successful conclusion of the defeat of the enemy on Luzon. You have swept them from all the Philippines and redeemed the promises of the American people to the loyal Filipino people. All Americans are happy that victory has been won with the lowest possible loss of lives. I am confident the powerful base we are now fashioning in the Philippines will play its full part in the final knock-out blow against Japan and restore the world to peace, freedom and sanity."

Secretary of War Stimson sent a message that reflected his long association with the Islands: "Your announcement that all Luzon has been liberated marks the achievement of a great military success. It has been brought about with a minimum of casualties. My congratulations to you and to all officers and men in your command for this most skillful and heroic accomplishment. From my own service in the Islands and my close association with their government, I have retained a high respect and warm friendship for the Philippine people. They have suffered cruelly under the Japanese occupation. I share their rejoicing at the liberation of the main island of their Commonwealth. Your great victory hastens the day when the last of the oppressors will have cleared Philippine soil."

The official headquarters record describes how MacArthur did indeed clear the last of the oppressors from the remaining islands: "Using the elements of the 8th Army under General Eichelberger, he instituted a series of amphibian thrusts with such lightning speed that the bewildered enemy, completely surprised, was successively overwhelmed. The islands of Panay, Cebu, Mindanao and the remainder of the Visayan and Southern groups were in rapid succession reconquered, liberated and restored to civil rule.

"This done, with the same brilliant tactics but using elements of General Blamey's Australian Army, he landed in succession on the north, east and south coasts of Borneo and reclaimed this great island with its almost limitless source of oil and other supplies."

When he went ashore at Borneo on June 10, 1945, with one of the assault waves, it was even more difficult than usual to keep him away from the front. I still recall vividly the expressions on the faces of the Australian soldiers as they rested along the side of the road waiting for orders to advance, staring at MacArthur as he calmly strode by. This was right at the front, and the advance troops were not sure when they were going to move forward themselves. Along came MacArthur, with no steel helmet and no arms and looking for all the world as if he were out for a walk on the parade ground, waving his hand in friendly greeting to them as he went by and saying: "Good morning, gentlemen." Lieutenant General Sir Leslie Morshead, the corps commander accompanying Mac-Arthur, suddenly stopped, explaining that we had arrived at the front line.

MacArthur smiled. "But I see some Australian soldiers," he protested, "fully a hundred yards ahead."

"General," said Morshead, "that is only a forward patrol, and even now it is under enemy fire. You cannot go beyond this point without extreme hazard. The enemy is right in front of it."

MacArthur said quietly: "You can't fight 'em, Morshead, if you can't see 'em. Let's go forward." As he advanced, Morshead turned to me, grinned, and said in an aside: "This is the first time I have ever heard of a commander-in-chief acting as the point."[1]

Shortly we came upon the bodies of some Japanese who had just been killed. A press photographer went ahead of MacArthur to take a picture of the bodies, but as he did, he fell with a sniper's bullet in his shoulder. Still MacArthur did not turn back until after he had carefully studied the enemy lines just ahead.

[1] "Point" is the military term for the extreme forward element in an advance.

Another thing that I remember clearly about the Brunei Bay inspection was that it included the most crowded jeep ride I have ever had in my life. We were still about two miles from the beach on our way back when a jeep came alongside us and stopped, and the driver asked MacArthur if he could give him a lift. MacArthur turned and counted those of us with him; there were twelve in all. "I am afraid you can't get all of us in," he said, "but let's try." Standing by the jeep, enjoying the shoving and squeezing as we tried to jam ourselves in, MacArthur waited until the last man was aboard. Somehow we made it, whereupon he eased himself into a tiny space left in the front seat. It was a heavy load—fourteen of us, all told—and I have never doubted since that the American jeep was the most versatile piece of equipment of World War II.

Three weeks later MacArthur was on hand when the second arm of his pincers closed on the east coast of Borneo. As we approached Balikpapan, our target area, roaring fires were burning when the pre-assault bombardment had touched off the oil refineries. MacArthur had instructed that a barge be sent alongside for himself and his staff at 9:30 in the morning. When that time came and passed with no barge appearing, he sent a signal of inquiry to Admiral Barbey, the amphibious commander. The reply that came back was: "Have delayed barge as beach is under enemy mortar fire and it is not safe for the commander-in-chief to proceed." MacArthur's retort was: "Send barge at once." Within five minutes the barge was shoved off, and we proceeded to the beach, where MacArthur inspected all the front-line positions.

About half a mile inland we climbed a hill overlooking the countryside around the town of Balikpapan. As an Australian officer and MacArthur studied a map, an enemy machine gun suddenly opened fire on the hill. Bullets whined about us, spurts of dust were kicked into the air. MacArthur and the Australian officer coolly continued to study the map until finally MacArthur folded it carefully and handed it to the Australian. Pointing to another hill near by, he said: "Let's go over there and see what's going on." As we went down the hill, with bullets still slicing the leaves above us, I overheard MacArthur say: "By the way, I think it would be a good idea to have a patrol take out that machine gun before someone gets hurt."

Meanwhile, a behind-the-scenes struggle was going on in Washington's military and diplomatic circles. MacArthur knew next to nothing about it, and though it concerned his theater crucially, he was not consulted until it was too late.

To understand the situation it is necessary to go back two months to the February day when MacArthur received word that Secretary of the Navy Forrestal was flying up from Leyte and invited the Secretary to drop in at his headquarters, which were then located at Tarlac, about a hundred miles north of Manila. Forrestal arrived with Cornelius Vanderbilt Whitney (no relation to me), then a colonel in the Air Corps. The Secretary was hot, tired, and dirty after the long trip involving travel by C-47, a liaison plane, and a jeep. MacArthur postponed lunch until Forrestal could clean up and refresh himself, and turned over his private room and bath to the Secretary. The conversation at the luncheon table was interesting primarily because of the issue MacArthur took with the Navy viewpoint that it would be some eighteen months after victory in Europe before Japan could be defeated. This conversation was recorded by Cornelius Vanderbilt Whitney in a book he later published entitled *Lone and Level Sands,* from notes he made at the time.

"The conversation immediately turned to the war in the Pacific," Whitney records. "The Secretary asked whether the General thought that military operations against Japan would become more and more costly as we approached the mainland of Japan.

"To this the General replied that operations against Okinawa, Kyushu and Honshu did not present undue difficulties as long as surprise and room to maneuver could be achieved. He did not expect the Japs to risk warfare in the open but thought that they would retreat to mountain caves and fortified positions. These positions could be effectively dealt with as long as there was space to maneuver.

"From this subject, the conversation led into the probability of our forces having to invade the mainland of China. The General was opposed to this notion, feeling that the Chinese army should be equipped by us to fight and that the fighting should be done by them. The supply line on the Yangsi River, however, should be attacked by our Navy and Air Force.

"The General evinced great respect for the Japanese artillery and mortar fire and felt that these would be more dangerous the closer we got to Tokyo. At Luzon these weapons had been used to great advantage. These, coupled with desperate defense of fortified caves and hideouts, were the Jap tactics to be expected.

"The Jap Air Force had taken a terrific beating at Luzon and no longer existed as a powerful force. We must expect trouble from the suicide pilots, but the General believed that the strength of the main line enemy air force had been crushed. In addition, the Japanese were confronted with a serious loss of aviation fuel which would render large scale air operations impossible.

"And what about the war on Luzon, itself? The General predicted its termination within two weeks and saw no immediate necessity to mop up enemy pockets either here or along the route to Australia.

"The Secretary then inquired concerning the lack of Japanese air action at Tokyo and Iwo Jima. MacArthur said this was due to his having spent his air force against Leyte and because of the continuous pressure put upon him from many quarters in the past two months. Of more than one thousand planes recovered in the vicinity of Clark Field, many were found intact but with empty fuel tanks, indicating that a large air force could no longer be maintained.

" 'And do you wish to hazard a guess upon the end of the war in the Pacific?' asked Secretary Forrestal.

" 'I predict,' said MacArthur, 'that it will terminate this year.'

"I could see the evident surprise in the Secretary's face, as current Navy thinking put a far more distant date on this event.

"General MacArthur added that the great pressure being put upon the Japanese from all sides would hasten their downfall. He said that the Oriental was a formidable opponent when he was operating according to plan. But when his plan was disrupted and he had to manufacture quick moves to deal with unpredicted pressures, he would not stand up long. Panic would supplant calm. MacArthur felt that this final phase of the war had now been entered and that collapse, when it came, would be sudden and unheralded, possibly within six months. (It actually took less than six months.)

"Mr. Forrestal was visibly impressed and yet unconvinced. He asked the General whether he could quote him in Washington, to which MacArthur said he had no objection.

"Shortly after this conversation, which, I judge, lasted a good hour, we rose from the table and passed into the staff room. Farewells were spoken, and we took our departure.

"I have given you only the highlights of this remarkable conversation. I say remarkable, because here was a man in position to know, predicting an early termination of the war, contrary to all naval thinking at the time." [2]

This conviction that Japan then faced early defeat was so completely shared by members of MacArthur's staff that the possibility of a bloodless occupation was the subject of serious discussion. Indeed, between January and March of 1945 the Eighth Army staff prepared a detailed plan, complete with all annexes, for the peaceful entry into Japan without any resistance whatsoever.

[2] From *Lone and Level Sands,* by Cornelius Vanderbilt Whitney (New York: Farrar, Straus & Young; 1951).

But the conviction was not shared unanimously in Washington. The behind-the-scenes struggle over Russian participation became more and more fervent. One school of thought held with MacArthur that Japan was already on the ropes and facing imminent defeat—the other that protracted fighting was inevitable unless the Soviet opened up against Japan's Manchurian forces on her Eastern front.

The conflict reached a decisive head on April 12 when a group of senior officers of the War Department's intelligence service presented to Marshall a strongly phrased study opposing the Soviet entry and, because of his well-known view that Japan was facing imminent collapse, urging that MacArthur be brought back to discuss the matter directly before the President.

"1. The entry of Soviet Russia into the Asiatic War would be a political event of world-shaking importance, the ill effect of which would be felt for decades to come," the report stated. Then it went on: "Its military significance at this stage of the war would be relatively unimportant.

"2. Many military experts believe that the United States and Great Britain, without further help, possess the power to force unconditional surrender upon Japan or to occupy the island and mainland possessions.

"3. It may be expected that Soviet Russia will enter the Asiatic War, but at her own good time and probably only when the hard fighting stage is over.

"4. The entry of Soviet Russia into the Asiatic War at so late a moment would shorten hostilities but little, and effect only a slight saving of American lives.

"5. It is not believed any diplomatic action we can take or fail to take, or any concession we make now or in the foreseeable future, will influence Soviet Russia to speed up or retard entry into the Asiatic War.

"6. Strong enough to crush Japan ourselves, the United States should make no political or economic concession to Soviet Russia to bring about or prevent an action which she is determined to take anyway.

"7. The entry of Soviet Russia into the Asiatic War would destroy America's position in Asia quite as effectively as our position is now destroyed in Europe east of the Elbe and beyond the Adriatic.

"8. If Russia enters the Asiatic War, China will certainly lose her independence to become the Poland of Asia; Korea, the Asiatic Romania; Manchukuo, the Soviet Bulgaria. Whether more than a nominal China will exist after the impact of the Russian armies is felt is very doubtful. Chiang may well have to depart and a Chinese government may be installed in Nanking which we would have to recognize.

"9. To take a line of action which would save few lives now, and only a little time—and simultaneously destroy our ally China, would be an act of treachery that would make the Atlantic Charter and our hopes for world peace a tragic farce.

"10. Under no circumstances should we pay the Soviet Union to destroy China. This would certainly injure the material and moral position of the United States in Asia.

"11. It should be reiterated that the United States Army is by no means united in believing it wise to encourage the Soviet Union to enter the Asiatic War.

"12. The President of the United States would be well advised, before he made any commitments to Russia in Asia which would clearly have dire political and moral consequences for the United States, to consult that particular American field commander who is steeped in every phase of the Asiatic War and in the political background of that struggle."

After reciting these courageous and prophetic conclusions, the officers' group then recommended to Marshall: "General MacArthur should be summoned to Washington immediately. The President should consider the all-important matter of Soviet Russia's entry into the Asiatic War with General MacArthur eye to eye. All other political and military personages should be excluded from the conferences."

It took rare courage and devoted patriotism to sign and submit such a report to the Chief of Staff of the Army, and every officer of that senior intelligence group should look with pride and satisfaction upon their far-sighted effort, as the country should honor them for it. They did all that they could—far beyond the call of duty—to stem a course which they foresaw could lead only to disaster. Had their views prevailed and their recommendations been adopted, the country might have been spared one of the most tragic blunders in its history.

It is significant—and hardly coincidental—that on the same day this report was submitted to General Marshall, the latter wired MacArthur for his views as to future Pacific war strategy. In it he outlined the two divergent schools of thought among the Pentagon planners and almost casually made reference to Soviet Russia's future entry into the war. "One school of thought," he said, "is that much more preparation is necessary than is possible with target dates of 1 December and 1 March for the main operations (Kyushu and Honshu). Hence a campaign of air-sea blockade and bombardment should be adopted which involves a Chosan operation and perhaps others such as a lodgement on Shantung or Korea or the islands in the Tsushima Strait area. . . . The other school of thought believes in driving straight into Japan proper as soon as the forces can be mounted from the Philippines and land-based air established in the Ryukyus. . . . Russia's entry into the war would be a prerequisite to a landing in the Japanese homeland by December. . . ."

On April 20 MacArthur, in reply, strongly urged a direct attack upon Kyushu for the installation of air forces to cover a decisive assault on Honshu. Completely ignoring the qualifying reference to Soviet Russia's entry into the war, he pointed out that: "The Japanese fleet has been reduced to practical impotency. The Japanese air force has been reduced to a line of action which involves unco-ordinated, suicidal attacks against our forces, employing all types of planes including trainers. Its attrition is heavy and its power of sustained action is diminishing rapidly." Then, in reiteration of his estimate of the imminence of Japan's collapse, Mac-Arthur expressed the opinion that with the proper utilization of our resources then available in the Pacific, a target date of 1 November (thirty days earlier than Marshall had specified) would be both feasible and best calculated to avoid dangerous weather conditions.

MacArthur's astonishment over the deal made to induce Soviet Russia to enter the war against already near-defeated Japan is probably best summarized in a recent public statement by General William L. Richie, then officer in charge of the Southwest Pacific area in the Operations Division of the War Department, general staff and liaison officer between Marshall and MacArthur. Richie, who not only saw all dispatches to and from MacArthur but made frequent official visits to MacArthur's headquarters during the war, recalls only three references by MacArthur to Russia and her part in the war. "The first reference," he said, "was in the autumn of 1942. The Germans at that time were knocking at the gates of Stalingrad, and Russia appeared to be in a very bad way. General Mac-Arthur expressed the hope that the Japanese would not launch an attack on Siberia and thereby force the Russians to hold back troops to protect their flank in Asia, instead of concentrating wholly on the war in the west.

"The second reference was in the fall of 1943. General MacArthur had started his offensive against the Japanese in New Guinea. He expressed the hope that the Russians would remain enough of a military threat in the Manchurian area to prevent the Japanese from sending reinforcements from there to the battle zone in the Southwest Pacific.

"The third time Russia was referred to by General MacArthur was in August of 1945. I had gone to the Southwest Pacific theater to brief the General on the results of the Potsdam conference. The subject of Yalta came up. General MacArthur was shocked at the concessions given and kept pressing for details. Again and again he asked: 'What else? What other concessions were given?' After he fully realized that the Russians had agreed definitely to come into the war against Japan, he turned to details of participation. General MacArthur wanted to know when they would attack, where they would attack. He wanted to know what could be done to get them going as soon as possible."

On July 5, 1945, MacArthur was saddened by word of the death of Prime Minister John Curtin of Australia. His eulogy was heartfelt: "He was one of the greatest of wartime statesmen, and the preservation of Australia from invasion will be his immemorial monument. I mourn him deeply." In addition to being a great patriot who invincibly stood for total defense of Australia's soil when some believed it necessary to compromise that principle, Curtin was a wise and able administrator who, more than any other Australian, was responsible for his nation's contribution of the full measure of its resources to the pursuit of total war. The revealing end-of-war statistics showed that Australia had contributed far more in reverse lend-lease than she had ever received. During the critical last six months of 1942 she not only contributed seventy per cent of all supplies consumed by United States forces in the Southwest Pacific area, but also sent large tonnages of vitally needed supplies to the South Pacific theater as well. During the last year of the war Australia was canning for the war effort 120,000 tons of meat per year and all the vegetables the American forces consumed, and providing 18,000 locally manufactured vehicles, more than 1,000,000 pairs of shoes, more than 300,000 blankets, and hundreds of thousands of automobile tires, as well as countless other essential items. On balance, Australia was contributing more than fifteen per cent of her productive resources to maintain American forces in the field—a record unsurpassed by any other Allied nation. For this magnificent record, MacArthur credited the sterling character of the Australian people, but even more he credited the splendid qualities of wartime leadership exemplified in Prime Minister Curtin.

The character of the Australian people was best exemplified in the famous and fabulous "Aussie" soldier. On August 21, as they were about to be relieved from his command, MacArthur formally expressed the admiration he felt for the Australian soldiers, sailors, and airmen. "Since the 18th of April 1942," he said, "it has been my honor to command you in one of the bitterest struggles of recorded military history—a struggle against not only a fanatical enemy under the stimulus of early victory but the no less serious odds of seeming impenetrable barriers of nature—a struggle which saw our cause at its lowest ebb as the enemy hordes

plunged forward with almost irresistible force to the very threshold of
your homeland. There, you took your stand and with your Allies turned
the enemy advance on the Owen Stanleys and at Milne Bay in the fall of
1942, thus denying him access to Australia and otherwise shifting the
tide of battle in our favor. Thereafter at Gona, Wau, Salamaua, Lae,
Finschhafen, the Huon Peninsula, Madang, Alexishafen, Wewak, Tara-
kena, Brunei Bay and Balikpapan your irresistible and remorseless attack
continued.

"Your airmen ranged the once enemy-controlled skies and secured
complete mastery over all who dared accept your challenge—your sailors
boldly engaged the enemy wherever and whenever in contact in con-
temptuous disregard of the odds and with no thought but to close in
battle, so long as your ships remained afloat.

"These, your glorious accomplishments, filled me with pride as your
commander, honored for all time your flag, your people and your race,
and contributed immeasurably to the advancement of the sacred cause
for which we fought.

"I shall shortly relinquish this command which throughout its tenure
you have so loyally and so gallantly supported. I shall do so with a full
heart of admiration for your accomplishments and of a deep affection born
of our long comradeship-in-arms. To you of all ranks I bid farewell."

But the Philippines were where the memories were. The beach where
MacArthur had landed at Lingayen Gulf was the same beach where he
had had barbed wire spread out in 1941 in futile defense against the Japanese invasion. It was on a Luzon road that he had come across a roadside
marker saying: "Major Logan, U.S.A., was killed on this spot 1898"; Major
Logan had been an aide to MacArthur's father when Arthur MacArthur
had landed at Lingayen forty-six years before. It was in Manila at dock-
side that Douglas MacArthur had welcomed back Arthur MacArthur, his
son, and his wife, Jean, and she had looked at the sky and said: "It's so
good to see *our* planes up there again." It was at Corregidor that he had
looked through field glasses across at Bataan and seen soldiers in retreat,
this time Japanese soldiers.

North Luzon—where he had directed Wainwright to dig in and hold
the enemy back while the rest of his weary forces side-slipped into Bataan; and where Wainwright had held. Manila—where they had tried to
talk him into taking down the flag over his headquarters because it was a
target for Japanese planes, and where he had said: "Take every normal
precaution, but let's keep the flag flying." Bataan—where he had said: "I
don't want to *see* your 155's, Jim; I want to *hear* them."

And, finally, the Philippines were all his again. On August 11 he an-nounced: "The entire Philippine Islands are now liberated and the Philip-pine campaign can be regarded as virtually closed. Some minor isolated action of a guerrilla nature in the practically uninhabited mountain ranges may occasionally persist, but this great land mass of 115,600 square miles with a population of 17,000,000 is now freed of the invader.

"The enemy during the operations employed 23 divisions, all of which were practically annihilated. Our forces comprised 17 divisions. This was one of the rare instances when in a long campaign, a ground force superior in numbers was entirely destroyed by a numerically in-ferior opponent. . . . Naval and Air Forces shared equally with the ground troops in accomplishing the success of the campaign. Naval bat-tles reduced the Japanese Navy to practical impotence and the air losses running into many thousands have seriously crippled his air potential. Working in complete unison, the three services inflicted the greatest dis-aster ever sustained by Japanese arms.

"The objects of the campaign were as follows: (1) To penetrate and pierce the enemy's center so as to divide him into north and south, his homeland to the north, his captured Pacific possessions to the south. Each halt could then be enveloped and attacked in turn; (2) The acquisition of a great land, sea and air base for future operations both to the north and to the south comparable to the British Islands in its use as a base for allied operations from the West against Germany; (3) The establishment of a great strangling air and sea blockade between Japan and the con-quered possessions in the Pacific to the south so as to prevent raw ma-terials from being sent to the north and supply or reinforcements to the south; (4) The liberation of the Philippines with the consequent collapse of the enemy's imperial concept of a greater East Asia Co-Prosperity Sphere and the re-introduction of democracy in the Far East; (5) The liberation of our captured officers and men and of internees held in the Philippines; (6) A crippling blow to the Japanese Army, Navy and Air Forces. All these purposes were accomplished."

The felicitations, the congratulatory messages, and the honors that were now heaped upon MacArthur were too numerous to count. But those that moved him most, perhaps because they were the most heartfelt, were the ones from the Philippines. Before representatives of the Islands' gov-ernment, President Osmeña presented him with the Medal of Valor, similar to the United States Medal of Honor, but created for this occa-sion and so high an honor that no one, American or Filipino, has won it since.

Manuel Roxas, who was later to become first President of the Philippine Republic, said then: "To those who know him well, what is even more remarkable than his extraordinary physical courage is his moral courage. Every problem that faces him, he decides not on the basis of whether it will be popular or not, not because of its possible effect on his own future, not in response to influential pressures, but solely and simply on what he judges to be right or what he judges to be wrong. Meticulous in carrying out the directives he receives, he is fearless in his outspoken frankness of view in the discussion period preceding a final decision. Emotionally sensitive to the rights of the lowly and absolutely devoted to the welfare of his nation, he is the very embodiment of the West Point tradition of 'Duty, Honor, Country.' "

And meanwhile, before the House of Representatives in Washington, Philippine Delegate Carlos Romulo eloquently explained something of the quality in MacArthur that so long stirred the hearts of the peoples of both nations. "He is a soldier," Romulo said, "and as a soldier he is one who apparently destroyed. He has not destroyed; he has built. Through his understanding of the simple faith of the simple people, he has salvaged understanding between two worlds. You of America, is it not a matter of national pride to learn that in a section of the world where white men have lost dignity and were being trampled under the advancing juggernaut of Japanese destruction, that one American remained in the hearts of eighteen million Filipinos as an emblem of all they most admire? The gulf between Orient and Occident was cleverly widened by Japanese propaganda, but Douglas MacArthur as an individual bridged that gulf, with no sudden protestation of friendship, but with a kindly faith expressed from the beginning in a nation and its people. His sympathetic understanding of the aspirations of the people—it is that that has made him a great statesman as well as a great soldier. . . . Men like him will eventually put an end to war. To America he is the hero-strategist who held the Stars and Stripes in its prideful place in the Far East. To us in the Philippines, he is you. He is America."

Then came the most signal honor of all, which was awarded to MacArthur as he was leaving the Philippines formally to take the surrender of Japan. It consisted of the first two Joint Resolutions passed by the post-war Congress of the Philippines.

The first conferred upon him honorary citizenship in the Philippines.

The second read: "That in reverent appreciation of General Douglas MacArthur, his name be carried in perpetuity on the company rolls of the units of the Philippine Army, and at parade roll calls, when his name is called, the senior non-commissioned officer shall answer 'Present in spirit'; and during the lifetime of the General he shall be accredited with a squad of honor composed of 12 men of the Philippine army.

"That coins and postage stamps, to be determined by the President, having the likeness of General Douglas MacArthur, shall bear the inscription

'DEFENDER—LIBERATOR.'"

Part II

JAPAN

". . . Have our country's flag unfurled in Tokyo's sun and let it wave in its full glory as a symbol of hope for the oppressed and harbinger of victory for the right."

City of Tokyo—September 8, 1945

CHAPTER I   "Today the guns are silent. . . ."

✍ "Fuji—how beautiful!" General Douglas MacArthur, the newly appointed Supreme Commander for the Allied Powers in Japan, woke from a cat nap as I nudged him gently and pointed to the famous Japanese landmark, rising majestically from its cloud-shrouded base. Despite the suspense of this flight in an unarmed, unescorted plane into the heart of the enemy's homeland, MacArthur had quietly slept through the last half-hour, and I awakened him only because I knew he would not want to miss the sight of Fuji.

He had seen the mountain many times before during his long career in the Far East. From his first glimpse of Japan in 1903, when he had accompanied his father on a mission to Japan, through his many other visits and up to his last trip there with President Quezon in 1937, his admiration for the mountain's natural grandeur had never ceased. MacArthur's sensibility to great natural features of geography stemmed from his earliest boyhood on our Western frontiers. The massive, brooding ranges of the Rockies were among his first visions. The West was an "outlander" region then, not yet tamed by the plow. It had a bigness, a vastness of silence, an impregnable mysticism of almost cathedral peacefulness which had left an indelible print upon his entire life.

And he knew that Fuji symbolized Japan. His first words after taking Manila had been echoed by the entire Army: "On to Fuji." Just as we had bragged in World War I of "watering our horses in the Rhine," so twenty-five years later we had boasted we would "pitch our tents in Fuji's shadows." Now, as we were almost there, MacArthur turned to me and said: "Court, did you ever have a dream come true?"

It had been a long time coming true. After his selection for the Supreme Command, and while the fighting was still going on in the Philippines, MacArthur had already prepared his plans for the great invasion, down to the last target beach for the last regiment. But he had also believed that no such massive invasion would be necessary, that his hold upon the Philippines, by splitting Japan's island empire in two, would force the enemy to his knees. He was sure that the deadly weapon of blockade would inevitably bring this about—as it did.

The dream started becoming actuality when, after the surrender terms had been accepted, MacArthur broadcast instructions in the clear to Tokyo to send a Japanese representative empowered to speak for the Emperor, the Imperial General Headquarters, and the Japanese government to Manila to secure directions concerning the surrender ceremonies. At MacArthur's order a sixteen-man delegation flew to Ie Shima, 750 miles from the Philippines, where they were met and brought to Manila. MacArthur had told them to use the recognition letters "BATAAN" for the landing at Ie Shima. The Japanese had replied that they would prefer to use the letters "JNP." MacArthur replied: "The letters are BATAAN." They used "BATAAN."

In Manila the Japanese representatives were received with chilly formality by Chief of Staff Sutherland. They did not get so much as a glimpse of MacArthur. They were required to deposit their long swords in an anteroom and were not permitted to wear them at the conference table. When they tried to hedge by saying that they were not certain that they understood the instructions, they were firmly told that the instructions were perfectly clear and that they were to abide by them. The instructions were to repair Atsugi Airfield, to remove any armed troops from the Tokyo Bay area and to take the propellers off all the Japanese aircraft on the field. Transportation was to be provided from the field to Yokohama, and that city's New Grand Hotel was to be given over to the Allies. The actual surrender ceremonies were to be aboard the U.S. battleship *Missouri* in Tokyo Bay.

The Japanese representatives received their orders with seeming Oriental impassiveness and departed for Japan. Their only argument was a mild protest that they might not be able to repair Atsugi Airfield in the few days before the scheduled arrival of the Supreme Commander. We did not at that time know the real cause for their worry, but we found out later. Atsugi was a training-base for Kamikaze pilots, and the members of that elite corps were quartered there and in the vicinity. These suicide fighters were awaiting their final missions and many of them had already received the solemn last rites for the dead. They not only refused to surrender, but even broke into the palace grounds searching for the recording that the Emperor had made to announce the Japanese surrender. Before they were subdued, they had killed the commanding general of the Imperial Guard Division and set fire to and machine-gunned the home of Prime Minister Kantaro Suzuki. This was the kind of atmosphere into which we were heading on that fateful afternoon of August 30, 1945.

MacArthur's unarmed entry into Japan was later described by Winston Churchill as the most daring and courageous venture of the entire war. It was indeed a daring venture. Our small security force accompanied by its commander-in-chief and other senior officers entered this nation in arms and faced over 2,500,000 still uncommitted, fanatical enemy soldiers, sailors, and airmen who had been organized, trained, and armed for a final stand in defense of Japanese soil. None knew better than MacArthur the nature of the gamble. But he had accurately assessed the Japanese character in the light of the formally undertaken surrender commitments. With an intuitive understanding of the Orient gained in a half century of service there, he knew it would pay off.

MacArthur betrayed no indication of concern over what kind of reception we would have. Much of the time during our seven-hour flight he spent pacing up and down the aisle of the C-54, deep in thoughts not of immediate danger but of long-range plans for a peaceful Japan. I still recall vividly the sight of that striding figure as he puffed on his corncob pipe, stopping intermittently to dictate to me the random thoughts that crowded his mind and were destined to become the basis of the occupation. I can see now in retrospect that those terse notes I took formed the policy under which we would work and live for the next six years.

First destroy the military power. . . . Then build the structure of representative government. . . . Enfranchise the women. . . . Free the political prisoners. . . . Liberate the farmers. . . . Establish a free labor movement. . . . Encourage a free economy. . . . Abolish police oppression. . . . Develop a free and responsible press. . . . Liberalize education. . . . Decentralize the political power. . . .

Thus the occupation of Japan was sketched out as a lone figure paced the aisle of an unarmed plane bound for the homeland of an armed and sullen enemy. There is little doubt that in doing so he recalled the examples—and the errors—of which he had read and reread of Cæsar and Alexander and Napoleon and other great captains who had experienced what he was about to experience. More especially he must have pondered the lessons that his own illustrious father, General Arthur MacArthur, had taught him, lessons learned out of his father's experience as Military Governor of the Philippines during the pacification of the Islands following their liberation from Spanish rule.

PART II: JAPAN

Actually Douglas MacArthur himself was no stranger to military occupations. During World War I his division, the famous "Rainbow," had occupied the Rhine sector from south of Bonn to Koblenz. It had linked with the British at Cologne in the north, with the French at Frankfurt in the south. He had at first hand witnessed what he regarded as basic and fundamental weaknesses in military occupation: the replacing of civil by military dominance; the inevitable loss of self-respect and self-confidence by the population of occupied territory; the ever-growing ascendancy of centralized dictatorial and arbitrary power as opposed to the localized and representative system of freedom; the lowering of the spiritual and moral tone of a people controlled by foreign bayonets; the gradual deterioration in the occupying forces themselves, as the disease of power slowly infiltrated their ranks and infected the troops with the poisonous implications that occupation meant some sort of race superiority. Often in conversations around the mess table I had heard Mac-Arthur express his doubts concerning military occupations in general principle, his belief that they frequently laid the basis for future wars, and his conviction that of all military assignments that of a military governor was the most difficult. Could he, for the first time in modern history, accomplish that miraculous phenomenon: a successful occupation of a defeated nation? With such hazards as he mentally anticipated, could he succeed? His very doubts were to be his best safeguard, his fears his greatest strength.

Now the plane swung down toward Atsugi. We circled the field at little more than treetop height, and as I looked out at the field and the flat stretches of Kanto Plain, I could see numerous anti-aircraft emplacements. It was difficult not to let my mind dwell on Japan's recent performances. The war had been started without a formal declaration; nearly everywhere Japanese soldiers had refused to give up until killed; the usual laws of war had not been complied with; deadly traps had frequently been set. Here was the greatest opportunity for a final and climactic act. The anti-aircraft guns could not possibly miss at this range. Had death, the insatiable monster of the battle, passed MacArthur by on a thousand fields, only to murder him at the end? I held my breath. But, as usual, he had been right. He knew the Orient. He knew the basic Japanese character too well to have thus gambled blindly with death. He knew and trusted that national spirit of traditional chivalry called *Bushido*.

The plane nestled down on the field and MacArthur, his corncob pipe still in his mouth, got out. He paused for a second or two to look about him. The sky was a bright blue, splotched with patches of fleecy clouds. The sun beating down on the airfield made the concrete runways and apron shimmer with the heat. There were several other U.S. planes on the field, and the few armed Allied troops in the area seemed a frighteningly small force. A handful of officers waited to greet him. The senior officer was Lieutenant General Robert Eichelberger, Commander of the Advance Occupation Force (he had asked MacArthur to give him two days to make sure that the area was secure; MacArthur had given him two hours). Eichelberger now strode forward to meet MacArthur at the bottom of the steps. They shook hands and MacArthur said in a quiet voice: "Bob, this seems to be the end of the road. As they say in the movies, this is the 'pay-off.'"

In the background was a string of the most decrepit vehicles I have ever seen—the best means of transportation that the Japanese could round up for the trip into Yokohama. MacArthur climbed into an American Lincoln of uncertain vintage. The other officers and aides found their places in a ramshackle motorcade. A fire engine that resembled the Toonerville Trolley started with an explosion that made some of us jump; then it led the way as the procession headed for Yokohama. That was when I saw the first armed Japanese troops in Japan proper.

All along the roadway to Yokohama they stood in a long line, their backs to MacArthur in a gesture of respect and for his better protection. There were two divisions of them, fully armed but now serving as a security force to protect the arriving conquerors. I must say that I regarded these formidable-looking troops with a wary eye. My misgivings were not put at rest by this display because I could not help wondering whether the Japanese intended it as a gesture of deference; whether they felt that a strong guard like this was really necessary; or whether there was some other deep-seated mysterious ulterior motive.

Yokohama seemed a phantom city. Shop windows were boarded up, blinds were drawn, and many of the sidewalks were deserted. Down empty streets we were taken to the New Grand Hotel, where we would stay until MacArthur made his formal entry into Tokyo. The New Grand Hotel is a magnificent establishment, erected after its predecessor was destroyed by the earthquake of 1923, and World War II had been kinder to the second building than the earthquake had been to the first. The manager and his staff all but prostrated themselves as they greeted us and showed us to the suite selected for MacArthur. We were tired and hungry, so we lost no time in going to the dining-room, where, amid the other American officers and almost entirely surrounded by solicitous hotel officials, we were seated and served a steak dinner.

I found it difficult to resist the impulse to snatch MacArthur's plate away from him that first night and make sure that his food had not been poisoned. I realized, however, that such action by me would not be appreciated, partly because MacArthur had no such fears but mostly because they were magnificent steaks. When I did voice my misgivings to him, he merely laughed and said: "No one can live forever."

I tried that night to take the precaution of having our own troops procure some eggs for MacArthur's breakfast; there was not one to be had in the hotel. I entrusted Major General Joe Swing and his 11th Airborne Division with the mission, but it produced exactly one egg. The incident led to one of MacArthur's most popular directives. As soon as this indication of the complete exhaustion of the Japanese food resources had been confirmed, he promptly issued an order forbidding the consumption by the occupation forces of local food. The order remained in effect throughout the occupation. Thereby MacArthur rejected the long-established custom of war, by which armies in military occupations have commandeered their food requirements locally. Thus the Japanese people were given their first glimpse of MacArthur's benevolent consideration for their well-being—a consideration which was to guide his actions throughout his six-year-long administration.

On the day following our arrival in Japan, as MacArthur plunged into the myriad of details in preparation for the signing of the surrender aboard the *Missouri*, we suddenly received word that General Wainwright and Lieutenant General Sir Arthur E. Percival, British commander at Singapore, had been freed from their prison camp near Mukden and had arrived in Manila. MacArthur immediately ordered that they be flown to Japan so they could be present in a position of honor on the *Missouri* next day. It was a poignant scene that night when, as we were having dinner in a small room that had been set aside for MacArthur and his staff, an officer came in and told us that Wainwright had just arrived at the hotel.

MacArthur jumped up from his chair, saying: "Show him in at once." As he strode for the door, it opened and Wainwright slowly walked in.

He never deserved his nickname "Skinny" more than he did then. Somewhere he had procured a new uniform, but it hung in folds. He seemed to have aged twenty years. He leaned on a cane as he walked. His gaunt close-cropped head seemed too large for his body. His cheeks were sunken and his neck scrawny and leathery. He managed a weak smile as MacArthur put both arms about him, but he choked up and was unable to say anything. MacArthur could only say: "Jim . . . Jim . . ." in a hoarse whisper.

When Wainwright sat down for dinner, we discovered that all through those long years in prison camp he had harbored a deep sense of mortification because he had been compelled to surrender Corregidor. He even expressed the belief that he would never be restored to active duty. MacArthur was shocked and amazed. "Why, Jim," he said, "you can have command of a corps with me any time you want it!" Wainwright's expression as he realized that he was not disgraced was a most gratifying sight.

September 2, 1945 had been fixed for the surrender ceremony aboard the *Missouri* in Tokyo Bay. On that fateful morning the world awaited MacArthur's words with mixed feelings—Japan with her back bared for the lash, and the rest of the world with complacent expectation of violent punishment. MacArthur was on his own that morning—without guidance, standing on the quarterdeck with only God and his own conscience to guide him.

The Japanese impression of what actually occurred was recorded by Mr. Toshikazu Kase, alumnus of Amherst and Harvard and a Japanese diplomat of twenty years' service with the Foreign Office, who accompanied Foreign Minister Mamoru Shigemitsu as a member of the surrender party, and is currently Japanese Ambassador-Observer to the United Nations. It was he who prepared the formal report of the surrender delegation to the Emperor, and I later asked him to record his observations and impressions for me. This he did, and I include his description in its entirety, because of its value and interest as a former enemy's-eye-view—of both the occupation and MacArthur.[1]

"It was a surprisingly cool day for early September," he wrote. "The sky was dull gray with clouds hanging low. We left Tokyo at about five o'clock in the morning. There were nine of us, three each from the Foreign Office, and the War and Navy Departments, besides the two delegates, Shigemitsu, the Foreign Minister representing the government, and General Umedzu, the Chief of Staff of the Army representing the Supreme Command. With the two delegates leading the procession, our cars sped at full speed on the battered and bumpy road to Yokohama. Along the highway, we could see nothing but miles and miles of debris

---

[1] Mr. Kase later used his account in his book *Journey to the Missouri* (New Haven: Yale University Press; 1950).

and destruction where there had once flourished booming towns containing a great number of munitions factories. The ghastly sight of death and desolation was enough to freeze my heart. These hollow ruins, however, were perhaps a fit prelude to the poignant drama in which we were about to take part . . . for were we not sorrowing men come to seek a tomb for a fallen empire? They were also a grim reminder that a nation was snatched from an impending annihilation. For were not the scenes of havoc the atomic bomb wrought a sufficient warning? The waste of war and the ignominy of surrender were put on my mental loom and produced a strange fabric of grief and sorrow. There were few men on the road and none, probably, recognized us. Our journey was kept in utmost secrecy in order to avoid publicity lest extremists might attempt to impede us by violence.

"To begin with, there was much ado in selecting the delegates. Nobody wanted to volunteer for the odious duty. The Prime Minister, Prince Higashikuni, was the Emperor's uncle and was considered unsuitable on that account. Next choice fell on Prince Konoye, who was vice premier and the real power in the government, but he shunned the ordeal. Finally, the mission was assigned to Shigemitsu, the Foreign Minister. On accepting the imperial command to sign the surrender document as principal delegate, he confided to me what an honor he felt it, since it was the mark of the sovereign's confidence in him. Shigemitsu, who had served twice before as foreign minister—namely, in the latter period of the Tojo Cabinet and through the duration of the succeeding Koiso Cabinet—is a man of confirmed peaceful views and during his twelve months' tenure of office did his utmost to prepare for an early termination of the war. His efforts, in which I assisted him to the best of my ability, were in fact, powerfully instrumental in expediting the restoration of peace. Such being the case, there was reason to believe that, unlike others who evaded the mission, hating it as unbearably onerous, Shigemitsu regarded it as a painful but profitable task. In his mind he was determined to make this day of national mortification the starting point for a renewed pilgrimage onward toward the goal, though dim and distant, of a peaceful state. If this day marked a journey's end it must also signify a journey's beginning. Only the traveler to grief must be replaced by the traveler to glory.

"Not so with General Umedzu, who reluctantly accepted the appointment as the second delegate. As this narrative will explain later, Umedzu opposed the termination of hostilities to the last moment. He was, moreover, a soldier born to command and not to sue. When he was recommended for the mission he grew, so it is reported, pale with anger and laconically remarked that if it was forced upon him, he would instantly commit harakiri in protest. It required the Emperor's personal persuasion to make him execute the duties with good grace.

"It may now sound somewhat silly, but as precautions were then deemed necessary, the appointment of the two delegates was not intimated to the press until the last moment. The names of the nine persons who accompanied them were not published at all as the service officers were against this, though these names had been communicated to and approved by the allied authorities. Such, indeed, was the temper of the times.

"This party arrived in Yokohama in less than an hour's time. It was on this day that the spearhead of the Eighth Army landed at the same port. Sentries with gleaming bayonets were heavily guarding the streets through which we rode slowly to the port area. All the cars had removed the flags on the bonnet and officers had left their swords behind, at the office of the prefectural governor where we rested awhile. We had thus furled the banner and ungirt the sword. Diplomats without flag and soldiers without sword—sullen and silent we continued the journey till we reached the quay.

"There were four destroyers with white placards hung on the mast marked A to D. We boarded the one marked B, which was the *Landsdown,* a ship which saw much meritorious service in the battle of the Pacific. As the destroyer pushed out of the harbor, we saw in the offing lines on lines of gray warships, both heavy and light, anchored in a majestic array. This was the mighty pageant of the allied navies that so lately belched forth their crashing battle, now holding in their swift thunder and floating like calm seabirds on the subjugated waters. A spirit of gay festivity pervaded the atmosphere.

"After about an hour's cruise the destroyer stopped in full view of the battleship *Missouri,* which lay anchored some eighteen miles off the shore. The huge 45,000-tonner towered high above the rest of the proud squadron. High on the mast there fluttered in the wind the Stars and Stripes. This was the same flag that was hoisted on the White House on the fateful day of the Pearl Harbor assault. The same flag was unfurled in Casablanca, Rome, and Berlin, commemorating each time the victorious entry of the American forces. Indeed, it was this flag that has lighted the marching step of America's destiny on to shining victory. Today this flag of glory was again raised in triumph to mark the Big Day. As we approached the battleship in a motor launch, our eyes were caught by rows of sailors massed on her broadside lining the rails, a starry multitude, in their glittering uniforms of immaculate white.

"Soon the launch came alongside the battleship and we climbed its gangway, Shigemitsu leading the way, heavily limping on his cane. For he walks on a wooden leg, having had his left leg blown off by a bomb outrage in Shanghai some fifteen years ago. It was as if he negotiated each step with a groan and we, the rest of us, echoed it with a sigh. As we, eleven in all, climbed onto the veranda deck (hurricane deck as it is called in England) on the starboard side, we gathered into three short rows facing the representatives of the Allied powers across a table covered with green cloth, on which were placed the white documents of surrender. The veranda deck was animated by a motley of sparkling colors, red, gold, brown, and olive, as decorations and ribbons decked the uniforms of different cut and color worn by the Allied representatives. There were also row upon row of American admirals and generals in somber khaki; but what added to the festive gaiety of the occasion was the sight of the war correspondents who, monkeylike, hung on to every clifflike point of vantage in most precarious postures. Evidently scaffolding had been specially constructed for the convenience of the cameramen, who were working frantically on their exciting job. Then there was a gallery of spectators who seemed numberless overcrowding every bit of available space on the giant ship: on the mast, on the chimneys, on the gun turrets —on everything and everywhere. . . .

"They were all thronged, packed to suffocation, representatives, journalists, spectators, an assembly of brass, braid, and brand. As we appeared on the scene we were, I felt, being subjected to the torture of the pillory. There were a million eyes beating us in the million shafts of 'a rattling storm of arrows barbed with fire.' I felt their keenness sink into my body with a sharp physical pain. Never have I realized that the glance of glaring eyes could hurt so much.

"We waited a few minutes, standing in the public gaze like penitent boys awaiting the dreaded schoolmaster. I tried to preserve with the utmost sangfroid the dignity of defeat, but it was difficult and every minute seemed to contain ages. I looked up and saw painted on the wall nearby several miniature Rising Suns, our flag, evidently in numbers corresponding to the planes and submarines shot down or sunk by the crew of the battleship. As I tried to count these markings, tears rose in my throat and quickly gathered to the eyes, flooding them. I could hardly bear the sight now. Heroes of unwritten stories, they were young boys who defied death gaily and gallantly, manning the daily thinning ranks of the suicide corps. They were just like cherry-blossoms, emblems of our national character, all of a sudden blooming into riotous beauty and just as quickly going away. What do they see today, their spirit, the glorious thing, looking down on the scene of our surrender . . . ?"

MacArthur walked briskly from the interior of the ship and stepped to the microphones.

"We are gathered here, representative of the major warring powers," he said, "to conclude a solemn agreement whereby peace may be restored. The issues, involving divergent ideals and ideologies, have been determined on the battlefields of the world and hence are not for our discussion or debate. Nor is it for us here to meet, representing as we do a majority of the people of the earth, in a spirit of distrust, malice or hatred.

"But rather it is for us, both victors and vanquished, to rise to that higher dignity which alone befits the sacred purposes we are about to serve, committing all our people unreservedly to faithful compliance with the obligation they are here formally to assume.

"It is my earnest hope and indeed the hope of all mankind that from this solemn occasion a better world shall emerge out of the blood and carnage of the past—a world founded upon faith and understanding—a world dedicated to the dignity of man and the fulfillment of his most cherished wish—for freedom, tolerance and justice.

"The terms and conditions upon which the surrender of the Japanese Imperial Forces is here to be given and accepted are contained in the instrument of surrender now before you.

"As Supreme Commander for the Allied Powers, I announce it my firm purpose, in the tradition of the countries I represent, to proceed in the discharge of my responsibilities with justice and tolerance, while taking all necessary dispositions to insure that the terms of surrender are fully, promptly and faithfully complied with."

"In a few minutes' time," Mr. Kase's description continues, "the speech was over and the Supreme Commander invited, with a stern gesture, the Japanese delegates to sign the instrument of surrender. Shigemitsu signed first, followed by Umedzu. It was 8 minutes past 9 when MacArthur put his signature to the documents. Other representatives of the Allied Powers followed suit in the order of the United States, China, the United Kingdom, the Soviet Union, Australia, Canada, France, the Netherlands, and New Zealand. As I saw them step up to the table, one after another, I could not help wondering anew how it was that Japan, a poor country, had the temerity to wage war against the combination of so many powerful nations. Indeed, it was Japan against the whole world. We fought valiantly with the rage and fury of Satan storming the iron walls of Heaven, setting our gallant army against the numberless armies of the mighty adversaries who were an immeasurable host commanding, as they fully did, the entire resources of the world. The contest was unequal from the first. The adventure was a product of brains fired by sheer madness. Like Satan's doomed legions, we fell from Heaven through chaos headlong into Hell.

"Firm we might have stood, yet fell. On this day of judgment as we came pleading guilty to the bar, we must, I told myself, steep ourselves in immutable determination to strive hard in atonement to regain the lost Paradise.

"When all the representatives had finished signing, MacArthur stepped forward and announced slowly: 'Let us pray that peace be now restored to the world and that God will preserve it always.' He then faced our delegation and curtly said: 'These proceedings are closed.' Whereupon we withdrew, filing out in the order of our arrival.

"At that moment, the skies parted and the sun shone brightly through the layers of clouds. There was a steady drone above and now it became a deafening roar and an armada of airplanes paraded into sight, sweeping over the warships. Four hundred B-29's and 1,500 carrier planes joined in the aerial pageant in a final salute. The ceremony was over."

There remained only a message to the people in the United States, which MacArthur now broadcast from the *Missouri,* lying in Tokyo Bay.

"Today the guns are silent. A great tragedy has ended. A great victory has been won. The skies no longer rain death—the seas bear only commerce—men everywhere walk upright in the sunlight. The entire world is quietly at peace. The holy mission has been completed. And in reporting this to you, the people, I speak for the thousands of silent lips, forever stilled among the jungles and the beaches and in the deep waters of the Pacific which marked the way. I speak for the unnamed brave millions homeward bound to take up the challenge of that future which they did so much to salvage from the brink of disaster.

"As I look back on the long, tortuous trail from those grim days of Bataan and Corregidor, when an entire world lived in fear; when democracy was on the defensive everywhere; when modern civilization trembled in the balance, I thank a merciful God that He has given us the faith, the courage and the power from which to mould victory. We have known the bitterness of defeat and the exultation of triumph, and from both we have learned there can be no turning back. We must go forward to preserve in peace what we won in war.

"A new era is upon us. Even the lesson of victory itself brings with it profound concern, both for our future security and the survival of civilization. The destructiveness of the war potential, through progressive advances in scientific discovery, has in fact now reached a point which revises the traditional concept of war.

"Men since the beginning of time have sought peace. Various methods through the ages have attempted to devise an international process to prevent or settle disputes between nations. From the very start workable methods were found in so far as individual citizens were concerned, but the mechanics of an instrumentality of larger international scope have never been successful. Military alliances, balances of power, leagues of nations, all in turn failed, leaving the only path to be by way of the crucible of war. We have had our last chance. If we do not now devise some greater and more equitable system, Armageddon will be at our door. The problem basically is theological and involves a spiritual recrudescence and improvement of human character that will synchronize with our almost matchless advances in science, art, literature and all material and cultural developments of the past two thousand years. It must be of the spirit if we are to save the flesh.

"We stand in Tokyo today reminiscent of our countryman, Commodore Perry, ninety-two years ago. His purpose was to bring to Japan an era of enlightenment and progress, by lifting the veil of isolation to the friendship, trade, and commerce of the world. But alas the knowledge thereby gained of Western science was forged into an instrument of oppression and human enslavement. Freedom of expression, freedom of action, even freedom of thought were denied through suppression of liberal education, through appeal to superstition, and through the application of force. We are committed by the Potsdam Declaration of principles to see that the Japanese people are liberated from this condition of slavery. It is my purpose to implement this commitment just as rapidly as the armed forces are demobilized and other essential steps taken to neutralize the war potential.

"The energy of the Japanese race, if properly directed, will enable expansion vertically rather than horizontally. If the talents of the race are turned into constructive channels, the country can lift itself from its present deplorable state into a position of dignity.

"To the Pacific basin has come the vista of a new emancipated world. Today, freedom is on the offensive, democracy is on the march. Today,

223

in Asia as well as in Europe, unshackled peoples are tasting the full sweetness of liberty, the relief from fear.

"In the Philippines, America has evolved a model for this new free world of Asia. In the Philippines, America has demonstrated that peoples of the East and peoples of the West may walk side by side in mutual respect and with mutual benefit. The history of our sovereignty there has now the full confidence of the East.

"And so, my fellow countrymen, today I report to you that your sons and daughters have served you well and faithfully with the calm, deliberate determined fighting spirit of the American soldier and sailor based upon a tradition of historical truth as against the fanaticism of an enemy supported only by mythological fiction. Their spiritual strength and power has brought us through to victory. They are homeward bound —take care of them."

"He is a man of peace," Kase wrote. "Never has the truth of the line 'peace has her victories no less renowned than war' been more eloquently demonstrated. He is a man of light. Radiantly, the gathered rays of his magnanimous soul embrace the earth, his footsteps paving the world with light. Is it not a piece of rare good fortune, I asked myself, that a man of such caliber and character should have been designated as the Supreme Commander who will shape the destiny of Japan? In the dark hour of our despair and distress, a bright light is ushered in, in the very person of General MacArthur.

"While the destroyer sped home, I wrote down hurriedly the impressions of the surrender ceremony which Shigemitsu took to the Throne immediately after our return to the Capital, as the Emperor was anxiously waiting for his report. At the end of this report, in which I dwelt at length upon the superb address of the Supreme Commander, I raised a question whether it would have been possible for us, had we been victorious, to embrace the vanquished with a similar magnanimity. Clearly, it would have been different. Returning from the audience, Shigemitsu told me that the Emperor nodded with a sigh in agreement. Indeed, a distance 'inexpressible by numbers that have name' separates us—America from Japan. After all, we were not beaten on the battlefield by dint of superior arms. We were defeated in the spiritual contest by virtue of a nobler ideal. The real issue was moral—beyond all the powers of algebra to compute.

"The day will come when recorded time, age on age, will seem but a point in retrospect. However, happen what may in the future, this

Big Day on the *Missouri* will stand out as one of the brightest dates in history, with General MacArthur as a shining obelisk in the desert of human endeavor that marks a timeless march onward toward an enduring peace."

Such was the first Japanese impression of MacArthur as he assumed his responsibilities of government. How different was this MacArthur philosophy from the stern, even brutal course that the Japanese had been led to expect by false government propaganda! How different from the arrogance of General Homma when he took Wainwright's surrender of Corregidor! How different from what the pronouncement of a Japanese commander would have been while taking the surrender of the United States in Washington, had the fortunes of war been reversed! But the applause from the masses of the world was in contrast to the chilly reaction in London and the State Department in Washington. It was obvious that MacArthur was going to have to "sell" them on this magnanimous approach. It was far indeed from the then prevailing plan of brute force, largely conceived in hate and dedicated to vengeance.

But on the Japanese people the result was electric, immediate, and unqualified. Just as he understood them, so they understood him. His philosophy was received with eagerness and, as understanding of its full meaning increased in the Japanese mind, with growing reverence. Thus was born the New Japan.

When MacArthur put his own signature on the surrender document, he used more than one pen, writing a few letters of his signature with each. One pen he handed to Wainwright, another to Percival; their thin figures stood at attention behind him in the place of honor.

The evening before the surrender ceremonies, when I had been with MacArthur discussing last-minute details, he had asked me for the loan of my pen. I had pulled it out—a Shaeffer which I had carried with me for years—and handed it to him. Assuming that he had merely wanted it for some personal correspondence, I had not given it further thought. But now that the ceremony was over and we were back in his temporary office in Yokohama, he suddenly took the pen out of his pocket and handed it to me with the rather casual remark: "Here, Court, is your pen. I used it to write the 'Mac' in my signature to the surrender document. I used Jean's pen to write the 'Arthur.' That pen I want to keep for Arthur to have some day."

Needless to say, I was deeply pleased at this thoughtful act. The pen was thereupon retired from active service and placed in a frame bearing

MacArthur's personal certification of the part it played in that moment of history. There it will remain as a constant reminder of a thoughtful commander and a historic occasion.

On his return from the *Missouri*, MacArthur found waiting for him a message from Secretary of War Stimson: "With the full realization of our Pacific victory," it read, "I send my warmest greetings and congratulations to you who have been its principal architect. Since the dark days of Bataan, I know that you have sought defeat of Japan not only as a military but as a personal duty which has been your single compelling purpose. . . . It seems both fitting and just that this enemy whom you have mastered completely on the battlefield should receive from you the orders which will destroy all his power to force war again upon peaceful nations."

To MacArthur this was a most heartening message. The accolade from the Secretary of War, referring to MacArthur as the "principal architect" of the Pacific victory, seemed to make all those heartbreaking days and nights of World War II melt away into insignificance. He sat down and composed his reply: "I am very grateful to you for your generous and moving message. Your unflinching support in the dark days and your complete understanding of the problems of the Orient were always a source of unfailing strength and inspiration not only to me but the entire command. May God be with you always."

On September 8 MacArthur, together with Admiral Halsey and General Eichelberger and several of us from his staff, drove through the rubble-strewn devastation along the twenty-two miles from Yokohama to Tokyo. At the American Embassy an honor guard from the 1st Cavalry Division awaited him. MacArthur strode to the terrace, where a soldier stood erect at the base of the flagpole, holding the same flag that had flown in Washington on Pearl Harbor day and over the *Missouri* in Tokyo Bay. He then summed up the successes of World War II as well as the hopes for future peace as he said: "General Eichelberger, have our country's flag unfurled, and in Tokyo's sun let it wave in its full glory as a symbol of hope for the oppressed and as a harbinger of victory for the right."

Chapter II   "In their hour of agony . . ."

With the American flag flying in Tokyo's sun again and with the sounds of the bugles hardly stilled, MacArthur inspected the American Embassy, which was to be his home throughout the occupation. Although Tokyo had been hurt as badly by the firebomb raids as Yokohama, the Embassy had come through the war virtually unscathed. A hole had been blown in the roof of the chancellery and a few pieces of furniture had been ruined by water, which still stood ankle-deep on some of the floors. Wading through this slush, MacArthur turned to Admiral Halsey beside him and said in a note of banter: "Now, Bill, aren't you ashamed?" Halsey retorted at once: "Don't blame the Navy for this, General. Blame the 20th Air Force. Blame Barney over there" (pointing to General Barney Giles).

Otherwise there was comparatively little damage. The building had not been occupied since Ambassador Joseph C. Grew had left just after Pearl Harbor, and MacArthur's footsteps echoed in the sparsely furnished rooms. In one of them he came upon a large portrait of George Washington, still hanging on the wall. MacArthur strode up to the portrait and said: "General, it's been a long time, but we finally made it."

MacArthur moved into the Embassy a few days later, to be followed shortly by Arthur and Mrs. MacArthur. Soon the bomb damage was cleaned up, walls and ceilings were repainted, and gardeners restored the beautifully landscaped grounds.

Slowly the old Embassy servants returned. One by one they tiptoed in the back way, timidly but at home in their surroundings. No word had gone out yet for them to return, but evidently no word was necessary. They went up into the attic, dug into some trunks, and reappeared in the Embassy staff kimonos that they had foresightedly packed away on the day that the war had begun.

So MacArthur settled down to one of the strangest jobs in the history of civilization. In the modern world there has been nothing comparable

227

to it. The Supreme Commander for the Allied Powers was to be a benevolent dictator of 80,000,000 people and a 147,690-square-mile area for as long as it would be necessary to restore Japan to her place among the free nations of the world. MacArthur himself summarized the situation he faced as follows:

"Never in history had a nation and its people been more completely crushed than were the Japanese at the end of the struggle. They had suffered more than a military debacle, more than the destruction of their armed forces, more than the elimination of their industrial bases, more even than the occupation of their land by foreign bayonets. Their entire faith in the Japanese way of life, cherished as invincible for many centuries, perished in the agony of their total defeat. The impact of defeat was probably greater than had ever been experienced in modern history. The extraordinary feudalism which had prevailed in this isolated land had resulted in almost mythological and fanatical belief in the invincibility of its arms and the superiority of its culture.

"Although lacking in almost all indigenous basic materials, it had prospered in the past century largely because of the thrift and industry of its people. It had discovered and practiced what might be called for lack of a better term the dignity of labor—that the human race was happier when it was working and constructing than when it was idling and intriguing. As a consequence although lacking in iron, coal, metals, cotton, oil and nearly all commodity essentials, it had nevertheless become a great industrial base. By trade and barter it imported the raw materials—the wool of Australia, the cotton of America, the rubber and tin and oil of Malaya and the East Indies—and with its cheap labor and transportation supplied the markets of the millions of the coolie class throughout Asia which could not afford the more costly manufactured goods of Europe and America.

"Its basic policy and purpose over the years had been to secure the bases which supplied its manufacturing plants. It had absorbed Formosa, Korea, Manchuria and was attempting to bring north China under its control. It had prospered and poured billions of its profits into these outlying areas. Indeed one of the contributing causes of the war had been its fear of the economic sanctions of the Allies initiated by President Roosevelt. Rightly or wrongly, it felt that such a course of paralyzing its industry would lead to internal revolution. It had hoped to seize and hold the bases contributing to its industrial empire and thus insure for all time its so-called 'greater East Asia co-prosperity sphere.'

"All during the war its people had been deluded into believing they were winning. . . . Now in one dreadful moment all this was to change. Ruin and disaster such as had never been dreamed possible had engulfed them. In their hour of agony, like all human beings, they turned to their religious faiths to bolster them. But even these failed them at the crucial moment. They, too, had become so absorbed by governmental control as to be almost an integral part of the fascist hierarchy of leadership."

No proconsul, no conqueror, no generalissimo ever had more power over his subjects than MacArthur had over the people of Japan. His authority was supreme. Its source lay in the Allied reply of August 11 to Japan's qualified acceptance of the Allied surrender terms: "With regard to the Japanese government's message accepting the terms of the Potsdam proclamation but with the understanding that the said declaration does not comprise any demand which prejudices the prerogative of His Majesty as a sovereign ruler," it said, "our position is as follows: from the moment of surrender the authority of the Emperor and the Japanese government to rule the state shall be subject to the Supreme Commander for the Allied Powers who will take such steps as he deems proper to effectuate the surrender terms." Upon receipt of this reply the Japanese had capitulated.

Yet despite his unprecedented power, MacArthur faced the challenge of his life in Japan. His unrivaled military genius was no longer a major factor. This was a problem of economics, of government, of political administration, involving every facet of civil knowledge—science, culture, production, manufacture, trade, education, and theology. It was indeed a new rendezvous with history. He would have to create a different nation upon the ashes left by war's destructive violence. Into a political, economical, and spiritual vacuum he would have to bring concepts of honor and justice and compassion drawn from his own teachings. And he well knew that no modern military occupation of a conquered nation had yet been a success.

But he lost no time in setting to work. The spectacle of him laboring at this task was an enlightening one. For a normal day with MacArthur in Japan was a combination of streamlined efficiency and the warmth and relaxation of home life in the Embassy, all in a routine that he had carefully worked out over the years to fit the pace of his seven-day work week.

As soon as MacArthur rose in the morning, which was usually about seven a.m., his room was invaded amidst the shrieks of seven-year-old Arthur and the barking of three dogs. For a few minutes the room was a near bedlam while father, son, and the dogs—named Brownie, Blackie, and Yuki—chased each other about. Usually at this time of day MacArthur was still in his beloved gray dressing-gown with a large black letter "A" superimposed over his heart, the symbol of an earlier time, when he had been a star baseball and tennis player and manager of the football team.

Eight a.m. was the time for family prayers. They were led by Mrs. Phyllis Gibbons, who became Arthur's tutor after MacArthur's troops rescued her from a Manila prison camp. Mrs. Gibbons conducted the service from the Anglican Book of Common Prayer, with MacArthur reading the Bible passage. The family then sat down to breakfast, with the three dogs squatting expectantly by MacArthur's chair. Breakfast was his heartiest meal of the day. It usually consisted of fruit, cereal, eggs, toast, and coffee; lunch and dinner for MacArthur were rarely more than soup, salad, and coffee. At half past eight Arthur left for his classes with Mrs. Gibbons.

MacArthur then started his day's work in his room, reading the early morning dispatches that had been sent up to him because of their importance. Meanwhile, at my office in the Dai Ichi Building, I read through the wire-service reports, telephoning him at the Embassy, to tell him of anything important. This "important" category included, during football season, the score of the major football games every Sunday morning.

By ten thirty a.m. the black 1941 Cadillac was waiting at the door. MacArthur appeared and stepped into the car, on schedule to the minute. The sedan rolled down the tree-lined driveway at the rear of the Embassy and onto the street. At two white sentry boxes two American soldiers, in starched uniforms and mirrorlike helmets, presented arms, while across the street in front of their police box two Japanese policemen stood at rigid salute. Sitting in the back seat of the car, MacArthur returned the salutes and nodded slightly in acknowledgment of the head-bobbing greeting of the Japanese who gathered across the street from the Embassy every day to watch him come and go. His hand resting in the strap beside the window and his eyes missing nothing, he rode down the hill from the Embassy, past the tile-roofed, pink-walled Okura Museum of Chinese Art, past another Embassy gate, where he returned another salute, and down to a level stretch of road where there was usually a sandlot baseball game in progress. He always watched the game with intense interest, but the Japanese boys soon became accustomed to the regular passage of the Supreme Commander and did not interrupt their game to watch.

At the main intersection Japanese policemen always turned the traffic light to green as MacArthur approached. The car rolled swiftly past the imposing Mantetsu Apartments, the rising concrete structure of the Finance Building, the fire-bombed ruins of the Navy Ministry, and the Sakurada Gate of the Imperial Palace, along the Imperial Moat, past the sycamore trees lining the Imperial Parkway, and up to the white-stone, six-story Dai Ichi Building.

Every morning a crowd of Japanese gathered here too, just to watch MacArthur get out of his car and go up the steps. Saluting the two sentries and nodding to the silently bowing Japanese, he strode quickly across the sidewalk and into the Dai Ichi Building. An elevator whisked him to his top-floor office. It was ten forty.

The office was large, walnut-paneled, and air-conditioned, but comfortable rather than luxurious. The room was dominated by a table-like desk covered with green baize. It was a military desk top, with no gadgets, but only such utensils as a letter-opener, some pencils, an "in" basket and an "out" basket. Behind it stood a well-worn brown leather swivel chair. The rest of the room had as much of a military look, with a cadet-gray rug, two plain leather couches, some chairs and a glass-front bookcase. On a little table by one of the chairs was a personal touch—a collection of MacArthur's pipes and a small glazed bowl containing his tobacco. On the walls were portraits of Washington and Lincoln; he had brought these with him from headquarters to headquarters along his island-hopping route from Brisbane to Tokyo. Under the Lincoln portrait was this quotation:

"If I were to try to read, much less answer all the attacks made on me, this shop might as well be closed for any other business. I do the very best I know how, the very best I can, and I mean to keep doing so until the end. If the end brings me out all right, what is said against me won't amount to anything. If the end brings me out wrong, ten angels swearing I was right would make no difference."

On the desk was no telephone, because MacArthur would have none in the office; instead there was a small buzzer for summoning his aides. As he arrived in the morning, two neat stacks of business awaited him. One contained the dispatches that had come in overnight which he had not yet seen and other important documents that demanded his immediate attention. The other stack contained all mail addressed to him personally. It was never opened for him. But one of his aides slit each envelope almost all the way across, so that he could open his voluminous correspondence with a minimum waste of time.

I usually joined him immediately after his arrival. Because I was head of the government section of SCAP, all of the pressing political problems found their way into my offices, which were situated down the corridor from those of the Supreme Commander. Promptly and with no time spent on idle pleasantries, MacArthur went through his mail first. Only at one time of the year did anything take precedence; that was on Sunday mornings in the fall, when the list of football scores was studied first. Throughout the season MacArthur kept a keen eye on Army's team. Coach "Red" Blaik, who was devoted to MacArthur and whom MacArthur held in deep affection, not only reported to him by letter on every detail of the season, but also frequently consulted him on strategy and players. MacArthur could quote the height, weight, year, and playing capabilities of every member of the varsity. One Sunday in the midst of the discussion of a particularly difficult and important problem having to do with occupation policy, he suddenly looked up from his papers and said: "I see the Army started its second-string backs yesterday. That's good generalship."

MacArthur always went through his mail rapidly, handing some of the letters to me for disposition and making a separate stack of those which he would answer himself. This he usually did in longhand on a plain, lined pad, to be typed by one of the office stenographers. He has seldom dictated to a stenographer. Frequently, though, he has dictated to a staff officer like myself, and I have invariably had difficulty in keeping abreast of his flow of words. He writes as he talks, in fully composed sentences, and does practically no revising.

During these morning sessions, right after clearing the desk of the most pressing problems and seeing the members of his staff who had policy matters to discuss, MacArthur usually began a rather tight schedule of appointments. On the Japanese side he was always available to the Prime Minister, the Chief Justice, the two heads of the Diet—representing the three branches of government—and a few other Japanese on special occasions. But every day brought a variety of U.S. church leaders, businessmen, politicians, editors, and administration officials to his office. An aide usually tried to brief MacArthur ahead of time on his visitor—and never ceased to be surprised at how much MacArthur knew about the man or the subject of the visit already.

As he did during the war, MacArthur tried to limit the number of visitors, because when he did see one, he always wanted to devote as much time to the discussion as was necessary. Many a visitor who expected to find a bustling executive granting a quick, curt interview was surprised to sink into a soft leather chair and have MacArthur do the same in another, lighting his pipe as leisurely as if he had nothing to do for the rest of the day.

These meetings assumed a familiar pattern: the visitor asked a few questions and MacArthur answered them; then the visitor fell silent as MacArthur held forth on the subject of their meeting. Sometimes he would talk fluently and eloquently on the subject for as much as an hour, while his visitor listened, too entranced to interrupt. As he talked, Mac-Arthur lit and relit his pipe, shaking his matchbox for emphasis. If the caller was an old friend from Washington, Manila, or the days of the island-hopping campaign, which already seemed so long ago, the talk could go on for the rest of the morning, despite the frequent entrances of an aide to hint that the visitor had long since used up the time allotted on the appointment calendar.

MacArthur usually planned to leave for lunch at two p.m. But if, as often happened, a visitor consumed more of the morning's working time than had been planned for, he stayed at his desk until all important decisions had been made. Such was the speed with which he worked, however, that it was rarely later than half past two before he went striding down the hall to the elevator, while an aide called the Embassy to let Mrs. MacArthur know that the general was on his way. When he had luncheon guests he would try to leave by one fifteen.

By this time the crowd outside the Dai Ichi Building silently awaiting his appearance had reached into the street and lined the moat on the opposite side. As MacArthur went down the steps, two at a time, the waiting lines edged forward slightly. But the Japanese always watched MacArthur's coming and going in the same reverent silence accorded the Emperor. Two sentries stood at the building's entrance and only one or two MP's held the crowds back. Any crank could have taken a shot at MacArthur or tossed a bomb. But he refused all suggestions from his staff that he be given greater protection. The fact of the occupation itself, he pointed out, was security enough. He had an abiding faith that "the Japanese people themselves will protect me against assassination."

His belief was borne out by the behavior of the crowds; not once during these four appearances a day for six years was there a hostile incident. Indeed, one day soon after the surrender a Japanese woman tried to show her respect by prostrating herself on the sidewalk in front of him. MacArthur went to her, picked her up, gently reproved her, patted her shoulder, and walked on to his car while, for once, the quiet was broken by a murmur of approval from the crowd.

Meanwhile a luncheon guest or two had already arrived at the Embassy. They were greeted by Mrs. MacArthur, who entertained them while waiting for the general, always keeping the conversation steered

233

clear of occupation policy. The callers were received in the Embassy's big dome-ceilinged reception room, with its French period furniture, decorated with the Japanese vases, screens, and prints which Mrs. MacArthur had bought on various shopping trips around Tokyo.

The Embassy was the first of several which President Hoover had planned to have built in various capitals of the world. As an engineer, Hoover had been interested in the design and construction of these buildings, while as President he had hoped to raise U.S. prestige by the buildings' impressiveness. The Embassy in Tokyo unfortunately used up the money allocated for ministerial residences, and Congress refused to appropriate any more; the Tokyo Embassy, President Hoover himself once laughingly told MacArthur, had since been known as "Hoover's folly."

The general's entrance was always sudden and unannounced. He strode quickly past the guests to Mrs. MacArthur, whom he greeted with "Jeannie," and a kiss. Then he shook hands with his guests, calling each by name and usually recalling a personal reminiscence. With no time wasted on chitchat, he said: "Let's go to lunch. You must be hungry; I know I am." There were never any cocktails.

The official dining-room of the Embassy looked out on the lawn, pool, and gardens. It contained a long table capable of seating up to thirty guests. On the wall behind MacArthur at the head of the table was a Japanese painting of two white cranes; over Mrs. MacArthur at the foot of the table was another painting, this one of a shimmering green waterfall. Apart from the guest of honor, all guests seated themselves where they wished. There were no place cards. When George Atcheson, MacArthur's diplomatic advisor made a mild protest at the beginning of the occupation that "protocol requires that diplomatic representatives be seated in a prescribed order," MacArthur said quietly but firmly: "Not at my table, George. If any question is raised as to my informality, you merely say that is the MacArthur protocol." The luncheon itself was usually simple but ample; a typical menu would include tomato soup, baked ham, sweet potatoes, corn, asparagus, ice cream and cookies, and coffee. MacArthur, however, always ate sparingly.

The conversation around the table usually started in small groups if there were a number of guests. At the outset MacArthur listened more than he talked; but just as happened in his office, the desultory talking gradually ceased as he launched into a discourse in answer to some question from one of his guests. Chairs were pushed back, coffee cups were refilled, and cigar and cigarette smoke rose into the air as MacArthur talked on and the luncheon guests listened with the same kind of absorp-

tion that characterizes most people who listen to him for any length of
time. Sometimes it was late afternoon before MacArthur and his guests
rose at the end of their luncheon.

On such occasions as this, MacArthur returned to his office immediately after lunch. When he had no luncheon guests, he was able to
take a short nap before going back to work. By the time he was behind the
baize-covered desk, it was piled high again with the reports, documents,
and memoranda that had been processed through his chief of staff's office,
which was on one side of his own, and those of his aides, which were
on the other.

Again he went through everything rapidly. Again he read all mail
addressed to him personally, depositing those letters which obviously
came from crackpots or cranks in the wastebasket, which he referred to
as "my 120-year file." His ability to comprehend quickly the principles of
a complicated document never ceased to astonish me. By his constant
probing for information, he sought to keep himself fully informed on any
subject that might even remotely bear upon his responsibilities.

I recall how Mr. William Henry Donald of Australia, a longtime
personal adviser to Generalissimo Chiang Kai-shek, called upon Mac-
Arthur en route home from the Los Baños internment camp on Luzon at
the end of World War II. I was present during the interview. It consisted
of a series of probing questions by MacArthur into every facet of the
Chinese situation. It lasted over three hours and drew from Mr. Donald a
most complete picture of Chinese political, economic, and social conditions, with a frank estimate of the strengths and weaknesses of the leading
personalities of the times. When he had finished I accompanied Mr.
Donald out. As soon as the door had closed behind us, the seventy-five-
year-old visitor turned to me and, with an expressive mop of his forehead,
said: "Whew! I never underwent such a cross-examination in my life."

As a result of such interviews MacArthur amassed a fantastic amount
of information. I can still clearly see the startled expression on the face of
Prime Minister Yoshida when on one occasion he called on MacArthur to
inform him about a political measure he was about to take. In the course
of the discussion MacArthur demonstrated as much knowledge of the
intricacies of Japanese politics as the Prime Minister himself.

The work usually went fast, but there was always a huge amount of it.
And frequently there were more visitors to be seen during this afternoon-
evening session. The firmest rule of MacArthur's office was that no work
be put over to the following day. He had no special spot on his desk for
business he could delay attending to. His capacity for prompt decision,

whether upon problems arising in the course of military campaign or civil administration, has always been his greatest forte. When he left his office in the evening, usually by eight or nine o'clock, but many times later, all of the problems of the occupation up to that hour had been decided. The rule applied on weekends and holidays just as it did on any other day, and those of us who worked closely with him were naturally expected to match his hours. I recall one Sunday when we had been working all evening on a particularly complicated problem. As MacArthur reached his decision, he looked up from his papers and across the room at a small clock on top of the bookcase. After focusing on the papers right in front of him for so long, his eyes could not immediately adjust to the distance. "What time is it, Court?" he asked me.

"It's ten thirty, sir," I said.

He pushed back his chair, rose, and stretched. "Well," he said with a smile, "what do you say if we take the rest of the weekend off."

Regardless of the time of his arrival home, MacArthur relaxed at the end of the day by having a moving picture shown in the reception room of the Embassy, to which the members of his staff living in the Embassy compound, the Embassy servants, and even the sentries standing guard outside were always invited.

With the exception of following sports in the press accounts, MacArthur's sole hobby lay in his work. He took no time off for golf or fishing or hunting or even attending sports events. Every minute of his free time, partly because there was so little of it, was devoted to his family.

The relationship between MacArthur and his son was a particularly affectionate and understanding one. Everything possible was done to see to it that Arthur had a normal life for a young boy. He had many playmates among the children of the staff officers and the SCAP administrators, and one or two of them were house guests at the Embassy nearly every weekend. Two or three afternoons a week friends of Arthur came to play with him, and the noisy rough-housing that went on around the Embassy grounds testified to a normal upbringing for the Supreme Commander's son. (His favorite game was cops and robbers.) During these years Arthur began to show his musical talent, especially at the piano and on a zither given him for Christmas in 1948. He also showed a keen mind in his classes, though he was having a little difficulty at that time with his spelling.

MacArthur's pilot, Colonel "Tony" Story, occasionally took Arthur down to the airport to let him handle the controls of his father's plane. Once when Tony and Arthur were ice skating, Arthur fell and broke his arm. I don't think that at any time throughout World War II MacArthur looked as worried as he did when he heard about that. He had X-rays of the arm taken from every possible angle and studied them himself, and he visited the hospital three times during the first few days that Arthur was there. The confusion in the hospital upon every visit of the Supreme Commander was complete, but MacArthur could not relax until he had personally seen that his son was progressing favorably.

Arthur was early in showing signs of individuality and self-assurance. He accompanied his mother on most of her official appearances, at museum openings, local parades, and especially baseball games. In the living-room at the Embassy was a piece of furniture known as "Arthur's table," on which he kept the results of that collector's instinct which all young boys have. One item in the collection was a tiny clay Japanese pipe that he had bought on a trip to Kyoto. On his return from the trip he had presented the pipe to his father and added: "If it's too small for you, I'll put it in my collection." His father had taken the hint.

It was only with great difficulty that a normal environment could be preserved in the home of the Supreme Commander. Mrs. MacArthur did her best to maintain this atmosphere by running the Embassy as much like a home as possible, by going shopping and sightseeing like any other American wife in Tokyo, and by ignoring the excited buzz that followed her everywhere she went. And she has always managed somehow to remain unaffected by the position into which she has been forced. On the day when Emperor Hirohito made his famous first call at the Embassy, Mrs. MacArthur was talking with Colonel Roger Egeberg, MacArthur's physician, who happened to be at the Embassy at the time. I remember that when I later asked Mrs. MacArthur if she had seen the Emperor, she replied: "Oh dear, yes. Doc and I peeked at him from behind the curtains."

But while his wife and son could try to live as nearly a normal life as possible, MacArthur himself could not. He knew that if he was to rule effectively over a people long steeped in the imperial tradition, he would have to command no less respect than that accorded their Emperor. This necessitated an aloofness befitting the authority he exercised. There were many small elements that added to the impressiveness of the Supreme Commander and the Supreme Command—the tall, specially chosen, and smartly dressed sentries at the Embassy and the Dai Ichi Building; the size and refined elegance of the American Embassy; the selection of the Dai Ichi Building for headquarters (*"Dai Ichi"* is Japanese for "number one"); the black sedan that made its regular trips unescorted across Tokyo by an undeviating route; the fact that no bodyguards of any kind were considered necessary. But MacArthur carefully tempered this impressiveness with a direct simplicity in his dealings with the Japanese that appealed to them as much as a certain amount of pomp impressed them. While he knew how to make the most of the Japanese love for heroes and idols, he also knew how to win their friendship as well as their respect.

MacArthur never had any part in the fun-poking that some Americans like to indulge in at the expense of Japanese attempts at speaking and writing English. I cannot recall that he ever used the word "Jap," so despised by all Japanese, despite even the provocation of the death march of Bataan. When Japanese tried to offer him impressive and costly presents, they were politely declined. But when Japanese sent flowers to the Embassy, they were warmly accepted, because MacArther knew that in the Orient a bouquet is regarded more as a thing of beauty than as a gift alone.

MacArthur saw to it that Japanese dignity, so important in the Orient, was protected from abuse by unthinking American soldiers. Any member of the occupation force who was convicted of abusing or molesting a Japanese was subject to extremely heavy fines and punishment. Fraternization was permitted, within the bounds of decency; and throughout the occupation, Army courtesy was stressed in dealing with all Japanese. As in the unprecedented directive that U.S. soldiers provide their own food instead of living off the land, a helping hand was everywhere extended to the broken and beaten nation, which had expected the heavy boot of a vengeful conqueror.

Many were the instances of compassion and courtesy MacArthur displayed toward the Japanese people. One in particular, which seemed insignificant at the time, came to have a significant influence upon occupation relations. On the day following the establishment of his headquarters in downtown Tokyo, directly across from the Imperial Palace, MacArthur was about to enter the elevator to proceed to his sixth-floor office when a little Japanese deferentially bowed himself out. MacArthur hailed him and insisted that he return to the elevator and ride up with him.

The incident was so inconsequential that nothing was thought of it at the time, but a week later a letter written in the Japanese language appeared in MacArthur's mail. Translated, it read: "I am the humble Japanese carpenter who last week you not only permitted but insisted ride with you in the same elevator. I have reflected on this act of courtesy for a whole week, and I realize that no Japanese general ever would have done as you did." The story of this little incident went the rounds of Japan and even became subject matter for a Japanese artist. Such incidents contributed materially to the unique relationship that later developed between MacArthur and the Japanese people.

A characteristic of MacArthur's which struck a responsive cord in the inner consciousness of the Japanese mind was his complete faith that in their midst he was safe from bodily harm at the hands of any would-be assassin. He went to and from his office by himself, often not even accompanied by an aide, and refused to permit security precautions to be taken to protect him even in those rare instances when threats of assassination were received. During one brief period two jeeps were assigned to cover his trip between the Embassy and his office; but when MacArthur discovered this security precaution, he ordered, with obvious impatience, that it be discontinued at once.

The fact that MacArthur never left the beat between his headquarters office and his Embassy home (except on those occasions when he visited the Korean battlefront); that he never followed the traditional routine of visiting Japan's scenic wonders; that he never sought the obeisance of the multitude by visiting the teeming centers of population—all deeply impressed the Japanese people. As a result, MacArthur was never taken for granted, even by the people of Tokyo, whose intense interest in seeing him in the flesh did not lag from the moment of his arrival to that of his departure.

All this was strange to the Japanese people, accustomed to witnessing the pomp and splendor and extraordinary security precautions which accompanied the Emperor, and sometimes even lesser lights, when they appeared in public. Yet they did not miss the faith it reflected in the stability of their society. It has been MacArthur's unfailing faith in the peoples of Asia through fifty years of recurring crises, and theirs in him, that has fashioned the unique bond between the two. More than all else, it promoted their faith in the United States—until his abrupt removal from his commands.

Despite his deliberate aloofness, MacArthur was at all times under the closest scrutiny by the Japanese people. They saw and marveled at his capacity for work as he maintained his daily routine unbroken through the weeks and months and years of his tenure in Japan, without taking time out for a vacation or other form of relaxation. And they saw in this complete dedication to his work a good omen for the future of Japan.

As the Japanese masses began to sense the benevolent nature of MacArthur's administration and witness his resolute insistence upon just treatment for them even against the great powers he represented, the people began to ask themselves: "What manner of man is this who came to our shores as a conqueror and so soon assumed the role of our protector?" They saw in the exemplary conduct of the occupation forces the mark of his leadership. It was a spiritual leadership, for he felt a deep sense of responsibility as guardian of these people so dramatically brought under his charge. He cautioned the troops from the start that by their conduct their country would be judged—that success or failure of their mission could well rest upon their poise and self restraint. Their general conduct was exemplary, many ancient customs of the Japanese gave way before the example they set, and admiration for them was aroused in Japanese hearts.

MacArthur scrupulously avoided any action that might be construed as interference by edict with Japanese culture or custom. On the contrary, he frequently made clear in public statements that at most the Japanese people should seek a healthy blend between the best of theirs and the adaptable best of ours, pointing out that there was much that we ourselves could draw from theirs to strengthen and improve ours. When the occupation was still new, MacArthur was encouraging delegations of Japanese to go to the United States and England to study the ways of the West. But what impressed the Japanese even more was his insistence that their purpose be not solely to obtain, but rather to exchange, ideas. This of course avoided any violence to Japanese dignity and thereby encouraged the voluntary absorption of desirable ideas from the West.

In such ways did MacArthur win the respect and, more important, the affection of the Japanese people. It was because of this devoted following that he was able to write a revolutionary and warmly human new chapter of world history.

CHAPTER III   "As victors, architects of a new Japan"

It would be impossible to exaggerate the magnitude and the complexities of the task which confronted MacArthur in that autumn of 1945. Here was a nation living in the twentieth century but feudalistic in virtually every other respect. Under an ancient and entrenched political system, Japan was ruled by an Emperor claiming absolute power by divine right as a direct descendant of the Sun Goddess. His dictatorial authority was exercised through a triple oligarchy of military, bureaucratic, and economic cliques. Fundamental human rights were nonexistent. The masses of the people—the peasants, the workers, and the small shopkeepers—were exploited arbitrarily and tyrannically. Even so-called "dangerous thoughts" were crimes against the states, and were relentlessly ferreted out and ruthlessly suppressed by a secret police net that extended into every home. In a three-year period before the war this secret police, the Kempei-Tai, had arrested nearly sixty thousand people for "dangerous thinking." Japan, as MacArthur himself put it, was "something out of the pages of mythology."

And now Japan had suffered an unparalleled disaster. Never in history had a nation and its people been more completely crushed than were the Japanese at the end of World War II. Not only had official propaganda constantly led the Japanese people into thinking that they were winning the war, but it was also used to whiplash them into patriotic frenzy by depicting all the Allies and especially the Americans as bloodthirsty barbarians. MacArthur in particular was invariably described in the most bestial terms. The first official suggestion that had reached the Japanese people to indicate that the foundations of their life might crumble under them came when the Emperor, at the moment of collapse, made an unprecedented broadcast containing one of the master understatements of the century: "The war has not been going par-

ticularly to our advantage." By the end of August, when the conquering Allies entered Japan, the image of the sadistic American soldier was
still vivid in the Japanese mind.

MacArthur wiped out this image with one gesture—when he stood
on the quarterdeck of the *Missouri* and, as Japan bared her back for the
lash, offered instead the hand of compassion: ". . . *rather it is for us, both
victors and vanquished, to rise to that higher dignity which alone befits
the sacred purposes we are about to serve. . . .*" But having thereby set
the tone of the occupation, he now faced the stupendous and fantastically
complicated job of building an entirely new nation upon the rubble of
the one he had had to help destroy.

It is characteristic of MacArthur that he applied to this stupendous,
complicated task a simple rule of method. He expressed it in an announcement during the first week of the occupation: "I am not concerned with
how to keep Japan down but how to get her on her feet again."

MacArthur took every opportunity to state and restate this philosophy. He wanted all to know and all to understand that while destroying
Japan's war-making potential and exacting just penalties for past wrongs,
he sought to build a bright and secure future for the people of Japan,
founded upon conditions of realism and justice, of individual liberty and
personal dignity.

His great passion was to see all policy in the occupation pass the
acid test of conformity to those principles for which our soldiers had
fought on the battlefield. As he later put it in an address opening the
Allied Council for Japan, "as success of the Allied occupational purposes
is dependent upon leadership as well as direction, as only through the
firm application of those very principles we ourselves defended on the
battlefield, may we, as victors, become architects of a new Japan—a Japan
re-oriented to peace, security and justice—this policy shall continue to
be the aim of my administration. Were it otherwise—were we but to insure the thoroughness of Japan's defeat, then leave it prostrate in the
ashes of total collapse, history would point to a task poorly done and but
partially complete. It is equally for us now to guide its people to rededicate themselves to higher principles, ideals and purposes, to help them
rise to the full measure of new and loftier standards of social and political
morality—that they firmly may meet the challenge to future utility in the
service of mankind."

Then MacArthur glanced meaningfully at Lieutenant General Kuzma
Derevyanko, the Soviet member of the Council, who sat just before him.
"In consummation of this high purpose," he went on, "we as victors in the

administration of the vanquished, stand charged to proceed in the full unity of purpose which characterized our common effort in the war just won." MacArthur probably surmised the futility of such an appeal, since the Soviet member had no greater discretion than has any other representative abroad under the Soviet system. But he felt obligated to make it.

The same challenge that presented these many problems also provided a stimulus that pervaded the entire staff. Most of our time in those early days was spent rapidly building up the organization of executives and experts, technicians and typists—civilian as well as military—that for the next years was to be known by the name formed from its initials, SCAP. By planeload and shipload they poured in from Washington, from nearly every state and possession of the United States and from other former theaters of war. Our offices quickly filled all the floors of the Dai Ichi Building and we were forced to requisition the Forestry and other buildings. Probably never before had so complicated an organizational structure grown so fast. Yet the confusions and foul-ups were surprisingly few, and the invigorating challenge of the great task seemed to inspire an activity and spirit that reminded me of those similar early days when we had finally been on our way back to the Philippines.

The organization included New Dealers from Washington and conservative businessmen on loan from American industrial concerns, Army veterans eagerly studying the history of government, and government experts trying to learn the ways of the Army. Meanwhile experts from every field with which the occupation was concerned came to Tokyo to give advice or temporarily lend a hand. Invariably they were impressed by the crusading spirit manifested everywhere in SCAP. Throughout the occupation I was pleased to hear from visitors who had also been in Germany that among the occupation personnel in Europe there was nothing to compare with the excitement and enthusiasm in Japan.

MacArthur himself set the tone of crusade and reform only thirty-two days after the surrender, when he issued what became popularly known as his "Civil Liberties Directive." All of Japan's existing laws restricting political, civil, and religious liberties were suspended; political prisoners were released; the infamous Kempei-Tai was abolished; and, in one of the most revolutionary changes, women were permitted to vote (in order, as MacArthur put it, "to bring to Japanese politics the spiritual influence of the Japanese home"). With the same dispatch he prodded the Diet into framing a liberalized election law, whereupon he called for a general election to be held on April 10, 1946.

This would be only seven months and seven days after the surrender, and MacArthur's selection of this early date emphasized the cardinal principle of his occupation policy: in place of military government he was substituting the existing civil government of Japan. There was wide criticism in Allied capitals of MacArthur's decision to hold a general election so soon. But these critics obviously did not realize that most of the legislators with whom MacArthur would have to deal had been practically handpicked by Tojo at the height of his power in 1942. The earliest possible date for a general election was therefore all-important.

None knew better than MacArthur that it would not suffice merely to prescribe by edict a pattern for Japanese reform or even to secure observance of occupation-induced change through fear of Allied force. For any change so induced would prove so unpalatable to the Japanese people that it would endure only so long as the pressure of force was maintained. Once that was lifted, prompt repeal might be expected. MacArthur understood too that the reformation of Japanese institutions, the substitution of realism for myths and legends in the building of Japanese public policy, and a revolution in Japanese spirit and thought, all essential if Allied objectives were to be achieved, could only be accomplished upon an enduring basis if they were fully responsive to the Japanese will. Here, he realized, was the key to the success of his mission. And this realization dominated all thought and action in his administration of Japan.

It was at this point that MacArthur made one of the fundamental decisions of the occupation. The revised election law had been drafted, debated, and enacted by the Diet with no assistance or advice and only gentle urging from the Dai Ichi Building. As passed by the Diet, it contained minor imperfections that might have led to some electoral abuses. MacArthur was aware of this, but refused to demand that the imperfections be corrected. The election law, he pointed out, was basically sound and democratic. "We must scrupulously avoid interference with Japanese acts," he said, "merely in search for a degree of perfection we may not even ourselves enjoy in our own country. This law as now enacted reflects Japanese thought and Japanese initiative and as such, however imperfect, will stand impervious to the strains nationalistic pressures may later place upon it. On the other hand, should we require a change, however slight, it will assume the attaint of Allied force and become marked for possible repeal once that force is lifted."

The crux of this policy, and therefore a major reason for the success of the occupation, was the manner in which MacArthur steered his course between letting the Japanese do it and not letting the Japanese get away with it. He never let himself or his staff forget that while the Allied directive to SCAP specifically stated that "control of Japan shall be exercised through the Japanese government," it also stated in terms of unmistakable bluntness: "You will exercise your authority as you deem proper to carry out your mission. Our relations with Japan do not rest on a contractual basis, but on an unconditional surrender. Since your authority is supreme, you will not entertain any question on the part of the Japanese as to its scope."

There were times when MacArthur had to make it clear that he intended to use this authority if it became necessary. An early instance came when he issued a so-called "purge" directive designed to implement the requirement of the Potsdam Declaration that all persons who had actively engaged in militaristic and ultra-nationalistic activities prior to the war should be removed from public office and excluded from political influence. This directive involved several state ministers in the Shidehara Cabinet. Evidently misguided by the reasonableness of MacArthur's early occupation policies, all of the cabinet members decided to resign en masse as a form of protest. The Prime Minister at the time was Baron Kijuro Shidehara, who because of illness sent his Foreign Minister, Shigeru Yoshida, to announce this decision to MacArthur. He also announced the decision to the press, which proclaimed it by banner headlines before Yoshida's call.

When Yoshida requested an appointment, MacArthur granted him one immediately. The Foreign Minister arrived at seven thirty in the evening and, while MacArthur listened impassively, detailed the cabinet's plan. All of the members, he said, would hand in their resignations to the Emperor. This was the method of resignation stipulated by the then existing prewar Japanese constitution, and by the same stipulation the Emperor was empowered to select someone for the formation of a new cabinet. Mr. Yoshida explained that it was furthermore planned that the Emperor would ask Baron Shidehara to select it.

MacArthur quietly heard Yoshida and then fixed him with a cold glance as he said: "Mr. Minister, I have the highest regard for Baron Shidehara, and I know of no one better qualified to carry out the terms of my directive, but if the cabinet resigns en masse tomorrow it can only be interpreted by the Japanese people to mean that it is unable to implement my directive. Thereafter Baron Shidehara may be acceptable to the Emperor for reappointment as Prime Minister, but he will not be acceptable to me."

The moment of silence that followed was an impressive one. Mr. Yoshida rose, bowing politely as he said that he would transmit the Supreme Commander's message to Baron Shidehara. I left MacArthur's office with him and accompanied him to the elevator. Although Mr. Yoshida understands English perfectly, I asked him, by way of making conversation: "You understand what the Supreme Commander said, do you not, Mr. Minister?"

"Mr. Yoshida looked at me significantly as the elevator door opened. "Too well," he said. "Too well."

The cabinet did not resign, with the exception of the members who had been disqualified by MacArthur's directive. But despite this warning from the Supreme Commander that he would not hesitate to use his authority when it was necessary, some of the Japanese politicians then in power still seemed to hope that they could successfully resist reform measures. They refined their peculiar type of polite political warfare to an art during the early days of the occupation. And the area in which a few Japanese political leaders evidently elected to force a showdown with the occupation authorities was in the discussions concerning the Japanese constitution.

Basic to MacArthur's reorientation of Japan was of course the need for a revision of the existing constitution. As the source of all law, it should not only encourage but make mandatory the growth of representative government. The existing (Meiji) constitution provided that the Emperor, as absolute sovereign, was the source of all political power and legal authority, with the administration of government conducted in his name by virtue of limited delegations. Thus the Japanese existed as an extremely regimented and exploited people governed by a hereditary dictatorship. That the concept of individual liberty was unknown to the people, who enjoyed the protection of no Bill of Rights, rendered the problem of revision less sensitive than otherwise it would have been. The masses of the people had everything to gain and nothing to lose.

MacArthur sensed the need to move swiftly toward the accomplishment of this all-important objective. For, to his astonishment, U.S. State Department thinking on the subject was reflected in his initial postwar directive from Washington; it provided that ". . . changes in the direction of modifying the feudal and authoritarian tendencies of the government are to be permitted and favored. In the event that the effectuation of such changes involves the use of force by the Japanese people or government against persons opposed thereto, you as Supreme Commander should intervene only where necessary to ensure the security of your forces. . . ." I recall vividly MacArthur's shock at reading this statement, which clearly implied that he was to stand passively by in the face of civil war in this already ruined nation. When shortly thereafter the State Department, at the Big Three foreign ministers' meeting in Moscow in December of 1945, surrendered the unilateral authority we were then excercising over Japan to an eleven-nation policy-making commission and gave the Soviet Union veto power over all policy incident to Japan, MacArthur realized the urgency of immediate action under the powers he then held.

I tell the story of our attempts to revise the constitution in detail because I think that besides the illustration it gives of the dedicated enthusiasm of the SCAP officers and besides its touches of humor, the account provides a dramatic example of MacArthur's policy in action. It may also make an interesting rejoinder to those who have heretofore considered the occupation as a fortuitous circumstance in which an all-powerful conqueror was able to impose his will upon a completely submissive, unquestioning government.

From the first meetings between MacArthur and successive Japanese prime ministers following the surrender, the Supreme Commander made it clear that the antiquated, restrictive and feudalistic constitution left over from the Meiji reign would have to be completely revised. He pointed out that only thereby might be built a firm foundation upon which a democratic society might safely rest. Always the Japanese Prime Minister would smile and agree politely; but always, upon later questioning, MacArthur would find that nothing had been done about it.

There were innumerable reasons for the delay, a favorite one being that there must have been some misunderstanding because Minister So-and-So had received an entirely different impression from some other SCAP member. But the most popular excuse was the one of a "difference in interpretation." MacArthur was determined that we would not force an American-written constitution down Japanese throats, so he continued, quietly but firmly to prod the Japanese into positive action.

In October 1945, a committee of Japanese political leaders was formed to draft the proposed revisions. It was established by Prime Minister Shidehara, given the title of the Constitutional Problem Investigation Committee and placed under the chairmanship of Dr. Joji Matsumoto, a state minister-without-portfolio. When its members sat down to work, they were bombarded with advice by the Japanese people. With no censorship, and in fact at MacArthur's urging, the constitution was debated at great length in the press of Japan, and every political party, including the Communist Party, advanced its own suggested revisions.

For three months, while SCAP staff members and MacArthur himself continued to remind Matsumoto and his colleagues of the need for speed,

247

the Constitutional Problem Investigation Committee worked on its draft of recommendations.

There evidently was a schism in the committee between the advocates of a conservative and those of a more liberalized constitution, but the committee in general was dominated by the wishes of Dr. Matsumoto, who was an extreme conservative. Finally, by the end of January, the committee unofficially presented SCAP headquarters with two documents, one entitled "Gist of the Revision of the Constitution" and the other "General Explanation of the Constitutional Revision drafted by the Government"; no formal submission of recommendations was ever made.

I had at that time recently taken on the duties of Chief of the Government Section, charged with the staff responsibility for the reorganization of the Japanese government and necessary revision of Japanese law. I of course passed both the "Gist" and the "Explanation" on to the members of my staff for their study, and it did not take them long to discover that the two documents recommended little more than word-changing of the old Meiji Constitution. For example, the emperor system was retained intact; the Emperor would by the proposed change become "supreme and inviolable" rather than "sacred and inviolable," and his power to rule the country as he had before was virtually unchanged. As for the "Bill of Rights" chapter of the constitution, the Matsumoto draft, far from increasing the rights of the people, seemed to reduce them. All were made subordinate to ordinary statutory law, for every constitutional grant was followed by the limitation "except as otherwise provided by law." Almost all of the other proposals for revision of the Matsumoto committee were so weak as to be of no importance, and in general would leave the constitution as flexible and open to repressive interpretation by the ruling classes as the Meiji Constitution had been. We could see at a glance that the proposed revisions amounted to no revision at all.

Meanwhile an appointment had been made for Foreign Minister Yoshida and me to discuss the Matsumoto draft on February 5. On February 2 a representative of the Foreign Office asked for a postponement of the conference. I suggested a postponement for one week. And this week was put to good use, for on February 3 MacArthur decided that the Japanese shilly-shallying had gone on long enough. The first general elections were only two months away, and he was determined that a presentable draft of revisions would be finished so that those elections would also constitute an unofficial plebiscite. If the Japanese continued to hedge and delay as they had for almost four months, the people would have no choice but to vote for or against what was nearly a carbon copy of the old Meiji Constitution.

Apparently the only way to make unmistakably clear to the Matsumoto committee that their recommendations were unacceptably reactionary was to prepare a draft of our own which could be used as the basis for future negotiations. When MacArthur came to his Dai Ichi Building office on the morning of February 3, he instructed me to have this done. I was to have full latitude in the initiation of the work except for the following prescriptions: (a) the emperor system would be preserved, though modified to bring it within constitutional limitations and subject to the ultimate will of the people; (b) war and war-making would be forsworn—a concept that had been proposed to MacArthur by Prime Minister Shidehara (about which more later); and (c) all forms of feudalism would be abolished.

With these instructions the government section set out to prepare a draft for consideration by the Japanese. I immediately appointed a steering committee led by my deputy, a brilliant officer, Colonel Charles L. Kades, and composed of two other members, Lieutenant Colonel Milo E. Rowell and Commander Alfred R. Hussey. All three were lawyers of distinction. With a willing, hard-working staff of assistants, they embarked on the momentous project.

Whereas the governments of nearly all the countries in the world had been built on years of tradition, articles, amendments, repeals, and the trial and error of experience, we were free to use the best of all these constitutions and discard the worst—and without the slightest necessity for playing partisan politics. While our final draft would consist of principles for a revised constitution and be so labeled, the only practical method of drawing up these principles was to do it in the form of an actual constitution.

For six days all other business of the section gave way to this project. The assistants to the members of the steering committee were split into groups of experts on the various subjects with which the constitution would concern itself. Lieutenant Colonel Frank Hays, for example, an able lawyer of long practice, worked out the section on the Diet; Commander Guy Swope, an accountant and government student and formerly a member of Congress and Governor of Puerto Rico, specialized on the cabinet section; the budget section was drafted by Major Frank Rizzo, an extraordinarily able engineer-turned-economist who became my successor after my departure from Japan. These specialists and others, with their assistants, drew up their proposals for a revised constitution and presented them to the steering committee members, who, article by article, prepared the final recommendations for constitutional reform.[1]

Our spirits were high. We worked with the enthusiasm natural to the challenge of our task, but also with a kind of dedication which came from the experience we had all so recently been through as combat officers. Everywhere we had seen the destruction and bloody death of war. Here was an opportunity to help an entire nation throw off the virus of militarism that had led to war.

We had arbitrarily set February 12, Lincoln's Birthday, for our deadline, and we made it. The draft had been approved by MacArthur with only one significant change, and mimeographed copies had been prepared for us to present to the Japanese committee members. Our meeting was to be at the home of Foreign Minister Yoshida, and we were met at his residence with low bows and smiles of apprehension. We were polite, but not cordial, businesslike but not brusque. We asked if our hosts could understand our English if we spoke slowly and clearly; and when they replied that they could, we requested that no interpreters be used, thereby reducing the opportunities for "misunderstanding."

While observing the amenities, I minced no words in informing the Japanese representatives that the Supreme Commander had found their proposals unacceptable. The Matsumoto draft, I said, fell far short of the broad and liberal reorganization of the Japanese governmental structure along democratic lines which the Allied Powers could regard as significant evidence that Japan had learned the lessons of war and defeat and was prepared to act as a responsible member of a peaceful community. I told them that the Supreme Commander had caused to be prepared a detailed statement of the principles he deemed basic and that we were presenting the statement to the Japanese government in the form of a draft constitution. I advised the committee to give this statement the fullest consideration and proposed that it be used as the guide in renewed efforts to prepare a revised constitution.

Then I took a chance. With no prior authorization from MacArthur, I told the Japanese that while there was no compulsion upon them to take further action, the Supreme Commander was determined that the constitutional issue should be brought before the people well in advance of the general election. He felt, I explained, that they should have full op-

---

[1] The major proposals and the discussions concerning them appear in Section III, Chapter V, of the official report entitled *Political Reorientation of Japan* (Government Printing Office).

portunity to discuss and freely express their will on constitutional reform. Therefore, I said, if the cabinet were unable to prepare a suitable and acceptable draft before the elections, General MacArthur was prepared to lay this statement of principle directly before the people.

The effect of this statement upon the Japanese representatives was immediately visible. Mr. Shirasu straightened up as if he had sat on something. Dr. Matsumoto sucked in his breath. Mr. Yoshida's face was a black cloud. I broke the ensuing silence by suggesting that the Japanese read our statement of principles here and now, adding that we would be glad to wait while they did so.

Mr. Jiro Shirasu, who lived with Mr. Yoshida, already appeared quite distraught as he ushered us to another section of the beautifully landscaped grounds that are part of the Foreign Minister's residence. There we sat down to wait. It was a clear and sunny day, and we enjoyed the beauty and serenity of Mr. Yoshida's garden as we talked among ourselves and waited. At the end of about an hour, I decided that we should rejoin our hosts, and we were rising as Mr. Shirasu reappeared.

He seemed flustered by the drastic changes in our draft, and it occurred to me that this was an opportune moment to employ one more psychological shaft. I did not know the impressive support that I was about to receive from an unexpected quarter.

As he mumbled apologies for keeping us waiting, I replied with a smile: "Not at all, Mr. Shirasu. We have been enjoying your atomic sunshine."

And at that moment, with what could not have been better timing, a big B-29 came roaring over us. The reaction upon Mr. Shirasu was indescribable, but profound.

When we seated ourselves across the patio from the committee members again, I could see that Mr. Shirasu's colleagues were as upset by our proposals as he was. I realized that, accustomed as they had been all their lives to ordering the affairs of their country pretty much their own way, they were finding it extremely difficult to be elastic, even though they must have known by now that they were impeding the progress of their country toward democracy.

By the time we had left Mr. Yoshida's residence shortly thereafter, we were fairly convinced that our proposed draft would be accepted as the basis for the revised constitution. But my gratification at this was tempered by the realization that I had committed MacArthur to a political maneuver which he might consider rash.

I had every reason to believe that my gamble would pay off, that the

Japanese committee members would not dare to let our statement of principles appear before the public as a draft that they opposed. Nevertheless, I did not wait to see what the results would be before reporting my action to MacArthur.

But I had known him long enough so that I should have realized what his answer would be. When I explained to him that he might well find himself out on a limb, that I had put him there and that he was free to repudiate my action before it was too late, he looked at me in shocked reproof. "Court," he said, "don't you know that I have never repudiated any action taken for me by a member of my staff? Right or wrong, whether I like it or not, I accept the situation as it stands and determine my next move from there." Nothing more was said on the subject.

Shortly thereafter I received the following letter from Mr. Shirasu, in which he said in part:

> . . . I venture to write you . . . my impressions about the way your draft was received by Dr. Matsumoto and others in the Cabinet.
>
> . . . Your draft came as a great surprise. He [Dr. Matsumoto] realizes that the object of your draft and his "revision" is one and the same in spirit. He is as anxious as you are, if not more, as after all this is his country, that his country should be placed on a constitutional and democratic basis for all as he has always deplored the unconstitutionality of the nation. He and his colleagues feel that yours and theirs aim at the same destination but that there is this great difference in the routes chosen. Your way is so American in the way that is straight and direct. Their way must be Japanese in the way that is roundabout, twisted and narrow. Your way may be called an Airway and their way a Jeep way over bumpy roads.
>
> He illustrated his point by the following drawing:

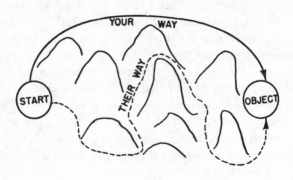

"As victors, architects of a new Japan"

I think I appreciate your standpoint well, [Mr. Shirasu continued] and I must confess I have a great admiration for it as I have for so many things American. I still am an ardent admirer of Lindberg's flight across the "uncharted" Atlantic for the first time and unaided. But alas! Lindbergs are so rare and far between even in America. I do not know if we ever had one in this country. . . .

I am afraid that I have already accelerated the paper shortage by writing this mumble but I know you will forgive me for my shortcomings for which my late father is also partly responsible.

Most sincerely yours,
JIRO SHIRASU

Three days later, on February 18, Dr. Matsumoto submitted what he called a "Supplementary Explanation concerning the Constitutional Revision." In it he suggested that "a juridical system is very much like certain kinds of plants, which transplanted from their native soil degenerate or even die. Some of the roses of the West, when cultivated in Japan, lose their fragrance." Dr. Matsumoto's argument continued that no reform or democratization of the government could succeed unless the people understood and accepted their responsibilities and that, therefore, no such democratization or reorganization was practicable or advisable, since the Japanese people had not changed. I noticed that he did not, however, mention my suggestion that our statement of principles be put before the people so that they could themselves decide.

A split quickly developed in the cabinet, with Foreign Minister Yoshida and Dr. Matsumoto standing pat against our suggested reforms and Prime Minister Shidehara advocating that they be accepted. An appointment had been scheduled for the Japanese representatives to meet with me on February 18 and inform me whether they had accepted our draft as the basis, but again I was asked for a postponement of forty-eight hours. I was somewhat appalled at their reason for requesting the delay: they had not even had our draft translated yet. But I decided to give them more than they asked for, and so told them that I would meet with them on February 22, Washington's Birthday.

On the morning of the 22nd, as the cabinet members entered my office, Dr. Matsumoto made an obvious last attempt to keep his draft as the basis for revisions. He opened the conference by saying: "We have accepted the ideas set forth in the draft of the new constitution [our proposal] but we are not sure that it presents a workable form." With that, after some further discussion, led largely by Prime Minister Shide-

253

hara, the latter said that they were prepared to present the draft to the Emperor. They presented it that afternoon. I learned later that to their utter astonishment the Emperor at once commanded that the draft be the basis for revision of the constitution, saying that "upon these principles will truly rest the welfare of our people and the rebuilding of Japan." This was his command, despite the fact that those very principles deprived the Emperor of all future political power, and caused the bulk of the property of the Imperial family to revert to the state.

On March 4 a new draft was handed to us for review. It had been patterned on the statement of principles which we had given the Japanese, and in general seemed acceptable.

But this document was in Japanese, and I could foresee more and more delays, as we translated it into English and then translated back into Japanese any suggestions we might have, and so on and on ad infinitum. The time fixed for the general elections was now but five weeks off. Time was therefore of the essence if the electorate was to be able to discuss the revision of the constitution in general principle.

The only solution seemed to be for the members of the steering committee, some translators, and the Japanese representatives to go into conference immediately and continue working without adjournment until a revised constitution had been agreed upon by both sides.

This we did. The new draft was taken up article by article. First the article was translated into English. The members of the steering committee then approved of it or explained why they did not approve. The discussion of the article continued until agreement was finally reached. Then the article, in its revised form, was translated back into Japanese. And then came a further complication, occasioned by the complexities of meanings of words in Japanese and English. The revised article in Japanese would have to be translated into English a second time, as a double-check to make sure that its exact meaning had not been lost or even obscured in the translation from English to Japanese. Only rarely did the phraseology come out of the Japanese exactly the same as it went in.

The session lasted all through the day, all that evening, all through that night, through the following morning, and until late in the afternoon. After half an hour on the first day, Dr. Matsumoto, the eldest member of the Japanese party by many years, asked to be excused. He returned home, and as each article of the draft was agreed upon, a copy went to him by special messenger for his approval. Promptly he approved them all. Meanwhile copies of each article were brought to me and to MacArthur; I stayed at my office in touch with the negotiators during the entire time, and I was in constant communication with MacArthur on points where the negotiators found difficulty in reaching agreement.

As the hours went by, coffee was brought into the conference room in five-gallon GI gasoline cans and K-rations were provided in place of lunch, dinner, breakfast, and the following lunch. The Japanese representatives, to whom this form of negotiation was unknown, showed signs of weariness; and so did our own steering committee members, for that matter. The plan, however, was working, and by midafternoon of the 5th all but a few sticky points had been cleared up. Thereupon the negotiators convened with me and we reached agreement even on those final principles.

By five thirty p.m. on March 5, MacArthur had been over the revised constitution and had approved it. By the next morning the cabinet had approved it too, and within a few hours MacArthur made this announcement:

"It is with a sense of deep satisfaction that I am today able to announce a decision of the Emperor and the government of Japan to submit to the Japanese people a new and enlightened constitution which has my full approval.

"The Japanese people thus turn their backs firmly upon the mysticism and unreality of the past and face instead a future of realism with a new faith and a new hope."

The approved draft of the constitution was publicized to the fullest extent. It was discussed everywhere, and refinements were offered from every quarter. But the Japanese people approved its principles overwhelmingly, as did the heads of every political party except the Communists. Throughout April the Japanese government carried out a program of education on the subject. A Society for the Popularization of the New Constitution was formed. With a special paper priority granted by SCAP, the society delivered a copy of the constitution to every Japanese home. Thus the April elections were an unofficial plebiscite on the revised constitution and, as MacArthur had foreseen, its strongest backers won the greatest public support.

After the elections the new constitution was presented to the Diet, where it received free and open debate all through the summer. The House of Representatives adopted it, with the basic principles intact but with many changes in form, in August. The House of Peers debated it for another month. And it was at length approved by both houses. November 3, the birthday of the Emperor Meiji, was fixed as the promulgation date, and the new constitution of Japan became effective six months thereafter. No constitution in history, including that of the United States, received such full and open debate before its adoption. In connection with this legislative action on the bill, I believe it is of interest to note that whereas the bill as submitted to the Diet provided for the gradual elimination of the peerage by the passing into extinction of all patents of nobility upon the death of those holding them, the Diet insisted that the corresponding titles, except those in the Imperial family, be revoked upon the effective date of the new constitution.

Though a new constitution, it was adopted as an amendment to the former one—at MacArthur's personal suggestion, in order to maintain the constitution's legal continuity. It is probably the most liberal constitution in history. It borrows freely from the constitutions of many lands. It divests the Emperor of all political power, leaving him as a constitutional monarch to serve as "the symbol of the state and unity of the people." It proclaims the popularly elected Diet as the highest organ of state power. It confers an enlightened bill of rights upon the people and provides adequate safeguards for their protection in the enjoyment of these rights. It separates the executive, legislative, and judicial branches of the government, directing each branch to co-ordinate with the others. It severs the long-established control of the ministry of justice over the courts; it grants to the courts, with the supreme court as their highest organ, the power to establish their own rules of judicial procedure within limits provided by law and to recommend directly to the national Diet their own budgetary requirements.

It provides for a central government based partially on the presidential system of the United States and partially upon the parliamentary system. Under its rules the prime minister is chief executive and is elected by the House of Representatives from among its membership for a term of four years. And here the new constitution has a provision of particular interest: should the house adopt a vote of nonconfidence in the government, or should it fail to adopt a vote of confidence proposed by the government, the prime minister has ten days in which to elect whether to resign and permit the House to elect his successor, *or dissolve the House of Representatives and call a new general election.* This provision has made for stability in the Japanese government, protecting it against capricious legislative action by members of the House who might find themselves forced to stand the expense of a new election.

Not only was the new constitution debated freely in the Diet for more than three months, but provision was also made for its amendment by a two-thirds vote of the people at a general election or a special referendum, thus making the Japanese people themselves the final judges and the ultimate protectors of their own liberties. Perhaps the most eloquent testimony to the popularity of the revised constitution is the fact that some of the very ministers who had been so shocked by our original draft were, by the time MacArthur left Japan, vying with each other for the credit of its adoption.

Had MacArthur not moved directly to solve the constitutional problem, Japan would undoubtedly have drifted aimlessly for years under the strictures and limitations of its old constitution, because of the inertia of the Far Eastern Commission sitting under the veto-power threat of the Soviet Union. Thus by timely action this threat was avoided, as was the threat to accomplish by bloodshed what, as MacArthur demonstrated, required only positive leadership to accomplish by peaceful means.

Yet critics from both extreme fringes—those who because of close ties with Japan's old order see nothing but evil from change of any kind and those pseudo-liberals who entertain the no less strange conviction that the basic character of political institutions may be permanently altered only by uprising of the masses—still occasionally assail the new constitution as a doubtful thing imposed upon the Japanese people by duress and force. While they do so, however, they carefully avoid attacking the instrument on its merit. They seemingly recognize that it is in fact the most liberal yet practical constitution of all time, embodying as it does the lessons from actual experience with human freedom through the ages.

One further and important point about the new Japanese constitution concerns the charge which has frequently been made, even by individuals and periodicals that should be better informed, that the famous "no war" clause was forced upon the government by MacArthur's personal fiat. The following facts will, I hope, finally answer and silence that charge.

Long before any thought had been given in the government section to writing down suggested principles for revising the constitution, the then Prime Minister Shidehara asked me for an appointment with the Supreme Commander in order to thank him for making penicillin available to him, which had miraculously cured his illness. This was at the time when Dr. Matsumoto's Constitutional Problem Investigation Committee was only just beginning to debate its draft, and SCAP officers were doing nothing more than making polite, periodic inquiries into the progress of the Matsumoto committee's deliberations.

The requested appointment was granted to Prime Minister Shidehara, and on his arrival at noon on January 24, 1946, I personally escorted him into MacArthur's office. I did not remain in the office, and so was not present during the discussion that followed. But I did go in to see Mac-Arthur immediately after Shidehara's departure at two thirty, and the contrast between the expressions on MacArthur's face before and after the interview told me immediately that something of importance had happened.

MacArthur explained what it was: Prime Minister Shidehara, after expressing his thanks for the penicillin, had proposed that when the new constitution was drafted, it contain an article renouncing war and the maintenance of a military establishment once and for all. By this means, Shidehara had said, Japan could safeguard itself against the re-emergence of militarism and police terrorism and at the same time offer convincing proof even to the most skeptic of the free world that Japan intended to pursue a future course of pacifism. Shidehara further pointed out that only if relieved from the oppressive burden of military expenditures could Japan have the slightest chance of providing the minimum necessities for its expanding population, now that all its overseas resources were gone. It was this that they had discussed for two and one-half hours. Shidehara's private secretary, Mr. Kuramatsu Kishi, has since thrown further light on Shidehara's views by stating that he had held them for a long time before communicating with MacArthur.

MacArthur could not have agreed more. For years it has been his burning passion to see war abolished as an outmoded means of resolving disputes between nations. Probably no living man has seen as much of war and its destruction as he. A veteran of twenty campaigns, a participant or observer in six wars, the survivor of a thousand battlefields, he has fought with or against the soldiers of practically every country of the world, and his abhorrence of war naturally reached its height with the perfection of the atomic bomb.

MacArthur's personal thoughts on the subject of war and how to outlaw it have become well known. It was because of his deep convictions on the subject of war that he was so delighted at Prime Minister Shidehara's suggestion. And when he instructed me to proceed with the preparation of a draft constitution, he admonished that it must include this principle: "War as a sovereign right of the nation is abolished. . . ." The principle was included in the draft prepared by the SCAP steering committee. And in the month-long discussions of the revisions between SCAP and the Matsumoto committee members, it was the war article alone that was never once objected to in any form by the Japanese.

It is now Article 9 of Chapter 11. It provides: "Aspiring sincerely to an international peace based on justice and order, the Japanese people forever renounce war as a sovereign right of the nation and the threat or use of force as means of settling international disputes. In order to accomplish the aim of the preceding paragraph, land, sea, and air forces, as well as other war potential, will never be maintained. The right of belligerency of the state will not be recognized."

MacArthur has always given his fullest support to this article of the constitution, and has defended it vigorously against the sniping attacks of cynics. For from a practical standpoint it pursued through Japanese initiative, rather than Allied compulsion, a course that was basic to Allied policy, first enunciated at Potsdam and thereafter specifically directed by the Allied powers as a primary objective of the occupation.

Upon his entry into Japan, MacArthur's basic directive required that Japan be at once disarmed and demilitarized. The directive stemmed from the Potsdam declaration that ". . . until there is convincing proof that Japan's war-making power is destroyed, points in Japanese territory . . . shall be occupied," and that "the Japanese military force, after being completely disarmed, shall be permitted to return to their homes, . . ." and finally that "Japan shall be permitted to maintain such industries as will sustain her economy . . . but not these which would enable her to rearm for war. . . ." The directive provided under Part III (1) Disarmament and Demilitarization, ". . . Japan is not to have an army, navy, air force, secret police organization or any civil aviation. Japan's ground, air and naval forces shall be disarmed and disbanded and the Japanese Imperial Headquarters, the General Staff . . . shall be dissolved. Military and naval material, military and naval vessels and military and naval installations, and military, naval and civilian aircraft shall be surrendered and shall be disposed of as required by the Supreme Commander." Hence, regardless of his own personal convictions, MacArthur was left no other course then to render Japan's war making potential impotent—spiritually and physically. What better method than to let the Japanese do it themselves?

Furthermore, even in peace, Japan's survival could only rest upon a sound and healthy industrial economy, as its full agricultural potential would never produce the minimum food requirements to sustain Japanese life. Its inadequacy of indigenous raw resources (Japan has but a token supply of iron, copper, manganese, chrome, tin, nickel, zinc, tungsten, rubber, petroleum, and hard coal within its post-defeat boundaries) renders its industrial plant largely dependent upon friendly trade abroad, particularly in Asia, whence such raw resources must be obtained. And that friendly trade rests in no small degree upon good will and confidence, always tempered by the realization that Japan's population pressures, rapidly increasing within the narrow confines of the four main islands, might well, under the impelling instinct for self-preservation, explode into new aggressions abroad were Japan provided the military capability to dominate less powerful neighbors. Further than this, MacArthur realized that in the light of modern weapons and techniques a Japan engaged in global war between the East and the West, whether on the side of victor or vanquished, would inevitably be ravaged and destroyed because of its geographical location.

True, when he withdrew the occupation forces from Japan to meet the requirements of the Korean war, MacArthur did provide for an internal Japanese security force—the National Police Reserve, as it was called. It consisted of four divisions, and he planned its progressive increase to an over-all strength of ten divisions. But this was solely designed to provide a core of defensive strength adequate to meet Communist-inspired local disorders or any casual encroachment upon Japanese territory by others, and a nucleus around which to build if any major threat to Japan's sovereign integrity should develop. MacArthur feels, however, that if Japan should rearm on a much broader scale, a distrust among her neighbors would be understandable. For such a rearmed Japan, under conditions of economic necessity brought about by population pressures, might well resort to arms once again to alleviate conditions of internal distress. As he has pointed out, "Japan cannot be expected to resist the overweening law of self-preservation."

Apart from these practical considerations, MacArthur saw in the Japanese constitutional proscription against war a vital step forward toward war's final abolition, now that scientific advances in mass killing and material destruction have raised the cost of victory possibly as high as the victor's own total destruction. He has long felt that the great masses of the human population oppose war and that their leaders who cling to its threat as a means toward political power are becoming increasingly apprehensive over war's disastrous probabilities—and that in time the futility of war will become universally accepted. Half in jest and half seriously, he refers to the front line as the safest place in the next war, if it comes, pointing out that the great industrial and population centers will bear the full brunt as well as initial shock of the struggle. He sees the scientist as grasping leadership from the theologian in the evolution of a universal moral code renouncing war as an arbiter between nations— a moral code not built necessarily upon an improvement in basic character, but rather from the universal realization that the unleashing of war's full potential violence may doom victor as well as vanquished.

These views MacArthur then entertained have since found increasing support in the march of events. Now no longer is the shooting down of foreign planes, the unprovoked molesting of foreign citizens, the enslavement or murder of prisoners of war, or indeed almost any invasion of the sovereign dignity and integrity of others considered a cause for war, as it once was. So fearful have the leaders of the free nations of the world become lest they provoke a major conflict that they now seem willing to accept almost any indignity—to go to any limit of appeasement of international troublemakers—rather than risk it. Thus they are beginning to accept MacArthur's warning from the quarterdeck of the battleship *Missouri*, in the immediate aftermath of victory, that war is now no longer a tenable solution for international disputes. And thus they seem to be drawing closer to the leadership Japan has taken by constitutional proscription.

Throughout the occupation of Japan and since, MacArthur at every opportunity has supported the Japanese constitutional proscription against war and encouraged firm adherence to it. "Some contemporary cynics," he told the people on New Year's Day 1950, "deride as visionary Japan's constitutional renunciation of the concept of belligerency and armed security. Be not overly concerned by such detractors. A product of Japanese thought, this provision is based upon the highest of moral ideals, and yet no constitutional provision was ever more fundamentally sound and practical. While by no sophistry of reasoning can it be interpreted as complete negation of the inalienable right of self-defense against unprovoked attack, it is a ringing affirmation by a people laid prostrate by the sword, of faith in the ultimate triumph of international morality and justice without resort to the sword. It must be understood, however, that so long as predatory international banditry is permitted to roam the earth to crush human freedom under its avarice and violence, the high concept to which you are pledged will be slow in finding universal acceptance. But it is axiomatic that there must be always a first in all things. In this historic decision, you are the first. The opportunity, therefore, is yours to exemplify before mankind the soundness of this concept and the inestimable benefit resulting from the dedication of all energy and all resources to peaceful progress. In due course, other nations will join you in this dedication, but, meanwhile, you must not falter. Have faith in my countrymen and other peoples who share the same high ideals. Above all, have faith in yourselves."

Yet MacArthur realized of course and frequently cautioned that the threat of predatory force might compel Japan to rearm sufficiently for its own defense. As he stated it in reply to an inquiry from the national commander of the AMVETS during the occupation, "Only a seer could answer the question you pose concerning the rearming of Japan, for the answer truly lies in the yet unpredictable future. Should the course of world events require that all mankind stand to arms in defense of human liberty and Japan come within the orbit of immediately threatened attack, then the Japanese too should mount the maximum defensive power which their resources will permit."

At the same time he warned against any oversimplification of the problem: "Pending a peace treaty, however," he said, "Japan remains under the policy control of the Allied powers, among whom there is much more apprehension over the prospect of a rearmed and remilitarized Japan than that Japan may fall prey to predatory forces bent upon freedom's destruction. The same rationalization is to be found even among the great masses of the Japanese people themselves who fear even more than external attack the resurgence of militarism and the return of police suppression. Consequently grave political as well as social and economic considerations must be faced in the light of the world situation."

Then MacArthur pointed out a service Japan was thus able to perform: "The great immediate purpose Japan can serve in the confusion which overrides all of strife-torn Asia is to stand out with striking and unruffled calmness and tranquillity as the exemplification of peaceful progress under conditions of unalloyed personal freedom. For thereby it will stand as a symbol of hope for less fortunate Asian peoples, wielding a profound moral influence upon the destiny of the Asian races."

Chapter IV Freedom's New Frontier

The occupation was barely a few months old when it became apparent to all that the Japanese people were not only treasuring their new-found freedom but were also learning how to use it. On April 10, 1946, blandly upsetting centuries of custom and tradition, nearly three fourths of the Japanese electorate went to the polls for Japan's first completely free election. Although it was only seven months since the beginning of the occupation, there were 2,781 candidates, representing 257 parties, campaigning for the 466 available seats in the Diet. The voters, numbering among them the newly enfranchised women in the surprisingly large number of over 13,000,000, injected fresh blood into the body politic. Hundreds of unknowns were elected to replace the old order of the Diet, eighty per cent of which had been hand-picked by Tojo during World War II. Whereas the previous Diets had been made up almost entirely of lawyers, industrialists, and professional politicians, the newly elected one contained but a small percentage from this class, including only six who could be called "politicians." The new membership also included 32 educators, 22 authors, 13 physicians, and 49 farmers. The average age of the members was two years younger than in previous Diets. In place of the one-party legislatures of Tojo's regime, the Diet elected in 1946 contained the representatives of no less than 33 political parties, in addition to 83 members who classed themselves as Independents. Thirty-eight women were elected to the House of Representatives. MacArthur summed up this spectacular performance in the statement on the elections which he issued on April 23, 1946:

". . . All men, since the beginning of time, have had the smouldering desire to achieve democracy—too few have had the unrestricted right to express that desire for it—fewer still to achieve it.

"It was Lincoln who said, 'The people are wiser than their rulers.'

The soundness of this statement is historically evident—and the Japanese people provide no exception. Given the opportunity for free expression of their popular will, they responded whole-heartedly; and, rejecting leadership dedicated to the political philosophies of the two extremes, both of the right and of the left, which experience has shown in practice inevitably lead to the same result—regimentation of the masses and the suppression of human liberty—they took a wide central course which will permit the ` evolvement of a balanced program of government designed best to serve their interests as a people. . . ."

One year and one month later the Supreme Commander could issue another congratulatory statement: ". . . From factories and shops and homes, from villages and farms and mines, the Japanese people streamed by the millions throughout the land to the polling places to discharge their new responsibilities of citizenship. There they voted for the candidates of their choice, freely and fearlessly without disorder and according to the rules as they understood them. In this atmosphere of freedom, marked by serious effort and honesty of purpose, no one can justly criticize their choice. This choice, for the first time in Japanese history, reflected the free will of the majority as against the totalitarian dictates of a minority. This is democracy!"

The Japanese deserved his tribute, for they had just put on another spectacular demonstration at the polls, a series of elections in anticipation of the enforcement of the new constitution on May 3. During an entire month the Japanese people went to the polls four times to choose a total of 205,062 officials. These 1947 elections showed graphically the promptness with which the Japanese had learned to understand the duties as well as the privileges of democracy. In place of the Home Minister, who had previously supervised all elections through his officials, 50,000 citizens representing every shade of political opinion supervised the 1947 elections in local committees throughout the land.

In a sense both the 1946 and the 1947 elections could be called not just an exercise of new-found freedom, but a vote of confidence in MacArthur as well. By the smooth-working efficiency of the election machinery and the victory of the moderate candidates the policies of MacArthur's occupation administration could be regarded as succeeding. But the field of his endeavors was far greater than that simply of political reform. A balance sheet of results accomplished by MacArthur in Japan could extend into many volumes of reports; but for purposes of simplification for the layman the most significant and interesting of them can be summarized as follows:

ECONOMIC

In the autumn of 1945 MacArthur found a nation whose material structure had been gutted by the massive violence of modern war, inhabited by a populace of 70,000,000 impoverished, bewildered and despairing Japanese at the point of mass starvation and entirely dependent upon an economy of almost hopeless scarcity. Essentially the economy of Japan was based upon a two-way trade. She imported the raw materials and, with cheap labor and transportation, supplied the markets of the millions of the coolie class throughout Asia who could not afford the more costly manufactured goods of Europe and America. So her policy had been to secure the bases that supplied her manufacturing plant. But she had lost the war, and in the process had lost her bases of supply, her markets, and virtually her entire merchant marine. The four islands that make up the country could scarcely keep alive a stopgap internal economy.

Besides, Japan could not hope to be self-sufficient agriculturally. Only sixteen per cent of the land was arable. What little rice was grown in the outlying districts stayed there because Japan's transportation system was hopelessly crippled as well. So desperate was the food situation in the early days of the occupation that only Army soup kitchen kept thousands from dying. And in the elections, some of the ballots bore two eloquent words on the space for write-in candidates: "More food."

MacArthur saw that he must move swiftly to prevent disaster. He well knew that all the social reforms he could effect would have little meaning to a starving people. As he later expressed it in his famous 1951 message before the joint session of Congress, "Word ideologies play little part in Asian thinking and are little understood. What the people strive for is the opportunity for a little more food in their stomachs, a little better clothing on their backs, a little firmer roof over their heads." At his urging, the breach was filled. Allied Army sources were tapped immediately for food, to be followed by imports of a total of 3,500,000 tons. This accomplished as much as any other single act of the occupation or any other gesture of American good will around the world—despite the fact that the Communists, unable to match this generosity themselves, spread rumors that the food was poisoned.

By the hundreds, unsolicited letters poured into SCAP headquarters, most of them addressed to MacArthur personally, to thank him for saving their lives. Meanwhile, from the very start of the occupation, when a full-sized Army foraging expedition had been able to locate only one egg, MacArthur had directed the occupying troops to provide their own food. The Japanese never forgot this magnanimity—of a conquering army refusing to live off the land and instead feeding the vanquished from its own resources.

An important principle, of course, lay behind this gesture, a principle that MacArthur explained in a strong appeal to the Appropriations Committee of the United States House of Representatives at a time when the committee had raised a serious question concerning the further subsidization by the United States of Japan's food deficits. "There is a popular misconception," he said, "that the achievement of victory in modern war . . . is solely dependent upon victory in the field. History itself clearly refutes this concept. It offers unmistakable proof that the human impulses which generated the will to war, no less than the material sinews of war, must be destroyed. Nor is it sufficient that such human impulses merely yield to the temporary shock of military defeat. There must be a complete spiritual reformation such as will not only control the defeated generation, but will exert a dominant influence upon the generation to follow as well. Unless this is done, victory is but partially complete and offers hope for little more than an armistice between one campaign and the next—as the great lesson and warning of experience is that victorious leaders of the past have too often contented themselves with the infliction of military defeat upon the enemy power without extending that victory by dealing with the root causes which led to war as an inevitable consequence."

MacArthur continued this message with a stern warning: "Under the responsibilities of victory the Japanese people are now our prisoners, no less than did the surviving men on Bataan become their prisoners when that peninsula fell. As a consequence of the ill treatment, including starvation of Allied prisoners in Japanese hands, we have tried and executed many Japanese officers upon proof of responsibility. Yet can we justify such punitive action if we ourselves, in reversed circumstances but with hostilities at end, fail to provide the food to sustain life among the Japanese people over whom we now stand guard within the narrow confines of their home islands?"

The Allies had won the war by successfully severing Japan's supply lines from abroad and destroying her merchant fleet as well as her navy. We had taken from her Manchuria, Korea, and Formosa, long contributors to Japanese maintenance. Besides, many millions of Japanese abroad had been repatriated to their home islands. Meanwhile the Allied blockade had been continued, extended, and intensified; trade and financial inter-

266

course with the rest of the world was so prohibited as to constitute economic strangulation. "To cut off Japan's relief supplies in this situation," MacArthur continued, "would cause starvation to countless Japanese—and starvation breeds mass unrest, disorder and violence." Then he made his final plea: "Give me bread or give me bullets." He got bread.

Meanwhile a large division of SCAP officers, under the able and resourceful direction of Major General William F. Marquat, was working desperately to restore Japan's shattered economy and make the country self-sufficient as soon as possible. Bombed-out factories were rebuilt, machinery was repaired, transportation and communications were revived and brisk trade was stimulated. But one of the first and biggest tasks was to give Japan a balanced budget.

The Japanese government's financial affairs were in an incredible confusion. During the war the militarists had asked for and received moderate appropriations, to which enormous special appropriations were immediately added. The brunt of taxes fell upon the poor, but few tax collectors expected to receive anywhere near the amount charged, and in fact an occasional tax agent was stoned out of town. An expert in the field of taxation, Harold Moss, was borrowed from the United States Treasury Department to assist in the complete revision of Japan's tax laws and procedures. Through great patience, wise guidance, and almost herculean effort—and with the counsel of a mission of distinguished tax experts, headed by Dr. Carl S. Shoup of Columbia University, which made a complete survey of Japan's tax situation—Moss helped the Japanese fiscal authorities to process through the Diet a comprehensive and modernized tax law. He then worked tirelessly and successfully in educating the public on the reasons behind the law and its implementation.

It is not very well known that MacArthur's original directive from Washington contained the specific injunction that he should not "assume any responsibility for the economic rehabilitation or the strengthening of the Japanese economy." He was forced to operate under this restriction for three years, and, of course, had he complied with the letter of it, Japan would have gone into economic oblivion. So, without assuming "any responsibility," he worked through the Japanese government, just as he did in reorienting the nation politically, to revive Japan's economic life and restore to her a free and healthy economy.

He placed major emphasis on transforming what he termed an "economic system of private socialism," under which ten Japanese families controlled about ninety per cent of all Japanese industry, into an economic system that would permit and encourage the development of free private competitive enterprise. While by no means opposed to big business itself, MacArthur believed that Japan's only hope depended upon that truly competitive free enterprise which had long been stifled by monopolistic control of the means of production and distribution. So it was that an early SCAP order broke up the feudalistic Zaibatsu monopoly. Using the argument that the only way to restore the nation's economy was to keep the Zaibatsu in business, these moguls of industry fought bitterly to hold their domains intact. But it was a futile battle against inevitable progress, and by SCAP directive the great trusts were broken. Members of the family dynasties were paid for their stock, but their incomes were limited and they were not thereafter allowed to impose their influence upon management. Although they professed outrage at the time, some of them later admitted surprise at not having been tried as war criminals.

MacArthur's economic reforms accomplished their goals more slowly than his other contributions to peacetime Japan, mainly because the war had so utterly destroyed the nation's economic life. But by New Year's Day 1947 he could tell the Japanese people that ". . . since the surrender, under the guidance of the occupation and with American help, Japan has been gradually restoring her shattered economy, and the curve is up, not down. The industrial output has now risen to over 45% of the prewar normal, and the improvement can be expected to continue. The relative stability, especially by comparison with more fortunately favored countries, and even under the blighting effects of practical blockade, has been one of the most amazing and encouraging features of the occupation."

The situation continued to improve. In 1948, for example, some 75 per cent of all Japan's imports were provided for by the United States. In 1949 this percentage had fallen to 60 per cent; in 1950 it was down to 43 per cent, and in 1951 to 26 per cent. Actually, on a per capita basis, the total financial aid received by Japan from the United States since the beginning of the occupation was one fourth of that extended to Germany —not counting the tremendously expensive Berlin Airlift. Yet the need for this American aid in Japan decreased steadily, so that in 1951 the United States was spending only half of what it had spent on Japan in 1949.

In the field of public finance, MacArthur secured the brilliant American banker Joseph M. Dodge to advise him. Then, after the worst dislocations of war had been substantially alleviated, he required that the Japanese government live within its income, warning that only in extreme cases would he permit supplementary appropriations to cover budgetary deficits. He did not prescribe either the sources or the amounts of public revenue, leaving that entirely to the political responsibility of the government. And he rejected every effort by the Japanese political leaders to induce him to accept the responsibility for tax legislation to bolster anticipated income. In answer to these efforts, he said publicly that "men since the beginning of time have understood through the crucible of bitter experience, that the power to tax is the power to destroy." The Japanese leaders and people responded magnificently to the budgetary limitations imposed upon the government, and for three successive years prior to MacArthur's departure adhered to budgets not only in true balance, but with substantial surpluses as well; public debt was kept down to less than two billion dollars.

Probably the healthiest shot in the arm that Japan's economy received was MacArthur's insistence that Japanese labor be given the right, for the first time, to organize and bargain collectively. This right was enthusiastically received by all Japanese workers, and within a year from the time the Diet passed a new labor law proposed by SCAP, there were 4,400,000 members in 17,000 unions in Japan. Everything possible was done to encourage this healthy phenomenon, with the double result that labor unions were less restricted in Japan than they were in the United States, and a greater percentage of Japanese industrial workers were organized than in many Western countries.

Labor in Japan was soon divided between a rightist J.F. of L. (Japan National Federation of Labor) and a leftist CIU (National Congress of Industrial Unions). Manifestations of worker unrest promptly took forms that could occur only in Japan: a chorus line went on half-strike by kicking only half as high as usual; some railway workers dramatized their grievance by blowing their whistles in chorus for a one-minute "shriek protest." On the other hand there was some tendency for organized workers to use their new strength to ask for even more of the same kind of paternalism that had been plaguing the labor movement since its infancy in the 1920's. Instead of demanding more wages, some Japanese workers were asking for and getting marriage and baby allowances written into their contracts. This was in the pattern of the traditional relationship between many of Japan's employers and workers. Japanese employees were treated as "members of the family," though generally as rather underprivileged members of the family.

To overcome this paternalism, and at the same time to safeguard against excesses in the opposite direction by powerful labor bosses, MacArthur sought to direct labor's course toward a recognition of its responsibility as an independent and vital force in modern Japanese society. He encouraged a labor leadership that would have the statesmanship to understand that labor's conflicts were never confined to the interests of workers and management alone, but that the interest of the general public was equally great. He tried to instill in the individual worker an independence and dignity which were responsive to the rights and liberties guaranteed by the constitution to all citizens, including the right to work and to enjoy the fruits of one's toil. In short, his goal for the trade labor movement was a legitimate and effective means whereby individuals as well as groups of workers could defend themselves against exploitation by government, management, or corrupt labor leaders. By planning and encouraging a program of education, he tried to plot a course toward a successful and healthy labor movement for the future of postwar Japan.

As might have been expected, the Communists seized upon this opportunity to make trouble for the occupation authorities. MacArthur was not surprised to see them infiltrating some of the labor unions, and following his principle of allowing as much political freedom as possible in postwar Japan, he was reluctant to curb them so long as they did not offset the orderly processes of government. But he *was* surprised at the rashness with which some Communist labor leaders acted when they decided to call a general strike. He waited patiently in the hope that more reasonable labor leaders would bring the situation under control by themselves. Finally, however, it became obvious that a general strike would indeed be attempted unless he personally put a stop to it.

It was a difficult and painful decision. He did not want to stand in the way of newly organized laborers attempting to assert their rights, even though in this case they were pawns in the hands of a few scheming bosses. He knew that he would be bitterly criticized abroad, especially in England and Russia, if he called off the strike by fiat. And he knew that he would take the chance that one or two local labor leaders might challenge his authority directly by taking their workers out on strike despite his intervention.

Yet he knew that the alternative was to let a few power-mad Communist labor leaders wreak economic disaster. He recognized this as a major challenge that he must firmly meet. They had asked for a showdown, and he would have to give it to them.

He ordered them to desist. But at the same time he issued to the Japanese people a statement clearly explaining his reasons. "Under the authority vested in me as Supreme Commander for the Allied Powers," he announced, "I have informed the labor leaders whose unions have federated for the purpose of conducting a general strike that I will not permit the use of so deadly a social weapon in the present impoverished and emaciated condition of Japan, and have accordingly directed them to desist from the furtherance of such action. I have done so only to forestall the fatal impact of such extreme measures upon an already gravely threatened public welfare. Japanese society today operates under the limitations of war, defeat and Allied occupation. Its cities were laid waste, its industries are almost at a standstill, and the great masses of its people are on little more than a starvation diet.

"A general strike, crippling transportation and communications, would prevent the movement of food to feed the people and of coal to sustain the essential utilities, and would stop such industry as is still functioning. The paralysis which would inevitably result might reduce large masses of the Japanese people to the point of actual starvation, and would produce dreadful consequences upon every Japanese home, regardless of social strata, or direct interest in the basic issue. Even now, to prevent actual starvation in Japan, the people of the United States are releasing to them large quantities of their own food resources. The persons involved in the threatened general strike are but a small minority of the Japanese people. Yet this minority might well plunge the great masses into a disaster not unlike that produced in the immediate past by the minority which led Japan into the destruction of war. . . ."

In this way MacArthur placed his case squarely before the people. And in this way he won the showdown with the Communists. The Japanese people, including the rank and file of labor, understood fully his purpose and supported it. The threatened general strike collapsed.

Defeated in open challenge, the Communists then tried the familiar tactic of massive infiltration. This time they concentrated upon the transportation and communications unions, and gained partial control of this large and important segment of labor. MacArthur readily saw the sinister nature of their maneuver; if the Communists obtained effective control of these unions, they would be in a position to paralyze two vital arteries of Japanese life at will, thus posing a dangerous threat to the survival of the government. Both the communications and the transportation systems of Japan had for many years been operated by the government, and so MacArthur moved to meet the threat by encouraging the enactment of a law bringing all government workers within the framework of a modernized civil-service system.

At his direction, I established in the government section a new division headed by the late Mr. Blaine Hoover, a distinguished United States civil-service authority. The division met with Japanese government officials and assisted them in the preparation of a law creating a National

Personnel Authority, comparable to the U.S. Civil Service Commission. By the provisions of this law all employees of the government would be bracketed within a civil-service system responsible solely to the Diet. Enlightened standards of employment, advancement, and retirement would be provided for these workers, and they would be given greater protection and broader opportunity than they had ever previously enjoyed. The law also provided for adequate grievance machinery, but the rights of collective bargaining and of striking were denied. The law was approved by the Japanese government officials and by MacArthur, and was thereupon placed before the Diet.

The announcement of the law immediately brought howls of righteous rage from abroad, especially from England and Russia, where the strike curb was heartedly condemned as anti-labor. Even some elements of the U.S. Government attempted covertly to obstruct this legislation. In view of this chorus of disapproval, MacArthur was agreeably surprised when, after a copy of the proposed law had been submitted by the State Department to the U.S. Civil Service Commission (apparently in the belief that the commission would support the British point of view), he was informed through non-official channels that the commission had ruled that it was "decidedly more liberal than the statutes pertaining to the United States Civil Service System." The estimate of our proposed law was made by none other than Commissioner Frances Perkins, one of the staunchest members of Franklin D. Roosevelt's first New Deal Cabinet. MacArthur, however, never was officially informed of this opinion.

Even inside SCAP there had been sharp differences concerning the law. MacArthur listened to the arguments of both sides in two sessions that lasted a total of twenty-one hours. When he was certain that he had the fullest information, he made his decision. He decided in favor of the proposed law.

From that point on, he refused to countenance any interference with its passage, even though criticism from abroad still found explosive expression. Once the legislation had had a chance to take effect, it was understood and accepted by the Japanese people. Under the statesman-like administration of particularly well-qualified Japanese commissioners, the law has worked very well. The Communists thereby lost their hold on the unions of the government workers, and never again during MacArthur's tenure did Communism become a serious factor in the Japanese labor movement. This has been no small contributing factor to the steady improvement of the economic health of Japan.

The Japanese are a proud, sensitive, and industrious race. They ask no alms from anyone and expect none. They seek only the inalienable right to live. The alternatives are as simple as they are few. Either Japan must have access to the raw materials needed to sustain its industrial plant and to markets in which to dispose of its manufactured products; or it must have provisions for voluntary migration of large masses of its population to less-populated areas of the world. Either solution rests upon the good will and statesmanship of others. Lacking such good will and if such statesmanship fails, Japan would be forced to desperation or to death. And as MacArthur has also said, "Men will fight before they starve."

RELIGION

Japan's recovery was as much a spiritual one as it was constitutional and economic. The catharsis of faith through which the Japanese people had to go was best described by MacArthur himself.

"For centuries," he said, "the Japanese people, unlike their neighbors in the Pacific basin—the Chinese, the Malayans, the Indians, and the whites—have been students and idolaters of the art of war and the warrior caste. They were the natural warriors of the Pacific. Unbroken victory for Japanese arms convinced them of their invincibility, and the keystone to the entire arch of their civilization became an almost mythological belief in the strength and wisdom of the warrior caste. It permeated and controlled not only all the branches of government, but all branches of life—physical, mental and spiritual. It was interwoven not only into all government process, but into all phases of daily routine. It was not only the essence, but the warp and woof of Japanese existence.

"Control was exercised by a feudalistic overlordship of a mere fraction of the population, while the remaining 70,000,000, with a few enlightened exceptions, were abject slaves to tradition, legend, mythology and regimentation. During the progress of war, these 70,000,000 heard of nothing but Japanese victories and the bestial qualities of Japan's opponents. Then they suddenly felt the concentrated shock of total defeat. Their whole world crumbled. It was not merely the overthrow of their military might—it was the collapse of a faith—it was the disintegration of everything they had believed in and lived by and fought for. It left a complete vacuum morally, mentally and physically.

"And into this vacuum flowed the democratic way of life. Then the American combat soldier came with his fine sense of self-respect, self-confidence and self-control. They saw and felt his spiritual quality—a spiritual quality which truly reflected the highest training of the American home. The falseness of their former teachings, the failure of their former leadership, the tragedy of their past faith were infallibly demonstrated in actuality and realism.

"A spiritual revolution ensued which almost overnight tore asunder a theory and practice of life built upon two thousand years of history and tradition and legend. Idolatry for their feudalistic masters and the warrior class was transformed into hatred and contempt, and the hatred and contempt for their foe gave way to honor and respect. This revolution of the spirit among the Japanese people represents no thin veneer designed to serve the purpose of the present. It represents an unparalleled convulsion in the social history of the world."

MacArthur is a devout Episcopalian. Because he was at his office in the Dai Ichi Building every morning, including Sundays, he did not attend church in Tokyo, though Mrs. MacArthur and Arthur did. But all his life MacArthur has been a practicing Christian. As a Christian he faced a normal temptation to convert by subtle but powerful pressures vast numbers of what many Christians might regard as "heathen" Japanese. Never had so great an opportunity for such a conversion presented itself. Unprecedented spiritual ruin had engulfed every Japanese. In their hour of agony, like all human beings they had turned to their religious faith for support, and at this crucial moment even their faith had failed them. Japan in September 1945 was a missionary's paradise.

But while a practicing Christian, MacArthur was not that kind of missionary. He has always had a sincere admiration for many of the basic principles underlying the Oriental faiths, which are much older than Christianity. He feels that in many essential respects there is no conflict between the two, and that one might well be strengthened by a knowledge and understanding of the other. That is why he decided not to attempt to force Christianity upon the Japanese, but rather to practice Christianity and to see to it that the occupation functioned in accordance with Christianity's highest principles. While not imposing conversion on anyone, he tried to give the Japanese the benefits of Christian concepts by exemplifying its highest values.

One of those values was freedom of religion, and one of MacArthur's earliest moves was to guarantee that every Japanese could worship as he wished. In order to accomplish this, it was necessary to abolish Japan's ancient and backward state-controlled, subsidized religion of Shintoism. By the precepts of this mythological holdover from primitive times, the

274

people were taught to believe that the Emperor was the High Priest of Shinto and that he derived his spiritual power from his Imperial ancestors, who had become gods. Shintoism preached that the Emperor was divine himself, and that the highest purpose of every subject's life was death in the service of the Emperor. This religion had been used opportunistically by the militarists who had led Japan into war, and it was still heavily subsidized by the state.

In a directive issued in November 1945 MacArthur ordered state subsidization of Shintoism to cease. And on New Year's Day 1946 he received an unexpected assist from the Emperor, who voluntarily and publicly renounced the concept of his own divinity. Almost hidden within a rather long Imperial rescript, the Emperor's statement read: "We stand by the people and we wish always to share with them in their moments of joys and sorrows. The ties between us and our people have always stood upon mutual trust and affection. They do not depend upon mere legends and myths. They are not predicated on the false conception that the Emperor is divine and that the Japanese people are superior to other races and fated to rule the world."

MacArthur was doubly gratified because of the completely voluntary nature of the Emperor's action. He publicly commented at once; "The Emperor's New Year's message pleases me very much. By it he undertakes a leading part in the democratization of his people. He squarely takes his stand for the future along liberal lines. His action reflects the irresistible influence of a sound idea. A sound idea cannot be stopped."

Thereafter, in accordance with his principle of religious freedom, MacArthur permitted Shinto priests to continue their teachings, so long as church and state were separated.

Meanwhile, though refusing to convert by force, MacArthur encouraged all possible Christian missionary work. At his request, for example, the Pocket Testament League distributed ten million Bibles in Japanese translation. And to a visitor in 1949 MacArthur said: "The more missionaries we can bring out here and the more occupation troops we can send home, the better."

Gradually, under his gentle guidance, a spiritual regeneration of Japan went on. He put it this way in a letter to the Brooklyn *Tablet:* "We shall, of course, do all in our power to encourage study of the historical development of the Christian concept. As a powerful corollary is the fact that its rudimentary understanding will come from the living example of the application of its immutable tenets to which every phase of occupational policy is attuned—of which every member of the occupation force is a daily practitioner. . . . There is thus penetrating into the Japanese mind the noble influences which find their origin and their inspiration in the American home. These influences are rapidly bearing fruit, and apart from the great numbers who are coming formally to embrace the Christian faith, a whole population is coming to understand, practice and cherish its underlying principles and ideals."

The fact that MacArthur's efforts toward the spiritual regeneration of Japan did no violence to religious freedom or to the sensibilities of those who followed the teachings and ritual of Buddha was illustrated graphically when the High Priest of the Buddhist faith in India bitterly assailed him in a public statement for trying to convert the Japanese people of the Buddhist faith to Christianity, implying that SCAP was employing some sort of "shotgun" conversion. To this charge the head of the Buddhist faith in Japan at once took sharp exception. "No," he said, "the Supreme Commander has made no effort to convert Japanese Buddhists to Christianity, but he has shown us in countless ways by his example where we Buddhists can materially strengthen our own faith."

EDUCATION

When MacArthur arrived, the Japanese school system was so tightly centralized that there was not a local school superintendant in the whole country. Textbooks, even those dealing with mathematics, were filled with militaristic and especially anti-American propaganda, and all were controlled and censored by the Ministry of Education in Tokyo. Not only were the press, radio, theater, and moving pictures governed by the strict authoritarianism of "thought control," but a great deal of Japan's entertainment was little more than propaganda.

But the most impressive task, and the most impressive performance, was in the field of textbooks. Their publication was taken out of the control of the Ministry of Education, and the preparation and printing of the books were opened to the Japanese publishing market for competitive bids. No texts were forced upon the Japanese people by MacArthur; to obtain SCAP approval, a Japanese textbook only had to show that the previous militarist, ultra-nationalistic propaganda had been removed. In the year 1950–1 alone, more than 250,000,000 new textbooks were printed for the schoolchildren of Japan.

MacArthur also made sweeping reforms to restore educational freedom for teachers. In a directive to the Ministry of Education, he stipulated: "Teachers and educational officials who have been dismissed, suspended, or forced to resign for liberal or antimilitaristic opinions or activities will be declared immediately eligible for . . . reappointment. Discrimination against any student, teacher or educational official on grounds of race, nationality, creed, political opinion or social position, will be prohibited. Students, teachers and educational officials will be encouraged in unrestricted discussion of issues involving political, civil and religious liberties."

A good measure of MacArthur's accomplishments in the field of education in Japan appeared in the American magazine *Life* for March 29, 1954. Theodor Geisel, the famous "Dr. Suess," author of American children's books, visited Japan in 1953 with an interesting survey test that he had devised. With the aid of 100 local teachers, he asked the Japanese children to show in a drawing what each wanted to be when he or she grew up. Out of the stacks of drawings, which included diplomats, streetcar conductors, teachers, doctors, umpires, wrestlers, and even a dilettante, only *one* student wanted to be an army or navy officer. He wanted to be MacArthur.

HEALTH

In 1945 Japanese medicine was twenty years behind that of the United States. Such diseases as smallpox, cholera, diphtheria, typhoid, and paratyphoid would spring into epidemics overnight. Tuberculosis was endemic nearly everywhere. Contrary to popular belief in the West, the Japanese were seriously lacking in modern hygiene; in all Japan there were exactly two sanitary engineers. The vast destruction of World War II had only made these conditions worse.

MacArthur immediately instituted an energetic program to combat this situation. He created a public-health section within the headquarters, directed by General Crawford Sams, a brilliant and energetic doctor who had been the first medical officer to become a paratrooper during World War II. Under his guidance a Ministry of Health and Welfare was established within the Cabinet, with agencies reaching down to all levels of local government. Public health was taught in the schools. Dietary deficiencies due to impoverishment or lack of balanced foods were corrected as far as possible. A nationwide sanitation program was set in motion. And, most important, Japan was given the largest mass immunization and vaccination treatment in the history of public health.

277

In order to curb smallpox, every Japanese was vaccinated not once but twice. That made 160,000,000 vaccinations, done in the course of a little more than three years. Medical history records nothing approaching this scale. The recent campaign in the United States for Salk anti-polio shots did not compare with it. More than 35,000,000 Japanese were vaccinated with a new agent known as BCG to control tuberculosis, reducing the number of cases by 79 per cent and TB deaths by 88 per cent within the immunized groups. Some 50,000,000 were dusted with DDT. Diphtheria inoculations reduced this disease by 86 per cent. Typhoid and paratyphoid were cut by 90 per cent. Even dysentery, for which there is no immunization agent, was reduced 86 per cent. Cholera was wiped out completely, with not a single case appearing in Japan after December 1946.

By a measure of such cold statistics, General Sams's public-health program saved 2,100,000 Japanese lives in the first two years of the occupation, through the control of communicable diseases alone. By a measure that goes beyond statistics, MacArthur did even more. His institution of so simple a public-health measure, for example, as free hot luncheons for schoolchildren not only had immediate results in terms of better health, but also brought a warm response from all the Japanese people. The Americans were in Japan, they saw, to build and not to destroy.

LAND REFORM

The one MacArthur accomplishment in Japan that will probably be ranked higher by the future historian than any other was the program he initiated to solve the problems arising from that country's ancient and feudalistic agrarian economy. In 1945 nearly half of all the arable land in Japan was worked by tenants under exorbitant sharecropper arrangements and in some areas even under near-slavery conditions imposed by dictatorial landlords. Before the year was out, MacArthur had set up a Natural Resources Section, headed by Colonel H. G. Schenk, a distinguished professor of geology whose dedication to the occupation was such that he refused to return to the classroom until his land-reform goals had been achieved.

MacArthur directed that immediate measures be taken to insure that those who tilled the soil of Japan would receive the fruits of their labor and that the hated and oppressive system of land tenure would be abolished. At his urging the Diet passed a series of laws under which the

278

government purchased land from the owners, at pre-set fair prices, and sold it to the tenants under long-term arrangements whereby the tenant had as long as twenty-five years in which to pay. Almost five million acres were thus transferred from landlord to tenant farmer, with all of this unprecedented program administered by popularly elected Japanese land commissioners in each community. By 1950 the Japan of landless, impoverished sharecroppers had been transformed to a Japan in which 89 per cent of the arable land was owned by free, independent farmers who worked their own property. MacArthur himself described it as "the most successful experiment of its kind in history."

The new class of capitalist landowners formed a strong barrier against the advance of Communism in rural Japan. Collectivism was of little interest to the Japanese farmer, who now owned, and was prepared to protect, a piece of land that was his alone. The success of MacArthur's land-reform program is indicated both by the fact that Communists everywhere made intense efforts to infiltrate the ranks of the 210,000 local land commissioners, as well as by the fact that their campaign of infiltration failed. The rural population would have no part of them.

Expiation

Probably nothing during his administration of the occupation gave MacArthur deeper concern than his obligation to act upon the judgment of the International Military Tribunal of the Far East. He quickly approved penalties adjudged against enemy field commanders or other military personnel who had permitted or committed atrocities against soldiers or civilians who had fallen under their custody during the war. He held to a rigid code delineating the responsibility for fair and humane treatment of an enemy, military or civilian, who fell under the power of a military commander, and he was outraged when this code was wantonly violated. He set forth this code in his review of the trial proceedings against General Tomoyuki Yamashita, who had been the Japanese military commander in the Philippines at the time of the sack of Manila in 1945:

"It is not easy for me to pass penal judgment upon a defeated adversary in a major military campagn. I have reviewed the proceedings in vain search for some mitigating circumstance in his behalf. I can find none. Rarely has so cruel and wanton a record been spread to public gaze. Revolting as this may be in itself, it pales before the sinister and far reaching implication thereby attached to the profession of arms. The soldier, be he friend or foe, is charged with the protection of the weak and unarmed. It is the very essence and reason for his being. When he violates this sacred trust, he not only profanes his entire cult, but threatens the very fabric of international society. The traditions of fighting men are long and honorable. They are based upon the noblest of human traits— sacrifice. This officer, of proven field merit, trusted with high command involving authority adequate to responsibility has failed this irrevocable standard; has failed his duty to his troops, to his country, to his enemy, to mankind; has failed utterly his soldier's faith. The transgressions resulting therefrom as revealed by the trial are a blot upon the military profession, a stain upon civilization and constitute a memory of shame and dishonor that can never be forgotten. Peculiarly callous and purposeless was the sack of the ancient city of Manila, with its Christian population and its countless historic shrines and monuments of culture and civilization which with campaign conditions reversed had previously been spared.

"It is appropriate here to recall that the accused was fully forewarned as to the personal consequences of such atrocities. On Oct. 24, 1944—just four days following the landing of our forces on Leyte—it was publicly proclaimed that I would hold the Japanese military authorities in the Philippines immediately liable for any harm which might result 'from failure to accord prisoners of war, civilian internees or civilian noncombatants the proper treatment and the protection to which they of right are entitled.' "

But despite MacArthur's outrage at such wanton violence to the military code, the principle of holding criminally responsible the political leaders of the vanquished in war was repugnant to him. He felt that to do so was to violate the most fundamental rules of criminal justice. He felt, and he so recommended, that any criminal responsibility attached to Japanese political leaders for the decision to wage war should be limited to an indictment for the attack on Pearl Harbor, since this was effected without a prior declaration of war as required by international law and custom. So he was pleased to be relieved of all responsibility having to do with the actual trial procedures before the International Military Tribunal, which started sitting in Tokyo January 4, 1946. MacArthur's obligations did not even include the selection of those to be tried. His only duties were to pass on the final judgments of the tribunal and to enforce the sentences.

The Potsdam Proclamation, which was the basis for the directive from which MacArthur took his orders as Supreme Commander, stated specifically that "stern justice shall be meted out to all war criminals, including those who have visited cruelties upon our prisoners." Accordingly, Japan's two largest and most modern prisons, one in Yokohama and the Sugamo Prison in Tokyo, soon housed hundreds of war criminals ranging all the way from former Prime Minister Tojo to Tokyo Rose. Such propagandists as the latter, together with many sadistic prison-camp guards and others of that stripe, were classed as minor war criminals and so tried. At Tojo's level were twenty-eight major Japanese political leaders who could be regarded as most responsible for formulating the policies that led to the war against the Allies. By the time the nine-month trial was over, two of the prisoners had died and one was declared insane. Tojo and twenty-four others were found guilty.

MacArthur would have been glad to have been relieved of the task he now had to perform—to pass on these judgments and to see to it that the sentences were carried out. Having no alternative, however, he endeavored to perform his duty in such a way as to write into the record another appeal against the utter futility of war and to impress upon the Japanese people that the judgments against their former leaders had not been made in a spirit of vengeance or vindictiveness.

He first conferred with the senior representatives of all the Allied Powers who had missions in Tokyo, in order to secure and consider their viewpoints. On November 24, 1948, after personally studying the legal review of the trial record, he closeted himself in his office and wrote: "No duty I have ever been called upon to perform in a long, public service replete with many bitter, lonely and forlorn assignments and responsibilities is so utterly repugnant to me as that of reviewing the sentences of the Japanese war criminal defendants by the International Military Tribunal for the Far East. It is not my purpose, nor indeed would I have that transcendent wisdom which would be necessary, to assay the universal fundamentals involved in these epochal proceedings designed to formulate and codify standards of international morality by those charged with the nation's conduct. The problem indeed is basically one which man has struggled to solve since the beginning of time, and which may well wait complete solution till the end of time.

"Insofar as my own immediate obligation and limited authority in this case is concerned, suffice it that under the principles and procedures described in full detail by the Allied Powers concerned, I can find nothing of commission or omission in the incidents of the trial itself of sufficient import to warrant my intervention in the judgments which have been rendered. No human decision is infallible, but I can conceive of no judicial process where greater safeguard was made to evolve justice.

"It is inevitable that many will disagree with the verdict; even the learned justices who composed the Tribunal were not in complete unanimity, but no mortal agency in the present imperfect evolution of civilized society seems more entitled to confidence in the integrity of its solemn pronouncements. If we cannot trust such processes and such men, we can trust nothing. I therefore direct the Commanding General of the Eighth Army to execute the sentences as pronounced by the Tribunal. In doing so, I pray that an Omnipotent Providence may use this tragic expiation as a symbol to summon all persons of good will to the realization of the utter futility of war—the most malignant scourge and greatest sin of mankind—and eventually to its renunciation by all nations. To this end, on the day of execution, I request the members of all the congregations throughout Japan of whatever creed or faith in the privacy of their homes or at their altars of public worship to seek divine help and guidance that the world will keep the peace, lest the human race perish."

His review was no sooner published than the pressure began to build to permit press photographs to be taken of the actual executions of the seven who had been sentenced to death. He refused, on the ground that such a spectacle would outrage the sensibilities of the Japanese and high-minded people everywhere in the world. The pressure was even turned on the Secretary of the Army to order the pictures taken, but MacArthur still refused, on the ground that he was acting in an international capacity in this case rather than as an officer of the United States. The matter was dropped. But in order to scotch any rumors that the executions had not actually taken place, MacArthur invited the members of the Allied Council for Japan—the United States, the British Commonwealth, China, and Russia—to act as official witnesses at the executions and certify to their accomplishment. All accepted, although somewhat reluctantly, and so certified.

The reaction of the Japanese people throughout this difficult period was a commendable one. During the trials a number of the prisoners themselves wrote letters to MacArthur or to the Tribunal, thanking them for the fairness with which the proceedings were being conducted. Such letters were even received from relatives of men who had been tried and sentenced to prison or executed. And when the last trial was over and the last sentence handed down, on November 12, 1948, MacArthur could take solace from the fact that, painful as his task had been, he had accomplished it with a minimum of ill will on the part of the Japanese.

Meanwhile SCAP was supervising the repatriation of more than six million Japanese soldiers, sailors, airmen, and civilian expatriates who flooded back into the homeland from the outposts reached during the campaign of conquest. Nearly all of them were permitted to resume their peacetime occupations, while more than one million slave laborers from Korea and China who had served as replacements were now shipped back to their homeland. At the same time political prisoners, most of whom had spent the war or a large part of it in jail for nothing more than "disloyal thought," were freed at MacArthur's order.

There remained an important segment of the Japanese population, in between those who were to be regarded as war criminals for their direction of Japan's aggressive policies and those humble soldiers who merely carried out orders and thus could be freed to go about their peacetime business. Just as there were unrepentant Nazis left to be ferreted out in Germany after V-E Day, just as it was necessary to clean out the collaborationists of occupied countries in Asia and Europe, so there were many Japanese who, while not being actual war criminals, shared some degree of contributing responsibility for the policies that led Japan into a war of conquest.

It was MacArthur's belief that though such persons should be barred for a time from any positions of power or influence, they should not be deprived of their civil rights and property or imprisoned in Japan as their counterparts had been in Germany. MacArthur's basic directive from Washington indicated that he should take into custody and hold for trial all such "militarists and ultranationalists." But he interpreted it liberally and tried, through nonpunitive methods, to permit a new leadership to arise in Japan, untainted by undesirable traits from the past. Moreover, in so far as possible, the implementation of this phase of occupation policy was left to the Japanese government. In all, 202,000 Japanese were purged from public life and political influence by final decisions handed down by Japanese review boards. Thus the Japanese people accepted both the principle and the practice of MacArthur's order, and no one purged became a martyr.

THE EMPEROR

While such political leaders as former Prime Minister Tojo and his colleagues were being tried as war criminals, there was considerable outcry from some of the Allies, notably the British and the Russians, to include Emperor Hirohito in this category. Indeed, the initial list of those proposed by the British to be charged with war crimes was headed by the Emperor's name. Realizing the tragic consequences that would follow such an unjust action, MacArthur stoutly resisted such efforts. Finally, when Washington seemed to be veering toward the British point of view, he advised that he would need at least one million reinforcements should such action be taken. He believed that if the Emperor were indicted as a war criminal, military government would have to be instituted throughout all Japan, and guerrilla warfare might break out. The Emperor's name was stricken off the list.

MacArthur's decision to resist the move to indict the Emperor early proved to be one of his wisest in the administration of Japan. It made a lasting impression upon the Japanese people, who understood that he had protected the Emperor's dignity and possibly his life, and they thereafter looked upon him as a symbol of protection against those animated solely by the base instinct of blind revenge. This in turn had a powerful influence upon the cooperation they extended to the occupation authorities thereafter. But, even more, the Emperor from the start became MacArthur's chief ally in the spiritual regeneration of Japan. Today in retrospect he credits the Emperor with a large share in the realization of the noble purposes to which MacArthur dedicated the occupation in his solemn pronouncements from the quarter deck of the battleship *Missouri*.

At the same time MacArthur saw to it that the Emperor's function was limited to that of a constitutional monarch. At his suggestion the revised Japanese constitution stipulated that the Emperor would exercise no political power, and that the power was thereafter vested in the people. Despite this, and despite the fact that the conservative cabinet members opposing this article of the constitution were persuaded to vote for it by the Emperor himself, many officials found it difficult to adapt themselves to the Emperor's new position.

A point of peculiar difficulty—and in some respects the greatest difficulty—arose in the revision of existing law to conform to the new constitution. The *lèse-majesté* provisions of the criminal code provided extreme penalties for any violation of the Emperor's person by word or by deed. MacArthur patiently explained to the Japanese political leaders that neither the President of the United States nor the King of England received the protection of special laws dealing with offenses against their persons. In the United States no legal distinction was drawn as to whether a murder victim was a private citizen or the President. But still the Japanese could not bring themselves to repeal the *lèse-majesté* provisions, and MacArthur was reluctant to issue a direct order for repeal.

Then, in early October 1946, just after the revised constitution had been adopted by the Diet, the public prosecutor of the city of Tokyo dismissed *lèse-majesté* charges against five individuals who had publicly criticized the Emperor and the emperor system. MacArthur seized the opportunity immediately and made a public statement that did much to clarify in Japanese minds the new constitutional position of the Emperor.

"The decision," he said, ". . . is a noteworthy application of the fundamental concept . . . that all men are equal before the law, that no individual in Japan—not even the Emperor—shall be clothed in legal protection denied the common man. It marks the beginning of a true understanding of the lofty spirit of the new National Charter which affirms the dignity of all men, and secures to all the right freely to discuss all issues, political, social and economic of concern to the people of a democratic nation. For the free interchange of ideas, the free expression of opinion, the free criticism of officials and institutions is essential to the life and growth of popular government. Democracy is vital and dynamic, but cannot survive unless all citizens are free thus to speak their minds. Such action, moreover, emphasizes the fact that from this land, broken and ravaged by war, there is emerging a free people and a free nation. As the Emperor becomes under this new constitution a symbol of the state, with neither inherent political power nor authority, the Japanese men and women are raised to a new status of political dignity and, in fact, will become the rulers of Japan. In his new role, the Emperor will symbolize the repository of state authority—the citizen. The dignity of the state will become the dignity of the individual citizen, and the protection accorded him as the symbol of the state ought to be no more or no less than the protection accorded the citizen. . . ."

It was largely in his own personal dealings with the Emperor that MacArthur set the tone of a just occupation policy. Shortly after his arrival in Japan, he was urged by some members of his staff to summon the Emperor to his headquarters as a show of power. MacArthur brushed the suggestion aside. "To do so," he explained, "would be to outrage the feelings of the Japanese people and make a martyr of the Emperor in their eyes. No, I shall wait and in time the Emperor will voluntarily come to see me." By thus adopting the patience of the East rather than the haste of the West, MacArthur won the affection of the Emperor's subjects instead of their hatred at the outset of the occupation.

The Emperor did indeed shortly request an interview. In cutaway,

striped trousers, and top hat, riding in his Daimler with the Imperial
Grand Chamberlain facing him on the jump seat, Hirohito arrived at the
American Embassy where MacArthur had offered to receive him in
secrecy. A photograph of the Emperor and MacArthur was taken only
after it was clear that the Emperor had no objection, and for the first time
in Japanese history a posed photograph of the Emperor was published in
the Japanese press. All other details of their thirty-eight-minute discussion, and in fact of all their subsequent periodic talks, were kept secret,
except that MacArthur has since revealed the tremendous and unexpected
impression made upon him by the Emperor immediately after his arrival
for their first Embassy meeting. "I come to you, General MacArthur," he
said through the court interpreter, "to offer myself to the judgment of the
Powers you represent as the one to bear sole responsibility for every political and military decision made and action taken by my people in the
conduct of the war." Nothing could have stirred MacArthur more than
this courageous assumption of a responsibility clearly belied by facts of
which MacArthur was fully aware. It established a close bond of understanding and a unity of purpose which was thereafter to serve both the
Allied Powers and the future of Japan.

MacArthur has told me that on subsequent visits their conversations
ranged over most of the problems of the world. A great deal of their
time together was spent with MacArthur explaining the underlying reasons for occupation policy while the Emperor listened attentively. The relationship between the two came rapidly to be one of mutual respect and
understanding. I remember MacArthur saying to me after one of these
conferences: "The Emperor has a more thorough grasp of the democratic
concept than almost any Japanese with whom I have talked."

Yet, when asked after the Emperor's first call when he intended to
return it, MacArthur replied with a tone of finality: "I shall never call
upon the Emperor until a treaty of peace is signed and the occupation
comes to a close. To do otherwise would be universally construed as an
acknowledgment of the equality between his position and that which I
occupy in representation of the Allied Powers—an equality which does
not exist." By thus keeping a firm but fair position between willful revenge
on the one hand and deference on the other, MacArthur earned for himself and the Allies Japanese friendship without thereby losing Japanese
respect. He often commented that when his policies were decried in
critical Allied circles as "too soft" from one side and "too tough" from the
other, he guessed that he was steering a fair and humane course.

THE PRESS

One of the groups that experienced the most difficulty in understanding the duties that accompany the privileges of freedom was that of the editors and publishers of Japan's newspapers and periodicals. Although Japanese publishers were traditionally subservient to centralized governmental control, one publisher early in the occupation became so intoxicated with his new-found freedom as to indulge in a fantastic campaign of propagating false anti-Allied atrocity stories. He did not stop until MacArthur was forced temporarily to suspend his newspaper's publication. This incident led to MacArthur's directing a comprehensive study of freedom of the press in Japan. The study led in turn to the adoption by all editors and publishers of a code of ethics modeled after that of the American Newspaper Publishers' Association. It still took a little while for the Japanese publishers to assimilate this new-found freedom to print what they wished without being controlled by the government, and for a time MacArthur still had to maintain some control until the press was able to assume its own full responsibility. The publishers gradually did, with the result that under the occupation Japan had its first entirely free press in the history of the country. That Japan's press has prospered under the code given it by MacArthur is indicated by the fact that the number of magazines published in Japan rose from 430 in 1946 to 699 in 1950; the number of newspapers rose from 55 to about 160 in the same period.

THE POLICE

MacArthur summed up both a diagnosis of Japan's past police problems and the prescription for remedying them in a message to Prime Minister Yoshida on September 16, 1947: "It has been a dominant characteristic of modern totalitarian dictatorships, as it was in Japan's feudalistic past, to establish and maintain a strongly centralized police bureaucracy headed by a chief executive officer beyond the reach of popular control," he said. "Indeed the strongest weapon of the military clique in Japan in the decade prior to the war was the absolute authority exercised by the national government over the 'thought police' and the Kempei Tai [secret police], extending down to prefectural levels of government. Through these media, the military were enabled to spread a network of political espionage, suppress freedom of speech, of assembly and even of thought, and by means of tyrannical oppression to degrade the dignity of the individual. Japan was thus in the fullest sense a police state. . . .

"It should be borne in mind that, in the final analysis, police power in the preservation of law and order in a democratic society does not attain its maximum strength through oppressive controls imposed upon the people from above, but rather does it find the infinitely greater strength in the relationship of a servant of, and answerable directly to the people. Thereby and thereby alone may it encourage respect for the people's laws through confidence and paternalistic pride in the policies as the law enforcement agency of the people themselves."

The Japanese police problems led to some of the longest discussions —not to say the most heated arguments—in SCAP offices during the entire occupation. The proponents of centralized control maintained that the Japanese people were temperamentally unequipped for the authority of decentralization and that for the time being, at least, there was a lack of resources at the community level to undertake such responsibilities. Geographically, they argued, Japan lent itself to the maintenance of public order by a centralized police system. Those who opposed, led by the government section, argued that local responsibility for exercise of the police power was inherently an aspect of local autonomy, provided for by the constitution, and without which the stature of local government could not possibly become dynamic and grow. MacArthur listened patiently to the arguments, both pro and con. But he had no difficulty making his decision, since it amounted to aligning himself against the proposal for the continuance of an all-powerful central government.

By his decentralization of the police power to invest the local community with the responsibility for its own protection in accordance with the constitutional provision for local autonomy, MacArthur struck one of his strongest blows for freedom in Japan. At one time he went so far as to express the view that, if we could leave Japan reoriented toward a structure of government firmly resting upon individual and community responsibility, even though it be no further advanced than was America a century and a half ago, he felt that a strong foundation would have been laid for the future of a free Japan.

MacArthur's philosophy was probably most clearly phrased by him in a public statement he issued following enactment by the Diet of a law providing that "local public entities shall have the right to manage their property affairs and administration and to enact their own regulations within the law." He took this occasion to point out: "Democracy cannot be imposed upon a nation. It is a thing of the spirit which to be lasting and durable must impregnate the very roots of society. It is not to be instilled from above. It must have its origin in the understanding and faith of the common people. It must well up from the people's will to be free, from their desire and determination to govern their own local affairs without domination by their strong men, by minority pressure groups or by entrenched bureaucracy. It is essential therefore that the people in every prefecture, city and village be given complete opportunity to express their will and by assuming full responsibility to learn procedure of democratic government. Such direct participation in local government will profoundly influence the shaping of national policies—will provide a checkrein against arbitrary governmental controls and a safeguard to individual freedom. . . . It is axiomatic that such experiences in government will develop the dynamic and enlightened leadership and initiative essential to the vigorous and progressive building of a democratic nation."

MacArthur never failed to align himself against the proponents of an all-powerful central government, which he felt stifled that sense of responsibility and dignity which must reside in the individual citizen if a nation is to achieve its maximum strength. He fully realized that on this issue there existed a basic conflict between those concepts which had guided the building of our own nation and those which traditionally had governed in Japan, as in most of Asia.

Our own nation had coalesced from a group of individual sovereign states into a federated unity when the states yielded to a centralized government the essential powers of a nation. Not so with the provinces which composed the Japanese Empire. They had not preceded but had followed the founding of the nation itself, and were subdivisions for administrative or other purposes. Never had they themselves been sovereign. But MacArthur had abiding faith that once a people had managed their own affairs, they would never voluntarily give up that authority. So has it proved in Japan. Japan will never again revert to a central autocracy unless its people are conquered and brought under the subjugation of a ruthless military force.

Possibly the new law which pleased MacArthur most was that which established the writ of *habeas corpus*. For this law, enacted by the Diet to bring the code of criminal procedure into harmony with the bill-of-rights provision of the new constitution, was a product entirely of Japanese initiative, without the slightest prodding or assistance from the government section. When it was thus introduced for the first time into the Japanese legal system, MacArthur was reminded that in 1901 the same protection had been first accorded the Filipino people under the administration of his father, General Arthur MacArthur, as Military Governor of the Philippine Islands. So it was that under the guidance of father and son this Anglo-Saxon guarantee against arbitrary detention was carried to the East as a safeguard for Asian peoples.

WOMEN

Of all the reforms wrought by MacArthur in Japan, none had such heartwarming results as that which changed the status of women. Almost overnight more than forty million people who had been virtual serfs achieved freedom and equal rights. Not since Lincoln has such a revolutionary change of status been accomplished on such a mass scale.

MacArthur insisted upon this move despite criticism from many quarters. From the first, when he asked for the enfranchisement of women in the general election, his view was opposed by many American and British "experts" on Japan who expressed the view that Japanese women were too steeped in the tradition of subservience to their husbands to act with any degree of political independence. Giving the vote to a woman, they argued, simply meant giving two votes to her husband. But MacArthur was unmoved by such predictions and continued to believe that women's suffrage would help lend stability and morality to Japanese politics.

The Japanese women proceeded in the first elections fully to bear out his faith. More than thirteen million women went to the polls. A result was that thirty-eight women were elected to the House of Representatives. Nearly 50 per cent of all women candidates for office were elected, in contrast with the election of only 15 per cent of all men candidates. Even by the standards of a Western country where women had voted for many years, this was a notable performance.

On the morning following that first election an extremely dignified but obviously distraught Japanese legislative leader requested and was given an appointment with MacArthur. Attired in a cutaway and striped trousers, the caller, who was one of a numerous group of Harvard Law School graduates in Japan, launched immediately into the subject that was troubling him so deeply.

"I regret to say that something terrible has happened, Your Excellency."

MacArthur listened politely but impassively.

"A prostitute, Your Excellency, has been elected to the House of Representatives."

MacArthur did not change his expression. "How many votes did she receive?" he asked.

The Japanese legislator sighed. "256,000," he said.

A twinkle appeared in MacArthur's eye. But he managed to keep from smiling as he said solemnly: "Then I should say there must have been more than her dubious occupation involved."

The Japanese women were embracing their freedom in many ways. They sought and found jobs in almost every business and profession, even including the local police forces; there were nearly 2,000 women police by 1951. More than 1,500,000 women joined labor unions. And, partly at the instigation of the new women Diet members, laws were passed giving women equal pay with men, limiting overtime for women, and providing adequate illness and maternity leave. In the schools, where the sexes had been segregated after the sixth grade and where girls had been educated at a lower level, even to including separate textbooks, equality of education was now established. Coeducation was installed in the high schools and state universities, and colleges for girls alone were opened for the first time.

Women also campaigned vigorously for equal *saké* and cigarette rations, and an end to concubinage and family contract marriages; they bought their own property, took time out from their housework to read *Blondie,* learned to square-dance, and even listened to radio soap operas. As part of the program for equality, laws concerning marriage, divorce, and adultery had to be changed. The male legislators who attempted to change the adultery law found themselves in a predicament they could not resolve: in order to punish a wife for adultery they would, by rights, also have to punish a husband for the same crime. After considerable pondering of this problem, the men resolved it by making adultery no longer a crime. Meanwhile, the courts were receiving their first divorce actions in which wives were taking the initiative—one in particular being a woman whose husband returned at the end of the war with a native wife and two children from Borneo.

MacArthur publicly expressed his gratification at the new role of women in Japan when he greeted a delegation of ten women leaders who were embarking to study the various aspects of women's participation in political, economic, and social affairs in America. Praising the women of Japan for their "magnificent response to the challenge to womanhood under a democracy," he pointed out that during the four years since their enfranchisement they had "fully justified my faith in the part Japanese women were destined to play in the transformation of a completely regimented society into one composed of individuals, each of whom of right is free, by demonstrating their capacity to assume coequal responsibilities of citizenship in a democratic state. . . . The rapid development of women's influence in community affairs without sacrifice to their position in the home is," he said, "one of the truly momentous developments in Japan's history. . . . From a condition of subservience to traditional domestic routine with little individuality in law, the women of Japan now share equally with men the sovereign responsibility of political direction. Never in history has there been a more far-reaching and dramatic transformation."

MacArthur pointed out that this transformation had not been accomplished through fiat or decree. The occupation had "simply helped eliminate obstacles to the emergence of this new and potentially dynamic force in Japanese life." To the women themselves, he added, "who accepted equality under the law without the slightest pause and are demonstrating a genuine eagerness to assume the corresponding responsibility in public affairs must be given full credit for the achievement." He said that in all fields their "great and good influence is being progressively felt," and that such influence "is a continuing challenge to the men of Japan to reach an ever higher order of responsible statesmanship in service to the nation." He concluded by reminding them of the uniquely vital responsibility of women in training youth to meet the exacting requirements of potential leadership. "Practical experience in civic affairs and in the stewardship of their newly won civil rights," he said, "will materially broaden the field of home training, with its reflection to be found in the character, the wisdom and the vision of Japan's future leaders."

But possibly no action MacArthur took during his administration had a more beneficial effect upon Japanese dignity and morale than when early in the occupation he ignored all precedents and moved to rekindle a spirit of healthy nationalism, pride, and self-respect in Japanese hearts. "To enhance the spiritual strength necessary to carry on in the pattern which your general welfare now demands, and in recognition of those advances you have heretofore made in establishing the sturdy base for a free political destiny," he said, "I now restore to you the unrestricted use and display of your national flag within your country's territorial limits.

And I do so with the fervent hope that this flag shall ever stand in future before the world as a symbol of peace, based upon those immutable concepts of justice and freedom universally sought by the human race; that it shall stand firm advocate for a concept of nationalism ever subordinate to the higher duty of obedience to the universal laws, written and unwritten, which establish the mutual obligations and responsibilities among peoples within the family of nations; and that it shall serve as a shining beacon to summon every Japanese citizen resolutely to the duty of building Japan's economic stature to ensure and preserve Japan's political freedom."

So, on the official level of directives, promulgations, and the implementation of official policy, MacArthur's SCAP rebuilt the structure of Japan. But MacArthur and the other Americans in Japan did a great deal more than that. In fact, an extremely interesting phenomenon occurred in the early days of the occupation. It was a source of surprise to most of us in SCAP that the GI's who had endured such vicious fighting against Japanese soldiers and that the Japanese civilians who had suffered so much from American bombings were able to get along together immediately after the war was over. MacArthur was not surprised. He realized that war and the constant threat of death teach a man a great deal about humility. And he said from the start that the combat soldiers would conduct themselves with infinitely more restraint than would their postwar, non-combat replacements.

A particularly enlightening example of this came when Shigeru Yoshida, the then Foreign Minister and later Prime Minister, had his first meeting with an occupation soldier. Yoshida was on his way from Tokyo to Yokohama on the day after MacArthur's arrival in Japan, when he was suddenly stopped by an American sentry. "I thought my time had come," Yoshida says in relating the story, "and I prepared to meet my Maker. But to my amazement, the soldier stuck his fist in the window next to me and with a friendly grin said: 'How about an American cigarette, buddy?' as he handed me a pack of cigarettes." This unknown, unsung GI made a great contribution to the mutual trust and faith between Americans and Japanese.

The Japanese talent for copying Western ways was never presented with more opportunities than during those early days of the occupation. While SCAP gave Japan the major political, economic, educational, religious, and other reforms enumerated previously in this chapter, the GI's made such equally important contributions to Japanese manners and mores as a picturesque slang, boogie-woogie, the geisha girls' favorite song: *You Are My Sunshine*, and a sign for a filling station outside Kyoto: "Last Chancu."

Partly because of such manifestations as these, but mostly because of the guiding hand of MacArthur, who understood the Japanese so well, the co-operation and partnership of occupier and occupied was a success from the start. In this case, Kipling erred; the twain *did* meet. So obvious was it to MacArthur that this was the first modern military occupation to succeed that only eighteen months after the surrender he announced that the Japanese people were then fully entitled to the restoration of full sovereign powers. His public statement was a political bombshell in the capitals of the Allies. The Japanese people, realizing that it was in opposition to the pronounced policies of the other Allied governments at the time and that MacArthur was in effect calling for an end to his unprecedented power, were no less astonished at first. But their surprise soon gave way to pride in their accomplishment and faith and trust in MacArthur. That the governments behind SCAP did not accept MacArthur's proposal did not diminish its soundness in the eyes of the Japanese.

Certainly the best summing up of Japan's progress and accomplishments under MacArthur was made by the Supreme Commander himself on New Year's Day 1951. In a message to the Japanese people, he not only summarized the results of five years of his administration, but also pointed out the spiritual bonds welded between victor and vanquished. The address also sets a standard for other nations to emulate if they would foster the good will of their neighbors and secure the blessings of enduring peace.

MacArthur credited the Japanese people with the magnificent way in which they were standing up before the gathering international storms. He reviewed their progress during the year just passed and called upon them, if necessity demanded, to "mount force to repel force" in concert with other free nations. "As the dawn of another year breaks upon new Japan," he said, "every Japanese citizen may review the past with satisfaction at progress achieved, and look forward with added self-assurance to the difficult tests which lie ahead. For this land in the past year has witnessed advances in every field of human and social endeavor and the Japanese citizen has undoubtedly emerged with added individual liberty and higher personal dignity. From this period of trial has, indeed, come a measure of the moral stature of the Japanese nation and people who have met the challenge of a flaming Asia with calm deliberation, unruffled composure and quiet determination.

"Politically, economically and socially, Japan has continued to make uninterrupted and significant progress toward the goal of national stability. Representative democracy in its added maturity now stands guardian over the rights and liberties of the people, and impressive strides have been made in the development of autonomous responsibility. Under the impetus which alone springs from the pursuit of free private competitive enterprises, production in agriculture and industry has achieved new post-war highs, and Japan has again been able successfully to operate under a government fiscal policy centering on a truly balanced budget, curtailment of subsidies and sound credit practices. For the first time since the war's end, the index of industrial production has exceeded the 1932–36 base level by an appreciable margin. In foreign trade, impressive and encouraging gains also were made, the volume of exports exceeding by 50% the volume achieved during the previous year, with the gap between imports and exports being further narrowed to a very heartening degree. Socially, progress has been no less notable. Despite increased international tensions, this land has been an oasis of tranquillity and progress. It has fully merited the respect and faith of men of good will everywhere and proved its right to equal partnership in the family of free nations of the earth."

"Your constitution," MacArthur continued, "renounces war as an instrument of national policy. This concept represents one of the highest, if not the highest, ideal the modern world has ever known and which all men must in due course embrace if civilization is to be preserved. This self-imposed limitation has meticulously guided your thought and action on the problem of national security, even despite the menace of gathering storms. If, however, international lawlessness continues to threaten the peace and to exercise dominion over the lives of men, it is inherent that this ideal must give way to the overweening law of self-preservation, and it will become your duty, within the principles of the United Nations in concert with others who cherish freedom to mount force to repel force. It is my fervent hope that such an eventuality will never come to pass, but should it, Japan's security would be the deep concern of all the other free nations of the Pacific area.

"I sincerely trust that this year will bring to New Japan the blessings of complete political freedom through a treaty effectively erasing the remaining scars of war, and that thereafter, a Japanese nation firmly rooted in immutable concepts of political morality, economic freedom and social justice evolved from a blend of ideas and ideals of the West and your own hallowed traditions and time-honored and universally-respected culture, may be counted upon to exercise a profound influence upon the course of destiny in Asia."

MacArthur could not know it at the time, but forces were already at work—in the United States and the capitals of western Europe—to make this his valedictory to the Japanese people as Supreme Commander for the Allied Powers.

CHAPTER V   Communism's Nemesis

✍ Sometimes it seemed to us in SCAP headquarters that while the enlisted man of the United States Army was MacArthur's strongest helper, his superiors in Washington were the worst hindrance. From the moment when he assumed his authority as Supreme Commander, MacArthur found himself under varying and conflicting pressures from Washington to put into effect any number of ill-advised programs in Japan. Policymakers at the highest governmental levels urged that another Morgenthau Plan be used on Japan to give our former enemy the *coup de grâce*. Similarly doubtful proposals from the Allies were passed along: British and Soviet officials were insistent upon the partition of Japan into spheres of Allied responsibility, as had been so disastrously permitted in Germany. The British demanded that the Emperor be tried as a war criminal. The Russians seconded this request, adding one that would make all Japanese prisoners of war into slave laborers. MacArthur refused to yield to these pressures. He could see the lesson of divided authority in Germany, and he intended to profit by that lesson even if the Washington officials could not.

Despite the fact that the United States provided seventy-five per cent of all occupations troops, Washington evidently wanted to divide the unilateral authority it then exercised with the British and the Russians. MacArthur was advised that plans for some kind of Allied commission on Japan were being drafted. MacArthur opposed this idea wholeheartedly. He felt that as the Pacific war had required a major United States military effort, the United States should unilaterally see it through until peace had been firmly restored. But in December 1945, Secretary of State James Byrnes went to Moscow, where a tripartite conference on the subject was held among the United States, Great Britain, and Russia. For reasons best known to the conferees, France and China were excluded. At this conference the unilateral authority of the United States was indeed surrendered in favor of an international authority acting through a policy-making body consisting of representatives of the eleven nations that had actually been engaged in the war against Japan. This body was seated in Washington and an advisory body consisting of representatives of the United States, the British Commonwealth, China, and the Soviet was seated in Tokyo.[1]

MacArthur concealed his irritation over such an ill-considered move, but he could not prevent his friends in positions of prominence and influence from protesting vigorously. At the end of December, however, a U.S. State Department officer speaking for the Far Eastern Commission, blandly announced   answer to such protests that MacArthur had been consulted regarding the Moscow conference and the subject to be discussed there and that he had made no objection. This was too much. MacArthur decided that to keep the record straight he was forced to speak up. He made the following ann uncement:

"The statement attribute .o the Far Eastern Commission officer, that I 'did not object to the nev Japan control plan before it was approved in Moscow' is incorrect. On October 31 my final disagreement was contained in my radio to the Chief of Staff for the Secretary of State advising that the 'terms in my opinion are not acceptable.' Since that time my views have not been sought. Any impression which the statement might imply that I was consulted during the Moscow conferences is also incorrect. I have no iota of responsibility for the decisions which were made there."

At the same time, however, MacArthur made it clear that despite these handicaps he would "see it through," because, he said, "I am here to serve and not to hinder or obstruct the American government."

In practice the Far Eastern Commission, largely because of its international composition and the veto power vested in four of its members, including the Soviet, moved so slowly in its deliberations that its positive action was generally confined to confirming steps which MacArthur had already taken months before on his own initiative. But it was the Allied Council which subjected MacArthur to some harassment. To cope with the situation he took the fullest possible advantage of the fact that under the Moscow agreement the Supreme Commander was specifically left as the "sole executive authority."

[1] It is difficult to reconcile this formal action taken at Moscow with President Truman's statement in his recently published memoirs: "Anxious as we were to have Russia in the war again Japan, the experience at Potsdam now made me determined that I would not allow the Russians any part in the control of Japan. I made up my mind that General MacArthur would be given complete command and control after victory in Japan."

The Allied Council for Japan was by its terms of reference solely advisory and consultative. On this fact MacArthur was to lean heavily in the years which followed. Although in complete disagreement with the principle of surrendering our unilateral authority over Japan and subjecting our freedom of action to the unwieldy framework of two international bodies, MacArthur set out to work in the closest possible co-operation with the council sitting in Tokyo. As he had suspected, however, his efforts in this direction were doomed to failure.

The Soviet delegate, Lieutenant General Kuzma Derevyanko, in particular sought from the start to utilize the Allied Council as a platform for propaganda speeches and statements and as a means of throwing obstacles in the path of orderly government in Japan. In fact, one of the first items on the agenda of the council was a critically worded request from Derevyanko for information on MacArthur's purge directives, carrying with it the implication that those responsible for the policies leading to the war were being protected. To counter this obvious propaganda device, MacArthur directed me to answer the query in such a manner that the Soviets would not repeat such tactics in the future. I thereupon gave the council a report that took three hours and that could have taken a full week if the Russian delegate had not finally capitulated with the admission that he had not intended to imply failure to implement the directive.

Another bit of harassment from the council was a request that every directive from SCAP be submitted to the council one week in advance. Obviously any such method of procedure would have utterly paralyzed occupation machinery, but because of his sincere desire to co-operate with the council even though it seemed only to be making work for his already overworked staff, MacArthur promised that wherever possible he would submit SCAP's major directives to the council two days in advance. He made it clear that he would do this for the council's information, not for its approval.

As the Soviet representative on the council continued in his attempts to turn that body into a captive Soviet organ of propaganda, MacArthur had no choice but to combat these attempts; and as a result the Allied Council was very soon reduced to complete impotence. Meanwhile, in Washington, where the Soviet delegate to the Far Eastern Commission was carrying out the same destructive program, that group of representatives became little more than a debating society; when a peace treaty was finally signed with Japan, it died a quiet death. Not one constructive idea to help with the reorientation and reconstruction of Japan had been offered by either the Far Eastern Commission or the Allied Council.

Part II: Japan

While MacArthur was having difficulties enough with Allied representatives in Tokyo, he was constantly forced to strain his patience and his powers of diplomacy to the utmost in dealing with the hordes of "visiting firemen," many of them self-styled experts on Asia, who happened to be passing through from Washington. The one who probably did the greatest amount of damage to the occupation program as well as to all United States prestige in Asia—by a single, unguarded statement—was a man whom MacArthur personally liked and admired. Kenneth Royall was Secretary of the Army when he passed through Tokyo in February 1949. While there, he held a select little cocktail party to which he invited a few newspaper representatives. Secretary Royall did not consult MacArthur before making his statement, and in fact when a press officer from SCAP, who at Royall's request had arranged for the correspondents to be present, appeared at the party with a friend, he was pointedly asked to leave. Whether Royall intended at the outset to make the remarks he did is a secret buried in the recesses of his own mind; certainly he could not have intended to produce quite the storm that followed his statement.

It was an informal affair, and the correspondents understood ahead of time that what the Secretary said was "not for attribution." This meant that what he said could be paraphrased or even quoted, so long as it was not attributed to him. Contrary to excuses made at the time, it was not an "off-the-record" session, and in fact specific stipulation was made that everything said at the cocktail party could be repeated after Royall had had five days to get out of town.

Royall also made the following remarks, according to the correspondents' accounts published after the stipulated time limit: "I don't know what our troops could do in Japan in the event of war. I am not certain we could hold Japan, nor am I certain it would be worthwhile as long as we have Okinawa and the Philippines." He added: "I think it might be better to pull out before the war started. . . . In any event, our west coast is not endangered. Our east coast is. So all priority must be given to plans to hold western Europe." This was in the same vein that had become so familiar to MacArthur throughout World War II. Royall even expanded on the theme. "The American Navy," the Army Secretary said, "could keep the west coast, Hawaii and probably the Philippines from any real danger."

As the party progressed, Royall made these further points: (1) "America is not obliged to stay in Japan. We don't owe the Japanese anything, not even as moral obligation. We had the right—and the duty—

to disarm them after the war, even though someone else may later cut their throats." (2) When asked if the United States should not defend Japan if only as a matter of prestige, Royall said: "If it is just a question of prestige, let's get our troops out now."

Asia's reaction to Royall's little cocktail party was fairly well summed up by an Australian newspaper headline, which read: "ALONE IN THE PA-CIFIC!" In the weeks and even months that followed these remarks, President Truman and General MacArthur both issued statements denying that the United States had any intention of suddenly pulling troops out of Japan. But despite these denials Royall's statement merely served to destroy a great deal of the confidence in the United States which Mac-Arthur had worked so hard to establish.

MacArthur was naturally surprised at such a blunder. But he was even more astonished when Royall, on his return to Washington, attempted through his aide to deny making any such statements and even to imply that they had actually been made by others in an attempt to focus more attention on the Asiatic theater. MacArthur did not protest publicly at the time, but his task was made a great deal more difficult by such ill-advised comments from official sources.

Secretary Royall obviously had no intention of obstructing Japan's recovery. Such, however, cannot be said of some other elements in the capitals of the Allies. Secretary of State Byrnes learned early during the tripartite negotiations in Moscow that it was the British who most wanted to dilute United States authority in Japan. The British, Secretary Byrnes said at a press conference after the Moscow meeting, "have been really more insistent upon greater participation than the Soviet government." In Tokyo, MacArthur found constant British efforts to exploit the Japanese people one of the principal obstacles to his program for restoring Japan's shattered economy.

Britain's primary purpose—and an understandable one—was to reduce Japan's competitive position in Asia. The strongest advocates of measures designed to put permanent restrictions upon Japan's industrial capacity, the British also sought desperately to bring Japan within the orbit of the "sterling bloc"; this would automatically impose price controls upon raw materials and finished products by placing limitations on the convertibility of local currencies. MacArthur refused to countenance placing Japan under such subservience to British finance, at least as long as the American people were subsidizing Japan's recovery with American dollars. The British did not give up easily, however, and it is a matter of historical interest that not many months before MacArthur was finally recalled from Japan in 1951, one of Britain's senior representatives informally told him that the British government was exerting every possible pressure upon Washington to have him removed from Asia.

But the British in turn could take lessons from the Russians. Although the Russians declared war on Japan only a week before the surrender, and although Russian fighting in the Pacific was confined to Manchuria and Korea, the Soviet government asked the American Ambassador in Moscow if a Soviet general could not be appointed Joint Commander-in-Chief with MacArthur in Tokyo. This request was naturally rejected, but the Soviets were nevertheless granted full coequal status with the other Allies as conquerors of Japan. Probably no greater prize was ever won more easily and with less cost in all history.

The Soviets lost no time in exploiting their prize. The Kremlin's representative in the Allied Council, Lieutenant General Kuzma Derevyanko, was a forty-three-year-old career soldier who looked like a professional wrestler and was able to speak very little English. Under his leadership, the Soviet representatives in Japan promptly set out to discover how much they could get away with.

Offering to supply Russian soldiers to the occupation force, they reneged when they found that MacArthur would not permit them to take over Hokkaido island, bordering Soviet territory and comprising one fifth of Japan. Thus MacArthur early won the enmity of the Soviet Union, but thus he forestalled an East Germany of Japan. Whenever Derevyanko found an opportunity to delay or interrupt the proceedings of the Allied Council, he leaped at the chance. Closely directed by the political commissars who always hovered at his elbow, Derevyanko did all he could to disrupt the council's business. Sometimes supported by his British Commonwealth counterpart, a former Australian radio commentator named MacMahon Ball, Derevyanko devoted most of his time on the council to making speeches in derogation of occupation policy and administration.

Actually, by virtue of its position as one of the conquerors, Soviet Russia was entitled to send a diplomatic "mission" under the terms of the agreement worked out with Secretary Byrnes and the British at Moscow. This she had declined to do, since such a mission would have to be accredited to SCAP. But she proceeded to use her office for the purpose of introducing all the "representatives" that she could into Japan. While none of the other Allied offices contained more than a small staff, the Soviet had four hundred men. Virtually every one of them could be presumed to be a trained espionage agent.

The Soviets were at that time accustomed to being treated to the diplomatic niceties in the United States and Europe, despite their own international behavior. But in Japan they found that they had an adversary who could speak their own diplomatic language.

When Derevyanko issued a loud protest accusing the Supreme Commander of noncompliance with the Potsdam Declaration and sent a note to that effect to MacArthur, he received the following blunt reply: "I have received your note of June 24 and have carefully considered its context in vain search for some semblance of merit and validity. Rarely indeed have I perused such a conglomeration of misstatements, misrepresentations and prevarications of fact. Without new or constructive thought, it is but a labored repetition of the line of fantastic propaganda which for some time has been emanating from centers within the orbit of Communist totalitarian imperialism.

"So complete is the unrealism of its premise that it offers no basis for rational discussion. Its plain purpose to support and encourage those few irresponsible Japanese bent upon creating mass confusion and social unrest leading to violence and disorder is a shameful misuse of diplomatic privilege which ill becomes the representative of a nation charged with a measure of responsibility in the democratic reorientation of Japan. I am accordingly left no other alternative than to disapprove its intemperate proposals, and indeed reject the complete context of the document itself." This was the kind of MacArthur diplomacy the Communists found in Japan. It served its purpose perfectly in keeping Soviet propaganda off balance by neutralizing most of it before it reached the Japanese people.

But at the propaganda level MacArthur found that he had to keep a wary eye on Washington as well as Tokyo. For the State Department usually reacted with a meek half-apologetic reply—if not complete silence —when the Soviet Ambassador took it upon himself publicly to denounce MacArthur and the administration of Japan. Usually an outbreak of Communist trouble-making in Japan would be carefully co-ordinated with an outburst from the Soviet Ambassador, and MacArthur found it necessary to deal with such world-wide propaganda maneuvers as summarily as he did in Tokyo.

And if the Soviets in Washington expected from him the same humble reaction to their propaganda tactics that they had been receiving from the United States State Department, they suffered a few nasty surprises. For example, an intemperate charge by the Soviet Ambassador that the occupation was being mismanaged was, as in practically every other case, virtually ignored by the State Department. But this is the answer publicly issued by MacArthur in Tokyo: "I have noted the statement of the Soviet ambassador before the Far Eastern Commission in derogation of American policy and action with reference to Japan. It has little validity measured either by truth or realism and can be regarded as mainly a continuation of the extraordinary irresponsibility of Soviet propaganda.

"Its basic cause is the complete frustration of the Soviet effort to absorb Japan within the orbit of the Communistic ideology. This effort has been incessant and relentless from the inception of the occupation. It has sought by every means within its power to spread discord and dissension throughout this country reduced by the disasters of war to an economy of poverty originally threatening the actual livelihood of the entire nation. It has hoped to so mutilate the masses that there would be imposed through the resulting despair and misery a godless concept of atheistic totalitarian enslavement. It has failed, due largely to the innate common sense and conservatism of the Japanese people, the concepts of democratic freedom implanted during the occupation and a progressive improvement in living conditions. The resulting rage and frustration have produced, as in the present instance, an unbridled vulgarity of expression which is the sure hallmark of propaganda and failure."

A few months later a Soviet attack in the Far Eastern Commission brought no reply whatever from the State Department. But it brought from MacArthur an answer that read, in part: "For the Soviet to prate of brutality, of labor freedom and economic liberty, is enough to make Ananias blush. At least his sin was not compounded by provocative hypocrisy."

And whenever the Soviet propaganda sniping became excessive, MacArthur used his biggest gun. He had only to ask: what became of those 300,000 Japanese soldiers captured by the Russians? This was the sorest point between the Japanese people and the Soviets. When the Kwantung army surrendered to the Russians in Manchuria at the end of World War II, 2,400,000 soldiers were taken prisoner, most of whom were kept in Soviet prison camps for four years, while every effort was made to indoctrinate them and deceive them with falsehoods about the United States. They were told that they could not be returned home because MacArthur would not send ships for them, and that food was being taken from the starving Japanese to feed the occupation forces.

When finally the first big batch of 95,000 prisoners were returned to Japan, many were so completely indoctrinated with Red propaganda that they were singing the *Internationale* and waving red flags. This Soviet trick backfired, however, when the returned Japanese discovered how badly they had been deceived. But what outraged the Japanese people was the fact that a large segment of the Kwantung army did not come back. More than 300,000 soldiers were not returned, and have not been accounted for to this day. So when MacArthur simply asked what had happened to them, he never failed to throw a wrench into the well-oiled gears of the Soviet propaganda machine.

In his personal dealings with the Soviet representatives in Japan, despite the countless and constant provocations, MacArthur maintained an attitude of fairness but firmness. Early in the occupation came an incident in which he established this policy in such a way that no Russian could misunderstand him—but also in a way that won the grudging respect of a Soviet officer who realized that he had met his match. The late Joseph Keenan, U.S. Chief Prosecutor at the Far East War Crimes trials, to whom I am indebted for this account, recalled it clearly because, as he put it, "It was my first lesson that the Soviets respected power and firmness—they recognized those qualities in General MacArthur and not alone behaved themselves in consequence, but held him in high esteem."

The Soviet concerned in the incident was the Russian representative on the prosecuting staff of the trials, Colonel General S. A. Golunsky, who in a point of military rank was probably the senior Communist representative in the Far East at the time. He headed a delegation of sixty-five aides and assistants, and an indication of his importance by Soviet measurement was that he was able to make decisions on the spot without submitting them to Moscow. One Sunday morning Prosecutor Keenan received a call from the Provost Marshal's office stating that the military police had picked up a Russian trying to leave Tokyo without a permit. He seemed upset, the caller told Keenan, and had asked that the Provost Marshal's office telephone him. Keenan had him brought to Mitsui House, where Keenan's quarters were.

The Russian was Golunsky, and he was indeed irate. He complained that he had been unceremoniously arrested by the American Military Police at a check point and that despite his rank and position he had been taken to the police station. He demanded an immediate written apology from MacArthur for this insult to his country.

Keenan, deeply perturbed, went to the Dia Ichi Building and laid the facts before the Supreme Commander.

MacArthur replied by asking: "Joe, do you ever try to leave Tokyo without properly executed orders?"

"No, sir."

"You may tell General Golunsky," MacArthur said, "that we have of

305

necessity carefully enacted rules and regulations applying to all personnel of the Allied forces. These regulations apply to all ranks from the privates to the general officers. They are enforced without partiality among the representatives of all nations. You may tell Golunsky that there are no discriminations for or against any nations or any nationals and that representatives of the Soviet Union will be treated exactly as anyone else. Tell him that as long as he obeys these regulations there will be no difficulties, but when infractions occur he may expect exactly the same results as today. Tell him," MacArthur added with finality, "there will be no apology, oral or written."

Keenan returned to Mitsui House and repeated the message exactly. Golunsky contemplated it impassively for a moment. Then he shook his head, broke into a wide smile, and pounded Keenan on the back. "What a man," he said. "He surely is a real leader."

MacArthur's uncanny ability to adapt himself to different peoples as well as to different situations never showed more clearly than in his dealings with the Russians in Japan. On a given morning at his office he could converse in the stylized civilities of Japanese diplomacy with the Prime Minister better than any other American; at lunch he could be a jovial host to a group of businessmen on a visit from the U.S.; and in the afternoon he could converse with General Derevyanko with a blunt forthrightness that would have shocked the Japanese Prime Minister or the U.S. businessmen, but which was precisely the language of Derevyanko. On one occasion, when Derevyanko called upon MacArthur to say good-by before returning to Moscow for a visit, he was treated to an hour's dissertation on what was wrong with Stalin and the whole fabric of Soviet foreign policy. "Now," MacArthur said, "you tell that to Marshal Stalin if you will." Derevyanko did not promise to do so, but he obviously appreciated this show of frankness.

It was a source of some amusement at SCAP, however, when Derevyanko did not return to Tokyo for nearly a year. When he did, MacArthur greeted him cordially. And by the same adaptability with which he had won the warm friendship of the Emperor by the most formal courtesy, MacArthur delighted Derevyanko with a jest suited perfectly to the Russian sense of humor: "Why, General Derevyanko! Delighted to see you back! When you failed to return sooner, I feared they had shot you!"

It seemed to us on MacArthur's staff that at every crisis with the Communists in Japan, the failure of Washington support seemed to reflect almost studied indifference. We constantly received reports of underground opposition to MacArthur and his occupation policies, with the focus of the opposition seeming to be in the State Department. Mac-Arthur was aware of this situation and was puzzled both by the pressures that seemed to operate against him and by the lack of explanation for them. Accustomed to dealing with people in an open and forthright manner, he found it difficult to believe that there actually were people in Washington conspiring against him. There were those of us on his staff, however, who were not so charitable and we viewed the situation with a growing uneasiness that gradually increased to actual alarm.

MacArthur had on numerous occasions invited Secretary of State Dean Acheson to visit Tokyo. But by the time Acheson was replaced by the new administration on January 20, 1953, the Secretary of State had visited Europe ten times and Asia not once. It seemed to MacArthur that any appreciation of the global importance of Asia had been surrendered to a type of North Atlantic isolationism. How much British hostility to the revitalizing of Japan had to do with this Washington attitude we could not assess at such a great distance and in the face of Washington's secretiveness. It was quite apparent, however, that British influence, both official and unofficial, was being more and more concentrated against Mac-Arthur's unflinching determination to protect American and Japanese interests from undue pressures or exploitation.

I recall during this period protesting to MacArthur against a particularly intemperate attack against him in a prominent London paper. He answered by pointing to the quotation from Lincoln which hung under his portrait over MacArthur's desk: ". . . *I do the very best I know how, the very best I can, and I mean to keep doing so until the end. If the end brings me out all right, what is said against me will amount to nothing. . . .*" And as I read the quotation again, MacArthur said: "Court, I have a very simple rule taught me by my father. 'Gather all the facts possible and then make your decision on what you think is right as opposed to what you think is wrong. Don't try to guess what others will think, whether they will praise or deride you. And always remember that at least some of your decisions will probably be wrong. Do this and you will always sleep well at night.'" It was difficult for those of us on his staff at that time, however, to rise quite so nobly above slanderous attacks by our Allies and the unexplained Washington refusal to defend American policy against these attacks.

While MacArthur dealt with the Soviets in Japan on the one hand, he had to deal with the Japanese Communists on the other. A major function of the Soviet "representatives" in Japan was liaison with the Communist Party. Its leader was Sanzo Nozaka, a slight, mustachioed man with a fondness for matching ensembles in his clothes and the slogan: "Communism is the course of the future." Nozaka concentrated much of his effort upon Japanese businessmen, arguing that "Japan must trade with the rest of Asia to survive, and all the rest of Asia is rapidly going Communist. Trust us," he told Japanese businessmen without cracking a smile, "and you will find that we favor business. We will reconstruct Japan and make it bright and happy." So long as Nozaka and his followers confined themselves to harmless blandishments like these, MacArthur refused to curb him. When members of his staff asked him why, he explained that after a generation of lies and repression of the freedom to speak, the only way the Japanese could build a healthy society of their own was by listening freely and learning how to choose between propaganda and truth.

His contention was borne out at first by the election results. In the 1946 elections the Communists, despite an intensive and militant campaign, won only 5 seats out of the 466 in the Diet. But, as in other lands, the Communists found that they could cause a great deal of trouble by massive infiltration of the labor unions. And once MacArthur had upset their drive to infiltrate and seize control of the unions of government employees, they set out to cripple Japan's economy. With the passage of the law creating the National Personnel Authority, their power in the communications and transportation industries was weakened. The Red threat against the orderly processes of government in Japan seemed dissipated—until the middle part of 1949. (It is interesting to consider in retrospect that it must have been about this time that the Soviets gave the green light to the coming Communist Korean attack.)

Communist troublemaking in 1949 came to a climax with a gigantic strike against Japan's railways, where the Communists still had a foothold in a large union. Not only did railway workers walk out, but switches were loosened, wires were cut, and derailments were attempted. Then Sadanori Shimoyama, president of the Japanese National Railways, was found lying across the tracks in Tokyo, murdered and with one arm and both legs cut off. All Japan reacted in horror. In a message to the Japanese people MacArthur hinted for the first time that it might be necessary to outlaw the Communist Party if its members' barbaric tactics continued to disrupt public order and threaten the national recovery. This message, which he gave on the third anniversary of the adoption of the new constitution, is an eloquent statement of his position vis-à-vis the Communists in Japan.

The Communist Party in Japan, he said, had openly assumed the role of "an avowed satellite of an international predatory force and a Japanese pawn of alien power policy, imperialistic in purpose and subversive in propaganda." The nature of the party's subversive acts, he added, "poses doubt as to whether it should longer be regarded as a constitutionally recognized political movement."

Summing up, MacArthur pointed out that "the issue is therefore clear and unequivocal—how far may the fundamental human rights be exercised unabridged without becoming the instrument of their own destruction. It is an issue which confronts all free peoples, forewarned that others have lost their liberties because blindly following an ideal they have failed to see the dangers inherent in reality. While it is the universal desire of all free men to preserve unabridged the exercise of their personal liberties, there is thus an issue projected into every law-abiding society which may not be ignored without hazarding the survival of liberty itself. I have the utmost faith that should coming events presage the need for definitive action here to preserve the public welfare against the destructive potential of this form of insidious attack, the Japanese people will proceed with wisdom, serenity and justice, without failing the integrity of their constitution."

Thus he served clear warning on the Communists while at the same time urging the Japanese government to act on its own initiative. He strongly felt that the Japanese should assume the political responsibility for this action. But in the absence of precedent among the free and democratic nations abroad and in the face of their rebellious minority at home, the Japanese leaders hesitated to act.

Events, however, forced action. Inflammatory speeches and press statements by the Communists became almost a daily occurrence, some of them carrying a thinly veiled challenge to the occupation itself. Mass demonstrations became commonplace and a few erupted into bloody riots. Sabotage increased on the railroads and elsewhere.

Realizing that he must act, MacArthur still declined to outlaw the entire Communist Party. Instead he decided to proceed against the erring leaders themselves by removing them from political influence, just as he had removed militarists and ultranationalists of the extreme right in the earlier days of the occupation period. He addressed a carefully worded note to the Prime Minister.

"It has been a fundamental purpose of the occupation," he wrote, "to assist the Japanese people to meet their commitments under the Potsdam Declaration, foremost of which requires the establishment in Japan of a new order of peace, security and justice upon which may firmly stand a peacefully inclined and responsible government. To such end the Japanese government is specifically enjoined in the Potsdam Declaration to 'remove all obstacles to the strengthening of democratic tendencies among the Japanese people.' In the implementation of this requirement, carried forward as one of the basic objectives of Allied policy as determined and prescribed by the Far Eastern Commission, the structure of the Japanese government has been redesigned, its laws and institutions where undemocratic have been revised, and those persons whose public record gives warning that their continued influence would be inimical to democratic growth have been removed and excluded from Japan's public affairs.

"The guiding philosophy of this phase of the occupation has been protective, not punitive. Its purpose and effect has been to provide assurance that the aims of Allied policy and the democratization of Japan would not be thwarted by the influence and pressure of anti-democratic elements. The area of its application for the most part has embraced those persons who because of position and influence bear responsibility for Japan's totalitarian policies which led to adventure and conquest and exploitation. Recently, however, a new and no less sinister groupment has injected itself into Japan's political scene, which has sought through perversion of truth and incitation to mass violence to transform this peaceful and tranquil land into an arena of disorder and strife as the means of stemming Japan's notable progress along the road of representative democracy, to subvert the rapidly growing democratic tendencies among the Japanese people. . . . Their coercive methods bear striking parallel to those by which the militaristic leaders of the past deceived and misled the Japanese people, and their aims, if achieved, would surely lead Japan to an even worse disaster. . . .

"Accordingly, I direct that your government make the necessary administrative measures to remove and exclude the following named persons, constituting the full membership of the Central Committee of the Japanese Communist Party, from public service and render them subject to the prohibitions, restrictions and liabilities of my directives of Jan. 4, 1946, and their implementing ordinances."

With this directive MacArthur sent a list of twenty-four persons, including every effective Communist leader in Japan. The prohibitions and restrictions he referred to were the same as those affecting some of the political leaders who had been purged between 1946 and 1948. Those so named were forbidden not only to hold public office but to engage in any form of political activity, such as being a member of a political party, public speaking, writing, or even engaging in private efforts to support a political cause. The directive required that their addresses or any change thereof be registered at all times with the government.

The expected cry went up that the Communist leaders, if so suppressed, would "go underground." Most of the twenty-four Communist
party leaders did indeed go underground, and that was that; they were
not heard from thereafter. They were no longer able to harangue their
followers or incite them to mass violence. And when MacArthur shortly
thereafter had to suppress the Communist press for flagrant misuse of its
freedom, Japan's Communist leaders were effectively silenced. The resultant quiescence in the Communist Party showed that the leaders were not
functioning anywhere near as effectively "underground" as some calamity
howlers had predicted.

Thus as the Communists in Japan made each move against Mac-
Arthur, he made a countermove against them. He stopped their attempted
general strike in the early stages of the occupation; when they tried to
infiltrate the leadership of the government's transportation and communications unions, he put those unions under civil-service status, which
denied them the strike weapon; he combated Communist infiltration of
the peasant class by a land-reform program which transformed the peasants into a strong new class of small capitalist landowners. By these moves
and by an effective educational program against its propaganda, Mac-
Arthur kept the Communist Party from gaining enough strength to paralyze Japan, as it had many other war-weakened countries. When the party
forced a showdown anyway, MacArthur curbed the leaders of the Communist conspiracy and thereby demolished it.

At the time when he was doing this he was subject to violent criticism
from abroad. It is interesting to note that within only a few months, the
criticism from the free nations was suddenly stilled and MacArthur was
instead hailed as the symbol of resistance to Red advance in the Far East.
The Communists had struck in Korea.

Part III

KOREA

". . . In humble and devout manifestation of gratitude to Almighty God for bringing this decisive victory to our arms, I ask all present to rise and join me in reciting the Lord's Prayer. . . ."

City of Seoul—September 29, 1950

CHAPTER I   The Red Challenge to Combat

◆ General MacArthur will always remember vividly how he received the news that war had started in Korea. It was early morning, Sunday, June 25, 1950, when the telephone rang in his bedroom in the American Embassy in Tokyo. Despite a muffler installed on the bell, it rang with the note of urgency that can sound only in the hush of a darkened room. MacArthur's hand reached out and lifted the receiver. There was the same note of urgency in the voice at the other end. It was a duty officer at headquarters.

"General," he said, "I am sorry to disturb you at this early hour, but we have just received a dispatch from Seoul, advising that the North Koreans have struck in great strength south across the 38th Parallel at four o'clock this morning."

It took only a moment for the import of the news to sink in. "Thank you," MacArthur said. "Call me as the situation develops." He hung up.

He rose, stepped into his slippers, put on his bathrobe, and started to pace the bedroom floor. It was the same gray West Point bathrobe that he had worn in his morning games with Arthur, the bathrobe with the large Army "A" sewed on the left breast. I have thought many times of his habit of clinging to this homely symbol of athletic prowess in the distant past, and have always realized that in that distant past he found a mighty reservoir of spiritual strength to meet the problems of the present.

He had won this Army letter at the Academy forty-nine years before, in varsity baseball. He had played on the Army team in its first baseball encounter with the midshipmen from Annapolis and had scored a run for West Point in that four-to-three game. Years later, while superintendent at the Military Academy, he had initiated the intramural-sports system that became the model for many of our great colleges and universities. It was he who had written the impressive words that adorn the entrance to the magnificent gymnasium building just off the plain:

PART III: KOREA

"UPON THE FIELDS OF FRIENDLY STRIFE, ARE SOWN THE SEEDS THAT, UPON OTHER FIELDS, ON OTHER DAYS, WILL BEAR THE FRUITS OF VICTORY."

He had led the American Olympic team which went to Amsterdam in 1928, and he was an unchallenged leader in the field of sportsmanship.

It was perhaps this belief in the value of athletics as a builder of character which had caused him to wear his "A," an honor relic of his youth, month in and month out for forty-nine years and more in the privacy of his home, and to dangle at the end of his watch chain the little gold footballs and baseballs, three of them, awarded him in those dim past days near the turn of the century. Although the ribbons and decorations of his war days are without parallel,[1] he never wears them. His uniform is unadorned, but that plain black "A" never leaves its place over his heart on his lounging-robe—because from it he gains the inner spiritual strength needed to guide him over difficult times.

MacArthur had need for that inner spiritual strength now. He has since told me of the multitude of conflicting thoughts which raced through his mind in that early morning hour as he paced the length of his bed-room. On receipt of his instructions his staff would even now be preparing to put into effect the well-laid plans for the evacuation by air and sea of some two thousand American citizens in South Korea. All that would be needed was the request from Ambassador John Muccio.

This was MacArthur's sole responsibility, since in 1948 the U.S. military occupation had ended and South Korea had become the concern of the U.S. State Department. But as he paced his bedroom floor, he tried to guess the answer to the larger questions: would the administration in Washington stop there? Would the United States merely evacuate American citizens or attempt as well as to resist this armed Communist aggression?

On the one hand, Secretary of State Dean Acheson had five months earlier, in a public speech, excluded South Korea from the areas in Asia which the United States could "guarantee . . . against military attack."

---

[1] No officer or enlisted man in the American Military Service has ever received such an array of awards for valor and distinction and sacrifice. The Medal of Honor; the Distinguished Service Cross three times; the Silver Star seven times; the Distinguished Service Medal of the Army five times; the Distinguished Service Medal of the Navy; the Distinguished Flying Cross; the Air Medal; the Bronze Star; the Purple Heart twice; the Distinguished Unit Citation four times; the Campaign Star fifteen times; the Foreign Service Campaign Stripe nine times; the "Resolution of Thanks" from Congress; and more than thirty of the highest foreign decorations and parliamentary thanks of the nations of the world.

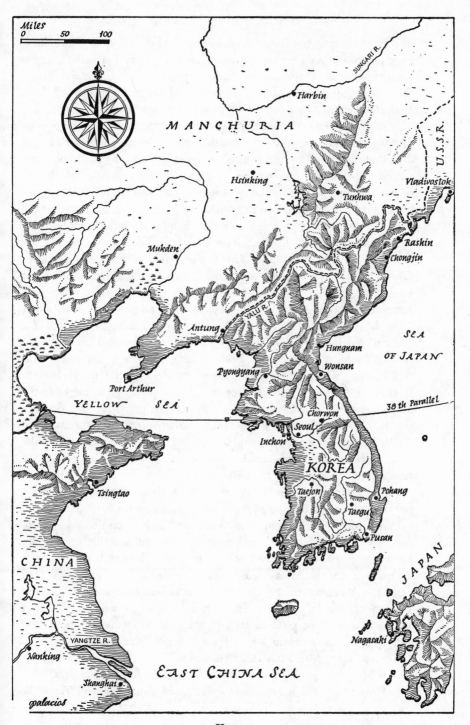

KOREA

And more recently the Joint Chiefs of Staff had drawn up a plan of strategic defense in Asia which was based on the assumption that under no circumstances would the United States engage in the military defense of the Korean peninsula. But on the other hand, MacArthur reflected, John Foster Dulles, visiting Korea as a personal representative of Acheson, had only six days before implied to the members of the South Korean legislature that America *would* defend South Korea if she were attacked. Could it be that the State Department had reversed its policy without bothering to notify the theater commander on whose shoulders would fall the responsibility for giving this policy practical implementation? It would not be the first time that this had happened. And MacArthur realized that the U.S., having in effect presided over the birth of this infant republic, did indeed have a moral obligation to respond if it called for help.

Here MacArthur paused in his pacing. Help with what? Ever since taking over the responsibility for South Korea, the State Department had seemed to guard the area jealously, as if it were some kind of private preserve, ignoring and disdaining any help or advice from MacArthur, who, though relieved of all responsibility for the area, naturally had a continuing interest in this country on his flank. There had been no consultation with him (probably because his complete disagreement was well known) when the State Department made its unilateral decision to limit South Korea's defensive force to light weapons and to organize the defenders along constabulary lines. The excuse given for this decision was that it was necessary to prevent the South Koreans from attacking North Korea—a curiously myopic reasoning that of course opened the way for the North Korean attack. It simply provided too much of a temptation for the Communists to resist.

And meanwhile, despite repeated warnings and requests for a force only strong enough to assure Japan's defense, the Joint Chiefs of Staff had denuded MacArthur's occupation forces until he had, on this June morning, only four divisions. Although every division still had three regiments, most regiments were reduced by a battalion, and most battalions by a company. Even MacArthur's corps headquarters had to be abolished. Had these two Washington agencies, the State Department and the Defense Department, co-ordinated on carefully laid plans to put the U.S. in a militarily impossible position in Asia, they could not have done better.

By now the bedroom was bathed in bright June morning sunlight. He looked up as Mrs. MacArthur entered.

"I heard you pacing up and down," she said. "Are you all right?"

MacArthur told her the news. Her face paled slightly. Then she immediately summoned up the courage that she had had to call upon so many times during their marriage. Through the years of Bataan and Corregidor, Australia and New Guinea, Leyte and Luzon, Jean MacArthur had had to watch her husband go off on his periodic and perilous front-line inspection trips. And though she had always understood the need for him to set an example of bravery for his troops, she had never been quite able to stifle the heart-sinking dread of each good-by. Now after five brief years of peace came the awful prospect of going through it all over again. And as Arthur came tiptoeing to the room in anticipation of jumping on his father's bed to wake him, she met him at the door and quietly explained the reason for the pacing figure with the preoccupied expression. MacArthur looked up, saw his son, came over to him, and silently put an arm around his shoulder for a moment. Then he thrust his hands back into the pockets of his gray robe and resumed his thoughtful pacing.

How, he asked himself, had the U.S. got itself into this mess? And what more could he have done to prevent it? Certainly if anyone in Washington had deigned to listen to his clear warnings, the situation would have been avoided. Ruefully MacArthur thought back to the days such a short time ago when the U.S. had been militarily more powerful than any combination of nations on earth. General Marshall, then Army Chief of Staff, had reported to the Secretary of War in 1945: "Never was the strength of the American democracy so evident nor has it ever been so clearly within our power to give definite guidance for our course into the future of the human race." Again and again MacArthur had tried to warn those in Washington who were rapidly frittering away this power in a bankruptcy of positive and courageous leadership toward any long-range objectives. But no one had listened, and now on this June day MacArthur actually had to ask himself: "What is U.S. policy in Asia?"

Had we had any policy in China? There our only accomplishment since World War II had been the Great Mistake. How George Marshall, a military man, could have made *the* mistake that is the nightmare of all soldiers—underestimating the enemy—MacArthur would never understand. Then, too, MacArthur had warned Washington that the results of this disaster would be felt far beyond the confines of China's borders, and he had asked for an increase in strength in Japan because of this envelopment of U.S. Pacific positions. His request had been turned down.

And now, with U.S. weakness in the Pacific enticing the Communists on, the military fortunes of America lay in the hands of men who understood little about the Pacific and practically nothing about Korea. While the State Department idealistically attempted to prevent the South Koreans from unifying the country by force, it inevitably encouraged the North Koreans to build their own offensive power. This fundamental error, MacArthur knew, is inescapable when the diplomat attempts to exercise professional military judgment. And the result in Korea was that 100,000 U.S.-trained constabulary troops, with few weapons besides their own rifles, were opposed by a Soviet-trained North Korean army of 200,000 men equipped with tanks, artillery, and every other type of heavy arms.

For a year before the North Korean attack MacArthur's headquarters had consistently informed Washington of this growing danger; the record shows more than 1,500 such warnings between June 1949 and June 1950, and one of these dispatches even suggested that June 1950 was the likely time for North Korea to cross the 38th Parallel. Like all the other warnings from MacArthur, these, too, had been ignored. The U.S. had seemed to be trying to maneuver itself into the diplomatic and military cul-de-sac in which it now found itself. Once again MacArthur asked himself: "What is the U.S. policy?"

Later that Sabbath day the call came. Ambassador Muccio asked that the evacuation plan be put into effect. Immediately MacArthur's office once again took on the atmosphere of a command post. With the speed and precision of a machine gun, the orders went out to the general staff, which immediately relayed them to the proper commanders. Within minutes, flights of transport planes were rising off runways in Japan and ships at sea were swinging about and heading full-draft toward Korean ports. The lives of some two thousand Americans rested upon the success of every one of the multitudinous elements in this operation. Meanwhile, the North Korean juggernaut was moving irresistibly southward, sweeping the lightly armed South Korean defenders before it.

Within the first few hours the pattern of the Communist pre-invasion preparations had come into clear focus. Along the 38th Parallel the North Koreans had posed a lightly armed constabulary force similar to that of their neighbors to the south. But the Communist constabulary force had only served to screen a powerful striking army, fully equipped with heavy weapons including Soviet tanks, which waited just beyond the first line of offense. When the North Korean constabulary units launched the attack across the border, they then swung right and left, while the heavy main force charged through the gap and struck violently toward the south.

Even then it was evident that this was far more than the "police action" that President Truman was so euphemistically to characterize it. In Korea, Communism had hurled its first challenge to war against the free world. Now was the time for decision. Now it was as clear as it would ever be that this was a battle against imperialistic Communism, far more than any localized clean-up of border-raiding North Koreans. Communism's alliances in Asia—including China—were no less known that June than they were six months later. Now was the time to calculate the inherent risks, to realize that this was a challenge to war by Asian Communism, and to make the decision whether or not to accept the challenge. As MacArthur sat down to breakfast that Sunday morning, he had already made all the decisions within his power. His next move waited on the broad and all-important decision to be made in Washington.

Chapter II   "Let's go to the front and have a look."

❧ As the hours wore on that Sunday morning of June 25, the same questions that MacArthur had pondered while pacing his bedroom were being asked in all the chancelleries of the world. What was U.S. policy? What would the U.S. do? Simultaneously two people who would have much to do with Korea in the future were now considering the problem in Tokyo. John Foster Dulles, who was then a consultant to the Secretary of State and is now himself Secretary of State, and John Allison, who was then deputy director of Far Eastern Affairs and is now U.S. Ambassador to Japan, had conferred with MacArthur and had visited Korea themselves. Together they now radioed Secretary Acheson: "We believe that if it appears the South Koreans cannot themselves contain or repulse the attack, U.S. force should be used, even though this risks Russian counter moves. To sit by while Korea is overrun by unprovoked armed attack would start a World War."

Only recently did MacArthur see this message for the first time. There could be no misconstruing the recommendation. It recognized what the history of the world has taught from the beginning of time: that timidity breeds conflict and courage often prevents it. It counseled leading from strength. It correctly emphasized that a failure to fight would be more likely to precipitate another world war than a decision to fight. And, even at this early hour, it fully recognized the inherent dangers. "U.S. force should be used," Dulles and Allison recommended, "*even though this risks Russian counter moves.*"

Meanwhile, momentous decisions were indeed being made with rapidity in Washington and at Lake Success. At the United States's request, U.N. Secretary General Trygve Lie called the Security Council delegates back from their weekends for a special session Sunday afternoon. The Russians, who were boycotting the U.N. in protest against membership of the Chinese Nationalists, did not have a delegate to cast a veto against the U.S. resolution and thus block it. This resolution, after reviewing the political origin of the government of South Korea and the steps that the United Nations had taken through its appointed "Temporary Commission on Korea" to promote and guide that government, charged that the action of the North Korean forces constituted a breach of the peace. Further, the resolution (1) called for the immediate cessation of hostilities and for the authorities of North Korea to withdraw forthwith their armed forces to the 38th Parallel; (2) requested that the United Nations Temporary Commission on Korea communicate its fully considered recommendations on the situation at once, observe the withdrawal of the North Korean forces to the 38th Parallel, and advise the Security Council upon compliance with its resolution; and (3) called upon all members to render every assistance to the United Nations in the execution of the resolution and to refrain from giving assistance to the North Korean authorities. With no Soviet veto, the Security Council adopted the resolution and called upon all U.N. members to "render every assistance to the U.N. in the execution of this resolution."

President Truman immediately interpreted the U.N. call to "render every assistance" as an authorization to assist the South Koreans militarily. Besides its radio connection, Washington maintained immediate contact with Tokyo by means of a "telecom," on which operators at both ends could "talk" with each other much as they could with two teletype machines. For the first time in his career MacArthur was summoned to a telecom conference. No one in Washington was quite ready yet to commit the U.S. completely, so the directive to MacArthur included only the use of the Navy and the Air Force. MacArthur was authorized and directed not only to assist South Korean defenses by whatever use he could make of these two arms, but also to isolate the Nationalist-held island of Formosa from the Communist Chinese mainland. The U.S. Seventh Fleet was turned over to MacArthur's operational control for this purpose, and MacArthur was specifically ordered to prevent any Nationalist attacks on the mainland as well as to defend the island against Communist attacks.

U.S. planes, it happened, were already in action over South Korea. This was because enemy aircraft had suddenly threatened MacArthur's operation to evacuate the two thousand Americans there, and MacArthur, after securing President Truman's authorization, had sent in U.S. war planes to protect the transports. Thus, the operation was concluded without the loss of a single man, woman, or child. Ambassador Muccio later wrote MacArthur: "Thanks to the speed, thoroughness, care and intrepidity with which the mission entrusted to your command was carried out, the evacuation by sea and air of some 2,000 persons, all at extremely short notice and in the face of danger, was a complete success. . . ." The success of the operation also elicited from the Joint Chiefs of Staff in Washington a message of thanks and praise, in which MacArthur also detected a note of relief, as though our part had been performed and we were well out of it.

But we were only just getting into it. On June 27 the United Nations Security Council met again and passed another resolution. In this one, after noting the events and particularly the failure of the North Korean authorities to desist from the attack and withdraw their military forces to the 38th Parallel, the Security Council concluded that "urgent military measures are required to restore international peace and security," and recommended "that the members of the United Nations furnish such assistance to the Republic of Korea as may be necessary to repel the armed attack."

Thus, step by hesitant step, the U.S. went to war against Communism in Asia. Busy as he was acting upon the multitudinous orders sent his way, MacArthur could not help but pause in amazement at the manner in which this great decision was being made. With no consultation of Congress, whose duty it is to declare war, and without even consulting the field commander whose advice and warnings had so long been ignored, President Truman, Secretary Acheson, and General Bradley agreed among themselves to enter the Korean war.

All the risks inherent in this decision—including the possibility of Chinese and Russian involvement—applied then just as President Truman and his advisers pointed out that they applied later. Had MacArthur been asked for his advice at the time of this decision, he would have pointed out clearly the risks, just as Dulles and Allison did that Sunday morning. And the men who decided among themselves to go to war in Korea would not have been able a year later to confess by implication that they had not realized the risk they had been taking.

Of course it never dawned on MacArthur in those early days of the Korean war that the administration would try to turn any such sophistry against him. And at the moment he was concerned with a far more pressing problem. Would U.S. air and naval forces be enough? Could the South Korean defenders, supported by these forces and supplied with armor, make a successful stand against the powerful Communist war machine that was rolling down upon them from the north? Or would U.S. ground troops have to be thrown into the battle after all South Korea was lost?

"Let's go to the front and have a look."

In World War II there had been only one way for MacArthur to learn such things. There was only one way now. He decided to go to Korea and see for himself.

On the night of June 28 he invited four correspondents to come to his Dai Ichi Building office. There he told them of his plan to visit Korea next day and offered to take them along with him. But he felt it necessary to warn them. "It will be an unarmed plane," he explained, "and we are not sure of getting fighter cover, not sure where we will land. If you are not at the airport, I will know you have other commitments."

One of the correspondents spoke up quickly to assure him that they would all be there. MacArthur smiled. "I have no doubt of your courage," he said. "I just wanted to give your judgment a chance to work."

By dawn the next morning rain and overcast completely surrounded Tokyo and Haneda Airport, and MacArthur's aides decided that the flight to Korea would have to be postponed. MacArthur was shaving when Mrs. MacArthur told him that his pilot, Colonel Anthony Story, was on the telephone. As MacArthur took the receiver and listened to the news, his jaw set in the familiar jutting line. Then he said simply: "We go."

It was still raining when we climbed into the unarmed *Bataan* and sent the spray flying as we roared down the Haneda runway on our hazardous way. We had every reason for being in low spirits. The news from Korea seemed even more disastrous than it had the day before. The capital city of Seoul had already fallen, and the South Korean government had moved to temporary headquarters at Taejon. As I watched MacArthur settle in his seat aboard the plane I could not help feeling deep sympathy for this great soldier who, with fifty years of service already behind him (half of it on foreign soil—the longest foreign service of any officer of the American Army), now faced, through no fault of his own, yet another military campaign. Once again it was a seemingly forlorn hope. Once again he had been thrust, virtually barehanded, into the breach against a heavily armed enemy—as on Bataan, as on Corregidor, as in New Guinea.

But as at Bataan and Corregidor and New Guinea, MacArthur was wasting no time on recriminations. In fact, those of us who had fought with him in World War II sensed the same MacArthur we had known then—responding to the challenge in a spirit not only of determination but of a resourcefulness born of long experience. Despite the gloom of the day and the even gloomier news dispatches, he remained completely calm and composed. As the plane rose above the murk of the overcast, he pulled out his famous long-stemmed corncob pipe, a trademark of World

War II which I had only rarely seen him smoke during the occupation. One of the correspondents commented on this, and MacArthur laughed. "I don't smoke this back there in Tokyo," he explained. "They'd think I was a farmer." When the message was relayed to him by the plane radio that the British fleet units in the area had been put under his command, MacArthur turned with no hesitation to his naval chief, Vice Admiral Charles Turner Joy, and gave him complete and explicit instructions for the intricate deployment of all these units.

Simultaneously his busy mind was contemplating the multitudinous ramifications of the events that had taken place in the past three days. As the *Bataan* droned ever nearer to Korea, he strode down the aisle and sank into the empty seat alongside Lieutenant General George E. Stratemeyer, his air chief. Together they discussed the almost insuperable problems of the air war over Korea as it was then being fought. Fighter pilots based in Japan found that Korea was at the extreme edge of their range and that their effective time over Korea was limited to about fifteen minutes. Even the longer-ranged bombers and transports were being curbed by the weather; the Communists had carefully chosen Korea's rainy season as their time for attack.

But a more important consideration than all of these, MacArthur realized, was the fact that as long as air operations were confined to the destruction of North Korean military targets south of the 38th Parallel, the North Korean forces maintained a distinct advantage. If North Korea remained an air sanctuary in which Communist forces could mobilize and maneuver and bring up supplies, MacArthur reasoned, he would not be giving to the South Korean defenders the "effective military assistance" that the U.N. had directed him to give. He concluded that his authority to destroy the North Korean military targets was permissive, not restrictive, and that implicit in his directive was the discretion normal to field command.

So he then and there instructed Stratemeyer to expand the field of operations for his air force and to include military targets north as well as south of the 38th Parallel. Here was no timid delay while authorization was obtained from Washington; here was the capacity for command decision and the readiness to assume responsibility which had always been MacArthur's forte. As a colleague told me of this decision a few minutes later, a glint of appreciation shone in his eyes and he spoke for all of us on the plane as he commented: "MacArthur at his best—a commander who fights to win."

As we passed over western Japan the weather cleared slightly and four Mustang planes came up to provide cover for us. But even then the *Bataan*'s radio was reporting heavy enemy strafing of the airfield at Suwon, twenty miles south of the already fallen city of Seoul. Over Korea a Russian-built Yak tried to slip past the four Mustangs escorting the *Bataan* and get a shot at us. But it was driven off.

The *Bataan* landed at Suwon through the clouds of oily smoke from two transports that had been bombed and strafed while unloading supplies only a few minutes before our arrival. Another attack could be expected momentarily, so we all hustled out of the plane and MacArthur ordered Story to return to Japan and come back to pick us up at five that afternoon.

Temporary headquarters of the U.S. military advisory group and survey team was in a schoolhouse in Suwon. There Brigadier General John H. Church, who had flown over from Tokyo only forty-eight hours before, was waiting for us. MacArthur listened patiently to a military briefing; but from my experience with him during World War II, I knew what was coming. It did. The briefing officer had barely put the pointer back on the rack below the map when MacArthur slapped his knee, stood up, and said: "Let's go to the front and have a look."

Those who had not tried to argue MacArthur out of risks like this before and therefore did not know the futility of it, tried to explain that nothing had ever been more fluid than the "front" in South Korea at that moment. Enemy tanks and spearheads were slicing through the thinly held South Korean lines everywhere, and even this temporary headquarters was dangerously near the onrushing North Korean forces. Furthermore, enemy airplanes were bombing and strafing almost at will along the few roads in the area. MacArthur heard them out and said quietly: "The only way to judge a fight is to see it yourself—to see the troops in action. Let's go."

In a black Dodge sedan and several jeeps we headed north toward the Han River. The little convoy moved slowly forward through the dreadful backwash of a defeated and dispersed army. The South Korean forces were in complete and disorganized flight. We reached the banks of the Han just in time to be caught up in the last rear-guard action to defend its bridges.

Seoul was already in enemy hands. Here, only a mile away, we could see the towers of smoke rising from the ruins of this fourteenth-century city. We halted for a moment, and then MacArthur took his corncob pipe from his mouth and jabbed its stem toward a hill a little way ahead. To Edward M. Almond, his chief of staff, he said: "What do you say we push

327

up there, Ned?" The motors groaned and the convoy ground ahead along the dusty road at the foot of the hill. There we got out and climbed to its top.

It was a dramatic, historic, and tragic scene. In the distance across the Han, Seoul burned and smoked in its agony of destruction. On the north side of the river we could clearly hear the crump of Red mortar fire as the enemy swooped down toward the bridges. Below us and streaming by both sides of our hill were the retreating, panting columns of disorganized troops, the drab color of their weaving lines interspersed here and there with the bright red crosses of ambulances filled with broken, groaning men. The sky was resonant with shrieking missiles of death, and everywhere were the stench and utter desolation of a stricken battlefield. Clogging all the roads in a writhing, dust-shrouded mass of humanity were the refugees. But there was no hysteria, no whimpering. Here were the progeny of a proud and sturdy race that for centuries had accepted disaster imperturbably. Watching them painfully plodding south, carrying all their worldly belongings on their backs and leading their terror-stricken but wide-eyed, uncrying children, I could not help feeling that something could be done to save the homeland of such a stubborn, sturdy race from Communist tyranny.

And on top of the hill, gazing down on this sight and these people, stood the man who must do it. I did not, of course, realize until he told me later that he was now planning how to do it. To those of us with him, he appeared to be only surveying the scene of disaster—his sharp profile silhouetted against the black smoke clouds of Seoul as his eyes swept the terrain about him, his hands in his rear trouser pockets and his long-stemmed pipe jutting upward as he swung his gaze over the pitiful evidence of the disaster that he had inherited. But, as he told me later, his mind was already encompassing an area far larger than the one he was studying atop this hill. He was forming a strategical maneuver such as could only be born of desperation.

This scene along the Han was enough to convince him that the defensive potential of South Korea had already been exhausted. There was nothing to stop the Communists from rushing their tank columns straight down the few good roads from Seoul to Pusan at the end of the peninsula. All Korea would then be theirs. First and foremost he must delay and then stop the enemy's headlong rush south. Even with U.S. or U.N. air and naval support, the South Koreans could not do so. Only the immediate commitment of ground troops could possibly save them. The answer MacArthur had come to seek was there.

"Let's go to the front and have a look."

But how could it be done? If he threw his occupation soldiers into this breach, what of Japan? Japan was where his primary responsibility lay; only a few hours before his most recent directive from Washington had reiterated that no action which he took to protect South Korea should prejudice the protection of Japan. Could he build a sufficient native force in Japan to deter Communist aggression against that country if he took elements of the pitifully thin American forces there and committed them in Korea?

It is fortunate that he had already thought out the answer to that part of the problem. MacArthur has never considered the Soviet Union as a potential threat to post-war Japan unless Japan should become Sovietized through Communist infiltration. Seizure of Japan by conquest, he has always felt, would give the Soviet a doubtful victory, for Japan's industrial facilities would be able to operate only as long as the flow of raw materials from abroad remained uninterrupted; once the Allies cut Japan's industrial lifelines at sea in World War II, her industry was immediately transformed from an asset to a liability. This the free nations could do against a Communist Japan as well.

But what if he did commit his occupation troops in Korea? Could he even get them there in time? The speed at which the enemy was racing southward, MacArthur realized, meant that he had not enough time even to build a massive beachhead at Pusan. And had he that time, all the forces that he could throw into South Korea would be outnumbered by almost three to one. This was the desperate situation for which MacArthur devised a desperate strategy.

He must use his occupation troops in South Korea, if Washington would agree. Completely outnumbered though he would be, he would rely upon strategic maneuver to overcome the odds against him. Because he would be unable to move this force as a unit across to South Korea in the few days left, he would employ his ground troops in a strategy that violated all accepted military doctrine and risked the destruction of his forces in detail. It was a risk he would have to take. And as his mind jumped ahead beyond the days to the weeks and months for which he had to plan his strategy, he conceived an even riskier but brilliant counterstroke that could in itself wrest victory from defeat.

MacArthur had stood on this hill only about an hour. But in that short time he had sketched out in his mind the outline of a strategy that would not only rescue the South Koreans but would defeat the North Koreans as well.

Raising his field glasses, he took another look at Seoul. In the last

329

hour the bridges, one by one, had been blown up. But as he lowered his glasses he pointed to a lone railroad bridge that still stood across the Han. North Korean tanks and trucks could grind across it. "Take it out," he ordered and turned, went down the hill, and climbed back into the black sedan. Backing and filling to turn in the narrow dirt road, the convoy headed back to Suwon.

The return trip was similar to the one we had taken north a little more than an hour before—the sedan and jeeps moving along like chips in the southward-flowing tide of a defeated nation. The vehicles were halted this time, however, by a direct enemy air attack. Once again, as in World War II, everyone dived for the ditches; and once again they looked back to see MacArthur striding slowly to the side of the road, where he stood erect and watched as the Communist planes screamed down to strafe the road. One jeep was knocked out of commission, but no one was hurt. Within a few minutes we were on our way again, south to Suwon.

At the temporary headquarters in the little schoolhouse a visitor was waiting for us. President Syngman Rhee had flown up from the government's provisional capital at Taejon. He himself had been attacked by an enemy plane en route and had escaped only after a hedge-hopping chase over hills that his pilot knew better than did the North Korean attackers. Now as these two rugged and indomitable fighters strode to meet each other and as MacArthur put both hands on Rhee's shoulders, I could not help being moved by the sight.

They had known each other ever since the days when MacArthur had been serving in the War Department before World War I and Rhee had been a student in the U.S. Over the long years since, they had formed a close attachment based upon mutual admiration, and MacArthur had always regarded Syngman Rhee's determined and uncompromising fight for Korean independence from Japanese rule as one of the sagas of the age. The two men had last been together in Seoul on August 15, 1948, when MacArthur had come over from Tokyo to make an address during the ceremonies inaugurating the Republic of Korea.

I recalled how, on that day two years before, MacArthur had stood in the blazing sun on the portico of the capitol building, facing the masses of Korean people below him, and had described the division of Korea at the 38th Parallel as one of the "greatest tragedies of contemporary history." This line was nothing more than what MacArthur called it—"an artificial barrier." And he had promised: "The barrier must and will be torn down. Nothing should prevent the ultimate unity of your people as free men of a free nation. Koreans come from too proud a stock to sacrifice their sacred cause by yielding to any alien philosophies of disruption." Now, two years later, the barrier against which MacArthur and Rhee had protested had served its purpose for screening the Soviets' aggressive preparations. And now these two doughty warriors were left to retrieve what others had lost.

MacArthur and Rhee retired to a room in the schoolhouse, where they conferred in private for an hour. In that conference MacArthur frankly pointed out the desperate nature of South Korea's situation, but promised all possible aid in her defense. The conference was followed by more briefings, which were periodically punctuated by machine-gun fire from enemy planes strafing the area, and by aerial combat high in the skies. The briefings showed how long and carefully the enemy had laid his plans before attacking.

The North Koreans had advanced across the 38th Parallel in an estimated strength of six infantry divisions and three constabulary brigades, spearheaded by approximately a hundred Soviet T-34 and T-70 tanks, with supporting units of heavy artillery. The main attack was along the Pochon-Uijongbu-Seoul corridor, with simultaneous attacks in the Ongjin Peninsula to the west, against Chunchon in the Eastern Mountains and down the east coast road, with amphibious landings at various South Korean coastal points. Only a major Communist design of aggression could account for the correlation of these many attacks and the superior amounts of weapons employed.

Opposed to this juggernaut were four divisions of ROK troops, completely lacking in armor and heavy artillery and with no supporting air force except for a few training-planes. So it was no surprise that the ROK forces had been overwhelmed all along the line.

For the moment all MacArthur could do was attempt to stiffen ROK morale, which he did by publicly calling upon the South Korean commanders to rally and reorganize their forces at all costs. To bolster their fighting spirit, he assured them that he would at once recommend to Washington that further assistance be extended. The shock of initial defeat, however, could not immediately be overcome. That very night North Korean elements crossed the Han, and the Suwon headquarters was forced to evacuate hastily to the south.

Indeed, even before his departure the entire Suwon area was under frequent air attack. It was well that MacArthur had ordered the *Bataan* to return to Japan instead of waiting on the airstrip, because only a few minutes before it returned to pick us up the field was bombed and strafed for the fifth time that day. Fortunately, however, the *Bataan* landed safely, and we hustled aboard and went roaring back down the runway. All of us on MacArthur's staff breathed a sigh of relief as we passed beyond the range of North Korean fighter planes. But MacArthur, who had watched out of the plane windows for action on the way over, was now deeply engrossed in the business of his report to the U.S. Joint Chiefs of Staff. Writing with a pencil in longhand on a pad of scratch paper, he composed the message that provided Washington with its first clear and complete report on the military situation.

"The South Korean forces," he wrote, "are in confusion, have not seriously fought, and lack leadership. Organized and equipped as a light force for maintenance of interior order, they were unprepared for attack by armor and air. Conversely they are incapable of gaining the initiative over such a force as that embodied in the North Korean Army. The South Koreans had made no preparation for defense in depth, for echelons of supply or for a supply system. No plans had been made, or if made were not executed, for the destruction of supplies or materials in the event of a retrograde movement. As a result they have either lost or abandoned their supplies and heavier equipment and have absolutely no system of intercommunication. In most cases the individual soldier in his flight to the south has retained his rifle or carbine. They are gradually being gathered up by an advanced group of my officers I sent over for the purpose. Without artillery, mortars and antitank guns, they can only hope to retard the enemy through the fullest utilization of natural obstacles and under the guidance of example of leadership of high quality. . . . The civilian populace is tranquil, orderly and prosperous according to their scale of living. They have retained a high degree of national spirit and firm belief in the Americans. The roads leading south from Seoul are crowded with refugees refusing to accept the Communist rule. . . .

"It is essential that the enemy advance be held or its impetus will threaten the over-running of all of Korea. The South Korean Army is entirely incapable of counteraction and there is a grave danger of a further breakthrough. If the enemy advances continue much further, it will threaten the Republic."

Then MacArthur made his recommendation: "The only assurance for holding the present line and the ability to regain later the lost ground is through the introduction of United States ground combat forces into the Korean battle area. To continue to utilize the forces of our air and navy without an effective ground element cannot be decisive. If authorized it is my intention to immediately move a United States regimental combat team to the reinforcement of the vital area discussed and to provide for a possible build-up to a two division strength from the troops in Japan for an early counteroffensive."

He concluded with a solemn warning: "Unless provision is made for the full utilization of the Army-Navy-Air team in this shattered area, our mission will at best be needlessly costly in life, money and prestige. At worst, it might even be doomed to failure."

Within twenty-four hours President Truman, through the Joint Chiefs of Staff, had authorized MacArthur to use ground troops. The number of combat elements which might be withdrawn from Japan without impairing that country's safety was left to MacArthur's discretion. Thus the United States accepted Communism's challenge to combat in Korea. Thus President Truman, Secretary Acheson, and General Bradley re-emphasized that they had made the decision to fight Asian Communism. The calculated gamble that the Soviet or the Chinese Communists might enter the war was as clearly understood and accepted by Washington at that time as it was by MacArthur. He naturally believed that he was backed by a strong American policy. Not by the wildest stretch of his imagination could MacArthur have conceived that his superiors would break with American tradition. That tradition has always been that, once American troops are committed to battle, the full power and means of their nation are mobilized and dedicated to fight for victory—and not for stalemate or compromise. And MacArthur set out to chart the strategic course which would make that victory possible.

Chapter III   Buying Time for Space—and Blood

One of MacArthur's favorite stories about his father concerns the time when the "Boy Colonel of the West," as he was known in the Union Army, found himself virtually surrounded by superior numbers of the enemy near Franklin, Tennessee. His commander rode out to look over the situation and was greatly alarmed.

"Arthur, I am deeply concerned," he said to the young colonel. "Kindly take ten minutes to give me an estimate of the situation and your plan to meet it."

The reply was immediate. "Sir, I do not need ten minutes. The situation is simple and apparent. The enemy is closing on me from three sides. My plan is to fight like hell."

His plan worked. The commanding general in his report credited in large part the Union victory at Franklin to the desperate resistance of this regiment, the 24th Wisconsin. At the battle's end, the young colonel was carried from the bloody field near the old Carter House, unconscious, with bullet holes through his chest and leg.

There were times during those dark early days of the Korean war when Douglas MacArthur must have felt that he had the enemy on *four* sides. But there was no question as to whether he was going to fight like his father. The reports from Korea continued to tell a grim story: the North Korean forces were moving irresistibly on, and South Korean resistance was now practically nonexistent. It had rapidly become a struggle in which the military advantages of surprise and superior weapons favored the enemy and the only hope left to MacArthur was time. Only through the speed of his defensive maneuvers could he slow the Communist advance before it enveloped all of Korea. MacArthur knew this, and was already moving with a dynamic speed probably never equaled in warfare. His moves were like lightning. His staff immediately went on a twenty-four-hour basis. Every ship, every plane, every train was commandeered. Never before have so many forces moved in such a short time from the peace and quiet of occupation duty by land, sea, and air transport to the violence of a battle area in another country. No mobilization to a battlefield under such conditions ever equaled it.

With precision and rapidity MacArthur was putting into effect the strategy that he had conceived as he stood on that hill overlooking Seoul and the Han. A desperate strategy it was, violating all the accepted rules of land warfare. He would commit his forces piecemeal, whether they be in squad, platoon, company, or battalion strength, as rapidly as he could get them to the front—even though he would thus risk their destruction in detail. His decision was based upon his unique understanding of the Oriental character—his belief that the discovery of American ground resistance in the battle area would chill the opposing commander and cause him to take precautionary and time-consuming measures. This would favor us with the all-important element of time.

Two rifle companies and a mortar platoon of the 24th Division were instantly dispatched by air to Korea with a mission to establish road blocks before the advancing enemy columns and otherwise to engage in harassing tactics. The road blocks were first established off Osan, just south of Suwon, which by then was in enemy hands. The effect of American ground troops, however small in number, resisting the enemy advance confirmed MacArthur's hopes. The enemy commander at once brought his advance to a stop to permit the laborious bringing up of artillery from across the river without benefit of the regular bridges, which our air by then had destroyed. He had no way of knowing either the strength of the American forces already committed and in their immediate support or what change in the battle situation their presence presaged. He decided, as MacArthur had divined, against taking any chance. So, instead of continuing to drive his tank columns forward, he deployed all of his forces across the difficult terrain in conventional line of battle. This fatal error gave MacArthur the first round in the duel of nerve and wit. For it provided him the time he needed to move an artillery battalion and infantry reinforcements forward to replace the small force initially committed, which was now, by virtue of the gallantry of its resistance against numerical odds as high as twenty to one, virtually destroyed. It had been a desperate gamble—probably one that no other commander would have taken. It had exacted a painful sacrifice from the men committed to this unequal battle, but it paid off in precious time, so essential if any tactic in the prevailing situation was to be successful. Of those first days of American fighting in South Korea, MacArthur reported:

"I threw in troops by air in the hope of establishing a locus of resistance around which I could rally the fast retreating South Korean forces. I had hoped by that arrogant display of strength to fool the enemy into a belief that I had greater resources at my disposal than I did. . . .

"We gained 10 days by this process before [the enemy] had deployed in line of battle along the 150 mile front from Suwon, as the pivotal point. By that time I had brought forth the rest of the 24th Division under [Major General William F.] Dean with orders to delay the enemy until I could bring the first cavalry division and the 25th Division over from Japan. Dean fought a very desperate series of isolated combats in which both he and a large part of that division were destroyed." [1]

By the time this had happened, the enemy commander had realized that MacArthur had outwitted him. He had been stopped not by massive American defensive force but merely by the appearance of force—by "that arrogant display of strength." He moved rapidly to make up for the time he had lost, but it was too late. The first round had gone to Mac-Arthur.

MacArthur had by this time established the Eighth Army in Korea, under the command of Lieutenant General Walton Walker, but the enemy still had enormous superiority in manpower and weight and quality of arms. Not only were the few Americans who had raced into the gap by plane outnumbered by twenty to one, but the North Koreans had Russian-manufactured medium and light tanks, 120-mm. mortars, and 122-mm. howitzers. The heaviest American weapon was the 105-mm. howitzer. Our light tanks proved to be no match for the North Koreans' Russian medium tanks, and even the fire from our much-heralded 2.36-inch "bazooka" and the 75-mm. guns was deflected by the 3-inch steel Russian turrets. Aided by his preponderance of manpower and weapons, the enemy was able simultaneously to exert heavy pressure against General Walker's men in the center and flow around them on both sides. While Walker held in the center, lightly armed South Korean police units fell back before the onslaught of North Korean attackers along the west side of the peninsula, so that the enemy was able to drive virtually unopposed toward the south in that area. On the west coast, as soon as the Communists had reached positions far enough south, they wheeled toward the east in what threatened to be a huge envelopment. Meanwhile, enemy columns were dashing down the east coastal road to form the sec-

---

[1] Fortunately, as we know now, General Dean was captured by the enemy, and has since been released in the prisoner exchange that was part of the truce of 1953.

ond arm of the envelopment. The target of both arms, of course, was Pusan.

MacArthur met this dual threat by sending the 1st Cavalry Division around to the east-coast port of Yongpo to stall the enemy drive there, and supplemented the action by directing the naval units under his command to approach as near as possible to the shore and bring the coastal roads under constant bombardment. He also sent the 25th Division through Pusan to strengthen Walker's left flank from the threatened western envelopment. But all of these could only be delayed moves until sufficient forces could be brought to the defense of South Korea.

It was on July 7 that MacArthur made his first major call for reinforcements. In a message to the Joint Chiefs of Staff he explained that the defenders were confronted with "an aggressive and well-trained professional army . . . operating under excellent top level guidance and demonstrated superior command of strategic and tactical principles." His immediate need, as he saw it, was for not less than four to four and one-half full-strength infantry divisions, airborne RCT complete with lift, and three medium-tank battalions, together with reinforcing artillery and service elements. It was in this message that MacArthur indicated that he was thinking far ahead of the immediate lines of defense in South Korea. His purpose also, he explained, was "fully to exploit our air and sea control and, by amphibious maneuver, strike behind his mass of ground forces."

It is interesting in the light of later developments in Korea to read in this same message of July 7, a little more than a week after the beginning of the war, a warning from MacArthur that his estimate of need was based upon military potential of North Korea itself. Should Soviet Russia or Communist China intervene, he added, "a new situation would develop which is not predictable now."

Despite his previous experiences with requests to Washington for reinforcements, MacArthur was surprised when this message of desperate need for the strength to implement Washington's decision was turned down by Washington. The reasons given were that a) no increase in any part of the services had been authorized; b) a suitable United States military posture in other parts of the world had to be maintained; and c) there was a shortage of shipping. What all this amounted to actually was the old faulty principle of "priorities," under which the Far East was placed near the bottom, if not at the bottom, of the list. That it reaffirmed the "Europe-first" principle which had lost us the Philippines and so hamstrung MacArthur's efforts to halt the Japanese advance in the Southwest Pacific was not so surprising as the circumstances under which this decision was being made. The all-important difference, of course, was that during World War II we had been fighting in Europe; now we were not. And it was obvious even to MacArthur at the other side of the world that the Soviet military dispositions in eastern Europe were defensive rather than offensive. Three days after his original request, he repeated it. Again he was turned down.

Meanwhile, on July 8, MacArthur was officially appointed Commander-in-Chief of the United Nations Forces in Korea, and thus a new headquarters was established—on paper. Actually, he continued to function through the same staff headquarters he had had as Commander-in-Chief of United States Forces in the Far East and as Supreme Commander for the Allied Powers, with only minor variations. However, this official appointment brought forth an exchange of messages which is interesting to look back upon now. Said the General to the President: "I can only repeat the pledge of my complete personal loyalty to you as well as an absolute devotion to your monumental struggle for peace and good will throughout the world. I hope I will not fail you." Replied the President to the General: "Your words confirm me . . . in my full belief in the wisdom of your selection."

While the President of the United States was supporting MacArthur mostly in the form of messages, the President of South Korea, Syngman Rhee, was coming to his support with actual troops. On July 15, President Rhee wrote MacArthur: "I am happy to assign to you command authority over all land, sea and air forces of the Republic of Korea during the period of the continuation of the present state of hostilities. . . ." Although South Korea was not a member of the United Nations, President Rhee readily surrendered his authority over his troops to the man who was fighting so desperately to protect Rhee's homeland from Communist tyranny. "The Korean army will be proud to serve under your command," Rhee wrote MacArthur, "and the Korean people and government will be equally proud and encouraged to have the over-all direction of our combined combat effort in the hands of so famous and distinguished a soldier, who also in his person possesses the delegated military authority of all the United Nations who have joined together to resist the infamous Communist assault on the independence and integrity of our beloved land. With continued highest and warmest feelings of personal regard."

Thus MacArthur was provided with a "world" of South Korean soldiers. But the complete lack of trained native officer material rendered these troops ineffective. MacArthur had a plan to meet this deficiency, a plan that simultaneously augmented the effective strength of our own divisions to nearly double its former force. Besides the four ROK divisions which were put into action, he ordered that South Korean troops be integrated into the ranks of U.S. units—man for man, with each American soldier bearing responsibility for training, example, and leadership of the native soldier next to him. This is the device that later became famous as the "buddy system." And MacArthur further ordered that such integration include the elimination of all differences in treatment between the two. The South Korean was to receive the same food ration, cigarette ration, candy ration, etc., and was encouraged to assume his full share of the attendant responsibility. At the time, General Walker and his staff received this policy with marked skepticism, but as soon as MacArthur detected the staff's obvious reluctance to implement it, he issued a peremptory order that the policy be carried out.

It took a very short time for Walker's staff and Walker himself to become convinced of the wisdom of the plan. Not only did it nearly double manpower and firepower, but it had the added and important effect of virtually transforming the South Koreans from dejected victims of defeat into proud and dignified soldiers. The "Roks," as the GI's called them, learned so fast that American patrol leaders actually began to pay them the supreme compliment of seeking their participation in the long and hazardous night patrols. In morale alone they became different men, and the camaraderie between them and their American colleagues reached the point where the GI's made a point of seeing that the South Koreans were not denied any of the American soldier's privileges. For example, under our contracts with the motion-picture producers the Army was required to make a nominal admission charge, which was turned over as rental of the picture then being shown. This would have raised difficulties for the Korean soldier, who was still paid in Korean currency at the standard Korean schedule of pay, had not the GI's found their own ingenious way around the rules. Before the movie started, and after the American troops were seated, the cashiers left their appointed places and the South Korean soldiers swarmed in. Language difficulties between the two disappeared much more quickly than expected; in fact, it was a very short time before the South Koreans were referring to all North Koreans as "Goddam Gooks," a term picked up from possibly less discriminating GI's.

MacArthur's system was so successful in South Korea that over eight thousand South Korean soldiers were sent to Japan to augment the 7th Division, which was then being readied for service. Thus, while only a trickle of soldiers was provided by Washington—under the excuse that troops were needed in Germany, where there was no war—MacArthur was able by this ingenious device to prevent the military disaster that surely would have resulted from Washington's "priority" policy. I later saw these South Korean 7th Division troops in action at Inchon. In poise, dignity, and fighting ability, they looked every inch the American soldier.

The increase in strength was further complemented by South Korean troops who fought as units. And the result was reflected in the battle of Yongdong on July 21, where, after a planned withdrawal from Taejon, our forces held off an all-out enemy assault for four days until over-whelming enemy reinforcements enabled them to penetrate our position and forced us into successive withdrawal farther south. The enemy was fighting not in a continuous line of deployment but in a series of columns of battalion and regimental size, probing main roads and mountain trails in a continuous effort to penetrate and outflank our positions. But, despite the fact that he still outnumbered us many times, the fighting effective-ness of the American–South Korean defenders had rapidly become suffi-cient to slow the enemy's race south to a walk. By mid-July, less than a month after the surprise attack across the 38th Parallel, a more or less stable line of defense had been established.

On July 19 President Truman radioed MacArthur a personal advance summary of a message he was sending to Congress later that day, in which he recited the events of the Korean campaign and related events in the Far East, with a discussion of the requirements of the nation in terms of increased military strength and the corresponding economic measures necessary to produce it. MacArthur replied with a personal note which typified a respect that he has always held, and never failed to em-phasize, for the office of the President, quite regardless of who occupied the office or what political party was in power.

To the members of that fringe who insistently attempt to discredit what MacArthur's leadership symbolizes by unwarranted personal attacks on what is termed his attitude toward Truman, I offer these words from his message: "It was a great state paper, in ultimate effect perhaps the most significant of modern times, for it means that the United States is determined that the Pacific areas shall be free. I am sure that the his-torian of the future will regard it as the focal and turning point of this era's struggle for civilization. I am proud and honored to serve under your leadership at so vital a moment. . . ."

And in the same message MacArthur gave the President a graphic account of the strategical situation thus far—an account that was written and sent to the President with such dispatch that large parts of it were embodied in Truman's message to Congress that afternoon. "With the deployment in Korea of major elements of the Eighth Army now accomplished," MacArthur wrote, "the first phase of the campaign has ended and with it the chance for victory by the North Korean forces. The enemy's plan and great opportunity depended upon the speed with which he could overrun South Korea once he had breached the Han River line and with overwhelming numbers and superior weapons temporarily shattered South Korean resistance. This chance he has now lost through the extraordinary speed with which the Eighth Army has been deployed from Japan to stem his rush. . . .

"The skill and valor thereafter displayed in successive holding actions by the ground forces in accordance with this concept, brilliantly supported in complete coordination by air and naval elements, forced the enemy into continued deployments, costly frontal attacks and confused logistics which so slowed his advance and blunted his drive that we have bought the precious time necessary to build a secure base. . . .

"It is, of course, impossible to predict with any degree of accuracy future incidents of a military campaign. Over a broad front involving continuous local struggles, there are bound to be ups and downs, losses as well as successes. . . . But the issue of battle is now fully joined and will proceed along lines of action in which we will not be without choice. Our hold upon the southern part of Korea represents a secure base. Our casualties despite overwhelming odds have been relatively light. Our strength will continually increase while that of the enemy will relatively decrease. His supply line is insecure. He had his great chance and failed to exploit it. We are now in Korea in force and with God's help we are there to stay until the constitutional authority of the Republic is fully restored."

Thus, only twenty days after MacArthur had been authorized to commit U.S. ground forces in South Korea, he was able confidently to assure the President and the American people that we were not going to lose in Korea. Overnight much of the gloom that the soothsayers had engendered in the public mind was dispersed.

The Communist enemy, attempting to discover how he had lost this first round, might have looked back to World War II and realized that he could have taken a lesson from General Homma. It was with just such a brilliant series of delaying-actions that MacArthur stood Homma off so long on Bataan.

Chapter IV Inchon—The Great Debate

📖 MacArthur had just taught the North Koreans the same lesson he had taught the Japanese on Bataan. And, had the Communists known it, they could have forearmed themselves by studying the lesson that MacArthur had taught the Japanese at Hollandia. In that first week of the Korean war, as MacArthur had stood on the hill overlooking Seoul and watched the backwash of defeat stream by him, he had planned not only the series of delaying-actions which had slowed the North Korean advance (as on Bataan) but also a strategic maneuver that would wrest the initiative away from the enemy (as at Hollandia).

Once again he had been handed a military situation that verged on disaster. Once again, with only a handful of troops and virtually no heavy arms, he faced hordes of the enemy who were not only formidably armed but were already on the verge of complete victory. Once again he was committed to a campaign in which it seemed that his only chance lay in massive defense. And once again he determined to defend by attack.

His plan, as he conceived it on that hill and developed the myriad details later at Tokyo headquarters, was for an envelopment that would at one stroke cut behind the enemy's rear, sever his supply lines, and encircle all his forces south of Seoul.

The target MacArthur selected for this landing was Inchon, twenty miles west of Seoul and the second-largest port in South Korea. The target date, because of the great tides at Inchon, had to be the middle of September. This meant that the staging for Inchon would have to be accomplished more rapidly than that of any other large amphibious operation in history. To add to its complexities, MacArthur knew beforehand that he would have considerable difficulty persuading Washington to undertake so daring a counterstroke. The best warning he had that the Joint Chiefs of Staff might disapprove of his plan was contained in a statement made

342

by General Omar Bradley to a Congressional committee on October 19, 1949, in which the JCS chairman had given his opinion that amphibious warfare was outdated and said that he could not foresee its use at any time in the future. Accordingly, MacArthur had to move with great caution in order that the Inchon landing should not be vetoed right at the start and U.N. forces thereby tied down in a hopeless defense or committed to the blood bath of a frontal counteroffensive.

But no such envelopment as he envisaged could be brought off without reinforcements. In Japan MacArthur had organized a "Police Reserve" designed to bring a hundred thousand Japanese under arms to control internal Communist pressures and secure the country against sudden seizure by the Soviet. Thus the U.S. 7th Infantry Division could be assembled as a nucleus for the amphibious force. By means of the U.S.–ROK "buddy system" that MacArthur had developed, the 7th Division was nearly back to the full strength it had had before Washington directives had stripped it nearly bare.

The 7th Division, however, could not do it alone. What was desperately needed was a Marine force especially trained and equipped for amphibious operations. In mid-July, when Lieutenant General Lemuel C. Shepherd, then Marine chief in the Pacific, visited MacArthur's headquarters, he agreed not only that there were Marines available for this landing but that an entire division could be delivered in Korea within six weeks. Therefore, on July 10 MacArthur asked the Joint Chiefs of Staff for the 1st Marine Division. Profiting by his experience with Washington's penchant for skeletonizing his forces, he carefully stipulated a division at full strength. He was turned down flat. He patiently tried again five days later, saying: "I cannot emphasize too strongly my belief in the complete urgency of my request." He was turned down again.

Meanwhile Lieutenant General Walton Walker and his forces in South Korea were fighting with their backs to the sea in what amounted to little more than an extended beachhead around Pusan. Only a miracle —or a brilliant counterstroke such as MacArthur planned—could keep that beachhead from slowly constricting upon Walker and his men. MacArthur had to take the chance of having his plan killed by the preconceived notions of General Bradley on the subject of amphibious warfare. It was now or never.

On July 23 he cabled Washington: "Operation planned mid-September is amphibious landing of a two-division corps in rear of enemy lines for purpose of enveloping and destroying enemy forces in conjunction with attack from south by Eighth Army. I am firmly con-

343

vinced that early and strong effort behind his front will sever his main lines of communication and enable us to deliver a decisive and crushing blow. . . ." He added the urgent warning: "The alternative is a frontal attack which can only result in a protracted and expensive campaign."

His plea was met with stony silence from the Joint Chiefs of Staff. Not for three weeks did the strategists in the Pentagon deign to discuss this subject with him. Meanwhile, MacArthur sensed that the ultimate decision might well depend upon the immediate play of events in Korea itself. Not having yet seen Pentagon timidity in the full flower to which it would later blossom, he believed that a large part of Washington's reluctance to take a seeming gamble was due to the rash of gloomy dispatches which had made the officials nearly as defeat-minded as most of the American press and people had become in recent weeks. MacArthur decided that it was time for another visit to the front.

On July 27 the *Bataan* was wheeled out onto the Haneda runway, and MacArthur roared off for another inspection trip. Landing at Taegu, he went directly to Walker's headquarters, where he received a formal briefing.

The military term for orderly retreat is "a retrograde movement." MacArthur found that Walker's staff had planned a whole series of retrograde movements, with details so complete as to establish dates on which successive phaselines in the rear would be reached. I remember watching MacArthur's face as these plans were outlined to him. Minute by minute his expression changed from attentiveness to surprise to amazement and then to consternation. Finally he spoke up, with a decided sharpness in his voice and a withering glance at the briefing officer. "These plans," he ordered, "will be scrapped at once." Future planning would emphasize advances rather than retreats. I cannot recall ever seeing him look as stern as he did when he summed up with: "The present line must be held at all costs."

Within forty-eight hours Walker had issued his now famous rallying-cry to his troops. "There must be no further yielding under pressure of the enemy," his order read. "From now on let every man stand or die." By such things can the tide of battle be reversed. The U.N. line of defense formed an arc that covered an almost unbelievable area. And so slim were Walker's resources that many times he could meet an infiltration or a direct assault only by pulling troops from another area and temporarily leaving that position completely exposed. But the line held.

Operating with thirteen divisions and with complete freedom of action to mass at any selected point for a local penetration, the North Ko-

344

reans closed in for what they thought was the kill. They had reason to believe so at Chinju, in particular, when a two-pronged attack sliced through the thin line of defenders and drove to within twelve miles of this keystone of the beachhead's left flank. But then, in a surprise counterattack, Walker's forces stopped them in their tracks. These units had decided that they would neither "stand or die"—they would advance. Their counterattack was highly successful. By August 11 the Communists had been driven back fifteen miles. For the time being, at least, the threat to the ports of Masan and Pusan was removed. MacArthur watched this and other such local operations with increasing admiration for Walker's generalship—and with obvious satisfaction; he had just such an operation in mind for "Johnnie" Walker, as he called him, when it came time for Inchon.

By mid-August the defense perimeter in Korea had stabilized, and so, apparently, had public opinion in the United States. Our forces had not, as had so widely been predicted, been driven into the sea. But, while MacArthur's pleas for reinforcements were receiving a little more attention in Washington, he still had not been informed of any definite decision on Inchon. Then, finally, the Joint Chiefs of Staff wired him that General J. Lawton Collins, Army Chief of Staff, and Admiral Forrest Sherman, Chief of Naval Operations, were coming to Tokyo to discuss this maneuver with him. It was evident immediately upon their arrival that the actual purpose of their trip was not so much to discuss it with him as to dissuade him from it.

Thus, at a little after five thirty p.m. on August 23, in the Dai Ichi Building, there occurred one of the most important strategy debates in American military history. It was also the most important strategy debate of the Korean war. The conferees included MacArthur, General Collins, and Admiral Sherman, as well as Marine Chief Shepherd; MacArthur's Air Commander, Stratemeyer; his Chief of Staff, Almond, already designated commander of the X Corps in the Inchon landing; Admiral Arthur D. Struble; Admiral C. E. Turner Joy; and a gathering of other staff officers and aides making up a veritable constellation of silver stars.

The conference room adjoined MacArthur's office, and its map-studded walls gave the blown-up geographic details essential to military planning. MacArthur sat at the head of the conference table, leisurely smoking his corncob pipe but missing nothing. Occasionally he jerked the pipe from his mouth and gestured with it as he interjected a question or a comment.

As at the Pearl Harbor conference with Roosevelt and Nimitz in

1944, the Navy presented its case first. A naval briefing staff argued that two elements—tide and terrain—made a landing at Inchon extremely hazardous. They referred to Navy hydrographic studies which listed the average rise and fall of the tides at Inchon at 20.7 feet—one of the greatest in the world. On the tentative target date for the invasion, the rise and fall would be more than 30 feet because of the position of the moon. When Inchon's tides were at full ebb, the mud banks that had accumulated over the centuries from the Yellow Sea were out of water in some places as far as two miles out into the harbor from the shore. And during ebb and flood these tides raced through "Flying Fish Channel," the best approach to the port, at speeds up to six knots. Even under the most favorable conditions "Flying Fish Channel" was narrow and winding. Not only did it make a perfect location for enemy mines but any ship sunk at a particularly vulnerable point could block the channel to all other ships.

On the target date, the Navy experts went on, the first high tide would occur at 6:59 in the morning, and the afternoon high tide would be at 7:19, a full thirty-five minutes after sunset. Within two hours after high tide most of the assault craft would be wallowing in the ooze of Inchon's mud banks, sitting ducks for Communist shore batteries until the next tide came in to float them again. In effect the amphibious forces would have only about two hours in the morning for the complex job of reducing or effectively neutralizing Wolmi-do, the 350-foot-high heavily fortified island which commands the harbor and which is connected with the mainland by a long causeway.

Assuming that this could be done, the afternoon's high tide and approaching darkness would allow only two and a half hours for the troops to land, secure a beachhead for the night, and bring up all the supplies essential to enable forces to withstand enemy counterattacks until morning. The landing craft, after putting the first assault waves ashore, would lie helplessly on the mud banks until the morning tide.

Beyond all this, the Navy summed up, the assault landings would have to be made right in the heart of the city itself, where every structure provided a potential strong point of enemy resistance. This was a most unfavorable situation for securing a beachhead, especially with the limited-time factors involved. Reviewing the Navy's presentation, Admiral Sherman concluded by saying: "If every possible geographical and naval handicap were listed—Inchon has 'em all."

MacArthur continued to puff on his pipe, saying nothing, as Collins presented his arguments. The Army, its Chief of Staff said, felt that Inchon was too far in the rear of the present battle area to have the neces-

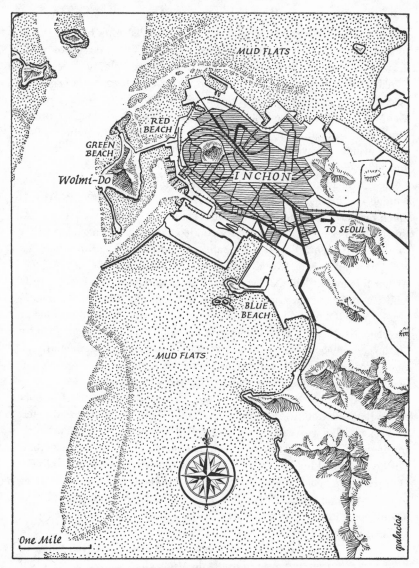

INCHON AND ITS HARBOR: LOW TIDE

sary immediate effect on the enemy. To accomplish this big maneuver successfully with the limited resources available would require withdrawing the 1st Marine Brigade, which was then holding a sector in Walker's hard-pressed defense line, and would thus further endanger his position. Collins was not at all sure—in fact, did not believe—that even if MacArthur captured Seoul he could make contact with Walker to the south. And furthermore, the Army Chief of Staff said, MacArthur might well run into overwhelming enemy force in the area of the capital city and suffer complete defeat.

Collins had an alternate proposal: to abandon the plan of the Inchon landing and instead aim for the west-coast port of Kunsan. This port was much farther south and presented few of Inchon's physical obstacles. At this point Sherman spoke up and seconded Collins in urging MacArthur to give up Inchon in favor of the safer plan of landing at Kunsan.

For a moment or two after Sherman and Collins had finished, Mac-Arthur remained silent. All eyes were upon him, and some of us virtually held our breaths as we waited for him to speak in defense of his much-abused plan. One could literally feel the tension rise in the room. One of the generals shifted a little uneasily in his chair; another drummed softly on the conference table with his fingertips. Wreaths of cigarette and pipe smoke floated across the big war maps that hung on the conference-room walls. If ever a silence was pregnant, this one was.

MacArthur started to talk in a casual, conversational tone. The bulk of the Reds, he said, were committed around Walker's defense perimeter. The enemy, he was convinced, had failed to prepare Inchon properly for defense. "The very arguments you have made as to the impracticabilities involved will tend to ensure for me the element of surprise," he said. "For the enemy commander will reason that no one would be so brash as to make such an attempt." His low, resonant voice rose imperceptibly to a convincing intensity as he added: "Surprise is the most vital element for success in modern war."

Then suddenly he was talking about a campaign that took place almost two centuries ago. The Marquis de Montcalm believed in 1759 that it was impossible for any armed force to scale the precipitous riverbanks south of the then walled city of Quebec, and therefore concentrated his formidable defenses along the more vulnerable banks north of the city. But General James Wolfe and a small force did indeed come up the St. Lawrence River and scale those heights. On the Plains of Abraham, Wolfe won a stunning victory that was made possible almost entirely by surprise. Thus he captured Quebec and in effect ended the French and Indian War.

Like Montcalm, the North Koreans would regard an Inchon landing as impossible. Like Wolfe, MacArthur could take them by surprise.

The Navy's objections as to tides, hydrography, terrain, and physical handicaps, MacArthur agreed, were indeed substantial and pertinent. But they were not insuperable. MacArthur smiled at his old friend Forrest Sherman as he added that his confidence in the Navy was complete, and that in fact he seemed to have more confidence in the Navy than the Navy had in itself. The Navy's rich experience in staging the numerous amphibious landings under his command in the Pacific during the late war, frequently under somewhat similar difficulties, left him with little doubt on that score.

Then he took up the proposal for a landing as Kunsan. It would indeed eliminate many of the hazards of Inchon, but it would be largely ineffective and indecisive. "It would be an attempted envelopment," he argued, "which would not envelop. It would not sever or destroy the enemy's supply lines or distribution center, and would therefore serve little purpose. It would be a 'short envelopment,' and nothing in war is more futile. Better no flank movement than such a one. The only result would be a hook-up with Walker's troops on his left. Better send the troops direct to Walker than by such an indirect and costly process."

In other words, this would simply be sending more troops to help Walker "hang on"; and hanging on was not good enough. MacArthur's voice rose again in emphasis as he predicted that no decision could be reached by such defensive action in Walker's perimeter. To fight frontally in a breakthrough from Pusan would be bloody and indecisive. The enemy would merely roll back on his lines of supply and communication.

But, he said, stabbing the air with his pipe, seizure of Inchon and Seoul would cut the enemy's supply line and seal off the entire southern peninsula. The vulnerability of the enemy was his supply position. Every step southward extended his transport lines and rendered them more frail and subject to dislocation. And the several major lines of enemy supply from the north converged on Seoul; from Seoul they radiated to the several sectors of the front. By seizing Seoul he would completely paralyze the enemy supply system—coming and going. This in turn would paralyze the fighting power of the troops that now faced Walker. Without munitions and food they would soon be helpless and disorganized, and could easily be overpowered by our smaller but well-supplied forces.

His voice was low and dramatically resonant as he said: "The only alternative to a stroke such as I propose would be the continuation of the savage sacrifice we are making at Pusan, with no hope of relief in sight.

Are you content to let our troops stay in that bloody perimeter like beef cattle in the slaughter house? Who would take the responsibility for such a tragedy? Certainly I will not."

Abruptly he switched to a global level. "The prestige of the western world hangs in the balance," he said. "Oriental millions are watching the outcome. It is plainly apparent that here in Asia is where the Communist conspirators have elected to make their play for global conquest. The test is not in Berlin or Vienna, in London, Paris or Washington. It is here and now—it is along the Naktong River in South Korea. We have joined the issue on the battlefield. Actually, we here fight Europe's war with arms, while there it is still confined to words. If we lose the war to Communism in Asia, the fate of Europe will be gravely jeopardized. Win it and Europe will probably be saved from war and stay free. Make the wrong decision here—the fatal decision of inertia—and we will be done. I can almost hear the ticking of the second hand of destiny. We must act now or we will die."

He paused for a moment or two and then said: "If my estimate is inaccurate and should I run into a defense with which I cannot cope, I will be there personally and will immediately withdraw our forces before they are committed to a bloody setback. The only loss then," he said with a sardonic smile, "will be my professional reputation."

But Inchon would *not* fail, he reiterated. Inchon would succeed. MacArthur's voice was a strident whisper as he concluded: "—And it will save 100,000 lives."

He had finished. The silence was so complete that across the conference room Admiral Sherman could be heard murmuring in undisguised admiration: "A great voice in a great cause."

MacArthur had talked for more than an hour without letup. Nothing more was said, and the spell was broken as the chairs were pushed back and we all rose to leave the room. Neither Collins nor Sherman made a definite commitment at the time, but on August 29, after their return to Washington, MacArthur received a wire from the Joint Chiefs of Staff: "We concur after reviewing the information brought back by General Collins and Admiral Sherman, in making preparations and executing a turning movement by amphibious forces on the west coast of Korea—at Inchon. . . ."

Had MacArthur waited until August 29 to get his preparations under way, he would have missed the September 15 deadline set by Inchon's tides. But he had not waited. The 7th Division was rapidly being assembled, as were the elements of the 1st Marine Division. Incidentally, Mac-

Arthur utilized the Kunsan suggestion in characteristic fashion: a part of the preliminaries to the actual assault on Inchon would be a feint at Kunsan, to throw the enemy off guard.

MacArthur also made a special trip to Korea to discuss his plan with Walker, who was naturally disturbed at the prospect of losing the 1st Provisional Marine Brigade from his already thin line. Walker wished that MacArthur would use the fresh troops to reinforce his perimeter instead of conducting the Inchon landing. But he had unlimited faith in MacArthur's strategic judgment, and as soon as he was convinced that MacArthur was invincibly determined upon the plan, he co-operated wholeheartedly.

In return, MacArthur reassured him to the extent of providing a regimental combat team from the 7th Division, to be in floating reserve off Pusan during the withdrawal of the Marine brigade. This combat team would literally be a floating reserve, waiting in ships off Pusan. It could rush into the gap of Walker's line, but only on MacArthur's express orders, if the need arose after the Marine brigade had pulled out. Otherwise it would steam for Inchon and become the last element to land there. Thus the same force would be available to Walker during his most hazardous period, but would also be able to dart in the other direction to support the Inchon assault. This was a dangerous maneuver, and one that could only be directed by men with iron nerves; MacArthur and Walker were that sort of men.

As delicate an operation was the withdrawal of the 1st Marine Brigade from the front lines. If it became known to the Communists, they might guess that a new operation was pending, and the Inchon movement would be imperiled. To help fool the enemy, the brigade was placed in general reserve for a time before it embarked from Pusan. But no operation of the size of Inchon could be performed without taking the chance of disclosure. In this connection it is to the credit of the many news correspondents at the front who could not fail to witness these troop dispositions and surmise the reason for them—as well as to the credit of their editors back home—that the projected counterattack was a secret well kept by many persons.

By a week before the target date, all the details of the master plan had been worked out. The troops that had come from Japan, the United States, and even the Mediterranean had virtually all arrived. Each unit had been assigned its separate responsibility, and those Marines and soldiers who were not already afloat along Korea's west coast were in the final stages of embarkation. It was at this eleventh hour that MacArthur received a message from the Joint Chiefs of Staff which chilled him to the marrow of his bones.

The message read: "We have noted with considerable concern the recent trend of events in Korea. In the light of the commitment of all the reserves available to the Eighth Army, we desire your estimate as to the feasibility and chance of success of projected operation if initiated on planned schedule. . . ." MacArthur read and reread the message with growing concern. What could have given rise to such a query at such an hour? Had someone in authority in Washington lost his nerve? Could it be the President? Marshall or Bradley? Or was it merely an anticipatory alibi if the operation should run into trouble? Whatever lay behind this mysterious, last-minute hesitancy, it clearly suggested the possibility that even after the millions of man-hours expended on this operation, Mac-Arthur might be ordered to abandon it. He immediately penciled a reply.

"I regard the chance of success of the operation as excellent," he wrote. "I go further in belief that it represents the only hope of wresting the initiative from the enemy and thereby presenting the opportunity for a decisive blow. To do otherwise is to commit us to a war of indefinite duration, of gradual attrition and of doubtful result, as the enemy has potentialities of build-up and reinforcements which exceed those of our own. Our stroke as planned would prevent any material reinforcements in build-up of the enemy in the present combat zone. The situation within the perimeter is not critical. It is possible that there may be some contraction, and defense positions have been selected for this contingency. There is no slightest possibility, however, of our forces being ejected from the Pusan beachhead.

"The envelopment from the north will instantly relieve the pressure upon the south perimeter and, indeed, is the only way that this can be accomplished. The success of the enveloping movement from the north does not depend upon the rapid juncture of the X Corps with the Eighth Army. The seizure of the heart of the enemy's distributing system in the Seoul area will completely dislocate the logistical supply of his forces now operating in South Korea and therefore will ultimately result in their disintegration. . . . The prompt junction of our two forces, while it would be dramatically symbolic of the complete collapse of the enemy, is not a vital part of the operation. . . ."

MacArthur concluded with his clinching argument: "The embarkation of the troops and the preliminary air and naval preparations are proceeding according to schedule. I repeat that I and all of my commanders and staff officers, without exception, are enthusiastic for and confident of the success of the enveloping movement."

After dispatching his reply, he waited with growing impatience and concern. Was it possible, he asked himself, that even now, when it was all but impossible to bring this great movement grinding to a halt, he would be forbidden the opportunity for turning defeat into victory simply because of timidity in some office thousands of miles away? With the target time approaching hour by hour, it seemed to MacArthur that he waited an eternity for the answer from Washington.

Finally a short, cryptic message arrived from the Joint Chiefs of Staff, announcing that in view of his reply they had "approved" the operation and "so informed the President." Did this mean that the President had had a change of heart on Inchon eve? MacArthur did not have time to ponder this one. The threat of a last-minute reversal was removed, and he had only just time to implement the final details of his plan. In fact, he would have to hurry to get to Inchon in time himself.

CHAPTER V   Inchon—The Great Victory

On the afternoon of September 12, 1950, a typhoon was brewing in the Sea of Japan. But despite the backlash of it which was sweeping along the coast, MacArthur took off from Haneda Airport in his new plane, the *SCAP*. He could not wait even for typhoons if he was to meet his new rendezvous with history at Inchon.

Only six of us accompanied him. Our departure was shrouded in the utmost secrecy, and not even written orders were issued until after the Inchon operation was completed. Because of the weather, however, we were forced to change our plans at the last minute, and the *SCAP* landed at Itazuke Airfield on Kyushu instead of at Fukuoka, as we had originally intended. One result was that the commanding officer at Itazuke did not know he had a distinguished visitor until MacArthur stepped down from his plane. But our surprised host was able nevertheless to provide us with transportation for the fifty-mile trip to our destination, the naval base at Sasebo. In fact, the Air Force even provided two blue military police jeeps to lead the convoy, and a new Chevrolet sedan for MacArthur. The sedan was complete with four stars on the front bumper, which seemed to dismay the sergeant driver of the five-star guest. "That's all we could find," he lamented. MacArthur was amused.

Despite the inconvenience and the tension of the occasion, MacArthur was relaxed throughout the two-hour trip and enjoyed the beautiful countryside of Kyushu. The sky had cleared, providing a blue backdrop for the creamy rose colors of a Japanese sunset. But as darkness descended on Kyushu, the charm of the countryside disappeared and our headlights emphasized the curtains of thick, yellow dust rolling up from Japan's country roads. Everything was coated with it by the time we reached the outskirts of Sasebo. As the convoy paused here, one of the members of the party stuck his head in MacArthur's car and, only half

354

joking, asked him if he didn't think SCAP should inaugurate a road-building program in Japan. MacArthur laughed, and said: "The trouble with you fellows is that you're getting soft."

So complete was the secrecy of our mission that even at Sasebo, our original destination, only the sentry at the naval base who waved us in and a few sailors who happened to see MacArthur climb out of his car to stretch his legs even knew that we were there. The executive officer of the base was at the officers' club at the time and never knew that MacArthur had come to Sasebo until after the Supreme Commander had left.

The *Mount McKinley* was to be MacArthur's flagship for Inchon. But she had been delayed by the typhoon, and because of the heavy seas had to be warped into the dock; it would be too dangerous to attempt to board her out in the harbor. We were forced to wait only about three hours, but at a time like this it seemed an eternity. We were all tired and hungry, as no dinner had been prepared for us behind the veil of secrecy and expectation that we would board the *Mount McKinley* immediately upon our arrival at the base. But someone had the bright idea that a ship's store nearby would provide our emergency needs, which it did. MacArthur, however, still appeared to be unperturbed. He waited in the base commandant's office, only occasionally betraying the slightest anxiety or impatience by getting up from his chair and resuming his familiar pacing.

It was nearly midnight before the *Mount McKinley*'s lines were made fast to the dock and we could go aboard. We lost no time in doing so, and the *Mount McKinley* quickly cast off.

We steamed out of Sasebo's harbor and were hit with the full force of the typhoon-lashed seas. The storm and the racing mountains of water came at us from the port quarter, giving the *Mount McKinley* a sickening combination of pitch and roll. The less said about that first night out, the better.

All the day of the 13th the storm continued to buffet our ship. By the second day out the seas had smoothed somewhat and we did not roll and pitch so heavily. A brisk breeze blew from starboard, off the Korean coast. As we rounded the tip of the Korean peninsula—where Walker and his men were fighting to hold the Pusan beachhead—our course changed; we swung into the Yellow Sea and steamed north for Inchon. The afternoon of the second day was bright and clear as we headed for our rendezvous with the rest of the assault armada.

That evening, as I stood at the port rail of the *Mount McKinley* and watched the sun go down beyond China over the horizon, I could think of nothing but the next morning, D-Day, when we would be threading our way over the shifting bars of "Flying Fish Channel," under the guns of Wolmi-do and skirting the edges of the deadly mud banks that stretched for as much as two miles across the harbor. All over the ship the tension that had been slowly building since our departure was now approaching its climax. Even the Yellow Sea rushing past the ship's sides seemed to bespeak the urgency of our mission.

Inchon, it happened, would mark my twentieth year in active service, and during that time I had accompanied MacArthur on every landing, including every visit to Korea, since Leyte. Only rarely on these occasions had he shown the slightest emotion. But Inchon was different. Never before had MacArthur embarked on so intricately complicated an amphibious operation. And never before had an operation been carried out with such reluctant approval by the military leaders in Washington. Even with all other considerations aside, it was impossible to measure the personal catastrophe that MacArthur faced should Inchon fail.

For a time his expression continued to show no sign of the conflicting emotions that were stirring deep inside him. His manner indicated that the decision had been made, the die cast, and that he faced the future imperturbably. But I was not surprised by what happened that evening.

We had retired early in preparation for a dawn rising. I judge that I had been asleep but a few moments when I awoke to the sound of knocking on my door. It was the Marine sentry who had been posted at the door of MacArthur's cabin.

"General MacArthur would like to see you, sir," he said. I threw on my bathrobe as I followed the sentry down the passageway to MacArthur's cabin. I entered to find him dressed in his robe, his hands thrust deep in the pockets and his brow wrinkled in meditation as he paced the length of the little cabin. He glanced up at me, said quietly: "Sit down, Court," and continued his pacing in silence.

It was a memorable night. The ship rolled gently beneath us as she entered the channel at the prearranged point and time and glided through the darkness toward the target. Faintly I could hear the muffled sound of her engines and the tread of the ship's crew going about their business. The only sound in the cabin was the familiar creak of a ship at sea and the bell of the ship's clock on the wall as it struck the half-hour. Before me MacArthur continued his silent striding, his carpet slippers whispering on the cabin rug. On my left I could see the framed photographs of his wife and son, his father and mother, and his brother—the same photographs that had surrounded him in his Tokyo bedroom, in his cabin aboard the *Nashville* at Leyte, in his temporary headquarters at Port

Moresby, and in his office in Manila. These were the symbols of family which meant so much to him and which always went with him, even to such temporary headquarters as a ship's cabin. But despite them MacArthur, at this troubled hour, was a lonely man. My greatest service to him would be not as an aide or adviser but as a friend—to talk with him, hear him think out loud, or share his silence.

What he wanted most was someone to listen to him as he weighed his thoughts, as he reviewed once more the infinite details as well as the grand design of Inchon. While I sat and listened, he continued his pacing and carried on a monologue that amounted to a kind of self-debate. On the one hand there were the many hazards that lay ahead; they had been graphically described by the Washington officials who had tried to talk him out of the operation. And on the other hand there was only his own reasoning to refute these objections. But did it? Was it still his best judgment that the element of surprise more than made up for the technical difficulties his men would face at dawn? Try as he would, he could not but conclude as he had a month earlier: the very fact of the difficulties was in his favor, for the reason that Inchon would be the last place in Korea where the enemy would expect him to attempt a landing—if the secret known now to so many had been kept. Had it been kept?

It had been his fervent argument of this logic that had won the reluctant support of the Joint Chiefs of Staff. So in a sense his responsibilities were greater on this mission than on any he had ever before directed. He alone would have to answer for victory—or for defeat. And certainly the odds of timing and terrain were greatly against him. As he reflected upon this fact, his mind turned naturally to the American boys who would have to pay with their lives and their blood if he *had* made a mistake. I recalled at that moment how at Leyte MacArthur had dwelt not upon the mighty armada he was leading back to the Philippines but upon "those fine American boys" who would die on the beaches. How much more cause he had to think of his men this time!

His hands thrust even more deeply into his bathrobe pockets, MacArthur frowned as he felt the physical pain of the memory of so many battlefields on which in fifty years of military service he had been forced to commit his men. And as he continued his remarkable soliloquy, he conjured up the scene of the mangled bodies, the bloody wounds, the shrieks of men who fought to live but were to die. In World War II, despite the disparity between the losses occasioned by his surprise landings and the bloody assaults made by the Navy and Marines against heavily fortified Japanese islands, MacArthur had had to watch thousands of young soldiers pay the supreme sacrifice for their country. He realized that there would be deaths in the morning, no matter how successful the landings; there is no such thing as a bloodless war. But the thought that he might by a mistake in judgment be committing hundreds of soldiers, sailors, and marines to slaughter sickened his soul.

He could not believe that this would happen. The same element of surprise that had saved the lives of so many thousands of MacArthur's men in World War II would, he was convinced, protect most of the thousands who now steamed in their blackened ships toward "Flying Fish Channel" and Wolmi-do.

Then he allowed himself to entertain one final doubt. Suppose he *was* faced with an alerted and well-prepared enemy with a force superior to his own—what then? He could not expect to extricate his forces without considerable loss. The narrow, treacherous channel, the tides, and the sucking mud of Inchon would all be against him. In fact, the entire assault fleet could be placed in greatest jeopardy, and it was possible that tomorrow, September 15, 1950, could go down in history as one of the great United States military disasters. No, there was no doubt about the risk. It was a tremendous gamble.

But to erase this doubt he had only to consider the alternative to Inchon. Right now, as he paced his cabin floor, General Walker and his men were fighting for their lives, hopelessly outnumbered by the hordes of Communists that had flooded into South Korea and had overrun all but the Pusan beachhead. Surely this calculated risk was better military strategy than a doubtful frontal counterattack against the massed enemy. In that there was no risk of slaughter; there was certainty of it.

Finally he stopped his pacing. He stood before the desk and looked at the pictures of his family while he spoke, still as if to himself. "No," he said, "the decision was a sound one, the risks and hazards must be accepted."

His expression changed. The worried creases disappeared from his brow as he turned to me. I rose and he put a hand on my shoulder. "Thanks, Court," he said. "Thanks for listening to me. Now let's get some sleep." He threw off his robe, climbed into his bunk, and reached to the table alongside to pick up his Bible.

As I swung the cabin door closed, I heard the ship's clock strike five bells; it was two thirty a.m. I went out and took a turn around the deck. The ship was blacked out from stem to stern. At their posts and battle stations the crew members were alert and silent, no longer exchanging the customary banter. At the bow I stood listening to the rush of the sea and watching the fiery sparklets of phosphorescence as I pondered the significance of this night—the dark ship plowing toward the target, the armada of other craft converging on the same area, all now past the point of no return. Through the thick night and the black seas this vessel was carrying MacArthur—to what? I thought back a month to his words at that meeting in the Dai Ichi Building: "I can almost hear the ticking of the second hand of destiny. We must act now or we will die." Within five hours 40,000 men would act boldly, in the hope that 100,000 others manning the thin defense lines in South Korea would not die. And below in his cabin the commander who was gambling with disaster to achieve an unprecedented victory was alone with his God.

Then I noticed a flash—a light that winked on and off across the water. I sought out the officer of the deck and from him learned that the channel navigation lights were on. Fearful of decoys, the ship's officers had carefully checked them and determined their authenticity. This was the first good omen. Evidently we *were* taking the enemy by surprise. The lights were not even turned off. I felt much relieved as I went to my cabin and turned in.

I could not have been asleep more than a couple of hours when a sudden thunder woke me. Our guns had opened up on Wolmi-do. This was the island which dominated Inchon harbor, and our landings could not proceed until it was reduced. I was trying to get back to sleep when the warning signal was sounded for enemy air attack.

Hurriedly dressing and going to the bridge, I learned that two enemy planes were attempting to bomb the cruiser just ahead of us. The pale lights of dawn had not yet dispersed enough of the darkness for me to follow the course of the action, but an officer reported that both planes were shot down before they could do any damage. I decided, however, that I had better awaken MacArthur because of this danger. When I went into his cabin and gently shook him, he woke, listened while I recounted the incident of the attack, and then turned over to resume his rest. "Wake me up again, Court," he said, "if they attack this ship." I gave up and went back on deck.

It was not long, however, before the red glow of sunrise and the increasing din of battle penetrated his cabin and woke him. He had a quick bite of breakfast and took his position on the *Mount McKinley's* bridge. From there, as daylight unfolded the scene before us, he scanned the shore lines of Inchon and Wolmi-do through his field glasses.

The water, which had changed from the deep blue of the open ocean to an olive green near the harbor, now showed shades of the silt-filled yellow from which the Yellow Sea gets its name. The closest streaks of yellow water swirled around Wolmi-do, the harbor island that had once been a peaceful summer resort and was now rocking under the bombardment of naval guns and aerial bombs. As MacArthur watched from the bridge, blue Corsairs swooped down from the clouds and added their bombs to the destruction. Through channels that even Korean pilots would not navigate except in broad daylight, and against tidal currents that raced past at speeds up to three and a half knots, destroyers had steamed up alongside Wolmi-do's guns and were bravely daring the beach defenders to open fire on them point-blank, in order to spot the location of coastal batteries for the bigger-gunned ships farther out in the harbor.

Already the bombardment was having its effect, and wreaths of dirty gray smoke were rising from the island. The naval guns were also scoring hits on Inchon itself, and their success was attested to by pillars of purple smoke that rose as high as five thousand feet. Against this rolling curtain of smoke the arcing, fiery trails of rockets could be seen as they streaked toward Inchon's beaches. It was a devastating amount of fire power; one statistic I recall was that two thousand rockets ripped into one beach in only twenty minutes before H-Hour. Even from our position out in the harbor we could see the immense explosions that were erupting all along Inchon's shores.

Now the endless circles of little landing craft started churning around and around the mother assault ships. As they did, MacArthur received the word that the enemy guns at Wolmi-do had been silenced. This was one of the best signs that Inchon was lightly defended and that he had indeed achieved the complete surprise on which he had gambled so much. But we could not relax yet. The first assault waves were now going up to the beaches of Wolmi-do. If the Marines, who were leading the invasion, were beaten off or even pinned down on the beaches for too long, that would mean that Inchon was protected by the enemy in force. It would take relatively few Communist defenders to slaughter these first waves of invaders while the rest were held back by the enormous mud banks.

Then, finally, the news came. At 8 a.m. an orderly climbed up to the bridge and handed MacArthur a slip of paper. His eyes swept it eagerly and his face broke into a broad grin. The message said that the first wave of Marines had landed and secured a beachhead without a single fatality. MacArthur turned to Admiral Doyle, the amphibious commander, and said: "Please send this message to the fleet: 'The Navy and the Marines have never shone more brightly than this morning.'"

Nor had MacArthur. Once again his genius for taking the enemy by surprise not only had won a magnificent victory but had also paid a small price in casualties. Like Wolfe defeating Montcalm by scaling the "impossible" cliffs of Quebec, MacArthur had defeated the North Koreans by landing at "impossible" Inchon.

And as Wolfe's victory led to the end of the French and Indian War, MacArthur's victory at Inchon led to the complete rout of the North Korean armies. As he had argued in the strategy debate in the Dai Ichi Building, the converging supply lines at Seoul were now at his mercy. Cut them and he would sever the jugular vein of the enemy. This he was now able to do.

By the time the tide had gone out of Inchon's harbor only an hour later, leaving some of the landing craft squatting on the mud banks, Wolmi-do had been fully secured. And late that afternoon, as soon as the tides rolled back in, MacArthur climbed into the gig of Admiral Struble, commander of the naval forces, and went ashore at Wolmi-do. There he made the discovery that the Communists had started an intense fortification of the island. As we studied these guns and dugouts, we realized how well MacArthur had timed his attack. Had he listened to those who wanted to delay the landing until the next high tides, nearly a month later, Wolmi-do would have been an impregnable fortress.

Next morning, on the following tide, MacArthur went ashore at Inchon itself, landing on a beach that actually had not been occupied yet. But the Communists had fled, and to get to the front lines MacArthur had to drive three miles beyond the city of Inchon. There he delighted two Marine commanders by awarding them the Army's Silver Star. He also inspected some North Korean prisoners of war and a Russian-built tank. By early afternoon he climbed along an improvised bridge to Struble's gig to make another inspection of Wolmi-do, where his jeep nearly ran onto an unexploded Russian shell. As the gig finally headed back to the ship, MacArthur rose and took a last look at the shore, where barges were unloading supplies, trucks and jeeps were moving forward along the coastal road, and troops were swinging confidently down the highway into Inchon. He turned back to Admiral Struble and the Marine commander, General Shepherd, and said simply: "Well done."

The force that had gone ashore at Inchon had been given the name of the X Corps and constituted a GHQ reserve under the command of MacArthur's chief of staff, Major General Edward Almond. The Marines and soldiers of X Corps immediately moved inland in predetermined directions toward predetermined objectives. One column headed for Seoul, with the more immediate mission to cut communications to the south and to seize Kimpo Airfield, the biggest in all Korea. The other column moved on toward Suwon, its mission being to recapture the air base there and to move on as the northern arm of the pincer movement MacArthur intended to apply against the trapped Communists in all of South Korea.

Events now happened with great rapidity. Kimpo Airfield was captured on the 17th, two days after the Inchon landings. One day after that, C-54's and C-119 "Flying Boxcars" came soaring in at the rate of one every eight minutes during the daylight hours. Only three days later the chain reaction of Inchon was felt all the way to the Pusan beachhead, where Walker noticed for the first time signs of growing weakness in the enemy camp.

He had been waiting for this, and promptly crossed the Naktong River in force. The enemy broke in disorder before his attack. Caught between our two pincers, the North Koreans tried to make an orderly retreat, but quickly broke into a rout. Red divisions and regiments ceased to exist as organized units. They abandoned their arms and equipment; tanks, artillery, trucks, and small arms littered the highways all over South Korea. The total of enemy prisoners of war rose to 130,000. In one brilliant stroke—and against the advice of all his superiors—MacArthur had turned defeat into victory and virtually recaptured South Korea.

About all that remained now was Seoul, which the enemy fought fiercely to defend in a face-saving gesture. But by September 28, less than two weeks after the Inchon landings, Seoul was liberated. Among the many messages of congratulations that came to MacArthur at this time were two that are of importance because their senders, just like the Communists who fought so bitterly in Seoul, realized the psychological importance of this victory throughout the Far East.

The first message was from President Syngman Rhee. "On this historical occasion of the liberation of Seoul," Rhee wired, "I wish to express to you on behalf of the Korean government and people deepest gratitude and everlasting warm memory for your brilliant leadership which has made this victory possible against great odds. Though battle still continues, outcome is certain. Of all your great achievements in a long life of extraordinary public service, I believe history will record your leadership of the U.N. forces in Korea as the most magnificent."

The second message was from another Asian leader, Generalissimo Chiang Kai-shek. He wired: "It gives the Chinese government as well as myself great gratification indeed to learn that under your magnificent planning and command the United Nations forces have recaptured Seoul. I send you hearty congratulations and am certain you will have complete victory." More than any Western politicians, these two leaders understood that the psychological impact from the liberation of a capital city meant more in Asia than the capture of a hundred lesser cities.

For the same kind of psychological advantage, but even more because of his dislike of military interference in civil government, MacArthur moved swiftly to have the government of Korea re-established in Seoul. Here again, as in his military strategy, he had established the precedent in the Philippines. But at this juncture he received an astonishing message from Washington. In an order that parroted the State Department's ill-concealed antagonism toward Syngman Rhee, the Joint Chiefs of Staff admonished that any plan for the restoration of his government "must have the approval of higher authority."

MacArthur, despite his amazement, replied instantly: "Your message is not understood. I have no plan whatsoever except scrupulously to implement the directives I have received. These directives envision support of the resolutions of the United Nations Security Council of 25 and 27 June, calling upon member governments to furnish 'such assistance to the Republic of Korea as may be necessary to repel the armed attacks and to restore international peace and security in the area.' In view of the fact the existing government of the Republic has never ceased to function and the position of the United States as stated in your message of July 7, 'Government of Republic of Korea is recognized by U.S. as responsible governing authority and only lawful government in Korea and is only Korean government whose legality has been recognized by U.N. authority . . . ,' with the concurrence of the cabinet, senior members of the legislature, the United Nations Commission and perhaps others of similar official category to domicile in Seoul as soon as conditions there are sufficiently stable to permit reasonable security. This of course involves no re-establishment of government nor indeed any change in government but merely a restoration of the existing government to its constitutional seat in order to facilitate the resumption of the civil process and to promote prompt and effective restoration of law and order in areas liberated from enemy control. Such action is not only very much desired by the American ambassador and all others concerned but appears to be implicit in my directives." That ended that, so far as Washington's attempt to undercut Rhee was concerned. And MacArthur ordered that on the 29th of September the city of Seoul be formally restored as the seat of the existing government.

On that day MacArthur flew to the newly opened Kimpo Airfield in the *SCAP,* where a five-starred sedan waited for him. Through the swirling dust of Korea's roads he drove from Kimpo to the Han River. Army engineers who had just completed a new pontoon bridge stood proudly at attention as he crossed it. In Seoul his motorcade rolled down Mapo Boulevard, where the rubble of the war had only just been cleaned away and where ROK soldiers saluted sharply as he went by.

Scarcely a house in Seoul failed to bear the scars of battle, and the sight of unburied dead in the midst of such desolation and destruction was heart-sickening. The tragedy of Seoul was alleviated only by the warm smiles of joy and gratitude on the faces of the South Koreans who recognized their liberator.

At the capitol building MacArthur saw Generals Walker and Almond for the first time since he had planned with them the co-ordinated operations for the Inchon landing and the great pincer movement. With obvious emotion he pinned the Distinguished Service Cross on both of these senior commanders who had so magnificently exploited the situation MacArthur had provided for them. Then a few moments to confer with Syngman Rhee—and the ceremony of handing back the capital city.

Here was another scene as impressive and stirring as it was historic. In the war-shattered assembly room where the ceremony was held sat row on row of heavily armed officers and men of both the U.N. and ROK armies. On both sides of the room the windows gaped brokenly, and the smell of death drifted through them. As I witnessed this occasion, my memory went back to the similar one in Malacañan Palace in Manila, when MacArthur had handed the seat of the government over to the civil authorities of the Philippines. Here too, as he had been at Malacanan, MacArthur was deeply moved. The mask that he was able to wear at times of danger and the eve of great battles did not serve him now. Emotion was visible on his face as he said:

"By the grace of merciful Providence, our forces . . . have liberated this ancient capital city of Korea. It has been freed from the despotism of Communist rule and its citizens once more have the opportunity for that immutable concept of life which holds invincibly to the primacy of individual liberty and personal dignity. . . ."

Then he said: "In humble and devout manifestation of gratitude to Almighty God for bringing this decisive victory to our arms, I ask that all present rise and join me in reciting the Lord's Prayer." The steel helmets and mud-caked fatigue caps came off as everyone rose to his feet. Together they recited the Lord's Prayer, and I remember that particles of glass tinkled down from the shattered roof of the assembly room as MacArthur concluded in a voice packed with deep emotion and the crowd murmured in unison: "Thine is the Kingdom, the Power and the Glory, for ever and ever. Amen."

My memory of Malacañan was even more poignant as MacArthur turned to Syngman Rhee and said virtually the same words he had spoken five years before to Sergio Osmeña: "Mr. President, my officers and I will now resume our military duties and leave you and your government to the discharge of the civil responsibility."

President Rhee seemed as moved by it all as MacArthur. He rose from the seat they had been sharing on the platform and clasped Mac-Arthur's hand. "We admire you," he said with tears flowing down his cheeks. "We love you as the savior of our race." And in their own way, when the ceremony was over, the people of Seoul echoed the sentiments of Syngman Rhee, as thousands of them lined the streets and clapped and waved their little paper flags and those who could speak English cried "God bless you!" as MacArthur rode slowly back to Kimpo to return to Tokyo.

Many were the congratulatory messages waiting for him at the Dai Ichi Building. The text of some of them is particularly interesting because of what was about to take place.

President Truman had wired: "I know that I speak for the entire American people when I send my warmest congratulations on the victory which has been achieved under your leadership in Korea. Few operations in military history can match either the delaying action where you traded space for time in which to build up your forces, or the brilliant maneuver which has now resulted in the liberation of Seoul. . . . I am particularly impressed by the splendid cooperation of our Army, Navy and Air Force. . . . The unification of our arms established by you . . . has set a shining example."

The Joint Chiefs of Staff had not a word to say about their part in endeavoring to kill Inchon, but conceded the soundness of the plan in a generous message: "The Joint Chiefs of Staff are proud of the great successes you have achieved. We realize that they would have been impossible without brilliant and audacious leadership and without the full coordination and the fighting spirt of all forces and all arms. From the sudden initiation of hostilities you have exploited to the utmost all capabilities and opportunities. Your transition from defensive to offensive operations was magnificently planned, timed and executed. You have given new inspiration to the freedom loving peoples of the world. We remain completely confident that the great task entrusted to you by the United Nations will be carried to a successful conclusion." General Marshall wired: "Accept my personal tribute to the courageous campaign you directed in Korea and the daring and perfect strategical operation which virtually terminates the struggle."

Of interest, too, is the message from the British Chiefs of Staff in London: "We send you our warmest congratulations on your brilliant victory. We have admired not only the skill with which you have conducted an extremely difficult rearguard action against odds over many anxious weeks, but equally the bravery and tenacity with which the forces under your command have responded to your inspiring and indefatigable leadership. We believe that the brilliant conception and masterly execution of the Inchon counterstroke which you planned and launched whilst holding the enemy at bay in the south will rank among the finest strategic achievements in military history."

Warmed and gratified by the unanimity of tone in these and many other similar messages, MacArthur pushed on to continue his exploitation of Inchon. First, on October 1, he broadcast a message to the enemy commander-in-chief, calling upon him to have his command lay down its arms and release all United Nations prisoners of war and civilian internees. "The early and total defeat and complete destruction of your armed forces and war-making potential is now inevitable," he warned. "In order that the decisions of the United Nations may be carried out with a minimum of further loss of life and destruction of property, I, as United Nations Commander-in-Chief, call upon you and the forces under your command, in whatever part of Korea situated, forthwith to lay down your arms and cease hostilities under such military supervision as I may direct —and I call upon you at once to liberate all United Nations prisoners and civilian internees under your control and to make adequate provision for their protection, care, maintenance and immediate transportation to such places as I indicate. . . . I shall anticipate your early decision upon this opportunity to avoid the further useless shedding of blood and destruction of property."

There was no reply, so MacArthur ordered the movement north to continue. Meanwhile he secured the east-coast port city of Wonsan. Thus he attempted simultaneously to close on the remnants of Communist troops fleeing toward North Korea, safeguard the Eighth Army from any attack by regrouped North Korean forces, and provide another badly needed port of entry for supplies and equipment for the U.N. forces who were rapidly liberating all the rest of the area that the Communists had invaded only a little more than five months before.

Inchon had turned the tide of war decisively. The North Korean forces that had attacked their South Korean neighbors were in full flight, and all that remained was to chase them down and finish them off. Nothing could prevent MacArthur and his U.N. forces from accomplishing this now— nothing, that is, so long as those in Washington and the capitals of the other U.N. nations had really meant what they said in their messages of congratulation, and so long as they too wanted the Korean war to end in victory.

Chapter VI   Formosa—Friendly Bastion or
Enemy Base

🖢 In hindsight and in the United States it is simpler than it was at the time in Tokyo to see the animosity against MacArthur that was rampant in Washington during the Korean war. But even reviewing and studying it today, I still find it difficult to understand. It seems clear that when President Truman, Secretaries Acheson and Johnson, and General Bradley met in the White House office and decided to go into the war, their intention at the outset was not to use American lives as pawns in lengthy bargaining sessions with the leaders of Asian Communism. I cannot believe— and neither can MacArthur—that these men plotted among themselves to kill 31,000 United States soldiers and spend 22 billion dollars only to ruin American prestige all over Asia.

But this was the actual result of the policies they adopted. Somehow their aims got twisted. Perhaps they were not thinking, but were only swinging blindly in the darkness of wishful ignorance when they struck back at the North Koreans in June 1950. Whatever their intention when they made their gesture of defiance, all Asia applauded. But then, when little by little America's posture turned from that of the powerful defender of the right to a timid appeasement of the wrong, Asian admiration turned to shocked disillusionment.

This MacArthur *could* see better from Tokyo than others could from Washington or Lake Success. But what surpassed his understanding was the reason why. It still does.

It took a little time for American courage and defiance of Communist aggression to become transformed into the kind of attitude that produced the losing stalemate at Panmunjon. But the signs of growing timidity in Washington were surprisingly fast in appearing, even ten thousand miles away in MacArthur's headquarters. The first clear indication he had that the United States might actually compromise with victory came in the handling of Formosa. MacArthur of course could not believe at first that the supposed leader of the world's nations would reverse all American history and adopt a foreign policy of vacillation and weakness. It took the strange Washington behavior over Formosa to suggest to him that this might unhappily be the fact.

The strategic importance of Formosa became universally recognized when the island was utilized so effectively by the Japanese as a staging depot and air base during World War II. Anyone who had been in the Philippines in December 1941 did not have to be reminded of how vulnerable the Philippines were to Japan's Formosa-based bombers. Much of Japan's campaign in the southwest Pacific and southeast Asia was launched from her Formosa bastions. MacArthur recognized that had Formosa been in Allied hands at the outset of World War II, our posture of defense would have been far more effective than it was.

So he was gratified when on June 28 the directive from Washington authorizing him to fight Communism in Korea also authorized him to defend Formosa against Communist aggression too. For the same reason, however, he was deeply concerned by the simultaneous orders, the effect of which was to defend the Communist forces and installations on the Chinese mainland against any attacks from the Formosan garrison. It was difficult for him to visualize the picture of American forces protecting Communists in China from attack while the latter were actively supporting the North Korean attack against the south in Korea—to assume the posture in effect of a defensive shield to protect a common enemy against our Chinese ally on Formosa. What he could see most clearly was the tremendous advantage this neutralization of Formosa gave to the Chinese Communists. They were thus given complete immunity from any counter measures, even the smallest harrying raid, while preparing coastal concentrations and building up forces for an attack against the island. They were also thereby promised United States naval protection for their entire coastline, so that they could release defending forces for employment anywhere else in Asia.

Busy as he was in Korea during those first few weeks of the war, MacArthur did not have the time to engage in the lengthy discussions that would inevitably follow should he attempt to point out to the State Department through the Joint Chiefs of Staff the faulty logic of such reasoning. But on July 29 the Joint Chiefs themselves came to the same realization and recommended to the Secretary of Defense that these directives be changed. After assessing Red China's capability of attacking Formosa under such advantageous conditions, the Joint Chiefs urged that the Nationalist government be permitted to employ its military forces in defensive measures in order to prevent Communist amphibious concentrations aimed at Formosa or the Pescadores. Such defensive measures, the Joint Chiefs' recommendation pointed out, could include attacks on military concentrations on the mainland and the mining of those mainland water areas from which a Communist assault could be staged.

On the same day they asked MacArthur to comment. He at once noted his concurrence with their recommendation, in this message: "There is deep resentment among senior Nationalist military and political leaders because of the restriction upon defensive operations from Formosa against the Chinese mainland. The cause of such resentment is given emphasis by recent Communist assaults upon Nationalist-held islands off the Chinese coast which, due to the restrictions, cannot be neutralized by counterattacks from Formosa against mainland supporting bases and concentration areas.

"The U.S. is thereby placed in the position of neither assuming a defense of these islands nor permitting the Nationalist government freedom to deploy its own military resources to such end. Furthermore, by denying the Nationalist garrison freedom within its own capabilities to destroy mainland air, sea and troop concentrations created to support amphibious operations against Formosa, the enemy is being given the distinct military advantage of being permitted openly to prepare for such a military operation in which our own forces, as well as the Chinese, are to be engaged. As a consequence, the restriction as presently imposed not only embodies elements of injustice against the Nationalist government, which gives rise to this resentment, but may prove to be one for which the U.S. will be forced to pay a heavy military price."

Here, for the first time and in a form that seemed harmless to all but a few farsighted military strategists, was the odd concept that was later to so cripple MacArthur in Korea—sanctuary for the enemy. Thus protected from any harassments from Formosa, the Red Chinese leaders moved two of their best field armies from their coastal defenses opposite Formosa to the staging areas north of the Yalu. And so, when the Red Chinese did decide to intervene in Korea, these two field armies spearheaded the attack and allowed the Chinese to smash against our Eighth Army in massive strength.

Who it was who won over President Truman's confidence and corrupted his logic to the extent of defying the experienced advice of his best military experts, has always been a well-kept Washington secret. Certainly the Secretary of Defense, Louis Johnson, did not favor this kind of appeasement. So the likely person to bear the enormous blame for this incalculable mistake would seem to be the then Secretary of State Dean Acheson, possibly acting under pressure from the British Foreign Office. And this supposition seems the more likely when considered in connection with the exchange of messages between Washington and Tokyo following MacArthur's concurrence with the Joint Chiefs' recommendation.

In the same wire in which he had supported the Joint Chiefs' stand on Formosa, MacArthur had added that he intended himself to go to the island on July 31 or thereabouts with a selected group of staff officers to make a brief reconnaissance of Formosa's defense potential. The Joint Chiefs, through whom virtually all messages to MacArthur were channeled, replied that certain policy matters in reference to Formosa were then under discussion with the State Department. Pending receipt of new instructions on these matters, the Joint Chiefs advised, MacArthur might "desire to send a senior officer to Formosa with the group on July 31st and go yourself later." That the suggestion was apparently the idea of the State Department rather than the Army was politely indicated at the end of the message, in which the Joint Chiefs directed him, if he felt it necessary to proceed personally on the 31st: "Please feel free to go, since the responsibility is yours."

MacArthur was somewhat puzzled by all this. But he was even more puzzled by the many conflicting reports that were coming from Formosa and other sources on the subject of military capabilities of the island for defense. As in World War II and as in Korea, the only way he could get a clear picture of the situation was to go and have a look himself. He explained this to the Joint Chiefs and told them that he would proceed to Formosa on July 31 as planned.

The flight was uneventful, except for a delay at its destination, when bad weather kept us circling Taipei's airfield for an hour and a half while Generalissimo Chiang Kai-shek and the members of his government waited below. I was struck with the fact that after all these years of fighting Japanese and Communist aggression side by side, as it were, these two comrades-in-arms had never actually met. Now, as they shook hands, MacArthur said: "How do you do, Generalissimo? It was nice of you to come down and meet me."

With no more ado, they climbed into a sedan and set off for a military briefing and a conference with the chief Chinese Nationalist leader with whom MacArthur would have to deal in the joint defense of the island. It was a busy day, but at the end of it MacArthur felt that he had obtained a general "feel" not only of the local military situation but on such intelligence from the mainland as had come out through Nationalist channels.

That evening we were guests at a formal dinner given by Generalissimo and Madame Chiang Kai-shek at their home. The Generalissimo's natural handicap in his inability to speak English on such social occasions was more than made up by his wife's charm as a hostess. She personally greeted by name every guest as he arrived, though she had never met most of us and probably had only heard of us through an official briefing for the occasion; how she did it I do not know. She made everyone at once feel the warmth of the hospitality of this great leader and his wife, who for so long have symbolized implacable resistance to the advance of Communism in the Far East.

I so enjoyed the cocktail which was served before dinner that I told Madame I should like to know how it was made. Two days after our return to Tokyo I received the following:

MADAME CHIANG'S COCKTAIL RECIPE

Put a piece of lemon peel, cut very thin, in a glass with ¼ teaspoonful of sugar and one tablespoon of water. Mix thoroughly until sugar is melted. Put in three cubes of ice, pour one jigger of Scotch. Add a dash of humour and stir in a big, warm welcome.

To anyone who would try this recipe, I would recommend the addition of at least a pinch of that invincible spirit which has left this gallant couple with a sense of humor, despite their harrowing experience as adversity closed on them from all around while they have struggled to hold aloft the torch of freedom in Asia.

It did not dawn on MacArthur that his visit to Formosa would be construed as being sinister in any way. The area in which he had military responsibility had been enlarged by the President so as to include Formosa, and MacArthur was accordingly attempting to make his own military estimate of the situation. But in order to forestall in advance any criticism that his trip had been other than military, he issued the following statement as soon as he returned to Tokyo:

"My visit to Formosa has been primarily for the purpose of making a short reconnaissance of the potentiality of its defenses against possible attack. The policy has been enunciated that this island, including the Pescadores, is not under present circumstances subject to military invasion. It is my responsibility and firm purpose to enforce this decision. My conferences here on all levels have been most cordial and responsive in every respect. Arrangements have been completed for effective coordination between the American forces under my command and those of the Chinese Government, the better to meet any attack which a hostile force might be foolish enough to attempt. Such an attack would, in my opinion, stand little chance of success. It has been a great pleasure for me to meet my old comrade-in-arms of the last war, Generalissimo Chiang Kai-shek. His indomitable determination to resist Communist domination arouses my sincere admiration. His determination parallels the common interests and purpose of Americans, that all people in the Pacific area shall be free —not slaves."

But despite his clear statement that it was a military and not a political trip, the cry immediately went up that MacArthur and Chiang Kai-shek had been plotting some kind of international deviltry at their meeting. It was not surprising that the Communist press and their fellow travelers erupted in screams of outrage over MacArthur's eulogy of the Generalissimo's resistance to Communism. For a few days there was a frenzy of irresponsible diatribe, but soon the Communist switch was pulled. As usual, the pack took off in some other direction.

What was surprising, however, was to hear echoes of this cry from the U.S. State Department. Secretary Acheson cabled William Sebald, the State Department officer on MacArthur's staff, urgently requesting a report on the details of MacArthur's talks at Formosa—"in the light," as he put it, "of their vital relationship to overall policy formulation," whatever that meant.

So nonpolitical had MacArthur's trip been that he had not even taken Sebald along with him. And so nonpolitical had the conferences on Formosa been that all Sebald could do was virtually repeat what MacArthur had already said in his statement.

"General MacArthur has advised me," Sebald wired Acheson, "that as theater commander his discussions with the Gimo and Chinese military authorities were entirely limited to arrangements for effective military coordination between the Chinese and American Forces respectively under Chinese National Government and his command, as envisaged by the President's statement and aide memoire, and that he was most meticulous in confining his discussions with Chinese Government officials to military problems of a technical nature. In reference to his main discussion General MacArthur has pointed out that he invited the Navy, Air and Army attaches of the Embassy [on Formosa] to be present and that Strong undoubtedly would be in position to report a consensus of their views.

"General MacArthur told me," Sebald continued, "as ancillary to his visit, in confidence his definite impression of deep resentment in Chinese official circles resulting from what was taken to be the attitude on the part of State Department representatives in Taipei of general hostility. Without entering into any discussion of the relative merits or demerits of issues which may be involved, General believes there has been very definite failure to establish a relationship based upon that degree of confidence and cordiality which is so essential to diplomatic success. General is especially concerned over adverse affect the continuance of such a situation might have upon his efforts to maximize the military coordination indispensable to the success of joint operation in defense of Taiwan."

Thus MacArthur tried as delicately as possible to report to Washington what was actually a nasty situation on Formosa, with U.S. representatives openly reflecting the hostility of the State Department to the Nationalist government. Even then MacArthur passed this information along only because of the effect he feared it would have on military co-operation between the United States and Nationalist forces in defense of Formosa.

Meanwhile MacArthur was following up his own survey of Formosa by sending a group from his headquarters to study and report in detail on the island's requirements for adequate defense. This group of experts went to Formosa on August 4, studied the island's military installations and personnel and equipment thoroughly, and returned to write a comprehensive report and make recommendations which formed the basis for subsequent military aid to the Chinese government.

By August 10 some of the misrepresentations had become so gross and obviously malicious that they were causing world-wide reaction. The situation seemed to be rapidly getting out of hand, and yet no attempt was being made in Washington even to answer some of the outright lies which were greatly disturbing many of the other U.N. governments.

In fact, some of the misrepresentations appeared to have been encouraged by various government officials in Washington. At least one reporter was flatly told, for example, that MacArthur had not even notified the President before he went to Formosa. As I have already pointed out, there was a considerable exchange of messages on the subject. Whether the Joint Chiefs of Staff, with whom it was MacArthur's responsibility to communicate, passed this important information to the White House or not, MacArthur could hardly know. But to leave Tokyo for whatever destination at so important a time without informing Washington would be unthinkable to MacArthur. It is difficult to conceive of the Joint Chiefs of Staff neglecting to tell the President that MacArthur had notified them of his intention to visit the island.

Formosa—Friendly Bastion or Enemy Base

One can only guess at where in Washington the slip-up occurred, but a logical conjecture might be that there was no slip-up at all—that the Joint Chiefs believed that the State Department would inform Truman and that the responsible State Department official purposely kept it from the President in order further to embarrass MacArthur. Aside from gross negligence on the part of both Joint Chiefs of Staff and the State Department, the only alternative answer to the mystery is the improbable one that the President himself, or a White House official close to him, was intentionally lying in accusing MacArthur of not informing Washington ahead of time.

In any case, MacArthur was forced himself to answer the false charges concerning his visit before grave harm was done to the U.N. military alliance which he headed. So on August 10 he issued this public statement:

"There have been so many misstatements made with reference to my recent trip to Formosa that in the public interest at this critical moment I feel constrained to correct them.

"1. This trip was formally arranged and coordinated beforehand with all branches of the American and Chinese governments.

"2. It was limited entirely to military matters, as I stated in my public release after the visit, and dealt solely with the problems of preventing military violence to Formosa, as directed by the President—the implementation of which directive is my responsibility. It had no connection with political affairs and, therefore, no suggestion was ever made from any source that a political representative accompany me.

"3. The subject of the future of the Chinese Government, of developments on the Chinese mainland, or anything else outside the scope of my own military responsibility was not discussed or even mentioned.

"4. Full reports on the results of the visit were promptly made to Washington."

Then MacArthur let fly with the full force of his resentment. "This visit," he said, "has been maliciously misrepresented to the public by those who invariably in the past have propagandized a policy of defeatism and appeasement in the Pacific. I hope the American people will not be misled by sly insinuations, brash speculations and bold misstatements invariably attributed to anonymous sources, so insidiously fed them both nationally and internationally by persons 10,000 miles away from the actual events, if they are not indeed designed, to promote disunity and destroy faith and confidence in American purposes and institutions and American representatives at this time of great world peril."

MacArthur's statement served its purpose of putting a stop to most of the outright lying on the subject of his Formosa visit. But an indication that the campaign of falsehoods had had its effect upon the President was contained in a most curious message which MacArthur meanwhile received. On August 5 the Secretary of Defense sent a directive which bore the notation that it had been approved by the President and the Secretary of State. It referred to the recommendations of the Joint Chiefs of Staff on July 29 that the Nationalists be permitted defensive action against Communist concentrations directed at Formosa, and to the fact that Mac-Arthur had concurred with this recommendation.

"You are to repel any attack upon Formosa and the Pescadores . . . ," the message continued. "Likewise you are to stop attacks from Formosa upon the mainland. No one other than the President as the Commander-in-Chief has the authority to order or authorize preventative action against concentrations on the mainland . . . the most vital national interest requires that no action of ours precipitates general war or gives excuse to others to do so."

MacArthur might have been insulted had he not been so surprised. The Joint Chiefs of Staff had made a recommendation and had asked him for his views. He had concurred with their recommendation. Neither he nor anyone else had even implied that a recommendation be put into action without the President's official sanction. Could this mean that MacArthur must be wary hereafter of giving an honest opinion, even on military matters, when it was requested by his superiors in Washington? If he recommended any course of action other than that originally conceived and approved in Washington, would he then be constantly accused of threatening to put his recommendations into actual practice?

His reply to this veiled hint was couched in terms that he hoped would calm whatever irritation had occasioned it. "The June 27th decision of the President to protect the Communist mainland is fully understood here," he wired, "and this headquarters is operating meticulously in accordance therewith . . . I understand thoroughly the limitations upon my authority as theater commander and you need have no anxiety that I will in any way exceed them. I hope that neither the President nor you has been misled by false or speculative reports, official or non-official, from whatever source."

As he sent this reply off to the Secretary of Defense, he pondered a painful question: Was he, after a lifetime of loyal service in the U.S. Army, actually being accused in Washington of insubordination? He could not believe it. But he also could not help wondering—what next? He was not to be kept long in suspense.

On August 17 he received an invitation from the commander-in-chief of the Veterans of Foreign Wars to send a message to be read at their forthcoming annual encampment. MacArthur had sent messages to many other veterans' organizations in the past, and he was glad to oblige in this instance. Besides, he saw here an excellent opportunity to attempt to reply to whoever was whispering malicious charges against him in Truman's ear. Since there are 1,350,000 members of the VFW and since a message from him to their national encampment would undoubtedly receive wide public circulation, MacArthur decided that this was an excellent opportunity to place himself on record as being squarely behind the President. Truman had explained his Formosa decision by saying: "The occupation of Formosa by Communist forces would be a direct threat to the security of the Pacific area and to the United States forces performing their lawful and necessary functions in that area."

MacArthur had approved of this statement wholeheartedly, and composed a message that not only supported it, but also explained the strategic reasoning behind it. I include it entirely, both because there has been so much discussion of the message and because only the full text will answer the silly charge that MacArthur was not following the letter of a policy first enunciated by the President himself.

"In view of misconceptions currently being voiced concerning the relationship of Formosa to our strategic potential in the Pacific," he wrote, "I believe it in the public interest to avail myself of this opportunity to state my views thereon to you, all of whom having fought overseas understand broad strategic concepts. To begin with, any appraisal of that strategic potential requires an appreciation of the changes wrought in the course of the past war. Prior thereto the western strategic frontier of the U.S. lay on the littoral line of the Americas with an exposed island salient extending out through Hawaii, Midway, Guam to the Philippines. That salient was not an outpost of strength but an avenue of weakness along which the enemy could and did attack us. The Pacific was a potential area of advance for any predatory force intent upon striking at the bordering land areas.

"All of this was changed by our Pacific victory. Our strategic frontier then shifted to embrace the entire Pacific Ocean, which has become a vast moat to protect us as long as we hold it. Indeed, it acts as a protective shield for all of the Americas and all free lands of the Pacific Ocean area.

377

We control it to the shores of Asia by a chain of islands extending in an arc from the Aleutians to the Marianas held for us and our free allies. From this island chain we can dominate by air power every Asiatic port from Vladivostok to Singapore and prevent any hostile movement into the Pacific. Any predatory attack from Asia must be an amphibious effort. No amphibious force can be successful without control of the sea lanes and the air over these lanes in its avenue of advance. With naval and air supremacy and modest ground elements to defend bases, any major attack from continental Asia toward us or our friends of the Pacific would be doomed to failure. Under such conditions the Pacific no longer represents menacing avenues of approach for a protective invader—it assumes instead the friendly aspect of a peaceful lake. Our line of defense is a natural one and can be maintained with a minimum of military effort and expense. It envisions no attack against anyone nor does it provide the bastions essential for offensive operations, but properly maintained would be an invincible defense against aggression. If we hold this line we may have peace—lose it and war is inevitable.

"The geographic location of Formosa is such that in the hands of a power unfriendly to the United States it constitutes an enemy salient in the very center of this defensive perimeter, 100 to 150 miles closer to the adjacent friendly segments—Okinawa and the Philippines—than any point in continental Asia. At the present time there is on Formosa a concentration of operational air and naval bases which is potentially greater than any similar concentration on the Asiatic mainland between the Yellow Sea and the Straits of Malacca. Additional bases can be developed in a relatively short time by an aggressive exploitation of all of World War II Japanese facilities. Any enemy force utilizing these installations currently available could increase by 100 percent the air effort which could be directed against Okinawa as compared to operations based on the mainland and at the same time could direct damaging air attacks with fighter type aircraft against friendly installations in the Philippines which are currently beyond the range of fighters based on the mainland. Our air supremacy at once would become doubtful.

"As a result of this geographic location and base potential, utilization of Formosa by a military power hostile to the United States may either counter-balance or over-shadow the strategic importance of the central and southern flank of the United States' front line position. Formosa in the hands of such a hostile power could be compared to an unsinkable aircraft carrier and submarine tender ideally located to accomplish offensive strategy and at the same time check-mate defensive or counter of-

378

fensive operations by friendly forces based on Okinawa or the Philippines. This unsinkable carrier-tender has the capacity to operate from 10 to 20 air groups of types ranging from jet fighters to B-29 type bombers, as well as to provide forward operating facilities for short range submarines. In acquiring this forward submarine base, the efficiency of the short range submarine would be so enormously increased by the additional radius of activity as to threaten completely sea traffic from the south and intersect all sea lands in the western Pacific. Submarine blockade by the enemy with all its destructive ramifications would thereby become a virtual certainty.

"Should Formosa fall and these bases thereafter come into the hands of a potential enemy of the United States, the latter will have acquired an additional 'fleet' which will have been obtained and can be maintained at an incomparably lower cost than could its equivalent in aircraft carriers and submarine tenders. Current estimates of air and submarine resources in the Far East indicate the capability of such a potential enemy to extend his forces southward and still maintain an imposing degree of military strength for employment elsewhere in the Pacific area.

"Historically, Formosa has been used as a springboard for just such military aggression directed against areas to the south. The most notable and recent example was the utilization of it by the Japanese in World War II. At the outbreak of the Pacific War in 1941, it played an important part as a staging area and supporting base for the various Japanese invasion convoys. The supporting air force of Japan's army and navy were based on fields situated along northern Formosa. From 1942 to 1944 Formosa was a vital link in the transportation and communication chain which stretched from Japan through Okinawa and the Philippines to southeast Asia. As the United States carrier forces advanced into the western Pacific the bases on Formosa assumed an increasingly greater role in the Japanese defense scheme. Should Formosa fall into the hands of a hostile power, history would repeat itself. Its military potential would again be fully exploited as the means to breach and neutralize our western Pacific defense system and mount a war of conquest against the free nations of the western Pacific.

"Nothing could be more fallacious than the threadbare argument by those who advocate appeasement and defeatism in the Pacific that if we defend Formosa we alienate continental Asia. Those who speak thus do not understand the Orient. They do not grasp that it is in the pattern of Oriental psychology to respect and follow aggressive, resolute and dynamic leadership—to quickly turn from leadership characterized by ti-

379

midity or vacillation, and they underestimate the Oriental mentality. Nothing in the last five years has so inspired the Far East as the American determination to preserve the bulwarks of our Pacific Ocean's strategic position from further encroachment, for few of its people fail accurately to appraise the safeguard such determination brings to their free institutions. To pursue any other course would be to turn over the fruits of our Pacific victory to a potential enemy. It would shift any future battle area 5,000 miles eastward to the coasts of the American continent, our own home coasts. It would completely expose our friends in the Philippines, our friends in Australia and New Zealand, our friends in Indonesia, our friends in Japan and other areas to the lustful thrusts of those who stand for slavery as against liberty, for atheism as against God.

"The decision of President Truman on June 27th lighted into a flame a lamp of hope throughout Asia that was burning dimly toward extinction. It marked for the Far East the focal and turning point in this area's struggle for freedom. It swept aside in one great monumental stroke all of the hypocrisy and the sophistry which has confused and deluded so many people distant from the actual scene."

After reading this statement over, MacArthur sent it off to the VFW with a satisfied feeling that he had thus firmly expressed himself in full support of the President's policy toward Formosa. He sent it through the Department of the Army ten days before the date set for the veterans' encampment. He heard nothing for a week. Then, suddenly, there arrived a message from the Secretary of Defense.

The wire was unusually formal and brusque, directing in the name of "President of the United States" that he withdraw his message to the VFW. The reason given was that "various features with respect to Formosa are in conflict with the policy of the United States." MacArthur was utterly astonished. He sent for a copy of the message and re-examined it, but still could find no feature that was not in complete support of the President. All he could do in this impossible situation was send the reply which he did.

"My message," he said, "was most carefully prepared to fully support the President's policy decision. . . . My remarks were calculated only to support his declaration and I am unable to see wherein they might be interpreted otherwise. The views were purely my personal ones and the subject had previously been freely discussed in all circles, governmental and private, both at home and abroad."

An equally baffling point was that after waiting more than a week the

Washington officials had now got themselves into a position where to censor the MacArthur statement would look far worse than doing nothing, since in that time the text of the message had already gone to press in the VFW magazine and other organs of the press. Such a move would only lend further emphasis to the message. MacArthur attempted to point this out in his answer to the Secretary of Defense. "The message has undoubtedly been incorporated in the printed agenda for the Encampment," he said, "and advance press releases thereof have already reached worldwide centers of circulation. Under these circumstances I am sure that it would be mechanically impossible to suppress the same at this late date, and I believe to attempt it under such conditions would be a grave mistake. Please, therefore, present my most earnest request to the President for reconsideration of the order given me in your message, as I believe that repercussions resulting from compliance therewith would be destructive and most harmful to the national interest."

In order to save time, he asked in the same message to the Secretary that if the decision remained unchanged, the following be sent to the commander-in-chief of the Veterans of Foreign Wars in his name: "I regret to inform you that I have been directed to withdraw my message to the National Encampment of Veterans of Foreign Wars." He soon received from Washington the cryptic note: "Your message to Clyde A. Lewis forwarded verbatim as requested."

MacArthur was left with only the mystery. Who had managed to construe his statement as meaning exactly the opposite of what it said? And how could this person have so easily deceived the President?

But in retrospect he has always felt, and the conclusion certainly seems logical, that his statement innocently ran afoul of plans being hatched in the State Department to succumb to British pressure and desert the Nationalist government on Formosa. Under ordinary circumstances MacArthur's statement would cause no international difficulties because it echoed and explained an already announced U.S. policy. But in the event that the State Department was conspiring with the British to hand over Formosa to the Communists, it is easy to see how the statement to the VFW would cause consternation.

Whether or not this was the case we shall no doubt never know, if only for the reason that the participants would naturally hesitate to admit it. On August 28, the day of the peremptory order to MacArthur to withdraw his message, the President formally endorsed a message in which Warren Austin, U.S. Ambassador to the United Nations, had explained, point by point, the position of the United States government on Formosa. It was somewhat apologetic in tone, and it contained the following highly suggestive clause:

"4. The action of the United States was expressly stated to be without prejudice to the future political settlement of the status of the island. The actual status of the island is that it is territory taken from Japan by the victory of the Allied Forces in the Pacific. Like other such territories, its legal status cannot be fixed until there is international action to determine its future. The Chinese Government was asked by the Allies to take the surrender of the Japanese forces on the island. That is the reason the Chinese are there now."

What is significant about this statement is simply that it is untrue. At Cairo on December 1, 1943, an agreement was entered into between the United States, China, and the United Kingdom, represented respectively by President Roosevelt, Generalissimo Chiang and Prime Minister Churchill. The agreement, which they all signed, reads in part as follows: "It is their purpose that Japan shall be stripped of all the islands in the Pacific which she has seized or occupied since the beginning of the first World War in 1914, and that the territories Japan has stolen from the Chinese, such as Manchuria, Formosa, and the Pescadores, shall be restored to the Republic of China."

That, and only that, was the reason why Formosa was given to China at the end of World War II. There was no further need to settle the question of who owned Formosa; as far as we were concerned, the Republic of China owned Formosa by the terms of the agreement at Cairo. The action of Secretary Acheson and his State Department advisers could only constitute a repudiation of an agreement by the crudest kind of dissembling. To suppose otherwise would be to assume that neither Acheson nor his advisers could remember one of the most important decisions made at the Cairo conference.

Changing the President's original directive defending Formosa was certainly not based upon any military reasoning. MacArthur's opinion of the strategic importance of Formosa was shared by the Joint Chiefs of Staff. On September 1 they officially recommended that the island and its disposition be kept out of any political horse-trading that the State Department might be contemplating at a forthcoming meeting of the foreign ministers. "The strategic consequences of a Communist-dominated Formosa," the Joint Chiefs advised, "would be so seriously detrimental to United States security that in the opinion of the Joint Chiefs of Staff, the United States should not permit the disposition of Formosa to be recommended in the first instance or decided by any commission or agency of the United Nations in which the United States has no voice."

But the pressure to betray our Nationalist Allies of World War II has never let up; it has, in fact, increased over the years. It started right after the war's end, when pseudo "liberals" argued that the Chinese Communists were really only "agrarian reformers"—a claim that has become one of modern history's bitterest jests. It was of course given its greatest impetus when General Marshall made the tragic mistake of using American prestige as a lever for forcing a "coalition government" on Chiang Kai-shek. And it manifested itself most vocally when MacArthur tried to implement the President's directive to defend Formosa by strengthening the alliance between Nationalist and U.S. military forces.

The arguments of this cynical school of thought have taken many forms. At first the claim was that Chiang's government was corrupt. Somehow the reasoning ran that rule by the Kuomintang was even worse than a Communist police state, and that therefore any change would be for the better. Who these people were, especially in the U.S. State Department, who would ally with the same Chiang against the Japanese but not against the Communists, was never clear. This wishful foolishness has been aided and abetted mostly by the British, especially by leaders of England's Labour Party, who have even toured Red China and written eulogizing books and articles about the new slave state.

In any event it has always been MacArthur's fervent hope that no such casuistry will long beguile American political leaders. As this is written, the United States is paying the price of the specious reasoning that compromise and timidity will fool the Asian Communists. Had the President—as well as his political advisers playing strategists and his military advisers playing politics—listened to the clear and simple warning of MacArthur five years ago, we would not today be frantically trying to stem the rush of Communism, directed against Indochina, Indonesia, Burma, and especially Formosa, that key island of our own defense system.

Chapter VII   The Enigma of Wake Island

✍ The Formosan problem, and particularly the suppression of his statement on it, gave MacArthur his first clear illustration of the devious workings of the Washington-London team. But he was about to get an even clearer illustration—at the famous Wake Island conference.

On October 12, George Marshall, who had succeeded Louis Johnson as Secretary of Defense, suddenly wired Tokyo that Truman would like to have an important conference with MacArthur. The President would like to confer at Honolulu on the following 15th, Marshall wired; but he added that "if the situation in Korea is such that you feel you should not absent yourself for the time involved in such a long trip, I am sure the President would be glad to go on and meet you at Wake Island." MacArthur unhesitatingly replied: "I would be delighted to meet the President on the morning of the 15th at Wake Island."

Wherever the meeting was to be held, MacArthur wondered at the purpose of it. Was the United States government planning some momentous diplomatic or military move in connection with the Korean war, a move so important that the President felt that he had to make so long and arduous a journey? Even if so, and if MacArthur's views on the subject were needed, why could not some one of the many Washington officials come out to talk with him about it? Certainly the President was not going to such drastic lengths simply to discuss routine details in connection with either Japan or Korea; he already had MacArthur's views in fullest detail on all matters affecting the Supreme Commander's responsibility, and could secure any further clarification he wished merely by asking for it. It must then be some new move of great importance, perhaps an attempt to capitalize upon the recent success of the Inchon landings by corollary diplomatic action to exploit that military victory and thus restore the peace.

384

The Enigma of Wake Island

Inchon—that gave MacArthur pause for a moment. His mind went back six years to a similar conference at Honolulu with President Roosevelt. That had been at a time when MacArthur had been winning a brilliant string of victories in New Guinea. The view had been expressed in many quarters that President Roosevelt had sought, by holding that meeting at that time, to capitalize upon the victories politically. But since the major result of the Honolulu conference had been that Roosevelt had followed MacArthur's advice and had rejected that of the Joint Chiefs of Staff to by-pass the Philippines, MacArthur has always refused to support this charge. His chief reaction to the entire conference was one of gratitude for Roosevelt's approval of the strategy that events later established to be the correct one.

But could this new Presidential call have ulterior political motives? Could this proposal for a dramatic mid-ocean meeting be as inexorably linked to the Congressional elections two weeks hence as the Inchon landings had been to the tides? It is well known that military victory has always lent powerful support to those seeking to secure or retain political power. Was it possible that the reason for a conference at Wake Island was to establish in the eyes of the voters a closer relationship between the administration and the victory just won? Despite the political logic of this assumption, MacArthur refused to accept it. He would countenance no slightest implication of criticism of the President.

In the many messages that followed concerning details of the meeting, none gave a hint as to the reason for it all. One of the details, however, provided a faint clue. It was mentioned that a planeload of White House correspondents would accompany the President's plane to Wake. A number of American correspondents in Tokyo had requested permission to accompany MacArthur. In view of the number of Washington correspondents attending, MacArthur assumed that the Tokyo representatives should be permitted to attend too, especially as his plane could accommodate a large representation without resort to other facilities. He passed their requests along to the Pentagon, and was surprised when the request was promptly and somewhat curtly disapproved.

We took off from Haneda in the *SCAP* on the afternoon of the 14th. It is an eight-hour flight from Tokyo to Wake, and during almost all of that time MacArthur paced restlessly up and down the aisle of the plane. He talked little, but it was easy to see that his mind was alternately on what lay in store for him at Wake Island and on the war he temporarily had to leave behind. MacArthur, more than most commanders, believes in keeping in the closest personal touch with events on the battlefield—as

385

witness his countless and hazardous trips to the front. So, more than to most commanders, the prospect of traveling two thousand miles from Korea for a conference that could be held by telecom or even telephone, was most distasteful to him. But the realization that the President was also taking time from his own important duties and indeed traveling an even greater distance made MacArthur feel that something really momentous was to be discussed at Wake Island the next day.

As the plane circled over the island, I recall thinking both of the battle the Marines had fought under General James Devereaux before being overwhelmed by the Japanese at the outbreak of World War II, and of MacArthur's reference in the message Truman had suppressed: ". . . an avenue of weakness along which the enemy could and did attack." A single runway traversed the length of the island. When the SCAP came to rest at the end of it, we were promptly shown to a Quonset hut that the Navy administrators of the island had thoughtfully made available for us.

Here MacArthur experienced some difficulty in adjusting himself to the time difference between Tokyo and Wake. The Wake Island time was three hours later than the Tokyo time by which he had arisen and scheduled his day. This meant that if he retired at midnight Wake time, it was only nine o'clock by his watch, which was still synchronized to Tokyo time. But as I watched him sitting there, puffing his pipe and trying to fathom the uncertainties of the day ahead, I realized that if he continued to go by his watch and waited up until his usual retiring time of midnight or one a.m., it would be three or four o'clock in the morning by Wake Island time—only two or three hours before the President's scheduled arrival at six. Also, tomorrow looked to me like a day for which MacArthur would need all the rest he could get.

I honestly believe that he would have stayed up until midnight or later by his watch, thereby getting no sleep at all before having to shave and wash up before meeting the President, had I not finally obtained what was from MacArthur a real concession. He turned in at eleven o'clock by his watch—which was two a.m. Wake time. Yet he rose without difficulty and seemed completely rested when I woke him an hour and a half later, to allow him sufficient time for bathing, shaving, dressing, and breakfasting before the President's scheduled arrival at six.

He looked as chipper as if he had slept twelve hours when he arrived at the end of the runway. He had to wait half an hour, however, for the President's delayed arrival. By this time a plane full of Presidential advisers and two others carrying thirty-five reporters and photographers had already alighted. Now they swarmed all over the field as the *Independ-*

ence came to a halt just beyond the *SCAP*. When the President stepped down, MacArthur held out his hand. Truman took it and grinned as he said: "I've been a long time meeting you, General."

MacArthur replied: "I hope it won't be so long next time." Little did he realize there was to be no next time.

After cordially shaking hands for the photographers, they climbed into a battered 1948 Chevrolet sedan, the best wheeled transportation available. Then, while the rest of us went directly to the Administration building, where the conference was to be held, the President and the general drove off to a Quonset hut which had been reserved for Truman, to wait there until the conference room had been prepared.

For half an hour they engaged in a private conversation behind closed doors, with no one else present. The complete details of this intimate conversation are their own secret, and when he was asked about them later during the Senate hearings in 1951, MacArthur said: "I would not feel at liberty to reveal what was discussed. . . ." But so much political capital has been made out of the Wake Island conference that I feel constrained to reveal at least these facts, as told me by MacArthur shortly thereafter.

Their private talk was a "relatively unimportant conversation." Early in it MacArthur expressed his regret that any misunderstanding had arisen over his message to the VFW on the strategic importance of Formosa. The President at once brushed the subject aside. "Oh!" he said, "think nothing more about that." So nothing more was said about Formosa, and most of the rest of the conversation was devoted to, of all things at this time, the fiscal and economic problems of the Philippines.

By seven thirty a.m. Truman and MacArthur had reached the Administration building, and at precisely seven thirty-six the conference got under way. The President sat at the head of the large table and the rest of the conferees sat around it. I had a "ringside seat," slightly to the right rear of the President and left of MacArthur, and was thus excellently located to observe the proceedings that followed.

From the start the disparity between the two staffs of "advisers" was striking; I was told later that it annoyed the President greatly. Besides myself, whom MacArthur brought along more as a companion than as an adviser, only MacArthur's aide-de-camp, Colonel Laurence E. Bunker, and his pilot, Lieutenant Colonel Story, were present. Truman, on the other hand, had brought the following coterie of advisers along with him: Admiral Arthur Radford, Commander of the Pacific Fleet; Army Secretary Frank Pace; Press Secretary Charles Ross; U.N. Ambassador Philip

PART III: KOREA

Jessup; Joint Chiefs Chairman Omar Bradley; State Department Far Eastern Chief Dean Rusk; and Special Adviser Averell Harriman. In the conference room also were numerous other Truman aides and aides' aides, even including his personal military aide, Major General Harry Vaughan. As the conference opened, Press Secretary Ross happened to notice that Colonel Bunker, MacArthur's aide-de-camp, was taking notes, whereupon he turned to MacArthur and told him that no record was to be made of the talks.

The President unfolded in front of him a sheet of paper which I should judge contained about a dozen questions. He opened the conference by saying that he had had a pleasant session with General MacArthur and that now we were all going to talk together. Wake Island's famous heat was beginning to make itself felt even this early, and the President removed his coat. MacArthur pulled out a briar pipe, asking: "Do you mind if I smoke, Mr. President?" Truman replied: "No. I suppose I've had more smoke blown in my face than any other man alive."

The first question concerned the rehabilitation of Korea, and the series that followed related to such matters as the Korean war, Japan, the Philippines, Indochina. After each question MacArthur gave his immediate and complete answer. When he had finished, the President quietly nodded his head and observed: "Well, that's just about the way I see it— anyone else want to comment upon that topic?" One, and only one near the bottom of the list, of these Presidential questions concerned the possibility of Red Chinese intervention in the Korean war. I shall come to that subject shortly.

As soon as the President had completed the agenda before him, he looked up and said: "I have no further questions to ask. Suppose we now adjourn until after luncheon, pending which representatives of both sides can meet to draw up a joint communiqué covering the meeting here." At this point MacArthur interjected: "If it is just the same to you, Mr. President, I would much prefer to finish up now and leave before lunch. There are many pressing matters awaiting my return to Tokyo." The President agreed. No further questions were asked, and the meeting adjourned, exactly one hour and thirty-six minutes from the time it had started.

Press Secretary Ross, Ambassador Jessup, and Charles Murphy, the President's legal aide, immediately went into a small adjacent office to prepare the communiqué. No one from MacArthur's staff was invited to assist in this little operation, and we waited in the conference room while the report was prepared and written. Periodically MacArthur pulled his watch from his pocket and consulted it, and I could see without his having

388

to say so that his mind was already back in Tokyo dealing with the many vital problems of the Korean war.

After a few minutes Truman and MacArthur went back to the Presidential Quonset hut and engaged in what might be called small talk. Far Eastern problems were not further alluded to. Instead the conversation drifted around to American politics. MacArthur asked the President whether he intended to run for re-election in 1952. The President, long accustomed to dodging this question in press conferences, immediately countered by asking MacArthur if he himself had any political ambitions. MacArthur had no need to duck the question. He promptly replied: "None whatsoever. If you have any general running against you, his name will be Eisenhower, not MacArthur."

The President chuckled. He expressed admiration for Eisenhower as a military man and friendship for him personally. "But," Truman said, "he doesn't know the first thing about politics." He paused a moment, and added: "Why, if Eisenhower should become President, his administration would make Grant's look like a model of perfection." The President seemed ready to go on at length in this vein, but MacArthur quickly swerved the conversation into other channels. Finally the draft of the communiqué was brought in.

It was an innocuous enough document, if somewhat misleading in the scope and importance it lent to the conference. MacArthur read it quickly, said he had no objection, and at the President's suggestion initialed it.

There remained only the courtesy of seeing the President off before we ourselves could be on our way. At the airstrip Truman surprised MacArthur by stepping up to the microphones that had been set up by the newsreel photographers and reading to the entire assemblage on Wake Island that early morning a citation awarding MacArthur an oakleaf cluster to the Distinguished Service Medal (the fifth time MacArthur had received the award).

"The President of the United States of America, authorized by Act of Congress, July 9, 1918, has awarded the Distinguished Service Medal (Fourth Oak Leaf Cluster) to

GENERAL OF THE ARMY DOUGLAS MACARTHUR

for distinguished service to the peoples of the United States and the Republic of Korea, and to the peoples of all free nations.

"Having been designated as the first field commander of United Nations armed forces, and directed, in the common interest, to repel an armed attack upon the Republic of Korea and to restore international peace and security in the area, he has given these forces conspicuously brilliant and courageous leadership and discerning judgment of the highest order. Having been compelled to commit his troops to combat under extremely adverse conditions and against heavy odds in order to obtain the time so imperatively needed for the build-up of his forces for the counter-offensive, he has so inspired his command by his vision, his judgment, his indomitable will and his unshakeable faith, that it has set a shining example of gallantry and tenacity in defense and of audacity in attack matched by but few operations in military history. His conduct has been in accord with the highest traditions of the military service of the United States, and is deserving of the enduring gratitude of the freedom-loving peoples of the world."

No one who witnessed this impressive scene and heard so laudatory an expression by a President of the United States to his field commander could have suspected that the same President, speaking before an audience in Chicago four years later, would answer the question: "Have you repented the firing of General MacArthur during your term of office?" with the statement: "The only thing I repent is that I didn't do it two years sooner."

As he was about to board the *Independence*, the President called me over to where he and MacArthur stood chatting. "General Whitney," he said, "you should have been a major general long ago. As soon as I get back to Washington I am going to see what I can do about having you made one." This seemed to please MacArthur immensely, and he acknowledged the President's remark by paying a very generous tribute to my service. True to his word, the President did upon his return to Washington see to it that my second star was soon forthcoming.

The *Independence* was barely in the air when MacArthur strode over to the *SCAP* and climbed aboard. We were airborne in five minutes. And it was not until then that I wondered if perhaps the fourth oakleaf cluster for the Distinguished Service Medal could be the real reason for President Truman's dramatic mid-Pacific conference. Certainly nothing else was accomplished that could not more conveniently have been done over the telecom. Not a question was asked of MacArthur on which Washington did not already have his full views. No new and momentous strategy of war or international politics was proposed or suggested at Wake Island.

But what Truman personally—and the Democratic Party—gained by that trip in terms of plain political advantage was inestimable. By this one stroke the President was able to establish a connection between his administration and the military strategy against which most of his military advisers had argued but which had won the great victory at Inchon.

He had not, however, managed to drape the mantle of MacArthur about his shoulders without misleading the American public. I have mentioned, for example, the brief exchange between MacArthur and Truman on the subject of Formosa. Imagine MacArthur's surprise when the President, first at the general conference and later to the press, made this statement: "General MacArthur and I have talked fully about Formosa. There is no need to cover that subject again. The general and I are in complete agreement."

MacArthur let this pass without challenge at the time, believing it to be an unfortunate method of expression. But when it was picked up and widely propagandized as signifying that he had altered his position on Formosa, and when no statement to correct this false impression was forthcoming from the President, MacArthur was forced on the 19th to deny publicly that he had changed his views concerning the strategic importance of Formosa in any way. He also stated categorically that "no policy discussion whatsoever was held at Wake Island with reference to Formosa." But for the time being, the President enjoyed the great political advantage of seeming to have persuaded MacArthur to reverse himself.

Evidently the administration's strategy at Wake Island was to attempt to make MacArthur little more than a political pawn from the start. I was as puzzled as he when Press Secretary Ross showed such anxiety at the sight of Colonel Bunker starting to take notes on the conference. In retrospect it seems to have been their plan at the time to maintain full control over every means of recording the conference. Neither of us realized until later that Bunker had very nearly upset this plan. We gave no thought to it, however, until months later when General Bradley sprang the surprise in an apparent effort to discredit MacArthur.

He produced sketchy "notes" of the conference which were alleged to have been surreptitiously taken. Without our knowledge, a secretary had evidently been placed behind a partially opened door to the conference room. This stenographer, lurking behind the door, could record only what she could hear through the small opening and what she could see by peeping through the keyhole, with the result that her account of the conference could at best be sadly inadequate. MacArthur did not even know of her presence, and when she made an appearance after the conference, he looked up in surprise and said: "Where did this lovely lady come from?" I am sure that had he known that she was there to record the proceedings, he would have been delighted to suggest that the young lady be seated at the conference table, where she could prepare an accurate record, without undue strain upon her eyes and ears.

Certainly the best example of how the administration used the Wake Island conference against MacArthur is shown by the President's charge that the General had given him assurance that the Chinese Communists would not enter the Korean war.

This is what the discussion on the subject amounted to: The question was low on the President's agenda. Truman asked: "What are the chances for Chinese or Soviet interference?"

MacArthur promptly replied that his answer would be purely speculative, but that his guess would be "very little." He then explained this viewpoint. Obviously he could only speak from a military standpoint, with its manifest limitations, on a question that revolved fundamentally around a political decision. But as a backdrop to his military speculation, MacArthur proceeded from the premise, as indeed all others present even better knew, that there was no evidence from Peiping even suggesting that Red Chinese intervention was under serious consideration. No such intimation had ever been communicated to him by the Defense Department, the State Department, or the Central Intelligence Agency, MacArthur's only sources of political intelligence on which alone such estimates could be made. Field intelligence in the limited area of battle could at best furnish no reliable clue, and actually it was badly handicapped in his area by the restrictions upon air reconnaissance ordered by Washington. Its scope was confined entirely to Korea itself—nothing beyond.

The assumption that Red China would not intervene was not questioned by the President himself, General Bradley, or any of those present from Washington, all of whom were there as conferees and each of whom would have been aware of political intelligence which even suggested the possibility that a decision to intervene in Korea was under serious consideration by the Chinese Communists. Their concurrence with MacArthur's guess, obviously to be drawn from their silence when the question was raised, was later to be supported by the Central Intelligence Agency, which formally reported on the day Walker launched the Eighth Army's drive to the Yalu, November 24, that "there is no evidence that the Chinese Communists plan major offensive operations in Korea."

To understand MacArthur's qualified guess that the Chinese Reds would not intervene in Korea, it is first necessary to understand certain military assumptions upon which he was naturally proceeding. It seemed to him at the time, as indeed it still does today, that if an enemy attacked our forces, we should retaliate. This would appear to be so simple an axiom that it did not even need to be stated. It would be difficult, if in fact possible, to mention a precedent in history in which a nation possessed of the strength to fight back instead openly proclaimed that it would not. Thus by no flight of the purest fancy could MacArthur imagine that if the U.N. forces were attacked by the Red Chinese, the political leaders would decide not to strike back. To him it followed as simply as night follows day that if the Chinese intervened in the Korean war, the U.N.—or certainly the United States, as in the first few hours of the North Korean attack—would respond with all of the military power and means available, as indeed his current directives strongly implied.

With our undisputed air and naval superiority we would at the very outset establish an effective blockade of the Chinese coast and launch destructive blows against Red China's Manchurian bases of supply. Such had been our immediate reaction to acts of war committed against us throughout history. Surely, for example, we were not pretending that the units of our Navy and Air Force were blockading and bombing the North Korean enemy only in South Korea, to the exclusion of North Korea. So self-evident a truth was it to MacArthur that it naturally never occurred to him to question President Truman and his advisers whether or not they actually intended to take such a course. To him it would be like asking if we intended to fight the enemy with guns or with bows and arrows.

Had someone suggested to MacArthur at that stage that we might suffer the Chinese Reds to strike us in full force and retaliate only by warding off the blow as it fell, without striking back on our own, he would not have believed any such preposterous notion. Furthermore—and this is what is important about MacArthur's assumption—he knew that the enemy's strategists realized as well as he did the might with which the U.N. forces could counterattack. The North Koreans and the Red Chinese were, after all, both Communist, and their aims were identical. Any prospective enemy military commander would regard as sheerest folly a peninsular campaign that so extended and exposed his bases and supply lines to destructive attack.

The Communist enemy, be he North Korean or Chinese, was at the time enjoying a sanctuary behind the Yalu for the simple reason that it was a war between North Korea and the United Nations. So far the U.N. political leaders had decreed that no U.N. planes would fly north of the Yalu into Manchuria. But the same planes *were* flying north of the 38th Parallel, and were bombing bases and supply lines all over North Korea. They were not bombing Manchuria for the same reason that they were not bombing China—because the U.N. forces were at that time not at war with China. If, however, the Chinese entered the Korean war in any force, it would be as logical to bomb their supply bases as it had been to bomb those in North Korea. All this was of course elementary; why it eluded the President and his military advisers MacArthur will never know.

But it could not have eluded the Chinese generals; of that MacArthur is sure. It naturally follows, then, that there can be only one circumstance under which the Chinese did finally decide to enter the Korean war: someone must have told them.

Someone must have told them what even MacArthur was not informed of before the Chinese intervened in Korea. Someone must have told them that even if the Red Chinese swarmed across the Yalu into North Korea in overwhelming hordes, even if they struck with no more warning than the Japanese had at Pearl Harbor, even if they slaughtered U.N. soldiers (nine out of ten of whom were American) on the battlefield and in the prisoner-of-war camps, the U.S. government would meekly submit to maintaining the same sanctuary in Manchuria, long after any possible reason for it existed.

Only with the knowledge that, by some quirk that verged on international poltroonery, the United States would continue to protect the enemy's bases and supply lines, would a Communist commander decide to throw the full weight of the Chinese armies into Korea. The Chinese commander-in-chief of the forces that entered North Korea is reported to have stated he had definite advance information that MacArthur's hands would be tied by this "sanctuary" doctrine. Otherwise, he is reported to have said, "I would not have dared risk almost certain destruction by crossing the Yalu in force. No competent commander," he added, "would have been such a fool."

MacArthur agrees and holds to the firm belief that had the Communist strategists not been given assurance that they could continue to enjoy the sanctuary of Manchuria, the Red Chinese armies would not have entered the Korean war. But ever since the conference there has been an ingeniously fostered notion that MacArthur flatly and unequivocally predicted to the President that under no circumstances would the Chinese Communists enter the Korean war. This is a prevarication.

It is of interest to note, though, that even if he had so predicted, he would have done little more than affirm the consensus at the conference. In fact, it was MacArthur alone who so much as raised a doubt on the subject. Not another whisper to the contrary was made by any of the corps of Presidential military advisers present at the conference.

394

The Enigma of Wake Island

So confirmed were they all that there would be no intervention that General Bradley asked MacArthur when he thought he could spare a division for Europe. MacArthur replied that the North Korean enemy might well be defeated in time for this to be done by Christmas. The plans for the political unity of Korea and its postwar government and rehabilitation were discussed as a matter of the immediate future. The President did not consider Chinese intervention worth more than a single question, and his advisers obviously did not consider it worth any extensive discussion. These advisers, with their political sources of information, were better able to give the President an authoritative estimate than was MacArthur, and everyone present knew it.

During the long pre-conference hours when MacArthur was trying to penetrate the enigma of the reason for the Wake Island conference, he rejected any idea that it rested on an insincere basis. He hoped that it would result in a better understanding by Washington of the problems in the field, and after he and the President had met and started to converse, he was sure that the conference would prove a constructive one. MacArthur liked Mr. Truman from the start, and was delighted with his engaging personality. He has never even to this day, so far as I know, criticized him personally.

And although Republican, probably as much by sentiment as anything else, MacArthur has always expressed admiration for the basic accomplishments of the Democratic Party, and appreciation of what he regards as its many great leaders over the years. Indeed, his criticisms have never been of parties but of concrete instances of mistakes and failures of whatever party.

It was only later, when Mr. Truman made his amazing charge that MacArthur had misled him on the possibility of Red Chinese intervention and when the scandalous method of preparing the "record" of the proceedings was exposed, that MacArthur realized that Wake Island was no longer an enigma—it was a sly political ambush.

CHAPTER VIII   The Wages of Appeasement

⚑ The controversy over Formosa and the political ambush at Wake Island made MacArthur realize that a curious—and sinister—change was taking place in Washington. The defiant rallying figure that had been Franklin Roosevelt in World War II was gone, and in his place was a group of figures of smaller stature who seemed more interested in temporizing than in fighting it through. Even the courageous decision of Harry Truman to meet aggression with force in Korea was apparently giving way to timidity and cynicism. Truman was evidently listening to a little group of advisers, under whose beguiling influence he found himself in the anomalous position of openly expressing his fears over calculated risks that he had willingly taken only a few months before.

This put the field commander in an especially difficult situation. Up to now MacArthur had been engaged in relatively uncomplicated warfare, more or less as warfare has been conducted down through the ages —the enemy attacks you, and you hit back with all your might; either his attack succeeds or your defense and counterattack defeat him. As in World War II, it had been a clear and simple test of MacArthur's military ability, albeit with an enormous handicap. And as in World War II, MacArthur had so far been able to demonstrate against the North Koreans the same strategical brilliance with which he had outsmarted and defeated the Japanese. I say "so far," because the Korean war, MacArthur could see now, was developing into something quite different from war as it had always been known.

Ever since the start of hostilities, Truman had referred to them as "a police action," while the members of the Joint Chiefs of Staff had decided upon their own term: "the Korean incident." MacArthur had thought this evasion a harmless euphemism. But he began to see that it marked a more serious kind of group self-deception which underestimated the entire nature of the conflict to which the government had committed U.S. fighting men.

In this display of deliberate wishful thinking the President and his clique of advisers were listening to the blandishments of some of the more timid politicians from other U.N. members. Extremely simplified, their argument seemed to be that more could be accomplished in Asia by appeasement than by moral resolution. Somehow President Truman had been made to believe that the leaders of Soviet Russia actually would temporize too, that they would upset the grand Communist design for eventual world domination and gamble the hard-won Communist gains in global atomic war over such a consideration as whether the U.N forces bombed a Manchurian power station or blew up a bridge across the Yalu. This argument assumed that the masterminds in the Kremlin were following a policy of expediency rather than long-range planning.

Some advocates of this specious logic went so far as to express fear that the Communists, who after all had committed aggression against us, might take it amiss if we pursued and destroyed North Korean forces instead of simply driving them back across the 38th Parallel, where they could reorganize for another attack. No sooner had U.N. soldiers begun probing northward from Seoul than a world-wide public debate erupted on the question of whether or not they should go beyond the 38th Parallel. From the standpoint of sound military doctrine, MacArthur saw that there was every reason why they should. The shattered remnants of the North Korean forces would have to be pursued into North Korea before they could be mopped up. Furthermore, there were known to be 100,000 North Korean replacements that had not even been committed. These troops certainly should not be permitted the time and the sanctuary to be trained, equipped, and thrown into battle.

The Joint Chiefs of Staff shared this view. In a directive dispatched to MacArthur on September 26, two days before the liberation of Seoul, they provided him with what they called "amplifying instructions as to further military action to be taken by you in Korea." These instructions stated unequivocally: "Your military objective is the destruction of the North Korean armed forces. In attaining this objective you are authorized to conduct military operations north of the 38th Parallel in Korea. . . . You will submit your plan for future operations north of the 38th Parallel to the Joint Chiefs of Staff for approval. . . ."

MacArthur replied on September 28: "Briefly my plan is: (a) Eighth Army as now constituted will attack across the 38th Parallel with its main effort on the Kaeson-Sariwon-Pyongyang axis with the objective of seizing

Pyongyang; (b) X Corps as now constituted will effect amphibious landing at Wonsan, making juncture with the Eighth Army; (c) 3rd Infantry Division will remain in Japan in GHQ reserve initially; (d) ROK Army forces only will conduct operation north of the line Chungjo-Yongwon-Hungnam; (e) Tentative date for the attack of the Eighth Army will not be earlier than 15 October and not later than 30 October. . . ." On September 30 the Joint Chiefs of Staff officially approved the plan. And six days later their approval was confirmed by a resolution of the United Nations General Assembly.

So far so good. There was none of the nonsense, later to be spread abroad, to the effect that our purpose was merely to drive the enemy out of South Korea and that MacArthur went beyond his authority when he ordered his troops across the 38th Parallel. His directive specifically ordered him to cross the parallel in pursuit of the North Korean forces, and not to be content only with driving them out of South Korea. He submitted his plan of operations, and it was officially approved; and this approval was backed by a resolution in the United Nations.

Yet just over the horizon lay the political cloud that was to befog military operations in Korea from then on. The first clear sign of it came on September 29, when Secretary of Defense Marshall sent MacArthur a worried query. ROK troops in the eastern sectors of the battle line had, without specific orders from the army commander, moved north across the 38th Parallel. There had been practically no resistance from the enemy, but there had evidently been some resistance among our Allies. The British in particular, it appeared, were urging that military operations cease at that geographical line. The situation had not been helped by some unguarded informal statements to correspondents at the front by a few staff officers of the Eighth Army who did not know of the directive from the Joint Chiefs.

MacArthur tried to put Marshall at ease by reiterating what he had already said a few days before. He added: "I am cautioning Walker against any involvement connected with the use of the term 38th Parallel, which line is not a factor in the military employment of our forces. The logistical supply of our units," MacArthur went on, "is the main problem which limits our immediate advance. In exploiting the defeat of the enemy forces, our own troops may cross the parallel at any time in exploratory probing or exploiting local tactical conditions. My overall strategic plan in North Korea is known to you. I regard all of Korea open for our military operations unless and until the enemy capitulates."

Meanwhile, as MacArthur pondered this evident international misunderstanding of our purpose in Korea, he decided that matters might be helped by some kind of clarification. So on September 30 he wired Marshall that in order to explain the U.N. position clearly, he intended, unless he received instructions to the contrary, to issue publicly on October 2 the following directive to the Eighth Army: "Under the provisions of the United Nations Security Council's Resolution of 27 June providing that we furnish such assistance to the Republic of Korea as may be necessary to repel the armed attack and to restore international peace and security in the area, the field of our military operations is limited only by the military exigencies and the international boundaries of Korea. The so-called 38th Parallel accordingly is not a factor in the military employment of our forces. To accomplish the enemy's complete defeat, your troops may cross this parallel at any time either in exploratory probing or exploiting local tactical conditions. If the enemy fails to accept my terms of surrender, our forces in due process of campaign will seek out and destroy his armed forces wherever they may be."

It was with some surprise that on the same day MacArthur received this reply from the Joint Chiefs of Staff: "We desire that you proceed with your operations without any further explanation or announcement and let action determine the matter. Our government desires to avoid having to make an issue of the 38th Parallel until we have accomplished our mission." While this message constituted a further evidence of the agreement of the Joint Chiefs of Staff with MacArthur's military plans, its implications made him raise his eyebrows. Was the administration trying to "put one over" on the U.N.? Judging by the fervor with which the British government had argued for stopping at the 38th Parallel, MacArthur could appreciate the President's natural inclination to present the other U.N. governments with a *fait accompli.*

The next indication of Washington–U.N. vacillation came after MacArthur had in effect completed his military mission. Despite the supply difficulties occasioned by the limitations on tonnage through the port of Inchon and the extensive repairs that had to be made to overcome the damage our bombers had done to the railroad from Pusan, Walker's troops pressed rapidly forward toward Pyongyang. Meanwhile Almond completed his operation of landing the X Corps at Wonsan, after running into trouble because of a heavy concentration of enemy mines guarding the approaches of that port. But by October 20 the co-ordinated maneuvers were proceeding satisfactorily, and MacArthur was able personally to witness what amounted to the *coup de grâce.*

As he watched from his plane, the 187th Regimental Combat Team of the 11th Airborne Division swung down out of the skies in their parachutes, twenty-five miles north of Pyongyang. Here was a typical MacArthur stroke, almost a duplicate of the one that "closed the gap" near Lae in New Guinea, or the jump in which the paratroopers of the same 11th Airborne Division enveloped Manila from the south, or the drop that recaptured Corregidor by placing troops in the very center of its fortifications and taking the island from the rear.

At Pyongyang this maneuver served to cut off the enemy's retreat, timed perfectly with the capture of the city by ground troops. Pyongyang was the enemy's capital, and its fall symbolized the complete defeat of the North Korean armies. Practically all organized resistance was brought to an end. For the first time in history, aggressive Communism had been decisively defeated on a battlefield, at a time, and against a force of its own choice. The prestige of the United Nations, and especially the United States, was at an all-time high in Asia.

And so, his military mission accomplished, MacArthur eagerly awaited the diplomatic action that would exploit it. But he waited in vain; nothing was done. He was astonished to see Allied diplomacy fail so completely to capitalize on this moment of triumph. The object of victory in battle is to pave the way for diplomacy to achieve peace. MacArthur expressed his surprise to General Walker. "The whole purpose of combat and war," he said, "is to create a situation in which victory on the battlefield can be promptly translated into a politically advantageous peace. Success in war involves political exploitation as well as military victory. The sacrifices leading to a military victory would be pointless if not translated promptly into the political advantages of peace.

"The golden moment to liquidate this war which has already been won militarily now presents itself. . . . But I am beginning to fear a tremendous political failure to grasp the glittering possibilities of ending the war and moving decisively toward a more enduring peace in the Pacific."

There was not much that MacArthur himself could do beyond what he had already accomplished by the military defeat of the North Koreans. He pointed out to the administration that the opportunity was fast fleeting. But the rest was up to Washington and Lake Success. Sixteen nations had by now contributed some military units to MacArthur's command; their troops were brave and willing, but their numbers were so small as to make only token additions to the over-all strength. Presumably negotiations with all sixteen of these nations consumed considerable time, but why the U.S. State Department had not foreseen this and made preparations much earlier was a mystery to MacArthur.

Thus there was only one thing left for him to do, and he promptly did it. He again summoned the North Korean commander to surrender. This time he was moved to include the sharp admonition to "liberate all United Nations prisoners-of-war and civilian internees and to make adequate provision for their protection, care and maintenance." He was so moved because our troops had in their advance found increasing evidence of the brutal murder of our captured men behind Communist lines. Literally hundreds of bodies of our soldiers were found, flung into roadside ditches like so much rubbish. Their hands had been tied behind their backs and their heads had been blown in by pistol shots behind the ear.

But MacArthur's summons was ignored.

Had the North Koreans any hope of continued resistance, MacArthur could have understood this refusal to consider any discussion of surrender. But by themselves the North Koreans could not hope to escape utter defeat. So there remained the chilling alternate possibility: were the Communists now deciding whether or not to throw the Red Chinese armies into the Korean war? MacArthur was as convinced now as he had been at Wake Island that no military strategist in his right mind would commit any army like China's in a war like Korea's against the combined land, sea, and air might of the United States. Could it be, then, that the Red Chinese leaders were attempting through one or another of the U.N. diplomats to determine if by any remote chance they could strike against the U.N. troops in Korea without being themselves attacked in turn?

Thus the war in Korea had reached a crucial point in much more than a military sense. This was the time, MacArthur firmly believed, when some government in the United Nations, or at least a so-called "neutral" government with representatives in or connections with the United Nations, assured the Chinese Communists that many of the U.N. government leaders—and possibly some officials in the United States as well—would see to it that the Chinese could attack in Korea without fear of any powerful retaliation.

A hint of this type of thinking came on October 22, in a message from the U.S. State Department. MacArthur was still puzzling over the State Department's inability—or refusal—to strike a diplomatic blow before it was too late, when his confusion was compounded by the October 22 request. He was asked to issue a statement to the effect that it was his purpose "not to interfere with the operations of the Siniho Hydroelectric Power Plant near Sinuiju in North Korea, nor alter such arrangements for the distribution of the electric power as existed on June 25, 1950," which was the day of the original North Korean aggression. This installation on the south bank of the Yalu supplied power not only to North Korea but also to industrial and munitions plants in Manchuria and Siberia. Both China and Russia utilized its power for manufacturing purposes as well as illumination throughout the area. It was a fundamental industrial resource for the entire region, and in any ordinary war it would have top priority as a military target.

MacArthur immediately replied through the Joint Chiefs of Staff that he did not believe it advisable "to issue any statement with reference to future operations of the Siniho Hydroelectric Power Plant, at least until it is under our control and we have had the opportunity to determine the disposition being made of its power output." If, he pointed out, this power was being "utilized in furtherance of potentially hostile military purposes through the manufacture of munitions of war, or there is a diversion of it from the minimum peaceful requirements of the Korean people, most serious doubts would at once arise as to our justification for maintaining a status quo."

He was not further pressed to issue so dangerous a statement. But the fact that he was asked to do so in the first place gave him cause for increasing concern. Little by little his weapons were being taken away from him. First he had been forbidden "hot" pursuit of enemy planes that had attacked our own. Then he had been denied the right to bomb the Manchurian hydroelectric plants along the Yalu. Then that order had been broadened even to include every plant in North Korea which was capable of furnishing electric power to Manchuria and Siberia. Most incomprehensible of all was the refusal of the Joint Chiefs of Staff to let MacArthur freely bomb the important supply center at Racin, which was not in Manchuria but in northeast Korea. Racin was a depot to which the Soviet Union forwarded supplies from Vladivostok for the North Korean Army. Try as he might, MacArthur could never elicit a sensible reason for this particular order.[1]

The next step in the unfolding of this calamitous drama came on the night of October 26. The Eighth Army had been continuing its northward advance. Two days earlier a regiment of the 6th ROK Division had arrived at the Yalu River near Changju, and the U.S. 24th Infantry Division

---

[1] At the Senate hearings in 1951 General Marshall excused the directive by saying that it would have been a waste of bombs anyway because the Communists would immediately pour more supplies across the border into it or set up another base—which, of course, amounts to an argument against aerial bombardment of any kind—and, extended to its logical extreme, is an argument against the airplane as a military weapon.

was rapidly approaching the river's mouth near Namsi-Dong. Widely separated U.N. columns, in classic pursuit formation, were making an almost uninterrupted advance toward the common objective—the Yalu River, boundary between North Korea and Manchuria. Then, on the night of the 26th, a squadron of the 8th Cavalry Regiment fell into an enemy ambush at Unsan. It was cut off and badly mauled.

A series of sharp enemy blows fell in rapid succession. The 2nd ROK Corps was hit as it advanced on the right flank of the Eighth Army. The enemy attack penetrated the three ROK divisions composing this corps and sent them reeling for a loss of ten or twelve miles. It was a local tactical enemy success, but by its location it threatened envelopment and destruction of all of the Eighth Army lead elements in the advance.

General Walker quickly revised his estimate that he could safely commit detached columns in an advance to the border. He ordered the 24th Infantry Division and the other forward elements to withdraw from the positions they then held to a line along the Chongchon River and to join the main body of the Eighth Army. All of them accomplished this withdrawal without incident, except the 7th ROK Regiment, which was intercepted by an enemy column newly arrived from Manchuria; the ROK regiment suffered heavy losses in men and equipment. Simultaneously most of the other U.N. units were feeling increasing enemy pressure. Then came the dread news: prisoners taken in the course of this period indicated for the first time that an estimated minimum of three divisions of Red Chinese had joined the battle.

So the great question was finally posed. Was this a Red Chinese reconnaissance in force, made across the Yalu as a defensive maneuver to obtain information on Eighth Army intentions? Was it the commitment of fresh North Korean units organized, trained, and equipped in Manchuria with a sprinkling of Chinese "volunteers"? Was it merely Red bluff? Or did it represent the jabs of a full-scale Red Chinese offensive?

The Red Chinese government had a ready "explanation" for this situation, which it announced to the world: the Chinese in North Korea were merely "volunteers" who had gone to the assistance of their Korean comrades. MacArthur had no trouble brushing this subterfuge aside. But the problem of determining what the captured Chinese represented was a much more difficult one. He felt that he could not ignore the assumption that Red China had determined upon a limited commitment of Chinese, and at the same time he certainly could not yet assume from the evidence at hand that the decision had been made in Peiping for all-out war in Korea. The logical source for information on any such policies decisions made in Peiping was, of course, Washington, and not the front line in Korea. But neither through the U.N. "neutrals," who usually professed authoritative knowledge of the goings-on inside China, nor through the much-heralded Central Intelligence Agency was there any reliable or useful knowledge to be gained on the subject. MacArthur was left to find out for himself.

But whatever the Red Chinese design, MacArthur's forces were ready for them.

General Walker, in a message to MacArthur, said: "There has never been and there is now no intention for this army to take up or remain in a passive perimeter or any other type of defense. Every effort is being made to retain an adequate bridgehead to facilitate the resumption of the attack as soon as conditions permit. All units continue to execute local attack to restore or improve lines. Plans have been prepared for resumption of the offensive employing all forces available to the army to meet the new factor of organized Chinese Communist forces. These plans will be put into execution at the earliest possible moment and are dependent only upon the security of the right flank, the marshalling of the attack troops and the restoration of vital supplies. . . ." Walker had already laid his plans for resuming the offensive.

And for a while it looked as if the officials in Washington too were refusing to be disturbed at the prospect of a Red Chinese attack. Before Inchon, MacArthur's directive required that should Chinese Communist forces appear on the Korean front, he should immediately assume a defensive position and request further instructions. But this directive had been modified shortly after Inchon. "Hereafter," he was told, "in the event of the open or covert employment anywhere in Korea of major Chinese Communist units, without prior announcement, you should continue the action as long as, in your judgment, action by forces now under your control offers a reasonable chance of success. In any case, prior to taking any military action against objectives in Chinese territory, you will obtain authorization from Washington." Not only did this modification require MacArthur to fight the Chinese if they came into the war so long as he believed there was "a reasonable chance of success," but it also indicated that he would be allowed to carry the fight to the Chinese as well; there was not much point in asking him to request permission for something that would automatically be denied.

MacArthur was encouraged, because he realized that the time might soon come when he would be called upon at a moment's notice to carry the fight into Manchuria by air. He felt, however, that a clear explanation of the situation at hand was needed in order that both the American people and the peoples of the other United Nations whose troops were fighting under his command would understand what confronted their soldiers, marines, airmen and sailors. He therefore issued a special communiqué on November 6. "The Korean war," he said, "was brought to a practical end with the closing of the trap on enemy elements north of Pyongyang and seizure of the east coastal area, resulting in raising the number of enemy prisoners-of-war in our hands to well over 135,000 which, with other losses mounting to over 200,000, brought enemy casualties to 335,000, representing a fair estimate of North Korean total military strength. The defeat of the North Koreans and destruction of their armies was thereby decisive.

"In the face of this victory for United Nations arms, the Communists committed one of the most offensive acts of international lawlessness of historic record by moving, without any notice of belligerence, elements of alien Communist forces across the Yalu River into North Korea and massing a great concentration of possible reinforcing divisions with adequate supply behind the privileged sanctuary of the adjacent Manchurian border.

"A possible trap was thereby surreptitiously laid, calculated to encompass the destruction of the United Nations forces engaged in restoring order and the processes of civil government in the North Korean border area. This potential danger was avoided with minimum losses only by the timely detection and skillful maneuvering of the United Nations commander responsible for that sector, who with great perspicacity and skill completely reversed the movement of his forces in order to achieve the greater integration of tactical power necessitated by the new situation and avert any possibility of a great military reversal.

"The present situation therefore is this. While the North Korean forces with which we were initially engaged have been destroyed or rendered impotent for military action, a new and fresh army faces us, backed up by a possibility of large alien reserves and adequate supplies within easy reach of the enemy but beyond the limits of our present sphere of military action. Whether and to what extent these reserves will be moved forward remains to be seen and is a matter of gravest international significance. Our present mission is limited to the destruction of those forces now arrayed against us in North Korea with a view to achieving the United Nations' objective to bring unity and peace to the Korean nation and people."

Despite the welter of restrictions placed upon him by Washington, there remained one weapon MacArthur could use against massive Chinese intervention. He ordered General Stratemeyer to employ ninety B-29's on the following morning to destroy the Yalu bridges and cut off this easy line of communication between Manchuria and North Korea, over which large armies of Chinese Reds could swarm. This action had never been forbidden him by the Joint Chiefs of Staff, but up to now MacArthur had avoided it because of the danger of accidentally missing the river and dropping bombs in Manchuria, which had been forbidden. Now, however, he had no choice but to cut off any easy avenues of Chinese entrance that he could. But he advised the Joint Chiefs of Staff of his orders before he retired on the night of the 6th.

He was awakened at two a.m. by a messenger bearing an urgent dispatch from Washington. The dispatch countermanded his order to Stratemeyer, and furthermore directed MacArthur "to postpone all bombing of targets within five miles of the Manchurian border until further orders."

MacArthur jumped out of bed and took the message to his desk, to read it under a stronger light than that provided by his bed lamp. Yet there it was, incredible as it seemed. Washington was extending to the enemy protection not only of the bridges which were the only means they had for moving their men and supplies across that wide, natural river barrier into North Korea, but also for a five-mile-deep area on this side of the Yalu in which to establish a bridgehead. It would be impossible to exaggerate MacArthur's astonishment. He took only time to cancel his order to Stratemeyer, pending further instructions, before sitting down to compose his reply.

In it he called attention to his previous warnings that there was a substantial movement across the bridges. "The only way to stop this reinforcement of the enemy," he said, "is the destruction of the bridges by air attack and air destruction of installations in North Korea which would facilitate the movement. . . . I feel that the operation is within the scope of the rules of war and the resolutions and directions which I have received. And I can accept the instructions rescinding my orders only under the gravest protest, as I feel that they might well result in a calamity of gravest proportions, for which I could not accept the responsibility. Urgently request reconsideration of your decision, or that the matter be brought to the attention of the President for his review."

All that resulted from this vigorous protest was a modification of the order to permit the bombing of the "Korean end of the Yalu bridges." At the same time MacArthur was cautioned to exercise extreme care to avoid violation of the Manchurian border and air space—that is, the sanctuary that had been granted to the enemy—because of the "necessity for maintaining the optimum position with regard to the United Nations policies and directives, and because it was vital to the national interests to localize the fighting in Korea."

Thus it was openly admitted by Washington that, so far at least, even this surreptitious attack by the Chinese Communists was not to be punished except by meek half-measures. At this stage, however, MacArthur could not but ascribe Washington's pusillanimity to the fact that the officials there continued to be beguiled by the Red Chinese claim that these troops in North Korea were actually "volunteers" and not official units of the Chinese Army. He refused to believe that if these first few Chinese soldiers were followed by a full-strength Red Chinese intervention, the officials of the United States and other U.N. countries would still elect to grant the Chinese this enormous advantage. In the weeks and months to come MacArthur was to learn much about the extent to which appeasement could go in Washington and Lake Success.

Meanwhile MacArthur's air chief, Stratemeyer, studied the conditions under which the bombing of the Yalu bridges was to be permitted and compared them with what we knew about the enemy concentrations of Chinese anti-aircraft installations on the north banks of the Yalu. He shook his head ruefully as he advised MacArthur: "It cannot be done— Washington must have known, it cannot be done." Nor has it since been done.

The reason why it could not be done was best detailed by Major General Emmett O'Donnell, Jr., head of the Far East Bomber Command, when he explained the situation at the Senate hearings in 1951. "We were not," O'Donnell testified, "allowed to violate Manchurian territory, and by violation of the territory I mean we were not allowed to fly over an inch of it. For instance, the Yalu has several pronounced bends like most rivers before getting to the town of Antung, and the main bridges at Antung we had to attack in only one manner. There was only one manner you could attack the bridges and not violate Manchurian territory, and that was a course tangental to the southernmost bend of the river. As you draw a line from the southernmost bend of the river to the bridge and that is your course, and these people on the other side of the river knew that, and they put up their batteries right along the line and they peppered us right down the line all the way. We had to take it, of course, and couldn't fight back.

"In addition to that, they had their fighters come up alongside; while

I didn't see them myself, the combat mission reports indicate that they would join our formation about two miles to the lee and fly along at the same speed on the other side of the river while we were making our approach, and just before we got to bomb-away position, they would veer off to the north and climb up to about 30,000 feet and then make a frontal quarter attack on the bombers just about at the time of bombsaway in a turn. So that they would be coming from Manchuria in a turn, swoop down, fire their cannons at the formation, and continue to turn back into sanctuary." Such were the overwhelming disadvantages enforced upon our airmen. Small wonder the question was asked time and time again: "On which side *are* Washington and Lake Success?"

Small wonder, too, that MacArthur expostulated to members of his staff: "For the first time in military history, a commander has been denied the use of his military power to safeguard the lives of his soldiers and safety of his army. To me it clearly foreshadows a future tragic situation in the Far East and leaves me with a sense of inexpressible shock. It will cost the lives of thousands of American soldiers and place in jeopardy the entire army. By some means the enemy commander must have known of this decision to protect his lines of communication into North Korea, or he never would have dared to cross those bridges in force."

But the decision on November 6 was never altered. Those bridges across the Yalu still stand. As MacArthur stated at the Senate hearings: "Their planks have echoed to the tramping feet of hundreds of thousands of men, and millions of tons of supplies and ammunition have crossed them, either to support the enemy or blast our own ranks." And even if someone in Washington had had the belated sense to rescind that order, it probably would have been too late. It was at this time, when the first clear warning call was sounded by MacArthur that Chinese troops in force might be entering North Korea, that the bridges played their most important role. As we know now, there followed twenty days during which the massive concentrations of Red Chinese did indeed tramp across these bridges—twenty days during which the near-disaster that followed could have been averted, twenty days in which, by a single decision in Washington, United States prestige in Asia was dragged from an all-time high to an all-time low. It was by all odds the most indefensible and ill-conceived and, in final analysis, disastrous decision enforced upon a field commander in the nation's history. Indeed, the blood of many American and other Allied soldiers, sacrificed upon the altar of that infamous decision, gives evidence of the prophetic nature of MacArthur's solemn warning in his reply of November 6: ". . . a calamity of major proportions for which I could not accept the responsibility."

The Wages of Appeasement

The principal architect of the policy that was so crippling our military operations in Korea had evidently begun to feel some pangs of conscience at this time. For on the day following the extraordinary directive and MacArthur's sharp protest, Secretary Marshall dispatched a message which seemed conciliatory in tone and which stated that MacArthur's concern over these alarming developments was fully understood and shared by the authorities in Washington.

Marshall said: "I have just talked with the President in Independence [where Truman was vacationing]. The discussions and decisions here are heavily weighted with the extremely delicate situation we have before the Security Council of the United Nations whose meeting tomorrow may have fateful consequences. We all realize your difficulty in fighting a desperate battle in a mountainous region under winter conditions and with a multinational force in all degrees of preparedness. I also understand, I think, the difficulty involved in conducting such a battle under necessarily limiting conditions and the necessity of keeping the distant headquarters closely informed of developments and decisions. However, this appears to be unavoidable, but I want you to know that I understand your problems. Everyone here, Defense, State and the President, is intensely desirous of supporting you in the most effective manner within our means. At the same time we are faced with an extremely grave international problem which could so easily lead into a world disaster." To this Marshall added a query: "Incidentally, for my own personal information, do you feel that the hydroelectric and reservoir situation is probably the dominant consideration in this apparently last minute move by the Chinese Communists, incited by the Soviets to protect their war interests in the Far East?"

MacArthur could not have agreed more that the situation in Korea was in grave danger of leading to world disaster—but for exactly opposite reasons to those advanced by Marshall. The danger was that by meeting naked force with appeasement we not only would perpetrate military disaster in Korea but would also invite Communism to make its bid for most of Asia. This was a far larger, more complex and long-range problem than could be dealt with in terms of a few power stations or reservoirs. Certainly Asian Communism's timetable did not depend upon whether U.N. planes knocked out a hydroelectric plant; and a naïve assumption that it did merely served to provide easier routes for conquest. In the brief time allowed him by the rush of events, MacArthur did his best to explain how much more far-reaching was the situation with which the U.N. was confronted.

"I do not believe that the hydroelectric system is the dominant consideration animating the Communist intervention in Korea," he wrote, "although it might well be contributory to such action. It is unquestionably being utilized as an argument to conceal the aggressive belligerency of the Chinese Communists. This view is supported by the fact that their activities in Korea throughout have been offensive—never defensive. . . . Moreover, from technical information available here, there appears to be a tendency to greatly overemphasize the industrial importance of the hydroelectric system which actually, following Soviet post-war looting, is clearly of insufficient consequences to become provocative of major war.

MacArthur went on to explain that "the motivating influences are far more fundamental than might be represented by immediate material considerations." In order to understand them, he pointed out, "one must examine the changes in Chinese character and culture over the past fifty years." Up until fifty years ago, MacArthur explained, China was "decompartmented into groups divided against each other. Their war-making tendency was almost non-existent." Not until the turn of the century, under the regime of Chiang-So-Lin, did China's nationalist urge begin. "This was further and more successfully developed," MacArthur wrote, "under the leadership of Chiang Kai-shek, but has been brought to its greatest fruition under the present regime, to the point that it has now taken on the character of a united nationalism of increasingly dominant aggressive tendencies.

"Through these past 50 years the Chinese people have thus become militarized in their concepts and in their ideals. They now make first class soldiers and are gradually developing competent staffs and commanders. This has produced a new and dominant power in Asia which for its own purposes has allied with Soviet Russia, but which in its own concepts and methods has become aggressively imperialistic, with a lust for expansion and increased power normal to this type of imperialism.

"There is little of the ideological concept either one way or the other in the Chinese makeup. The standard of living is so low and the capital accumulation has been so thoroughly dissipated by war that the masses are desperate and avid to follow any leadership which seems to promise alleviation of local stringencies. I have from the beginning believed that the Chinese Communists' support of the North Koreans was the dominant one. Their interests at present are parallel to those of the Soviet, but I believe that the aggressiveness now displayed, not only in Korea but in Indo-China, and Tibet and pointing toward the south, reflects predominantly the same lust for the expansion of power which has animated every would-be conqueror since the beginning of time.

"Quezon once said to me in the darkest days of Bataan, 'I have no fear that we will not ultimately defeat the Japanese, nor do I feel any dread of ultimate conquest by them. My great fear is the Chinese. With their increasing militarism and aggressive tendencies, they are the great Asiatic menace. They have no real ideologies, and when they reach the fructification of their military potential, I dread to think what may happen.' He has been shown to be almost prophetic by developments since he spoke."

Secretary Marshall's reply was brusque, completely unresponsive, and served to demonstrate his knowledge of Asia. "I think you misunderstood my query regarding hydroelectric installations," he wired. "I was referring only to the sudden developments of the past week."

At about this time the British government came up with an ingenious solution to the problem of combating Red Chinese intervention: give the Communists a slice of North Korea to serve as a "buffer" area, and as evidence of the U.N.'s good intentions. In the face of such foolhardy advice—and growing indications that the U.S. State Department might heed this advice—MacArthur made another effort to warn Washington of the disastrous course ahead.

"The widely reported British desire to appease the Chinese Communists by giving them a strip of Northern Korea," he said, "finds a most recent precedent in the action taken at Munich on 29 September 1938 by Great Britain, France and Italy, wherein the Sudetenland, the strategically important Bohemian mountain bastion, was ceded to Germany without the participation of Czechoslovakia and indeed against the protest of that government. Within ten months following acquisition of that vital strategic bastion, Germany had seized the resulting impotent Czechoslovakia, declaring it had ceased to exist as a sovereign state and that the Reich forces would thereafter preserve order."

MacArthur further pointed out that our own State Department, in a public document entitled "Post War Foreign Policy Preparation," realized and pointed out that this was a typical case in which "the weakness of peaceful efforts toward just settlements in the face of determined aggression was unmistakably demonstrated." Trying to point out that the State Department was blinding itself to axioms that it had already advocated, MacArthur said: "This observation of the State Department points unmistakably to the lessons of history. There is no known exception which would cast doubt upon the validity of this concept. In the case of the United Nations, such action would carry within itself the germs of its own ultimate destruction, or it would bear its own weaknesses, requiring that it limit the imposition of its decisions and order upon the weak, not the strong. It would be a tribute to aggression to encourage that very international lawlessness which it is the fundamental duty of the United Nations to curb."

MacArthur knew that this might be his last chance to reiterate his warning before it was too late. He could visualize those Red Chinese soldiers massing above the Yalu, and possibly already swarming across the bridges that the State Department and the diplomats of other U.N. members were refusing to let him destroy. If so, there would soon be no time left in which to plead for a realistic understanding of the situation. So MacArthur couched this warning in the strongest possible terms: "To give up a portion of North Korea to the aggression of the Chinese Communists would be the greatest defeat of the free world in recent times. Indeed, to yield to so immoral a proposition would bankrupt our leadership and influence in Asia and render untenable our position, both politically and militarily. It would not curb deterioration of the present situation into the possibility of a general war, but would impose upon us the disadvantage of having inevitably to fight such a war if it occurs, bereft of the support of countless Asiatics who now believe in us and are eager to fight with us. Such an abandonment of principle would entirely reverse the tremendous moral and psychological uplift throughout Asia and perhaps the entire free world, which accompanied the United Nation decision of June 25th, and leave in its place the revulsion against the organization bordering on complete disillusionment and distrust.

"From a military standpoint, I believe that the United States should press for a resolution in the United Nations condemning the Chinese Communists for their defiance of the United Nations' orders by invading Korea and opening hostilities against the United Nations' forces, calling upon the Communists to withdraw forthwith to positions north of the international border on pain of military sanctions by the United Nations should they fail to do so. I recommend with all the earnestness that I possess that there be no weakening at this critical moment and that we press on to complete victory which I believe can be achieved if our determination and indomitable will do not desert us."

Fervent arguments these were, and they were supported by facts that MacArthur could not yet know. At this fleeting stage of the Korean war he stood in a no-man's-land of time, while he sought to determine whether he was on the verge of completing a war or being thrust into an entirely new one. The unknown quantity was the intention of Peiping. Were those Chinese troops across the Yalu stationed there to protect Manchuria, with only occasional reinforcements of them being used to add to the strength of the North Korean armies? Or had Peiping decided upon all-out war?

Again this was a question more easily answered in the capitals of the world than on the battlefield. But no help was forthcoming from Washington. The Central Intelligence Agency could hardly be said to have helped answer the great question. It compiled, for example, a National Intelligence Estimate on November 24, more than a month after the first Red Chinese units had been discovered on Korean soil. This estimate did not reach MacArthur's headquarters until December 12, nearly three weeks after the Chinese had struck in full force; and, in any case, all the CIA could offer was the statement that "available evidence is not conclusive as to whether or not the Chinese Communists are as yet committed to a full scale offensive effort." Beyond that, the estimate pointed out that "there has been no suggestion in Chinese propaganda or official statements that the Chinese support of North Korea has a limited objective such as protecting power plants, establishing a buffer zone on the border, or forcing the U.N. forces back to the 38th Parallel"—facts that MacArthur not only had long since known but had also reported to Washington himself.

The more he pondered this question, the more he realized that at this juncture, in so far as his immediate tactical plans were concerned, it was academic. He actually had no alternative but to continue his advance. Certainly he could not break and run. A possible move would have been to draw his forces together in a location where he could use natural obstacles to assist in defense, and dig in with a supposedly impregnable perimeter across Korea. This alternative has since been advocated by many self-appointed military strategists who expressed seeming wisdom after the fact but who should have known better. There *was* no terrain with natural obstacles surpassing the great obstacle of the Yalu River itself. And even if there had been, all of MacArthur's troops taken together would not have provided him with sufficient defense in depth against the overwhelming superiority in numbers of the Chinese armies.[2]

There remained one alternative to advancing, and that was to call for more reinforcements to meet any such new onslaught. MacArthur had already tried this. And he had been refused. American troops, by the

[2] Later a line like this was established and held near the 38th Parallel. By that time U.N. forces had nearly trebled in strength.

curious logic of the strategists at home, were needed more in other parts of the world where there was no fighting going on—nor any imminently threatened.

MacArthur consulted with his field commanders and with his staff. He reviewed his orders from Washington: "*In the event of the open or covert employment anywhere in Korea of major Chinese Communist units, without prior announcement, you should continue the action as long as, in your judgment action by forces now under your control offers a reasonable chance of success. . . .*" He concluded that the best possible "posture of security" was actually to continue his "operation on the offensive" through implementation of Walker's plan of attack. This would deny the enemy the selection of the time and place of attack. The drive north would be simultaneously a mopping-up of the defeated North Korean forces and a reconnaissance in force to probe the intentions of the new Chinese forces. And if the primary function of this drive should turn out to be the latter and finally spring the Red trap, MacArthur's troops would have the necessary freedom of action to escape its jaws. Anticipating just this situation, he directed that a program be prepared in complete detail for disengagement and withdrawal from action if indeed it developed that Red China was entering the Korean war in determined force.

All on MacArthur's staff agreed with this plan. It was submitted to the Joint Chiefs of Staff in Washington. They too approved. At the Senate hearings six months later, MacArthur said: "The disposition of those troops, in my opinion, could not have been improved upon had I known the Chinese were going to attack." That disposition was meticulously planned for a twofold purpose: (1) if the Chinese were not coming into Korea, the drive would finish the Korean war; (2) if the Chinese were coming in, the U.N. troops were in a far better position to cope with the unfathomable uncertainties that would follow than they would be had they dug in along an immobile line of too thin defense.

Meanwhile, behind the curtain of fright thrown up along the Yalu by Washington, the Chinese Communists were surging into positions for the big attack. Under the cover of darkness and the deadly pattern of anti-aircraft defense permitted them by the U.N. restrictions, they poured more than 200,000 troops into North Korea between November 6 and November 26. Those were the twenty days of use of the Yalu bridges against which MacArthur had tried so valiantly, but in vain, to warn Washington. It was time for action rather than further exchanges with Washington. So MacArthur gave Walker the go-ahead.

Chapter IX   Springing the Red Trap

🔰 On November 24, 1950 MacArthur flew to Eighth Army headquarters on the Chongchon River in Korea, to be greeted by two generals and a dachshund. The generals were Walton Walker, commander of the Eighth Army, and Frank Milburn, commander of the First Corps; the dachshund was Ebbe, Milburn's pet and the mascot of his division. The occasion for MacArthur's visit was to launch the drive north to the Yalu.

He had given his original go-ahead signal to Walker on November 15. But supplies had not yet caught up with Walker's rapid advance, and the jump-off date had had to be postponed. By the 24th, the day of Mac-Arthur's visit, the supply situation was still unsatisfactory. But MacArthur and Walker both felt that they could wait no longer. Patrols were finding it increasingly difficult to maintain contact with the enemy, leaving a wide gap in information on his order of battle as well as capability and intentions. The limitation on air reconnaissance, combined with the enemy's adeptness at concealment, were making the job of intelligence increasingly difficult.

But, most important, if the Chinese were coming into Korea in force, every day of delay on our part allowed more thousands of them to cross the Yalu bridges. And every day brought on the winter weather, which would freeze the Yalu and let thousands more across. Had MacArthur been allowed to take out those bridges, he could have wound up the war in Korea before the ice highways formed across the river. But since this decisive weapon had been denied him, his only hope was to strike before Chinese superiority in numbers became too great.

Besides, it must be remembered that at this stage everyone was still in doubt whether or not large forces of Chinese actually were to be committed to Korea. With no air reconnaissance over Manchuria, with no way to safeguard his troops by knocking out the bridges, with no intelligence information on the subject from Washington, MacArthur could only proceed with a reconnaissance in force—and hope that it turned out to be instead a mopping-up operation against only the North Koreans, with but a scattering of Chinese "volunteers."

Winter was in the air when the *SCAP* set down at Sinanju airstrip. MacArthur greeted the officers who had come to meet him, squatted down to pat the dachshund, entered a jeep, and headed for the command post. After a military briefing, he took off again in the jeep and spent the rest of his five-hour visit touring the front.

At one sector, as he was talking to General John B. Coulter, the IX Corps commander, MacArthur happened to recall the part of the Wake Island discussion in which, responding to Bradley's inquiry, he had said that he believed he could return some troops to the United States by Christmas. He also thought of the frequency with which the State Department, reflecting British pressure, had asked him to give public assurance to the Communists that the U.N. command had no designs on territory beyond the Yalu—assurances that he had declined to give for fear they might be misinterpreted as reflecting weakness. And he thought of the veteran troops who that morning were being sent into indeterminate battle in the face of the onrushing bitterness of winter weather. Then, half in jest but with a certain firmness of meaning and purpose, he said to Coulter: "If this operation is successful, I hope we can get the boys home by Christmas."

Those of us present certainly understood what he meant. Such was his method of reassuring the Chinese Reds that we had no designs of conquest beyond the Yalu; of reassuring his troops that there was a definite limit to the campaign ahead; and of reassuring Bradley that he had not forgotten the request of the Joint Chiefs to release troops from Korean duty as soon as possible. None regarded the remark as predicting the result of the battle, least of all MacArthur. But a few days later, when the Chinese struck in such force as to stop the advance, it was completely twisted and misinterpreted as a powerful propaganda weapon with which to bludgeon MacArthur.

By midafternoon the *SCAP* was airborne again, and we had settled back in our seats for the three-hour return flight to Tokyo—when MacArthur instructed the pilot, Lieutenant Colonel Story, to head for the mouth of the Yalu River. The rest of us looked at each other in open surprise. Even had our plane been armed and accompanied by a heavy fighter escort (there were a few fighters hovering over us), this would have been an extremely hazardous undertaking. As it was, the *SCAP* would be a sitting duck for enemy anti-aircraft fire or air interception. But most of us knew better by now than to argue with MacArthur about taking risks; to the mention of these dangers he simply replied that there was no substitute for a personal reconnaissance of the approaches into North Korea from the Yalu. Furthermore, he wanted to study the terrain features and look for any enemy activity. Besides, he said, the very audacity of the flight itself was its best protection.

We at least tried to get him to put on a parachute, only to bring a laugh as he replied: "You gentlemen wear them if you care to do so, but I'll stick with the plane." While none of the rest of us would countenance putting one on after that remark, I noticed that many a longing look was cast in the direction of the unused parachutes piled near the tail of the plane as we approached the enemy border.

When the mouth of the Yalu appeared below us, MacArthur told Story to turn east and follow the course of the river at an altitude of about five thousand feet. At this height we were sufficiently low to observe in detail the entire area of international no-man's-land all the way to the Siberian border. We could easily make out the snow-covered roads and trails; but not one gave a sign of any extensive use. If a large force or massive supply train had passed over this border, its imprints had already been well covered by the intermittent snowstorms of the Yalu Valley. All that spread before our eyes was an endless expanse of utterly barren countryside, its jagged hills, yawning crevices, and all but the black waters of the Yalu locked in the silent death-grip of snow and ice. MacArthur was right; it would be better to stay with the plane than parachute into this merciless wasteland.

On his return to Tokyo, he found a disquieting message waiting for him. It was from the Joint Chiefs of Staff, and it said: "There is a growing concern within the United Nations over the possibility of bringing on a general conflict should a major clash develop with Chinese Communist forces as a result of your forces advancing squarely against the entire boundary between Korea and Manchuria. . . . Proposals in United Nations may suggest unwelcome restriction on your advance to the north since some sentiment exists in United Nations for establishing a demilitarized zone between your forces and the frontier in the hope of thereby reducing Chinese Communist fear of United Nations military action against Manchuria. . . .

"The consensus of political and military opinion at a meeting held Thursday with the Secretaries of State and Defense, the Joint Chiefs of Staff and other officials, was that there should be no change in your mission, but that immediate action should be taken at top governmental level to formulate a course of action which will permit the establishment of a unified Korea and at the same time reduce risk of more general involvement. On the assumption that your coming attack will be successful, exploratory discussions were had to discover what military measures, which you might in any event wish to take, might lend themselves to political action which would reduce the tension with Peiping and the Soviet Union and maintain a solid United Nations front."

Then came the alarming part: a suggestion that after advancing to a position at or near the Yalu, MacArthur might secure the position, using ROK forces to "hold the terrain dominating the approaches from the Valley of the Yalu." The limit of his advance in the northeast, this proposal went on, would be fixed at Chongjin.

There it was again, the foolish and fainthearted notion that by displaying timidity in advance we would somehow humor the Red Chinese into altering whatever plans they may or may not have made for entering the Korean war. MacArthur replied at length and at once. "It is believed that the suggested approach would not only fail to achieve the desired result, but would be provocative of the very consequences we seek to avert. In the first place," he said, "from a military standpoint my personal reconnaissance of the Yalu River line yesterday demonstrated conclusively that it would be utterly impossible for us to stop upon terrain south of the river as suggested and there be in position to hold under effective control its lines of approach to North Korea. The terrain ranging from the lowlands in the west to the rugged central and eastern sectors is not adaptable to such a system of defense were we, for any reason, to sacrifice the natural defense features of the river line itself, features to be found in no other natural defense line in all of Korea. Nor would it be either militarily or politically defensible to yield this natural protective barrier safeguarding the territorial integrity of Korea."

But there was more to this than military tactics alone. MacArthur pointed out: "Moreover, any failure on our part to prosecute the military campaign through to its public and oft-repeated objective of destroying all enemy forces south of Korea's northern boundary as essential to the restoration of unity and peace to all of Korea, would be . . . regarded by the Korean people as a betrayal of . . . the solemn undertaking the United Nations entered into on their behalf, and by the Chinese and all of the other peoples of Asia as weakness reflected from the appeasement of Communist aggression. . . ."

Then MacArthur tried once again to dispel the illusion that Asian

Communist strategy depended upon the output of a few power plants. "Study of the Soviet and Peiping propaganda line," he said, "discloses little to suggest any major concern over the potentiality of United Nations control of the southern banks of the Yalu River. Even what has been said concerning the hydroelectric facilities in North Korea is for the most part a product of British-American speculation, finding little reflection in any Soviet or Chinese utterances. Indeed, our information on these facilities and the disposition abroad of their power output fails to confirm that dependence upon this source of power is a major factor in the basic causes giving rise to the Chinese aggressive moves in Korea. Thus, despite the fact that those hydroelectric facilities at Chongjin brought under control of the X Corps had been closed down completely for a full month prior to the arrival of our forces, with much of the vital machinery and other equipment removed and dispersed and are not yet restored to operation, no suggestion of complaint has emanated from Soviet or Chinese sources over the deprivation of power consequent thereto. In view of these factual considerations one is brought to the conclusion that the issue of hydroelectric power rests upon the most tenuous of grounds. . . .

"Our forces are committed to seize the entire border area," MacArthur went on, "and indeed in the east have already occupied a sector of the Yalu River with no noticeable political or military Soviet or Chinese reactions. We have repeatedly and publicly made it unmistakably clear that we entertain no aggressive designs whatsoever against any part of Chinese or Soviet territory. It is my plan, just as soon as we are able to consolidate positions along the Yalu River, to replace as far as possible American forces with those of the Republic of Korea and publicly announce orders affecting: (1) The return of American forces to Japan; (2) The parole of all prisoners-of-war to their homes; (3) The leaving of the unification of Korea and the restoration of the civil processes of government to the people, with the advice and assistance of the United Nations authorities. I believe that the prompt implementation of this plan as soon as our military objectives have been reached will effectively appeal to reason in the Chinese mind. If it will not, then the resulting situation is not one which might be influenced by bringing to a halt our military measures short of present commitments. By resolutely meeting those commitments," MacArthur concluded, "and accomplishing our military mission as so often publicly delineated, lies the best—indeed the only— hope that Soviet and Chinese aggressive designs may be checked before these countries are committed from which, for political reasons, they cannot withdraw."

419

Much of this MacArthur had said before, and as he wrote the message he must have wondered how many times he might be required to say it again. I am here recording most of that lengthy message for the first time, only partly in answer to those detractors who have seemed up to now not to have been aware of the fact that MacArthur was, in November of 1950, giving any consideration to the possibility of Chinese intervention. The more important purpose in including the sometimes necessarily long messages between MacArthur and the Joint Chiefs of Staff is to delineate for the historical record the thinking at the time both in Washington and in Tokyo. A great deal of apologetic evasion of this documentation has gone on even in supposedly objective official Army historical studies, in an obvious attempt to shift the blame for ensuing events from where it belongs. Many of the dispatches during this period, incidentally, are published here for the first time, almost five years after the event—through no fault of MacArthur. They were all available in Washington. At great pains he has answered lengthy questionnaires sent to him; virtually everything he has said, however, has been ignored.

As of November 26, 1950, MacArthur had sent Washington his last warning. On the following day the Red Chinese struck.

While restrictions on air reconnaissance had hampered MacArthur's intelligence, the enemy had operated under no such handicap. The Chinese intelligence proved to be excellent, and the first blow came at the weakest point in the Eighth Army line. This was the juncture between the American and South Korean forces—and not, as some professed experts later asserted, between the Eighth Army and the X Corps; the rugged spinal mountain range between these two latter forces would have been virtually impassable for any sizable attack.

Simultaneously other units of the Chinese armies unleashed attacks that mounted in tempo all along the Eighth Army line. It rapidly developed that our troops were being hit by as many as seven Chinese field armies. Much of this force had of course been released for this employment by the Presidential directive five months earlier which had promised protection of the Chinese mainland from Formosa by the Seventh Fleet. And the bulk of all seven armies had in only twenty days thundered across the privileged Yalu River bridges which MacArthur had sought in vain to destroy. The assault against the ROK forces on the right of the Eighth Army was so strong that the South Koreans broke before it, exposing the right flank of the remainder of the Eighth Army line to punishing attacks and possible encirclement. The Red trap was sprung.

But MacArthur and Walker were ready for it. This is a fact that cannot be stated too forcefully. MacArthur was greatly saddened, as well as angered, at this despicably surreptitious attack, a piece of treachery which he regarded as worse even than Pearl Harbor. But he was *not* taken by surprise. His troops did *not* rush blindly north into a massive ambush, as claimed by some detractors. The push north had been carefully designed to be effective either as a mopping-up operation or as a reconnaissance in force; and now it had unhappily become the latter. But the plans were already made for this development, and Walker at once ordered them executed.

There followed a series of delaying actions. As in all such situations, not every unit was able to follow the letter of the plan. There were, as always, losses; and there were also examples of personal heroism which equaled those of our highest military traditions. The U.S. 2nd Infantry Division and the Turkish contingent, for example, conducted magnificently the rear-guard action to which assigned, which enabled the rest of the army swiftly to break contact and avoid a flanking movement by the enemy.

Meanwhile MacArthur informed Washington of the bitter news and announced his necessary decision to "pass from the offensive to the defensive, with such local adjustments as may be required by a constantly fluid situation." The Joint Chiefs of Staff approved his decision and added that "any directive in conflict therewith is deferred." A new war thus started in Korea.

Once MacArthur had come to grips with the enemy, his intelligence was able to determine what had not been known up to then. He at once reported to the Joint Chiefs of Staff: "All hope of localization of the Korean conflict to enemy forces composed of North Korean troops with alien token elements can now be completely abandoned. The Chinese forces are committed in North Korea in great and ever increasing strength. No pretext of minor support under the guise of voluntarism or other subterfuge now has the slightest validity. We face an entirely new war.

"Interrogation of prisoners-of-war and other intelligence information established the following enemy order of battle, exclusive of North Korean elements, as reported by commanders in the field: 38th, 39th, 40th, 42nd, 66th, 59th, and 20th Chinese Communist field armies. The North Korean fragments, approximately 50,000 troops, are to be added to this strength. The pattern of Chinese strategy is now quite clear. Immediately after the Inchon operation, the center of gravity of the Chinese forces was moved northward in China, with heavy concentrations of their troops in Manchuria and surreptitious movement by night infiltration of their organized forces into North Korea under protection of the sanctuary of neutrality. After checking the United Nations advance toward the Yalu late in October, following the destruction of the North Korean forces, the Chinese partially broke contact before launching a general offensive in order to build up in overwhelming strength, presumably for a spring offensive. Their ultimate objective was undoubtedly a decisive effort aimed at the complete destruction of United Nations forces in Korea.

"At the present moment the freezing of the Yalu River increasingly opens up avenues of reinforcement and supply which it is impossible for our air potential to interdict. It is quite evident that our present strength in forces is not sufficient to meet this undeclared war by the Chinese with the inherent advantages which accrue thereby to them. The resulting situation presents an entirely new picture which broadens the potentialities of world-embracing considerations beyond the sphere of consideration by the theater commander. . . ."

It was patently impossible to stem the tide of enemy advance with the troops MacArthur had in Korea at the time. He had asked for reinforcements so many times, and had been refused so many times, that he coupled his plea this time with a request that he be allowed to use the only other major source available. At the outbreak of hostilities in Korea half a year earlier Chiang Kai-shek had immediately offered his finest corps of 33,000 veteran regulars, with more if needed. At that time MacArthur had had more than his hands full training and orienting South Korean soldiers into his U.N. armies, and he had agreed that the Nationalist Chinese soldiers should wait until a more propitious date. Then, as the opportunity arose for the employment of Nationalist soldiers in Korea, Washington demurred—not for military reasons, but for fear that this too might hurt the sensibilities of the Red Chinese.

Now, however, with the Red Chinese in full onslaught against the U.N. forces, the speciousness of that argument had been revealed. So MacArthur wired the Joint Chiefs of Staff on November 29, urgently recommending that "the theater commander be authorized to negotiate direct with the Chinese government authorities on Formosa for the movement north and incorporation into United Nations command of such Chinese units as may be available and desirable for reinforcing our position in Korea." He carefully pointed out that the previous argument of fear of the Red Chinese was "no longer valid," and stressed the urgency of the situation.

To this he received a particularly vacillating reply. His recommendation, Washington said, was under consideration, but despite the urgency,

Springing the Red Trap

a firm answer would be delayed because it involved "worldwide consequences." The message went on to say that: "we shall have to consider
the possibility that it would disrupt the united position of the nations
associated with us in the United Nations, and leave the United States
isolated. . . . It may be wholly unacceptable to the commonwealth
countries to have their forces employed with Nationalist China. . . .
Our position of leadership in the Far East is being most serious compromised in the United Nations. The utmost care will be necessary to avoid
the disruption of the essential Allied line-up in that organization. . . ."

MacArthur could have told Washington—and, in fact, had done so
long ago—that "our position of leadership in the Far East is being most
seriously compromised." And it would continue to be, so long as the
United States abetted the Asian policies of such nations as the British,
who evidently were willing to sabotage the U.N. effort in Korea rather
than fight alongside Nationalist Chinese. Indeed, the British preferred the
farcical diplomatic position of officially recognizing a nation and fighting
its armies at the same time, as it had with Communist China. MacArthur
believed, however, that there was a length to which even the most timid
politicians would not go. It was clear to the simplest mind that if military
restrictions upon him were not lifted, Korea was doomed without substantial reinforcements. The only immediate source for these reinforcements
was Formosa. MacArthur was convinced that he was being subjected to
no more than an exasperating delay. Eventually reason would prevail; he
felt it had to.

The lights in the study of the American Embassy burned even later
than usual on the night of December 1. MacArthur was holding one of the
most important conferences of the war. Secretly, with few besides their
chiefs of staff and pilots knowing it, Walker and Almond had flown in
from the front. The only others present at this conference with MacArthur
were Admiral Joy and Generals Stratemeyer, Hickey, Willoughby,
Wright, and myself. The military situation on both fronts was carefully
explored. And despite the pessimism of the "experts" on the newspapers
and in the Pentagon, both Walker and Almond were optimistic. Walker
felt that he could hold at least the Pyongyang area. Almond, who had not
as yet been subjected to the full force of the enemy's counteroffensive in
the northeast, felt that the 1st Marine Division could press forward to the
corridor that the enemy had used in the west and attack him from the
rear.

Walker agreed that he did desperately need reinforcement, but he
felt that he would prefer not to give up the tactical advantage which the

PART III: KOREA

X Corps could give him by maintaining pressure on the enemy's flank, instead of joining forces with him. All present fully understood the seriousness of the situation, but there was complete accord on the strategy for the immediate future. The meeting broke up after midnight on a note of confident resolution. Walker and Almond caught a few hour's sleep and left early in the morning to rejoin their commands. MacArthur at once communicated his decisions to Washington.

Red Chinese pressure, however, intensified even more than expected, as a constant stream of fresh reinforcements poured from Manchurian sanctuary across the protected Yalu bridges. Hit hardest was the X Corps, which was forced to withdraw to the Wonsan-Hamhung area. There was bitter, bloody fighting as the X Corps withdrew, but it was accomplished with skill and valor and with no disproportionate losses. The Eighth Army was forced to pull back too; and it too disengaged from the enemy in as orderly a fashion as can be accomplished in a withdrawal action.

It took nerves of steel for Walker and Almond to fight the kind of battle which had been decided upon at the strategy meeting in Mac-Arthur's Embassy study. But disengaging the enemy was the only tactic that would save the forces in Korea from fruitless loss and provide the basis for an eventual counterattack. The sole purpose, as MacArthur had outlined it, was to reach a point where the U.N. armies could suddenly turn on the enemy and punish him. "Much as we wish to hold on to all of the ground we won in combat," he told Walker, "our primary consideration must be the safety of the command and that safety can only be secured by reducing the enemy's relativity of military strength. We ourselves can expect no substantial reinforcement. He has unlimited reinforcements at his command. This leaves supply the only vulnerable point in his armor. We must draw him south in order that his supply difficulties will increase in proportion as ours decrease."

A most frequently repeated piece of advice freely offered MacArthur at the time echoed an earlier British suggestion that MacArthur establish a defense line across the so-called "waist" of Korea—a line roughly running from Pyongyang to Wonsan. The idea was to pull all of his troops, the Eighth Army as well as the X Corps, together into this defense line and sit there waiting for the enemy onslaught. So great did the pressure on Tokyo and Washington become to adopt this tactic that MacArthur felt constrained to point out to the Joint Chiefs of Staff the fallacies in the argument.

In a message on December 3, he said: "There is no practicability, nor could any benefit accrue thereby, to attempt to unite the forces of the

Eighth Army and the X Corps. Those forces are completely outnumbered and their junction would, therefore, not only not produce added strength but would actually jeopardize the free flow of movement that arises from the two separate logistical lines of naval supply and maneuver.

"As I previously reported, the development of a defense line across the waist of Korea is not feasible because of the numerical weakness of our forces as considered in connection with the distances involved; by the necessity of supplying the two parts of the line from ports within each area; and by the division of the area into two compartments by the rugged mountainous terrain running north and south. Such a line is one of approximately 150 miles. If the entire United States force of seven divisions at my disposal were placed along this defensive line, it would mean that a division would be forced to protect a front of approximately 20 miles against greatly superior numbers of an enemy whose greatest strength is a potential for night infiltration through rugged terrain. Such a line no doubt would have little strength, and as a defensive concept would invite penetration with resultant envelopment and piecemeal destruction. Such a concept against the relatively weaker North Korean forces would have been practicable, but against the full force of the Chinese Army is impossible.

"I do not believe that full comprehension exists of the basic changes which have been wrought by the undisguised entrance of the Chinese Army into the combat. Already Chinese troops to the estimated strength of approximately 26 divisions are in line of battle with an additional minimum of 200,000 to the immediate rear and now in the process of being committed to action. In addition to this, remnants of the North Korean army are being reorganized in the rear, and there stands, of course, behind all this the entire military potential of Communist China.

"The terrain is of a nature to diminish the effectiveness of our air support in channelizing and interrupting the enemy supply system; it serves to aid the enemy in his dispersion tactics. This, together with the present limitation of international boundary, reduces enormously the normal benefit which should accrue to our superior air force. With the enemy concentration inland, the Navy potential is greatly diminished in effectiveness: amphibious maneuver is no longer feasible and the effective use of Naval gunfire support is limited. The potentials, therefore, of our combined strength are greatly reduced and the comparison more and more becomes one of relative combat effectiveness of ground forces. . . .

"This small command actually under present conditions is facing the entire Chinese nation in an undeclared war, and unless some positive and immediate action is taken, hope for success cannot be justified and steady attrition leading to final destruction can reasonably be contemplated. . . ."

This was the situation which MacArthur and his field generals were forced, with virtually no further help, to retrieve. On the same evident theory that it was better to lose the war than to fight alongside Nationalist Chinese, U.N. member governments refused to consent to the use of the fresh, eager troops offered to MacArthur by Chiang. No sizable reinforcements were promised from any other source, either. In a press conference in the White House, President Truman hinted once that he might make atomic weapons available to the U.N. command in this uneven battle, but Britain's Socialist Prime Minister Attlee hurried to Washington and put a stop to that within forty-eight hours.

Yet retrieve this near-disastrous situation in Korea is what MacArthur, his officers, and his troops did. Walker's withdrawal of the Eighth Army was accomplished with such speed that it led to many comments by ignorant correspondents that the troops were running in full flight. That this was the opposite of the truth was shown later when a well-organized Eighth Army turned on the Chinese and slaughtered them in great numbers. Almond's X Corps had to fight in its retreat, and some of its units, particularly the Marines, put up valiant defenses which will add as much to the luster of the Marine Corps as Tripoli, Iwo Jima, and Inchon. Their heroism was typified by Major General Oliver P. Smith's reference to the brilliant withdrawal from the Chosen Reservoir area: "Retreat, hell! We're just attacking in a new direction."

Not only was the X Corps, consisting of 105,000 men, quickly evacuated through the port of Hungnam in an "Inchon landing in reverse," but more than 100,000 cilivian refugees were brought out with the troops; they had co-operated with the X Corps, which they regarded as an army of liberation, and they had now pleaded frantically for evacuation to the south to escape what they regarded as certain death at the hands of the North Koreans and the Chinese Communists. More than 350,000 tons of munitions and supplies were brought out too. Nothing of military value was left to the enemy.

Thus was accomplished one of the most successful military maneuvers in modern history. No American army had ever been compelled to face such odds. No incident in recent wars is remotely comparable to this successful retrograde movement. Probably the most eloquent testimony to its success was the simple statement MacArthur made during the Senate hearings five months later: "The losses that we had in that withdrawal

426

were less than the losses we had in our victorious attack at Inchon."

It had been an unsurpassed co-ordination of ground, sea, and air. On December 25 MacArthur received a message from the President. "I wish to express my personal thanks," it read, "to you, Admiral Joy, General Stratemeyer, General Almond and all your brave men for the effective operation—it is the best Christmas present I've ever had." In less than a month MacArthur had reached up, sprung the Red trap, and escaped it. With his forces regrouped, he was now ready to resume the offensive.

CHAPTER X   Fighting in a Policy Vacuum

⚑ On the wall of MacArthur's office in the Dai Ichi Building hung a framed copy of a translation from Titus Livius' *History of Rome*. The passage quoted an observation by a Roman general of 2,100 years ago. Lucius Æmilius Paulus, the Supreme Commander in the war against the Macedonians, had addressed an assemblage of people from the steps of the Roman Senate in 168 B.C. as follows:

"In every circle and truly at every table, there are people who lead armies into Macedonia; who know where the camp ought to be placed; what posts ought to be occupied by troops; when and through what pass that territory should be entered; where magazines should be formed; how provisions should be conveyed by land and sea; and when it is proper to engage the enemy, when to lie quiet. And they not only determine what is best to be done, but if anything is done in any other manner than what they have pointed out, they arraign the Consul as if he were on trial before them. These are great impediments to those who have the management of affairs. . . .

"I am not one of those who think that commanders ought at no time to receive advice; on the contrary, I should deem that man more proud than wise, who regulated every proceeding by the standard of his own single judgment. What then is my opinion? That commanders should be counselled, chiefly, by persons of known talent; by those who have made the Art of War their particular study, and whose knowledge is gained from experience; by those who are present at the scene of action, who see the country, who see the enemy; who see the advantages that occasions offer, and who, like people embarked in the same ship, are sharers of the danger.

"If, therefore, anyone thinks himself qualified to give advice respecting the war which I am to conduct, which may prove advantageous to the

428

public, let him not refuse his assistance to the State, but let him come with me into Macedonia. He shall be furnished with a ship, a horse, a tent; even his travelling charges shall be defrayed. But if he thinks this too much trouble, and prefers the repose of city life to the trials of war, let him not, on land, assume the office of a pilot. The City, in itself, furnishes abundance of the topics of conversation; let it confine the passion for talking within its own precincts, and rest assured that we shall pay no attention to any councils but such as shall be framed within our camps."

During the period immediately following Red Chinese intervention in Korea, MacArthur found himself contemplating the advice of Lucius Æmilius Paulus more often than at any time before. For now that he and his generals had successfully accomplished their painful and difficult mission of avoiding the Red trap in Korea, MacArthur was forced into an equally exasperating paper battle with Washington.

He was still subject to the basic policies and directives which had covered his operations against the North Korean Army. But the situation was completely changed. The hitherto victorious U.N. forces were thrown into a totally new and different war against the vast military potential of Red China. What MacArthur needed now, as much as more men and arms and supplies, was a clear definition of policy to meet this new situation.

He had long since proposed the tactics and strategy which in his opinion were best suited to the situation, and they had been disapproved. He was prepared to go on searching for other means and methods, in the hope that at some time in the future, before it was too late, one of them might be accepted. But to find these new ways and means he needed first to know what exactly U.N. policy for this new situation was.

From Tokyo at that time it looked to MacArthur, and indeed to all of us on his staff, as if Washington really did not know what course to pursue. Certainly this was indicated in the content as well as the tone of its messages. It was right after the successful evacuation of the X Corps from Hungnam when MacArthur received a particularly chilling dispatch from the Joint Chiefs of Staff.

"It appears from all estimates available," said the J.C.S., "that the Chinese Communists possess the capability of forcing United Nations forces out of Korea if they choose to exercise it. The execution of this capability might be prevented by making the effort so costly to the enemy that they would abandon it, or by committing substantial additional United States forces to that theater, thus seriously jeopardizing other commitments including the safety of Japan. It is not practical to obtain

429

significant additional forces for Korea from other members of the United Nations."

Then came a statement which was later to be echoed by General Bradley's famous crack that the Korean struggle was "the wrong war, at the wrong place, at the wrong time and with the wrong enemy," which was so to confuse the entire issue. "We believe," the J.C.S. message read, "that Korea is not the place to fight a major war. Further, we believe that we should not commit our remaining available ground forces to action against Chinese Communist forces in Korea in face of the increased threat of general war. However, a successful resistance to Chinese–North Korean aggression at some position in Korea and a deflation of the military and political prestige of the Chinese Communists would be of great importance to our national interest, if they could be accomplished without incurring serious losses.

"Your basic directive . . . requires modification in the light of the present situation. You are now directed to defend in successive positions . . . subject to the primary consideration of the continued threat to Japan, [and] to determine in advance our last reasonable opportunity for an orderly evacuation. It seems to us that if you are forced back to position in the vicinity of the Kum River and a line generally eastward therefrom, and if thereafter the Chinese Communists mass large forces against your positions with an evident capability of forcing us out of Korea, it then would be necessary under these conditions to direct you to commence a withdrawal to Japan." The message concluded with a request for MacArthur's views "as to the above outlined conditions which should determine a decision to initiate evacuation," and added ominously: "particularly in the light of your continuing primary mission of defense of Japan, for which only troops of the Eighth Army are available."

MacArthur read the message in utter dismay. It showed clearly the confusion and contradiction in which the Pentagon minds seemed to be weltering. On the one hand, it would be nice if we could accomplish "a successful resistance to Chinese–North Korean aggression at some position in Korea"; but on the other hand, "Korea is not the place to fight a major war." Was it, then, a policy that we would meet Communist aggression in Asia only if we could do it without too much trouble? Surely not; but what else could the Joint Chiefs of Staff mean? One had to be expert at divination to make sense out of much of the correspondence from Washington during this period, but from a long experience of translating such messages, MacArthur was able to perceive at least two main theses:

Fighting in a Policy Vacuum

(1) The administration had completely lost the "will to win" in Korea. President Truman's resolute gesture of defiance which had so thrilled free Asia had gradually been tempered as the threat of Chinese intervention increased, and had now deteriorated almost into defeatism. Washington planning was not directed toward methods of counterattack but rather toward the best way to run; not toward any solution of the problem of reinforcement, even with Nationalist Chinese troops, but toward unrealistically expecting the impossible from the battered, weary men who had gone in to fight one war, had won it, and were now trying to fight a much bigger one. To MacArthur this was an especially appalling attitude; to expect the Eighth Army, currently accomplishing the near-impossible against vastly superior Red Chinese forces, to be responsible for the defense of Japan as well was preposterous.

(2) But the most repugnant aspect of the message was a seeming intention of the Joint Chiefs not only to give up without a hard fight but also to attempt to evade the responsibility for this shameful decision. The implied evacuation of Korea was properly a political decision, not a military one. The thought of defeat in Korea had never been entertained by MacArthur—so long as he would be allowed to use his military might against the enemy's. Indeed, it was his view that, given this authorization, he could not only save Korea but also inflict such a destructive blow upon Red China's capacity to wage aggressive war that it would remove her as a further threat to peace in Asia for generations to come. If, however, the U.N. and the U.S. preferred to multiply this threat by meekly lying down and letting the Juggernaut roll on, it must be a political decision, which would be made in Washington, not Tokyo. Everything in his heart and soul rebelled against such a solution.

I have seen MacArthur in moments of great sorrow and distress; but I cannot recall when I have seen heartache etched so vividly on his countenance and in his every attitude as at this time when the realization of official defeatism in Washington and Lake Success struck him with full impact. It was at this time, too, that he had sustained a great personal loss. General Walton Walker, his old friend "Johnnie" Walker, after surviving five months of extremely dangerous fighting from Pusan to the Yalu, had been killed in a freak jeep accident.

It had been Walker who had held out, with some of the most courageous and brilliant generalship in military history, at the very bottom of Korea until MacArthur could save him by slicing behind the enemy at Inchon. It had been Walker who had almost always greeted MacArthur on his visits to the front with cheerful confidence and rugged determination. Only a few days earlier Walker had predicted that the Eighth Army would by no means be defeated by the Chinese hordes.

He had been killed two days before Christmas. It was a difficult time, during a sustained withdrawal and at the verge of striking the counter-blow, to change commanders. But MacArthur knew whom he wanted for this extremely difficult task, and he had Chief of Staff Collins telephoned in Washington immediately to ask for General Matthew Ridgway. Mac-Arthur had known Ridgway for a long time, and admired his aggressive fighting qualities. Collins at first demurred, but MacArthur was insistent, and that evening received word that Ridgway was leaving for Tokyo at once.[1]

It was with a sense of personal as well as official bereavement that MacArthur sat down late in the evening of December 30 and composed his reply to the J.C.S. message on the evacuation of Korea. This reply is probably MacArthur's most important single comment on the Korean war. It not only defined the situation in the war, but outlined the specific meas-ure he had advocated to turn the tide. It pointed out the policy vacuum in which he found himself and pointed up the danger of remaining in that vacuum too long. It predicted the dangerous future risked by U.N.–U.S. political timidity not alone in Korea but in all of Asia. And such was the accuracy of his forecast that, unlike most day-to-day messages, it reads even better now than it did then. In setting it down in full for its historical importance, I have myself italicized those passages which, had they had the desired effect in Washington, might have averted a situation we find confronting us in Asia today. In fact, their importance as guideposts for U.S. policy has been increased rather than diminished by the passage of events.

"Any estimate of relative capabilities in the Korean campaign," Mac-Arthur wrote, "appears to be dependent upon political-military policies yet to be formulated vis-à-vis Chinese military operations being con-ducted against our forces. It is quite clear now that the entire military resource of the Chinese nation, with logistic support from the Soviet, is committed to a maximum effort against the United Nations command. In implementation of this commitment a major concentration of Chinese force in the Korean-Manchurian area will increasingly leave China vul-nerable in areas whence troops to support Korean operations have been drawn. Meanwhile, under existing restrictions, our naval and air potential are being only partially utilized and the great potential of Chinese Na-

---

[1] MacArthur also asked that General James Van Fleet be kept in readiness and fully briefed should either he or Ridgway be a casualty.

tionalist force on Formosa and guerrilla action on the mainland are being ignored. Indeed, as to the former, we are preventing its employment against the common enemy by our own naval force.

"Should a policy determination be reached by our government or through it by the United Nations to recognize the state of war which has been forced upon us by the Chinese authorities and to take retaliatory measures within our capabilities, we could: (1) blockade the coast of China; (2) destroy through naval gun fire and air bombardment China's industrial capacity to wage war; (3) secure reinforcements from the Nationalist garrison in Formosa to strengthen our position in Korea if we decided to continue the fight for that peninsula; and (4) release existing restrictions upon the Formosan garrison for diversionary action (possibly leading to counter-invasion) against vulnerable areas of the Chinese mainland.

"I believe *that by the foregoing measures we could severely cripple and largely neutralize China's capability to wage aggressive war and thus save Asia from the engulfment otherwise facing it.* I believe furthermore that we could do so with but a small part of our overall military potential committed to the purpose. There is no slightest doubt but that this action would at once release the pressure upon our forces in Korea, whereupon determination could be reached as to whether to maintain the fight in that area or to affect a strategic displacement of our forces with the view to strengthening our defense of the littoral island chain while continuing our naval and air pressure upon China's military potential. I am fully conscious of the fact that this course of action has been rejected in the past for fear of provoking China into a major war effort, but we must now realistically recognize that China's commitment thereto has already been fully and unequivocably made and that nothing we can do would further aggravate the situation as far as China is concerned.

"Whether defending ourselves by way of military retaliation would bring in Soviet military intervention or not is a matter of speculation. I have always felt that a Soviet decision to precipitate a general war would depend solely upon the Soviet's own estimate of relative strengths and capabilities with little regard to other factors. . . . If we are forced to evacuate Korea without taking military measures against China proper as suggested in your message, it would have the most adverse affect upon the people of Asia, not excepting the Japanese, *and a material reinforcement of the forces now in this theater would be mandatory if we are to hold the littoral defense chain against determined assault.*

"*Moreover, it must be borne in mind that evacuation of our forces*

433

from Korea under any circumstances would at once release the bulk of the
Chinese forces now absorbed by that campaign for action elsewhere—
quite probably in areas of far greater importance than Korea itself. . . .

"I understand thoroughly the demand for European security and
fully concur in doing everything possible in that sector, but not to the
point of accepting defeat anywhere else—an acceptance which I am sure
could not fail to insure later defeat in Europe itself. The preparations for
the defense of Europe, however, by the most optimistic estimate are
aimed at a condition of readiness two years hence. The use of forces in
the present emergency in the Far East could not in any way prejudice
this basic concept. To the contrary, it would ensure thoroughly seasoned
forces for later commitment in Europe synchronously with Europe's own
development of military resources."

Suppressing the bitterness that welled within him, MacArthur gave
the cold, professional estimate requested by the Joint Chiefs of Staff. "So
far as your tactical estimate of the situation in Korea is concerned, under
the conditions presently implied, viz: no reinforcements, continued restrictions upon Chinese Nationalist action, no military measures against
China's continental military potential, and the concentration of Chinese
military force solely upon the Korean sector, would seem to be sound. The
tactical plan of a successively contracting defense line south to the Pusan
beachhead is believed the only possible way which the evacuation could
be accomplished. In the execution of this plan it would not be necessary
for you to make an anticipatory decision for evacuation until such time as
we may be forced to that beachhead line."

The answer he received from the Joint Chiefs of Staff not only contained dismal news, but also made a much more obvious attempt to put
the onus for evacuation on his shoulders. The message started by saying
that "the retaliatory measures you suggest have been and continue to be
given careful consideration." But, it went on gloomily, "there is little possibility of policy change or other eventuality justifying the strengthening
of our effort in Korea. Blockade of China coast, if undertaken, must await
either stabilization of our position in Korea or our evacuation from Korea.
However, a naval blockade off the coast of China would require negotiations with the British in view of the extent of British trade with China
through Hong Kong; naval and air attacks on objectives in Communist
China probably can be authorized only if the Chinese Communists attack
United States forces outside of Korea and decision must wait that eventuality. Favorable action cannot be taken on the proposal to obtain Korean reinforcements from the Chinese Nationalists garrison on Formosa,

in view of improbability of their decisive effect on the Korean outcome and their probable greater usefulness elsewhere. . . ."

All one could do was smile sadly at such arguments. It was evidently more important to protect British profits in Hong Kong than to save American—and British—lives in Korea by means of a blockade. Possibly their most glaring inconsistency lay in the suggestion that military retaliation against Red China would be in order only if it attacked our forces *outside* of Korea—the attack within Korea for some strange reason not being deemed sufficient justification. By what mental process could such a distinction possibly be conjured up?

The Joint Chiefs of Staff directed, "in the light of the foregoing and after full consideration of all pertinent factors," that MacArthur "defend in successive positions as required by the Joint Chief of Staff's message . . . inflicting maximum damage to hostile forces in Korea, subject to primary consideration of the safety of your troops and your basic mission of protecting Japan." Then came the booby trap: "Should it become evident in your judgment that evacuation is essential to avoid severe losses of men and matériel, you will at that time withdraw from Korea to Japan."

MacArthur refused so easily to be taken in. He shot a query right back, asking for clarification. "In view of the self-evident fact," he said, "that my command as presently constituted is of insufficient strength to hold a position in Korea and simultaneously protect Japan against external assault, strategic dispositions taken in the present situation must be based upon over-riding political policy establishing the relativity of American interests in the Far East. There is no doubt but that a beachhead line can be held by our existing forces for a limited time in Korea, but this could not be accomplished without losses. Whether such losses were regarded as 'severe' or not would to a certain extent depend upon the connotation one gives the term. . . . The troops are tired from a long and difficult campaign, embittered by the shameful propaganda which has falsely condemned their courage and fighting quality in misunderstood retrograde maneuver, and their morale will become a serious threat to their battle efficiency unless the political basis on which they are asked to trade life for time is quickly delineated, fully understood and so impelling that the hazards of battle are cheerfully accepted.

"The issue really boils down," he went on, "to the question whether or not the United States intends to evacuate Korea, and involves a decision of highest national and international importance, far above the competence of a theater commander guided largely by incidents affecting the tactical situation developing upon a very limited field of action. Nor is it a decision which should be left to the initiative of enemy action, which in effect would be the determining criteria under a reasonable interpretation of your message. My query therefore amounts to this: is it the present objective of United States political policy to maintain a military position in Korea indefinitely, for a limited time, or to minimize losses by the evacuation as soon as it can be accomplished?"

I clearly recall the expression of puzzled exasperation on MacArthur's face when he sent this message to Washington. How on earth could he put the question any more clearly? How could he work his way out of this policy vacuum? Did Washington and the U.N. intend to stay in Korea or get out? If the former, we could stay, but only if we ceased granting the enemy military favoritism. If we wanted to get out, we should get out now and stop wasting lives.

The conclusion that MacArthur had put on his query summoned up the dark memories of Corregidor and Bataan. Under the extraordinary conditions imposed on it, he had reiterated, the military position of the command in Korea was untenable over the long term. But, he said, "it can hold for any length of time, up to its complete destruction, if overriding political considerations so dictate."

Yet even despite this straightforward request for an answer, Washington continued to duck the question. That the query was indeed read in Washington, at some time or other, was indicated only by the use made of it later, when Secretary Marshall employed MacArthur's answers on the machinery of evacuation in an attempt to indicate that MacArthur had himself advocated evacuation, which he had not.

Not only did MacArthur at no time recommend evacuation, but he sought throughout this period to find out whether or not the Joint Chiefs of Staff did or did not. Throughout a series of messages which followed on the details of possible evacuation, however, MacArthur was still unable to get a straightforward answer. A good example of the exchange was the query to MacArthur to designate at what phase line a directive for evacuation should be issued. He at once replied: "There appears to be no reason why your directive should not be issued at any time, unless there is some possibility of policy change or other external eventuality favorable to the strengthening of our effort in Korea." No directive was issued.

Then, suddenly, MacArthur received a clear statement of U.S.-U.N. policy in Korea—or at least the closest approximation to it that he realized he would ever get under the circumstances. Army Chief of Staff Collins and Air Force Chief of Staff Vandenberg had come to Tokyo to discuss the problem. The preliminary meeting had been marked by much hemming and hawing on the subject, and even from the officials in person MacArthur was unable to get his answer. On January 14, just before a full-dress conference between his staff and the visiting Joint Chiefs, a long dispatch arrived from President Truman.

It was a personal message, and it said: "I wish in this telegram to let you have my views as to our basic national and international purposes in continuing the resistance to aggression in Korea. We need your judgment as to the maximum effort which could reasonably be expected from the United Nations forces under your command to support the resistance to aggression which we are trying to rapidly organize on a world-wide basis. This present telegram is not to be taken in any sense as a directive. Its purpose is to give you something of what is in our minds regarding the political factors."

The President then spelled out the situation as he saw it and gave a frank statement of the policy desired. "1. A successful resistance in Korea would serve the following important purposes: (a) To demonstrate that aggression will not be accepted by us or by the United Nations and to provide a rallying point around which the spirits and energies of the free world can be mobilized to meet the worldwide threat which the Soviet Union poses. (b) To deflate dangerously exaggerated political and military prestige of Communist China which now threatens to undermine the resistance of non-Communist Asia and to consolidate the hold of Communism on China itself. (c) To afford more time for and to give direct assistance to the organization of non-Communist resistance in Asia both outside and inside China. (d) To carry out our commitments of honor to the South Koreans and to demonstrate to the world that the friendship of the United States is of inestimable value in time of adversity. (e) To make possible a far more satisfactory peace settlement for Japan and to contribute greatly to the post-treaty security position of Japan in relation to the continent. (f) To lend resolution to many countries not only in Asia but also in Europe and the Middle East, who are now living within the shadow of Communist power, and to let them know that they need not rush to come to terms with Communism on whatever terms they can get, meaning complete submission. (g) To inspire those who might be called upon to fight against great odds if subject to a sudden onslaught by the Soviet Union or by Communist China. (h) To lend urgency to the rapid build-up of the defenses of the Western world. (i) To bring the United Nations through its first great effort in collective security and to produce a free world coalition of incalculable value to the national security inter-

437

ests of the United States. (j) To alert the peoples behind the Iron Curtain that their masters are bent upon wars of aggression, and that this crime will be resisted by the free world.

"Our course of action at this time should be such as to consolidate the great majority of the United Nations. This majority is not merely part of the organization, but is also the nations whom we would desperately need to count on as allies in the event the Soviet Union moves against us. Further, pending the build-up of our national strength, we must act with great prudence insofar as extending the area of hostilities is concerned. Steps which might in themselves be fully justified and which might lend some assistance to the campaign in Korea would not be beneficial if they thereby involved Japan or Western Europe in large scale hostilities.

"We recognize, of course, that continued resistance might not be militarily possible with the limited forces with which you are being called upon to meet large Chinese armies. Further, in the present world situation, your forces must be preserved as an effective instrument, for the defense of Japan and elsewhere. However, some of the important purposes mentioned above might be supported, if you should think it practical and advisable, by continued resistance from offshore islands of Korea, particularly Cheju-Do, if it becomes impractical to hold an important position in Korea itself. In the worst case, it would be important that, if we must withdraw in Korea, it be told to the world that that course was forced upon us by military necessity and that we shall not accept the result politically or militarily until the aggression has been rectified. In reaching a final decision about Korea, I shall have to give constant thought to the main threat from the Soviet Union and to the need for a rapid expansion of our armed forces to meet this great danger.

"The entire nation is grateful for your splendid leadership in the difficult struggle in Korea, and for the superb performance of your forces under the most difficult circumstances."

MacArthur read the message through twice. Here, at last, was an exposition of what he and his men were supposed to be fighting for and the aims they were supposed to achieve. In the national interest and to serve the purposes enumerated, MacArthur was to hold a position in Korea— even if it meant fighting from the off-shore islands around the peninsula. If it were necessary to withdraw temporarily from the mainland, Truman had said, the fighting would go on. Here was none of the vacillation that had characterized the flurry of messages from the other Washington officials in the past two months. Here was the first statement: "*We shall not accept the result [withdrawal from Korea] politically or militarily until the aggression has been rectified."* MacArthur's answer was simply: "We will do our best."

He walked into the next office, where the conference with Collins and Vandenberg was about to start. He carried the message from President Truman with him, and as he took his seat at the table, he opened the proceedings by reading it. As he did, I could see from the expressions of Collins and Vandenberg that they had been taken by surprise. MacArthur finished, tossed the message on the table, and stabbed at it with his finger as he said: "That, gentlemen, finally settles the question of whether or not we evacuate Korea. There will be no evacuation."

Collins spoke up to argue that MacArthur had misinterpreted the President's message. But MacArthur held to his understanding of it, despite fervent protests by Collins. Then Vandenberg, who had listened silently to the exchange, spoke up. He agreed, he said, with MacArthur.

Thus the policy vacuum was partially filled. MacArthur still faced a desperate and seemingly impossible situation, with limitations on his freedom of action which constituted what he later termed "fantastic favoritism" for the enemy, with few if any reinforcements from the U.S. or other U.N. countries and a denial of his request to use the Nationalist Chinese troops. But one thing he did now have: a mission. He set out to accomplish it.

CHAPTER XI   The Press of a Free Nation

✍ "I have always been able to take care of the enemy in my front—but I have never been able to protect myself from sniping in the rear."

This remark by MacArthur, made in the winter of 1951, neatly summarized a particularly difficult problem he was having at a time when he could least afford to have it. For during the most critical days, when Red Chinese armies were swooping down upon our exhausted troops with full force, MacArthur was subjected to the most violent barrage of criticism from the many fringe elements of the press that it has been his misfortune to experience during his entire career. At the very time when these correspondents and their editors at home could be contributing most to their country's struggle by supporting it, they seemed to be taking out their personal frustration upon the one man who was doing the most to avert the disaster they so feared and predicted.

If the Korean war was different in kind from any which the United States had fought in the past, its press coverage was curiously different too. MacArthur learned this most clearly in the matter of censorship. He had many reasons for the decision he took at the outset of the Korean war to forbid press censorship. Some of his reasons stemmed from past campaigns, when he had seen such controls applied with rigidity but never with any degree of success. They invariably resulted in distortion and sometimes in plain falsehoods. As for Korea, it would be even more difficult to censor news from the battlefront unless censorship were also applied to all of Japan, since that country was the hub from which Korean news disseminated throughout the world. And Japan was the home base for many war correspondents in Korea, who could by-pass military censors with ease if they did not wish voluntarily to abide by the word and the spirit of the regulations.

The Pentagon officers looked aghast at this revolutionary decision; but beyond mildly questioning its wisdom they did not intrude upon what was regarded as the domain of the field commander's responsibility. Mac-Arthur established at army and corps headquarters and set up in Japan the mechanics for advising correspondents on the application of voluntary censorship; he left the rest to the judgment and patriotism of the correspondents and their editors and publishers.

Then came the curious result. Strong opposition to this kind of freedom of the press was raised by the press itself. Some of the same men who had criticized MacArthur during World War II for the necessary censorship he had had to impose under orders from Washington now seemed to have no difficulty in arguing that they preferred censorship. They even went so far as to imply that by not imposing censorship MacArthur was responsible for any breaches of security which they themselves would make.

MacArthur, on the contrary, was pleased with the manner in which most correspondents were accepting individual responsibility for self-censorship. There had been some wild and hysterical distortion, but this was very much the exception to the general rule, and it was almost entirely traceable to those few who would always warp the truth in order to secure sensational headlines or who would unerringly follow a propaganda line; military censorship would worsen rather than better this situation. It had had some adverse effect upon public and troop morale, but even in its worst excesses it had not compromised military security—mainly because most of the distortion, innuendo, and propaganda came from sources at home rather than at the front.

MacArthur explained the situation clearly in his November 1 report to the United Nations Security Council. "Despite heavy pressure to the contrary," he wrote, "no military censorship has been instituted by the United Nations Command throughout the Korean campaign. Reliance for security against the premature publication of information helpful to the enemy has instead rested upon voluntary censorship by editors and correspondents. This policy has resulted in the most complete and prompt public dissemination of information on the course of operations of any military campaign in history, without as far as is known a single security breach of a nature to assist the enemy. This may be said to the great and lasting credit of the press of the free world and its responsible publishers, editors and correspondents. In evaluating the issue between compulsory and voluntary censorship, one must understand that the sole purpose of either is to safeguard against the premature publication of information on plans and operations which would assist the enemy to develop countermeasures. No form of censorship can prevent espionage, nor can it properly be employed to control undue emphasis given to the outcroppings of emotional strain which must, as in the present campaign, find its correction in the balance achieved through maturity gained with battle experience. Nor is it the proper instrument for the avoidance of factual error. Correspondents assigned to cover military operations are the selected representatives of responsible publishers and editors, and their ability to assume the responsibility of self censorship has been amply and conclusively demonstrated in the course of the Korean campaign. In the many military campaigns in which I have engaged, most of which were covered by a rigid form of news censorship, I have never seen the desired balance between public information and military security so well achieved and preserved as during the Korean campaign."

After the Chinese Communists had entered the war, however, the correspondents and their editors worried more and more about one of their number inadvertently breaching security. And the issue reached a crisis when the British news agency Reuter's carried a dispatch that contained an implication of the projected evacuation from Hungnam. The editors of the American wire services, already in a great state of excitement, were thereby triggered into demanding full details of the operation from their correspondents. Most of these queries came in the form of "rocket" (i.e., reprimanding) messages. The fact that a British news agency was the offender only served further to aggravate the editors and publishers of the American press.

Seeing the intense pressure under which the correspondents were forced to operate in this circumstance, MacArthur called a conference to see what he could do to help. The meeting, which was held in the office of MacArthur's chief of staff, was attended by representatives from Reuter's, the Associated Press, the United Press, and the International News Service. The burden of the meeting was reported to the Defense Department by MacArthur's Public Information Office on December 15.

"Security and methods of preserving same were discussed fully," the report read. "Agencies except INS stated that home offices believed voluntary censorship could and would work. All agencies admitted breaches of confidence and security followed the same pattern; that is, fringe statement was made by one service. This was then broadened either stateside or locally. A rocket to another agency states story broken. This latter agency then broke all security and confidence. This is what happened with Associated Press breaking innocuous writer's statement from here. At conference all agencies stated they were on the spot by rockets from their home office demanding full story, regardless security, based on fact another agency broke it. They admit home pressure is severe. They further state that client papers pressurize their home wire offices. AP representative says, 'I suggest that the only way you can get to first base is by having some responsible men in Washington call in the heads of the big agencies and papers and talk to them. . . . There is a vast range of ignorance among the men who would be perfectly willing to cooperate, but they do not know they are not cooperating. Washington has failed in that leadership, that background.'

"INS representative says, 'One of the main bones of contention between our bureau here and our home office is the continued question we have received time and time again, "Can't you do something to make sure that security regulations which you observe and which apply to us are also observed by all the rest?"' It is believed cooperation with the press can and will work at this level; however, as in any organization, it is necessary that orders and instructions come from the top. It it believed essential that this matter be taken up at Defense Department level with the ANPA level, and by that we mean not only the publishers but the managing editors who are the working level and their counterparts in radio and the wire services. It is believed that if they are security conscious and realize that they have as much at stake in this critical period of our history as the fighting men at the front, they would cease rockets which demand security breaches. It is recommended that high level conference be called soonest on the subject. Local bureau chiefs believe most of the demands made on them are because of a failure by their home offices to appreciate gravity of security breaches."

Such a conference was held on December 18, in the office of Secretary of Defense Marshall. Representatives of the editors, publishers, and broadcasters of the country were present.[1] And the result of the meeting was expressed in the following message which MacArthur received: "Fully conscious of importance of maximum protection armed forces, but feel security of information from the combat area is the responsibility of the military. That responsibility cannot be passed to any other agency or group within the combat zone or without. If the military feels some further action is necessary to maintain maximum security, that action should be consistent with a minimum interference with flow of news to

---

[1] Edwin S. Friendly and Cranston Williams of the American Newspaper Publishers Association; Ben McKelway and Jack Lockhart of the American Society of Newspaper Editors; Robert McLean, president, and Frank Starzel, general manager, of the Associated Press; Lyle C. Wilson, Washington manager of the United Press; Barry Faris, editor-in-chief, and William K. Hutchinson, Washington Bureau chief, International News Service; Justin Miller, president, and Ralph W. Hardy and Robert K. Richards of the National Association of Broadcasters.

all media free to inform the democratic nations. The military likewise has the reponsibility to provide the maximum information consistent with security, and to give adequate guidance and facilities for news gathering and handling in discharging this responsibility."

MacArthur read this message with astonishment. It did not even attempt to answer the problem expressed in the message of his public information officer in requesting the conference. In a personal note to a friend later, he commented: "This was so irresponsive to the query I wished to place before the group that I have wondered whether my message was ever shown them." The dispatch from the Pentagon not only was a complete repudiation of the freedom of the press in war, which MacArthur had assumed to be a principle worth the tireless efforts he had devoted to defending it, but it was a repudiation also of every argument which had been advanced against military censorship throughout World War II.

Under the circumstances, MacArthur felt that he was left with no recourse other than to institute censorship again. He established it, however, at the army level alone, thus obviating the necessity of enforcing it within Japan. But, as he added in the aforementioned note, "I believe that in due course my view will prevail, and if it does the freedom of the press will be fortified by new strength—a strength based upon its acceptance of the moral responsibility to work with rather than be controlled by the military in the dissemination of war news. The power of censorship is difficult to curtail once it is enforced. Many nations of the world now under rigid censorship in peace attest to this fact. My view is that the press should explore and carefully consider the sharing of responsibility before it agrees that its power of free expression be suppressed by the rigidity of military censorship."

By now MacArthur probably should not have been as surprised as he was when the establishment of censorship immediately brought cries from the press that he was unduly stringent and arbitrary and was suppressing news to which the reading public was entitled. Since hosts of censors were needed to implement such a massive program as is entailed in military censorship, errors of judgment unquestionably were many times made, but by and large the program worked amazingly well. Still this did not protect MacArthur from being attacked by the press for not saving what the press itself had refused to defend.

It was when the attack against him spread from the irresponsible to the responsible segments of the press that he was most disappointed. Then he felt that he had no alternative but to set the record straight.

444

"I have just seen the United Press report of your editorial concerning military censorship of Korean war news," he wrote to *Editor and Publisher,* January 17, 1951, "and am amazed at the degree to which you seem to be misinformed. The censorship rule enjoined upon the correspondents reporting on ground operations in Korea by the commanding general, Eighth Army, are lifted almost bodily out of those set forth in the Basic Field Manual Regulations for Correspondents accompanying United States Army Forces in the Field, dated 21 January 1942, and which governed the exercise of military censorship throughout the past war and which presumably were drawn up with the advice and acquiescence of the press itself.

"I am informed that studies made by the local correspondents' association have failed to detect any substantial variance whatsoever and that the rules are accepted by the predominant majority as reasonable, if censorship at all is to be enforced. In your editorial as reported here, you failed to particularize upon those requirements you characterize as 'the most stringent censorship ever clamped over United States news corre spondents.' But you do mention specifically in this connection the ban upon articles that will 'injure the morale of our forces or our Allies' or 'that embarrass the United States, its Allies or neutral countries.' These restrictions are verbatim from Article 134 of the referenced field manual, and are established to guide the commander in the field in the exercise of his censorship responsibility. They are not novel to this war or this theater, but were rigidly applied throughout the past war."

Editor and Publisher printed MacArthur's message and replied shamefacedly: "We'll plead guilty to not knowing that most of the general's censorship regulations were taken from the manual prepared in 1942. But we're not embarrassed, because we were not alone. There were a lot of other people who did not know it either." That was the end of that objection.

As the war went on, and especially as the U.N. forces had to withdraw temporarily before the numerical superiority of the Red Chinese, it became more and more apparent that the real danger of the press in Korea was not from the exposure of military secrets but from another direction entirely. During this period in the winter of 1950–1, MacArthur found himself bitterly arraigned and harassed by some segments of the press in England, France, and the United States, aided by a few sensation-seekers among the war correspondents at the front who seemed more intent upon finding a whipping boy than in aiding the defenses against the big onslaught.

445

In cleverly worded propaganda articles, attributed to anonymous sources but calculated to create the impression of the highest official authenticity, they attempted not only to blame MacArthur personally for Red China's entry into the war, but also to disparage the courage and fighting qualities of his men. MacArthur watched with growing concern as these irresponsible writers indulged in a field day of vilification and distortion.

The particular correspondents involved were not numerous but exceedingly voluble. At first MacArthur naturally expected that at least their offensive slanders against U.S. fighting men would be answered by Washington. But when only silence reigned on the Potomac, the fantastically exaggerated "news dispatches" from the front increased in stridency as well as falsity. What concerned MacArthur most about all this was the danger of its alienating public opinion and confidence in the troops in Korea, and he continued to be dismayed when no attempt was made in Washington to answer loose charges which the officials of the Pentagon knew were lies.

Meanwhile MacArthur himself was beginning to receive direct inquiries from responsible leaders of the American press. Ordinarily he would not have taken all the time necessary to go into this problem; but Washington's mysterious silence left him no alternative. Every fresh smear lowered the morale of his troops that much more, to the extent, in fact, that GI's were circulating protest petitions. The entire course of the Korean war threatened to be misrepresented to such an extent that the American people as well as our Allies would be left in a welter of confusion. So MacArthur decided that, despite the heavy duties of this crucial time in the war, he must answer some of the most vicious attacks upon his troops.

Arthur Krock of the *New York Times* had just wired him to inquire about a news item appearing in his paper under the by-line of James Reston. "Answering criticisms of military action beyond the 38th Parallel or Pyongyang," Krock's query read, "some officials here saying for non-attribution but for publication that every time such stoppoint was suggested, you replied you would not accept responsibility for security of your troops if decision was made; that this faced authorities with the dilemma of taking risks replacing you with elections coming on or letting you proceed against their political and diplomatic judgment and against some high military judgments also."

MacArthur's reply to Krock effectively destroyed that particularly poisonous rumor. "There is no validity whatsoever to the anonymous gossip to which you refer," he wrote. "Every strategic and tactical movement made by the United Nations Command has been in complete accord with United Nations resolutions and in compliance with the directives under which I operate, every major step having been previously reported and fully approved. I have received no suggestion from authoritative source that in the execution of its mission the command should stop at the 38th Parallel or Pyongyang, or at any other line short of the international boundary. To have done so would have required revision of the resolutions of the United Nations and the directives received in implementation thereof. It is historically inaccurate to attribute any degree of responsibility for the onslaught of the Chinese Armies to the strategic course of the campaign itself. The decision of the Chinese Communist leaders to wage war against the United Nations could only have been a basic one, long premeditated and carried into execution as a direct result of defeat of their satellite North Korean armies."

This rumor, which had been so naïvely repeated by the *Times'* Reston, is a perfect case in point to illustrate the sniping to which MacArthur was subject from always unidentified officials in the U.S. State Department. Their tactics then—and evidently still—were to feed to selected representatives of the press a propaganda line that bore the mark of Washington officialdom while at the same time hiding behind the shield of anonymity. How far they would deviate from the truth is indicated particularly in this instance, as can be seen from the following message which had been sent from Secretary Acheson to MacArthur's diplomatic adviser, William Sebald, on December 7, 1950.

"View advanced in number of other countries," Acheson's message read, "both Asia and Europe, according to reports reaching Department, that Chinese Communists onslaught Korea was merely responsive to imagined threat presented by United Nations offensive. This theory doubtless advanced in part as result natural human tendency when faced by unpalatable reality and hard decision to find formula reducing situation to more comfortable dimensions and relieving one's self of need facing hard facts. As such, theory possibly impossible extirpate from credulous minds. Nevertheless, Department considers it important when you encounter such explanation you make clear it is wholly at variance with the facts. It is unanimous considered judgment Joint Chiefs of Staff, supported by information from field commanders, the present Chinese offensive planned and staged over considerable period of time and that what happened is that two offensives collided.

"Obviously it is fantastic to suppose that offensive involving half million men could have been prepared impromptu. Owing fact considerable displacement Chinese Communist units began a year ago, involving movement north of Lin Piao's Fourth Field Army, it is impossible to say when concentration for purpose of assault on Korea began, but reports reaching us May and June (prior to North Korean attack upon South Korea) from travelers arriving Hong Kong revealed railway traffic both north and south Hangkow clogged with troop trains moving north. Appearance on Korean front of Chinese Communist troops of Korean ancestry, as individuals and units, began during initial Korean assault and long before return to 38th Parallel, indicating Peiping would in any case feel free to assert itself in Korea regardless military situation.

"Department now in receipt of unpublished report by neutral Asian journalist in Communist China written before offensive, which discloses that Communist China had by third week in November completed preparations for mass advance against United Nations forces in Korea designed to drive them back the length of the Peninsula regardless of the risk of general war and had secured pledge of Soviet assistance in event reverse suffered. Report contains eye-witness account of feverish movement of troops in readiness for invasion as early as second week in October and of preparations for air raid defense in major north China cities recalling Jap days. This report paralleled from many other sources."

What makes this a perfect example of the deviousness of the anti-MacArthur coterie in the State Department is the timing as well as the complete falsity of their rumor-mongering. As can be seen from the foregoing message, the Secretary of State, the Joint Chiefs of Staff, and MacArthur were in fundamental accord. Yet at the same time that Secretary Acheson was making the official conclusion of the Department known to its representatives throughout the world, his aides within the Department were leaking information to Reston and other favored correspondents in an attempt to mislead the public into believing an untrue explanation of the reasons for Red China's intervention in the Korean war.

No doubt it was the same clique which saw to it that none of the information on which Acheson based his conclusions ever reached MacArthur's headquarters. It is of further interest, incidentally, that some of this information, in particular the reports on large troop movements north, was available and presumably considered before the decision to go to war in Korea. The risk of Red Chinese intervention, therefore, must have been knowingly accepted at the time.

During those hectic weeks MacArthur had to take the time also to answer other defamations made against him by irresponsible correspondents at the front, aided and abetted by other such unpatriotic elements at home. So he replied, in much the same vein in which he had to Arthur Krock, to David Lawrence, publisher of *U.S. News and World Report;* to Hugh Baillie, president of the United Press; to Ward Price of the London *Daily Mail* and its associated papers; to the Tokyo Press Corps; and to Barry Faris, managing editor of the International News Service. So many slanders had been spread abroad by now that MacArthur had a whole new list of them to answer in his message to Mr. Faris.

"The entire effort," he said, "to distort and misrepresent the causes leading to the existing situation in Korea represents one of the most scandalous propaganda efforts to pervert the truth in recent times. . . . It is clearly apparent from the record that the United Nations command at no time has deviated from the policies and directives given it. This has been publicly confirmed within the past few days not only by President Truman and Foreign Minister Bevin but from many other authoritative sources. Any impression that as United Nations Commander I am more than an agent to implement policies determined upon a much higher level is perfectly fantastic. . . .

"The statement that agreement was made at Wake Island to a British proposal that the United Nations forces stop forty miles south of the international boundary is a pure fabrication. There was no mention made of such a proposal at Wake Island. As a matter of fact, when the Wake conference took place our troops were barely across the 38th Parallel, and no proscription whatsoever upon their movement was ever enjoined upon the command, other than that it should not violate the international border. Apart from this, it would be naïve indeed to believe that such an imaginary line would have influenced in the slightest degree the Chinese Communists in their monumental decision.

"The suggestion that I have ever personally deprecated the fighting qualities of the Chinese troops finds no substantiation in truth. Quite the contrary is the case. Nor does the statement that the Eighth Army and X Corps were uncoordinated rest upon any higher credibility. Their activities were coordinated in most complete detail by general headquarters, as is customary in the conduct of widely separated operations such as those involved. They were operating in different geographic compartments, one supplied from the east coast of Korea and the other from the west coast. Their coordinated power with reference to the enemy has always been completely cooperative and in mutual support. The use or non-use of the atom bomb is not a question which falls within the scope of my authority unless expressly delegated by the President."

PART III: KOREA

It seemed, however, that beyond tacitly supporting these untruths about the Korean campaign with silence, some elements in the administration were prepared to go even further. After MacArthur's attempt in his message to Mr. Faris to set the record straight, he received on December 4 a copy of a Presidential directive addressed to all overseas commanders. "In view of the present international situation," it read, "and until further notification, no speech, press release, or other public statement concerning foreign policy or military policy will be released without clearance from the Department of the Army. Overseas army commanders will exercise extreme caution in public statements, will clear all but routine statements with the Department of the Army and will refrain from direct communication on foreign or military policy with newspapers, magazines or other publicity media in the United States. Purpose of above not intended to curtail flow of information to the American people but to assure that information released is in accord with the policies of the United States Government."

MacArthur had little trouble guessing that this directive, supposedly sent to all theaters, was aimed squarely at him; and in fact Marshall later admitted it. Thus Washington refused not only to defend American fighting men in Korea against calumny, but refused to let MacArthur defend them either. So much did some bureaucrats in the Pentagon and State Department wish to discredit MacArthur that they seemed to care little if in the process they destroyed public confidence in the entire war effort as well. MacArthur nevertheless accepted this dictum and was meticulously guided by it. As he said later at the Senate hearings, "No more subordinate soldier has ever worn the American uniform."

The first test of this directive occurred on December 8, 1950, when MacArthur transmitted to the Department of the Army a message that Major General Charles A. Willoughby, chief of MacArthur's intelligence service, wished to send to the New York *Herald Tribune* in reply to an editorial of that paper which had sharply criticized the intelligence service of the United Nations command. The message was entirely temperate in tone and objective in content, and its sole purpose was to correct the errors in fact on which the *Herald Tribune* editorial seemed to be based.

It explained what the *Tribune* should have known long since—that is, that the war against North Korea had been won and that the campaign which had won it was not intended to defeat the Chinese Communists as well. It explained, as I have in a previous chapter, that because of the lack of any intelligence information in Washington and because of the restrictions placed upon air reconnaissance in Korea, the only method of

450

determining the intentions of the Chinese Communists was through the November 24 attack. "There was only one way to find out, and it is a soldier's way under the offensive mission of the United Nations Forces, and that was to attack," Willoughby wrote. The attack did indeed spring the Red trap, he pointed out, long before the Red Chinese intended it to be sprung, and probably thereby saved the Eighth Army from destruction.

Willoughby added that his intelligence had certainly not been unaware of troop movements in China and Manchuria. "The transfer of Lin Piao's Fourth Field Army, aggregating 500,000 men alone, from South China, from Hainan and off-shore Formosan areas, was trailed from one railroad terminal to the next. Its arrival in Manchuria and successive deployment along the Yalu River was also known. The only 'estimate,' if that vague term could be applied, was speculation in Tokyo as well as in London and Washington (and presumably in the editorial chambers of the *Herald Tribune*) on if and when the Chinese would intervene. . . . One can hardly blame the United Nations Field Command for the Chinese coming en masse at their own time and place. That monumental decision was beyond the local military intelligence surveillance; it lay behind the Iron Curtain and in the secret councils of Peiping."

Willoughby concluded by saying: "These facts are sent to you in the public interest, and it is hoped that you would publish them. It is time for distinguished newspapers such as yours to appeal to calmness and reason, avoiding hysterical accusations or deductions. In this as always you can render a valuable public service."

MacArthur felt that Willoughby's statement was an objective clarification of the situation and that releasing and publishing it was distinctly in the public interest. What was his astonishment, then, when he received the following cryptic reply from Washington: "Your objections to editorial criticizing intelligence service is understandable. However, because of difficult and delicate discussion now in progress, it is felt that we should avoid entering any controversies in the press. The editorial represents the writer's opinion. Your proposed refutation could be quoted out of context to the detriment of your own intentions. Therefore it is necessary to disapprove your statement." Someone in Washington evidently was determined that the true facts about the Korean war would not be known—unless it could be that the Pentagon's fear of the Chinese Communists had extended to fear even of the New York *Herald Tribune.*

It was puzzling, to put it mildly, to receive at the same time that this statement was disapproved a request from the same Department of the

Army that MacArthur set the record straight in connection with a report to be published in the *Christian Science Monitor*. "Following CBS broadcast of last night for your information," the message from the Department of the Army read: "Boston exclusive special. In tomorrow's morning edition of the *Christian Science Monitor*, there will be the sensational story of the darkest pages in American history. The *Monitor* will say that while sources in this country are merely hinting at disaster in Korea, sources in the field are experiencing some of it already. . . . The *Monitor* will also reveal that one United Nations division left all its artillery and supplies in the field; that only about half of that division reached Seoul, where it was examined and declared unfit for combat. From another source, I learned that the Chinese soldiers are so short of ammunition that they had to stop to search the bodies found on the battlefield. The *Monitor* story tomorrow will give you a picture of the mechanized army fleeing in jeeps and trucks from an overwhelming horde of poorly equipped Chinese who were following on mules, ponies and camels. . . ."

This story, fantastic almost to the point of being humorous, had finally jolted the Washington officials out of their self-imposed inertia. MacArthur was urgently importuned to make a statement "extolling heroic stand made by the principal covering force for withdrawal of Eighth Army." The message to MacArthur went on to say: "Story in *Christian Science Monitor*, though not yet seen, will break confidence in eyes of the public in troops and give columnists chance for field day unless statement to press from your headquarters is issued soonest possible time."

What the subtle distinction was between the New York *Herald Tribune* and the *Christian Science Monitor*—why one should be answered and the other should not—MacArthur could not tell. Nor did he waste any time trying to fathom the puzzle of why within twenty-four hours Washington had both relegated him to silence and urged him to talk. Instead he reviewed the situation and submitted to the Pentagon for clearance a proposed communiqué that he hoped would restore the proper perspective to the over-all course of events in Korea and reassure the American people.

Almost as if to compound the confusion, Washington promptly disapproved the communiqué it had asked him for. It did not, said the Department of the Army, conform with "the intent of the President."

The *Christian Science Monitor* was thereby permitted to publish unchallenged one of the most ridiculous accounts of the Korean war. It is interesting to note that Gordon Walker, the *Monitor's* only correspondent in Korea at the time this fantastic story was printed (though not under his byline), was later selected by the *Monitor* to review Major General Charles A. Willoughby's book, *MacArthur, 1941–1951*. In his review Walker blandly stated: "One cannot but wonder at his flat statement that Washington turned down MacArthur's request for Chinese Nationalist reinforcements in Korea, after the General himself testified before Congress in 1951 that the addition of such divisions to his command would have been 'like an albatross around our necks.'"

There is no more truth in this statement than there is in the picture that the *Monitor* had previously painted of mechanized U.S. troops fleeing before Chinese mounted on camels. It is instead a revealing example of quoting out of context to achieve the exact opposite of the truth. In the Senate hearings in 1951, MacArthur was asked by one of the Senators whether it had been his opinion at the outset of the Korean war that the Chinese Nationalist troops would have been "like an albatross around our necks." MacArthur had, in answer to that question—as the *Monitor* must have known—clearly explained that at the beginning of the Korean war, when both the Nationalist and the South Korean troops were poorly trained and ill-equipped, when Red China was not directly involved in the Korean war and the commitment of elements from the Formosan garrison might conceivably have provoked such involvement, this had been the case. But as soon as the South Koreans had been integrated into the U.N. command and the Nationalist soldiers had been better trained, and as soon as the Red Chinese had in fact entered the Korean war against us, exactly the opposite was the case. Thus the *Monitor* must answer guilty either to the charge of deliberate distortion or to that of atrociously inaccurate reporting.

Attacked by the press on paper almost as fiercely as he was by the North Korean and Chinese Communists in the field, supported not at all by the officials in Washington and in fact betrayed by some of them, MacArthur found that there was little he could do to prevent the maliciously false account which was spread abroad by some of the less respectable elements of the American and European press.

Then suddenly MacArthur received an unexpected assist—unexpected in the sense that it was a Washington leak in reverse of the usual order. For this time there was leaked to the press the truth concerning events in Korea—truth that broke the Pentagon's silence and openly challenged the distortions and falsehoods which were rapidly undermining public confidence in American arms.

In an article appearing in the January 26, 1951, issue of *U.S.*

News and World Report, Mr. David Lawrence had skillfully developed the facts under the heading: "What Really Happened in Korea." By the question-and-answer method he had elicited from an unnamed source on "the army's top level staff in Washington" the facts concerning military developments following Red China's entry into the Korean war, which fully confirmed MacArthur's statements and demolished the lies that had been fabricated concerning those events.

MacArthur was grateful for this development. He saw in it a vitally needed public service on the part of both the editor and his informant. He would have liked the source to have been named for the added authenticity it would have lent to his clarifying statement but he knew he could not ask or expect more. If the leadership of the Pentagon were committed to a policy of silence in the face of the public abuse the Army was receiving from the press, he was glad indeed that one of the Pentagon officers had risen to such a degree of patriotic resentment as to cause him to break through that silence to defend the courage and integrity of the American soldiers committed in Korea and the quality of the generalship which had directed those operations.

When in February the United Nations forces confounded the calamity howlers by turning northward and resuming the offensive, the scapegoat-hunters of the press could not very well continue their attacks against MacArthur's troops. So they now concentrated their fire upon him personally. Their new tactic was to spread the following propaganda line: MacArthur had personally invited the Chinese Communists into the Korean war by his "arbitrary" crossing of the 38th Parallel; MacArthur's authority in command of the Korean operation had been sharply curtailed; the Joint Chiefs of Staff had in effect assumed field command, operating through Ridgway and by-passing MacArthur in the chain of command; MacArthur was therefore on the verge of retiring or resigning.

As any study of the press at the time will show, this was more than a mere rumor started by a few correspondents. It was a carefully outlined campaign of propaganda, and it was supported by some anonymous sources within the Pentagon itself. So loudly was the refrain repeated that the campaign assumed major proportions and became embarrassing even to the administration. MacArthur held his silence. But on February 16 the President finally put an end to the insinuations and "dope stories" by denying them flatly at his press conference. MacArthur's crossing of the 38th Parallel, Truman stated categorically, was based on a strategic decision fully concurred in by Washington.

This Presidential statement was supplemented by one from the Pentagon. Joint Chiefs Chairman Bradley announced that: "General Mac-

Arthur is in full command in Korea. He has absolute control of the Korean war operations, and Washington has taken over none of the direction. It would be impossible," Bradley added, "to run a war from a distance of 7,000 miles. The general in command of the theater must be responsible and have freedom of action. He is on the spot and knows the situation better than anyone back here could know it." And Bradley's clarification was complemented by another from the White House. "General Mac-Arthur," a spokesman said, "has the President's complete confidence. He has done a great job in the Far East. It is expected that he will remain in command until peace has been restored in Korea and a Japanese peace treaty has been signed."

Even as this is being written, certain elements of the American press, whose violent opposition to MacArthur over the years has seemed almost pathological, react bitterly against any charge or implication that the interests and security of the United States have been or are being compromised by spies and saboteurs. For instance, on the matter of the assumption that prior to its decision to enter the war for Korea Red China had been assured there would be conventional retaliation against its supply lines and bases of attack north of the Yalu (Chapter VII), the *Washington Post* at once set up an editorial straw-man and proceeded to demolish it. The assumption, the *Post* editorially lamented, "amounts virtually to a charge of treason at responsible military and civilian leaders in Washington." Of course nothing of the sort was said in the reference which the *Post* quoted upon which to rest its point, nor could it be rationally implied therefrom.

There can be no doubt in any reasonable mind that Red China was informed that if it entered the war it need not fear the conventional counterstroke by our forces. MacArthur thought they had the benefit of such prior knowledge, as evidenced by the statement in his letter to Senator Byrd of April 19, 1953: ". . . By one process or another it was conjectured by, or conveyed to, the Red Chinese that even though they entered the fray in large force it would be under the sanctuary of being relieved from any destructive action of our military forces within their own area."

General Van Fleet thought so, as he testified before the Senate Interior Security Subcommittee on September 29, 1954: ". . . he [the enemy] would not have entered Korea if he did not feel safe from attack in North China and Manchuria. . . . My own conviction is there must have been information to the enemy that we would not attack his home bases."

General Almond thought so, as he testified before the Senate Internal Subcommittee on November 23, 1954: ". . . The things as they

455

happened looked very strange insofar as the assurance upon which the enemy appeared to operate. I think it would have been a very hazardous thing for the Chinese to enter North Korea in the abundant numbers in which they did if they had thought their bases of rice or ammunition or any other base would be subject to attack."

But the *Washington Post* editorially proposes not to think so.

It is not to say that there may not have been those treasonably inclined within the ranks of our own government (as experience suggests the contrary), to point to the international character of our military operations and the broad field this provided for treasonable activity. Beyond this one need go no further in search for the source than recent revelations, which the *Washington Post* may not lightly shrug off, that as far as at least one of our allies, Britain, is concerned, the arch traitors Burgess and MacLean undoubtedly kept Red China fully informed on the secret plans and policies of the allies in the conduct of the Korean war.

For it is established that both were in the service and pay of the Soviet at the time and each could have had ready access to the secret files bearing upon the war. Burgess, after an assignment to the Far Eastern section of the British foreign office all during the Chinese debacle leading to the recognition of Red China by the British government, went from there to the post of second secretary to the British Embassy in Washington, where he remained until a few days after MacArthur's relief from command in the Far East. MacLean was the head of the American section of the British foreign office during that same period of time. If they did not report to their Kremlin masters fully upon our secrets in the conduct of the war against the Communists in Korea, what then could have been their treasonable purpose? It must be presumed that they did so.

Furthermore, any assumption that our security was vulnerable to compromise rests upon other evidence than Red China's decision to commit major force to battle on the peninsula. On several occasions General Walker complained bitterly to MacArthur that his operational plans, which were always telegraphed to Washington under the highest secrecy classification, were being leaked to the enemy, thereby giving the latter a constant awareness of his battlefield strategy. The exact source of such leaks mattered only insofar as knowledge of it would provide the basis for their being plugged. For the tragic consequences were the same, regardless of source. MacArthur understood. He had long been helplessly aware that even his top-secret dispatches to Washington came under the scrutiny of unauthorized persons. He protested, but to no avail.

The Press of a Free Nation

Finally on December 30, 1950, at possibly the most crucial phase of the war against Red China in Korea, one of MacArthur's top-secret dispatches to Washington giving intelligence on the order of battle was in part published verbatim in the same *Washington Post*, under the byline of a prominent columnist. MacArthur vigorously expressed his concern in a message to Washington on January 6. "The leakage of highly classified messages dispatched to the department from this headquarters and subsequently published in the press either textually or in substance gives me increasing concern," his message read. ". . . An intolerable situation is created under which an irresponsible columnist . . . achieves access to the secret dispatches of this command dealing with military operations against the enemy. His very acquisition and possession of such secret dispatches is unquestionably a criminal act for which he should be vigorously prosecuted by the government in the public interest." Then MacArthur pleaded that "measures be taken to ensure that future security measures are adequate to safeguard the secret dispatches of this headquarters from public disclosure." Washington apparently did nothing.

Access to these secret dispatches may have come from traitors within our own ranks or the ranks of others allied with us. In the absence of concrete information to the contrary, however, they can be presumed to have come from Britain's Burgess and MacLean, known to have had the capability, the motive, and the will to engage in such treasonable activities. The editorial lament of the *Washington Post* is therefore not only unsupported by fact or logic, but it discloses a most arbitrary determination to remain blind to reality.

MacArthur has always believed that there are certain fundamental decencies, whether written or not, which the press must always regard as one of the responsibilities that go with freedom of the press. They were not always observed in Korea.

Because of his position over so many years, MacArthur has long since become accustomed to the abuse that seems always to go with fame. It would not occur to him in such terms, but this is one of the penalties of greatness. In the face of most such attacks he is silent, making exceptions only where a record of history may be distorted.

But at least he is able to do that. In Tokyo, in 1950 and in 1951, he was not. Then he could only wonder at the curious antics in Washington. It was almost as if the highest officials there were conspiring against him. It would not be long now before MacArthur would discover that, in fact, they were.

CHAPTER XII   Valedictory to the Battlefield

◢ The rolling might of the Red Chinese enemy seemed almost irresistible in those painful days as 1950 turned into 1951. By the hundreds of thousands they continued to pour down out of their privileged sanctuary and up against the thinly manned U.N. defense lines. The U.N. forces had completed their withdrawal now and had turned to fight again. But even though the enemy was slaughtered by the thousands, they still came on.

So MacArthur read with mixed emotions the statement made by General Ridgway after his arrival at the front and his inspection of his new command. The Eighth Army, Ridgway said, would hold its current line north of the city of Seoul, at roughly the 38th Parallel, and would repulse any enemy attempt to dislodge it. These were brave words from a brave general—MacArthur's kind of general, as Walker had been, a general who was not afraid of the enemy and stood there defiantly and said so. But MacArthur's satisfaction was tempered by the realization that there might still be further withdrawals necessary before the counter-offensive could begin.

There unfortunately were. Ridgway had misjudged his ability to hold. On New Year's Day the enemy had launched a general offensive in tremendous force, successfully making penetrations of up to twelve miles. In conjunction with an enveloping drive in the west, it forced the Eighth Army into another withdrawal. By January 4 the enemy had reoccupied Seoul, and by January 7 the Eighth Army had retired to new positions roughly seventy miles south of the 38th Parallel. Until then, incidentally, there had been many wishful predictions made in Washington and at Lake Success to the effect that the Chinese Communists would voluntarily halt their advance at the 38th Parallel. That rosy bubble was now burst.

For two weeks a desperate and uneven struggle had gone on, while the Red Chinese threw everything they had into an effort to drive the U.N. forces out of Korea, and the press of the United States and most of Europe cried hysterically that the U.N. armies "are going to be pushed into the sea!"—a dire prediction that was solemnly repeated on the floor of Congress.

Meanwhile Ridgway was fighting as magnificently as Walker had, and the Eighth Army line was holding. But the seriousness of the situation, and the tendency of the Eighth Army still to adhere to the concept of evacuation, can be gathered from the following exchange between the command post and headquarters:

RIDGWAY TO MACARTHUR: ". . . During any evacuation, which may be ordered, concentration of troops, shipping, installations, and civilian personnel in Pusan area, would present particularly inviting target for atomic attack. . . . I suggest for your consideration that Central Intelligence Agency be requested to initiate without delay a strong effort to ascertain Soviet capabilities and probable intentions with respect to this form of attack upon us, either openly with its own forces, or by employing Chinese Communists."

MACARTHUR TO RIDGWAY: "When all factors are fully considered, it does not seem likely that use of the munition you mention would be initiated by the Soviet on a tactical target."

Two days later MacArthur and Ridgway were conferring together in Korea. MacArthur had flown over to stop any further talk of evacuation and personally give him the go-ahead for the counteroffensive. At the same time, in an attempt to calm some of the jitters caused by exaggeratedly pessimistic predictions in the press and in an attempt also to reorient public thinking, MacArthur took the occasion to make a statement to the correspondents who assembled at Army headquarters. "There has been a lot of loose talk," he said, "about the Chinese driving us into the sea, just as in the early days there was a lot of nonsense about the North Koreans driving us into the sea. No one is going to drive us into the sea. This command intends to maintain a military position in Korea just as long as the statesmen of the United Nations decide we should do so. . . . Considering that the entire military might of Communist China is available against this relatively small command, only by maneuver may it avoid the hazards inherent in the great odds which it now faces. In this it is performing in a highly satisfactory manner."

Shortly thereafter, Ridgway's first probing patrols started north in battalion strength. The Eighth Army was on the way back.

The patrols met light to moderate enemy resistance, and the rest of the Eighth Army followed on their heels. MacArthur's strategic plan was to push steadily forward until he reached the line where a balance was achieved in the relativity of supply. As the Eighth Army moved forward, he ordered Ridgway: "Keep advancing . . . until contact with the main line of resistance is established."

By February 3 Ridgway had reached Haengsong, with the next stop the Han River, just short of Seoul. And at that point he wired MacArthur that, because of the terrain in the eastern area, which "is exceedingly rugged, and in part well wooded and deficient in roads," and because "there is no good defensible position north of the Han," he was not planning to make any all-out effort to capture Seoul and its environs.

This posed MacArthur with a dilemma. He placed far greater stress on the factor of supply than Ridgway apparently did. In this barren, rugged land the campaign was largely one of supply, and our predominant air superiority, by constantly bombing the enemy's supply lines, was adding enormously to his natural difficulties in sustaining his front line. The Seoul area was a vital supply hub which must be seized for our own purposes and denied the enemy for his; that was the main reason why MacArthur had planned his Inchon landing. In addition there was always the distinct psychological advantage inherent in possession of the ancient capital city. Therefore, he had no intention of holding the Eighth Army south of the Han River. Yet he understood fully that Ridgway's caution was natural because of the heavy blow the army had sustained when he had sought to hold the Seoul area before. For those reasons, as well as his confidence in and affection for Ridgway, MacArthur worded his reply very carefully.

"I am in complete accord with your general plan," he wrote. "I interpret your objective to be such an advance with concomitant pressure by your own forces as will develop the enemy's main line of resistance and enable you to use your superior fire power with the greatest degrees of effectiveness. The Han River would seem to be merely incidental in the accomplishment of your purpose, and need not be a definite objective one way or the other, i.e., if you develop enemy main line of resistance south of the river you would not attempt to push further. If, on the other hand, you reach the river without serious resistance, you would continue your probing further northward until you develop his line or the fact that he does not have such a line. As far as Seoul is concerned, the reoccupation of Kimpo Airfield and the Harbor would unquestionably be of marked value, and if they present an easy prey, they should be taken. Their use by us would greatly relieve the supply difficulties and increase the power of your air support. The occupation of Seoul itself would, of course, present certain diplomatic and psychological advantages which would be valuable, but its military usefulness is practically negligible.

"Your performance of the last two weeks in concept and in execution has been splendid and worthy of the highest traditions of a great captain. My best to you always. Before long I hope to drop in on you for a personal chat."

Here was one of the marks of leadership; MacArthur thus got his conflicting views across to Ridgway without doing violence to sensibilities which had been suffering acutely in the difficult campaign. Ridgway accepted MacArthur's viewpoint without question and proceeded diligently to pursue it.

By February 11, MacArthur was able to report to Washington: "Until I develop the enemy's main line of resistance, or the fact that there is no such line south of the 38th Parallel, it is my purpose to continue ground advances. . . . It is evident that the enemy has lost his chance for achieving a decisive military decision in Korea. . . ." But beyond that, just as in June of 1950, MacArthur had already been laying his long-range plans for turning from defense to offense in a dazzling series of strokes just as he had at Inchon.

As at Inchon, he would go for their supply lines. First, by constant and ubiquitous thrusts at widely scattered points but only for limited objectives, he would gradually regain the Seoul line for a base of future operations. Then he would clear the enemy rear, all across the top of North Korea, by massive air attacks. And then he would employ an ingenious weapon: if he could not attack the massed enemy reinforcements across the Yalu, and if he could not even destroy the bridges over which they came, he would keep them back by making the south bank of the Yalu impassable. He would sow across all the major lines of enemy supply and communication a defensive field of radioactive wastes, the by-products of atomic manufacture. Then, reinforced by Chiang Kai-shek's Formosan troops if he was permitted them, with simultaneous amphibious and airborne landings at the upper end of both coasts of North Korea, he would close the gigantic trap. It would be Inchon all over again, except on a far larger scale.

The first phase of this strategy was working well. By March 14, Ridgway's men were nearing the 38th Parallel. But then the old question came back to plague MacArthur. In capitals of U.N. countries and even in Washington as well, the debate started again over whether or not the U.N. forces should cross the 38th Parallel. To MacArthur the situation was virtually the same as when he had been driving the North Koreans back in this area; militarily the 38th Parallel was meaningless. The question actually was a larger one, and one that could be answered only by policy decisions in Washington and at Lake Success. If the strategy just outlined accomplished its purpose, as the Inchon strategy had done, what then? Would the U.N. political leaders fail to capitalize on the military victory? Or would the Chinese Communists simply retire into their sanctuary across the Yalu, regroup, and flood back again against the U.N. troops, as soon as they had found a path through the radioactive barrier? Could Korea become, by Communist design and U.N. blindness, a bloody open drain into which the best of American manhood was to be poured, perhaps for many years?

MacArthur believed even more deeply than before that Red Chinese aggression in Asia could not be stopped by killing Chinese, no matter how many, in Korea, so long as her power to make war remained inviolate. And he was gratified to learn that in Washington the Joint Chiefs of Staff had finally overcome their illusion that fighting back against China would bring on global war, enough so that they had recommended to the Secretary of Defense a strategy that paralleled in many respects what MacArthur had urged long before.

On January 12 they had proposed that the following measures among others be taken against China:

"Prepare now to impose naval blockade of China and place into effect as soon as our position in Korea is stabilized, or when we have evacuated Korea. Remove now restrictions on air reconnaissance on China's coastal areas and of Manchuria. Remove now the restrictions on operations of Chinese Nationalist forces and give such logistic support to those forces as will contribute to effective operations against the Communists. . . ."[1]

MacArthur's pleasure at having some of his recommendations endorsed by the Joint Chiefs, even this late, was enhanced by the knowledge that General Ridgway, after seeing the situation at first hand, had im-

---

[1] At the Senate hearings later Secretary Marshall attempted to argue that this was not a support of MacArthur's argument for the reason that the Joint Chiefs recommended that these measures be taken only if it were necessary to evacuate Korea. This claim is disproved by the wording of the recommendation: ". . . As soon as our position in Korea is stabilized, or when we have evacuated Korea . . ." But the most interesting thing about Marshall's claim is the fallacy of the argument itself—that these measures would have a different effect upon the Communist leaders of China depending upon whether we happened to be in or out of Korea at the time. Such fallacies appeared to dominate Washington thinking from the time when the Chinese Reds struck.

mediately written a strong personal note to Collins, as one old friend to another, urging him to allow Chinese Nationalist troops to reinforce the tired men of the Eighth Army. But again nothing was done. The Joint Chiefs' recommendation was turned down. And so had been Ridgway's personal request for Nationalist reinforcements.

MacArthur did not realize at this state that, so far as he personally was concerned, the entire problem was shortly to become academic. The tragedy was moving inexorably into its final act.

At the time they seemed like a series of wholly unconnected incidents. But the relationship of each to the other was important and unrevealed, right up to the final scene. The first incident occurred on March 20, when MacArthur wrote a letter to Congressman Joe Martin, minority leader of the House of Representatives. His letter was in reply to a query Martin had sent him.

"In the current discussions of foreign policy," Martin had written, "and overall strategy, many of us have been distressed that, although the European aspects have been heavily emphasized, we have been without the views of yourself as Commander-in-Chief of the Far Eastern Command. I think it is imperative to the security of our nation and for the safety of the world that policies of the United States embrace the broadest possible strategy, and that in our earnest desire to protect Europe, we do not weaken our position in Asia. Enclosed is a copy of an address I delivered in Brooklyn, New York, on February 12, stressing this vital point and suggesting that the forces of Generalissimo Chiang Kai-shek on Formosa might be employed in the opening of a second Asiatic front to relieve the pressure on our forces in Korea. . . . I would deem it a great help if I could have your views on this point, either on a confidential basis or otherwise. Your admirers are legion, and the respect you command is enormous. May success be yours in the gigantic undertaking which you direct."

MacArthur carefully read the note and the accompanying speech. He saw that it recognized the point he had been stressing for years—the tendency in shaping national policy for the administration to focus nearly all of its attention on Europe, with only minor concern for Asia, the inability to realize that Asia would in time become the nerve center of civilization's progress and that disaster in Asia portends disaster in Europe. He replied to Congressman Martin at once. He had always felt it a duty frankly to reply to every Congressional inquiry into matters connected with his official responsibility. This had been a prescribed and routine practice when he had been Chief of Staff of the Army from 1930 to 1935 under Republican President Hoover and Democratic President Roosevelt; and it still is the practice, since in no other way could the nation's lawmakers intelligently cope with the nation's problems.

"My views and recommendations," MacArthur wrote, "with respect to the situation created by Red China's entry into war against us in Korea have been submitted to Washington in most complete detail. Generally these views are well known and clearly understood, as they follow the conventional pattern of meeting force with counterforce, as we have never failed to do in the past. Your view with respect to the utilization of the Chinese forces on Formosa is in conflict with neither logic nor this tradition. It seems strangely difficult for some to realize that here in Asia is where the Communist conspirators have elected to make their play for global conquest, and that we have joined the issue thus raised on the battlefield; that we here fight Europe's war with arms while the diplomats there still fight it with words; that if we lose the war to Communism in Asia, the fall of Europe is inevitable, win it and Europe most probably will avoid war and yet preserve freedom. As you pointed out, we must win. There is no substitute for victory."

MacArthur signed the letter, dispatched it, and promptly forgot all about the interchange—little realizing the important part it would play in the drama to follow.

The next incident occurred on the following day, when MacArthur received a message from the Joint Chiefs of Staff. It read: "Presidential announcement planned by State shortly that, with the clearing bulk of South Korean aggressors, United Nations now preparing to discuss conditions of settlement in Korea. Strong U.N. feeling persists that further diplomatic efforts towards settlement should be made before any advance with major forces north of the 38th Parallel. Time will be required to determine diplomatic reaction and permit new negotiations that may develop. Recognizing that parallel has no military significance, State has asked Joint Chiefs of Staff what authority you should have to permit sufficient freedom of action for next few weeks to provide security U.N. forces and maintain contact with the enemy. Your recommendations desired."

What exactly MacArthur was supposed to recommend he could not tell. His opinion as to methods for bringing the war to a close were certainly well known in Washington by now, and he did not propose to take part in any discussion of methods for weaseling on the original U.S. pledge to restore Korea to the proper authorities. There was one thing he did want to reiterate to Washington, though: that there were more than

464

enough restriction placed upon his freedom of action already, without adding more.

So he replied to Washington with an urgent request that "no further military restrictions be imposed upon the United Nations command in Korea." But in view of the obvious Washington sensitivity to the problem of crossing the 38th Parallel, he did instruct Ridgway not to cross the line in force without previous aurthority from him. "If press forces you to discuss question," he said, "evade direct reply by saying matter is for my decision." MacArthur did not want any sensation-seeking correspondents at the front to upset the delicate negotiations that were evidently going on among the U.N. representatives.

Ridgway replied that he would follow these instructions carefully, and outlined in brief his plan for immediate future operations. To this MacArthur responded giving his approval, and adding: "Will see you at Seoul Airfield Saturday."

Little did MacArthur realize that this trip to Korea would prove his last opportunity to see his U.S. troops on the Korean front in action. But when that day dawned, as if guided by an unseen hand, he followed the unusual procedure of releasing a statement prior to his departure, reviewing the military problem of Korea. Although he did not then know it, it was to be his valedictory—a valedictory addressed to his troops, to the enemy, and to the world, a large part of which he represented as United Nations Commander.

To the free world the MacArthur who made this statement on March 24 was a heroic figure who in the Korean war alone had been given a nearly impossible military situation and had retrieved it not once but twice. To the enemy he was a figure of implacable opposition who had managed to destroy their best-laid plans ever since the first Communist emerged from hiding in Japan immediately after World War II; and now he had, against fantastic odds and with equally fantastic handicaps, shattered the military prestige of Asian Communism on the battlefield. That MacArthur was also about to become a towering figure of tragedy no one but a few plotting bureaucrats could at that time know.

Yet MacArthur's statement made an excellent valedictory, even though he had no idea that it was to serve this purpose. It summed up both the events of the Korean war and the lessons from it; while tracing the course of the immediate past, it charted a clear course for the future.

"Operations continue according to schedule and plan," he said. "We have now substantially cleared South Korea of organized Communist forces. It is becoming increasingly evident that the heavy destruction along the enemy's lines of supply, caused by our round-the-clock massive air and naval bombardment, has left his troops in the forward battle area deficient in requirements to sustain his operations. This weakness is being brilliantly exploited by our ground forces. The enemy's human wave tactics have definitely failed him, as our own forces have become seasoned to this type of warfare; his tactics of infiltration are but contributing to his piecemeal losses, and he is showing less stamina than our own troops under the rigors of climate, terrain and battle.

"Of even greater significance than our tactical successes has been the clear revelation that this new enemy, Red China, of such exaggerated and vaunted military power, lacks the industrial capacity to provide adequately many critical items essential to the conduct of modern war. He lacks the manufacturing base and those raw materials needed to produce, maintain and operate even moderate air and naval power, and he cannot provide the essentials for successful ground operations, such as tanks, heavy artillery and the refinement science has introduced into the conduct of military campaigns. Formerly, his great numerical potential might well have filled this gap, but with the development of existing methods of mass destruction, numbers alone do not offset the vulnerability inherent in such deficiencies. Control of the sea and the air, which in turn means control over the supplies, communications and transportation, are no less essential and decisive now than in the past. When this control exists, as in our own case, and is coupled with an inferiority of ground fire power as in the enemy's case, the resultant disparity is such that it cannot be overcome by bravery, however fanatical, or the most gross indifference to human loss.

"These military weaknesses have been clearly and definitely revealed since Red China entered upon its undeclared war in Korea. Even under the inhibitions which now restrict the activity of the United Nations forces and the corresponding military advantages which accrue to Red China, it has shown its complete inability to accomplish by force of arms the conquest of Korea. The enemy, therefore, must by now be painfully aware that a decision of the United Nations to depart from its tolerant effort to contain the war to the area of Korea, through the expansion of our military operations to his coastal areas and interior bases, would doom Red China to the risk of imminent military collapse. These basic facts being established, there should be no insuperable difficulty in arriving at decisions on the Korean problem if the issues are resolved on their own merits, without being burdened by extraneous matters not directly related to Korea, such as Formosa or China's seat in the United Nations. The Korean nation and

466

people, which have been so cruelly ravaged, must not be sacrificed. That is the paramount concern. Apart from the military area of the problem where issues are resolved in the course of combat, the fundamental questions continue to be political in nature and must find their answer in the diplomatic sphere."

MacArthur added one more offer to the enemy field commander to talk military terms for possible surrender. "Within the area of my authority as the military commander, however," he said, "it should be needless to say that I stand ready at any time to confer in the field with the commander in chief of the enemy forces in the earnest effort to find any military means whereby realization of the political objectives of the United Nations in Korea, to which no nation may justly take exception, might be accomplished without further bloodshed."

So it was that MacArthur attempted to strike at the morale of the enemy. All unknowing, he also struck consternation into the ranks of a group of diplomats in Washington. Among those who had been intent upon appeasing Red China, this defiance of the enemy, in the finest tradition of American history, was apparently the wrong thing to do. In the tirade of criticism which was raised against MacArthur's statement, the section that was seized upon was his offer to the enemy field commander to talk military terms. The argument was made that he had disrupted some magic formula for peace on which the United States had already secured international agreement and which it was about to announce. MacArthur has since asked and waited in vain for any record or other proof to indicate that any such plan for restoring peace to Korea had been drafted, and the complete lack of evidence can only mean that this claim was a fabrication.

Actually, far from MacArthur's ken, a sinister element in the last act of the tragedy had been taking place. It seems reasonable to assume that in some parts of the U.N. and the U.S. State Department, and in some very high places elsewhere in Washington, men were scheming to change the status of Formosa and the Nationalists' seat in the United Nations. That this plot was definitely afoot, and that it had reached the top echelons of the administration, is suggested by what happened to a Joint Chiefs of Staff policy statement on this subject when it got into the office of Secretary of Defense Marshall.

The statement read: ". . . The present military situation in Korea may be conducive to a satisfactory resolution of the immediate overall problem by political action. Specifically, it may be possible to take political action to end the aggression, to conclude the fighting and insure against its resumption. Such a resolution of the situation, however, must provide for a termination of hostilities in Korea only under circumstances which would make possible the ultimate attainment of our objective without forfeiture of, or prejudice to, our general position with respect to the U.S.S.R. and with specific respect to Formosa and to seating the Chinese Communists in the United Nations."

This recommendation, which reflected MacArthur's argument, drew an extremely interesting comment. In a letter dated March 31 to the Secretary of State, less than two weeks before MacArthur's recall, the Secretary of Defense wrote: "I am in general agreement with the terms, conditions and arrangements enumerated in the Joint Chiefs' memorandum. However, I believe that the questions of Formosa and Chinese Communist membership in the United Nations, as well as other general, political and security factors referred to, would be fitting topics in the consideration of the basic terms of settlement of the Korean situation, and might be taken up in discussions between our two departments on the overall question of Korea." Marshall, incidentally, later testified at the Senate hearing that he did not mean to approve of this appeasement of the Chinese Reds; he just wanted to make sure that the idea was given proper consideration—a piece of sophistry reminiscent of the double-talk that went on during the attempt to force Chinese Communists into Chiang Kai-shek's Cabinet. The men who had "let the dust settle" in China were now letting the blood settle in Korea.

What had happened was that by sheer accident, in his statement and in its reference to settling the war without reference to Formosa or the United Nations seat, MacArthur had cut right across one of the most disgraceful plots in American history. Or was it not accident, but intuition? This I do know: had MacArthur fully realized the hornets' nest he would stir up, he still would not have been deterred.

And then came a final development. Without realizing the unfortunate timing, Congressman Martin released the full text of MacArthur's note to him on the subject of fighting Red China to win. In the atmosphere in which many of the U.N. diplomats, more particularly the British, had been operating, no doubt the phrase that galled them most was: "There is no substitute for victory." It was the British particularly who raised the most strident cry for MacArthur's scalp, both in their press and through their diplomatic representatives who seemed to have so much influence in Washington. They sized up the political implications involved in this action and fully exploited it by strong representations to the United States against the position MacArthur had taken as "calculated to spread the war"—an old argument which had been used to brush off every suggestion, following Red China's commitment to war against us, that we fight to win.

The curtain was set to rise on the final act of the tragedy.

CHAPTER XIII   "Jeannie, we're going home at last."

◆ Wednesday, April 11, 1951, dawned in New Japan with the breath of early spring in the air. And as the sun rose, as it had since time immemorial, upon this land of the chrysanthemum with its deep shadows and brilliant hues, with its majestic peaks and low-lying valleys, its winding streams and inland seas, its cities and towns and rolling plateaus, all with their natural beauty enhanced by man-made lacquer-red bridges and temple-studded horizons, the people went about their appointed tasks with customary calm and industry. From the low-backed farmers tilling the soil to the begrimed workers building industry and commerce; from the shopkeepers and tradesmen to the vast army of clerical assistants; from the children romping on the city streets and country roads to their mothers on their daily rounds of the market places and shops, the same expressions of serenity and confidence lighted every countenance. For were not the prying eyes and ears of the secret police gone; and had not those hated agents of the landlords ceased to exact their toll of sweat and toil; and was not every youth relieved from the command of the militarists that he prepare bravely to die for the Emperor; and was not the small shopkeeper now relieved from the levy of tribute by those who monopolized all business; and had not the women assumed a place of independence and dignity within the body politic; and had not the workers, freed from the shackles of exploitation and slavery, now assumed the dignity of voice in their own conditions of employment; and did not every citizen now have the right to worship as he chose, to work where he pleased, to speak freely his mind, and to be governed only as the majority so willed; and above all else was not "Macassa Gensui" there to fortify their faith that if they worked hard, practiced thrift, and clung to their liberties, all would be well for New Japan?

MacArthur arrived at his office at the usual time and, as was his practice, called for overnight reports on Korean operations. The war was then proceeding at a satisfactory pace. Our forces had retaken the city of Seoul and had driven the enemy back to the 38th Parallel. As he studied these reports, he instructed an aide to make the necessary arrangements to permit him to fly to Chorwon the coming Saturday. Chorwon was still in enemy hands, but MacArthur was confident in his own estimate that this important town would again be ours before his arrival. Then he settled down to the routine of his administrative tasks, leaving early for a luncheon engagement at the Embassy.

Suddenly this atmosphere of calm and serenity and progress was rent as though by a thunderclap. The radios all over Japan brought upon the land a hushed silence as a special bulletin from Washington broke through all programs to announce: "The President has just removed General Mac-Arthur from his Far Eastern and Korean commands and from direction of the occupation of Japan."

And in the U.S. Embassy, the inevitable tragedy reached its climax. There the MacArthurs had two luncheon guests, Senator Warren Magnuson of Washington and William Sterns of Northwest Airlines. The meal was proceeding quietly and the conversation was still devoted to the amenities, when from her end of the table Mrs. MacArthur looked over the General's shoulder and through the door to see the anguished face of a MacArthur aide-de-camp, Colonel Sidney Huff. She excused herself quietly, rose from the table, and left the room. There were tears in Huff's eyes when she came up to him. He told her quickly and simply the news that he had just heard on the radio. MacArthur was abruptly and brutally removed from command, with no other reason given than a doubt that he would be able to "support the policies of the administration."

The General was laughing heartily at a remark made by one of his guests when she walked into the room behind him and touched his shoulder. He turned and she bent down and told him the news in a voice so low that it was not heard across the table.

Here was the payment of a great nation for a longer and more distinguished military service than that of any other man in American history. Here was the reward for victory in three wars. The inexorable tragedy was finished.

MacArthur's face froze. Not a flicker of emotion crossed it. For a moment, while his luncheon guests puzzled on what was happening, he was stonily silent. Then he looked up at his wife, who still stood with her hand on his shoulder. In a gentle voice, audible to all present, he said:

"Jeannie, we're going home at last."

Within a short time the meal was concluded. It was not rushed; but

471

with the sense of tragedy which pervaded the scene, none present had further stomach for food or light conversation. MacArthur, however, maintained a mask of calm throughout.

When the guests had departed, he called me on his bedroom phone. "Court, have you heard the news?" came from the other end of the line as I picked up the receiver. The voice sounded almost as though he were referring to the outcome of an important football game. "Yes, General," I replied. "I will be right over." On my way to the Embassy I tried desperately to think of what I should say—what I could say—to comfort this man in the moment of anguish I knew too well had descended upon him. But try as I might, I could not produce the right words for the moment. When I arrived, I resolved the dilemma by merely taking his hand in mine and saying what came from my heart: "I am sure, General, it will turn out all for the best."

To my amazement, MacArthur wanted only to discuss the problems that would confront *me* after his departure. But I cut him short. Almost incredulously I asked: "Why, General, you don't think for one minute that you are going to leave here without me, do you? I accompanied you into Japan and I shall certainly accompany you out."

MacArthur gently replied: "But, Court, I am sure that Washington would not approve orders for you to accompany me." I had a ready answer for that one. "General," I said, "I have served on active duty sufficient years to fulfill the statutory requirement to retirement, subject only to the approval of the Defense Department, and I am sure that when I submit my request for retirement this evening, it will encounter no opposition in Washington." It did not.

Thus the one man in those many millions who retained his outward calm and composure was the victim himself of this infamous purge. None could fail to see that this was, indeed, MacArthur's finest hour, the hour of mental crucifixion and martyrdom. Yet, behind his soldier's mask of unruffled calm, there must have passed with the speed of light the memory of the past fifty years—happy years among his people and bitter, lonely ones in their service abroad, years filled with their triumphs and their reverses, glorious and devoted years he had so unstintingly given to his country and the service of mankind. And he must have pondered why he had thus become the first captain in all history to be so shamefully treated, and by the hand of the leader of those for whom he was even then fighting in a forlorn hope against desperate odds resulting from our self-imposed military disadvantages.

But true to his military training, MacArthur lost no time in ungainful reflection. There was work to be done. The cables soon confirmed the radio broadcast by the official cryptic orders from the President: ". . . you will turn over your commands effective at once. . . ." Having read that, MacArthur automatically ceased to be Supreme Commander in Japan, ceased to be Commander-in-Chief of the United Nations Forces in Korea, ceased to be in command of our land, sea, and air forces everywhere else in the Far East. His removal from these responsibilities had been brought about without so much as affording him the opportunity to bid farewell to his troops. Nor could he transfer his duties to his successor, normal procedure even in the relief of a corporal from his duty assignment. The President had specifically made his relief from command "effective at once."

No one has questioned the right of Mr. Truman, as President, to remove MacArthur, although millions have questioned his judgment. But the form his action took established a new and incredible low in military precedent and procedure. To a soldier of MacArthur's service, distinction, and professional attainment, it was punitive to the fullest extreme and no evidence has since appeared to even suggest that it was not so intended. So diametrically opposed to MacArthur's own philosophy even in the treatment of an enemy, it outraged the sensibilities of the Japanese and other Orientals, just as it did those of the American people. Quite apart from the method of implementing his decision, moreover, Mr. Truman, by one irresponsible and reckless blow, destroyed a strong and vital link between those ancient myths and legends of the East and the enlightened realism of the West when he removed MacArthur, then standing as a mighty symbol to bulwark the forces of freedom against the furthur advances of Communism in Asia. By so doing, he destroyed as well much of the faith in our ways and institutions which MacArthur had done so much to build in Asian hearts and minds and left a bewilderment in Japan scarcely surpassed by that in the wake of war's crushing defeat.

The Communist leaders, their sycophants, and fellow travelers, of course, exulted. Ever since the removal of MacArthur from a position of influence in Asia, Communism has progressively strengthened and become an increasingly powerful threat to freedom and peace. He had been the one they most feared, and the one they most hated—and yet the one they most respected.

In Japan public reaction to MacArthur's summary removal was charged with historic significance. As he went to his offices for the last time to withdraw his personal papers on the evening of that fateful day of his removal, thousands of Japanese were silently waiting, despite the rain, for his arrival. The upturned faces all had the same somber, distressed look and one could see the grief and resentment which dominated their bewilderment. That was his last visit to his headquarters of nearly six years, his last opportunity to withdraw personal papers and take a farewell look upon the scene of such tireless effort and vital decisions. He did so as an officer without military assignment—with no longer the rights and dignity of command.

During the ensuing days before his departure, the question was asked time and time again by the Japanese people: "Why does the greatest nation on earth thus treat its most distinguished son?" And throughout the length and breadth of the land, Japanese hearts welled up in gratitude and tribute to this man who had done so much to lead Japan from the brink of destruction.

Echoing the popular refrain, the two leading Japanese newspapers, with a combined circulation of more than eight million, editorially lamented: "The removal is a great disappointment to the Japanese, especially when the peace settlement is so near. Japan's recovery must be attributed solely to his guidance. We feel as if we had lost a kind and loving father . . ." (*Asahi Shimbun*) and "MacArthur's dismissal is the greatest shock since the end of the war. He dealt with the Japanese people not as a conqueror but a great reformer. He was a noble 'political missionary.' What he gave us was not material aid and democratic reform alone—but a new way of life, the freedom and dignity of the individual. . . . We shall continue to love and trust him as one who best understood Japan's position. . . . We wanted your further help in nurturing our green democracy to fruition. We wanted your leadership at least until a signed peace treaty had given us a sendoff into the world community . . ." (*Mainichi Shimbun*).

In the Imperial Palace the question was solemnly debated between the Emperor on the one hand, and old retainers still steeped in the tradition of feudalism on the other: should the Emperor call upon MacArthur before his departure? The Emperor strongly wished to do so, but his retainers argued that MacArthur was now a private foreign citizen without official position or authority in Japan, and that it was below the Emperor's station to make such a call. The Emperor, however, was obdurate in the face of these arguments. Finally, sensing defeat, the retainers offered to compromise their views if MacArthur would return the Emperor's call, and sent a feeler to his aide to ascertain whether he would do so. When the situation was brought to MacArthur's attention, he quietly said: "Send word to the Emperor that it is wholly unnecessary for him to call upon me prior to my departure, and that in any event, the pressure upon me at this time is too great to permit me to return his call."

Upon receipt of this message, the Emperor made his final decision. He instructed that MacArthur be asked to receive him on Sunday, the day prior to his scheduled departure. The Emperor arrived at the appointed hour, and as he took MacArthur's hand in both of his, tears streamed unchecked down his cheeks. The ensuring private meeting between these two men was the most poignant of all the farewells MacArthur had to say in Japan.

On the morning of MacArthur's departure the Japanese people fully reflected their gratitude for all of the blessings which had come from his benign leadership and guidance. Before sunrise that same populace which six years before in fear born of desperation had concealed itself before the arrival of this hated and much-feared conqueror from the West, a million strong, bearing Japanese and American flags, now lined the streets from his Embassy home to the Haneda Airport to give him a silent tribute and tearful farewell as a benevolent and beloved leader.

The following day the House of Representatives of the National Diet passed a resolution of tribute and thanks of the nation; it was sponsored by the three major political parties, the leaders of which, with the Prime Minister for the government, in an unprecedented alliance, eloquently extolled MacArthur's inestimable service to the Japanese people in their hour of greatest agony and emphasized the void left in the wake of his departure. This tribute by the conquered to the conqueror established for the guidance of historians the contemporary judgment of the Japanese people and their leaders upon MacArthur's role in the history of Japan. The new frontier of freedom MacArthur had forged in this beautiful land of the chrysanthemum was now to come under the spiritual stewardship of the Japanese people. MacArthur had gone, but they would go forward firmly and proudly erect in the light he had left.

The citizens of Kanagawa Prefecture, embracing the great port city of Yokohama, some three months before had already put into words that which was latent in many Japanese hearts. On the base of a bronze bust which Japan's leading sculptor had been commissioned to create, they had foretold the verdict of history—

"GENERAL DOUGLAS MACARTHUR—LIBERATOR OF JAPAN"

Part IV

AMERICA

"In war, there is no substitute for victory!"
City of Washington—April 19, 1951

CHAPTER I   Homeward Bound

⚓ "Court, please arrange the trip so that we will arrive in San Francisco and New York after dark to enable us to slip into a hotel without being noticed." I looked with astonishment at MacArthur as he gave me these instructions, and suddenly for the first time realized the humiliation that seared his soul as a result of the foul and shocking blow by which his long and devoted service to the nation had been so abruptly terminated. So deep was this humiliation that it deprived him of a true understanding of public reaction at home. For he had only a general idea of the thousands of supporting cables which had accumulated from world-wide sources. He had read none of the press accounts of the popular indignation aroused by the President's curt order. He knew nothing of the great pressure on the telephone circuits from people trying to get through to Tokyo to register their personal resentments and extend expressions of sympathy and understanding. His time in the four-day interval had been consumed in the multitudinous personal details of preparing for his departure.

Then my mind went back to the content and implication of the President's message and dwelt upon that phrase: ". . . you are authorized to have issued such orders as are necessary to complete desired travel to such place as you may select. . . ." This was the treatment accorded to the one great World War leader who had not taken time off from duty to return home to receive a hero's welcome and the nation's tribute for his World War victories, to the "principal architect" of the Pacific victory as Stimson had so aptly described him, to a soldier after fifty years of devoted service, half on foreign soil, to the recipient of all the nation's highest honors. No other American soldier had ever received such a list, and none had served abroad so long. I have never seen the order committing Napoleon to exile, but I dare say that it exuded greater warmth and was couched in terms reflecting higher honor than that which authorized MacArthur to

479

spend the public funds necessary to take him to an oblivion of his own selection.

Because he was no longer Supreme Commander for the Allied Powers, MacArthur had the name *SCAP* taken from his plane, and *Bataan* restored. The *Bataan* took off from Haneda airport near Tokyo early on the morning of April 16, 1951. As I looked down I saw the upturned faces of those thousands of Japanese who jammed the airbase. They were still waving farewell, and I could feel rather than see that their lips still formed the traditional Japanese expression at parting: "Sayonara, Sayonara"—good-by and Godspeed. Then MacArthur motioned toward the horizon and remarked: "It will be a long, long time, Court, before we see her again." There stood Mount Fuji, still snow-covered, rising majestically into the sky as if to claim the right over mortal man to bespeak the final farewell. That was the last MacArthur will probably ever see of Japan or Japan of him. But the good he did in Japan will live on into eternity.

As our plane passed over the coastline and headed into the vast Pacific, it would have been strange indeed had not my mind dwelt momentarily upon the great difference in the setting which greeted us on the day of our arrival, August 30, 1945, and this day of our departure, nearly six years later. Then we had found a hostile and resentful, if despairing, Japanese nation and people without a friend in the entire world. Today we had just left a new nation reclaimed from the ashes of defeat and destruction and dedicated to peace and progress within the family of nations—and a populace whose heart wept at the great national and personal loss. I felt, though, as I had felt from the moment I had first heard of Truman's order, that in the over-all scheme of things, quite apart from the vulgar and cruel manner in which the action was taken, in so far as MacArthur personally was concerned, his relief at this time might in final balance save him from great future mental torture.

He had long since completed his mission to Japan and he had stabilized our position in Korea, regaining the approximate area of what was formerly delineated as South Korea by driving the Chinese Red armies back to a line of theoretical stalemate. There was little more that he could do, unless a radical change in U.N. war policies should take place, and no promise whatsoever was held out for this. Ahead therefore would have been nothing but the frustration which would have tried the soul of any commander, more particularly that of Douglas MacArthur, whose credo for fifty years had been to fight to win.

Chapter II   "There is no substitute for victory."

The *Bataan* roared straight across the Pacific, past the International Date Line, past Midway Island just over the horizon, and finally over the bluffs of Diamond Head, where we circled and landed at Honolulu's Hickam Air Force Base. There we were guests of Admiral Radford, the then Commander-in-Chief of the Pacific Theater and now Chairman of the Joint Chiefs of Staff.

And there we began to experience some of the warmth of the sentiment of peoples outside of Japan for this almost legendary leader who was approaching his native shores for the first time in nearly fourteen years. There too we learned, from friends who had come on from the United States, something of the emotion with which the American people were waiting to pay tribute to MacArthur as he set foot on American soil. But we had not the slightest idea of the strange odyssey on which he was shortly to be projected and of which this was in a sense the first leg. He was, although he did not know it, approaching another rendezvous with history. The American people were to make him understand that he returned from his country's wars abroad with a respect, an admiration, and an affectionate devotion probably never exceeded in contemporary times by mortal man.

We paused only for an overnight rest before taking off again for San Francisco. It was dark when our plane swung in over the Golden Gate, and a panoply of glittering lights spread out below us. I studied Mac-Arthur's face as he approached his homeland after so many years away. What his deep and conflicting emotions were at this moment can only be guessed, but his principal thought was of his son, who was thirteen and had never seen his native land. Arthur's dark eyes were opened wide in wonder at the sparkling panorama unfolding before him. He watched it all in silent awe as his father put his arms around his shoulders and said gently: "Well, Arthur, my boy, here we are home at last."

PART IV: AMERICA

The plane had no sooner come to a stop than all three MacArthurs were caught up in an indescribable scene of pandemonium. From acres of parked cars an army of surging humanity forced its way past the police lines and swarmed around the erect figure in the familiar cap, his charming wife and wide-eyed boy. Governor Warren of California and Mayor Robinson of San Francisco greeted the MacArthurs with a warmth far beyond the call of official courtesy. But what brought tears to my eyes was the riotous reception of the thronging crowds.

MacArthur's welcomers all but mobbed him at the airport, lined the route into San Francisco, and were packed block-deep around his hotel to give him a thunderous ovation as he arrived there. In the weeks and months which followed I was to see him again and again receive this same outpouring of the American heart, as we later toured the length and breadth of the land. The settings may have been different, but the spirit was everywhere the same. The cheers and the tears, the light in the eyes, and the fervent expression of friendship were identical in California and in New York, in Illinois and in Texas, in Massachusetts and in Mississippi. It was one great powerful manifestation of the American public's belief that MacArthur had been brutally wronged by the manner of his dismissal, that he deserved the greatest hero's welcome of all, that—to put it bluntly—MacArthur was right and Truman wrong.

The few old friends whom MacArthur had time to receive in his hotel suite in San Francisco on the evening of his arrival told him that the question being asked most often was whether or not he intended to regard this rare tribute as political support should he desire to seek the Presidency. Not only did MacArthur have no such desire, but he was disturbed at this injection of politics into a situation that to him was nothing more than a gratifying evidence of the people's appreciation of his military service and their friendliness toward him.

Accordingly, when next morning he was officially greeted by the mayor in a ceremony at the City Hall—and by what looked like every man, woman, and child in San Francisco—he did his best to scotch any such rumor. After acknowledging the mayor's tribute to him, MacArthur said: "I was just asked if I intended to enter politics. My reply was no. I have no political aspirations whatsoever. I do not intend to run for political office, and I hope that my name will never be used in a political way. The only politics I have is contained in a single phrase known well to all of you—'God Bless America!'" With this specific and categorical statement he was able to put a halt to the talk that he was running for President—though only for a short interlude, since there was no stopping the growing popular clamor that he run, nor the sniping by enemies who still feared that he would.

The warm, friendly atmosphere of San Francisco's welcome was momentarily chilled on the day after MacArthur's arrival by a telephone call from the Pentagon. A Public Relations officer in the Department of the Army directed that MacArthur submit his contemplated speech to Congress for scrutiny by the Department before it was delivered. MacArthur was almost as angered as he was astonished by this order. There was no light he could regard it in other than of an arrogant act of unprecedented censorship. He felt sure that it was unauthorized as well. He therefore immediately challenged the legality of the directive, at which the Department of the Army quickly backed down, admitting in its apology that the order had been a mistake by one of the Department's administrative officials.

MacArthur had all but finished his speech on the flight from Tokyo to San Francisco, but he went over it again while, on April 18, his plane completed the last leg of the journey to Washington. He had received countless greetings from cities and towns all over America, many of them asking that he stop briefly, or at least circle at low altitude, as he crossed the country. But our time schedule would not permit this, since as it was we would not reach Washington until late at night. Indeed, it was after midnight when the *Bataan*'s wheels finally touched ground at National Airport.

Despite the late hour a crowd estimated at twenty thousand was waiting. They staged a near riot in their efforts to get closer to MacArthur. It took heroic assistance by the police to find us a way through this frenzied throng of well-wishers to the car that waited to take the MacArthurs to the hotel. On hand also was a curious delegation of official greeters. Generals Marshall, Bradley, Collins, and Vandenberg and Admiral Sherman, the very men who had supported the President's vindictive action, were there to blandly welcome him home. MacArthur greeted them courteously, but the irony of the situation did not escape him.

At the Statler Hotel the Presidential suite had been reserved for the MacArthurs and was already banked with flowers from friends and well-wishers. Although it was after one a.m. when the door closed on the last visitor, MacArthur sat down once more for a final polishing of the speech he would have to deliver next day.

He well realized that this was to be one of the most important statements of his long career. Simultaneously it would have to be a report from the front that he had just left, a judicious estimate of the entire situation with which the free world was still confronted, a reasoned and dispassionate explanation of the methods by which he believed that disaster in the Pacific could be avoided, a refutation of the many misrepresentations that had been made, and, last but certainly not least, a personal valedictory to the nation and the people he had served so long. The valedictory note on which he chose to end his speech, incidentally, did not occur to him until those pre-dawn hours while he sat at the writing-desk of the Statler suite, making the final revisions on the address he would deliver in only a few hours.

The morning of the 19th was not only one of the most important but also one of the most dramatic occasions in his whole life. Our motorcade filed by the cheering thousands lining Pennsylvania Avenue, and, promptly at noon, a committee from both Houses ushered MacArthur into the Chamber of the House of Representatives amidst deafening applause. As MacArthur stood on the rostrum just forward of the Speaker of the House and the President of the Senate and waited for the applause to cease, I realized that he would be seen and heard by many millions besides this assemblage, through the electronic miracle of television.

I had been courteously provided a chair facing the audience and just to the right of Speaker Rayburn, and I could observe both the Congressional reactions and MacArthur's face as he quietly began.

"I stand on this rostrum," he said, "with a deep sense of humility and great pride—humility in the wake of those great American architects of our history who have stood here before me, and pride in the reflection that this forum of legislative debate represents human liberty in the purest form yet devised. Here are centered the hopes and aspirations and faith of the entire human race." MacArthur then made clear that, despite the urgings of many friends that he use this occasion to give the administration its richly deserved castigation, he was speaking only as a steward and that he was giving a high-level, nonpartisan accounting to the people.

"I trust therefore that you will do me the justice of receiving that which I have to say as solely expressing the considered viewpoint of a fellow American. I address you with neither rancor nor bitterness in the fading twilight of life with but one purpose in mind, to serve my country." The hush that had fallen over the great chamber as MacArthur spoke was now broken by a thunderclap of applause from both sides of the aisle. MacArthur then proceeded to develop the issues and to emphasize that they were of far more than regional nature.

"The issues are global," he warned, "and so interlocked that to con-

sider the problems of one sector oblivious to those of another is but to
court disaster for the whole. While Asia is commonly referred to as the
gateway to Europe, it is no less true that Europe is the gateway to Asia,
and the broad influence of one cannot fail to have its impact upon the
other."

He explained the revolutionary changes which time had produced on
the Asiatic scene, pointing out that "the peoples of Asia found their opportunity in the war just past to throw off the shackles of colonialism and
now see the dawn of new opportunity, of heretofore unfelt dignity and
the self respect of political freedom."

Asia, MacArthur reminded Congress, mustered "half of the earth's
population and 60% of its natural resources," and Asians "are rapidly
consolidating a new force, both moral and material, with which to raise
the living standards and erect adaptations of the design of modern progress to their own distinct cultural environment. Whether one adheres to
the concept of colonialism or not, this is the direction of Asian progress
and it may not be stopped. It is a corollary to the shift of the world economic frontiers as the whole epicenter of world affairs rotates back toward the area from which it started. In this situation it becomes vital that
our country orient its policy in consonance with this basic revolutionary
condition, rather than pursue a course blind to the reality that the colo-
nial era is now passed and the Asian peoples covet the right to shape
their own free destiny. What they seek now is friendly guidance, understanding and support, not imperialist direction; the dignity of equality,
not the shame of subjugation."

MacArthur then discussed in detail the strategic relationship of the
Pacific area to the security of the United States, the position of Formosa,
and the historic transformation of China. He paid tribute to the Philippines and extolled the progress made by the people of Japan in the wake
of war's near-total destruction. He carefully delineated his recommendations for winning the war in Korea, answering the spurious charge that
he was a warmonger who wished to spread the area of the conflict into
other lands; from the deck of the U.S.S. *Missouri* five and a half years
earlier, he pointed out, after accepting Japan's surrender, he had warned
that because of the scientific advance in the destructiveness of weapons,
war must be abolished if civilization is to survive.

But when war is here, he reiterated, it must be fought to win. Solemnly surveying the legislators seated before him, he warned of the dangers of further appeasement. "War's very object is victory, not indecision,"
he said. "In war, there is no substitute for victory."

PART IV: AMERICA

MacArthur had no idea at the time of the emotions that would be aroused by the note on which he chose to finish his report to his country. But it has become a national byword, and is already one of the best-remembered utterances of American history. "I am closing my fifty-two years of military service," he said. "When I joined the Army, even before the turn of the century, it was the fulfillment of all my boyish hopes and dreams. The world has turned over many times since I took the oath on the Plain at West Point, and the hopes and dreams have all since vanished, but I still remember the refrain of one of the most popular barracks ballads of that day, which proclaimed most proudly that old soldiers never die; they just fade away. And like the old soldier of that ballad, I now close my military career and just fade away, an old soldier who tried to do his duty as God gave him the light to see that duty. Good-by."

486

Chapter III   Revitalizing the Nation

The din of one of the most thunderous ovations in the history of Washington, D.C., was still ringing in our ears when the MacArthurs and I returned to the Presidential suite of the Statler. There was time only for a few calls by old friends and comrades-in-arms before MacArthur had to leave to make his scheduled arrival in New York.

What followed was a rigorous test of MacArthur's stamina. The surging mass of eager humanity which struggled for a glimpse of him at La Guardia Field on his arrival was complemented by the throngs which lined the streets and greeted him with a deafening and progressive roar of applause as his car moved toward the Waldorf-Astoria, where accommodations had been arranged for him. My astonishment at the mass fervor of his welcoming was compounded when I saw the amount of "mail" which was awaiting him at the Waldorf. There were more than 150,000 letters and 20,000 telegrams, and they continued to pour in by the sackload.

On the next day New York gave MacArthur its official welcome. And never before had it given such a welcome to anyone in the history of the city. The crowds were variously estimated by police at from seven to ten million people. No one could of course fail to be moved by the stupendousness of this great phenomenon of American history—the deafening clamor that echoed and re-echoed in the caverns which New York's skyscrapers make of its streets, the swelling crescendo as the motorcade neared its destination at City Hall, and the constant shower of paper from above which literally clouded the atmosphere like a blizzard and covered our car as though under drifts of snow. But more than that, as I rode in the front seat of MacArthur's car, I was impressed by the people themselves along the way—men, women, and children, rich and poor, black and white, of as many differing origins as there are nations on the earth, with their tears and smiles, their cheers and handclaps, and most of all their heart-lifting cries as the car approached: "There he is! THERE HE IS!!"

When it was all over and we returned to the contrasting silence of the Waldorf, I wondered, as I would time and time again: what did it all mean? Was it a popular call to some form of duty yet undone? Did it, as so many of MacArthur's friends and well-wishers argued, carry political connotations? But when I voiced these questions, MacArthur rejected any such idea. He saw in this great phenomenon merely a manifestation of the people's confidence and faith, an expression for which he had the utmost gratitude, and a sentiment of which he would be ever mindful.

But now the hue and cry was over and MacArthur could, as he had so aptly put it in his Congressional address, "just fade away." He was not, however, to be granted this privilege quite yet. He had scarcely become settled in his new apartment home in the Waldorf when he was formally asked to appear before a hearing to be conducted by a joint session of the Senate Committees on Armed Services and Foreign Relations, to inquire into "the military situation in the Far East" and his relief from his assignment in that area.

MacArthur did not relish this ordeal, and he had hoped that he might avoid it entirely. But he knew that he had no alternative except to appear. He did so, however, with simplicity and directness. When some of his friends urged that he prepare a comprehensive statement, reiterating his case and indicting the administration, he refused. Despite the argument that such statements were common practice at Congressional inquiries, MacArthur simply replied: "No, the committees apparently only want me to amplify certain phases of my address to Congress. I am prepared to answer any questions they may ask me concerning the area of my responsibilities in the Far East."

He prepared for this inquiry just as he had prepared for the conference at Wake Island, which is to say that he prepared not at all. He went to Washington, as he had to Wake Island, with only the information that he carried in his head. He intended to answer any questions asked, to the best of his ability from personal knowledge; and if he did not know the answer, he intended frankly to say so.

But he rarely had to say so. His appearance before the Joint Committee was a revelation to the Senators who questioned him, to the handful of observers allowed behind the doors of the closed session, and to the hundreds of thousands who read the transcript of the hearings as it was released, after censorship, each day. MacArthur appeared to be tireless. For three days, with no documents, he answered questions that covered the whole scope of Asian history and U.S. foreign policy and military power, lucidly, unequivocally, and with no hesitation. Time and time again, members of the committee from both parties expressed to me their amazement at his tremendous reservoir of strength, which permitted him to go on and on without the slightest sign of fatigue.

The members were even more impressed by his broad grasp of the Far Eastern situation and his penetrating analysis of the course of events. At the start some efforts were made to trip him with loaded questions by a few who thought to inject politics into the inquiry. With good nature but unmistakable firmness, MacArthur took them all in stride, managing meanwhile to maintain a nonpartisan position. The efforts to trap him were soon abandoned.

Nearly every member of the Joint Committee, regardless of political affiliation or agreement with the policies MacArthur advocated, expressed his admiration of the manner in which he conducted himself on this occasion under such trying circumstances. Their separate opinions were well summed up by Senator Richard Russell, the Democratic chairman of the committee, who presided over the inquiry with impartiality and statesmanship. "General MacArthur," Senator Russell said, "I wish to state to you that the three days you have been here with us are without parallel in my legislative experience. I have never seen a man subjected to such a barrage of questions in so many fields and on so many varied subjects. I marvel at your physical endurance. More than that, I have been profoundly impressed by the vastness of your patience and the thoughtfulness and frankness with which you have answered all the questions that have been propounded. We have certainly drawn freely on your vast reservoir of knowledge and experience, not only as a great military captain, but as a civilian administrator of 80 million people."

MacArthur returned to New York and took no further interest in the inquiry. He did not read a line of the testimony given by the others, or even the press accounts of the proceedings. He felt that he had given the committee his complete viewpoint on the topics concerned, and that if anyone differed with his viewpoint, it was his privilege. During that period, as the hearings continued for five more weeks, I was subjected to a barrage of questions from the press. I answered those queries which concerned a subject I felt had been misrepresented; but I made no other effort to keep abreast of the proceedings, and MacArthur did not wish me to do so. Only recently have I read the entire transcript, in preparation for the writing of this book.

On his return to New York, and on every day that followed, Mac-

Arthur received countless invitations to appear in cities and towns all over the nation, to receive awards or plaques or degrees or other honors. He politely declined them all, however, because he believed that at last he *could* keep the promise to himself to "just fade away."

But now that he was back home for the first time in many years—and now that he had some leisure for the first time in that period—MacArthur was able to study U.S. domestic policy at close hand. He was not encouraged by what he saw. He had returned home convinced that the current U.S. Far Eastern policy would inevitably lose all of Asia to Communist imperialist aggression. When he surveyed our domestic administration, he realized that the same moral dry rot that infected U.S. Korean policy was also eating away at our conduct of affairs at home.

I repeat that MacArthur had no political motivations whatever. Furthermore, he never regarded the public expression of faith and trust in him—the expression which led him to make the decision he did to speak out—as having any political significance. It was simply that he felt a compelling need to warn of the dangers he saw menacing the land and the people he loves. And since many of these people had proclaimed, by their tears and cheers and ear-splitting ovations, that they believed in him and in what he stood for, he felt that not to warn them was to betray them.

He determined therefore to embark upon a crusade—a lone crusade that was probably without parallel—to do what he could to save the freedom of representative government in America. For the past five and a half years MacArthur had been advocating the principles of the America he had known in his stewardship of Japan. It was a shock to him to discover that some of those principles were being more honored in the breach than in the observance right here at home. If only for that reason alone, MacArthur felt that he should embark upon his lone crusade.

MacArthur is a lifelong Republican. But he would not have changed his course if he had felt that a Republican administration was leading the nation toward disaster. In his speeches during this crusade he quoted from many great Americans of the past whose philosophy, it seemed, had temporarily been forgotten; and it happened that he quoted from as many Democratic leaders as Republican, from men like Jefferson and Jackson as much as from Lincoln. In order to avoid political implications as to his itinerary, MacArthur arranged to visit both Republican and Democratic centers of population all over the country; his tour took him into Illinois, Wisconsin, Texas, Tennessee, Virginia, Florida, Ohio, Pennsylvania, Massachusetts, Michigan, and Washington.

490

His speech on April 26, 1951, before a wildly cheering crowd at Soldier Field in Chicago, served as a proper introduction for the crusade. "I have endeavored since my return home to keep the issue on a higher level than partisan politics," he said. "The lives of your sons call for this measure of consideration. For the enemy bullets have no respect for political affiliation and strike down the son of a Democrat just as surely as the son of a Republican. Although my public life is now closed and I no longer carry any responsibilities of the national administration, I feel my responsibility of national citizenship no less deeply."

He conceived of it as a crusade to revitalize the nation. It was a blunt-spoken, hard-hitting crusade. And it provided the first summing-up of MacArthur's views, which have so often been distorted, on domestic, foreign and military policy. For anyone who has asked himself where MacArthur stands on these issues, I recommend a close study of his speeches during those thirteen months from the spring of 1951 to the spring of 1952. I quote here only the major guideposts for such a study.

DOMESTIC POLICY

Before the Texas legislature in Austin on June 13, 1951 MacArthur said: "My correspondence reflects a growing lack of faith by a large segment of our population in the responsibility and the moral fiber of our own process of government. Truth has ceased to be a keystone to the arch of our national conscience, and propaganda has replaced it as the rallying media for public support. Corruption and rumors of corruption have shaken the people's trust in the integrity of those administering the civil power. Government has assumed progressively the arrogant mantle of oligarchic power, as the great moral and ethical principles upon which our nation grew strong have been discarded or remolded to serve narrow political purposes. The cost of government has become so great and the consequent burden of taxation so heavy that the system of free enterprise which built our great material strength has become imperiled. The rights of individuals in communities have rapidly been curtailed in the advance towards centralized power and the spiritual and material strength amassed through our original concept of a federation erected upon the local responsibility and autonomy of its several components, shows marked deterioration."

Where the real dangers lay in the conduct of domestic affairs MacArthur saw clearly, as he pointed out in Houston the following day: "It

491

is not from the threat of external attack that we have reason for fear," he warned. "It is from these insidious forces working from within. It is they that create the basis for fear by spreading false propaganda designed to destroy moral precepts to which we have clung for direction since the immutable Declaration of Independence became the great charter of our liberty. The campaign to pervert the truth and shake or confuse the public mind, with its consequent weakening of moral courage, is not chargeable entirely to Communists engaged in a centrally controlled worldwide conspiracy to destroy all freedom. For they have many allies, here as elsewhere, who, blind to reality, ardently support the general Communist aims while reacting violently to the mere suggestion that they do so.

"There are those who subvert morality as a means to gain or entrench power. There are those who, believing themselves liberals, chart a course which can but lead to our destruction. There are those cynically inclined whose restless impulse is ever seeking change. There are those who are constantly trying to alter our basic concepts of freedom and human rights. There are those who seek to prevent others from speaking their minds according to the dictates of their conscience. There are those who plan to limit our individual right to share in the sovereign power of the people. There are those who seek to subvert government from being the guardian of the people's rights, to make it an instrument of despotic power. There are those who seek to make the burden of taxation so great and the progressive increase so alarming that the spirit of adventure, tireless energy and masterful initiative which built the material strength of the nation will become stultified and inert. There are those who seek to to change our system of free enterprise which, whatever its faults, commands the maximum energy from human resource and provides maximum benefits in human happiness and contentment. There are those who seek to convert us to a form of socialistic endeavor, leading directly to the path of Communist slavery."

MacArthur repeated this theme many times, notably in a rousing speech before the Michigan legislature on May 15, 1952. He cited Lincoln's warning that "If this nation is ever destroyed, it will be from within, not from without." And he challenged President Truman's failure to take this peril seriously—a failure that was shared by many others in the nation, of whom President Truman was only the foremost spokesman. "We must not underestimate the peril," MacArthur said. "It must not be brushed off lightly. It must not be scoffed at, as our present leadership has been prone to do by hurling childish epithets such as 'red herring,' 'character assassin,' 'scandal monger,' 'witch hunt,' 'political assassination,' and like terms designed to confuse or conceal the real issues and intimidate those who, recognizing the gravity of the dangers, would expose them to the light of public scrutiny and understanding."

What was sadly lacking in the conduct of domestic affairs, Mac-Arthur was convinced, was the kind of spirit of which he spoke on June 15, 1951, as he stood bareheaded before the Alamo in San Antonio, Texas. He extolled "that small band of Texans [who] stood and died rather than yield the precious concepts of liberty." He called upon the nation to regain their faith and their courage. "It is in their spirit that our nation has met and overcome the successive crises which have beset its progress, and it is in [their] spirit that we must meet the problems which now dominate human thought. The great issue of the day is whether we are departing from that spirit in the shaping of national policy to meet the challenge of the time. Are we failing it? Are we lacking the spiritual courage to adjudge issues upon the simple test of what seems right and what seems wrong? Are we content to compromise basic principle to appease the savage instincts underlying ruthless aggression, to cower before the verbal whiplash of an international bully? These are the questions now agitating and disturbing the public conscience.

"Had your heroes who fought here, and others who through the generations have matched their heroic example, failed this simple but immutable test—had they been bound by extraordinary limitations withholding the power essential to achieve victory—liberty would long ago have perished. Had they followed counsels of timidity and fear, this great nation might well have disappeared."

There was one place where that spirit was not lacking, and that was in the heart of Douglas MacArthur. On July 25, 1951 he took the occasion of being in Boston to discuss forthrightly a most controversial subject: taxes. Here it was that men with the same spirit 178 years earlier had forthrightly expressed *their* opinions on a tea tax by dumping all the tea in Boston Harbor. Harking back to days of America's early greatness, MacArthur praised the adventurous spirit "which despite risks and hazards carved a great nation from almost impenetrable wilderness; which established the pattern for modern industrialization and scientific development; which built our own almost unbelievable material progress and favorably influenced that of all others; which through the scientific advance of means of communication closed the international geographic gaps to permit rapid and effective trade and commerce among the peoples of the world; which raised the living standard of the American people beyond that ever before known; and which elevated the laborer, the

493

farmer and the tradesman to their rightful station of dignity and relative prosperity. "This adventurous spirit is now threatened," MacArthur warned, "by an unconscionable burden of taxation."

It was, he said, "sapping the initiative and energies of the people, [leaving] little incentive for the assumption of the risks which are inherent and inescapable in the forging of progress under the system of free enterprise. . . . More and more we work not for ourselves but for the state. In time, if permitted to continue, this trend cannot fail to be destructive. For no nation may survive in freedom once its people become the servants of the state. . . . Nothing is heard from those in supreme executive authority concerning the possibility of a reduction or even limitation upon these mounting costs [of government]. No plan is advanced for easing the crushing burden already resting upon the people. To the contrary, all that we hear are plans by which such costs progressively may be increased. New means are constantly being devised for greater call upon the taxable potential, as though the resources available were inexhaustible."

Much of the danger, he knew, came from too much concentration of power in the executive. In his administration of Japan MacArthur had seen at first hand the pernicious consequences of such highly centralized political power, and he therefore felt strongly the need for the nation to regain its political self-reliance. In Cleveland on September 6, 1951 MacArthur pointed out this danger. "Under the stress of national emergencies during the past two decades," he said, "there has been a persistent and progressive centralization of power in the federal government, with only superficial restoration to the states and the people as emergencies subsided. This drift has resulted in an increasingly dangerous paternalistic relationship between federal government and private citizen, with the mushrooming of agency after agency designed to control the individual. Authority specifically reserved to the states by constitutional mandate has been ignored in the ravenous effort to further centralize the political power. Within the federal government itself there has been a further and dangerous centralization.

"For example, the Department of State, originally established for the sole purpose of the conduct of foreign diplomacy, has become in effect a general operating agency of the government, exercising authority and influence over many facets of executive administration formerly reserved to the President or the heads of other departments. The Department of State indeed is rapidly assuming the character of a prime ministry, notwithstanding that its secretary is an appointed official, neither chosen by nor answerable directly to the people."

494

Striking back at those in Washington who, behind the mask of official anonymity, were threateningly questioning his right as an officer of the Army to criticize public authority and policy, MacArthur then sternly warned: "This drift toward totalitarian rule is reflected not only in this shift toward centralized power, but as well in the violent manner in which exception is taken to the citizen's voice when raised in criticism of those who exercise the political power. There seems to be a determination to suppress individual voice and opinion, which can only be regarded as symptomatic of the beginning of a general trend toward mass thought control. Abusive language and arbitrary action, rather than calm, dispassionate and just argument, ill becomes the leadership of a great nation, conceived in liberty and dedicated to a course of morality and justice. It challenges the concept of free speech and is an attempt at direct suppression through intimidation of the most vital check against the abuse of political power—public criticism. If long countenanced by free men, it can but lead to those controls upon conviction and conscience which traditionally have formed stepping stones to dictatorial power."

Another disease that had infected the body politic, MacArthur knew, was the growing tendency of the federal government to make the states financial wards of the administration. He singled out this malady before a cheering audience which composed the Mississippi legislature on March 22, 1952. Indicting those bureaucratic officials who had thus usurped the political powers expressly reserved by the Constitution to the states, MacArthur said: "By the devious method of expenditure progressively beyond income and increasing taxation to keep pace with expenditure, these political leaders have been rapidly exhausting the remaining revenue-producing potential of the citizenry. This has rendered the states and other communities increasingly dependent upon the federal government. It places the state in the position of a supplicant."

FOREIGN POLICY

It seemed to MacArthur that our foreign policies were confused, vacillating, and too subject to foreign pressures. In the Boston speech in which he discussed taxation, he said: "We compound irresponsibility by seeking to share what liquid wealth we have with others. In so doing we recklessly speak of the billions we set aside for the purpose as though they were inconsequential. There can be no quarrel with altruism. Such has ever been a predominant quality making up the nobility of the Ameri-

495

can character. We should do all in our power to alleviate the suffering and hardships of other peoples, and to support their own maximum effort to preserve their freedoms from the assaults of Communist imperialism. But when this effort is carried beyond the ability to pay, or the point that the attendant burden upon our people becomes insufferable, or places our own way of life and freedom in jeopardy, then it ceases to be altruism and becomes reckless imprudence.

"I have yet to see evidence that such vast outlays were preceded by the slightest concern for the ultimate effect they will have upon our own liberties and standards of life. . . . It is said that we must give boundlessly if we are to be assured allies in an emergency. I reject the reasoning. . . . The survival of the free world is infinitely more dependent upon the maintenance of a strong, vigorous, healthy and independent America as a leavening influence than upon any financial aid which we might provide under our own existing stringencies."

As dangerous to our conduct of foreign affairs as financial imprudence was the administration's concentration upon one half of the world, to the almost utter neglect of the other. In a speech before an enormous crowd in Seattle on November 13, 1951, MacArthur emphasized the new horizons beyond the Pacific. "To the early pioneer the Pacific coast marked the end of his courageous westerly advance," he said. "To us it should mark but the beginning. To him it delineated our western frontier. To us that frontier has been moved across the Pacific horizon. For we find our western defense geared to an island chain off the coast of continental Asia, from which with air and sea supremacy we can dominate any predatory move threatening the Pacific Ocean area. Our economic frontier now embraces the trade potentialities of Asia itself; for with the gradual rotation of the epicenter of world trade back to the Far East whence it started many centuries ago, the next thousand years will find the main world problem the raising of sub-normal standards of life of its more than a billion people. The opportunities for international trade then, if pursued with the vision and courage of the early pioneer, will be limitless. . . .

"Such possibilities seem, however, beyond the comprehension of some high in our governmental circles, who still feel that the Pacific Coast marks the practical terminus of our advance and the westerly boundary of our immediate national interests—that any opportunity for the expansion of our foreign trade must be found mainly in the area of Europe and the Middle East. Nothing could more surely put a brake upon our growth as a strong and prosperous nation. Intentionally or not, it would yield to industrialized Europe the undisputed dominion over the trade and commerce of the Far East. More than this, it would in time surrender to European nations the moral, if not political, leadership of the Eastern hemisphere. Nothing could more clearly attest a marked recession from that far-sighted vision which animated the pioneer of 100 years ago. . . .

"There should be no rivalry between our East and our West—no pitting of Atlantic interests against those of the Pacific. The problem is global, not sectional. The living standards of the people of the Oriental East must and will be raised by a closer relativity with that of the Occidental West. Only the Communists and their blind disciples advocate the lowering of the one to achieve the raising of the other—the Karl Marx theory of an international redistribution of wealth to achieve a universal level. To others the course is clear. There must be such a development of opportunity that the requirements for a better life in the Oriental East may be filled from the almost unlimited industrial potential of the Occidental West. The human and material resources of the East would be used in compensation for the manufactures of the West. Once this elementary logic is recognized, trade with the Far East may be expected rapidly to expand under the stimulus of American vision, American enterprise and American pioneering spirit. The pioneer of the 20th Century has in all respects as broad an avenue of advance as did the pioneer of the 19th Century."

The greatest failing of all, MacArthur attempted to point out in his crusade, was that far from having a foreign policy that was right or wrong, the United States seemed in fact to have no foreign policy at all. In his Boston speech he asked: "Is there wonder that men who seek an objective understanding of American policy thinking become completely frustrated and bewildered? Is there wonder that Soviet propaganda so completely dominates American foreign policy? And, indeed, what is our foreign policy? We hear impassioned appeals that it be bipartisan—violent charges that sinister efforts are being made to obstruct and defeat it —but I defy you or any other man to tell what it is. It has become a mass of confused misunderstandings and vacillations. It has meant one thing today, another tomorrow. It has almost blown with every wind, changed with every tide. The sad truth is that we have no foreign policy.

"Expediences as variable and shifting as the exigencies of the moment seem to be the only guide. Yesterday we disarmed, today we arm—and what of tomorrow? We have been told of the war in Korea, that it is the wrong war, at the wrong time and in the wrong place. Does this mean that they intend and indeed plan what they would call a right war, at a right time and in a right place? . . . Do we intend to resist by force Red aggression in Southeast Asia if it develops? These are questions that disturb us, because there is no answer forthcoming."

MILITARY POLICY

Perhaps a main reason for the confusion of United States foreign policy was the kind of Atlantic isolationism which pervaded the administration. In his Austin, Texas, speech MacArthur attacked this administration delusion. "Europe's very survival," he said, "is dependent upon our gaining a decisive victory in Asia where Communism has already thrown down the gage of battle. By confining their concern so assiduously to one area and ignoring the global nature of the Communist threat and the need to stop its predatory advance in other areas, they have become the 'isolationists' of the present time. And it is a form of isolation which offers nothing but ultimate destruction. Our first line of defense for Western Europe is not the Elbe, it is not the Rhine—it is the Yalu. Lose there and you render useless the effort to implement the North Atlantic Pact or any other plan for regional defense."

On October 17, 1951, in an address before the annual convention of the American Legion at Miami, Florida, MacArthur said:

"It has become necessary to help the free nations of Western Europe prepare against the threat of predatory attack by Communist forces now occupying Eastern Europe, and generally throughout the world our policy has been enunciated to extend a helping hand to others whose freedom is threatened and who have the will but lack the entire resources essential to their own defense. The soundness of this concept will depend upon the wisdom with which it is administered. Recklessly and abnormally applied, it could encompass our own destruction. This country obviously lacks the resources militarily to defend the world. It has the resources, however, reasonably to assist in that defense.

"But such assistance must be contributory to, rather than in place of maximum local national effort. It should be extended only upon conditions that assistance to others be really for defense and be so limited as not to deplete our own resources to the point of imperiling the survival of our own liberties, and that those we would assist be animated by the same love of freedom as we and possess the will and determination to pledge their own lives and full resources to secure their own defense. . . .

"There are, however," MacArthur warned, "many disturbing signs to the contrary. There are many of the leaders and peoples of Western Europe who mistakenly believe that we assist them solely to protect ourselves, or to secure an alliance with them should our country be attacked. This is indeed fallacious thinking. Our potential in human and material resource, in alignment with the rest of the Americas, is adequate to defend this hemisphere against any threat from any power or any association of powers. We do desire to retain our traditional friends and allies in Europe, but such an alliance must rest upon spiritual bonds fabricated from a mutuality of purpose and a common heritage of principle—not an alliance to be secured at a price.

"There are other disturbing signs that some of the people we seek to bolster are showing a lack of the will to master their own full resources in their own defense. There appear to be many among them who feel that their defense is and should be our sole responsibility, and that beyond a token military collaboration they should confine their own energy and resources to the building up of their civilian economies. The startling thing is that such viewpoints are not lacking in support among our own leaders. Apparently some of them, more in line with the Marxian philosophy than animated by a desire to preserve freedom, would finance the defense of others as a means of sharing with them our wealth.

"This wealth, accumulated by our own initiative and industry under the incentives of free enterprise, would then serve as the means of covering socialist or Communist deficits abroad. The ultimate effect, whatever the intent, would be to reduce our own standard of life to the level of universal mediocrity.

"We have committed ourselves to contribute six ground divisions to Western Europe, notwithstanding that only a small fraction of the great masses of its people have been called to the colors. Indeed, if the human resource and industrial potential of the Western European nations were effectively employed for defense, there would be minimum need for American ground forces or even great quantities of American munitions —air and naval power, yes, but little honest need for ground troops unless it be solely for morale purposes."

In Korea, General Bradley, the Chairman of the Joint Chiefs of Staff, had testified that the United States was relying upon a passive defense. This, MacArthur pointed out in his Austin, Texas, speech, is a doctrine "which in all history has never won a war—a doctrine which has been responsible for more military disaster than all other reasons combined. Does experience teach us nothing?"

What we were doing, in fact, was allowing ourselves to fall for a

499

gigantic hoax. "There is no slightest doubt in my mind," MacArthur continued, "but that the Soviet has been engaging in the greatest bulldozing diplomacy history has ever recorded. Without committing a single soldier to battle, he has assumed direct or indirect control over a large part of the population of the world. His intrigue has found its success not so much in his own military strength, nor indeed in any overt threat of intent to commit it to battle, but in the moral weakness of the free world.

"It is a weakness which has caused many free nations to succumb to and embrace the false tenets of Communist propaganda. It is a weakness which has caused our own policymakers, after committing America's sons to battle, to leave them to the continuous slaughter of an indecisive campaign by imposing arbitrary restraints upon the support we might otherwise provide them through maximum employment of our scientific superiority, which alone offers hope of early victory. It is a weakness which now causes those in authority to strongly hint at a settlement of the Korean conflict under conditions short of the objectives our soldiers were led to believe were theirs to attain and for which so many yielded their lives."

And why were we thus engaged in a futile military maneuver? Because, claimed the Joint Chiefs of Staff, we were not prepared. Here indeed was a clear lesson for the future, as MacArthur pointed out in his speech at Cleveland. "We have just passed another anniversary of the end of the war with Japan," he said. "Six years ago with a few strokes of the pen a calm descended upon the battlefields of the world and the guns grew silent. Military victory had been achieved for our cause, and men turned their thoughts from the task of mass killing to the higher duty of international restoration, from destroying to rebuilding, from destruction to construction. Everywhere in the free world they lifted up their heads and hearts in thanksgiving for the advent of peace in which ethics and morality based upon truth and justice might thereafter fashion the universal code. Then more than ever in the history of the modern world a materially strong and spiritually vibrant leadership was needed to consolidate the victory into a truly enduring peace for all of the human race. America, at the very apex of her military power, was the logical nation to which the world turned for leadership. It was a crucial moment—one of the greatest opportunities ever known.

"But our political and military leaders failed to comprehend it. Sensitive only to the expediences of the hour, they dissipated with reckless haste that predominant military power which was the key to the situation. Our forces were rapidly and completely demobilized, and the great stores of war matériel which had been accumulated were disposed of with irresponsible waste and abandon. The world was thus left exposed and vulnerable to an international Communism whose long-publicized plan had been to await just such a favorable opportunity to establish dominion over the free nations.

"The stage had, perhaps unwittingly, been set in secret and most unfortunate war conferences. The events which followed will cast their shadow upon history for all time. Peoples with long traditions of human freedom progressively fell victims to a type of international brigandage and blackmail, and the so-called Iron Curtain descended rapidly upon large parts of Europe and Asia. As events have unfolded, the truth has become clear. Our great military victory has been offset, largely because of military unpreparedness, by the political successes of the Kremlin. Our diplomatic blunders increased as our senseless disarmament became a reality. And now the disastrous cycle is completed as those same leaders, who lost to the world the one great chance it has had for enduring universal peace, frantically endeavor by arousing a frenzy of fear throughout the land to gear anew our energy and resources, to rebuild our dissipated strength and to face again a future of total war.

"Our need for adequate military defense with world tensions as they were and are, is and should have been completely evident even before the end of the war. By what faith then can we find hope in those whose past judgments so grievously erred—who deliberately disarmed in the face of threatening Communism? Can they now be blindly trusted, as they so vehemently demand, to set an unerring course to our future well-being and security? There are those of us who from neither partisan affiliation nor political purpose think not."

And at the root of this military fallacy lay a strange new function of our armed forces. In his Boston speech MacArthur spotlighted this curious change that seemed to have taken place. "I find in existence a new and heretofore unknown and dangerous concept," he said, "that the members of our armed forces owe primary allegiance and loyalty to those who temporarily exercise the authority of the executive branch of the government, rather than to the country and its Constitution, which they are sworn to defend. No proposition could be more dangerous. None would cast greater doubt upon the integrity of the armed services. For its application would at once turn them from their traditional and constitutional role as the instrument for the defense of the republic into something partaking of the nature of a prætorian guard, owing sole allegiance to the political master of the hour.

"While for the purpose of administration and command the armed services are within the executive branch of the government, they are accountable as well to the Congress, charged with the policy-making responsibility, and to the people, ultimate repository of all national power. Yet so inordinate has been the application of the executive power that members of the armed services have been subjected to the most arbitrary and ruthless treatment for daring to speak the truth in accordance with conviction and conscience."

It was in this same speech that MacArthur made his only reference to his recall. "I hesitate to refer to my own relief from the Far Eastern Commands," he said, "as I have never questioned the legal authority underlying such action. But the sole reasons publicly stated by the highest of authority clearly demonstrates the arbitrary nature of the decision.

"The first reason given was that, contrary to existing policy, I warned of the strategic relationship of Formosa to American security and the dangers inherent in this area's falling under Communist control. Yet this viewpoint has since been declared by the Secretary of State, under oath before Congressional Committees, to have been and to be the invincible and long-standing policy of the United States.

"The second reason given was that I communicated my readiness to meet the enemy commander at any time to discuss acceptable terms of a cease-fire arrangement. Yet, for this proposal I was relieved of my command by the same authorities who since have received so enthusiastically the identical proposal when made by the Soviet government.

"The third and final reason advanced was my replying to a Congressman's request for information on a public subject then under open consideration by the Congress. Yet both Houses of Congress promptly passed a law confirming my action, which indeed had been entirely in accordance with a long existing and well recognized, though unwritten, policy. . . . And this formal enactment of basic policy was approved without the slightest dissent by the President."

There was one other military note in MacArthur's crusade, and that one threw his political backers into consternation. In his speech to the Michigan legislature he said: "The history of the world shows that republics and democracies have generally lost their liberties by way of passing from civilian to quasi-military status. Nothing is more conducive to arbitrary rule than the military junta. It would be a tragic development indeed if this generation was forced to look to the rigidity of military dominance and discipline to redeem it from the tragic failure of a civilian administration. It might well destroy our historic and wise concept which holds to the supremacy of the civil power." This single statement blasted all the plans which MacArthur's followers had made to draft him for high political office. But MacArthur was undisturbed, since he had no desire to enter politics.

"The Hearts of a People"

The theme of MacArthur's crusade—and indeed the main reason for it—was his belief that the people, if they could be stirred into realization of our national wrongs, would right them. He stated this belief most clearly in his Cleveland address. "During the five months since my return," he said, "I have been encouraged to believe that our citizens will not complacently tolerate further incursions against their cherished liberties and will move to correct the drift away from truly representative government. I have found this encouragement in the rare opportunity to search the faces of millions of my fellow countrymen. Therein I have been given understanding of the meaning of Abraham Lincoln when he said: '. . . To the salvation of the union there needs but one single thing— the hearts of a people like yours. When the people rise in a mass in behalf of the liberties of the country, truly it may be said that nothing can prevail against them.'

"I have seen in the faces of the American people that to which Mr. Lincoln prophetically referred. I have clearly seen that the soul of liberty is still living and vibrant in the American heart. It is neither Democratic nor Republican, but American. It will assert itself by constitutional processes and will mount invincible force in the battle to save the republic. The people still rule." And, as MacArthur said at Seattle, "I have faith that the American people will not be fooled."

His crusade to revitalize the nation showed in his own words that MacArthur the soldier was also a sound civil administrator. He had demonstrated this brilliantly in action in Japan as well. And it happened that just four months following his relief from the administration of that country, MacArthur had occasion to sum up his entire political philosophy—in answer to a communication from Japan's Prime Minister, Shigeru Yoshida. These, he wrote to Prime Minister Yoshida, are the principles of good government by which Japan should be guided.

"Public morality is the touchstone to the people's faith in the integrity of the governmental process.

"Restraint and frugality in the use of the public purse produces economic stability, encourages individual thrift and minimizes the burden of taxation.

503

"Avoidance of the excessive centralization of political power safeguards against the danger of totalitarian rule with the suppression of personal liberty, advances the concept of local autonomy and develops an acute consciousness in the individual citizen of his political responsibility. Undue paternalism in government tends to sap the creative potential and impair initiative and energy in those who thereby come to regard governmental subsidy as an inalienable right.

"The preservation inviolate of the economic system based upon free, private, competitive enterprise alone maximizes the initiative, the energy and in the end the productive capacity of the people.

"The vigorous and faithful implementation of the existing land laws providing land ownership for agricultural workers and the labor laws providing industrial workers a voice in conditions of their employment is mandatory if all these important segments of Japanese society are to enjoy their rightful dignity and opportunity, and social unrest based upon just grievance is to be avoided.

"The Bill of Rights ordained by the Constitution must vigilantly be preserved if the government would be assured of the people's full support. Public criticism should be encouraged rather than suppressed as providing a powerful check against the evils of maladministration of the political power. Freedom of speech as an inalienable right should never be challenged unless it directly violates the laws governing libel and slander.

"The courts must function as the champion of human justice, and the police power be exercised with primary regard to individual rights.

"Without sacrifice of the principles of justice, the devious advances of international Communism must be firmly repelled as a threat to internal peace and national security. To such end, so long as international tensions exist in Asia, adequate security forces should be maintained to safeguard Japan's internal peace against any threatened external attack."

As MacArthur said in the conclusion of his letter to the Prime Minister, "A Japan erected firmly upon such a form of political principles and policy, as well as setting a sure course to your own free destiny, could not fail to exercise a profound and beneficial influence upon the course of events in continental Asia . . . and contribute immeasurably to the spiritual and material advance of civilization."

The same principles of good government, though in this case written down for the particular needs of the Japanese nation, would with few changes apply to the United States. For almost thirteen months MacArthur, spurred on by no purpose other than that of love of his country and rewarded by nothing save the realization that he was doing all he could to save that country from deterioration, covered the length and breadth of the land, crying out in a lone voice against the dangers that lay ahead. What effect his crusade had on the elections the following year, in which Truman's administration was repudiated, no one can accurately measure. How many of the millions of people who heard and cheered MacArthur during this crusade dropped their complacency and worked for a cleaner, better government, MacArthur cannot know. He did, however, as he finished his crusade, know the one thing he needed to know; and that was simply that he had done what he could. He had raised the danger signals which called time for a change.

The Reverend Norman Vincent Peale, noted churchman, lecturer, and author, wrote an introduction to *Revitalizing a Nation*, which was published by the Heritage Foundation and embodied excerpts from MacArthur's public statements. In his introduction Dr. Peale had this to say:

"No man of our time is more authentically the voice of real America than Douglas MacArthur. To the millions who lined the streets of our great cities to cheer and weep as he passed by, he is the personification of American tradition and history.

"As he rode up great avenues 'midst vast throngs, the people through misty eyes saw in him the noble leaders of the past—Washington, Lee, Grant. And when he addressed the Congress of the United States, once again Americans heard the great truths which many, starved for them, never expected to hear again, and those who never heard them before wept unashamedly.

"In this stalwart, romantic figure, the great hopes, dreams and ideals of our country come to life again. He stimulates renewed faith that the land of Washington, Jefferson and Lincoln still lives in the hearts of the people.

"I shall never forget the light on General MacArthur's face, and the deep feeling in his voice when he said to me, 'They are wonderful people—the American people—quick, impulsive, generous, whole-hearted! You can always trust them and believe in them, for in their hearts they are good and true; in a crisis, they will do the right thing.'

"In the present crisis, this book outlines the sound, spiritual and practical thought of a great man who from a position of lofty eminence sees clearly the dangers facing us and gives of his rich wisdom to guide us. What he has to say reaches the spiritual side of our lives with a power found in the words of few of our leaders. Out of a lifetime experience of leadership and unsurpassed achievement, General MacArthur has gathered wisdom and insight into the great principles upon which our republic was founded and only upon which it can endure."

Then Dr. Peale urged that MacArthur's public statements be read to the children, "so that the noble, incomparable sentences of our greatest master of English speech may fall like music upon their ears; that they too . . . may hear enunciated the immortal principles of God and country. These words will live in their hearts . . . forever."

CHAPTER IV   In Retrospect

✠ When the first cold notice of his recall reached MacArthur in Tokyo, he had not the slightest notion of why the President had taken such action. Now, after a complete investigation by a Senate committee, after countless attempts at an explanation by administration figures involved, and after talks with Americans throughout the length and breadth of the United States, MacArthur still does not know.

Of course it is a larger problem than the relief from command of one officer, no matter how important his position. The roots of the problem lie much deeper, and the question can be answered only in terms of the great issue of how the Korean war should have been fought.

Of Truman it may be said that he acted with boldness and decision, however one might rate his judgment, when the North Korean armies struck into the weakly defended south, and by so doing at once commanded the support of the American people and the admiration, as well, of other peoples, particularly in Asia. Had he held to so firm a course when Red China threw down the gauntlet, countless American casualties might have been avoided, the pattern of contemporary events could have been cast in a much more secure and serene mold, and the threat of a new world war would have diminished. But he failed to reject the counsels of fear then thrust upon him; he instead heeded the ill-founded warnings that if we reacted normally and aggressively we would precipitate a world war. And he committed us instead to a course of "passive defense," from which could come only bloodshed with neither victory nor enduring peace.

Those who bore ultimate responsibility for American military and political policy could not, indeed, have served the enemy's cause better than through the formulation and implementation of this extraordinary decision. For it set at the international boundary of Korea a limit upon our military operations which screened from our counterattack or aerial

507

observation the enemy's maneuvers in support of his peninsular campaign. It denied us any right of intrusion upon this sanctuary, even in hot pursuit of enemy aircraft disengaging from combat with our own planes, and prohibited any countermeasures against enemy anti-aircraft batteries emplaced along the north banks of the Yalu to harass our air operations south of the border. It protected the enemy's lines of communication and supply to his peninsular forces by denying us the right by any reasonable means to destroy vital arterial bridges spanning the Yalu or his bases of attack and supply to the north. It facilitated Red Chinese intervention by so doing, and permitted the build-up of a massive Chinese force which, treacherously and without prior notice of belligerency, struck the Eighth Army while advancing to mop up the North Korean remnants. It denied us reinforcement to strengthen our lines even from trained Chinese troops standing by uncommitted on the island of Formosa, while at the same time employing our Seventh Fleet to deny those troops the right to make diversionary attacks upon the common enemy on the Chinese mainland, which would have reduced the pressure upon our beleaguered forces in Korea. It denied us the right to blockade Red China against the importation of supplies essential to sustain its military operations against us. It refused to countenance the employment of our naval and air striking power against Red China's arsenals and other war-sustaining industries, then subject to ready reduction under the weight of our air and naval supremacy, and without which Red China could not have sustained military operations against our forces in Korea, or military adventures elsewhere.

The cumulative effect of these limitations and inhibitions upon the employment of our dominant naval and air potential was to relegate our ground forces in Korea to a costly, unproductive, bloody, and stalemated war of attrition. Because MacArthur could not ask his troops to die for such an indecisive purpose without raising his voice in vigorous protest, he was summarily relieved of his command after, under his leadership and direction, it had regained the initiative against Red China's opposing armies and was even then inflicting crushing and costly local defeats upon them.

Thereafter, at the Soviet's behest, we entered into protracted truce negotiations with the enemy commander, during which, although we discontinued our offensive tactics, we sustained even more casualties than we had suffered during the previous period of active and bitter combat while MacArthur was still in command. Eighty thousand added American casualties—the equivalent of more than five full American infantry divisions—many thousands from within the silence of the grave, sadly attest to this fact. MacArthur estimated that he could have won the war with Red China with less than half this loss had his advice been accepted. These truce talks, with the accompanying easing of our military pressure upon the Red Chinese, permitted them to build up their air power to the point where it could take a much heavier toll of Allied life, to build up their anti-aircraft batteries to the point where they could multiply our own air losses, while at the same time shifting their axis of movement of manpower and supplies to the south as the means of strengthening Communist operations in the reduction of Indo-China and other target areas in southeast Asia. When I told MacArthur of the signing of the Korean Armistice he exclaimed: "This is the death warrant for Indochina."

All of these developments were clearly foreseen by MacArthur, who repeatedly warned of their inevitability in the wake of any appeasement of our Red Chinese enemy. "In war," he said, "a great nation which does not win must accept all of the consequences of defeat."

Final judgment upon Korean war decisions, although still awaiting events now in the making, has steadily crystallized toward an overwhelming conviction that MacArthur was right and Truman wrong. MacArthur's viewpoint was dictated by his professional judgment, well tested by historic lessons across the panorama of time; Truman's by his rejection of such judgment in the service of what he believed to be the political expediency of the time. MacArthur understood, what Truman did not, that the admixture of military strategy with political expediency can produce national disaster. And he sought to avoid it. He felt, as experience has long taught, that once the diplomats have failed to preserve the peace, it becomes a responsibility of military leadership to devise the strategy which will win the war. Of the soundness of MacArthur's professional acumen it is well to record for the future historian the contemporary estimates expressed after the curtain fell even by those who were hostile to him.

President Truman: "General MacArthur's place in history as one of our greatest commanders is fully established. The nation owes him a debt of gratitude for the distinguished and exceptional service he has rendered our country in posts of great responsibility."

General Marshall: "He is a man for whom I have tremendous respect as to his military abilities and military performances."

General Bradley (who later admitted that MacArthur might have been right): "I would not say anything to discredit the long and illustrious career of General MacArthur."

General Collins: "I think he is one of the most brilliant military leaders that this country has ever produced. Throughout his career he has been brilliantly successful."

General Vandenberg: "I have great admiration for him."

Admiral Sherman: "I would say that he was in the forefront among the strategists with respect to the coordinated use of land, sea and air forces."

General Carl Spaatz, retired Chief of Staff of the Air Force and one of the world's most authoritative strategists, recently summarized in these words the issue raised when our extraordinary military policy denied MacArthur the right to fight to win:

"Korea," he said, "could have been the right war in the right place. That it did not turn out so can be blamed, in retrospect, on the political limitations placed on the United Nations' objectives, not on the original decision to fight. . . .

"Given the wisdom of hindsight, it now appears that our best opportunity to stop the spread of Communism in Asia was presented to us when the Chinese Communist army crossed the Yalu. This was clearly an act of aggression by Mao Tse-tung fully committing Red China to war and inviting the consequences of that commitment. The United Nations would have been justified in using all the power at its command—land, sea and air—against all the resources under Mao's control, all the way back to the heart of China. History will record the tragic consequences of the U.N. failure to fight Mao with everything we had then and there. When the fighting was stopped in Korea, the Chinese Army had been badly mauled even though its supply lines and resources beyond the Yalu had not been molested. What had started as the first real setback to the Communist march toward domination of Asia, thanks to prompt intervention of U.N. troops spearheaded by the military forces of the U.S., ended in the gratuitous release of Chinese forces and supplies for the fight in Indo-China."

The American people are steadily coming to comprehend the relationship between the reasons for MacArthur's summary removal from the Far Eastern scene and the series of tragic events which have since come to pass and those clearly threatened for the future. As contemporary judges upon the great issues of their time, they are giving increasing expression to the theme voiced by Hugh Gregg, the brilliant young Governor of New Hampshire. When MacArthur was made an honorary citizen of that state, Gregg referred to him as "a man who demonstrated the ultimate in courage and devotion to country, when, at the height of his career, he refused to compromise his ideals. He did not remain silent," Gregg went on, "when the soldiers of many nations, but principally his fellow Americans, were being sacrificed in a wasteful war which they were not permitted to win—an involuntary stalemate from which he knew no real peace could ever be fashioned. Fearlessly, he spoke out in a firm voice which hurled its thunderous accents across the seas and around the world. The foresight then displayed by this outspoken leader is now bitterly apparent. A tragedy of our own making, with maybe more misery to come—all because we failed to resolve the Korean fighting by the complete crushing of the communist armies to the point where further aggression in the Far East would have been impossible. Millions of freedom loving peoples everywhere still want the guidance of this greatest military leader—the one man whom the communists fear most."

Those elements of the press which tended to support Washington in the great debate at the time are now taking a second look at their position, and some are coming to understand how untenable it was. To mention only the Alsop brothers, long lusty critics of MacArthur, they have recently had the moral courage and objectivity, after personally studying the Far Eastern scene and the play of events three years after his recall, to pronounce his cause right after all.

"One of the things the Indo-Chinese crisis is doing is to vindicate the judgment of General Douglas MacArthur," the Alsops wrote in their syndicated column of June 13, 1954. "The free world would not now be menaced with a catastrophe in Asia if MacArthur had won his fight against the artificial limits on the Korean War.

"Back in 1950, from the false perspective of Washington, the arguments against MacArthur's views sounded convincing to many. Speaking personally, one of these reporters discovered for himself how farsighted General MacArthur had been during a visit to Asia last year.

"MacArthur was in fact right in three different ways and on three different levels. He was right, first, in proclaiming that there was 'no substitute for victory.'. . . MacArthur was right, second, in his view that the Korean war was a crucial test which it was necessary to win at all costs and risks. Indo-China is the proof.

"Because General MacArthur's policy was rejected, the Communists were able to fight our armies to a standstill in Korea. The truce then automatically transferred the strategic storm center of Asia from the relatively manageable contest in Korea, to the extremely unmanageable contest in Indo-China. Because we did not win the first test, we seem to be about to lose the second and many others after that. The danger in Indo-China is the direct result of the failure in Korea.

"Third and finally, MacArthur was right in feeling as he obviously did that the time of the Chinese intervention in Korea was the right time for a showdown in the world struggle between the Soviet and the free halves of the world. In the simplest terms, the United States already possessed decisive air-atomic striking power, while Soviet air-atomic power was still virtually nil in 1950–51. The Communist enemy had then proved his aggressive intentions. Our one major weapon then had its fullest value. That value was already being impaired by the Soviet air-atomic build-up. Logic demanded a showdown without further delay.

"Indo-China is again the proof. It is not generally known, but it is the chilling fact that Soviet air-atomic striking power has for the first time begun to influence American policy in the present crisis. The Joint Chiefs of Staff have not been influenced. That will no doubt come a year or two later. Then the Soviet air-atomic build-up will have gone much further. Then the peril of the United States will be total, which is not yet the case. . . ."

As this is written, Charles J. V. Murphy, the noted military analyst, has just summed up in *Fortune* the current strategic thinking within the Pentagon. "Long reflection," he says, "has persuaded the Joint Chiefs of Radford's regime that the Korean War should have been fought to a real decision, that the war which General Omar Bradley described as 'the wrong war, at the wrong place, at the wrong time, and with the wrong enemy' was in fact the best possible place to challenge communist power without risk of a general war. China is still, and for some time will remain, critically dependent upon the Soviet Union for its major weapons. For Russia to support China in a war in which no artificial restraints were imposed on U.S. action would put an impossible strain upon the Trans-Siberian Railway. Korea offered the U.S. a chance to engage the highest forms of Soviet air power, and on most advantageous terms, in a war of attrition over China, which, pressed home, might well have destroyed the Mao regime and severely shaken the prestige and power of the Soviet Union."

Whether President Truman and his advisers realized it or not, the roots of the tragedy of MacArthur's recall went far deeper than questions of military and political strategy. Indeed, the basic cause went as far back as the early 1920's. That was when the Communist conspiracy against the United States was first launched, on the heels of the Bolshevik

Revolution in Russia. It happened that simultaneously Douglas MacArthur had become one of the most popular heroes in the United States.

By the same token that these accomplishments marked MacArthur as a symbol of American opportunity, they also marked him as prime target for all those, especially the Communists, who were intent upon radical change in the basic concepts of the American system. What gave him even greater priority as the Communist target was his stalwart and outspoken advocacy even then of those principles and ideals which have guided America's destiny since the birth of the Republic.

Strange as it may seem, the well-publicized incident of the "Bonus March" in 1932 has a definite bearing upon the recall of MacArthur from his post in Korea in 1951.

The Bonus March of 1932 was conceived by certain Western veterans of World War I as an honest and dramatic appeal to the government to provide a veterans' bonus. But it was unfortunately seized upon by the Communists as a tailor-made device for exploiting the prevailing world-wide economic panic into mob violence against the government in Washington.

As the Bonus March moved east, its leadership gradually became infiltrated with a hard core of Communist agitators. The Communists also managed to swell the marchers with a heavy percentage of criminals, men with prison records for such crimes as murder, manslaughter, rape, robbery, burglary, blackmail, and assault. This motley crew had no sooner arrived in Washington than its members showed, by acts of violence so severe that the civil police were unable effectively to cope with them, that the purpose of its leadership was to flout the orderly processes of government. In fact, a secret document which was captured later disclosed that the Communist plan covered even such details as the public trial and hanging in front of the Capitol of high government officials. At the very top of the list was the name of Army Chief of Staff MacArthur.

With the situation out of hand, the government of the District of Columbia appealed to the federal government to help. At President Hoover's request, Secretary of War Patrick J. Hurley sent MacArthur the following order: "The President has just now informed me," it read, "that the civil government of the District of Columbia has reported to him that it is unable to maintain law and order in the District. You will have United States troops proceed immediately to the scene of disorder. Co-operate fully with the District of Columbia police force which is now in charge. Turn over all prisoners to the civil authorities. In your orders insist that any women and children who may be in the affected area be accorded every consideration and kindness. Use all humanity consistent with the due execution of the order."

MacArthur put troops on the scene immediately. Mob violence was broken up and the chief trouble-makers dispersed.

Secretary of War Hurley reported the actual events as follows: "General MacArthur," he said, "gave detailed instructions to Brigadier General Perry Miles, who was in command of the troops, how to handle the situation without firing on the rioters. Miles, in turn, orally passed on the same detailed instructions to his subordinates. In the face of the showers of brickbats and clubs, not one officer, not one enlisted man of the Army fired a single shot. *No one gave any order at any time, either oral or written, to fire on the veterans or marchers.* . . . The Army used no weapon other than a few tear gas bombs. After having thrown a volley of brickbats at the troops at the first camp (significantly called "Communist Camp"), the marchers broke and ran. Every soldier engaged in the service of suppressing the bonus riot in Washington, from General MacArthur to the lowest private in the ranks, conducted himself with skill, patience and courage."

Secretary Hurley then quoted from MacArthur's report to him at the time. "The mission given them [the troops] has been performed loyally and efficiently," the report read. "They have not fired a shot, and have actually employed no more dangerous weapons than harmless tear gas bombs. Even these were not used in heavy concentrations nor for periods of more than a few minutes each. Any contention that injury to individuals was caused by them is entirely without foundation.'" That report, incidentally, was prepared by then-Major Dwight D. Eisenhower, who was one of the two staff officers accompanying MacArthur at the time.

Despite such clear refutation, however, the Communists and their dupes, innocent and otherwise, have continued to parrot the falsehood that MacArthur ordered U.S. soldiers to fire upon other Americans, and to use this lie as the foundation for an equally fallacious charge that he would someday become "the man on horseback," and would attempt to become some kind of American dictator. And these same groups, noting well MacArthur's defiance of Communism everywhere, have sought continuously to discredit his every action.

They found a ready, though initially innocent, ally in the "Europe-first" cliques in the War and State Departments in Washington at the time of the outbreak of World War II. Together, for their separate reasons, these two groups sought to block acceptance of MacArthur's view that Europe and Asia—the Atlantic and Pacific—were equally important in the contemplation of our national interest and security. Together they attempted to discredit MacArthur in every way and thwart even his efforts against the enemy in World War II and Korea. Together they fostered the tragic notion that appeasement instead of defiance would win in Asia. Together they were responsible for MacArthur's recall.

CHAPTER V   Political Overtures

✠ Ever since 1919, when MacArthur returned from Europe as a brigadier general with a distinguished record in World War I, various groups have sought to launch him as a Presidential candidate. Though gratified by these expressions of confidence in his character and ability, he never took the movements seriously. He realized that any leadership, whether political or military, is impotent without the support of public confidence and faith; and he measured such evidences of acclaim only in so far as they helped to demonstrate public support in the military leadership which he could give the nation.

Not only did MacArthur do nothing to encourage any of these political movements, but he felt that he was not called upon to make any decision with regard to them one way or the other. In World War II, for example, he took notice of a campaign to draft him for the Presidential candidacy only to the extent of issuing a polite but firm refusal to have any part of it. The first time, in fact, that he was forced to give any serious thought at all to the question was in 1944.

MacArthur was in the midst of the details of the operation that would bring him back upon Philippine soil when a direct invitation was extended to him. With no warning whatsoever, an officer representing himself to be an emissary from Thomas E. Dewey arrived at MacArthur's headquarters. His mission, he said, was "to inquire whether you would agree to accept the Republican nomination for the vice-presidency on the Dewey ticket." If he would accept, Dewey, it was said, would in effect delegate to him control over the armed forces in the conduct of the war.

Ordinarily MacArthur would not have had to think for a minute before declining such an offer; he was not interested in the vice-presidency. But what gave the offer its element of attraction was the promised authority over the allocation of U.S. armed forces. He was convinced that he could provide a more realistic balance between the Atlantic and Pacific operations and bring a much earlier victory over Japan, without delaying in the slightest the Allied victory over Germany and the rest of the Axis. So he asked for time in which to ponder this invitation. And ponder it he did with the utmost seriousness.

But he realized that, despite the slimness of the resources allowed him, his over-all strategy against Japan was well on its way to being achieved. The time was actually a little too late. Had such a bid been made a year earlier, he might have accepted it. But now, if a Dewey-MacArthur ticket should win in the autumn of 1944, MacArthur would not have the opportunity for making the necessary changes in strategy and troop allocation until 1945. Meanwhile the injection of his name into the political campaign would mean his immediate removal from command. That would in turn disrupt the orderly conduct of the strategy against Japan, which was reason enough in itself for deciding against running for any office at this time. So MacArthur replied that, while grateful for the offer, he could under no circumstances leave his field command until victory over Japan had been achieved.

The talk of MacArthur's running for the Presidency, however, would not die until he was forced to issue a public statement asking for its cessation. He stated categorically that he was not interested and that he would under no circumstances become a candidate for political office. All he wanted, he said, was to get on with fighting the war in his present role or any other that might be assigned him. This served to stop most of the speculation then going on—and incidentally occasioned considerable happiness in the White House. Australia's then Prime Minister Curtin later told MacArthur he had been in President Roosevelt's office when Steve Early had brought in the press dispatch embodying MacArthur's statement; the President, Curtin said, had read it with great glee and obvious relief.

MacArthur was allowed to forget politics for the next three years, but as the time for the 1948 campaign drew near, the urgings of his supporters inevitably multiplied. MacArthur was at this time busy enough with the administration of Japan, and when many of his friends in the United States asked him to permit his name to be entered in Wisconsin's Presidential primary (his consent being required by the laws of the state), he at first paid little attention to the whole idea. As the time for this particular primary approached, however, the pressures on him to allow his name to be entered increased manifold. And as these pressures reached public notice, they began to meet with the violently outspoken opposition of the traditionally anti-MacArthur forces in the nation.

MacArthur began to watch closely and with some concern the bitter diatribes hurled at him simply because some friends had taken it upon themselves to suggest him openly for political office. He maintained his silence, however; by virtue of his position, an action that alienated any large groups against him might also alienate them against the firm and positive American posture in the Far East which he advocated. Then happened a curious incident which more than anything else influenced MacArthur's decision at that time.

A bitterly scurrilous attack was launched against him by William Z. Foster, then head of the Communist Party in the United States (and now under federal indictment for advocating the overthrow of the U.S. government by force and violence). The attack was launched in the July 27, 1947 issue of the *Daily Worker*, under the screaming headline: "IS GEN. MACARTHUR THE MAN ON HORSEBACK?"

· Foster first recounted a fanciful story concerning plans to project MacArthur into the political arena. "It is plain, therefore," Foster went on, "that the democratic forces must begin to pay attention to General MacArthur. . . . It would be folly for them to stand aside and allow the people, unwarned, to fall victims to the deluge of reactionary demagogy that will mark the triumphal return of MacArthur. To be fore-warned is to be fore-armed. The time to begin to put the American people on guard against the reactionary effects of MacArthur's sudden plunge into the political struggle, is right now, not after he has arrived and is being paraded and feted and glorified. . . .

"General MacArthur is a main political hope and instrument of the most dangerous fascist-minded and warmongering elements in the United States. He must not be allowed to develop unchallenged the political offensive that he and his backers are planning for next year. . . . This country needs no man on horseback to ride his way into this most vital of national elections."

MacArthur did not know about this opening gun fired at him by the leader of the Communists in the United States, nor the volley that followed in the *Daily Worker*, until specimens were sent to him by friends. He then noted the attack with amusement. But as the signal was immediately picked up by those other members of U.S. politics and press who, usually with pretended innocence, so often parrot the Communist line, and as the opening volley became a thundering barrage of everything from innuendo to libelous vilification, MacArthur's amusement slowly turned to anger.

He had no more desire than formerly to become a politician. He well knew that he could not successfully run for high office without returning to the United States, and he had only recently requested friends not to carry out their proposed plans for effecting that return by means of an invitation to testify before a Congressional committee. His job in Japan was still too important, he felt, for him to interrupt it for what would amount to little more than a warm display of public good will which would serve no useful purpose.

But as the Wisconsin deadline drew near, MacArthur realized that the ever-mounting campaign of abuse against him by the Communists and their open or covert supporters was an attempt to blackmail him into staying out of the race entirely. If he were to let his name be entered in the primary, the Communists were threatening, they would do their evil best to besmirch his accomplishments and everything he stood for. This much, evidently, the Communists feared the political might of his name. The more he thought of their presumption, the more irate he became. And it was for this reason that he finally made his decision.

On March 9, 1948, he arrived at his Dai Ichi Building headquarters at the usual time and sent for me. As I entered his office, he handed me a sheet of tablet paper on which he had scribbled the following in pencil:

"I have been informed that petitions have been filed in Madison, signed by many of my fellow citizens of Wisconsin, presenting my name to the electorate for consideration at the primary on April 6th. I am deeply grateful for this spontaneous display of friendly confidence. No man could fail to be profoundly stirred by such a public movement in this hour of momentous import, national and international, temporal and spiritual. While it seems unnecessary for me to repeat that I do not actively seek or covet any office and have no plans for leaving my post in Japan, I can say, and with due humility, that I would be recreant to all my concepts of good citizenship were I to shrink because of the hazards and responsibilities involved from accepting any public duty to which I might be called by the American people."

I finished reading it and glanced up at MacArthur. He was smiling and there was a twinkle in his eye. "Court, please have it published," he said. "That will be my answer to Mr. Foster."

MacArthur never entertained any illusions that even the people of his own state of Wisconsin, beyond a few devoted friends, would support his candidacy in the face of the tremendously active campaigning by Dewey and Stassen (one of whose hardest-working helpers was Senator Joseph McCarthy). Indeed, the size of the vote that he did receive surprised him. But his main purpose was accomplished: as always in dealing with Communist bluster, firm defiance quickly silenced it. The slander that had been directed at MacArthur by the Communists and their fellows so long as MacArthur did not answer, quickly vanished as soon as their bluff was called.

It was not long before MacArthur found, however, that the 1948 political campaign was not quite over for him. On May 29 he received a formal invitation from Senator Styles Bridges, chairman of the Senate Appropriations Committee, to appear and testify on Far Eastern problems before that committee. The invitation was issued at the height of an extremely active and vocal campaign to get MacArthur to become an active candidate for the Presidency, and the pressures upon him from many different directions were almost overwhelming. The burden of the argument was that he simply could not in good faith decline such an invitation at such a time.

MacArthur studied the invitation most carefully, as well as General Marshall's forwarding comments (which were not difficult to construe as a transmittal of a message, rather than any order to return). But he knew that unless he wished to find himself thrust into the political campaign, he could not do otherwise than decline. He realized that his unprecedented reply might jar legislative sensibilities. But he tried to obviate this by answering with complete frankness and honesty.

"No man could fail to appreciate the friendly and generous spirit prompting the invitation of your distinguished committee," he wrote to Senator Bridges. "It reflects a high order of devotion to the public interest that you ignore much discussed political implications in order to insure that the views of none which might contribute to the sound orientation of American policy go unheeded. You may be sure that I have wished earnestly ever since the end of the war for the opportunity to return to my native land, but the heavy pressure of my duties here and the paramountcy of the public interest have left me no justification for so doing from motives unofficial or personal in character.

"In normal circumstances I should respond at once to your present invitation as a citizen and servant of the Republic and sit in with you frankly to state my views, whether they might parallel or cut across already determined policies or concepts being advanced by others. But the existing circumstances are not normal, and my return at this time, however sincere its purpose, would be misunderstood and condemned by many as politically inspired, and much that I might be obligated in good conscience to say would lose its effect under the impeaching process of doubt thereby aroused in the public mind. Furthermore, on the question of appropriations affecting the Far East, concerning which my views specifically are requested, the basic policies are already determined and in effect, leaving only the detail yet to be resolved as to this theater. I have already directly and through representatives expressed my views on such detail and there is little that I could add to what has already been said thereon and is now before the Congress.

"Apart from this, it would be peculiarly repugnant to me to have it felt that I sought to capitalize to political advantage, as many have frankly urged, the public good-will which might manifest itself upon my first return to American soil following the Pacific war. For such good-will would find its inspiration in the victory which crowned our Pacific war effort to which countless gallant Americans, living and dead, contributed by unfailing and invincible devotion. Usurpation by me of such good-will to serve a political end would be a shameful breach of their faith and a betrayal of the mutual trust on which was erected the cornerstone to the Pacific victory. On the other hand, following settlement of the political issues to be resolved next month, I should feel free to place myself fully at your disposal should you still desire clarification of my views on this or any other matter affecting the public interest."

Although this reply to Senator Bridges was evidently a grievous blow to the MacArthur-for-President supporters who had urged issuance of the invitation, MacArthur's frankness and sincerity removed the sting from his unprecedented action, and the chairman and members of the committee sympathized with his point of view. Among the general public too there was some recognition of this reply for what it was—a staunch and morally upright refusal to capitalize on the Pacific victory for personal political advantage. Although he did not think of it at the time, this reply was also as firm a refutation as could possibly be made to the foolish—and malicious—charges that MacArthur would be a "man on horseback."

Again politics were forgotten for another three years, except for the politics that played a part in the manner of MacArthur's recall. Then, toward the end of 1951, I received a telephone call from Senator Robert A. Taft, who said that he was most anxious to call on MacArthur. Taft planned to be in New York the following morning, so I suggested that he and I breakfast together in the apartment I was occupying in the same hotel. We could then pay a visit to MacArthur at the time when I usually call on him to go over the day's business, which is nine a.m. Senator Taft agreed, and joined me for breakfast at half past seven the following morning.

We had an enjoyable meal, during which I took occasion to recount an anecdote of the Korean war which peculiarly concerned the Senator. During a period in the war when the events were being subjected to an inordinate amount of distortion, Senator Taft had with his usual thoughtfulness sent MacArthur a message of encouragement and warm support. Coming at the time it did, the message cheered MacArthur greatly. I still recall clearly his smile as he read Taft's letter and turned to me and told a little story.

At the time of Napoleon's retreat from Moscow, Marshal Ney, who was directing the rear-guard action, lost many stragglers who were cut down by civilian farmers armed with pitchforks and knives. Ney therefore issued the most stringent orders against straggling. "Napoleon visited headquarters one day," MacArthur said, "and he and Ney set off to ride the rear line. In the course of this trip far to the rear, they came across a grizzled old sergeant, with the insignia and trappings of the Grenadier Guards, along with two privates who had dropped out of the column. Ney started to give them a terrible tongue-lashing, but Napoleon cut in and said quietly: 'Sergeant, you know the orders against straggling. What would you and your two companions do if you were suddenly set upon by the populace?'

"The sergeant pulled himself erect, saluted with his hands across his chest, and said: 'Sire, we'd form square!' "

MacArthur grinned again. "Court, he said, "do you suppose Bob Taft and you and I could form square?"

At MacArthur's apartment the two greeted each other with the utmost warmth and cordiality. MacArthur at once said: "Senator, I have been a Republican all of my life and I want you to know that while I do not intend actively to campaign, you will have my fullest support for the Republican nomination." Taft thanked him, and MacArthur went on to say: "You have given the Republican Party during its past lean years such a dynamic leadership that you have become known to the country as 'Mr. Republican,' and I feel that for the party to fail to rally to you now for the coming crucial test would be like changing a general when all the preparations for combat have been made under his guidance and the battle is just about to be joined. It would be an inconceivable betrayal." Taft was deeply moved by this viewpoint, one which I heard MacArthur express many times thereafter when the subject of politics arose in the privacy of his home.

During the months that followed, MacArthur continued to demonstrate that he meant it. He did not actively campaign, and Taft never asked him to do so. But he did everything in his power to discourage the rising pressures put upon him to declare himself a candidate. In the state primaries where law required his consent for the filing of his name, he refused. In others, where his consent was not required and where friends entered his name for him, he asked that it be withdrawn. And to those who asked him in private conversations, he reiterated that, win, lose, or draw, he was invincibly for Taft because he felt that Taft had deserved the loyalty of the Republican Party.

While MacArthur continued to discourage attempts to put him on any ticket, even including a MacArthur-Taft ticket, talk of a Taft-Mac-Arthur slate, however, increased as convention time drew near. The proposal gained even greater impetus when Taft publicly announced that if he were elected President he would at once call MacArthur to over-all command of the armed forces. This statement naturally pleased Mac-Arthur, since he had long felt sure that he could provide the nation with a greater measure of security at far less cost than the vast amounts then being expended and, even more important, that he could restore to American arms the will to win. But while he stood ready to serve in such a military capacity if called upon, he continued to refuse all offers to project him into politics.

Early in June of 1952, however, Senator Taft asked me to a private luncheon with him at his Georgetown home. At this meeting I made it clear that MacArthur's support of Taft was as unswerving as ever, and that MacArthur could under no circumstances be persuaded to permit his own name to be put up for the Republican nomination. Taft replied to this by asking whether there was any chance of getting the general's agreement to a Taft-MacArthur ticket. I replied that I was sure he would react adversely to the idea of being vice president, since he would not look with favor at the prospect of being tied down presiding over the Senate.

Taft had already guessed this, and had a countersuggestion. Calling my attention to the powers inherently vested in the President to assign any duties to the vice president that he wished, Taft said that his intention was not only to turn over to MacArthur responsibility for the national security, but also to ensure that the vice president had a strong voice in the formulation of foreign policy bearing upon the national security. Our discussions on this subject continued at some length, and finally resulted in the following memorandum, which we penciled in duplicate at the table in the library of Taft's home.

"If Senator Taft receives the Republican nomination," the memorandum read, "in the course of his acceptance he will announce his intention to appeal to General MacArthur's patriotism to permit his name to be presented to the convention as his [Taft's] choice for running mate. Senator Taft will at the same time inform the convention that if Mac-Arthur consents, if elected he will deputize the general to assume responsibility for the national security as deputy commander-in-chief of the Armed Forces and give him a voice in the formulation of all foreign policy bearing upon the national security."

I warned Senator Taft under no circumstances to speak to MacArthur about this until Taft actually became the Republican nominee. I felt sure that, faced with any premature suggestion of this kind from Taft, MacArthur would decline the offer firmly. And my estimate of his reaction was partially correct. When, on my return to New York, I attempted to broach the subject tentatively, MacArthur was horrified. While he would have welcomed the task of improving our national defense, he visualized himself having to take valuable time from that job for one which he would not at all relish, presiding over the Senate. I pleaded with him, however, to make no decision until the issue actually developed, and won his consent to that extent at least.

Several days later we were discussing another subject entirely when MacArthur suddenly fixed me with a penetrating glance as he asked some pertinent questions: How deeply did Taft seem to wish MacArthur to join him on the ticket? To what degree did Taft believe that such a combination would add political strength to the Republican slate? I answered the questions promptly and easily, since Taft had been most explicit on all facets of the matter. And I was pleased at this indication that MacArthur had, if only tentatively, been exploring the subject. I hastened to point out to MacArthur the strength that the political authority of the vice-presidency would bring to his efforts to improve the nation's security. He said no more at the time, and I took the hint. I let the subject rest, in the hope that time and contemplation might accomplish what persuasion could not.

A few days later Taft found it necessary, despite my warning, to call MacArthur directly and ask for some kind of assurance that he might accept this offer if it were made. MacArthur had apparently given the matter considerably more thought, because his initial reaction to it had been tempered to the extent that he gave his hesitant agreement to the proposition—but only on the understanding that he was not to enter actively into the political campaigning that was going on before the convention, and that if at any time Taft felt that someone else would add more strength to his ticket he should feel entirely free to choose that person.

Taft was as enthusiastic about the whole idea as MacArthur was reluctant, and never thereafter altered his desire to have MacArthur as his running mate. On one occasion I recall his phoning me to disclaim the truth of a report that he had offered the second place to another person as an inducement for a block of delegates. Nor did MacArthur thereafter relax his firm support of Taft, despite the repeated urgings of his would-be backers that he announce himself available.

Indeed, it was only because of his feeling for Taft that MacArthur allowed himself to take part in the one occasion in his life which he regards as being actively political. That was the night on which he delivered the keynote address before the Republican national convention on July 7, 1952.

When he was first approached on the subject, in a telephone call by Guy Gabrielson, Chairman of the Republican National Committee, MacArthur promptly demurred. He pointed out that his appearance on such an occasion would be misconstrued. He regarded his views as neither Republican nor Democrat, but they were nevertheless clear and definite, and he could not see how he could on the one hand maintain the impartial note that the position of keynote speaker demanded without pronouncing political doctrine in which he did not believe. More than that, he had a genuine fear that his personal followers might attempt doubtful political exploitation of his position as the keynote speaker. Predictions were loosely being bandied about that his mere appearance at the convention would stampede it into giving him the nomination by acclamation. The very prospect of this dismayed him, both because of his reluctance to run for office and because of the suggestion of disloyalty to Taft. So he was determined to reject the invitation to appear at the convention, even before it was extended.

But then Taft telephoned MacArthur and asked him with great earnestness to accept if the National Committee asked him to be the keynoter. Again MacArthur reluctantly yielded to Taft's entreaties, this time on the condition that in preparing his address he would be the sole judge of what he was to say. The invitation was extended to him by the National Committee on the following day, and MacArthur's conditions were agreed to. He did, however, ask Gabrielson to go over his finished draft when he had completed it, in order to avoid infringement upon any rules and precedents of the Republican Party and to test its content for impartiality.

The address was scheduled for eight p.m., July 7, so we left La-Guardia airport at three p.m. New York time. For the first time on such a public occasion MacArthur wore civilian clothes. During his earlier crusade, in which he had spoken frankly to the American people as a nonpartisan citizen and soldier, MacArthur had worn his uniform because it seemed to him proper for the occasion. For this one, however, it seemed to him improper, since he was taking part in partisan politics for the first time.

It was five o'clock Chicago time when we arrived at Midway airport, where we were met by a small delegation from the National Committee. MacArthur was still greatly concerned over the possibility of a demonstration for him getting out of hand, and he had specifically requested that every effort be made to permit us to arrive and depart with as little ostentation as possible. We were therefore whisked to the Stock Yard Inn, where Mr. William Prince, president of the concern that operated nearby Convention Hall, had put his private suite at MacArthur's disposal. Thus we were able to avoid a trip through the city itself.

What followed in the next few hours is as eloquent testimony as should be needed to the fact that MacArthur would never lift a finger to obtain the Presidential nomination. After a three-hour wait for the business of the convention to reach the stage for the keynote speech, we were finally notified that it was time to start for the hall. We walked past a file of Chicago police, lining the street all the way to the entrance to the convention floor. There we were met by a delegation selected by the chairman to conduct MacArthur to the rostrum.

Then, as we entered the hall and moved slowly down the aisle, the entire body of the convention erupted into an ovation such as I have rarely before heard. Everyone in the hall rose, and the applause, cheering, and shouting reached such a crescendo that the din was like a physical thing pressing against my ears. I am sure that nearly everyone who witnessed the spectacle of the uproarious welcome given to MacArthur on that occasion, whether actually on the scene or watching and listening to this tremendous display on television, would agree that if a delegate had at that moment placed the name of MacArthur in nomination, he would have become the Republican standard-bearer immediately by acclamation. I wondered then if the thought occurred to MacArthur, but in any case neither of us had any time to dwell on the thought as we pushed our way through the milling throngs that crowded the aisle, yelling, jostling to get a better look, and reaching out to touch him as he went by. Long after he had reached the podium and had stood facing the assemblage, waiting for quiet to be restored so he could speak, the ovation went on and on.

A measure of silence was finally restored, and MacArthur's voice filled the commodious hall, seeming even more vibrant than usual over its public address system. His keynote speech attempted to be a valedictory to the cause for which he had made his recent trip around the country—a valedictory in the sense that he was now turning that crusade over to others, getting them to enlist "all sound and patriotic Americans irrespective of party" to a dedication of "their hearts and minds and fullest effort" to restore the spiritual and temporal strength of the nation.

The speech was also a severe indictment of the Truman administration's policies, both foreign and domestic. But while MacArthur placed the blame where it was due, he at the same time sounded a note of optimism for the future. "Our failures in domestic policy can be overcome," he declared, "for government takes its tone, character, even its general efficiency from its leadership. Sound leadership can restore integrity to the public service; can economize in the public administration; can eliminate disloyal elements from public authority; can purge our educational system of subversive and immoral influence; can restore to youth its rightful heritage; can strengthen the fabric of our free economy; can raise the dollar to its true value; can reduce the tax burden upon individual and industry; can regain the course of constitutional direction; can recapture personal liberties now impaired; can correct social inequities; can strengthen the position of both worker and owner in private industry, even while protecting the public interest; can fortify the initiative, energy and enterprise of the farmer so as to ensure the adequacy of the production of food in lean years and its distribution in those of plenty, without being crippled by the unwarranted interference and domination of government; and can rearm the nation without undue burden upon the people. The correction of domestic evils and lapses would not be too difficult provided that the will to do so firmly exists."

MacArthur struck hard at foreign policy. "Foreign policy has been as tragically in error as has domestic policy," he charged. "We practically invited Soviet dominance over the free peoples of Eastern Europe with our strategic dispositions of Soviet force at the close of the European war; we deliberately withdrew our armies from thousands of square miles of hard-won territory, permitting the advance of Soviet forces to the west to plant the red flag of Communism on the ramparts of Berlin, Vienna and Prague, capitals of Western civilization; we recklessly yielded effective control over vast areas of uranium deposits without which the Soviet might never have developed the threat of atomic power; we foolishly permitted the encirclement of Berlin by Soviet forces, rendering almost inevitable the tragically high cost we have had to pay to secure open lines of supply and communication between our zones of occupation there and in West Germany; we authored, sponsored and approved policies under which the German industrial plant was subjected to major post war dismantling and destruction; we turned over to the Soviet for slave labor hundreds of thousands of German prisoners of war in violation of every humanitarian concept and tradition; we failed even to protest the murder by the Soviet of the flower of the Polish nation; and even after victory had been achieved, we continued to supply the Soviet with quantities of war matériel despite the clear and inescapable warnings of the Soviet threat to future peace."

Here MacArthur challenged directly the spending program under the Truman policy. "The Administration," he said, "is obsessed by the idea that we can spend ourselves into a position of leadership abroad, just as it believes we can spend ourselves into prosperity at home. Both are based upon illusory promises. Both challenge economic and social truths deeply rooted in the experience of mankind. World leadership can only rest upon world respect. Such respect is one of those spiritual ideals which do not result from gifts, propaganda, salesmanship or any artificial means. It is not for barter to the highest bidder. It is not within the orbit of international trade. It is influenced solely by the soundness of ideas by which we better our own way of life, and strengthen the dignity of our own citizenry. Only through the exemplification of sound ideas, which in the crucible of experience have produced for us a better and more serene life, may we contribute in fullest measure to the well-being of others. The higher our own standard and more stable we become, the greater our appeal to less fortunate people and the more they will look to us and our ways for guidance and leadership. This applies equally to those behind the Iron Curtain and those blessed by the concept of human freedom. For the whole record of civilization has proved that the tyranny has not as yet been devised which can long resist a sound idea."

MacArthur returned to an optimistic note with a call for national unity, and urging of the Republican Party to carry on its crusade and a reaffirmation of his faith in the American people. "Despite stresses and strains," he said, "the fine basic character of the American people remains unimpaired. It offers hope that, under the inspiration of a strong, moral leadership, the people—all the people—will hurl back insidious efforts to sow the seeds of suspicion, distrust and hatred calculated not only to stir up racial or religious strife between the several segments of our society, but to destroy the unity and common understanding which has been the cornerstone to our growth as a nation. The very survival of our liberties and, indeed, our civilization is dependent upon citizenry of all races, creeds and colors standing firmly and invincibly together with a singleness of purpose, a mutuality of faith and a common prayer—God Bless America. It is this spiritual unity which offers assurance that the coming crusade to rechart the nation's course towards peace and security and prosperity will find an aroused countryside ready and eager to march. That crusade rests upon the humanitarian aspirations of mankind, its constitutional rights, and the moral necessity for happiness. It demands a purification of the nation's conscience and a refortification of its will and faith. Therein lies the Republican party's challenge to leadership."

The convention erupted again. This time the cheering and applause were accompanied by a spontaneous demonstration from the floor. MacArthur watched for a few moments, then waved to the delegates and withdrew. His exit was through a rear door, in order to avoid any further demonstrations. We returned to Mr. Prince's suite at the Stock Yard Inn, where we waited a short while before it was time to leave for the airport. Literally dozens of delegates and political leaders seized this opportunity to plead with MacArthur to stay in Chicago.

And what is to my mind the most eloquent testimony that MacArthur would not connive for the Presidency is the fact that he refused to stay. The ovations he had received both before and after his keynote speech could not have but convinced him that he need only help his backers a very little in order to secure the nomination. He was convinced at this time that Senator Taft had lost his chance, because of the outcome of the dispute over Texas delegates. This meant not only that there was no longer any practical purpose to be served by continuing his unwavering support of Taft, but also that the position of MacArthur as a possible compromise nominee was greatly enhanced—if he wanted it. Meanwhile leaders of the party, even including former President Herbert Hoover, were calling to ask him to stay in Chicago and lend only the support of his presence, if he would offer no other help, to those who wished him to have the nomination.

MacArthur turned it all down, politely but firmly. He would continue to support Bob Taft for the nomination.

Instead he went out to Midway airport, got aboard a regular scheduled airline flight to New York, and returned home. On the following morning he had one more opportunity to become the compromise candidate if he wished. In the dramatic moments before the first ballot, tremendous pressure was brought to bear upon Taft to withdraw in favor of MacArthur. I was with MacArthur in his apartment when a telephone call from Taft came through to him. Taft explained the situation. He said it had been proposed that he, Taft, should withdraw before the voting started and present MacArthur's name. He wanted MacArthur's views, implying his own willingness to withdraw if MacArthur thought it should be done. MacArthur's reply was:

"Bob, you are the leader. You make any decision you think proper and I will support it. I am behind your banner to the end. Win or lose I am with you. If you think you have a chance stand by your own nomination."

Taft was deeply moved. He said he felt duty bound to his legion of supporters to see the thing through the first ballot. "I will phone you then," he said, "to discuss the situation before the second ballot. The first will not be decisive."

He was wrong. There was no second ballot.

So it was that MacArthur passed up every opportunity offered him to win the nomination. But the simple truth is that MacArthur has never really wanted to be President. One of his principal motivations in this decision was a belief that it was not the proper time for the nation to turn to solely military leadership. He agreed wholeheartedly with the statement made by General Eisenhower in January of 1948: "It is my conviction that the necessary and wise subordination of the military to civil power will be best sustained and our people will have greater confidence that it is so sustained when lifelong professional soldiers, in the absence of some obvious and overriding reasons, abstain from seeking high political office." And MacArthur had been not a little surprised when, as the convention drew near, Eisenhower suddenly changed his mind. MacArthur still felt that the same reasons applied as when Eisenhower had originally stated them. Much as MacArthur would have liked the opportunity to put his plans for the improvement of national defense in action, I am convinced that a great part of his motivation in being willing to accept the position of vice president and deputy commander-in-chief was his respect and affection for Taft, his firm conviction that the party owed him its loyal support and his desire to help him win the Presidency.

It was a very great personal loss to MacArthur when Senator Taft died a year later. MacArthur expressed that loss, typically and eloquently, in a letter which he then penned to Mrs. Taft. It probably best reflects the spiritual tone to the political relationship that existed between the two.

DEAR MRS. TAFT [he wrote],

It is difficult for me to write this letter—there is so much I would like to say—yet words are so inadequate to convey the depth of my feeling. First, and above all else, Mrs. MacArthur and myself want you to know how real and how sincere and understanding is our sympathy for you in your inestimable personal loss. We know that the gaps created by death can never be completely bridged although a merciful God has ordained that time tends to smooth the way.

I think you know of the close political relationship between your husband and myself. I felt he was the indestructible bulwark upon which we could base the welfare and future of our beloved country. Now that he has gone, I have an indescribable feeling of national loss that leaves me for the first time in a mood of pessimism for the future. I can only hope that something of his greatness may mantle the shoulders of those who succeed him. It is my most earnest hope that at least one of your sons will set his steps along the path of his father and grandfather and that he will long have the wise guidance, the loving counsel and the inspirational companionship of a mother who so magnificently contributed to his father's immortality.

With great respect and regard,
Most faithfully,
DOUGLAS MACARTHUR

Saddened as MacArthur was by the death of his great friend, I am sure that he would have felt it his obligation to carry on for both in the discharge of the heavy responsibilities he would have faced if the Taft-MacArthur ticket had been elected. For MacArthur would, of course, now be President of the United States.

CHAPTER VI   Still Waters and—Silence

✄ "I guess I shan't be wearing it again, Court, until they carry me to Arlington Cemetery," MacArthur quietly replied as I asked him why his orderly was packing his uniform and worn and faded cap which had witnessed so many campaigns in the Far East. I was startled at the note of finality in both the tone and nature of his reply. Yet I was soon to learn that it did not imply a retirement from responsibility—merely a change in the direction of responsibility. For before the day was over—it was the day following his keynote address to the Republican National Convention —he was formally to accept the long-standing bid of James H. Rand to become Chairman of the Board of Remington Rand and turn his tireless energies and acute mind toward new horizons.

Back in the fall of 1949, Jim Rand had sent an emissary to Tokyo to confer with MacArthur concerning the possibility of acquiring his services upon completion of his duties in the Far East. MacArthur had carefully studied the history of the company and was deeply impressed by its aggressive international program and outstanding leadership in the adaptation of the principles of electronics to business and scientific devices. MacArthur's professional mind, trained in engineering, immediately foresaw in the evolution of electronics a tremendous and yet untapped potential. All this stimulated his interest and fired his imagination, and he determined to make such an alliance when he had completed his service to the nation.

Once he had finished his crusading tour across the country, winding up with his keynote address before the Republican National Convention, MacArthur felt that there remained little more that he could do as a private citizen bereft of public authority, so on August 1 he entered upon his duties as Chairman of the Board of Remington Rand. From the ensuing business career he has derived infinite satisfaction and happiness and formed a warm and close association not alone within the circles of his own company but with the leaders of American science and industry as a whole, and today, in an entirely new career, he stands as one of the most influential business executives in the world.

His broad grasp of industrial problems, as well as his vision into the future, are reflected in his impromptu statement at the conclusion of the recent annual stockholders' meeting of Remington Rand, which had been called to pass upon a proposed merger with the Sperry Corporation.

"In ultimate result," MacArthur said, "I am sure the stockholders of this company have never held a more important meeting than this one. By their approval of the merger with Sperry, they have opened up an entirely new vista of opportunity. The industrial world is at the threshold of an era of pioneering scientific progress. Vast panoramas will unfold before us of a magnitude and diversity not as yet fully comprehended. There will be no artificial boundaries to progress in this great new industrial field. It will have no lost horizons. Its limits will be as broad as the creative genius and imagination of man. The old methods and solutions will no longer suffice. We must have new thoughts, new ideas, new concepts. And by your votes today, you have wisely decided that Sperry Rand shall be in the forefront of this dynamic evolution."

He was elected Chairman of the Board of Sperry Rand, the new corporation.

On another occasion MacArthur had expressed his views on U.S. business and industry. His major address before the National Association of Manufacturers in December 1954 was a memorable speech. He deprecated as artificial any concept of divergence between the profession of arms and the techniques of industry. He pointed to the inescapable interdependence of the one upon the other. "It is an unassailable truth," he said, "that the science of industry has become a major element in the science of war. The successful conduct of a military campaign now depends upon industrial supremacy. As a consequence, the armed forces of a nation and its industrial power have become one and inseparable. The integration of the leadership of one into the leadership of the other is not only logical but inescapable. It has become indisputably clear that it is no longer the standing armies now in being, nor the naval and air forces which range freedom's vast frontiers, which stay the bloody specter of willful aggression, but rather a realistic appreciation of our massive potential of industrial power which is so capable of rapidly mounting the means to retaliate and to destroy. Industry has thus become the leavening influence in a world where war and the threat and fear of war would otherwise distort the minds of men and violently react upon the peaceful progress of the human race."

Assaying the role of American industry in defense and diplomacy and in the preservation of world peace, MacArthur said: "In the mighty and almost limitless potential of American industry, the brilliance and rugged determination of its leaders; the skill, energy and patriotism of its workers —there has been welded an almost impregnable defense against the evil designs of any who would threaten the security of the American continent. It is indeed the most forceful and convincing argument yet evolved to restrain the irresponsibility of those who would recklessly bring down upon the good and peace-loving peoples of all the nations of the earth the disaster of total war."

Then MacArthur launched into a stirring defense of the capitalistic system. Though no offspring of this system himself, he had long been annoyed by the silence of those whose defense of that system should have been vigorous and bold, but which had instead been pallid, ineffectual, and even at times apologetic. Such people seemed to have a tendency to shrink from any public association with the name, as though it actually bore the stigma which Communist propaganda tries to impute to it. MacArthur regards it as a mighty force which has created the high standard of life which our people enjoy, and one that must be passed on unimpaired to the American generations that will follow. It was therefore natural that he looked to the capitalistic system for his principal topic of discussion as he faced the nation's industrial great and demanded that it be brought out into the open and treated as something of which we were proud, not ashamed.

"Belabored by the Communists, their fellow travelers and the socialists, the capitalistic system has even been tacitly repudiated by some capitalists themselves," he warned. "Succumbing to propaganda, they have wavered in their loyalty to a theory and a practice which has both served them well and built this nation far beyond the wildest dreams of its architects. It has never failed to maximize the fruits of human energy and creative enterprise. It has never failed to provide the sinews for victory in war and has become now the one great hope in the struggle for peace. Was there ever greater hypocrisy than that which flows from those who castigate private capitalism as an evil to be renounced by human society, while avidly seeking to ensnare its benefits—those who regard American dollars as the panacea for all economic ills, while denouncing and condemning the source of such wealth—those who seek American goods, while scoffing at and deriding the very institutions by which these goods are produced?

"The past twenty years have witnessed an incessant encroachment upon the capitalistic system through the direction of our own public policy. This has left our free economy badly bruised and severely tried. The assault has taken various forms. For political expediency and even baser purposes, efforts have constantly been made by those in power or those seeking to be in power to provoke distrust and strife between industrial owners and industrial workers, between management and labor—to breach the community of purpose and effort which so logically must exist between these two great segments of our industrial economy. The effect of this has been to produce a sense of unrest and antagonism where a firm and confident alliance, built upon a mutuality of faith and understanding and a community of purpose, will not only serve the interests of both, but further the well-being of that third great economic segment, the consuming public.

"Another and yet more serious form of assault upon the capitalistic system has been the increasingly oppressive government levies upon both capital and profit. The principle underlying such levies has not been to equalize the burden of meeting the legitimate costs of government by a just and uniform assessment, but has followed instead a conspiratorial design, originally evolved by Karl Marx, to first weaken and then destroy the capitalistic system. Thus, many of our tax laws amount in practical effect to a series of graduated penalties upon the efficiency and the thrift which produces profit and accumulates capital—penalties which strike at the very roots of the incentive to labor, to create and to cheerfully accept the risks and hazards of enterprise in the traditional American pioneering spirit. . . . If the capitalistic system—free enterprise—is to be preserved to the future generations of our people, the course of government must now be sharply re-oriented and America's industrial leadership must assume an invincible and uncompromising defense of that system. Only thereby may there be fostered and preserved adequate incentive to encourage the thrift, the industry and the adventure which brought our nation to its present pre-eminence among all of the other nations of the earth and which alone can carry it forward in peace and security and progress."

It is not by choice that MacArthur's time and talents have been devoted during the recent years to private rather than national problems. Just as his counsel went unheeded at the moment of vital decision after

Red China committed itself to war against our forces in Korea, his view-point on the struggle for Asia has been unsought—except, strangely enough, by the leaders of Asia themselves; their faith in him withstood the shock after the tragedy of events, and when in this country they never fail to pass by to pay their respects and commune again with what they regard as a mighty reservoir of wisdom, understanding, and strength. At home he has been invited to participate in no briefings concerning the global military situation, nor has he been furnished with any information thereon. And despite the flow of events which have demonstrated with tragic clarity the wisdom of his policy recommendations, only once has he been officially approached on Korean War matters under public inquiry. Senator Byrd by letter asked his comment on charges that ammunition shortages had impeded the war effort. In his reply to Senator Byrd under date of April 19, 1953, MacArthur pointed out that ammunition shortages had handicapped operations in Korea from the beginning—that at one time General Walker, in his Pusan defense, had been forced to ration his guns to five rounds per day.

"I was never consulted, directly or indirectly," he said, "with refer-ence to the supply program. Its scope and volume, its appropriations and production schedules were prepared solely by Washington authorities, the function of my command being limited entirely to routine reporting of my needs and necessities."

Then MacArthur pointed to the controlling cause of our unhappy situation in Korea. "The overriding deficiency incident to our conduct of the war in Korea," he said, "was not in the shortage of ammunition or other matériel, but in the lack of the will for victory, which has pro-foundly influenced both our strategic concepts in the field and our sup-porting action at home. This lack undoubtedly must bear responsibility for the extraordinary failure to anticipate and provide the means by which victory might have been made possible. This led us into the fatal error of becoming bogged down in positional warfare on terrain which, with the abandonment of a war of maneuver, necessitated a tremendously increased expenditure of ammunition to protect our lines from enemy in-filtration or collapse. . . .

"Underlying the whole problem of ammunition and supply," he warned, "has always been the indeterminate question as to whether or not the Soviet contemplates world military conquest. If it does, the time and place will be at its initiative and could not fail to be influenced by the fact that in the atomic area the lead of the United States is being diminished with the passage of time. So, likewise, is the great industrial potential of the United States as compared with the Communist world. In short, it has always been my belief that any action we might take to resolve the Far Eastern problem now would not in itself be a controlling factor in the precipitation of a world conflict. It is quite probable that the Soviet masses are just as eager for peace as our own people. They probably suffer the delusion that there are aggressive intentions against them on the part of the capitalist world and that they would welcome an imaginative approach which would allay this false impression. The Soviet is not blind to the dangers which actually confront it in the Far East in the present situation. We still possess the potential to destroy Red China's flimsy industrial base and sever her tenuous supply lines from the Soviet. This would deny her the resource to support modern war and sustain large military forces in the field. This, in turn, would greatly weaken the Communist government of China and threaten the Soviet's present hold upon Asia. A warning of action of this sort provides the leverage to induce the Soviet to bring the Korean struggle to an end, without further bloodshed. It would dread risking the eventuality of a Red China debacle and such a hazard might well settle the Korean War and all other pending global issues on equitable terms just as soon as it realizes we have the will and the means to bring them to a prompt and definite determination. Such an end would justify the sacrifice of our countrymen we have asked to die in that far-off land—would rejoice the Korean people whose nation we are pledged to redeem—would validate the principle of collective security upon which rests our present foreign policy—and would ensure us the respect and faith of the peoples of Asia now and for all time."

Few will now dispute the soundness of MacArthur's thesis, but none in high authority appear to have had the moral courage to take the bold approach to the problems, created by the Soviet's saber-rattling and blustering diplomacy, which offers hope of eliminating international tensions and restoring normalcy and moderation to international affairs.

MacArthur perhaps gave his final military message to the Association of Graduates of West Point at the Founders' Day Dinner of 1953. "Napoleon once said," he remarked, "that military organization and tactics should be revised at least every ten years. He recognized that in the evolution of military science nothing would remain static and that new techniques would become indispensable to attain the changeless goal of victory. Down through the ages, the character of war, but not its purpose, is a constant record of change. From the elephant of Hannibal's day to the modern tank and airplane, the story is always the same—the tactics in one war are always deficient in the next, but the endless purpose remains immutable—victory.

"But, now, oblivious to the lessons of military history and the American tradition, a new concept has arisen which tends to disavow victory as the combat objective and to advocate in its stead a new kind of tactic on which to base the battle. The result can be nothing but failure, nothing to repay the terrible human sacrifice of war. We of the military shall always do what we are told to do. But if this nation is to survive, we must trust the soldier once our statesmen fail to preserve the peace. We must regain our faith in those lessons and traditions which have always sustained our victorious march through the military perils which have beset our past. We must recapture the will and the determination to win, come what may, once American arms have been committed to battle. We must reject the counsels of fear which strange and alien doctrines are attempting to force upon us. We must proclaim again and again and again an invincible adherence to the proposition that in war, there can be no substitute for victory."

In September of the same year MacArthur received a welcome message from Prime Minister Yoshida of Japan. It read:

"Peace Treaty was signed the day before yesterday. My heart and the hearts of all Japanese turn to you in boundless gratitude, for it was your firm and friendly hand that led us, a prostrate nation, on the road to recovery and reconstruction. It was you who first propounded the principles for a fair and generous peace which we now have at long last. In the name of the Japanese government and people I send you our nation's heartfelt thanks." Nothing could more truly demonstrate the tremendous moral force which America has had in Asia in the person of this extraordinary man.

MacArthur was later to be reassured that the government and people of Korea remembered too his strong and rigorous support in *their* agony and despair. For as the fifth anniversary of the victory at Inchon rolled around he was to hear from them through their indefatigable leader, President Syngman Rhee.

"My government and people," the message read, "express their undying gratitude for your great leadership on the occasion of fifth anniversary of liberation landing at Inchon. This daring military exploit so reminiscent of the storming of Quebec by General Wolfe on the same day in 1759 saved Republic of Korea and freedom on this peninsula. Had your sage advice been followed subsequently, it would also have won the war and stopped the advance of Communism in Asia. Inchon will always remain one of the great triumphs of military history and a supreme credit to your military genius. All free Koreans join in wishing you good health and undiminished energy in the continuing struggle to defeat Communism and preserve the world in democracy and freedom. As we prepare to face the Red hordes once again, we are inspired by the example of your dauntless courage, your dedication to the liberty of all men and your matchless military and political wisdom. We pledge to you that the spirit of Inchon shall never die. Syngman Rhee."

To this stirring message MacArthur replied: "I am deeply moved by your message and grateful indeed to your government and the people of Korea. Their indomitable will to be free has become the inspirational beacon of liberty in the Far East. The determination to risk death rather than accept despotic domination is reminiscent of the birth of liberty everywhere. It is in truth the basic spiritual foundation upon which has been laboriously built the very fabric of all civilization. You have been pledged a free and united Korea. If that pledge is not redeemed, the light of freedom will have begun to fade. The concept of collective security will become shattered. Korea is the touchstone and we watch with bated breath the final outcome. May God preserve you and your gallant men. I only wish I could again be with you. MacArthur."

General MacArthur chose the dedication of a monument and memorial park by the city of Los Angeles to deliver a plea for peace which echoed around the world. It would have been dramatic at any time, couched as it is in the prose of a master. But coming at a moment in the world's history when war seemed a fearful possibility, his words fell with terrific impact.

One of his most habitual critics, the New York *Herald Tribune,* had this to say of the speech:

"There are occasions when the simplest and most familiar things stand out as if they had been seen for the first time. So it is with this declaration that war has become an anachronism which neither side can win and in which all may perish. This has been known. Undoubtedly, as General MacArthur stated so feelingly, it is known by plain people everywhere, behind the iron curtain as well as in the free countries.

"Yet seldom, if ever, has this fact—so meaningful for the world—revealed itself with such somber logic and such compelling force.

"Words have a way of remaining the same, when the things they describe change radically. Thus war, as the General pointed out, covers a phenomenon which is fundamentally different from that which it covered in other epochs. In a single lifetime the target has ceased to be the individual man; it has become men by the dozens, the thousands, the hundreds of thousands—and today potentially men by the millions. Can there be any question but that a new kind of thinking must be summoned to meet this new condition?

"An old ethical question has been converted to one of common sense and of plain necessity. In this General MacArthur finds the chief hope of ending war forever. Philosophers are now reinforced by the most palpable and incontrovertible facts. What had been apprehended by a few is now starkly plain to the many. The many could decide—and General MacArthur believes it within the realm of possibility that they will decide—to end war completely before it ends us all.

"The soldier who has denounced 'little wars' and insisted there is no 'substitute for victory' finds his place as the great advocate of peace. General MacArthur retreats from none of his controversial positions of the past. But in this extraordinary appeal he transcends controversies to take his stand upon the absolutes. Never has he seemed a grander figure.

"From that height one returns to immediate problems such as the Red threat to Formosa. There is no hope for solving it by a simple abolition of war. Neither is there any hope, as MacArthur states, for solving it by a simple resort to war. Therein lies the paradox of our time. And therein, too, lies the hope.

"Patience and understanding may yet bring the kind of peace which extends and grows until it is the great peace that is without war. When that day comes, General MacArthur's words will stand as a beacon that led mankind toward its goal."

The old soldier—veteran of twenty campaigns, hero of three great wars—indeed, as the *Herald Tribune* said, "never . . . seemed a grander figure" as he stood before the people of Los Angeles, assembled to honor his seventy-fifth birthday, and denounced the institution of war as a direct threat to the survival of the human race and called for its abolition.

"Many in this brilliant audience," he pointed out in measured tones, "were my comrades-in-arms in the days of used-to-be. They have known war in all its horror and, as veterans, hope against its recurrence. How, we ask ourselves, did such an institution become so integrated with man's life and civilization? How has it grown to be the most vital factor in our existence? It started in a modest enough way as a sort of gladiatorial method of settling disputes between conflicting tribes. One of the oldest and most classical examples is the Biblical story of David and Goliath. Each of the two contesting groups selected its champion. They fought and based upon the outcome an agreement resulted. Then, as time went on, small professional groups known as armies replaced the individual champions. And these groups fought in some obscure corner of the world and victory or defeat was accepted as the basis of an ensuing peace. And from then on, down through the ages, the constant record is an increase in the character and strength of the forces with the rate of increase always accelerating. From a small percentage of the populace it finally engulfed all. It is now the nation in arms.

"Within the span of my own life I have witnessed this evolution. At the turn of the century, when I entered the Army, the target was one enemy casualty at the end of a rifle or bayonet or sword. Then came the machine gun designed to kill by the dozen. After that, the heavy artillery raining death upon the hundreds. Then the aerial bomb to strike by the thousands—followed by the atom explosion to reach the hundreds of thousands. Now, electronics and other processes of science have raised the destructive potential to encompass millions. And with restless hands we work feverishly in dark laboratories to find the means to destroy all at one blow.

"But, this very triumph of scientific annihilation—this very success of invention—has destroyed the possibility of war being a medium of *practical* settlement of international differences. The enormous destruction to both sides of closely matched opponents makes it impossible for the winner to translate it into anything but his own disaster.

"The Second World War, even with its now antiquated armaments, clearly demonstrated that the victor had to bear in large part the very injuries inflicted on his foe. Our own country spent billions of dollars and untold energies to heal the wounds of Germany and Japan. War has become a Frankenstein to destroy both sides. No longer is it the weapon of adventure whereby a short cut to international power and wealth—a place in the sun—can be gained. If you lose, you are annihilated. If you win, you stand only to lose. No longer does it possess the chance of the winner of a duel—it contains rather the germs of double suicide. Science has clearly outmoded it as a feasible arbiter. The great question is—does this mean that war can now be outlawed from the world? If so, it would mark the greatest advance in civilization since the Sermon on the Mount. It would lift at one stroke the darkest shadow which has engulfed mankind from the beginning. It would not only remove fear and bring security—it would not only create new moral and spiritual values—it would produce an economic wave of prosperity that would raise the world's standard of living beyond anything ever dreamed of by man. The hun-

541

dreds of billions of dollars now spent in mutual preparedness could conceivably abolish poverty from the face of the globe. It would accomplish even more than this; it would at one stroke reduce the international tensions that seem so insurmountable now to matters of more probable solution. For instance, the complex problems of German rearmament, of preventive war, of satellite dominance by major powers, of Universal Military Service, of unconscionable taxation, of nuclear development for industry, of freer exchange of goods and people, of foreign aid and, indeed, of all issues involving the application of force. It would have equally potent political effects. It would reduce immeasurably the power of leaders of government and thus render more precarious totalitarian or autocratic rule. The growing and dangerous control by an individual over the masses —the socialistic and paternal trends resulting therefrom—is largely by virtue of this influence to induce war or to maintain peace. Abolish this threat and the position of Chief Magistrate falls into a more proper civic perspective.

"You will say at once that although the abolition of war has been the dream of man for centuries every proposition to that end has been promptly discarded as impossible and fantastic. Every cynic, every pessimist, every adventurer, every swashbuckler in the world has always disclaimed its feasibility. But that was before the science of the past decade made mass destruction a reality. The argument then was along spiritual and moral lines, and lost. It is a sad truth that human character has never reached a theological development which would permit the application of pure idealism. In the last two thousand years its rate of change has been deplorably slow compared to that of the arts and the sciences. But now the tremendous and present evolution of nuclear and other potentials of destruction has suddenly taken the problem away from its primary consideration as a moral and spiritual question and brought it abreast of scientific realism. It is no longer an ethical equation to be pondered solely by learned philosphers and ecclesiastics but a hard-core one for the decision of the masses whose survival is the issue. This is as true of the Soviet side of the world as of the free side—as true behind the Iron Curtain as in front of it. The ordinary people of the world, whether free or slave, are all in agreement on this solution; and this perhaps is the only thing in the world they do agree upon. But it is the most vital and determinate of all. The leaders are the laggards. The disease of power seems to confuse and befuddle them. They have not even approached the basic problem, much less evolved a working formula to implement this public demand. They debate and turmoil over a hundred issues—they bring us to the verge of despair or raise our hopes to utopian heights over the corollary misunderstandings that stem from the threat of war—but never in the chancelleries of the world or the halls of the United Nations is the real problem raised. Never do they dare to state the bald truth, that the next great advance in the evolution of civilization can not take place until war is abolished. It may take another cataclysm of destruction to prove to them this simple truth. But, strange as it may seem, it is known now by all common men. It is the one issue upon which both sides can agree, for it is the one issue upon which both sides will profit equally. It is the one issue —and the only decisive one—in which the interests of both are completely parallel. It is the one issue which, if settled, might settle all others.

"Time has shown that agreements between modern nations are generally no longer honored as valid unless both profit therefrom. But both sides can be trusted when both do profit. It becomes then no longer a problem based upon relative integrity. It is now no longer convincing to argue, whether true or not, that we can not trust the other side—that one maverick can destroy the herd. It would no longer be a matter depending upon trust—the self-interest of each nation outlawing war would keep it true to itself. And there is no influence so potent and powerful as self-interest. It would not necessarily require international inspection of relative armaments—the public opinion of every part of the world would be the great denominator which would ensure the issue—each nation would so profit that it could not fail eventually to comply. This would not, of course, mean the abandonment of all armed forces, but it would reduce them to the simpler problems of internal order and international police. It would not mean Utopia at one fell stroke, but it would mean that the great road block now existing to the development of the human race would have been cleared.

"The present tensions with their threat of national annihilation are kept alive by two great illusions. The one, a complete belief on the part of the Soviet world that the capitalist countries are preparing to attack them; that sooner or later we intend to strike. And the other, a complete belief on the part of the capitalistic countries that the Soviets are preparing to attack us; that sooner or later they intend to strike. Both are wrong. Each side, so far as the masses are concerned, is equally desirous of peace. For either side war with the other would mean nothing but disaster. Both may well, without specific intent, ultimately produce a spontaneous combustion.

"I am sure that every pundit in the world, every cynic and hypocrite, every paid brainwasher, every egotist, every trouble-maker, and many

543

others of entirely different mould, will tell you with mockery and ridicule that this can be only a dream—that it is but the vague imaginings of a visionary. But, as David Lloyd George once said in Commons at the crisis of the First World War, 'We must go on or we will go under.' And the great criticism we can make of the world's leaders is their lack of a plan which will enable us 'to go on.' All they propose merely gravitates around but dares not face the real problem. They increase preparedness by alliances, by distributing resources throughout the world, by feverish activity in developing new and deadlier weapons, by applying conscription in times of peace—all of which is instantly matched by the prospective opponent. We are told that this increases the chances of peace—which is doubtful—and increases the chances of victory if war comes—which would be incontestable if the other side did not increase in like proportion. Actually, the truth is that the relative strengths of the two change little with the years. Action by one is promptly matched by reaction from the other.

"We are told we must go on indefinitely as at present—some say fifty years or more. With what at the end? None say there is no definite objective. They but pass along to those that follow the search for a final solution. And, at the end, the problem will be exactly the same as that which we face now. Must we live for generations under the killing punishment of accelerating preparedness without an announced final purpose or, as an alternative, suicidal war; and trifle in the meanwhile with corollary and indeterminate theses—such as limitation of armament, restriction on the use of nuclear power, adoption of new legal standards as propounded at Nuremberg—all of which are but palliatives and all of which in varying form have been tried in the past with negligible results? Dangerous doctrines, too, appear—doctrines which might result in actual defeat; such doctrines as a limited war, of enemy sanctuary, of failure to protect our fighting men when captured, of national subversive and sabotage agencies, of a substitute for victory on the battlefield—all in the name of peace. Peace, indeed, can be obtained at least temporarily by any nation if it is prepared to yield its freedom principles. But peace at any price—peace with appeasement—peace which passes the dreadful finality to future generations—is a peace of sham and shame which can end only in war or slavery.

"I recall so vividly this problem when it faced the Japanese in their new Constitution. They are realists; and they are the only ones that know by dread experience the fearful effect of mass annihilation. They realize in their limited geographical area, caught up as a sort of No Man's Land between two great ideologies, that to engage in another war, whether on the winning or the losing side, would spell the probable doom of their race. And their wise old Prime Minister, Shidehara, came to me and urged that to save themselves they should abolish war as an international instrument. When I agreed, he turned to me and said, 'The world will laugh and mock us as impractical visionaries, but a hundred years from now we will be called prophets.'

"Sooner or later the world, if it is to survive, must reach this decision. The only question is, when? Must we fight again before we learn? When will some great figure in power have sufficient imagination and moral courage to translate this universal wish—which is rapidly becoming a universal necessity—into actuality? We are in a new era. The old methods and solutions no longer suffice. We must have new thoughts, new ideas, new concepts, just as did our venerated forefathers when they faced a New World. We must break out of the strait jacket of the past. There must always be one to lead, and we should be that one. We should now proclaim our readiness to abolish war in concert with the great powers of the world. The result might be magical.

"This may sound somewhat academic in view of the acuteness of the situation in the Far East. Strategically, the problem there has developed along classical lines—the familiar case of a concentrated enemy in a central position deployed against scattered allies. Red China, inherently weak in industrial output for modern war but strong in manpower, engaged on three fronts—Korea, Indo-China and in civil war with Nationalist China. Fighting on all three simultaneously meant defeat, but individually the chances were excellent. The hope for victory depended on getting a cease-fire on some fronts so that the full potential of its limited military might could be thrown against the remaining one or ones. That is what has happened and is happening. First was the cessation of the civil-war action by the isolation in the Formosa area which practically immobilized National China, one of the allies. Red China then concentrated against Korea and Indo-China. But even the double front was too much for its strained resources. So a cease-fire was obtained in Korea. This immobilized the so-called United Nations Forces and the South Koreans and left Red China free to concentrate on the third front—Indo-China and the French. Successful there, the Reds now turn back to the old first front located in Formosa. As Napoleon Bonaparte once said: 'Give me allies as an enemy so that I can defeat them one by one.'

"Militarily the situation demonstrates the inherent weakness of the theory of collective security—the chain is no stronger than its weakest link, and what is even more vital—its full power can only be utilized when all links are brought simultaneously into action. The diverse interests of allies always tend toward separation rather than unity.

"Whatever betides the ultimate fate of the Far East—and indeed of the world—will not be settled by force of arms. We may all be practically annihilated—but war can no longer be an arbiter of survival."

MacArthur at seventy-five is the embodiment of the truism that you are only as old as you feel. He looks and acts as though he were but middle-aged. His hair is only slightly grayed; his carriage is still as straight as that of any West Point cadet; his ears are as sharp as his eyes; and he can stand in a receiving line before or after a speech for as many hours as he once stood on a parade ground or reviewing stand, and with no fatigue.

There is a reason for this. His practice is "to live every day of your life as though you expected to live forever." In his famous seventy-fifth-birthday speech he elaborated on this credo.

"The poet said," he remarked with a smile, "that youth is not entirely a time of life—it is a state of mind. It is not wholly a matter of ripe cheeks, red lips or supple knees. It is a temper of the will, a quality of the imagination, a vigor of the emotions, a freshness of the deep springs of life. It means a temperamental predominance of courage over timidity, of an appetite for adventure over love of ease. Nobody grows old by merely living a number of years. People grow old only by deserting their ideals. Years may wrinkle the skin, but to give up interest wrinkles the soul. Worry, doubt, self-distrust, fear and despair—these are the long, long years that bow the head and turn the growing spirit back to dust. Whatever your years, there is in every being's heart the love of wonder, the undaunted challenge of events, the unfailing child-like appetite for what comes next, and the joy and the game of life. You are as young as your faith, as old as your doubt; as young as your self-confidence, as old as your fear; as young as your hope, as old as your despair. In the central place of every heart there is a recording chamber; so long as it receives messages of beauty, hope, cheer and courage, so long are you young. When the wires are all down and your heart is covered with the snows of pessimism and the ice of cynicism, then, and then only, are you grown old."

The MacArthur family life is an idealistic one. Simple, of quiet elegance and of complete unity and devotion. A deep feeling of kinship, of spirituality, and of destiny runs through MacArthur and through his son as well. The understanding which they share so deeply is exemplified in a prayer, written by MacArthur himself, which father and mother and son have repeated together many times in their morning devotions. When he wrote it many years ago during the early days of the desperate campaigns in the Far East in World War II, MacArthur gave it the title "A Father's Prayer."

"Build me a son, O Lord, who will be strong enough to know when he is weak, and brave enough to face himself when he is afraid; one who will be proud and unbending in honest defeat, and humble and gentle in victory.

"Build me a son whose wishes will not take the place of deeds; a son who will know Thee—and that to know himself is the foundation stone of knowledge.

"Lead him, I pray, not in the path of ease and comfort, but under the stress and spur of difficulties and challenge. Here let him learn to stand up in the storm; here let him learn compassion for those who fail.

"Build me a son whose heart will be clear, whose goal will be high; a son who will master himself before he seeks to master other men; one who will reach into the future, yet never forget the past.

"And after all these things are his, add, I pray, enough of a sense of humor, so that he may always be serious, yet never take himself too seriously. Give him humility, so that he may always remember the simplicity of true greatness, the open mind of true wisdom, and the meekness of true strength.

"Then, I, his father, will dare to whisper, 'I have not lived in vain.'"

And thus I close this book. MacArthur has assuredly given our country a last full measure of devotion, as he sought to do his duty as God gave him the light to see that duty. The thunderous roars, the violent storms, the incredible tumult of stress and strain that belonged to times that used-to-be have passed and gone. Still waters, now—and silence—and a "peace that passeth all understanding."

Index

INDEX

INDEX